THE
PORTABLE MBA
IN FINANCE AND ACCOUNTING

Second Edition

The Portable MBA Series

Published:
The Portable MBA, Eliza G. C. Collins and Mary Anne Devanna
The New Portable MBA, Eliza G. C. Collins and Mary Anne Devanna
The Portable MBA in Marketing, Alexander Hiam and Charles Schewe
The Portable MBA in Finance and Accounting, Second Edition, John Leslie Livingstone
The Portable MBA in Management, Allan R. Cohen
The Portable MBA in Entrepreneurship, Second Edition, William D. Bygrave
The Portable MBA in Economics, Philip K. Y. Young
The Portable MBA in Investment, Peter L. Bernstein
The Portable MBA in Strategy, Liam Fahey
The Portable MBA Desk Reference, Paul A. Argenti
Real-Time Strategy: Improvising Team-Based Planning for a Fast-Changing World,
    Lee Tom Perry, Randall G. Stott, W. Norman Smallwood
New Product Development: Managing and Forecasting for Strategic Success,
    Robert J. Thomas
*Total Quality Management: Strategies and Techniques Proven at Today's Most
    Successful Companies,* Stephen George and Arnold Weimerskirch
*Market-Driven Management: Using the New Marketing Concept to Create a Customer-
    Oriented Company,* Frederick E. Webster
Psychology for Leaders, Dean Tjosvold

Forthcoming:
The Portable MBA in Marketing, Second Edition, Alexander Hiam and Charles Schewe
The Portable MBA Desk Reference, Second Edition
The Portable MBA in Entrepreneurship Case Studies, William D. Bygrave and
    Dan D'Heilly

THE
PORTABLE MBA
IN FINANCE AND ACCOUNTING

Second Edition

John Leslie Livingstone, Editor

John Wiley & Sons, Inc.
New York • Chichester • Weinheim • Brisbane • Singapore • Toronto

Copyright © 1997 by John Wiley & Sons, Inc.
Published by John Wiley & Sons, Inc.

Library of Congress Cataloging-in-Publication Data:
The portable MBA in finance and accounting/ [edited by] John Leslie
    Livingstone. — 2nd ed.
        p.   cm.
    Includes bibliographical references and index.
    ISBN 0-471-18425-X (alk. paper)
    1. Business enterprises—Finance.   2. Accounting.
I. Livingstone, John Leslie.
HG4026.P665   1997
658.15—dc21   97-14095
                                                            CIP

Printed in the United States of America

10   9   8   7   6   5   4   3   2

CONTENTS

PART THREE: MAKING KEY STRATEGIC DECISIONS

PREFACE

Do you know how to perform these vital business tasks?

- Do a breakeven analysis
- Prepare a budget
- Interpret financial statements
- Figure out return on investment
- Compute the cost of capital
- Use a computer spreadsheet for financial analysis
- Put together a business plan
- Legitimately minimize your firm's income taxes
- Decide whether to incorporate your business
- Manage exposure to foreign currency
- Take your company public
- Evaluate an acquisition target
- Select the most profitable long-term investments
- Collect on a loan to a firm in Chapter 11 bankruptcy
- Measure productivity
- Manage financial risk using derivatives
- Use information technology for competitive advantage

These are some of the important topics explained in this book. It will enable you to pick up the basics in finance and accounting without having to incur the considerable time and expense of a formal MBA program.

The first edition of this book was published in 1992. It was an immediate success, and has sold more than 60,000 copies. In addition, it has been translated into Chinese,

French, Indonesian, Portuguese, and Spanish. We are pleased that so many readers have found it useful. Now, the entire book has been updated, and new chapters have been added on computers and information technology, analyzing income statements, and managing financial risk.

The book consists of practical and valuable "how to do it" information, applicable to an entire range of businesses as small as the newest start-up and as large as long-established Fortune 500 corporations. It covers both the perspective of "what do the numbers mean" as well as the more qualitative and intuitive aspects of financial planning and control.

The various chapters have been written by an outstanding team of leading professors from well-known business schools across the United States, as well as seasoned practitioners in the fields of finance, accounting, and law. The authors are experts, with national recognition, and they have been drawn from all over the United States, literally from coast to coast: from Boston to San Diego, and from Palm Beach to Seattle. The authors include Harvard Business School professors, a partner in one of the "Big 6" international accounting firms, a lawyer who specializes in an entrepreneur clientele, a hugely successful businessman, a much sought-after mergers and acquisitions adviser, a prominent venture capital investor, and several top business consultants. In each case, they are masters of their subjects.

There is a comprehensive array of key topics in finance and accounting in this book. It can be read, and reread, with a good deal of profit. Also, it can be kept handy on a nearby shelf, in order to pull it down and look up questions as and when they occur. This book will help you learn how to deal with finance and accounting experts on their own turf, and in their own jargon. You will know what questions to ask, and you will understand the replies that you receive, without being intimidated or confused.

Who can benefit from this book?

- Managers who want to sharpen their business skills.
- Engineers, chemists, scientists, and other technical professionals preparing to take on increased business management responsibilities.
- People operating their own businesses, or people who are thinking about going into business for themselves.
- Businesspeople in nonfinancial positions who want to learn some or all of the basic techniques of finance and accounting.
- MBA alumni who majored in marketing, or human resources, or manufacturing, or general management, and who now need specialized knowledge in finance and accounting.
- MBA alumni who have been out several years and could use an update.

Whether you belong in one, two, or none of these categories, you will find that this book has much of value to offer you. Frankly, most finance and accounting books are intimidating, technically complex, or simply dull. This book emphasizes clarity to nonfinancial readers, the use of many helpful examples, and a bright, interesting style of writing.

ACKNOWLEDGMENTS

A book like this results only from the contributions of many talented people. I want to thank the authors of the chapters that make up this book for their clear, informative explanations of the powerful concepts and tools of finance and accounting. Thanks are also due to Jim Childs, Publisher, Professional & Trade Division, and Bob O'Sullivan, Editorial Assistant, of John Wiley & Sons. My deepest appreciation goes to my wife, Trudy, and our son, Robert, who gave me the inspiration and the encouragement to undertake this exciting project.

John Leslie Livingstone
Palm Beach, Florida

PART I
Understanding the Numbers

1 UNDERSTANDING FINANCIAL STATEMENTS

Michael L. Fetters

Linda Weber's expertise as a gardener was a source of wonder to all who knew her. Each year she had increased the amount of land tilled until she had overwhelmed her friends with vegetables, and her freezer could hold no more. She decided to build a farmer's stand and sell her produce. Compulsively, she kept in a box her receipts for the lumber, tools, wiring, and so on.

Business at the farmer's stand went extremely well. In fact, one might describe the scene as frenetic. Unsure about pricing, Linda decided to set her prices at one half of the prices at local supermarkets. Low prices would be an excellent incentive for people to drive to her stand. Linda succeeded beyond her wildest expectations and had to hire high school kids to help run her stand.

At the end of the growing season, Linda had dreams of a pile of cash for her efforts. Although she did not begin the enterprise for the money, she had worked hard and expected to have surplus cash in her safe. She wanted to take this cash and rent more land as well as a truck in order to haul her vegetables to farmers' markets around the city. In this way, she could sell more, build a more diverse base of customers, and develop a demand that might eventually help her own a store rather than a stand.

As she counted her cash, she became painfully aware that there wasn't as much as she had hoped. When compared to a salary offer she had received at the beginning of the growing season, she was way behind. What had happened? Where was the cash? What would she have to change in order to meet her goals for the next growing season?

STATEMENT OF CASH FLOWS

Linda contacted her friend Joyce, a business manager, who suggested she go back through her records. She pulled out the shoebox where she had kept records of her cash outflows for the stand, employees, and utilities and collected her daily cash register tapes. With this data, she would try to trace her business's cash flow.

Joyce helped Linda establish categories to classify her costs; these included the farmer's stand, seed, organic fertilizer, wages, supplies, utilities, tools, and "other." Soon columns were set up and cash outflows were grouped under the appropriate categories. The checkbook and reconciled bank statements were examined to identify the sources of cash. Although cash came primarily from customer sales, Linda had also invested some personal savings and taken out a bank loan for the growing season. This loan, plus interest, had been repaid. The information collected is presented in Exhibit 1.1.

After Linda had collected the information, Joyce rearranged the cash flow by activity. This format is presented in Exhibit 1.2.

The ease with which she understood the logic of the cash flow statement surprised Linda (she had thought accounting was difficult). She needed cash to get her business going and this information was collected in the financing section. Her start-up investment in tools, tractors, and stand were included under investment activities, and the cash generated by operations was at the top of the form. But she

EXHIBIT 1.1   Linda's Farm Stand, cash flows: First growing season.

Outflows	
Seed	$ 1,000
Fertilizer from stables	1,500
Wages	20,000
Farmer's stand	5,000
Tools including small tractor	10,000
Supplies (bags)	1,000
Utilities	2,000
Other (includes loan interest)	2,000
Loan repaid	10,000
Total outflows	52,500
Inflows	
Personal savings	5,000
Loan received	10,000
Cash from sales	40,000
Total inflows	55,000
Net cash inflow	$ 2,500

EXHIBIT 1.2 Linda's Farm Stand, statement of cash flows by activity: First growing season.

Cash activities: Operations		
Inflow from sales		$40,000
Outflows		
Seed	1,000	
Fertilizer	1,500	
Wages	20,000	
Supplies	1,000	
Utilities	2,000	
Other (includes loan interest)	2,000	27,500
Net inflow from operations		12,500
Cash activities: Investment		
Outflows		
Farmer's stand	5,000	
Tools/tractor	10,000	(15,000)
Cash Activities: Financing		
Inflows		
From personal savings	5,000	
Bank loan received	10,000	
Outflows		
Repayment of bank loan	(10,000)	5,000
Net cash inflow		$ 2,500

was not sure what should go in the "cash activities: operations" section. For instance, it seemed to her that the tractor was used in operations so shouldn't it be shown in operations? Joyce explained that the cash flow for the tractor and tools would benefit many seasons of operations, not just a few. It was a major investment of $10,000 in the operating assets of the business. The core of the operating section focused on the normal cash inflows and outflows caused by the day-to-day operation of the farm stand. Cash inflows were from customers and cash outflows were for typical daily business expenditures, such as seed, fertilizer, and wages.

Although Linda still had some nagging questions, overall she felt pretty comfortable with the format. The reason she did not have as much money as expected was not because of a poor cash flow from operations but because she had purchased major equipment. She reasoned that if she continued the operations at the same level next year, she could expect to have a larger net cash inflow. In order to be sure, she decided to make some projections using the cash statement format from the first growing season. These projections, also known as pro forma statements, are shown in Exhibit 1.3. (Quite simply, pro formas are the financial representation of management predictions. They present the expected financial state of the company after the forecast period.)

EXHIBIT 1.3   **Pro forma—Linda's Farm Stand, projected cash flows: Second growing season (operations stay the same).**

Operations		
Cash inflow		$40,000
Cash sales outflow		
Seed	$ 1,000	
Fertilizer°	5,000	
Wages	20,000	
Supplies	1,000	
Utilities	2,000	
Other	2,000	31,000
Net inflow from operations		9,000
Cash activities: Investment tools[†]		(500)
Cash activities: Financing		–0–
Expected net cash inflow		$ 8,500

° Includes $2,500 she owes from first growing season plus $2,500 expense expected for the second growing season.
[†] Additional tools purchased.

Now Linda's cash flow looked much better. The pro forma model even allowed her to play "what if" games. If she raised her prices to 62% of the supermarket prices, cash inflow from customers would increase from $40,000 to $50,000, assuming demand was unaffected by this price increase. Net cash flow from operations would climb to $19,000 and expected net cash inflow would be $18,500.

Linda looked at a second scenario. If she did not haul the fertilizer herself, but subcontracted this work, the cash outflow for fertilizer would be $6,000 and then her net flow would be $7,500. Perhaps, she could get by with less labor.

Linda still had some doubts about her cash flows. For instance, she still owed $2,500 for the fertilizer she had used during her first growing season. Using the cash flow statement format, the $2,500 expense would not be acknowledged until the second growing season. Linda also wondered about the tractor, tools, and farm stand. How would they show up in her operating results? Her cash flow statement was a valuable document, but it didn't seem to capture the whole picture.

INCOME STATEMENT AND BALANCE SHEET DEVELOPMENT

From Exhibit 1.2, Linda understood that while her operations had generated a decent cash flow, her investment activities had significantly reduced her net cash position. She wondered how this would affect her expansion plans, and how she could use this information to plan the next season's operations.

Again, Joyce offered some advice: She suggested that Linda create an income statement and a balance sheet. Joyce explained that the income statement differs from cash flow: Income statements try to match effort and accomplishment within one period (in this case a growing season); cash flow matches cash inflows and out-flows. Joyce noted that while cash flow from operations did not include any expense for Linda's tractor or tools during the first season, these items were an important part of the effort to produce crops. Furthermore, during that season, Linda owed $2,500 for fertilizer to the manager of the stables and $1,000 to an organic farmer from Maine. The organic farmer had flown down to advise Linda on organic farming and expansion of her operations. Although integral to opera-tions, these items were not a part of the cash flow statement for the first season.

Exhibit 1.4 represents Linda's income statement for the first growing sea-son. Linda saw the logic of the accounting information: It showed sales to cus-tomers and the costs which produced those sales. Linda liked the idea that expenses and revenues were not tied solely to cash flow. If she did something to effect the operations in the first growing season, it would be captured on the income statement for that season. For instance, she had used $4,000 worth of fertilizer and that is what she saw on the income statement.

EXHIBIT 1.4   Linda's Farm Stand, income statement: First growing season.

Sales		$40,000
Expenses		
Seed	$ 1,000	
Fertilizer°	4,000	
Wages	20,000	
Supplies	1,000	
Utilities	2,000	
Other	2,000	
Consultant°	1,000	
Depreciation°		
Equipment	1,000	
Farmer's stand	1,250	33,250
Net income		$ 6,750

° These items differ from the Statement of Cash Flows. Fertilizer expense is the sum of the $1,500 which had been used and paid for and the $2,500 which had been used but not as yet paid for. The consultant's advice helped this growing season, but the bill for these services had not been paid. Finally, depreciation is the allocation of the cost of major assets to the operating periods they benefit. The $1,000 for equipment depreciation is one-tenth of the $10,000 cost of the tractor and tools, which are expected to last ten years. The $1,250 depreciation for the stand represents one year's use of the stand, which has an expected service life of four years.

Expenses associated with the use of the farm stand, tools, and tractor were also included in the income statement. Linda had determined that the farm stand would benefit her operations for four years and the tractor and tools would yield ten years of benefits. The costs associated with these benefits should be shown within these time frames. Joyce had explained that this association is represented by depreciation. As these assets were used up, the original investments in these assets should be allocated to the periods of wear and tear. Depreciation was $1,250 for the farm stand and $1,000 for the tractor and tools. Although they were not cash outflows, Linda liked the idea that income calculations included a cost associated with the wear and tear on her major assets.

Linda also thought an income statement would be helpful in reviewing her choice of price, which she had set significantly below the supermarket price. After all, if her sales did not cover all her costs, in the long run, she would not survive.

Now for the balance sheet. She needed to know what she had to start with for the second growing season. As she understood the balance sheet, it contained a listing of her assets, liabilities, and investments at a particular date. Assets were the resources owned or controlled by her business. They were good things to have because she could use them to help make a future profit. Liabilities were commitments to pay out assets (typically cash) or to render services to creditors. Liabilities seemed to be necessary in order to help fund the business's assets.

The final category on the balance sheet was owner's equity. This represented the owner's investment in the company and took two forms: Direct investment by the owner or a positive income flow. Linda understood direct investment. She had invested $5,000 of her own cash to get the farm stand going: This was owner's equity. However, she was a little fuzzy about the positive income flow notion. Joyce explained that revenues bring assets into the business and expenses are outflows of assets to help generate revenues. If revenues were greater than expenses, assets would increase, benefiting the owner. The increase in the owner's assets means that the owner's equity has increased. If revenues were less than expenses, the owner's equity would decrease. Increases of owner's equity caused by profitable operations (when revenues exceed expenses) are called retained earnings: These earnings are reinvested in order to fund the growth of the business.

Linda now felt that she had mastered the owner's equity concept, and she hoped that actually creating a balance sheet would solidify her understanding of this statement. First, she listed her assets. Cash, farmer's stand, and tractor and tools were the only assets of her farm stand business. She thought about listing the land she farmed but that was really her family's land, and she was just using it in her business. Maybe someday her growing operations would include land, but not now. She also had a file for bills. At the end of the growing season, she owed $2,500 to the stables for fertilizer used during the first growing season and $1,000 payable to the organic farming consultant. Linda listed her assets and liabilities. She still was not sure what to do with owner's equity, but she knew it had to help balance her balance sheet. After all, something called a balance sheet should balance!

Joyce looked at Linda's balance sheet and explained that assets are listed at their purchase cost, minus depreciation where appropriate. She stressed that assets are not shown at today's estimated value but at the price paid for them. Thus, the farm stand is shown at $3,750: The original cost of $5,000, less $1,250 of depreciation during the first growing season. Joyce also noted that both assets and liabilities are separated into current items (used or paid within one year) and long-term items (used or paid after one year). Linda felt comfortable with the concept of asset and liabilities and the form of her balance sheet (Exhibit 1.5). However, Linda was surprised that the owner's equity equaled just the amount needed to balance her balance sheet. She asked Joyce why this had occurred.

EXHIBIT 1.5   Linda's Farm Stand, balance sheet: End of the first growing season.

Assets			
Current assets			
Cash			$ 2,500
Long-term assets			
Farm stand at cost	$ 5,000		
Less: Accumulated depreciation°	(1,250)	$3,750	
Tractor/Tools at cost	10,000		
Less: Accumulated depreciation°	(1,000)	9,000	12,750
Total assets			$15,250
Liabilities			
Current liabilities			
Payable to stables manager	$ 2,500		
Payable to organic farming consultant	1,000		
Total liabilities			3,500
Owner's Equity			
Original investment	$ 5,000		
Retained earnings	6,750		
Total owner's equity			11,750
Total liabilities and owner's equity			$15,250

° Accumulated depreciation is simply the sum of the yearly depreciation expensed to date. At the end of the second growing season, accumulated depreciation for the farm stand would be $2,500 (2 seasons at $1,250 per season). The balance sheet at the end of the third year would list $3,750 as accumulated depreciation for the farm stand.

Joyce reviewed the concept of owner's equity with Linda, explaining that owner's equity consists of two items: the owner's original investment plus any profitable operations. The original investment by Linda was $5,000, and operations had generated $6,750 of profit (Exhibit 1.2). The $5,000 is original investment or contributed capital and the $6,750 is retained earnings. Together, they total $11,750 of owner's equity.

In summary, the balance sheet lists assets at cost and shows how these assets are financed: either by creditors (liabilities) or owner's investment. For Linda's operations, most of the financing was done by owner's investment. Of the total assets, 77% ($11,750) were financed by contributed capital or profitable operations. Linda was proud of this, but she did see a problem highlighted by the balance sheet. She had $2,500 of cash and $3,500 worth of liabilities. Where would the extra $1,000 cash come from? Next year's operations would have to take that into account. Since those bills were due soon, she better start her planning process immediately.

PLANS: PRO FORMA FINANCIAL STATEMENTS

Cash flows are critical to remaining in business, but do not necessarily measure operating results. Income statements match effort and accomplishment that result from the operations of a business. Balance sheets are a list, at a point in time, of an entity's assets and how they are funded (liabilities and owner's equity). These financial statements made sense to Linda and she knew they would be useful in organizing her analysis and evaluation of her business. Further, she could use these three financial statements to help her plan for the next growing season.

Her pro forma cash flow statement would help her evaluate her cash flow activities after the first growing season. She realized she could use pro forma income statements and balance sheets, as well as cash flow statements, to estimate what her farm stand's financial position would be after implementation of her expansion. These pro formas would help her organize her plan and present the expected results in a logical manner.

First, she listed all her projected changes in operations.

1. Prices would increase to 90% of local supermarket prices.
2. She would purchase and resell organically grown produce from farmers who lived farther from the metropolitan location than she did.
3. She would truck her vegetables to farmers' markets located within the city, in order to expand her customer base.

These three changes would generate many effects on her business. For instance, if she was going to sell more, she might have to increase her stand size, her employee hours, and the size of her crop. Two of her projected changes would require a truck. Linda saw that her stated changes would have a ripple effect and decided that she might want to do variations on these changes. She had been experimenting with a new computer spreadsheet: This forecasting would be a perfect application for the spreadsheet.

Linda made projections for each of her proposed changes: She showed their effect on cash flow, income from operations, and the balance sheet at the end of the second growing season. She found it useful to organize all of her projected changes into one list, which showed the dollar amount of each change and the reason for the change.

Sales: $130,000	In her second year of operation, Linda expected a substantial increase in her sales. For that reason, she planned to plant more, purchase produce from other organic farmers for resale, and raise her prices to 90% of supermarket prices. She reasoned she could do this because she was better known than last year; if she trucked her vegetables to market, the price incentive would not have to be as great; and she was buying produce for resale, so she would need higher prices to make a profit.
Seed: $3,000	Prices and amounts would be higher because of her planned expansion.
Fertilizer: $8,000	The amount doubled because she was going to pay the stable to deliver the organic fertilizer. She would no longer clean the stables and haul the fertilizer.
Wages: $30,000	Included a truck driver and increased help.
Utilities: $2,200	Minimal change because the stand was big enough to support the additional sales.
Other: $4,000	Doubled because of gas and insurance for the truck.
Depreciation: Equipment and truck: $7,000	This was much higher because of the truck depreciation.
Farmer's stand: $1,250	It would not have to be expanded to do the additional business. Same amount depreciated as last year.

Using these projections and following her previous reporting format, Linda developed the following financial statements (Exhibits 1.6, 1.7, and 1.8). As the numbers flashed upon her computer screen, Linda gulped. She had expanded her operations, yet ended up with a negative cash balance. Why did this happen? She quickly realized that her investment in a major asset would

EXHIBIT 1.6   Linda's Farm, projected financial statements: Second growing season.

Statement of Cash Flows

Cash inflows		$130,000
Cash outflows—harvest		
Seed	$ 3,000	
Produce	50,000	
Fertilizer°	10,500	
Wages	30,000	
Supplies	1,500	
Utilities	2,200	
Other	4,000	
Consultant[†]	1,000	102,200
Cash from operations		27,800
Cash outflows—investments		
Truck	40,000	(40,000)
Net outflow		(12,200)
Beginning cash		2,500
Projected negative ending cash balance		$ (9,700)

° Includes $2,500 owed from last growing season.
† From last growing season's commitment.

EXHIBIT 1.7   Linda's Farm, projected financial statements: Second growing season.

Income Statement

Sales		$130,000
Expenses		
Seed	$ 3,000	
Produce	50,000	
Fertilizer	8,000	
Wages	30,000	
Supplies	1,500	
Utilities	2,200	
Other	4,000	
Depreciation		
Truck	6,000	
Farmer's stand	1,250	
Other	1,000	106,950
Net income		$ 23,050

**EXHIBIT 1.8   Linda's Farm, projected financial statements:
End of second growing season.**

Balance Sheet

Assets		
Current		
Cash—negative		$ (9,700)
Long term: at cost less depreciation		
Farm stand	$ 2,500	
Tractor/tools	8,000	
Truck	34,000	44,500
Total assets		$ 34,800
Liabilities		–0–
Owner's equity		
Beginning owner's equity	11,750	
Retained earnings (provided by		
operations—second growing season)	23,050	
Ending owner's equity—projected		$ 34,800

use up all her cash, and she would have to finance the asset. However, she had expected that tripling her sales would increase her cash by far more than it had. She decided to go back and look at each of her business strategies: Raising prices, selling other farmers' materials, and trucking produce to farmers' markets.

First, she looked at the price changes. By her calculations, her prices were, on average, about 65% of supermarket prices. If nothing changed but her pricing policy (and the unavoidable increases in fixed expenses), the projected income statement and cash flow for the second growing season would be quite good (Exhibit 1.9). By raising her prices and keeping her costs essentially level, she could have an excellent summer.

Therefore, she reasoned, her projected cash flow problems must have developed by purchasing and reselling other farmers' produce and/or her trucking operations. Although she thought these were separate business strategies, they were closely related. If she was going to inspect the produce she was buying, she might as well pick it up in a truck. If she was going to buy enough to be a worthwhile customer of the other farmers, she would not only have to sell more at her farm stand but also sell produce at the farmers' markets.

Exhibit 1.10 represents Linda's next iteration of her cash projections from operations, incorporating her two additional management strategies. She pre-

EXHIBIT 1.9   Linda's Farm Stand, projected income and cash flow statements: Second growing season pricing policy change.

| | Income Statement | | Cash Flow | |
	Previous Year	Projected	Previous Year	Projected
Sales	$40,000	$56,000	$40,000	$56,000
Seed	(1,000)	(1,100)	(1,000)	(1,100)
Fertilizer	(4,000)	(6,000)	(1,500)	(8,500)
Wages	(20,000)	(21,000)	(20,000)	(21,000)
Supplies	(1,000)	(1,000)	(1,000)	(1,000)
Utilities	(2,000)	(2,200)	(2,000)	(2,200)
Other	(2,000)	(2,500)	(2,000)	(2,500)
Depreciation	(1,000)	(1,000)		
Consultant	(1,000)			(1,000)
Farmer's stand	(1,250)	(1,250)		
Total expenses/ outflows	(33,250)	(36,050)	(27,500)	(37,300)
Net from operations	$ 6,750	$19,950	$12,500	$18,700

sents columns for projected price increase only, projected full plan (all three changes), and an incremental column to highlight the difference in results between the two projections. The full plan increased Linda's cash by $9,100, which did not seem like a lot for the addition of $40,000 in assets and the hard work necessary to triple sales. Although she tripled sales, her cash from operations only increased by approximately 50%. Maybe her income would look better, but she doubted it. After all, depreciation was included in the income statement.

Exhibit 1.11 shows Linda's projected income statement. From these projections, Linda began to see some additional considerations—possibly problems. The monetary rewards reaped in the second growing season from her proposed operations would not compensate sufficiently for her increased effort and risk. She projected only a $3,100 increase in profits. Linda had not expected such a low return for the risk of expanding her business. Her incremental investment would be $40,000 and her incremental income would be $3,100; only a 7.7% return ($3,100/$40,000). She suddenly began to understand the short-run management versus long-run management issues. If managing for the short run, she would keep operations about the same, raise prices, and things would probably go smoothly. If managing for the long run, she would need to look at market penetration, product recognition, and potential for long-run growth in profits and cash flow. If she moved now with her organic produce, she would be the first significant presence in her area. This would be bound to have some favorable long-run consequences, even if the short-run rewards were meager.

EXHIBIT 1.10 Linda's Farm Stand, projected statement of cash flows—operations: Second growing season.

	Projected Prices Only	Projected Full Plan	Increment
Inflow			
Sales	$56,000	$130,000	$74,000
Outflows			
Seed	(1,100)	(3,000)	(1,900)
Fertilizer	(8,500)	(10,500)	(2,000)
Produce	–0–	(50,000)	(50,000)
Wages	(21,000)	(30,000)	(9,000)
Supplies	(1,000)	(1,500)	(500)
Utilities	(2,200)	(2,200)	–0–
Other	(2,500)	(4,000)	(1,500)
Consultant	(1,000)	(1,000)	–0–
Total outflows	(37,300)	(102,200)	(64,900)
Net increase in cash	$18,700	$ 27,800	$ 9,100

Before she made her final decision, Linda would have to go back over her projections and make sure she was comfortable with her assumptions. She would change some of them to see how sensitive her income statement and statement of cash flows were to her assumptions. And, she would expand her analysis from a one-year time span to a five-year time horizon. Whatever she decided, she now

EXHIBIT 1.11 Linda's Farm Stand, projected income statement: Second growing season.

	Projected Prices Only	Projected Full Plan	Increment
Sales	$56,000	$130,000	$74,000
Expenses			
Seed	(1,100)	(3,000)	(1,900)
Fertilizer	(6,000)	(8,000)	(2,000)
Produce	–0–	(50,000)	(50,000)
Wages	(21,000)	(30,000)	(9,000)
Supplies	(1,000)	(1,500)	(500)
Utilities	(2,200)	(2,200)	–0–
Other	(2,500)	(4,000)	(1,500)
Depreciation	(1,000)	(7,000)	(6,000)
Farm stand	(1,250)	(1,250)	–0–
Total Expenses	(36,050)	(106,950)	(70,900)
Net from operations	$19,950	$ 23,050	$ 3,100

knew the scope of her cash needs and the impact of her strategies on her financial statements.

A CHECKLIST FOR FINANCIAL STATEMENTS

Linda developed a memory helper (MH) that she placed next to her computer. Listed on this MH were things she wanted to remember about financial statements. Her list is as follows.

Cash Flow Statements
- A format to make order out of checkbook chaos—deposits are inflows, checks are outflows
- Cover a period of time
- Divide into three sections: Operations, investing, and financing
- Are not net income measurements

Income Statements
- Income equals revenues minus expenses
- Efforts are matched to accomplishments
- Cash sales and credit sales are considered revenues
- Expenses occur when cash is paid, when major assets are used (depreciation), or when material is used that was bought on credit (e.g., organic fertilizer)
- Income statements are for a period of time
- You can have income and still be short of cash
- Income should be a major source of owner's equity

Balance Sheets
- Assets equal liabilities plus owner's equity
- Liabilities and owner's equity are two ways to finance assets
- Assets are shown at original costs, not their current value
- Current assets will be used or turned into cash within one year
- Current liabilities will be paid within one year
- Retained earnings is not a pool of cash but accumulated income amounts that have been reinvested in assets

EMERGING BUSINESS AND INDUSTRY DATA

Fifteen years after Linda had started her farm stand, she was on the verge of taking her local business regional. Early in her budding career, she had gambled and expanded her organic farming operations in spite of her initial projections of small profits. The gamble paid off. She had gone from one farm stand to four grocery stores, which featured organically grown produce from all over the world. Her stores were expensive, but her food was perceived as "healthy." People did not have to worry about chemicals in or on her products.

Business was excellent and she had just been approached to open up new stores in four neighboring states. Although she had borrowed some money from a local bank, she had developed her business largely through her own operations and savings. If she was going to expand again, moving quickly to penetrate the market, she would need a major infusion of capital. She was not quite sure how the capital markets would evaluate her efforts to date, or how they would evaluate her future plans. She called Joyce who told her to grab her most recent set of financial statements and come down to her office. This was an important decision, partly because Linda now wanted Joyce to join the business.

Linda's most recent financial statements represented a typical year for her business. Sales had grown about 10% annually for four years. In the most recent year, sales had jumped 33% as people became more concerned about the food they ate. As Linda laid her statements on the desk (Exhibits 1.12 and 1.13), Joyce put a collection of percentages and other numbers on the desk (Exhibit 1.14). These were numbers that Joyce had calculated from two major supermarket chains in the United States. Albertson's was a high-end grocery store. Expensive food was sold, and high-quality service and shopping area were provided. Winn Dixie was a low-cost, bargain-oriented supermarket chain. Joyce proposed that she and Linda go through each of the ratios and numbers from the benchmark companies and calculate the same numbers for Linda's past operations. Joyce would then explain how the numbers might be put together by an outside creditor or potential investor.

CASH ASSESSMENT

Joyce explained that the analysis of a company's cash position had many different components: These are divided into a company's ability to meet its short-term cash needs (solvency), a company's financial flexibility (capital structure), and a company's annual cash flow (statement of cash flows).

In the short term, the availability of cash to pay bills is essential to a company's survival. Insufficient cash resources means bankruptcy. There are many ways to measure a company's ability to meet short-term cash needs. Joyce explained that analysts would look at many financial indicators and then make an overall evaluation of a company's solvency position. Joyce began by describing the current account indicators on the balance sheet: Working capital (current assets − current liabilities) and the current ratio (current assets/current liabili-

EXHIBIT 1.12   Linda's organic markets.

INCOME STATEMENT
Periods ending 31 August

	19X1	19X2
Sales	$30,000,000	$40,000,000
Cost of goods sold	19,500,000	25,600,000
Gross profit	10,500,000	14,400,000
Operating expenses	9,000,000	12,300,000
Operating income	1,500,000	2,100,000
Interest expense	100,000	120,000
Income before taxes	1,400,000	1,980,000
Taxes	420,000	594,000
Net income	$ 980,000	$ 1,386,000

BALANCE SHEET
As of 31 August

	19X1	19X2
Assets		
Current		
Cash/short-term investments	$ 500,000	$ 900,000
Receivables	360,000	580,000
Inventories	2,600,000	3,900,000
Prepaid expenses	40,000	60,000
Total current assets	3,500,000	5,440,000
Property, plant & equipment (net)	3,000,000	3,800,000
Total assets	$ 6,500,000	$ 9,240,000
Liabilities		
Current		
Accounts payable	$ 1,817,000	$ 2,420,000
Short-term credit	200,000	200,000
Misc. payables	200,000	137,000
Total current liabilities	2,217,000	2,757,000
Long-term debt	200,000	200,000
Owner's equity	4,083,000	6,283,000
Total assets and owner's equity	$ 6,500,000	$ 9,240,000

ties) are indications of short-term cash position. Assuming that current liabilities will be paid by current assets, the excess of current assets over current liabilities is an indicator of a company's short-term safety position. It indicates a company's ability to meet short-term commitments.

Linda and Joyce now compared the financial analysis completed on Linda's organic market to the benchmark firms (Exhibits 1.14 and 1.15).

EXHIBIT 1.13   Linda's organic markets, statement of cash flow: Periods ending 31 August.

	19X1	19X2
Cash from operations	$350,000	$486,000
Investing activities		
Property, plant, & equip.	(300,000)	(900,000)
Financing activities		
Issue common stock	100,000	814,000
Increase in cash during the year	$150,000	$400,000

EXHIBIT 1.14   Financial data from Benchmark Companies, 19X2.

	High-quality store ALBERTSON'S°	Low-price store WINN DIXIE°
Cash assessment		
Working capital	$194,000,000	$426,000,000
Current ratio	1.17	1.35
Quick ratio	.14	.17
Accounts receivable turnover	128.	81.8
Inventory turnover	9.1	11.0
Payables turnover	14.5	16.3
Long-term debt/Owner's Equity	56%	17%
Times Interest Earned	13	26
Cash operations	$793,000,000	$416,000,000
Cash operations/cash investments	1.19	1.09
Profitability assessment		
Return on Owner's Equity (ROE)	24%	19%
Return on Assets (ROA)	11.2%	9.8%
Profit margin	3.7%	2%
Asset turnover	3.0	4.9
Total Assets/Owner's Equity	2.1	1.97
EPS	$1.84	$1.69
Price/Earnings ratio	18	20.1
Gross profit margin	25.6%	23%
Operating income margin	6.4%	2.2%
Income before tax margin	6%	3.0%

° Information calculated from company's SEC 10-K report.

Clearly her working capital was not as big as Albertson's or Winn Dixie's, but they were much larger companies. Linda's working capital was positive and growing. Linda decided that it would be more useful to compare her current ratio with those of the two benchmark companies. When she did so, her figures were in the same range as the supermarkets'. She maintained a more conservative number for 19X2 and there had been improvement in her numbers. Albert-

EXHIBIT 1.15   Linda's organic market, financial data.

	19X1	19X2
Cash assessment		
Working capital	$1,283,000	$2,683,000
Current ratio	1.58	1.97
Quick ratio	0.41	0.52
Accounts receivable turnover	83.3	69
Inventory turnover	7.5	6.6
Payables turnover	10.7	10.6
Long-term debt/Owner's Equity	4.9%	3.2%
Times interest earned	15	17.5
Cash operations	$ 350,000	$ 486,000
Cash operations/Cash investments	1.17	0.54
Probability assessment		
Return on Owner's Equity	24%	27.2%
Return on Assets	15.1%	15%
Profit margin	3.27%	3.46%
Asset turnover	4.6	4.33
Total Assets/		
Owner's Equity	1.59	1.47
EPS		
Gross profit margin	35%	36%
Operating income margin	5%	5.3%
Income before tax margin	4.67%	4.95%

son's and Winn Dixie could probably afford a lower short-term safety margin because of high volume and high turnover of food.

Next, prospective creditors and investors would examine a more conservative short-term ratio: the *quick ratio*. Cash, marketable investments (those easy to sell), and accounts receivable are summed and divided by current liabilities to obtain the quick ratio. This ratio excludes inventory, because inventory frequently takes a long time to be converted into cash. Analysts want to look at the safety margin in a worst-case scenario: that is, a situation where nobody wants the current inventory. Along with these static measures (the current and quick ratios are calculated using only balance sheet items), analysts may also look at activities that measure the length of time it takes to sell inventory, collect accounts receivable, and receive payment for inventory purchases. These three ratios are "activity" ratios and are labeled inventory turnover, accounts receivable turnover, and accounts payable turnover, respectively. They are calculated by combining information from the income statement (a dynamic flow statement) and the static balance sheet.

Evaluation must consider the interconnections among the ratios. For instance, if a company has a low current ratio, but very rapid inventory and account receivable turnovers, it might be in better liquidity position than a company with a high current ratio but very low (slow) turnovers. If a company has a rapid inventory turnover, then the quick ratio may be too conservative an estimate of liquidity: The worst-case scenario in which inventory cannot be sold is inappropriate. Inventory may be converted into cash quickly enough to cover current liabilities.

For example, say a small company has the following current position:

Current Assets		**Current Liabilities**	
Cash	$10,000	Accounts payable	$120,000
Accounts receivable	60,000		
Inventory	80,000		

If accounts receivable and inventory turnovers are slow, then clearly this company is in a difficult short-term position. Its quick ratio of 0.583 highlights the firm's possible jeopardy. However, if accounts receivable and inventory turnovers are quite rapid (accounts receivable within 30 days and inventory within 30 days), then this company could quite easily meet its short-term commitments. In this case, the current ratio of 1.25 is more indicative of the company's ability to meet its current obligations. This example shows why investors look at many indicators to assess cash and liquidity positions.

Linda compared her accounts receivable and inventory turnovers to the benchmark companies and found her turnovers low. She expected her turnovers were to be not quite as good as Winn Dixie's, but to approximate Albertson's. However, there was some cause for concern. Her inventory turnover dropped substantially from 19X1 to 19X2. Further, she might have to extend more credit to maintain her status as a high-quality, high-price store. If she had to implement such a credit strategy, her receivables would increase and turnover would slow. The future cash from credit sales would not be realized as quickly. Although she would have to explore these possibilities and develop some answers for her inventory turnover slowdown, overall, her current cash position was pretty solid.

Looking at her payables turnover, she saw she was a bit slow compared to the benchmark companies. Payables turnover (cost of goods sold/payable to inventory suppliers) is a measure of how long a company takes to pay its accounts payable. However, her suppliers were pleased with her payment record, and she wanted to continue financing some of her current cash needs with supplier credit. She preferred supplier credit to a bank loan because to date, the former carried no interest cost.

As discussed earlier, a company can fund growth in its operations through money borrowed from creditors, additional owner investments, or cash generated by operations. A company's financial flexibility may be measured by several ratios, but Joyce recommended that they keep it simple and focus on only two: long-term debt/owner's equity and times interest earned. Long-term debt/owner's equity measures how much of other people's money management is using to earn money for the owners. The higher this ratio, the more debt being used to finance the business: The more debt used to finance assets, the less the owner has to finance. As long as management can earn a higher return than the interest it pays on the debt, the owner's profit will increase.

However, risk of business failure increases with higher levels of debt financing. If operations decline, there may not be sufficient cash flows to meet the required interest and principle payments associated with the debt instruments (for example, notes and mortgage payables). In such situations, debt instruments have to be renegotiated. The creditors have a measure of control over the company and can force bankruptcy proceedings.

The company's ability to meet existing or projected fixed payments is measured by times interest earned (income before taxes plus interest expense/interest expense). It represents a safety margin—it gauges how much earnings could decrease and still cover the required interest payments. The higher the leverage, the higher the interest expense, and this cuts into a company's pretax earnings. Too much leverage will be highlighted by a low times interest earned ratio.

Linda and Joyce noted that Linda's company had used far less debt to finance its expansion than her comparison companies had. Her times interest earned was within the range of the benchmark companies, and her long-term debt/owner's equity ratio was negligible. Clearly, she had tremendous financial flexibility with respect to long-term cash needs. The numbers indicated that she could expand her operations with substantial long-term debt and still have a reasonable level of debt/owner's equity.

A firm's cash position can be evaluated by judging if cash generated from operations is sufficient to cover the cost of operations. A potential investor would determine if cash from operations is positive or negative. If negative a company needs to have other means of generating cash to meet current obligations because operations are a drain on cash. If a company throws off a lot of cash from its operations, then it is generating a regular cash flow that could be used to meet short-term obligations and help expand the business.

Here again Linda's numbers look fine. Her cash from operations was positive and essentially covered her expansion. From a cash assessment perspective, Linda had felt that she was doing well, and this analysis supported her instincts. With the exception of the decline in inventory turnover, she felt that external investors and creditors would probably view her short-term cash position and long-term funds position as quite strong. Now she needed to look at her company's profitability assessment.

PROFITABILITY ASSESSMENT

The second major area of analysis is operations. Is the company profitable? How is management using assets? What effect does the financing strategy have on operations? These are all questions to which analysts seek answers. Joyce found that the best way to do this analysis was to begin with something called the Du Pont chart. The chart begins with return on owner's equity (ROE); a measure of management's success with the owner's investment. This can be split into components that allow focus on various aspects of ROE. Linda suggested they keep it simple, and Joyce obliged with the following chart (Exhibit 1.16).

ROE is dichotomized into return on assets (ROA) (NI/TA) and financial leverage (TA/OE). These ratios are used to explore management's handling of the firm's accumulated assets and the effects of its financing methods on ROE.

At first, Linda thought ROA was a pretty simple concept. A company had a certain dollar amount invested in assets and it earned net income with these assets. NI/TA measured the return on management's investment, while ROE measured the return on the owner's investment. However, the concept of financial leverage (TA/OE) gave her some difficulty. Joyce explained that assets can be funded either through loans from creditors (liabilities) or investment from owners (owner's equity). On the balance sheet, Assets equal Liabilities plus Owner's Equity. TA/OE is a way to measure how assets are financed. The smaller the owner's equity, the higher the amount of liabilities that were used to finance assets. Management has used other people's money to produce earnings for the owners. This is termed financial leverage and the greater the leverage, the higher TA/OE will be. Joyce pointed out that this ratio is multiplied by ROA to calculate the owner's return. Thus, TA/OE acts as a financing multiplier to raise the owner's return (ROE).

EXHIBIT 1.16   Du Pont chart.

To illustrate the effects of financial leverage, Joyce set up the following example.

	Company A	Company B
Total assets	$1,000,000	$1,000,000
Net income	200,000	200,000
Liabilities	500,000	250,000
Owner's equity	500,000	750,000

ROAs for Companies A and B are equal at 20 percent ($200,000/$1,000,000). However, the financial leverage measures (TA/OE) are quite different. Company A has a TA/OE of 2 ($1,000,000/$500,000); Company B has a TA/OE of 1.3 ($1,000,000/$750,000). When Joyce multiplied the ROAs and TA/OEs to calculate the ROE, Linda could see the impact of financial leverage. Company A's ROE is 40% (20% × 2); Company B's ROE is 26% (20% × 1.3).

Next, Linda and Joyce looked at operating efficiency (NI/Sales) and asset turnover (Sales/TA). These components allow a more in-depth study of how management generates return on assets. NI/Sales looks at how much profit was generated out of each sales dollar, while Sales/TA is a measure of asset utilization.

The benchmark companies can be used to further explore the relationships highlighted in the Du Pont chart. Winn Dixie has a lower ROE (19%) than does Albertson's (24%). The first dichotomy shows that Winn Dixie is slightly more conservatively financed than Albertson's (1.97 TA/OE versus 2.12 TA/OE, respectively). Albertson's must generate a far better ROA in order to have a higher ROE. Albertson's ROA (11.2%) is higher than Winn Dixie's (9.8%), providing evidence of the success of Albertson's operations.

Why were Albertson's operations so successful? Was it operating efficiency, total asset turnover, or a combination of both? Winn Dixie has a better asset turnover (4.9 versus 3.0), which Linda had expected. After all, Winn Dixie is a low-price grocer, whereas Albertson's strategy is to attract people through high quality. But look at the profit margin! Albertson's net income/sales was near 3.7% but Winn Dixie's was only 2%. Winn Dixie's better use of its assets was not great enough to overcome Albertson's profit margin advantage. Linda was anxious to see how her company would compare to these two companies. She expected to be closer to Albertson's numbers because her operating strategy more closely resembled Albertson's.

Linda first put her information into the Du Pont chart format that Joyce had outlined (Exhibit 1.17). Linda's organic market stores did quite well in terms of ROE and ROA; in fact, they were outstanding! The site selections for her stores and her early entry into the market had really paid off. Her only problem was the small declines in her ROE and asset turnover. However, she did have an increase in her profit margin, and she could see that if her TA/OE stayed at the 19X1 level, her ROE would stay at roughly the 24% level.

This chart really helped Linda make the connection between her financial numbers and her management decisions. She could see the value of electronic spreadsheets, for now she could play with the components of ROE, equate these manipulations to operating policies, and evaluate strategies. At the same time, she would get a sense of how potential creditors would view her operations, to date, as well as her plans for the future.

Joyce then suggested a more in-depth look at operations. She proposed that Linda compare various profit calculations to sales, and then compare these new margins to her benchmark companies. Linda compared her gross profit, operating profit, and income before tax margins to Albertson's and Winn Dixie. The comparisons between Albertson's and Winn Dixie were striking. Consistent with its high-quality, high-price profile, Albertson's gross profit margin was larger than that of Winn Dixie. This difference was more striking when operating margins were examined. Albertson's was 6.4% and Winn Dixie's was 2.2%. Operating expenses from the quality chain must have been controlled better (gross profit − operating expenses = operating income) than those for the low-cost, low-price Winn Dixie chain.

Linda felt her business strategy was closer to Albertson's than that of Winn Dixie. Her company was a high-quality, relatively high-price grocery store, specializing in organically grown food. What she discovered is that while her gross margin was much better than Albertson's, Albertson's had done a better job of controlling operating expenses (selling, general, and administrative) because their operating income margin was substantially higher than Linda's. (Albertson's 6.4% versus Linda's 5.3%). She needed to take a closer look at operations and be able to explain why her percentages differed from a chain with a similar business strategy.

EXHIBIT 1.17   Linda's Du Pont chart: 19X2.

Joyce thought Linda should also be cognizant of earnings per share (EPS) and the price/earnings (P/E) ratio. Linda calculated her EPS for 19X2 (net income/average number of common shares outstanding): It was $1.39. EPS is similar to ROE, in that it is a measure of return to the owners. Net income available to the stockholders is divided by a surrogate for owner's investment (average number of common shares outstanding for the year). Joyce noted that a company's P/E ratio, defined as the market price of a common share/EPS, indicates the stock market assessment of that company. A high P/E ratio means a favorable assessment; a low P/E ratio shows a less favorable assessment. Although Linda found this information interesting, she did not feel it was pertinent to her because she and her family were the sole investors in her company. Thus, there was no stock market assessment of Linda's company. Linda knew, however, that this knowledge would be useful in the future, if she continued to expand her company.

Linda's session with Joyce had not only helped Linda understand prospective investors' and creditors' viewpoints, but also had helped her to understand her own company. She could now follow the effects of her operating strategies on financial statements and conduct ratio analysis. She could perform sensitivity analysis on her operations to determine the outcome of critical management actions. Her accounting knowledge had helped her systematically review her performance and plan her operations. She realized that accounting was a powerful tool: It had helped her with past business decisions and would be critical in her current decision process.

FOR FURTHER READING

Anthony, Robert N., James S. Reece, and J. Hertenstein, *Accounting Text and Cases,* 9th ed. (Homewood, IL: Irwin, 1995).

Fraser, Lyn M., *Understanding Financial Statements,* 2d ed. (Englewood Cliffs, NJ: Prentice Hall, 1988).

Helfert, Eric A., *Techniques of Financial Analysis,* 7th ed. (Homewood, IL: Irwin, 1991).

Higgins, Robert C., *Analysis for Financial Management,* 2d ed. (Homewood, IL: Irwin, 1989).

Porter, Gary A. and Curtis L. Norton, *Financial Accounting,* alternate ed. (Orlando, FL: The Dryden Press, 1995).

Stickney, Clyde, *Financial Reporting and Statement Analysis,* 3d ed. (Orlando, FL: The Dryden Press, 1996).

2 ANALYZING BUSINESS EARNINGS

Eugene E. Comiskey
Charles W. Mulford

A recent study by a special committee of the American Institute of Certified Public Accountants (AICPA) concluded the following about earnings and user needs:

> Users want information about the portion of a company's reported earnings that is stable or recurring and that provides a basis for estimating sustainable earnings.[1]

While users may want information about the stable or recurring portion of a company's earnings, firms are under no obligation to provide such an earnings series. However, there are generally accepted accounting principles (GAAP) requirements for separate disclosure of selected nonrecurring revenues, expenses, gains, and losses on the face of the income statement or in notes to the financial statements. Further, there are Securities and Exchange Commission (SEC) requirements calling for the disclosure of material nonrecurring items.

The prominence given the demand by users for information on nonrecurring items in the above AICPA report is, no doubt, driven in part by the recent explosive growth in nonrecurring items. The acceleration of change, together with a passion for downsizing, rightsizing, reengineering, and so forth, has fueled this growth. The issuance by the Financial Accounting Standards Board (FASB) of a number of new accounting statements, which require recognition of previously unrecorded expenses and more timely recognition of declines in asset values, has also contributed.

A very limited number of firms do provide, on a voluntary basis, schedules that show their results with nonrecurring items removed. Raychem Corporation's 1995 Annual Report (p. 20) provides one such example. Only that portion of the

EXHIBIT 2.1   Raychem Corporation pretax income before nonrecurring items years ended June 30 (in millions).

	1993	1994	1995
Core business			
"Ongoing" pretax income	$136	$143	$146
One-time license fees	9	—	—
Provision for restructuring and divestitures	—	—	(24)
Gain on sales of assets	4	—	5
Severance, plant consolidations, and other charges	(17)	(6)	(9)
Core business pretax income	$132	$137	$118

schedule dealing with "core" income is reproduced, shown in Exhibit 2.1. The line, "Ongoing pretax income," shows results with nonrecurring items of revenue or gain and expense or loss excluded. On this basis, Raychem has a rising earnings trend, as opposed to an up-and-down series with the nonrecurring items included.

In contrast to the Raychem example above, the task of developing information on a firm's recurring (sustainable) results, remains the responsibility of the statement user. It is true that companies do provide, to varying degrees, the raw materials for this analysis. However, the formidable task of creating the finished product is left to the user. The goal of this chapter is to help users develop background and skills that will make it possible to perform this critical aspect of earnings analysis.

THE NATURE OF NONRECURRING ITEMS

It is difficult to provide a definitive definition of nonrecurring items. "Unusual" or "infrequent in occurrence" are characteristics often cited in defining nonrecurring items. Kieso and Weygandt, in their very popular intermediate accounting text, use the term *irregular* items to describe what most mean by nonrecurring.[2] For our purposes, irregular or nonrecurring items are revenues or gains and expenses or losses that are not reasonably consistent contributors to results, either in terms of their presence or amount. This is how we use the term *nonrecurring items* throughout this chapter.

From a security valuation perspective, nonrecurring items could be characterized as items having a smaller impact on share price than recurring elements of earnings. Some items can often be identified as nonrecurring simply by their very nature, for example, restructuring charges, litigation settlements, flood losses, product recall costs, embezzlement losses, and insurance settlements. Other items may appear consistently in the income statement, but vary widely in sign (income versus expense, gain versus loss) and amount. For example, the following gains on the disposition of flight equipment were reported in recent years by Delta Air Lines:[3]

1992	$35 million
1993	65 million
1994	2 million
1995	0 million
1996	2 million

These above gains have averaged about $25 million over the past 10 years and ranged from a loss of $1 million (1988) to a gain of $65 (1993). The more recent five years typify the variability in the amounts for the entire 10-year period. It would be difficult to call these gains nonrecurring, but they are certainly irregular in amount. There are at least three different ways to handle this line item in revising results for the purpose of identifying sustainable or recurring earnings: (1) Simply eliminate the line item based upon its highly inconsistent contribution to results; (2) include the line item at its average value ($25 million for the period 1987 to 1996) for some time period; or (3) attempt to acquire information on planned aircraft dispositions that might make possible a superior prediction of the contribution of gains on aircraft dispositions that might make possible a superior prediction of the contribution of gains on aircraft dispositions to future results. The last may appear to be most appealing, but may prove to be difficult to implement due to lack of information, and it may also be less attractive when viewed from a cost-benefit perspective. In general, we would recommend either removing the gains or simply employing a fairly recent average value for the gains in projecting earnings.

Recent results of The Goodyear Tire and Rubber Company provide a striking example of the impact of nonrecurring items on the evaluation of earnings performance. Listed in Exhibit 2.2 are pretax results from the 1995 Annual Report (p. 24) of Goodyear, with and without losses on foreign exchange.

As with Delta Air Lines, it may seem questionable to characterize as nonrecurring exchange losses that appear repeatedly. However, in line with the definition of the key characteristics of nonrecurring items above, Goodyear's foreign-exchange losses are both irregular in amount and unlikely to be consistent contributors to results in future years. Across the period 1993 to 1995, the reduction in foreign exchange losses contributed to Goodyear's pretax results, by $35.5 million in 1994 and $60.2 million in 1995. The only way that the foreign exchange line could contribute a further $60.2 million in 1996 would be for a foreign exchange gain in the amount of $42.8 million ($60.4 − $17.4) to be produced—not a very likely prospect.

Other examples of *irregular* items of revenue or gain and expense or loss abound: temporary revenue increases or decreases associated with the Gulf War

EXHIBIT 2.2   The Goodyear Tire and Rubber Company, results with and without foreign-exchange losses years ended December 31 (in millions).

	1993	1994	1995
Income before income taxes, extraordinary item, and cumulative effect of accounting change	$784.9	$865.7	$925.8
Add back foreign-exchange losses	113.1	77.6	17.4
Income exclusive of foreign-exchange losses	$898.0	$943.3	$943.2
Percentage income increase:			
Income as reported		10.3%	6.9%
Income exclusive on foreign-exchange losses		5.1%	0.0%

("Sales to the United States government increased substantially during the Persian Gulf War. However, sales returned to more normal levels in the second half of the year . . ."[4]); temporary revenue increases associated with expanded television sales due to World Cup soccer; temporary increases in loan loss provisions resulting from economic downturns and problems in the financial services industry; and temporary increases in warranty expense produced by special problems with selected automobiles or products, for example, the Pentium chip.

Identification of nonrecurring or irregular items is not a mechanical process; it calls for the exercise of judgment and involves both line items as well as the period-to-period amounts of individual income statement items.

THE PROCESS OF IDENTIFYING NONRECURRING ITEMS

Careful analysis of past financial performance, aimed at removing the effects of nonrecurring items, is a far more formidable task than one might suspect. The task would be fairly simple if most nonrecurring items were prominently displayed on the face of the income statement; but, this is not the case. Recent work suggests that less than a quarter of nonrecurring items are likely to be found, individually disclosed, in the income statement.[5] Providing guidance to enable location of the remaining two-thirds is one of the goals of this chapter.

Our experience with this search activity suggests a sequence that appears to have a high cumulative yield of nonrecurring items in terms of both materiality and search cost. Search cost, mainly analyst time, is an important consideration because financial analysis is an economic activity that should be conducted in an efficient manner. Further, time devoted to this task is not available for another and, therefore, there is an "opportunity" cost to consider. The discussion and guidance that follows is organized around the recommended search sequence outlined in

EXHIBIT 2.3   Efficient search sequence for nonrecurring items.

Search Step	Search Location
1.	Income statement
2.	Statement of cash flows—operating activities section only
3.	Inventory note—assuming that the inventories exist, are significant, and that the firm employs the last-in, first-out (LIFO) method
4.	Income tax note
5.	Other income (expense) note in cases where this balance is not detailed on the face of the income statement
6.	MD&A of Financial Condition and Results of Operations—a Securities and Exchange Commission requirement and therefore available only for public companies
7.	Other notes that occasionally reveal nonrecurring items:

Note	Nonrecurring items revealed
a. Property and equipment	Gains and losses on asset sales
b. Long-term debt	Foreign currency and debt retirement gains and losses
c. Foreign currency	Foreign currency gains and losses
d. Restructuring	Current and prospective impact of restructuring activities
e. Contingencies	Prospective revenue or expense
f. Quarterly financial data	Nonrecurring items in quarterly results

Exhibit 2.3. Following only the first four steps in this search sequence is likely to locate almost 60% of all nonrecurring items.[6] Continuing through steps 5 and 6 will typically increase this location percentage. However, the 60% discovery rate is undoubtedly higher if the focus were only on *material* nonrecurring items. The nonrecurring items disclosed in other locations (beyond steps 1 to 4) are far fewer in number and likely to be less material than those found through steps 1 to 4.

NONRECURRING ITEMS IN THE INCOME STATEMENT

Examination of the income statement, the first step in the search sequence, requires a thorough understanding of the design and content of contemporary income statements to aid in the location and analysis of nonrecurring components of earnings. This calls for a review of the generally accepted accounting principles (GAAP) that determine the structure and content of the income statement. Locating nonrecurring items in the income statement is a highly efficient, cost-effective process. Many nonrecurring items will be prominently displayed on separate lines in the statement and be readily recognizable. Further, leads to other nonrecurring items disclosed elsewhere may be discovered during this process. For example, a line item summarizing items of other income (expense) may include an associated note reference detailing its contents. These notes should always be reviewed, step 5 in the search sequence, because they will often reveal nonrecurring items.

Examples of the two principal income statement formats under current GAAP are presented in Exhibits 2.4 and 2.5. The income statement of Toys 'Я' Us, Inc. (1995 Annual Report, p. 8) is a "single-step" design and that of General Signal Corporation (1995 Annual Report, p. 22) is in the "multistep" format. An annual survey of financial statements conducted by the American Institute of Certified Public Accountants (AICPA) reveals that about a third of the 600 companies in its survey use the single-step format and the other two-thirds the multistep. The distinguishing feature of the multistep statement is that it provides an intermediate earnings subtotal designed to reflect pretax operating performance. In principle, operating income should be composed almost entirely of recurring items of revenue and expense, which result from the main operating activities of the firm. In practice, it is common for numerous material nonrecurring items to be included in operating income. For example, where present, "restructuring" charges, one of the most popular nonrecurring items of the 1990s, is virtually always included in operating income.

The Toys 'Я' Us single-step income statement does not partition results into intermediate subtotals. For example, there is no preliminary result identified as "operating income." Rather, all revenues and expenses are separately totaled and "income before income taxes" is computed in a single step, simply as

EXHIBIT 2.4   Consolidated statement of earnings:
Toys 'Я' Us, Inc. (in millions)

	Year Ended		
	Jan. 29 1994	Jan. 28 1995	Feb. 3 1996
Net sales	$7,946.1	$8,745.6	$9,426.9
Costs and expenses:			
Cost of sales	5,494.7	6,008.0	6,592.3
Selling, advertising, general, and administrative	1,497.0	1,664.2	1,894.8
Restructuring and other charges	—	—	396.6
Depreciation and amortization	133.4	161.4	191.7
Interest expense	72.3	83.9	103.3
Interest and other income	(24.1)	(16.0)	(17.4)
Total	7,173.3	7,901.5	9,161.3
Earnings before taxes on income	772.8	844.1	265.6
Taxes on income	289.8	312.3	117.5
Net earnings	$ 483.0	$ 531.8	$ 148.1

Note: Per share amounts omitted.

EXHIBIT 2.5   Statement of earnings: General Signal Corporation year ended December 31 (in millions).

	1993	1994	1995
Net sales	$1,354.2	$1,527.7	$1,863.2
Cost of sales	959.0	1,109.5	1,308.0
Selling, general, and administrative expenses	259.3	292.3	354.4
Transaction and consolidation charges	13.2	—	20.1
Merger breakup fee and other special items	(33.0)	(46.2)	—
Total operating costs and expenses	1,198.5	1,355.6	1,682.5
Operating earnings	155.7	172.1	180.7
Interest expense, net	16.6	11.8	24.3
Earnings from continuing operations before income taxes	139.1	160.3	156.4
Income taxes	41.0	56.2	56.3
Earnings from continuing operations	98.1	104.1	100.1
Earnings (loss) from discontinued operations, net of income taxes:			
Operations	(31.5)	2.4	—
Disposal	—	(25.8)	(64.0)
Earnings before extraordinary charge and cumulative effect of accounting change	66.6	80.7	36.1
Extraordinary charge	(6.6)	—	—
Cumulative effect of accounting change	(25.3)	—	—
Net earnings	$ 34.7	$ 80.7	$ 36.1

Note: Per share amounts omitted.
SOURCE: General Signal, annual report, December, 1995, p. 22.

total expenses deducted from total revenues. However, the General Signal multistep income statement provides an intermediate profit subtotal identified as "operating earnings."

Nonrecurring Items Located in Income from Continuing Operations

Whether a single- or multistep format is used, the composition of income from continuing operations is the same. It includes all items of revenue or gain and expense or loss with the exception of those (1) identified with discontinued operations, (2) meeting the definition of extraordinary items, and (3) resulting from the cumulative effect of changes in accounting principles. Because it excludes only these three items, one can find in income from continuing operations all other nonrecurring items of revenues or gains and expenses or losses in this key profit subtotal.

The Nature of Operating Income

Operating income is designed to reflect the revenue or gain and expense or loss that are a product of the fundamental operating activities of the firm. However, notice that the 1993–1995 operating earnings of General Signal include at least four nonrecurring charges. In this case, operating income, as reported, is not that measure of "sustainable" earnings called for in the quote, from the AICPA Special Committee on Financial Reporting, with which we opened this chapter. Even at this early point in the operations section of the income statement, non-recurring items have been introduced that will require adjustment in order to arrive at an earnings base "that provides a basis for estimating sustainable earnings."[7] Be aware that "operating income" in a multistep format is an earlier subtotal than "income from continuing operations."

Nonrecurring Items Included in Operating Income

A review of current corporate annual reports readily reveals that General Signal's situation is not at all unusual. A sample of nonrecurring items included in the operating income section of multistep income statements is provided in Exhibit 2.6. There are more instances of nonrecurring expenses and losses than of nonrecurring revenues and gains. This may simply suggest that operating activities are far less likely to produce favorable than unfavorable nonrecurring items.

However, fundamental accounting conventions such as the historical-cost concept and conservatism may also provide part of the explanation. Many of the nonrecurring expense or loss items involve the recognition of declines in the value of specific assets. Restructuring charges have been among the most common items in this section of the income statement in recent years. These charges involve asset writedowns and liability accruals that will be paid off in future years. Seldom is revenue or gain recorded as a result of writing up assets. Further, unlike the case of restructuring charges, the favorable future consequences of a management action would rarely support current accrual of revenue or gain.

Nonrecurring Items Excluded from Operating Income

"Other income (expense)" items, typically reported immediately below the operating income subtotal, are usually less closely associated with the basic operating activities of the firm. A sampling of nonrecurring items found, in "other income and expense" category of the multistep income statements of a number of companies, is provided in Exhibit 2.7.

A comparison of the items in two exhibits reveals some potential for overlap in these categories. The first should be dominated by items closely linked to company operations. The nonrecurring items in the second should fall outside the operations area of the firm. Notice that the USX litigation charge (Exhibit

EXHIBIT 2.6   Nonrecurring items of revenue or gain and expense or loss included in operating income.

Company	Nonrecurring Item
Expenses and losses	
Amdahl Corporation (1995)	Purchased in-process development
Argosy Gaming Company (1995)	Flood costs
CommNet Cellular, Inc. (1995)	Writedown of plant and equipment
Fruit of the Loom (1995)	Impairment writedown of goodwill
Gaylord Container Corporation (1994)	Asset writedowns from plant relocation
Heart Technologies, Inc. (1992)	Product recall costs
Hitox Corporation (1994)	Inventory valuation charge
Interlinq Software Corporation (1996)	Writeoff of capitalized software costs
Meredith Corporation (1994)	Writedown of film assets
Micron Technology, Inc. (1996)	Restructuring charge
On The Border Cafes, Inc. (1994)	Injury claim settlement (airplane crash)
Osmonics, Inc. (1993)	Embezzlement loss
Pinkerton Security and Investigation (1993)	Investment writedown
Southwest Airlines Company (1993)	Merger expenses
Universal Foods Corporation (1992)	Lease termination and related costs
USX Corporation (1993)	Litigation charge (antitrust action)
Worthington Foods, Inc. (1991)	Writedown of nonoperating assets
Revenues and gains	
Air Products and Chemicals, Inc. (1993)	Insurance settlement
Boise Cascade Corporation (1993)	Sales of assets
H.J. Heinz Company (1995)	Gain on sale of confectionery business
Ingersoll-Rand Company (1993)	Restructure of operations benefit

SOURCES: Companies' annual reports. The year following each company name designates the annual report from which each example was drawn.

2.6) is included in operating income but that a lawsuit loss of Sun Microsystems (Exhibit 2.7) is pushed out of operating income and down into the "other income (expense)" category. The antitrust character of the USX charge must be viewed as more operations-related than the securities-related settlement of Sun Microsystems. However, the Baxter litigation settlements related to product-related suits, and the Global Industries Ltd. fire loss on a marine vessel, were both excluded from operating income. Each of these items would seem to be closely tied to the operations of these two firms, and therefore more properly included in operating income. The goal of the operating income subtotal should be to capture core operating profitability. Clearly, the range and complexity of nonrecurring items creates difficult judgment calls in implementing of this concept of operating income.

Unlike the multistep format, the single-step income statement does not include a subtotal representing operating income. As a result, the task of identifying core profitability is somewhat more difficult. Nonrecurring items of rev-

EXHIBIT 2.7   Nonrecurring items of revenue or gain and expense or loss excluded from operating income.

Company	Nonrecurring Item
Expenses or losses	
Baltek Corporation (1995)	Foreign currency loss
Champion Enterprises (1995)	Environmental reserve
Cryomedical Sciences, Inc. (1995)	Settlement of shareholder class action suit
Gibson Greetings, Inc. (1995)	Loss on derivative transactions
Global Industries (1993)	Fire loss on marine vessel
Hollywood Casino Corporation (1992)	Writeoff of deferred preacquisition costs
Imperial Holly Corporation (1994)	Work force reduction charge
Sun Microsystems (1993)	Securities class action lawsuits
Trimark Holdings, Inc. (1995)	Litigation settlement
Revenues or gains	
Amtran, Inc. (1992)	Gain on sale of takeoff/landing slots
Artistic Greetings, Inc. (1995)	Unrealized gains on trading securities
Ferro Corporation (1993)	Foreign currency transaction gain
Freeport-McMoRan, Inc. (1991)	Insurance settlement (tanker grounding)
Lin Broadcasting Corporation (1992)	Litigation settlement
Meredith Corporation (1994)	Sale of broadcast stations
New England Business Service, Inc. (1996)	Gain on sale of product line
Noble Drilling (1991)	Insurance on rig abandoned in Somalia
Pollo Tropical, Inc. (1995)	Business interruption insurance recovery

SOURCES: Companies' annual reports. The year following each company name designates the annual report from which each example was drawn.

enue or gain and expense or loss are either presented as separate line items within the listing of revenues or gain and expense or loss or included in an "other income (expense)" line.

Nonrecurring Items Located under Income from Continuing Operations

The region in the income statement under income from continuing operations has a standard organization that is the same for both the single- and multistep income statements. This format is outlined in the following table.

Standard Income Statement Format

Income from continuing operations	$000
Discontinued operations	000
Extraordinary items	000
Cumulative effect of changes in accounting principles	000
Net income	$000

The income statement of General Signal, shown in Exhibit 2.5, illustrates this format. Each of the special line items—discontinued operations, extraordinary items, and changes in accounting principles—is discussed, along with illustrative examples, in the following sections.

Discontinued Operations

The discontinued operations section is designed to enhance the interpretive value of the income statement through separation of the results of continuing operations from those that have been, or are in the process of being, discontinued. Only the discontinuance of operations that constitute a separate and complete segment of the business are to be reported in this special section.

Examples of operations that have been viewed as separate segments, and therefore classified as "discontinued operations," are provided in Exhibit 2.8.

EXHIBIT 2.8   Examples of discontinued operations.

Company	Principal Business	Discontinued Operation
Atlantic American Corp. (1995)	Insurance	Retail furniture
Chiquita Brands (1991)	Fresh fruits, vegetables, and processed foods	Meat segment
Clorox Corporation (1995)	Branded consumer products	Bottled water and frozen foods
Ecolab, Inc. (1992)	Cleaning, sanitizing, and maintenance products and services	Lawn care (Chem-Lawn)
Ethyl Corporation (1993)	Chemicals	Insurance Company
General Electric Company (1993)	Diversified manufacturing and financial services	Aerospace business
Gleason Corporation (1995)	Gear machinery and equipment	Metal stamping and fabricating
International Technology (1995)	Environmental management	Pollution control manufacturing
Kodak (1993)	Imaging	Chemical business
Maxco, Inc. (1996)	Manufacturing, distribution, and real estate	Automotive refinishing products
Owens-Illinois, Inc. (1993)	Packaging products	Glass tableware
Quaker State Corporation (1992)	Petroleum products and related activities plus insurance	Coal operations
Texfi Industries, Inc. (1995)	Textile manufacturer	Commodity yarn, corduroy, and diaper fabric production
Thomas Nelson, Inc. (1996)	Publishes books, music and produces specialty gift items	Christian-lifestyle magazines and radio networks
Waverly, Inc. (1995)	Publisher of books and periodicals	Printing operations

SOURCES: Companies' annual reports. The year following each company name designates the annual report from which each example was drawn.

Extraordinary Items

Income statement items are considered extraordinary if they are *both* (1) un-usual and (2) infrequent in occurrence.[8] Unusual items are not related to the typical activities or operations of the firm. Infrequency of occurrence simply implies that the item is not expected to recur in the foreseeable future.

In practice, the joint requirement of "unusual and nonrecurring" results in very few items being reported as extraordinary. Generally accepted accounting principles do require that gains or losses associated with two particular transac-tions be classified as extraordinary without the need to satisfy the tests of their being both unusual and nonrecurring: (1) gains and losses from the extinguish-ment of debt,[9] and (2) gains or losses resulting from "troubled debt restructur-ings."[10] Included in the latter case are either the settlement of obligations or their continuation with a modification of terms.

A tabulation of extraordinary items, based upon an annual survey of 600 companies conducted by the American Institute of CPAs, is provided in Exhibit 2.9. This summary highlights the relative rarity of extraordinary items under cur-rent reporting requirements. Debt extinguishments represent the largest por-tion of the disclosed extraordinary items. Extraordinary items associated with operating loss carryforwards have now been eliminated under the new require-ments of Statement of Financial Accounting Standard No. 109, "Accounting for Income Taxes."[11] This leaves only from four to six *judgmental* extraordinary items per year among the 600 companies surveyed.

The small number of gains and losses classified as extraordinary is consis-tent with their definition. However, this adds to the challenge of locating all non-recurring items as part of a thorough earnings analysis. Few nonrecurring items will qualify for the prominent disclosure that results from display in one of the special sections, such as for extraordinary items, of the income statement. A review of recent annual reports highlights the variation in practice resulting from

EXHIBIT 2.9   Frequency and nature of extraordinary items.

	1991	1992	1993	1994
Debt extinguishments	33	60	79	59
Operating loss carryforwards	20	17	9	—
Litigation settlements	1	2	1	—
Other	4	5	6	—
Total extraordinary items	58	84	95	59
Companies presenting extraordinary items	55	81	91	59
Companies not presenting extraordinary items	545	519	509	541
Total companies	600	600	600	600

SOURCE: American Institute of Certified Public Accountants, *Accounting Trends and Techniques* (1995), p. 426.

application of the "unusual and nonrecurring" test to determine extraordinary items. Exhibit 2.10 presents a number of nonrecurring transactions, some of which were and some were not treated as extraordinary. The similarity between the two groups highlights the degree of judgment involved in applying the classification rules. For example, Raychem[12] reported a charge from a class-action litigation settlement as extraordinary and Scientific-Atlanta[13] did not. Each case involved a class-action securities suit. As each appears to be nonrecurring, the classification decision must have turned on whether the charges were unusual. It becomes more difficult to consider such items as unusual in today's litigious environment. Raychem's 1993 Form 10-K lists ten different legal proceedings.[14] However, they are all related to the operation of the business, not to relations

EXHIBIT 2.10   Extraordinary item classification decisions.

Item or Event	Company
Reported as extraordinary	
Settlement of class action litigation	Raychem Corporation (1992)
Gain on insurance settlement due to damage to building from San Francisco earthquake	American Building Maintenance (1989)
Insurance settlement due to deprivation of use of logistics and drilling equipment abandoned in Somalia due to civil unrest	Noble Drilling Corporation (1991)
Gain on insurance settlement resulting from a drilling rig being subject to theft and vandalism	Noble Drilling Corporation (1989)
Gain on downward revision of obligation to United Mine Workers of America Combined Benefit Fund	NACCO Industries (1995)
Loss from accidental melting of radioactive substance in the steelmaking operation	NS Group (1992)
Gain from settlement with the government of Iran over the expropriation of Phillips' oil production interests	Phillips Petroleum (1990)
Not reported as extraordinary	
Settlement of securities class action litigation	Scientific-Atlanta (1994)
Gain from a settlement with the government of Iran over the expropriation of Sun oil production interests	Sun Company (1992)
Hurricane loss	Alexander & Baldwin, Inc. (1992)
Flood costs	Argosy Gaming (1993)
Insurance claim settlement (airplane crash)	On The Border Cafes (1994)
Gain from insurance settlement as a result of the loss of Rowan Gorilla I jack-up, which capsized and sank while being towed to the North Sea	Rowan Companies (1988)
Loss provision for costs associated with cleanup of oil spill in Valdez Alaska	Exxon (1989)

SOURCES: Companies' annual reports. The year following each company name designates the annual report from which each example was drawn.

with investors in Raychem. Material losses from these cases are more likely to be classified as part of operating results.

American Building Maintenance treated the results of a natural disaster, an earthquake, as extraordinary, but Alexander Baldwin, Inc., did not classify its loss from a natural disaster, a hurricane, as extraordinary. Again, in the Bay Area of San Francisco, the location of American Building's loss, it would seem difficult to consider earthquakes as unusual. However, an earthquake of the magnitude of the one in 1989 is clearly an exceptional event.

The last examples in the two classifications, Phillips Petroleum Co. and Sun Company, Inc., represent the sharpest contrast because the gains they reported appear to be identical. That is, each company received settlements from the government of Iran as a result of the expropriation of oil production interests during the Iranian revolution.

The judgmental character of the definition of extraordinary items, combined with the growing complexity of company operations, results in the diversity in classification revealed in Exhibit 2.10. The task of locating all nonrecurring items of revenue or gain and expense or loss is aided only marginally by the presence of the extraordinary category in the income statement, because it is employed so sparingly. Location of most nonrecurring items calls for careful review of other parts of the income statement, other statements, and notes to the financial statements.

Changes in Accounting Principles

Changes in accounting principles, for example, the adoption of newer accounting standards for income taxes and postretirement benefits, and changes in estimates, such as an increase in useful lives used in computing depreciation, are the principal types of changes that affect earnings analysis.

In changing from one accepted accounting principle to another, the most common reporting treatment is to show the cumulative effect of the change, on the results of prior years, as a single total, net of taxes, in the income statement for the year of the change. Less common is the retroactive-effect approach whereby statements of prior years are restated on the new accounting basis. The effect on years prior to those presented in the annual report for the year of the change, usually three years, is treated as an adjustment to retained earnings of the earliest year presented. Recent accounting standards have sometimes required one of the two methods of reporting a change in principle, and in other cases either has been permitted.

Accounting changes in recent years have been dominated by the requirements to adopt a series of new Financial Accounting Standards Board statements. Information on accounting changes, both in accounting principles and in estimates, is provided in Exhibits 2.11 and 2.12. This information is drawn from the annual financial statement survey conducted by the American Institute of

EXHIBIT 2.11   Accounting changes.

Subject of the Change	Number of Companies			
	1991	1992	1993	1994
Pension actuarial assumptions	151	121	224	274
Investments (SFAS No. 115)	—	—	21	108
Income taxes				
SFAS 109 adopted	16	244	233	89
SFAS 96 adopted	16	—	—	—
Postemployment benefits	—	21	87	80
Postretirement benefits	39	198	176	44
Depreciable lives	4	6	6	6
Inventories:				
LIFO discontinued	3	4	6	1
LIFO adopted	2	3	1	1
Capitalization of cost				
formerly expensed	3	2	—	1
Other	3	—	2	2
Reinsurance contracts	—	—	7	2
Reporting entity	1	5	5	1
Depreciation method	5	3	3	—
Other—described	18	17	21	28

SOURCE: American Institute of Certified Public Accountants, *Accounting Trends and Techniques* (1995), p. 43.

Certified Public Accountants. The distribution of adoption dates results because some firms adopted the new statement prior to its mandatory adoption date. For example, the latest that Statement of Financial Accounting Standard (SFAS) No. 109 could be adopted was for fiscal years beginning after December 15, 1992, or calendar 1993 for firms with a December 31 year-end.

EXHIBIT 2.12   Separating the current period and cumulative impact of a change in accounting principle: Federal-Mogul Corporation (millions of dollars).

	1993	1992
Incremental annual expense	$ 6.6	$ 7.6
Income tax benefit	(2.4)	(2.7)
	4.2	4.9
Cumulative effect of		
accounting change		135.7
Income tax benefit		(47.6)
	—	88.1
Net effect of SFAS 106	$ 4.2	$ 93.0

SOURCE: Federal-Mogul Corporation, annual report, December 1993, p. 33.

Most recent changes in accounting principle have been reported on a cumulative-effect basis. The cumulative effect is reported, net of tax, in a separate section of the income statement. The cumulative effect is the impact of the change on the results of previous years. The impact of the change on the current year, that is, year of the change, is typically disclosed in a note describing the change and its impact. However, it is not disclosed separately on the face of the income statement. An example of disclosure of the separate effects (current and prior year) of the adoption of SFAS 106, *Employers' Accounting for Postretirement Benefits Other Than Pensions,* by Federal Mogul Corporation, is provided in Exhibit 2.12.

The incremental effect of the adoption of SFAS 106 is properly excluded, that is, added back to results, if the objective is to compare 1992 results with those of 1991 on a consistent basis. However, if the goal is to arrive at a sustainable earnings base for purposes of forecasting future results, then the incremental annual expense is part of future results and should not be removed. The cumulative effect would still be added in developing a sustainable earnings series.

Changes in Estimates

Whereas changes in accounting principles are handled on either a cumulative-effect or retroactive restatement basis, changes in accounting estimates are handled on a prospective basis only. The impact of a change is included only in current or future periods; retroactive restatements are not permitted. For example, in its 1993 fourth quarter, Delta Air Lines implemented two changes in estimates: (1) an extension of the useful life of its flight equipment to 20 from 15 years and a reduction in their estimated residual values to 5% from 10% of cost, and (2) an increase in the expected long-term rate of return on pension assets of from 9 to 10%. Delta reported that "flight equipment that was not already fully depreciated is being depreciated on a straight-line basis to residual values (5% of cost) over a 20-year period from the dates placed in service."[15] Delta disclosed that the changes in useful life and residual value estimates reduced the level of depreciation for 1993 by $34 million. Since the change affected only the fourth quarter of 1993, the size of the impact for the next full year would have been four times this amount, or $136 million. Prospective application of the change in estimate involved computing future depreciation based upon the new useful life and residual value estimates. Depreciation expense for 1993 was simply $34 million less than it would have been under the prior useful life and residual value assumptions. No separate identification of the impact of the change appeared in the 1993 income statement.

The increase in the pension return assumption reduced operating expenses by $13 million for the single quarter in 1993 for which the change was effective. This amounts to an expense reduction of $52 million on an annualized basis: $13 million reduction per quarter × four quarters = $52 million. Pension expense is reduced by an amount equal to the return assumption multiplied by pension fund assets. If the assumed rate of return is increased, then so is the pension return deducted in arriving at a net pension expense. The annualized effects of Delta's two estimate changes, $136 million from the depreciation change and $52 million from the pension return change, should have added $188 million to 1994 pretax results.

The implications for earnings analysis of changes in accounting principles, for example, a switch from accelerated to straight-line depreciation, versus changes in estimates differ. A change in accounting principle reported on a cumulative-effect basis places a clear nonrecurring item in the income statement. However, a change in estimate, for example, Delta's extension of the useful life of its flight equipment, simply shifts the amount of an expense or revenue item to a different level on an ongoing basis. A comparison of Delta's financial performance in 1993 (year of the change) to that of 1992 must place 1993 net income on the same basis as 1992 net income. Therefore, 1993 net income should be reduced by the combined after-tax benefit of the depreciation and pension changes. However, a projection of Delta's 1994 net income, as distinguished from a comparison of 1993 with 1992, should employ 1993 net income with a further adjustment to put the benefits of both the depreciation and pension changes on a full-year basis.

NONRECURRING ITEMS IN THE STATEMENT OF CASH FLOWS

After the income statement, the operating activities section of the statement of cash flows is an excellent secondary source of disclosure of nonrecurring items (step 2 in the search sequence). The diagnostic value of this section of the statement of cash flows results from two factors: (1) Gains and losses on the sale of investments and fixed assets must be removed from net income in arriving at cash flow from operating activities, and (2) noncash items of revenue or gain and expense or loss must be removed from net income. All cash flow associated with the sale of investments and fixed assets is to be classified in the investment section of the statement of cash flows. This requires removal of the gains or losses, which are typically nonrecurring in nature, on the sale of such items in arriving at cash flow from operating activities. Similarly, many nonrecurring expenses or losses do not involve a current-period cash outflow. This requires that such items be adjusted out of net income in arriving at cash flow from operating activities. Such adjustments, assuming that they are not simply combined in a miscellaneous balance, often highlight nonrecurring items.

The partial statement of cash flows of Eagle-Picher Industries, Inc., as shown in Exhibit 2.13, illustrates the disclosure of nonrecurring items in the operating activities section of the statement of cash flows. The nonrecurring items would appear to be (1) the provisions for asbestos litigation, (2) the provision for environmental claims, (3) the cumulative effect of the accounting change, and (4)

EXHIBIT 2.13   Nonrecurring items disclosure in the statement of cash flows: Eagle-Picher Industries, Inc. consolidated statements of cash flow (in thousands).

	1993	1994	1995
Operating activities			
Net income (loss)	$(1,157,368)	$ 48,749	$(944,171)
Adjustments to reconcile net income (loss) to net cash provided by operating activities:			
Provision for asbestos litigation	1,135,500	—	1,005,511
Provision for environmental and other claims	41,436	—	—
Cumulative effect of accounting change	12,578	—	—
Depreciation and amortization	24,955	26,143	28,708
Changes in assets and liabilities:			
Receivables	(10,764)	(11,544)	(17,914)
Inventories	(4,098)	(13,676)	(1,665)
Deferred income taxes	(12,137)	(14,000)	(18,900)
Accounts payable	5,539	11,326	(3,373)
Other	2,015	(1,905)	(6,235)
Net cash provided by operating activities	$ 37,676	$ 45,093	$ 30,456

SOURCE: Eagle-Picher Industries, Inc., annual report, November 1995, p. 16.

the gain on the sale of an investment. The Eagle-Picher income statement also disclosed, on separate lines, each of the nonrecurring items revealed in the operating activities section. The provisions for both asbestos litigation and environmental claims, along with the cumulative effect of the accounting change, are added back to net income because they represent obligations that have been accrued but not yet paid. The gain on sale of the investment is deducted from net income in the computation of cash from operating activities because all cash from such transactions must be classified in the investing activities section.

Examples of nonrecurring items disclosed in the operating activities section of a number of different companies are presented next. Frequently, nonrecurring items appear in both the income statement and operating activities section of the statement of cash flows. However, none of the nonrecurring items in the schedule in Exhibit 2.14 was separately disclosed in the company income statement. The operating activities section is a very productive source of information on nonrecurring items.

NONRECURRING ITEMS IN THE INVENTORY DISCLOSURES OF LIFO FIRMS

The carrying values of inventories maintained under the LIFO method are often significantly understated in relationship to replacement cost. For public compa-

EXHIBIT 2.14   Nonrecurring items in the operating activities section of the cash flow statement but not in the income statement.

Company	Nonrecurring Item
Apogee Enterprises; Inc. (1996)	Gain on sale of a business
Avon Products, Inc. (1993)	Translation losses
Biomet, Inc. (1996)	Gain on sale of securities
Cyprus Amax Minerals Company (1995)	Gain on sales of assets
IBP, Inc. (1993)	Loss on disposal of properties
Internet Corporation (1995)	Writedown of equipment and goodwill
Jacob's Engineering Group, Inc. (1994)	Gains on disposals of property and equipment
Martin Color Fi, Inc. (1995)	Inventory writedown
Modine Manufacturing Company (1995/96)	Gain on sale of business
Scott Paper Company (1993)	Gains and losses on asset sales
Sherwin-Williams (1993)	Provisions for disposition of operations and for environmental remediation
SCI Systems, Inc. (1993)	Unrealized foreign exchange losses
Tiffany & Co. (1995)	Gain on sale of subsidiary, impairment loss, and loss on disposal of fixed assets
Zycad Corporation (1993)	Gain on sale of Synopsys stock

SOURCES: Companies' annual reports. The year following each company name designates the annual report from which the example was drawn.

nies, the difference between the LIFO carrying value and replacement cost (frequently approximated by FIFO) is a required disclosure under Securities and Exchange Commission regulations.[16] An example of a substantial difference between LIFO and current replacement value is found in a summary of the inventory disclosures of Handy and Harman in Exhibit 2.15.

A reduction in the physical inventory quantities of a LIFO inventory is called a *LIFO liquidation*. With a LIFO liquidation, a portion of the firm's cost of sales for the year will be made up of the carrying values associated with the liquidated units. These costs are typically lower than current replacement costs, resulting in increased profits or reduced losses.

As with the differences between the LIFO cost and replacement value of the LIFO inventory, Securities and Exchange Commission regulations also call for disclosures of the effect of LIFO liquidations.[17] The following disclosure in

EXHIBIT 2.15   LIFO inventory valuation differences: Handy and Harman (in thousands).

	1994	1995
Precious metals stated at LIFO cost	$32,450	$28,870
LIFO inventory—excess of year-end market value over LIFO cost	$139,068	$141,458

SOURCE: Handy and Harman, annual report, 1995, p. 26.

EXHIBIT 2.16   Nonrecurring gains from LIFO liquidations: Wyman-Gordon Company (in thousands).[18]

	1992	1993	1994	1995
Lower quantities	$18,388	$5,469	$2,050	$7,567
(Inflation) deflation	2,448	4,450	1,085	(1,393)
Net increase to income from operations	$20,836	$9,919	$3,135	$6,174

SOURCE: Wyman-Gordon, annual report, 1995, p. 27.

Exhibit 2.16, from the statements of Wyman-Gordon Company, illustrates compliance with this requirement.

The 1992 impact of the LIFO liquidation is quite dramatic. The $18,388,000 increase in 1992 income from operations amounted to 67% of the $27,275,000 of income from operations for the year. Even though Wyman-Gordon reported LIFO liquidations for each of the years 1991 to 1993, an analysis of sustainable earnings should consider the profit improvements from the liquidations to be nonrecurring. The LIFO-liquidation benefits result from reductions in the physical quantity of inventory. There are obvious limits on the ability to sustain these liquidations in future years; the inventory cannot be reduced below zero. Moreover, the variability in the size of the effect on profits of the liquidations argues for the nonrecurring classification. The profit improvement resulting from the LIFO liquidation amounts to nothing more than the realization of an undervalued asset. It is analogous to the gain associated with the disposition of an undervalued security, piece of equipment, or plot of land.

A statement user cannot rely on the disclosure requirements of the Securities and Exchange Commission when reviewing the statements of nonpublic companies, especially where an outside accountant has performed only a review or compilation.[19] However, one can infer the possibility of a LIFO liquidation through the combination of a decline in the dollar amount of inventory across the year combined with an otherwise unexplainable improvement in gross margins. Details on the existence and impact of a LIFO liquidation could then be a subject for discussion with management.

NONRECURRING ITEMS IN THE INCOME TAX NOTE

Income tax notes are among the more challenging of the disclosures found in annual reports. However, mastering this challenge is worth the effort because they can be a rich source of information on nonrecurring items. Fortunately, our emphasis here on the persistence of earnings permits us to focus only on a subset of the information found in tax notes.

EXHIBIT 2.17   Reconciliation of statutory and actual federal income taxes: Biogen, Inc. (in thousands).

	1991	1992	1993
Income tax at statutory rates	$2,532	$13,577	$12,116
Foreign income tax (benefit) at other than U.S. rates	56	(655)	(253)
Utilization of net operating loss carryforwards	(2,510)	(14,070)	(11,159)
Effects of losses not currently utilizable	—	2,562	1,187
Other	182	206	309
Reported income tax expense	$ 260	$ 1,620	$ 2,200

SOURCE: Biogen, Inc., annual report, December 1993, p. 29.

Under the requirements of current GAAP related to tax disclosures, the location of nonrecurring tax items calls for mastery and review of only two elements of the tax notes. The first is a schedule that reconciles the actual tax expense or credit with the amount that would have resulted if all pretax results had been taxed at the statutory federal rate. The tax disclosures shown in Exhibit 2.17 of Biogen, Inc. provide an illustration of this schedule.

Notice that Biogen's tax expense is substantially reduced in each of the years 1991 to 1993 due to the utilization of losses from earlier years. Current U.S. tax law permits net operating losses to first be carried back, providing a refund of prior taxes, for 3 years and then, if not fully utilized, to be carried forward for 15 years, providing a shield against future tax payments. Biogen's carryforward benefits have a very substantial favorable impact on its current profitability. For example, the net operating loss carryforward benefits in 1992 and 1993 amount to 37% and 34%, respectively, of net income. However, these benefits are not a sustainable element of operating results. Biogen's tax note discloses the availability of $89 million of unused net operating loss carryforwards, plus $11 million of tax credit carryforwards. As a result, near-term projections of results should continue to assume that profits will be substantially shielded from taxation. However, the amount of unused net operating loss and tax credit carryforwards will not last forever and should be closely monitored.

A strong indicator of nonrecurring tax benefits is an unusually low effective tax rate. This condition should first be noticed upon initial review of the income statement, step one in the search sequence outlined in Exhibit 2.3. The percentage relation between Biogen's tax provision and its income before taxes for 1991 to 1993 are shown in Exhibit 2.18.

Another source of nonrecurring tax benefits are tax reductions and tax credits offered by foreign governments to encourage investment and to increase employment in their countries. The tax reconciliation schedule of C. R. Bard,

**EXHIBIT 2.18   Effective tax rate: Biogen, Inc.
(dollars in thousands)**

	1991	1992	1993
Total income tax provision	$ 260	$ 1,620	$ 2,200
Income before income taxes	7,446	39,931	34,617
°Effective tax rate	3.5%	4.1%	6.4%

°The actual tax provision divided by earnings before income taxes.
SOURCE: Biogen Inc., annual report, December 1993, p. 28.

Inc. (see Exhibit 2.19) provides an illustration. The substantial reductions in Bard's effective rate will be maintained only if Bard continues to conduct operations in Ireland and Puerto Rico, if the associated laws remain in effect, and if Bard's eligibility for these tax benefits continues. This series of "ifs" means that an important element of Bard's future net income is subject to an additional element of uncertainty.

Expanding somewhat on the C. R. Bard example, we examine information from the 1995 annual report of Digital Equipment Corporation. Digital's tax reconciliation schedule details tax benefits from the taxation of manufacturing operations in Puerto Rico (operations discontinued in fiscal 1993), Ireland, and Singapore. It discloses the nature of these arrangements as follows:[20]

> Ireland: The income from products manufactured for export by the corporation's manufacturing subsidiary in Ireland is subject to a 10% tax rate through December 2010.
>
> Singapore: The income from certain products manufactured by the corporation's manufacturing subsidiary in Singapore is taxed at approximately 15% through December 1995.

These data on Digital's tax benefits reveal that all the arrangements are for limited periods of time. Continuation of this boost to profitability is obviously not assured.

**EXHIBIT 2.19   Effective tax rate reduced by operations
in Ireland and Puerto Rico: C. R. Bard, Inc.**

	1992	1993	1994
Tax based on statutory rate	34%	35%	35%
State income tax net of federal income tax benefits	2	3	2
Operations taxed at less than statutory rate, primarily Ireland and Puerto Rico	(10)	(11)	(10)
Justice Department settlement		7	
Other, net	4	3	4
Effective tax rate	30%	37%	26%

SOURCE: C. R. Bard, Inc., annual report, December 1994, p. 25.

In addition to net operating loss carryforwards and tax benefits offered by foreign governments, a variety of other tax-law features produce nonrecurring tax expenses or tax benefits. These include:

1. Tax reductions from other loss carryforwards and various tax credits and tax credit carryforwards such as capital loss carryforwards, research and development tax credits, alternative minimum tax-credit carryforwards, and foreign tax credits.
2. Tax increases or decreases resulting from revaluations of deferred tax assets and liabilities as a result of changes in income tax rates.
3. Tax increases or decreases resulting from the resolution of disputes with tax authorities.
4. Tax increases or decreases attributable to changes in the deferred tax valuation allowance based upon (a) realization of previously unrecognized deferred tax benefits or (b) revised estimations of the likelihood of realization of deferred tax assets.

NONRECURRING ITEMS IN THE "OTHER INCOME (EXPENSE)" NOTE

An "other income (expense), net" or equivalent title, line item, or section is commonly found in both the single- and multistep income statement. In the case of the multistep format, the composition of other income and expenses is sometimes detailed on the face of the income statement. In both the multistep and single-step formats, the most typical presentation is a single line item with a supporting note, if the items included in the total are material. Even though a note detailing the contents of the other income and expense may exist, guidance is typically not provided as to its specific location. A note often exists even in the absence of a specific note reference. Where present, "other income (expense)" notes tend to be listed close to the end of the notes to the financial statements.

Small Net Balances May Obscure the Presence of Large Nonrecurring Items

Even if their net amount is small, the composition of other income and expense balances should be explored. For example, a small net balance may result from nonrecurring expense items offsetting recurring items of income. An illustration of this point is the "Other Income (Expense)—Net" note found in the 1993 annual report of 3Com Corporation displayed in Exhibit 2.20. In 1992, there was an apparent temporary increase of about $2 million (nonrecurring element) in the level of the provision for doubtful accounts. The $1.7 million in "Other" is a

EXHIBIT 2.20   Details of an other income (expense) note: 3Com Corporation (in thousands).

	1993	1992	1991
Interest income	$3,602	$5,080	$6,143
Provision for doubtful accounts	(1,995)	(3,683)	(1,691)
Other	(2,284)	(1,744)	(2,570)
Total	$ (677)	$ (347)	$1,882

SOURCE: 3Com Corporation, annual report, December, 1993, p. 34.

combination of losses on property and equipment dispositions and foreign-exchange transactions. These should also be viewed as nonrecurring. As a result, a net line-item balance of only $347 thousand masks nonrecurring charges of about $3.7 million. Thus, one should always look for details on the composition of other income and expense, even where its net amount is small.

"Other Income (Expense)" Notes Typically Include a Mix of Recurring and Nonrecurring Items

The 3Com note in Exhibit 2.20 details the composition of a single "other income (expense)" income statement line item. In contrast, Dresser Industries provides some of the detail on the face of the income statement and then discloses the balance in a note. As with 3Com above, the balance is a mix of recurring and nonrecurring items. Both the income statement display and note information of Dresser are provided in Exhibit 2.21.

From the Dresser Industries income statement disclosure, nonrecurring gains of about $287 million on investments are evident. The note disclosure reveals further nonrecurring candidates in the form of the "gain on business disposal," "retirement medical benefit plan curtailment," "gains on sales of assets," and the "foreign exchange" line items. In addition to these disclosures, there is also commentary on the "other income" category in MD&A of financial condition and results of operations. The value of this section of the annual report of public companies, as an aid in locating nonrecurring items, is discussed next.

NONRECURRING ITEMS IN MANAGEMENT'S DISCUSSION AND ANALYSIS (MD&A)

MD&A of financial condition and results of operations is an annual and a quarterly Securities and Exchange Commission reporting requirement. Provisions of this

EXHIBIT 2.21   Income statement and note disclosures of "other income (expense)" elements: Dresser Industries (in millions).

	1993	1994	1995
From income statement			
Other income (deductions)			
Interest expense	$(27.4)	$ (49.3)	$(47.4)
Interest earned	16.0	31.1	21.6
Gain on sale of interest in Western Atlas	—	275.7	—
Gain on affiliate's public offering	—	11.0	—
Other, net	19.3	(3.4)	6.3
Total other income, net	$ 32.3	$299.3	$(19.5)
From note			
Composition of "Other, net"			
Gain on business disposal	$ —	$ 7.1	$ —
Retiree medical benefit plan curtailment	12.8	—	—
Gains on sales of assets	4.8	3.1	7.5
Foreign exchange gain (loss)	1.7	(13.6)	(1.2)
Total "Other, net"	$ 19.3	$ (3.4)	$6.3

SOURCE: Dresser Industries, Inc., annual report, October 1995. Information obtained from *Disclosure, Inc., Compact D/SEC: Corporate Information on Public Companies Filing with the SEC* (Bethesda, MD: Disclosure, Inc., September, 1996).

regulation have a direct bearing on our goal of locating nonrecurring items. As part of the MD&A, the Securities and Exchange Commission requires registrants to:

> Describe any unusual or infrequent events or transactions or any significant economic changes that materially affected the amount of reported income from continuing operations and, in each case, indicate the extent to which income was so affected. In addition, describe any other significant components of revenues and expenses that, in the registrant's judgment, should be described in order to understand the registrant's results of operations.[21]

Responding to the preceding means firms have to identify and discuss items that may have already been listed in other financial statements and notes. In reviewing the MD&A with a view to locating nonrecurring items, attention should be focused on the section dealing with results of operations. Here is presented a comparison of results over the most recent three years, with the standard pattern involving discussion of, for example, 1996 with 1995 and 1995 with 1994.

Locating nonrecurring items in MD&A is somewhat more difficult than locating these items in other places. Typically, the nonrecurring items in MD&A are discussed in text and are not set out in schedules or statements.

A small number of firms do summarize nonrecurring items in schedules within MD&A. The information on nonrecurring items in Exhibit 2.22 is from the 1995 annual report of Unocal Corporation. This schedule summarizes, in a

EXHIBIT 2.22   Nonrecurring items included in MD&A of financial condition and results of operations: Unocal Corporation (in millions).

	1993	1994	1995
Net earnings excluding special items	$347	$ 300	$297
Special items:			
Cumulative effect of accounting changes	(130)	(277)	—
Impairment of long-lived assets (SFAS No. 121)	—	—	(53)
Litigation	(30)	(43)	(37)
Environmental remediation provisions	(10)	(99)	(26)
Writedowns of assets	(12)	(44)	(12)
Asset sales	66	8	71
Provision for abandonment and remediation of the Guadalupe oil field	—	(16)	—
Restructuring costs	—	(15)	—
Other	(18)	33	20
Net earnings (loss) including special items	$213	$(153)	$260

single location, the after-tax impact of the listed nonrecurring items on Unocal's results for 1993 to 1995. All of these items would have been located by completing steps 1 to 5 of the search sequence outlined in Exhibit 2.3.

The presentation within the MD&A of information on nonrecurring items in schedules is still a fairly limited practice but may be on the rise.[22] Though helpful for the task of locating nonrecurring items, such schedules must be viewed as useful complements to, but not substitutes for, a complete search process. A review of the scope of items presented in such schedules reveals that the displays are sometimes limited to only a subset of nonrecurring items. A sampling of omissions of nonrecurring items from MD&A schedules of nonrecurring items is provided in Exhibit 2.23. These omissions probably reflect issues of materiality as well as the judgmental aspect of the nonrecurring designation.

NONRECURRING ITEMS IN OTHER SELECTED NOTES

The preceding discussion has illustrated the location of nonrecurring items through steps 1 to 6 of the search sequence outlined in Exhibit 2.3. Generally, most material nonrecurring items will have been located by proceeding through these first six steps. Occasionally, however, additional nonrecurring items will be located in other notes. It is possible for nonrecurring items to surface in virtually

EXHIBIT 2.23   Sample omissions from MD&A schedules of nonrecurring items.

Company	Nonrecurring Items Omitted
Amoco Corporation (1995)	Foreign exchange gains and losses
Carpenter Technology (1991)	LIFO liquidation gains
Deere & Company (1994)	LIFO liquidation gains
Doskocil Companies (1993)	Impact of a strike Insurance gain
Halliburton Company (1994)	Foreign currency losses
Maxus Energy Corporation (1993)	Gains on sales of assets

SOURCES: Companies' annual reports. The year following each company name designates the annual report from which each example was drawn.

any note to the financial statements. Three selected notes, which frequently contain other nonrecurring items, are now discussed: foreign exchange, restructuring, and quarterly and segment financial data.

Foreign Exchange Notes

Foreign exchange gains and losses can result from both transactions, for example, accounts receivable or payable denominated in foreign currencies, and translation exposure from foreign subsidiaries. They can also result from the use of various currency contracts such as forwards, futures, options, and swaps employed for purposes of both hedging and speculation. It is not uncommon to observe foreign exchange gains and losses year after year in a company's income statement. However, it is also the case that the amount and nature, a gain versus loss, of these items will typically be very irregular.

To illustrate, a portion of a note titled "foreign currency translation" from the 1993 annual report of Dibrell Brothers, Inc. is reproduced here:

> Net gains and losses arising from transaction adjustments are accumulated on a net basis by entity and are included in the Statement of Consolidated Income, Other Income—Sundry for gains, Other Deductions—Sundry for losses. For 1993, the transaction adjustments netted to a gain of $4,180,000. The transaction adjustments were losses of $565,000 and $206,000 for 1992 and 1991, respectively, and were primarily related to the Company's Brazilian operations.[23]

The gain and losses disclosed appear as adjustments, reflecting either their noncash or nonoperating character, in the operating activities of Dibrell's statement of cash flows. The effect of the 1993 currency exchange gain is also referenced in Dibrell's MD&A as part of the comparison of earnings in 1993 to those in 1992.[24]

While appearing in each of the last three years, Dibrell's foreign-currency gains and losses are far from stable—two years of small losses followed by a year

EXHIBIT 2.24   Contribution of foreign currency gains to pre-tax income from continuing operations: Dibrell Brothers, Inc.

Pretax income from continuing operations	
1993	$58,259,560
1992	43,246,860
Increase	$15,012,700
Foreign currency gains and losses	
1993 gain	$4,180,000
1992 loss	565,000
Improvement	$4,745,000
Contribution of improvement in foreign currency results, 1993 over 1992, to 1993 pretax income from continuing operations: $4,745,000/15,012,700	32%

with a large gain. One way to gauge the significance of these exchange items is to compute their contribution to the growth in income before income taxes, extraordinary items, and cumulative effect of accounting changes. This computation is outlined for 1993 in Exhibit 2.24.

Dibrell's currency gain made a major contribution to its profit growth in 1993. This would explain the fact that a separate note to the financial statements is devoted to its discussion and disclosure. Following the recommended search sequence should have turned up this item at step 2, the statement of cash flows, or step 6, MD&A. If search failures occurred at steps 2 and 6, then examination of the foreign exchange note represents a backup procedure to ensure that the important information contained in this note is available in assessing Dibrell's 1993 performance.

Restructuring Notes

The 1990s have been dominated by the corporate equivalent of a diet program. Call it streamlining, downsizing, rightsizing, redeploying, or strategic restructuring—the end result is that firms have been recording nonrecurring charges of a size and frequency that are unprecedented in our modern economic history. The size and scope of these activities ensures that they leave their tracks throughout the statements and notes. Notes on restructuring charges are among the most common of the transaction-specific notes.

The 1993 restructuring charge of Kimball International illustrates the variety of locations in which the charge and related commentary appear. The Kimball charge reduced operating income by $2,850,000, or 5.8%, in 1993. In the absence of the restructuring charge, Kimball would have had a small increase in operating income of $287,000. Kimball's restructuring charge was extensively

**EXHIBIT 2.25   Restructuring charge disclosures:
                  Kimball International, Inc.**

Location of Disclosure	Page in Annual Report
Separate line item in income statement	22
Separate line item in the statement of cash flows, operating activities section	23
Separate note to the financial statement devoted to the restructuring charge	26
Disclosed and discussed in the MD&A	18
Disclosed with quarterly financial information	29
Disclosed in an 11-year summary of operations	32
Disclosed in the management letter to shareholders	2

SOURCE: Kimball International, Inc., annual report, June 1993.

disclosed because of its material effect on operating income. A summary of this disclosure is provided in Exhibit 2.25.

Restructuring notes sometimes add *prospective* information to the current-period information in the income statement and statements of cash flows. This contributes to improving the quality of earnings expectations. A portion of a restructuring note of The Times Mirror Company is reproduced here:

> The restructuring charges over this three-year period (1991–93) have totaled $325.2 million, or $196.5 million after taxes, principally for severance and payroll-related costs for staff reductions and for expected losses on leased facilities. . . . The restructuring efforts have helped to improve operating results in newspaper publishing and are expected to improve results at the professional publishing companies over the longer term.[25]

While current results were reduced significantly by these restructuring charges, the company projected a favorable effect on future earnings from them. Another restructuring firm, Armstrong World Industries, also projected a favorable impact on future results: "Cash outlays for the 1993 restructuring charges will occur primarily throughout 1994 and should be fully recovered within two to three years."[26]

Quarterly and Segmental Financial Data

Quarterly and segment financial disclosures frequently disclose nonrecurring items. In the case of segment disclosures, the goal is to aid in the evaluation of profitability trends by segments. For example, BF Goodrich Company disclosed the impact of restructuring charges on the operating income of its aerospace and specialty chemicals segments.[27] Firmwide restructuring charges for the affected years were already disclosed in the BF Goodrich income statements. Moreover, breakdowns of the restructuring charges by segment were also provided in MD&A and in a separate restructuring note.

Quarterly financial data of Intermet Corporation disclosed the effect on earnings for the fourth quarter of 1994 of retirement pay and benefits for its previous chairman and vice chairman, as well as severance pay for the planned termination of salaried employees. The only other disclosure of these items was in MD&A.[28]

SUMMARIZING THE EFFECT OF NONRECURRING ITEMS ON SUSTAINABLE EARNINGS

The analysis to this point lays important groundwork, but it is not complete. Still required is a device to assist in summarizing information discovered on nonrecurring items so that new measures of sustainable earnings can be developed. A worksheet designed to summarize nonrecurring items is introduced and its use illustrated in the balance of this chapter. Two different company case studies are employed to illustrate both use and interpretation of the worksheet.

THE SUSTAINABLE EARNINGS WORKSHEET

The sustainable earnings worksheet is shown in Exhibit 2.26.[29] Instructions for completing it follow:

1. Net income or loss is recorded on the top line of the worksheet.
2. All identified items of nonrecurring expense or loss, which were included in the income statement on a pretax basis, are recorded on the "add" lines provided. Where a prelabeled line is not listed in the worksheet, a descriptive phrase should be recorded on one of the "other" lines and the amounts recorded there. In practice, the process of locating nonrecurring items and recording them on the worksheet would take place at the same time. However, effective use of the worksheet calls for the background provided earlier in the chapter. This explains the separation of these steps in the chapter.
3. When all pretax, nonrecurring expenses, and losses have been recorded, subtotals should be computed. These subtotals are then multiplied by 1 minus a representative combined federal, state, and foreign income tax rate. This puts these items on an after-tax basis so that they are stated on the same basis as net income or net loss.
4. The results from step 3 should be recorded on the line titled "tax-adjusted additions."

EXHIBIT 2.26   Adjustment worksheet for sustainable earnings base.

	Year	Year	Year
Reported net income or (loss)	___	___	___
Add			
Pre-tax LIFO liquidation losses	___	___	___
Losses on sales of fixed assets	___	___	___
Losses on sales of investments	___	___	___
Losses on sales of other asset	___	___	___
Restructuring charges	___	___	___
Investment writedowns	___	___	___
Inventory writedowns	___	___	___
Other asset writedowns	___	___	___
Foreign currency losses	___	___	___
Litigation charges	___	___	___
Losses on patent infringement suits	___	___	___
Exceptional bad-debt provisions	___	___	___
Nonrecurring expense increases	___	___	___
Temporary revenue reductions	___	___	___
Other	___	___	___
Other	___	___	___
Other	___	___	___
Subtotal	___	___	___
Multiply by			
(1 – combined federal, state tax rates)	___	___	___
Tax-adjusted additions	___	___	___
Add			
After-tax LIFO liquidation losses	___	___	___
Increases in deferred tax valuation allowances	___	___	___
Other nonrecurring tax charges	___	___	___
Losses on discontinued operations	___	___	___
Extraordinary losses	___	___	___
Losses/cumulative-effect accounting changes	___	___	___
Other	___	___	___
Other	___	___	___
Other	___	___	___
Subtotal	___	___	___
Total additions	___	___	___

(Continued)

EXHIBIT 2.26   *(Continued).*

	Year	Year	Year
Deduct			
Pretax LIFO liquidation gains	——	——	——
Gains on fixed asset sales	——	——	——
Gains on sales of investments	——	——	——
Gains on sales of other assets	——	——	——
Reversals of restructuring charges	——	——	——
Investment writeups (trading account)	——	——	——
Foreign currency gains	——	——	——
Litigation revenues	——	——	——
Gains on patent infringement suits	——	——	——
Temporary expense decreases	——	——	——
Temporary revenue increases	——	——	——
Reversals of bad-debt allowances	——	——	——
Other	——	——	——
Other	——	——	——
Other	——	——	——
Subtotal	——	——	——
Multiply by			
Times (1 – combined federal, state tax rate)	——	——	——
Tax-adjusted deductions	——	——	——
After-tax LIFO liquidation gains	——	——	——
Reductions in deferred tax valuation allowances	——	——	——
Loss carryforward benefits from prior periods	——	——	——
Other nonrecurring tax benefits	——	——	——
Gains on discontinued operations	——	——	——
Extraordinary gains	——	——	——
Gains/cumulative-effect accounting changes	——	——	——
Other	——	——	——
Other	——	——	——
Other	——	——	——
Subtotal	——	——	——
Total deductions	——	——	——
Sustainable earnings base	══	══	══

5. All after-tax nonrecurring expenses or losses are next added separately. These items will typically be either tax items or special income statement items that are disclosed on an after-tax basis under GAAP, for example, discontinued operations, extraordinary items, or the cumulative effect of accounting changes. The effects of LIFO liquidations are sometimes presented pretax and sometimes after-tax. Note that a line item is provided for the effect of LIFO liquidations in both the pretax and after-tax additions section of the worksheet.

6. Changes in deferred-tax-valuation allowances are recorded in the tax-adjusted additions (or deductions) section only if such changes affected net income or net loss for the period. Evidence of an income-statement impact will usually take the form of an entry in the income tax rate–reconciliation schedule.

7. The next step is to subtotal the after-tax additions entries and then combine this subtotal with the amount labeled "tax adjusted additions." The result is then recorded on the "total additions" line at the bottom of the first page of the worksheet.

8. Completion of page 2 of the worksheet, for nonrecurring revenues and gains, follows exactly the same steps as those outlined for nonrecurring expense and loss.

9. With the completion of page two, the sustainable earnings base for each year is computed by adding the "total additions" line item to net income (loss) and then deducting the "total deductions" line item.

ROLE OF THE SUSTAINABLE EARNINGS BASE

The sustainable earnings base provides profitability information from which the distorting effects of nonrecurring items have been removed. Some analysts refer to such revised numbers as representing "core earnings."

Sustainable is used in the sense that earnings devoid of nonrecurring items of revenue or gain and expense or loss are much more likely to be maintained in the future if previous operating conditions persist. *Base* implies that the sustainable earnings provide the most reliable foundation or starting point for projections of future results. The more reliable such forecasts become, the less the likelihood that frequent earnings surprises will result. Chevron Corporation captures the essence of nonrecurring items in the following:

> Transactions not considered representative of the company's ongoing operations. These transactions, as defined by management, can obscure the underlying results of operations and affect comparability between years."[30]

EXHIBIT 2.27   Adjustment worksheet for sustainable earnings base: Acme-Cleveland Corporation (thousands of dollars).

	1990	1991	1992
Reported net income	$5,113	$(2,963)	$5,319
Add			
Pretax LIFO liquidation losses			
Losses on fixed-asset sales			
Losses on sales of investments	1,377		
Losses on sales of other assets			
Restructuring charges			1,750
Investment writedowns	3,384		
Inventory writedowns			
Other asset writedowns			
Foreign currency losses	313		
Litigation charges			
Losses on patent infringement suits			
Exceptional bad-debt provisions			
Nonrecurring expense increases		800	
Temporary revenue reductions			
Other			
Other			
Other			
Subtotal	$5,074	$ 800	$1,750
Multiply by			
(1 − combined federal, state, foreign rates)	60%	60%	60%
Tax-adjusted additions	$3,044	$ 480	$1,050
After-tax LIFO liquidation losses			
Increases in deferred tax valuation allowances			
Other nonrecurring tax charges			
Losses on discontinued operations		6,035	
Extraordinary losses			
Losses/cumulative-effect accounting changes			
Other			
Other			
Other			
Subtotal		6,035	
Total additions	$3,044	$ 6,515	$1,050
Deduct			
Pretax LIFO liquidation gains			
Gains on fixed asset sales	$ 422	$ 25	$ 241

(Continued)

EXHIBIT 2.27   *(Continued).*

	1990	**1991**	**1992**
Gains on sales of investments	423	1,137	
Gains on sales of other assets	352		919
Reversals of restructuring charges			
Investment writeups (trading account)			
Foreign currency gains		61	150
Litigation revenues			
Gains on patent infringement suits			
Nonrecurring expense decreases			
Temporary revenue increases			
Reversals of bad-debt allowances			
Other			
Other			
Other			
Subtotal	$1,197	$ 1,223	$1,310
Multiply by			
(1 − combined federal, state, foreign rates)	60%	60%	60%
Tax-adjusted deductions	$ 718	$ 734	$ 786
After-tax LIFO liquidation gains	137	224	2,484
Reductions in deferred tax valuation allowances			
Loss carryforward benefits—from prior periods	2,050		1,700
Other nonrecurring tax benefit			
Gains on discontinued operations			
Extraordinary gains			
Gains/cumulative-effect accounting changes			
Other			
Other			
Other			
Subtotal	2,187	224	4,184
Total deductions	$2,905	$ 958	$4,970
Sustainable earnings base	$5,252	$ 2,594	$1,399

CASE ONE: APPLICATION OF THE SUSTAINABLE EARNINGS WORKSHEET TO ACME-CLEVELAND CORPORATION

This first illustration of the application of the sustainable earnings base worksheet uses the financial statements of Acme-Cleveland Corporation.[31] A completed worksheet is provided in Exhibit 2.27. Further, a summary of the results of the nonrecurring items search process is provided in Exhibits 2.28 and 2.29. This search sequence is based upon the experience of the authors, supported by a large-scale study of nonrecurring items by Choi.[32] The tax rate assumed in the analysis in the Acme-Cleveland worksheet was a combined 40%. This is a blend of state, federal, and foreign taxes. This rate was arrived at by removing some nonrecurring increases from Acme-Cleveland's three-year average effective rate of 48%. Further, all identified nonrecurring items were recorded on the worksheet without regard to materiality. We believe this to be the best procedure to follow. A materiality threshold could exclude a series of immaterial revenues or gains and expenses or losses that, in combination, could distort a firm's apparent profitability.

EXHIBIT 2.28   Summary of nonrecurring items search process: Acme-Cleveland Corporation.

Step and Statement Location	Nonrecurring Items Discovered
1. Income statement	Provision for facility consolidation (1992)[1]
	Provision for asset writedown (1990)[1]
	Loss on discontinued operations (1991)[1]
	Extraordinary items (1990 and 1992)[1]
2. Statement of cash flows	Provision for asset writedown (1990)[2]
	Loss on disposal of minority equity investments (1990)[1]
	Gains on property, plant, and equipment (1990–92)[1]
3. Inventory note (LIFO firm)	LIFO liquidation benefits (1990–92)[1]
4. Income tax note	Tax benefits of tax loss carryforwards, disclosed in the income statement as extraordinary items (1990 and 1992)[1]
5. Other income note	Gains on sales of minority equity investments (1990 and 1991)[1]
	Gains from sales of unused land and buildings (1990 and 1992)[1]
6. MD&A	Provision for facility consolidation (1992)[2]
	Provision for asset writedown (1990)[3]
	Tax benefits of tax loss carryforwards (1990 and 1992)[2]
	Loss on discontinued operations (1991)[2]
	LIFO liquidation benefits (1990–93)[2]
	Unusual warranty costs (1991)[1]
7. Other notes disclosing nonrecurring items:	
Foreign currency	Translation and transaction gains (1991 and 1992) and losses (1990)[1]
Facility consolidation	Provision for facility consolidation (1992)[2]
Discontinued operations	Loss on discontinued operations (1991)[3]
Provision for asset writedown	Provision for asset writedown (1990)[4]

Note: The superscripts 1, 2, 3, 4 indicate in how many search locations the nonrecurring item was found: for instance, "provision for asset writedown" was found in the income statement (first location); in the cash flow statement (second location); in MD&A (third location); and in "other notes" (fourth location).

EXHIBIT 2.29   Efficiency of the nonrecurring-items search sequence: Acme-Cleveland Corporation.

	Incremental Nonrecurring Items Discovered			
	(1) All Nonrecurring	(2) Cumulative	(3) All Material[a]	(4) Cumulative
Step and Search Location	**Items**	**% Located**	**Items**	**% Located**
1. Income statement	5	25	4	36
2. Statement of cash flows	4	45	1	45
3. Inventory note	3	60	1	54
4. Tax note	0	60	0	54
5. Other income note	4	80	4	91
6. MD&A	1	85	1	100
7. Other notes	3	100	0	100
Total nonrecurring items	20	100%	11	100%

[a]5% or more of either the amount or the change in net income or loss, on a tax-adjusted basis.

Comments on the Acme-Cleveland Worksheet

From a strictly bottom-line perspective, the reported net income or loss of Acme-Cleveland for 1990 to 1992 would suggest a profitable year (1990), followed by a loss year (1991), followed by a year of recovery (1992). However, the complete restatement represented by the worksheet conveys a quite different message. The income series reveals a decline in fundamental profitability over the period 1990 to 1992. The number and magnitude of nonrecurring items in the Acme-Cleveland income statements alone should suggest a lack of reliability of the unanalyzed earnings data. However, until a comprehensive identification of nonrecurring items has been completed and summarized, the operating performance over the three-year period is difficult to discern. This is the value of the search process and sustainable earnings base worksheet.

Exhibit 2.29 presents information on the efficiency of the search process. The meaning of each column in the Exhibit is as follows.

Column 1: The number of nonrecurring items located at each step in the search process. This is based on all twenty nonrecurring items without regard to their materiality.

Column 2: The cumulative percentage of all nonrecurring items located through each step of the search process. Eighty percent of the total nonrecurring items were located through the first 5 steps of the search process. All nonrecurring items were located by step 7.

Column 3: Same as column 1 except that only material nonrecurring items were considered.

Column 4: Same as column 2 except that only material nonrecurring items were considered.

For the case of Acme-Cleveland, Exhibit 2.29 reveals that 91% of all *material* nonrecurring items were located through the first five steps of the search sequence. This result is achieved very efficiently because most of the nonrecurring items are located either in statements or schedules, with little requirement to read more time-consuming text. Further, locating nonrecurring items in text is subject to a greater risk that a nonrecurring item will simply be overlooked.

CASE TWO: APPLICATION OF THE SUSTAINABLE EARNINGS WORKSHEET TO EVANS & SUTHERLAND COMPUTER CORPORATION

The Evans & Sutherland case expands upon Acme-Cleveland by not only providing the completed worksheet but also the text of selected financial statements and associated disclosures where nonrecurring items were located. With the exception of the income statement, only that portion of the financial statement or note that discloses a nonrecurring item will be presented. This information is presented in the order in which it appears in the recommended search sequence—Exhibit 2.3.

Comments on the Evans & Sutherland Worksheet

The Evans & Sutherland worksheet records 24 nonrecurring items to 20 in the case of Acme-Cleveland (see Exhibit 2.30). The first five steps in the search sequence located 83% of all material nonrecurring items and 92% of only those judged to be material in amount (see Exhibits 2.31 and 2.32). The same numbers were 80% and 91%, respectively, for Acme-Cleveland. Reported results of Evans & Sutherland were a profit of $4.1 million, a loss of $3.7 million, and then a sharp increase in profit to $20.8 million, in 1993, 1994, and 1995, respectively. After removing all nonrecurring items, the sustainable earnings series is lower and less volatile, with a profit of $1.7 million, a loss of $.8 million, and then, again, a sharp profit increase to $4.9 million. This analysis suggests that the return to profitability in 1995 results from basic operating improvement and is not simply a product of an array of nonrecurring gains that were included in 1995 net income. However, it would be a challenge to make this determination without completing the sustainable earnings base worksheet.

EXHIBIT 2.30   Adjustment worksheet for sustainable earnings base Evans & Sutherland Computer Corporation (thousands of dollars).

	1993	1994	1995
Reported net income or (loss)	$4,093	$(3,700)	$20,811
Add			
Pretax LIFO liquidation losses			
Losses on sales of fixed assets	101	69	
Losses on sales of investments			
Losses on sales of other asset			
Restructuring charges	7,900	8,212	
Investment writedowns			
Inventory writedowns	114	4,316	7,988
Other asset writedowns			
Foreign currency losses	291		53
Litigation charges			
Losses on patent infringement suits			
Exceptional bad-debt provisions			
Nonrecurring expense increases			
Temporary revenue reductions			
Writeoff of acquired research and development			705
Other			
Other			
Subtotal	8,406	12,597	8,746
Multiply by			
(1 – combined federal, state tax rates)	60%	60%	60%
Tax-adjusted additions	5,044	7,558	5,248
Add			
After-tax LIFO liquidation losses			
Increases in deferred tax valuation allowances			
Other nonrecurring tax charges			
Losses on discontinued operations			
Extraordinary losses			
Losses/cumulative-effect accounting changes			
Other			
Other			
Other			
Subtotal			
Total additions	$5,044	$7,558	$5,248

(Continued)

EXHIBIT 2.30   *(Continued).*

	1993	1994	1995
Deduct			
Pretax LIFO liquidation gains			
Gains on fixed asset sales		93	
Gains on sales of investments	6,238	4,009	7,126
Gains on sales of other assets			
Reversals of restructuring charges			
Investment writeups (trading account)			
Foreign currency gains		266	
Litigation revenues			3,750
Gains on patent infringement suits			
Temporary expense decreases			
Temporary revenue increases			
Reversals of bad-debt allowances			
Gain on sale of CDRS			23,506
Other			
Other			
Subtotal	6,238	4,275	34,475
Multiply by			
Times (1 – combined federal, state tax rate)	60%	60%	60%
Tax-adjusted deductions	3,743	2,565	20,685
After-tax LIFO liquidation gains			
Reductions in deferred tax valuation allowances			
Loss carryforward benefits from prior periods			
Other nonrecurring tax benefits	1,275		
Gains on discontinued operations			
Extraordinary gains		1,859	327
Gains/cumulative-effect accounting changes	2,267		
Research and development tax credits	160	226	124
Other			
Other			
Subtotal	3,702	2,085	451
Total deductions	7,445	4,650	21,136
Sustainable earnings base	$1,692	$(792)	$4,923

**EXHIBIT 2.31   Summary of nonrecurring items search process:
Evans & Sutherland Computer Corporation.**

Step and Statement Location	Nonrecurring Items Discovered
1. Income statement	Restructuring charges (1993 and 1994)[1]
	Writeoff of acquired R&D (1995)[1]
	Gain from sale of CDRS (1995)[1]
	Gain on sale of marketable securities (1993–1995)[1]
	Extraordinary gains (1994 and 1995)[1]
	Cumulative effect of accounting change (1993)[1]
2. Statement of cash flows	Provision for inventory writedowns (1993–1995)[1]
	Extraordinary gains (1994 and 1995)[2]
	Gain on sale of CDRS (1995)[2]
	Gains and losses on disposal of fixed assets (1993–1995)[1]
	Gains on sales of marketable securities (1993–1995)[2]
3. Inventory note, if using LIFO	Uses weighted average method
4. Income tax note	Federal tax refund from prior years (1993)[1]
	Research and development tax credits (1993–1995)[1]
5. Other income note	No other income (expense) note
6. MD&A	Restructuring charges (1993 and 1994)[2]
	Writeoff of acquired R&D (1995)[2]
	Gain on sale of CDRS (1995)[3]
	Extraordinary gains (1994 and 1995)[3]
	Cumulative effect of accounting change (1993)[2]
	Litigation settlement (1995)[1]
	Inventory writedown (1995)[2]
	Gains on sales of marketable securities (1993–1995)[3]
7. Other notes disclosing nonrecurring items:	
Foreign currency	Transaction gains and losses (1993–1995)[1]
Marketable securities	Gains on sales of marketable securities (1993–1995)[4]
Inventories	Inventory writedown (1995)[3]
Long-term debt	Extraordinary gains on retirement (1994 and 1995)[4]
Commitment and contingencies	Litigation settlement (1995)[2]
Restructuring charges	Restructuring charges (1993 and 1994)[3]
Business sold and acquired	CRDS gain (1995)[4]
Quarterly financial data	Extraordinary gains (1994 and 1995)[5]

Note: The superscripts 1, 2, 3, 4 indicate in how many search locations the nonrecurring item was found: for instance, the "Gain on the sale of CDRS" was found in the income statement (first location), statement of cash flows (second location), MD&A (third location), and in a note on business sold and acquired (fourth location).

Selected Evans & Sutherland Computer Corporation Annual Report Data

Only financial statements and related disclosures where nonrecurring items were located are reproduced in Exhibits 2.33 and 2.34. (Reference should be made to Exhibit 2.31 for listings of the nonrecurring items discovered in each location.) Information is listed in search-sequence order.

EXHIBIT 2.32   Efficiency of the nonrecurring-items search sequence: Evans & Sutherland Computer Corporation.

	Incremental Nonrecurring Items Discovered			
	(1) All Nonrecurring Items	(2) Cumulative % Located	(3) All Material[a] Items	(4) Cumulative % Located
Step and Search Location				
1. Income statement	10	42	8	67
2. Statement of cash flows	6	67	2	83
3. Inventory note	0	67	0	83
4. Tax note	4	83	1	92
5. Other income note	0	83	0	92
6. MD&A	1	88	1	100
7. Other notes	3	100	0	100
Total nonrecurring items	24	100%	12	100%

[a]5% or more of either the amount or the change in net income or loss, on a tax-adjusted basis.

1. Income Statement

EXHIBIT 2.33   Income statement: Evans & Sutherland Computer Corporation, years ended December 29, 1995, December 30, 1994, and December 31, 1993 (in thousands).

	1993	1994	1995
Net sales	$142,253	$113,090	$113,194
Cost of sales	65,678	60,626	62,768
Gross profit	76,575	52,464	50,426
Expenses:			
Marketing, general, and administrative	40,154	32,874	30,714
Research and development	31,757	27,890	19,406
Restructuring charges	7,900	8,212	—
Writeoff of acquired research and development	—	—	705
	79,811	68,976	50,825
Gain from sale of CDRS			23,506
Operating earnings (loss)	(3,236)	(16,512)	23,107
Other income (expense):			
Interest income	2,738	2,710	4,752
Interest expense	(2,613)	(1,902)	(1,477)
Gain on sale of marketable securities	6,238	4,009	7,126
Miscellaneous	(296)	311	72

(Continued)

EXHIBIT 2.33   *(Continued).*

	1993	1994	1995
Earnings (loss) before income taxes, extraordinary gain, and cumulative effect of change in accounting principle	2,813	(11,384)	33,580
Income tax expense (benefit)	1,005	(5,825)	13,096
Earnings (loss) before extraordinary gain and cumulative effect of change in accounting principle	1,826	(5,559)	20,484
Extraordinary gain from repurchase of convertible debentures, net of income taxes of $209 in 1995 and $1,115 in 1994	—	1,859	327
Cumulative effect of change in accounting for income taxes	2,267	—	—
Net earning (loss)	$4,093	$(3,700)	$20,811

Note: Note references and earnings per share amounts omitted.
SOURCE: Evans & Sutherland Computer Corporation, annual report, December, 1995, p. 20.

2. Statement of Cash Flows—Operating Activities Section

EXHIBIT 2.34   **Statement of cash flows: Evans & Sutherland Computer Corporation, years ended December 29, 1995, December 30, 1994, and December 31, 1993 (in thousands).**

	1993	1994	1995
Cash flows from operating activities:			
Net earnings (loss)	$4,093	$(3,700)	$20,811
Adjustments to reconcile net earnings (loss) to net cash provided by (used in) operating activities:			
Depreciation and amortization	13,344	10,280	8,741
Provision for writedown of inventory	114	4,316	7,988
Gain on repurchase of convertible debentures		(2,974)	(536)
Gain on sale of CDRS	—	—	(23,506)
Provision for warranty expense	1,121	348	470
Loss (gain) on disposal of fixed and other assets	101	69	(93)
Other amortization	1,094	424	1,209
Restructuring charges	7,900	8,212	—
Gain on sale of marketable securities	(6,238)	(4,009)	(7,126)
Other, net	287	99	158
Changes in operating assets and liabilities net of effects of purchase/sale of businesses:			
Receivables	17,197	7,426	(6,117)
Inventories	(13,278)	(772)	(7,695)

(Continued)

EXHIBIT 2.34   *(Continued).*

	1993	1994	1995
Costs and estimated earnings in excess of billings on uncompleted contracts, net	8,685	(8,789)	8,530
Prepaid expenses and deposits, and other assets	(175)	(241)	(423)
Accounts payable and accrued expenses	(6,137)	(10,713)	(3,912)
Customer deposits	6,954	691	(3,472)
Income taxes payable	(4,463)	(3,760)	12,169
Deferred income taxes	(2,507)	(1,541)	414
Net cash provided by (used in) operating activities	$28,092	$(4,634)	$ 7,610

SOURCE: Evans & Sutherland Computer Corporation, annual report, December, 1995, p. 22.

3. Inventory Note

The inventory note is not listed here because Evans & Sutherland does not use the LIFO inventory method. Only the LIFO method creates the potential for nonrecurring items associated with liquidations of inventory quantities. The inventory note did contain information on nonrecurring items from other sources and is treated in step 7, following.

4. Income Tax Note

Of the information in the Evans & Sutherland tax note, only the tax reconciliation schedule (Exhibit 2.35) is reproduced. This is typically the only portion of the tax disclosures that would reveal nonrecurring items.

5. Other Income (Expense) Note

None was provided by Evans & Sutherland.

6. Management's Discussion and Analysis of Financial Condition and Results of Operations (MD&A)

Nonrecurring items were disclosed at several locations in the MD&A. Income statements, with all items expressed as a percentage of sales, for 1993 to 1995 were presented (annual report, p. 12). These statements disclosed the following: restructuring charges, writeoff of in-process R&D, extraordinary gains, and the cumulative effect of the accounting change. The 1995 income from a litigation settlement was first discovered in the MD&A under the discussion of net sales:

EXHIBIT 2.35   Tax reconciliation schedule: Evans & Sutherland Computer (in thousands).

The actual tax expense differs from the tax expense (benefit) as computed by applying the U.S. federal statutory tax rate of 35% for 1995, and 34% for 1994 and 1993, to earnings before income taxes as follows:

	1993	1994	1995
Tax at U.S. federal statutory rate	$963	$(3,871)	$11,753
Research and development tax credits	(160)	(226)	(124)
Foreign taxes	139	352	124
Losses (gains) of foreign subsidiaries	1,577	(1,461)	217
Federal and state tax refunds from prior tax years	(1,275)	—	—
Earnings of foreign sales corporation	(343)	(123)	(344)
State taxes (net of federal income tax benefit)	96	(511)	1,075
Other, net	8	15	395
	$1,005	$(5,825)	$13,096

SOURCE: Evans & Sutherland Computer Corporation, annual report, December, 1995, p. 30.

"Sales in 1995 included $3.7 million in the settlement with Thomson" (annual report, p. 13). Inventory writedown, but only for 1995, was disclosed under discussion of costs and expenses. The gain on the sale from CDRS was prominently disclosed under a separate caption. Gains on the sale of marketable securities were also disclosed under an "other income, net." The extraordinary gains were also disclosed (all in the annual report, p. 13).

7. Other Notes with Disclosures of Nonrecurring Items

a. Foreign Currency Translation

Transaction gains and losses are included in miscellaneous income (expense) for the period in which the transaction occurs and amounted to net gains (losses) of $(53) in 1995, $266 in 1994, and $(291) in 1993 (annual report, p. 26).

b. Marketable Securities

Realized gains and losses on securities for 1994 and 1995 were presented in this note (annual report, p. 27).

c. Inventories

Inventories totaling $10,767 were written off during 1995 of which $7,467 was charged to cost of sales and $3,300 to the CDRS sale (annual report, p. 27).

d. Long-term Debt

During 1995 and 1994, the Company repurchased $2,360 and $16,691, respectively, of convertible debentures on the open market. These purchases resulted in extraordinary gains of approximately $536 and $2,974, respectively. These extraordinary gains are shown net of income taxes in the accompanying consolidated statements of operations (annual report, p. 29).

e. Commitments and Contingencies

In September 1995, the Company reached a settlement agreement with Thomson Training & Simulation (Thomson). Under the agreement, the Company received $3,750 from lost revenues for breach of a working agreement by Thomson (annual report, p. 35).

f. Restructuring Charges

In the fourth quarter of 1994, the Company incurred a restructuring charge of $8,212. . . . In the fourth quarter of 1993, the Company incurred a restructuring charge of $7,900 (annual report, p. 35).

g. Quarterly Financial Information

The extraordinary gains were also disclosed here.

h. Businesses Sold, Acquired, and Spin-off

Details on the sale of CDRS were provided in this separate note.

On April 12, 1995, the Company sold CDRS to Parametric Technology Corporation (PTC), a Massachusetts Corporation. The proceeds from the sale net of direct expenses of $1,591 was approximately $31,488 resulting in a gain of $23,506 summarized as follows:

Proceeds		$31,488
Assets and liabilities sold:		
Accounts receivable	$ (961)	
Inventory	(466)	
Net property, plant, and equipment	(1,228)	
Liabilities	387	(2,268)
Provision for expenses		(2,414)
Writeoff of inventory		(3,300)
		$23,506

SUMMARY

This chapter provides background information designed to build the skills necessary to identify nonrecurring items of revenue or gain and expense or loss. The search sequence outlined in Exhibit 2.3 is an efficient procedure to follow in an attempt to locate all material nonrecurring items. In recent years, the number of nonrecurring items found in many annual reports has been very large. The sustainable earning base worksheet was introduced, and illustrated with two case studies, to provide a systematic procedure for accumulating and processing information on nonrecurring items. The sustainable earnings series developed with the worksheet provides information that is essential in gauging trends in operating performance, and it is also the most reliable point from which to build an earnings expectation or forecast for coming periods.

FOR FURTHER READING

Bernstein, L., *Financial Statement Analysis: Theory, Application, and Interpretation,* 5th ed. (Homewood, IL: Richard D. Irwin, Inc., 1993).

Comiskey, E., C. Mulford, and H. Choi, "Analyzing the Persistence of Earnings: A Lender's Guide," *Commercial Lending Review* (Winter 1994–95).

Mulford, C. and E. Comiskey, *Financial Warnings* (New York: John Wiley & Sons, Inc., 1996).

Special Committee on Financial Reporting of the American Institute of Certified Public Accountants, *Improving Business Reporting—A Customer Focus* (New York: American Institute of Certified Public Accountants, 1994).

White, G., A. Sondhi, and D. Fried, *The Analysis and Use of Financial Statements* (New York: John Wiley & Sons, Inc., 1994).

ANNUAL REPORTS TO SHAREHOLDERS REFERENCED IN THIS CHAPTER

Acme-Cleveland Corporation (1992)

Air Products and Chemicals, Inc. (1993)

Alexander & Baldwin, Inc. (1992)

Amdahl Corporation (1995)

American Building Maintenance (1989)

Amoco Corporation (1995)

Amtran, Inc. (1992)

Apogee Enterprises, Inc. (1996)

Argosy Gaming Company (1995)

Artistic Greetings, Inc. (1995)

Atlantic American Corporation (1995)

Avon Products, Inc. (1993)

Baltek Corporation (1995)

Bard, C.R., Inc. (1994)

Biogen, Inc. (1993)

Biomet, Inc. (1996)

Boise Cascade Corporation (1993)

Carpenter Technology Corporation (1991)

Champion Enterprises (1995)

Chevron Corporation (1995)

Chiquita Brands International, Inc. (1991)

Clorox Corporation (1995)

CommNet Cellular, Inc. (1995)

Cyprus Amax Minerals Company (1995)

Deere & Company (1994)

Delta Air Lines, Inc. (1993 and 1996)

Dibrell Brothers, Inc. (1993)

Digital Equipment Corporation (1995)

Doskocil Companies (1993)

Dresser Industries (1995)

Eagle-Picher Industries, Inc. (1995)

Ecolab, Inc. (1992)

Evan & Sutherland Computer Corporation (1995)

Exxon Corporation (1989)

Federal Mogul Corporation (1993)

Ferro Corporation (1993)

Freeport-McMoRan, Inc. (1991)

Fruit of the Loom, Inc. (1995)

Gaylord Container Corporation (1994)

General Electric Company (1993)

General Signal Corporation (1995)

Gibson Greetings, Inc. (1995)

Gleason Corporation (1995)

Global Industries Ltd. (1993)

Goodrich, BF Company (1993)

The Goodyear Tire and Rubber Company (1995)

Halliburton Company, Inc. (1994)

Handy and Harman (1995)

Heart Technologies, Inc. (1992)

Hitox Corporation (1994)

H.J. Heinz Company (1995)

Hollywood Casino Corporation (1992)

Hormel, Geo. A & Company (1993)

IBP, Inc. (1993)

Imperial Holly Corporation (1994)

Ingersoll-Rand Company (1993)

Interlinq Software Corporation (1996)

Intermet Corporation (1995)

International Technology (1995)

Jacob's Engineering Group, Inc. (1994)

Kimball International, Inc. (1993)

Kodak (1993)

Lin Broadcasting (1992)

Martin Color Fi, Inc. (1994)

Maxco, Inc. (1996)

Maxus Energy Corporation (1993)

Meredith Corporation (1994)

Micron Technology, Inc. (1996)

Modine Manufacturing Company (1995/96)

NACCO Industries (1995)

New England Business Service (1996)

Noble Drilling, Inc. (1991)

NS Group, Inc. (1992)

On The Border Cafes, Inc. (1994)

Osmonics, Inc. (1993)

Owens-Illinois, Inc. (1993)

Phillips Petroleum Company (1990)

Pinkerton Security and Investigation (1993)

Pollo Tropical, Inc. (1995)

Quaker State Corporation (1992)

Raychem Corporation (1992 and 1995)

Rowan Companies (1988)

SCI Systems, Inc. (1993)

Scientific-Atlanta, Inc. (1994)

Scott Paper Company (1993)

Sherwin-Williams (1993)

Southwest Airlines Company (1993)

Sun Company, Inc. (1992)

Sun Microsystems (1993)

Texfi Industries (1995)

Thomas Nelson, Inc. (1996)

3Com Corporation (1993)

The Times Mirror Company (1993)

Tiffany & Co. (1995)

Toys 'Я' Us, Inc. (1995)

Trimark Holdings, Inc. (1995)

Unocal Corporation (1995)

Universal Foods Corporation (1992)

USX Corporation (1993)

Waverly, Inc. (1995)

Worthington Foods, Inc. (1991)

Wyman-Gordon Company (1995)

Zycad Corporation (1993)

NOTES

1. *Improving Business Reporting—A Customer Focus*, The American Institute of CPA's Special Committee on Financial Reporting (November 1993), p. 4.

2. Donald E. Kieso and Jerry J. Weygandt, *Intermediate Accounting*, 8th ed. (New York: John Wiley & Sons, Inc., 1995), pp. 145–53.

3. Delta Air Lines, 1996 Annual Report, pp. 50–51.

4. Geo. A. Hormel & Company, 1993 Annual Report, p. 58.

5. Choi, Hyun-Dol, *Analysis and Valuation Implications of Persistence and Cash-Content Dimensions of Earnings Components Based on Extent of Analyst Following*, unpublished Ph.D. thesis, Georgia Institute of Technology (October 1994), p. 80.

6. Ibid. It should be noted that the authors of this chapter served as committee member and committee chair for Dr. Choi's thesis guidance committee.

7. *Improving Business Reporting—A Customer Focus*, The American Institute of CPA's Special Committee on Financial Reporting (November 1993), p. 4.

8. Accounting Principles Board Opinion No. 30, *Reporting the Results of Operations* (July 1973), paragraph 20.

9. SFAS No. 4, *Reporting Gains and Losses from the Extinguishment of Debt* (March 1975).

10. SFAS No. 15, *Accounting by Debtors and Creditors for Troubled Debt Restructurings* (June 1977).

11. SFAS No. 109, *Accounting for Income Taxes* (February 1992).

12. Raychem Corporation, 1993 Annual Report, p. 22.

13. Scientific-Atlanta, 1994 10-K Report, pp. 17 and 22.

14. Raychem Corporation, 1993 10-K Report, pp. 4–5.

15. Delta Air Lines, 1994 Annual Report, p. 27.

16. SEC, Regulation S-X, Rule 5-02.6.

17. SEC, Staff Accounting Bulletin No. 40.

18. Wyman-Gordon changed its fiscal year in 1994. As a result, 1992 and 1993 are full years ending on December 31; 1993 is a five-month period ending on May 28, 1994; and 1995 is a full year ending on June 3, 1995.

19. Reviews and compilations represent a level of service below that of an audit. With compilations, it is typical that only an income statement and balance sheet are provided. Neither notes nor a statement of cash flows are part of the disclosures.

20. Digital Equipment Corporation, 1995 Annual Report, Information obtained from *Disclosure, Inc., Compact D/SEC: Corporate Information on Public Companies Filing with the SEC* (Bethesda, Md.: Disclosure, Inc., September, 1996).

21. United States Securities and Exchange Commission, Regulation S-K, Subpart 229.300, Item 303(a)(3)(i).

22. Other companies providing similar presentations include Amoco Corp.; Carpenter Technology; Chevron Corp.; Deere & Company, Inc.; Halliburton Co., Inc.; Maxus Energy Corp.; Raychem Corp.; and UNOCAL Corp.

23. Dibrell Brothers, Inc., 1993 Annual Report, p. 35.

24. Dibrell Brothers, p. 14.

25. The Times Mirror Company, 1993 Annual Report, p. 23.

26. Armstrong World Industries, 1993 Annual Report, p. 41.

27. BF Goodrich Company, 1993 Annual Report, p. 16.

28. Intermet Corporation, 1995 Annual Report, p. 8.

29. An earlier version of this sustainable earnings worksheet was published in E. Comiskey, C. Mulford, and H. Choi in *The Commercial Lending Review* (Winter 1994–95), pp. 4–23.

30. Chevron Corporation, 1995 Annual Report, p. 24.

31. Acme-Cleveland has subsequently been acquired.

32. H. Choi, "Analysis and Valuation Implications of Persistence and Cash-Content Dimensions of Earnings Components Based on Extent of Analyst Following," unpublished Ph.D. thesis, Georgia Institute of Technology, October 1994, chaps. 5 and 6.

3 COST-VOLUME-PROFIT ANALYSIS

John Leslie Livingstone

Eileen opened her restaurant a year ago, and was successful right from the start. Her "Healthburgers" satisfied the need for food that was healthy as well as fast. Healthburgers were made from soybeans, and contained no meat, fat, chemical additives, or cholesterol. Eileen served the patties broiled (not fried), on whole-wheat buns, free of preservatives, fat, and sugar, with lettuce and tomato slices. For food that was so wholesome, healthburgers were surprisingly delicious. As a result, business was brisk, and satisfied customers packed the seating section, or ordered healthburgers to go at the drive-through window.

Healthburgers sold for $1.95, and the ingredients cost Eileen 75 cents per burger, including the paper wrapping. The $1.95 selling price less the $0.75 cost of ingredients is $1.20. This $1.20 is called the *contribution* because it is the amount that the sale of each healthburger contributes toward paying the monthly costs of doing business and earning a profit. These monthly costs of doing business were as follows:

Employee wages	$12,000
Rent	3,600
Utilities	2,400
Depreciation of equipment	1,200
Advertising	2,000
Repairs and maintenance	1,300
Insurance, dues, and subscriptions	700
Miscellaneous expenses	800
Total	$24,000

Sales averaged 1,000 healthburgers a day (30,000 a month). Monthly profit was as follows:

Sales: 30,000 healthburgers @ $1.95	$58,500
Less cost of ingredients @ $0.75	22,500
Contribution: 30,000 @ $1.20	36,000
Less monthly costs of doing business	24,000
Monthly profit before income taxes	$12,000

Note that we could have shortened the profit calculation by going directly to the contribution approach, as follows:

Contribution: 30,000 @ $1.20	$36,000
Less monthly costs of doing business	24,000
Monthly profit before income taxes	$12,000

It may seem to be a small point, but the "contribution analysis" method is very useful for several purposes, as we shall soon see.

The situation had been very comfortable for Eileen. But recently, two new fast food restaurants had opened nearby, with attractive menus and good value for the money. The vigorous competition had driven healthburger sales down to 800 a day (24,000 a month). Monthly profit was cut to the following:

Contribution: 24,000 @ $1.20	$28,800
Less monthly costs of doing business	24,000
Profit before income taxes	$4,800

Monthly profit fell from $12,000 to $4,800, which is a drop of $7,200. This $7,200 is the decline of healthburger sales by 6,000 units (30,000 less 24,000) times the contribution of $1.20 per unit. Therefore we can quickly compute the result of each further drop of 1,000 units per month in healthburger sales: namely, 1,000 times $1.20, or $1,200. If sales fell by another 4,000 units, the further decrease in profit would be $4,800 (4,000 times $1.20), which would wipe out the entire monthly profit of $4,800.

In every competitive business it is essential to understand the response of costs and profits to changes in unit volume. For Eileen, this information is shown in Exhibit 3.1, which is a computer spreadsheet displaying all monthly unit volumes from 0 to 40,000 units. Also shown are dollar sales revenue, ingredient costs, contribution, and the resulting monthly profit or loss (as the case may be). Although the computer prepared these figures very quickly and easily, Exhibit 3.1 does contain a wealth of vital information that is well worth the time required to study it in depth. We now do so.

EXHIBIT 3.1   Healthburger cost-profit-volume spreadsheet.

A	B	C	D	E	F	G	H
	A Times $1.95	A Times $0.75	(B – C)		(D – E)	(C + E)/A	(F/A)
Units Sold	Dollar Sales	Ingredient Costs	Contribution	Monthly Costs	Pretax Profit	Total Cost Per Unit	Pretax Profit Per Unit
0	0	0	0	24,000	(24,000)	N/A	N/A
1,000	1,950	750	1,200	24,000	(22,800)	24.75	−22.80
2,000	3,900	1,500	2,400	24,000	(21,600)	12.75	−10.80
3,000	5,850	2,250	3,600	24,000	(20,400)	8.75	−6.80
4,000	7,800	3,000	4,800	24,000	(19,200)	6.75	−4.80
5,000	9,750	3,750	6,000	24,000	(18,000)	5.55	−3.60
6,000	11,700	4,500	7,200	24,000	(16,800)	4.75	−2.80
7,000	13,650	5,250	8,400	24,000	(15,600)	4.18	−2.23
8,000	15,600	6,000	9,600	24,000	(14,400)	3.75	−1.80
9,000	17,550	6,750	10,800	24,000	(13,200)	3.42	−1.47
10,000	19,500	7,500	12,000	24,000	(12,000)	3.15	−1.20
11,000	21,450	8,250	13,200	24,000	(10,800)	2.93	−0.98
12,000	23,400	9,000	14,400	24,000	(9,600)	2.75	−0.80
13,000	25,350	9,750	15,600	24,000	(8,400)	2.60	−0.65
14,000	27,300	10,500	16,800	24,000	(7,200)	2.46	−0.51
15,000	29,250	11,250	18,000	24,000	(6,000)	2.35	−0.40
16,000	31,200	12,000	19,200	24,000	(4,800)	2.25	−0.30
17,000	33,150	12,750	20,400	24,000	(3,600)	2.16	−0.21
18,000	35,100	13,500	21,600	24,000	(2,400)	2.08	−0.13
19,000	37,050	14,250	22,800	24,000	(1,200)	2.01	−0.06
20,000	39,000	15,000	24,000	24,000	0	1.95	0.00
21,000	40,950	15,750	25,200	24,000	1,200	1.89	0.06
22,000	42,900	16,500	26,400	24,000	2,400	1.84	0.11
23,000	44,850	17,250	27,600	24,000	3,600	1.79	0.16
24,000	46,800	18,000	28,800	24,000	4,800	1.75	0.20
25,000	48,750	18,750	30,000	24,000	6,000	1.71	0.24
26,000	50,700	19,500	31,200	24,000	7,200	1.67	0.28
27,000	52,650	20,250	32,400	24,000	8,400	1.64	0.31
28,000	54,600	21,000	33,600	24,000	9,600	1.61	0.34
29,000	56,550	21,750	34,800	24,000	10,800	1.58	0.37
30,000	58,500	22,500	36,000	24,000	12,000	1.55	0.40
31,000	60,450	23,250	37,200	24,000	13,200	1.52	0.43
32,000	62,400	24,000	38,400	24,000	14,400	1.50	0.45
33,000	64,350	24,750	39,600	24,000	15,600	1.48	0.47
34,000	66,300	25,500	40,800	24,000	16,800	1.46	0.49
35,000	68,250	26,250	42,000	24,000	18,000	1.44	0.51
36,000	70,200	27,000	43,200	24,000	19,200	1.42	0.53
37,000	72,150	27,750	44,400	24,000	20,400	1.40	0.55
38,000	74,100	28,500	45,600	24,000	21,600	1.38	0.57
39,000	76,050	29,250	46,800	24,000	22,800	1.37	0.58
40,000	78,000	30,000	48,000	24,000	24,000	1.35	0.60

COST BEHAVIOR

It is important to understand how costs respond to changes in unit volume. Exhibit 3.2 displays this information, taken from the spreadsheet in Exhibit 3.1. First, we see that the monthly costs do not respond to changes in volume. They remain at $24,000 per month for all levels of volume. These are known as *fixed costs* because they remain fixed with respect to volume. Of course, these costs may fluctuate for reasons other than changes in volume. For example, the rent may be increased by the property owner, or more money may be spent on advertising because of fiercer competition, or wage costs may drop because an experienced worker leaves and is replaced by an inexperienced, lower-paid employee. So fixed costs are fixed only with respect to unit volume, and not in any other respects.

Also, it is important to bear in mind the limits of recent experience. Eileen has operated the restaurant for only one year. It was an immediate success, and unit volume in the very first month was 16,000 healthburgers. Since then, the unit volume increased to 30,000 but never higher. Therefore the range of actual experience is limited to unit volumes of 16,000 to 30,000. The chart in Exhibit 3.2 shows cost estimates for unit volumes below and above this range, but these costs are only theoretical estimates and are not as dependable as the costs that have actually been experienced in practice.

The unit volume between 16,000 and 30,000 is known as the *relevant range* because it has been experienced in practice. Therefore it provides more reliable cost information than any zone outside of this known range. For example, if

EXHIBIT 3.2   Healthburger cost chart.

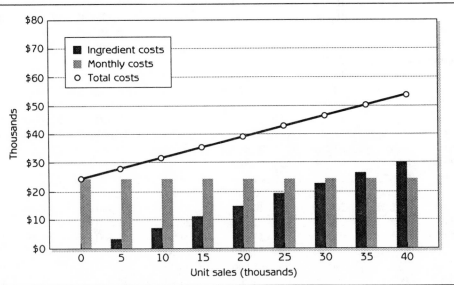

monthly volume was as low as 5,000 units, perhaps fewer employees would be needed and some cost savings could be achieved by cutting the employee hours. Then the total fixed costs may be less than $24,000 at or below unit volume of 5,000. By the same token, at unit volume above 35,000, it may become necessary to add staff, thereby increasing wage costs. In that case, fixed costs would exceed $24,000 at or above unit volume of 35,000. But this is based upon assumption and not upon actual experience.

Of course, if wages did in fact behave as assumed, then the monthly costs would not be fixed beyond the relevant range. They would respond in step fashion, not smoothly in direct proportion to unit volume but in "lumps" that occurred at certain trigger levels of unit volume. This is known as a *step* or *semi-fixed* cost.

Fixed costs do not respond to volume, but usually relate to time. In fact, fixed costs are sometimes called "period costs" because they are related to the passage of time. This is the case for rent, insurance, and dues and subscriptions, which are based on $X per month or per year. That is why fixed costs are incurred even at zero volume, because rent and other time-related costs have to be paid, even if no units are being sold. Some fixed costs may not be related to time but are discretionary instead. For example, consider advertising. Management makes a decision, at its discretion, on how much to spend on advertising. This decision may take several factors into account, but in the last analysis, the amount to be spent is set at the discretion of management.

In addition to fixed costs, Exhibit 3.2 also shows the cost of ingredients, which vary in direct proportion to unit volume. Each extra healthburger sold costs $0.75 for the ingredients required. The cost of ingredients increases (or decreases) in direct proportion to unit volume. Costs that respond in direct proportion to changes in unit volume are known as *variable costs,* because they vary directly with volume. Again, the concept of relevant range applies: We can place reliance upon actual experience, but we must be cautious when speculating outside of the range of experience.

Caution is also in order because variable costs may change not only in relation to volume, but also for other reasons. For instance, the cost of healthburger ingredients may rise due to increased costs for tomatoes caused by drought. Or a switch may be made in the wrapping to use recycled paper for environmental reasons, which could lead to some difference in the cost of wrapping paper.

In order to ascertain total costs, we must combine the fixed and the variable costs. Exhibit 3.2 shows the line for total costs, which is the sum of the monthly and the ingredient costs. This total-cost line increases with volume, due to the variable costs included, but it does not increase as fast as volume, due to the fixed-cost component. The fact that total cost does not grow as fast as volume has some profound effects, as we now explore.

COST-PROFIT-VOLUME ANALYSIS

The total cost charted in Exhibit 3.2 can be compared with sales revenue in order to arrive at profit for each level of unit volume. This is shown in Exhibit 3.3.

In Exhibit 3.3, the total-cost line starts at $24,000 (for zero volume) and rises as volume grows. The sales-revenue line begins at zero (when unit sales are zero, sales revenues are likewise zero). But total costs grow more slowly than sales, and thus the sales-revenue line catches up with—and then overtakes—total costs. As long as total costs are greater than sales revenue, losses are incurred. But after sales revenue exceeds total costs, profits are earned.

At the point where sales revenue just catches up with total costs, there is neither profit nor loss. This is known as the *breakeven point.* As shown by the spreadsheet in Exhibit 3.1 and also the chart in Exhibit 3.3, the breakeven point occurs at unit volume of 20,000 per month. At this volume, total sales revenue is $39,000, ingredient costs are $15,000 (making the total contribution $24,000), and fixed costs are $24,000. The total costs are $39,000, and the resulting profit is zero. At all unit volumes less than the breakeven point, losses are incurred, as the chart indicates. But, as the chart reveals, profits are earned at all unit volumes above breakeven.

The breakeven point may be computed (as in the spreadsheet of Exhibit 3.1) or plotted (by drawing a graph as in Exhibit 3.3) or it can be calculated by formula as follows:

Profit = Revenues − variable costs − fixed costs

Profit = contribution − fixed costs

EXHIBIT 3.3   Healthburger cost-volume-profit chart.

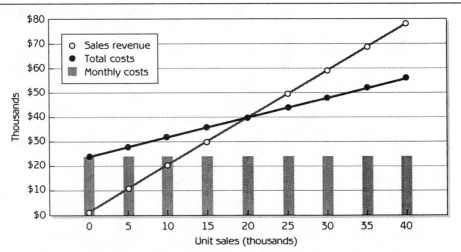

Setting profit equal to zero, for breakeven:

$$\text{Zero} = \text{Contribution} - \text{fixed costs}$$
$$\text{Contribution} = \text{Fixed costs}$$
$$\text{Contribution per unit} = \text{Fixed costs/\# units to breakeven}$$
$$\text{\# units to breakeven} = \text{Fixed costs/contribution per unit}$$
$$= \$24,000/(\$1.95 - \$0.75)$$
$$= \$24,000/\$1.20$$
$$= 20,000 \text{ units}$$

This formula makes it easy to answer relevant questions: For example, what would be the breakeven point if fixed costs increase to a level of $27,000 per month? The new breakeven point is 22,500 units (27,000/1.20). Or, how many units must be sold to earn a profit of $6,000 per month? Adding the fixed costs of $24,000 and the desired profit of $6,000, the new total contribution required is $30,000. Then $30,000 divided by the unit contribution of $1.20 is 25,000 units.

Breakeven analysis is a most practical and useful technique. For instance, Eileen's volume has fallen from 30,000 a month to 24,000. It would be important for her to know the volume at which she would break even. Or at what volume would she be losing $3,000 a month? This answer is $21,000 ($24,000 − $3,000) divided by $1.20, or 17,500 units.

It is especially helpful for people considering opening a new business to use cost-volume-profit (CVP) analysis. If, for example, you are exploring the purchase of a franchised type of business, you will soon find that the franchisors will be reluctant to give you any projections of the profits you can expect to earn (because they are afraid of being sued in case the business fails to produce these results). While they do not want to give out this information, you really do need to know what kind of profits you can reasonably earn. How do you overcome this obstacle?

Usually you can get information from the franchisor and other franchisees about unit prices, and about the costs of doing business (both fixed and variable). With this information, you can calculate breakeven volume, and also the unit volumes required to earn various levels of monthly or yearly profits. Next, you can estimate how realistic, and how difficult, it may be to reach these unit-volume targets. Franchisors and other franchisees are usually quite willing to discuss unit volumes whereas they are reluctant in the extreme to reveal profit information. With an understanding of breakeven and CVP analysis, you can quite easily compute the necessary profit information from the available facts on costs and selling prices.

To summarize, breakeven volume in units is determined by the following formula:

$$\frac{\text{Fixed costs} + \text{Target amount of profit}}{\text{Unit contribution}}$$

Breakeven analysis is a widely used and helpful technique, but like all techniques, there are some cautions to keep in mind when applying it. Note that it is only as good as the information that goes into it. Accurate results depend on obtaining current and accurate information on selling price, variable costs, and fixed costs. If any of these elements is subject to change, then the breakeven analysis will need to be revised.

CONTRIBUTION ANALYSIS

We have seen that the essence of breakeven and CVP analysis is the notion of *contribution* toward fixed costs and profit. This valuable notion allows us to simplify the breakeven chart of Exhibit 3.3 into the contribution-profit chart shown in Exhibit 3.4.

In Exhibit 3.4, the dark bars represent the monthly fixed costs, and the sloping line depicts the contribution at each level of volume. The light bars are the monthly profits. As the contribution increases with volume, it covers a larger portion of the fixed costs, thus reducing the losses incurred at all levels of volume below breakeven. Right at the point of breakeven volume, the contribution is

EXHIBIT 3.4   Healthburger contribution-profit chart.

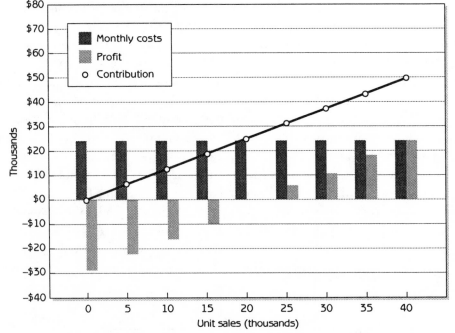

just sufficient to compensate for the monthly fixed costs, and therefore there is neither a profit nor a loss. Above the breakeven point, the contribution exceeds the fixed costs by a growing amount at each level of volume. The result is that profit is also increased at each level of volume.

The contribution approach can be useful in many practical business situations. One example is when a special order is received.

A Special Order

The president of a local bank stopped by to see Eileen. He asked if she would like to supply 1,000 healthburgers for the annual company picnic next month. "Of course," he added, "with such a huge order, we will certainly expect to pay a lot less than your regular price of $1.95 per burger. In fact, Burger Queen has already offered us a price of $1.25. Can you match that price?"

Eileen knew that she could not make all of the 1,000 extra burgers during the restaurant's regular business hours of 11 A.M. to 11 P.M. and that she would need to schedule overtime hours for some of the work. She estimated that it would need two people for four hours, which would cost $60 in wages. It seemed wise to think through this offer very carefully, so she said "Thank you for giving me an opportunity to make a bid. Could I get back to you in about an hour with a final answer?" "Of course, Eileen. Call me at the bank," replied the president.

What should Eileen do? Contribution analysis will provide the information she needs to make a sound decision. At the special price of $1.25, less the ingredient costs of $0.75, the contribution per burger will be $0.50. For 1,000 burgers this adds up to $500 in total. Subtract the extra wage costs of $60, and the remaining contribution towards fixed costs and profit is $440. Clearly Eileen would be well advised to accept the offer from the bank, which makes her better off by $440.

If necessary, just how low a price could Eileen charge on this special order? Note that the order increases fixed costs by $60. Therefore it must have a contribution of at least $60 to be a breakeven proposition. A contribution of $60 on 1,000 burgers translates into 6 cents per burger as the required contribution per unit. Variable (ingredient) cost per burger is $0.75, and therefore a 6 cent contribution per burger would indicate a price of $0.81 to breakeven. The calculation using the breakeven formula is as follows:

$$\text{Breakeven volume} = \text{Fixed costs/unit contribution}$$
$$1{,}000 \text{ units} = \$60/\text{unit contribution}$$
$$\text{Unit contribution} = \$60/1{,}000$$
$$= 6 \text{ cents}$$

On a total basis, this result would be:

Sales revenue: 1,000 times $0.81	$810
Less ingredients: 1,000 times $0.75	750
Less extra wage costs	60
Remaining profit	$0

It is appropriate to point out two important factors relating to contribution analysis in general, and in particular to the decision before Eileen. First, she should be very sure that the special order does not involve any other extra costs. Of course, any extra costs would have to be taken into account. It is all too easy to overlook extra costs in a new situation and in a situation where one may be eager to jump in. As an example of possible extra cost, who will transport the 1,000 burgers to the picnic, what cost will that entail, and who is responsible for paying that cost?

Second, will the decision have any indirect consequences? We have assumed that the special order is separate, independent, and a "one shot" event that will have no impact on regular business. If this is not true, then any indirect effects must be considered. For example, say that Eileen has been supplying 200 burgers a week to the cafeteria at the nearby high school at the regular price. The high school principal learns that the bank paid only $1.25 rather than $1.95 per burger, and demands that the school price should also be cut to $1.25. If Eileen has to agree to that request, her sales revenue will be reduced by $4,200 a year (200 burgers times 30 weeks per school year times the price reduction of $0.70 per burger). Her yearly profit will also be down by $4,200, and the profit of $390 on the bank annual picnic does not even come close to compensating for this lost $4,200.

It is plain that consequences can be serious, and they may be unintended or even unforeseen. Contribution analysis should therefore be used with care, and with diligent attention to qualitative as well as quantitative factors.

Short and Long Run

In particular, note that contribution analysis is a short-run approach. Consider once more the bank's special order for the 1,000 healthburgers. The special order at $1.25 each less the ingredient cost of $0.75 leaves a contribution of $0.50 per burger. But monthly fixed costs are $24,000 and at this time, average monthly unit volume is running at 24,000 healthburgers. This means that average fixed cost per burger is $1 ($24,000/24,000), and the 50-cent contribution will not cover this $1 fixed cost per burger.

Does this mean that Eileen was wrong in accepting the order? No, our contribution analysis was valid and led to the right decision *in the short run*. But, in the long run, all costs (fixed as well as variable) must be covered in order to make profits and remain in business. Therefore, on an occasional exception basis, it is fine to accept special orders based on contribution analysis. But it should not become a regular way of life: In that case it leads to disaster.

Price Discrimination

With respect to granting cut prices to some customers, but not to others, there is a need to avoid price discrimination. Like several other forms of discrimination, discrimination on the basis of price may be illegal under state laws and under the federal Robinson-Patman Act. However, it is legitimate to practice price discrimination under certain mitigating conditions, for instance if the lower price can be justified by lower costs of manufacture, sales, or delivery.

Over the long run, a business must sell its products at a price sufficient to pay back all costs (fixed as well as variable) and also to provide a reasonable profit. Therefore, a useful rule of thumb to remember is that contribution analysis is fine for occasional short-run decision purposes, but in the long run, fixed costs cannot be left out of consideration.

MULTIPLE PRODUCTS

In order to keep things straightforward, up to now we have considered only a single-product situation. But breakeven analysis can also be applied to multiple products. Assume that the typical order at Eileen's restaurant consists of:

	Selling Price	Variable Cost	Contribution
Healthburger	$1.95	$0.75	$1.20
Onion Rings	1.20	0.40	0.80
Beverage	1.00	0.30	0.70
Combined	$4.15	$1.45	$2.70

The contribution per order is now $2.70. Then the breakeven volume becomes $24,000 fixed cost/$2.70 contribution, which is 8,889 units. Or, if the target profit is $6,000, then the required volume will be ($24,000 + $6,000)/$2.70, or 11,111 units.

This is valid so long as the typical order remains unchanged. But if there is a change in the mix (say customers lose their taste for onion rings) or a change in the price or variable cost of any of the items, then the contribution per order is altered. With this change in the contribution, there will be a corresponding change in the breakeven volume. In other words, there is a breakeven volume for any given product mix, and a different mix will result in a different breakeven.

Next, we leave breakeven analysis and consider another aspect of fixed costs.

ECONOMIES OF SCALE

Consider what happens to the cost per burger as volume grows. The ingredient cost of $0.75 must be incurred on each burger, regardless of whether the monthly volume is 5,000 units or 40,000 units. But the fixed costs of $24,000 per month can be spread over more and more burgers as volume increases. If 6,000 burgers are sold this month, then the fixed cost per burger averages $4 ($24,000/6,000). If 12,000 burgers are sold this month, then the fixed cost per burger averages $2 ($24,000/12,000). If 24,000 burgers are sold, then the fixed cost per burger averages only $1 ($24,000/24,000).

This can seem confusing. As far as *total costs* are concerned the total fixed costs do not respond to changes in volume, and they tend to stay fixed in regard to volume. Total variable costs change in direct proportion to fluctuations in volume, and this is why they are known as variable. But, on a *per-unit* basis, the fixed cost *per unit* decreases as volume grows (because there are more units to share the total fixed costs, and thus each unit has a smaller fixed-cost component). The variable cost *per unit* tends to stay the same as volume changes (even though total variable costs increase as volume increases). In the case of health-burgers, the variable cost of $0.75 for ingredients is incurred for each burger, no matter whether it is the first one sold or the 40,000th one. This may seem confusing, but the key to understanding it is to be clear what is being considered: total cost or cost per unit.

As more and more burgers are sold, their average fixed cost per unit declines. Of course, the variable cost per unit for ingredients remains at $0.75 (don't get confused at this point: The *total* variable cost for all units increases as volume expands. But the variable cost *per unit* stays the same over the relevant range of volume). With fixed cost per unit going down, and variable cost per unit unchanged, then the total cost per unit will fall as volume grows. This is an example of economies of scale. When unit cost is falling but unit selling price is steady, profit per unit increases with volume. Therefore economies of scale tend to be linked with increasing profit per unit as volume grows.

The term "economies of scale" is mostly used by economists. Accountants normally refer to "cost leverage" to mean the same thing. Which of these two terms is used may tell us whether we are hearing an economist or an accountant.

Exhibit 3.5 shows the healthburger cost and profit per unit in chart form, based on the numbers from the last two columns of Exhibit 3.1. Note the rapid decline in unit costs in the range between 1,000 and 15,000 units per month. At 1,000 units, the fixed cost per burger is a lofty $24 ($24,000/1,000)! But at 15,000 units the fixed cost per burger is only $1.60 ($24,000/15,000).

Economies of scale occur when unit costs decrease as volume increases. Economies of scale usually come about due to the existence of fixed costs: Recall

EXHIBIT 3.5   Healthburger per unit cost-profit chart.

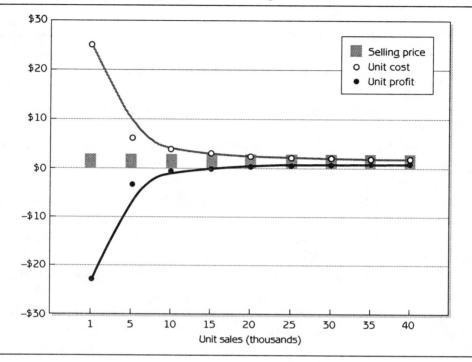

that variable costs per unit do not change as volume increases, therefore they do not give rise to economies of scale. But fixed costs per unit do drop as volume increases, and this results in economies of scale.

The existence of significant economies of scale can have a major impact on the size of the businesses in an industry. If there are significant economies of scale, then the larger the firm, the more profit it can earn per unit of output. The very largest firms will be the lowest-cost producers. At the extreme, one giant firm could be the lowest-cost producer in its industry, and it could drive all of the less efficient competitor firms out of business by undercutting their high prices.

Would this not be beneficial? Eliminating all but the single most efficient firm represents the survival of the fittest competitor, and its customers will now be paying the lowest possible price. On the other hand, the survivor firm will become a monopolist, with the power to raise its prices (and profits) due to the absence of competition. Then the benefits of economies of scale will still be reaped by the firm, but may no longer be passed on to its customers. In that case, the public may be the losers.

Economies of scale can raise important issues of public policy, and are dealt with in our antitrust laws and various other areas of government regulation of business. One of these areas is known as predatory pricing.

PREDATORY PRICING

In recent years a legal battle raged between two of the nation's largest tobacco companies. The Brooke Group Inc. (previously known as Liggett Group, Inc.) accused Brown & Williamson Tobacco Corporation of predatory pricing in the wholesale cigarette market. At trial in federal court, the jury decided that Brown & Williamson had indeed engaged in predatory pricing against Brooke. The jury awarded damages of $150 million to be paid to Brooke by Brown & Williamson. However, the presiding judge threw out this verdict. Since then, Brooke filed an appeal, and the case continued.

Predatory pricing cases are not unusual, and damage awards as large as $150 million are not unheard of. *Predatory pricing,* as the name implies, is a tactic where the predator company slashes prices in order to force its competitors to follow suit. The purpose is to wage a price war and inflict upon the competition losses of such severity that they will be driven out of business. After destroying the competition, the predator company will be free to raise prices so that it can recover the losses it sustained in the price war and also rake in profits that will greatly exceed normal earnings at the competitive level. This final result is harmful to competition, and therefore predatory pricing has been made unlawful.

In order to determine whether a firm has engaged in predatory pricing, the courts need a test that will supply the correct answer. One of the usual tests is whether there is a sustained pattern of pricing below average variable cost. If the answer is yes, this indicates predatory pricing. Let us examine the logic underlying this widely used test.

First, recall that contribution is the margin between selling price and variable cost. Contribution goes towards paying fixed costs and providing a profit. Now, if price is less than variable cost, contribution is negative. In that case, the firm cannot fully cover its fixed costs and certainly it will suffer losses. Therefore, it makes no sense for the firm to charge a price that is below variable cost, unless the firm is engaging in predatory pricing in order to destroy other competing firms. That is why pricing below variable cost is considered to be consistent with predatory pricing.

We should bear in mind that the variable cost used in the test is that of the alleged predator, and not that of the alleged victim. The reason is that the alleged predator may be an efficient low-cost producer, whereas the alleged victim may be an inefficient high-cost producer. Therefore, a price below the alleged victim's variable cost may be above that of the alleged predator, in which case it could be a legitimate price and simply a reflection of the superior efficiency of the alleged predator. The antitrust laws are designed to protect competition, but not competitors (especially those competitors who are inefficient).

Of course, this is only one indicator of predatory pricing, and all of the relevant evidence must be considered. It is also appropriate to note that there should be a pattern of sustained pricing below variable cost. Prices that are slashed only sporadically or occasionally are probably legitimate business tactics, such as "loss leader" pricing to attract customers, or clearance sales to get rid of obsolete goods.

Predatory pricing is an important topic and has been the subject of major lawsuits in a wide variety of industries. In turn, as a common test for predatory pricing, variable cost is also a very important topic that all successful business people will benefit by thoroughly understanding.

Predatory pricing is usually thought of in a regional sense, or perhaps on a national scale. But it can also occur on an international basis. In that case, it is known as "dumping."

Dumping

If a foreign company is the predator, there is no inherent difference in the tactics or the goal of predatory pricing. Pricing below variable cost would still remain a valid test. However, our law imposes a stricter test on foreign than on domestic companies. The legal test for dumping does not involve variable cost. Rather it focuses on whether the foreign company is selling its product here at a price less than the price in its home market.

Dumping is simply predatory pricing by a foreign company. So the logic that supported using variable cost as a test for predatory pricing would also support using the same test for dumping. But the test actually used is the domestic selling price (usually higher than variable cost). This test makes it easier to prove dumping than to prove predatory pricing. It favors the domestic firms and is harder on the foreign company. This may be a matter of politics as well as one of economics.

Perhaps the best-known cases of dumping have involved the textile industry and the steel industry. Another recent case of dumping concerned Japanese auto companies accused by U.S. competitors of dumping minivans in this country. Also, the Japanese makers of flat screens for laptop computers (active matrix liquid crystal displays) were alleged to have sold their products in the United States at prices below those in the home market.

It is not always easy to ascertain the home market selling price. Even if there are list prices or catalog prices in the home market, there may be discounts or rebates that are difficult to detect. Therefore, instead of using the home market selling price as the test, the production cost may be used instead. This is reasonable, because chances are that the production cost is below the home market selling price. Therefore a dumping price below production cost is virtually certain to also be below the home market selling price. But bear in mind that production cost includes both fixed and variable costs, and is therefore above variable cost. Also, bear in mind that it may be arguable as to what should be included in production cost. For example, some may consider it to include interest expense on money borrowed to purchase manufacturing material inventories. Others may believe that interest is not part of production cost.

If it is determined that dumping has indeed taken place, then the U.S. International Trade Commission (ITC) will impose an import duty on the foreign product involved. This duty will be sufficiently high to boost the U.S. selling price up to the same level as the home market price.

Dumping is an important subject area, with a large potential impact on businesses and industries in our economy. In turn, production cost is also of great importance and is a subject that successful businesspersons will find it profitable to understand.

THE SHUTDOWN POINT

We now return to Eileen and the healthburger restaurant. The competition has intensified, and unit volume has dropped down to 15,000 healthburgers in the latest month. At this volume, Exhibit 3.1 indicates that a loss of $6,000 is incurred. Eileen has become discouraged and wonders whether she should close down.

If the restaurant is closed down for several weeks, or even months, most of the monthly costs will still be incurred so long as there is an intention to reopen again, and not just abandon the business. It will be necessary to keep paying the rent due under the lease, to continue insurance coverage, and to keep the equipment repaired and maintained. Some employees may be laid off, but it is probably wise to keep at least a core group on the payroll. Eileen carefully examines all of the costs, and finds that she can cut the monthly costs of $24,000 down to $18,000 if the restaurant is temporarily shut down.

Now the decision is clearer. Staying open at monthly volume of 15,000 units incurs a loss of $6,000 per month. But if the restaurant is shut down, the monthly cost is $18,000. It is definitely better to stay open. However, Eileen must keep a close watch on her available cash. Whether she stays open (at a cost of $6,000 per month) or shuts down (at a cost of $18,000 per month) there is a question of how long can the business incur losses and still survive? The answer depends on how big a war chest of cash is available. When the cash runs out, the end will come quickly.

Returning to the decision about shutting down, at what volume is Eileen better off to close than to remain open? Exhibit 3.1 shows that at a monthly volume of 5,000 units, the loss amounts to $18,000, which is the same amount as the monthly cost for a temporary shutdown. This is the shutdown point, where it is a matter of breakeven between being open or closed: Either way, the loss is $18,000.

Fortunately, the shutdown decision did not materialize for Eileen, as business picked up again and continued to be good. Therefore, we leave Eileen to live long and prosper, and turn our attention to a different company in a different industry.

BANANA COMPUTER CORPORATION

Banana Computers was started in a home garage by two highly innovative engineers with excellent business intuition. The firm grew fast and became a $7 billion corporation after only 10 years of existence. Its product is a personal computer system, and Exhibit 3.6 shows the sales in dollars and units and operating costs.

Thinking back to Eileen's restaurant, how did we know that the cost of ingredients was $0.75 or that monthly fixed costs were $24,000? Someone must have figured that out and kindly given us that useful information. But in real life, we need to understand how to do this for ourselves. Banana Computer Corporation will provide this opportunity.

The numbers in Exhibit 3.6 do not give us the information about fixed costs per period or variable costs per unit. But they do provide the basis for finding this out. This may be done as follows.

COST ESTIMATION

It is usually helpful to chart this type of information, as has been done in Exhibit 3.7. Each dot on the chart is one year of unit sales and operating cost information from Exhibit 3.6. For example, the 2001 unit sales of 3,138 are paired with

EXHIBIT 3.6   Banana Computer Corporation.

	Sales ($ million)	Unit Sales (,000)	Operating Costs ($ million)
1991	335	92	260
1992	583	163	464
1993	983	301	830
1994	1,516	509	1,387
1995	1,918	681	1,728
1996	1,902	699	1,577
1997	2,661	1,008	2,219
1998	4,071	1,619	3,375
1999	5,284	2,198	4,523
2000	5,558	2,503	4,641
2001	6,600	3,138	5,544
2002	7,500	3,654	6,302

EXHIBIT 3.7   Banana Computer Corporation, cost-volume chart.

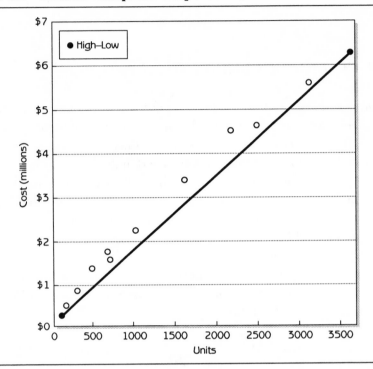

the 2001 operating cost of 5,544 to form the dot that appears near the top right corner of the chart, one before the most northeast dot.

After plotting all 12 of these dots (for the years 1991 to 2002), we next study the relationship between the operating costs and the unit volume, as indicated by the pattern of the dots.

In Exhibit 3.7, the dots are roughly along a line, which implies that there is a consistent relation between cost and volume. The next task will be to find this line, because it will tell us the fixed and variable costs.

If the dots did not approximate a line (which may be straight or curved) but were more widely scattered, then it is likely that:

1. Other factors instead of (or in addition to) volume are the drivers of costs, or
2. Production operations may be in a volatile state, and must be allowed to settle down before any stable cost relationships with volume can be found, or
3. There are serious errors in the cost or unit volume data that we have used, and the data should be thoroughly checked.

In these cases, further study is required. But fortunately the dots in Exhibit 3.7 are well behaved, so we may proceed to estimate the fixed and variable cost pattern. There are three different methods to do this.

The High-Low Method

First is the *high-low* approach, which simply is a straight line connecting the highest and the lowest dots, as shown in Exhibit 3.7. This line is used as follows to estimate the fixed and variable costs from the information in Exhibit 3.6 or 3.7:

	Unit Volume (,000)	Operating Costs ($ million)
High	3,654	6,302
Low	92	260
High less Low	3,562	6,042

The volume increased by 3,562 thousand units while the costs went up by $6,042 million. For each increase of 1,000 units, costs increased by about $1.7 million ($6,042 million/3,562 thousand). Therefore, the variable costs are $1.7 million per 1,000 units, which is $1,700 per unit.

For the high volume of 3,654 thousand units, the variable costs would total $6,211 million (3,645 times $1.7). Now, as previously shown, the actual total cost of the 3,654 thousand units was $6,302 million. Total cost less variable cost leaves fixed cost, so fixed costs are $91 million ($6,302 less $6,211). To recap, the high-low line has estimated fixed costs at $91 million a year and variable costs at $1.7 million per thousand units ($1,700 per unit).

The high-low approach has the virtue of simplicity, but it is very crude and imprecise. Note that there were 12 years of information, but this method used only two years: the highest and the lowest. The remaining 10 years of information were totally neglected, which is why this method is so crude and imprecise. Information is valuable, and there is no excuse for throwing it away. From Exhibit 3.7, we can see that quite a few of the dots lie away from the "high-low" line, which illustrates the inexact nature of this approach. It should be used only when there is absolutely no other way to proceed (for example, if only two years of data can be obtained). A better method is the "eyeball" technique.

The Eyeball Technique

The *eyeball technique* also fits a line to the dots, but it is done by judgment. Usually, a transparent ruler is placed over the dots, and adjusted by eye to find the best fitting line. Exhibit 3.8 illustrates the results of this technique.

The eyeball line is clearly more representative of all the dots than the high-low line was. It can be seen that more of the dots now lie on or near the line, so it is more accurate than the high-low line.

From the eyeball line, the fixed and variable costs can be estimated in exactly the same way as was done with the high-low line, by reading the relevant numbers off the chart. This is shown on the next page.

EXHIBIT 3.8   Banana Computer Corporation, cost-volume chart.

	Estimated Unit Volume (,000)	Estimated Operating Costs ($ million)
High	3,654	6,650
Low	92	600
High less Low	3,562	6,050

The volume increased by 3,562 thousand units while the costs went up by $6,050 million. For each increase of 1,000 units, costs increased by about $1.7 million ($6,050 million/3,562 thousand). Therefore, the variable costs are $1.7 million per 1,000 units, which is $1,700 per unit.

For the high volume of 3,654 thousand units, the variable costs would total $6,212 million. Now, as shown above, the total cost of the 3,654 thousand units was $6,650 million. Total cost less variable cost leaves fixed cost, so fixed costs are $438 million ($6,650 less $6,212). To recap, the eyeball line has estimated fixed costs at $438 million per year, and variable costs at $1.7 million per thousand units ($1,700 per unit). While the variable costs are similar under both methods, there is a large difference in the estimated fixed costs which were $91 million under the high-low method, and are $438 million by the eyeball approach.

The eyeball approach is superior to the high-low method. But it can be arbitrary or subjective in some cases, because it depends on individual judgment. A method which can be more objective is known as regression analysis.

Regression Analysis

Both the high-low method and the eyeball approach are ways to fit a line to a group of dots. *Regression analysis* is also a method of fitting a line to dots, by the use of mathematics. It finds the line to which the dots as a whole are closest (as technically measured by minimizing the sum of the squared distances of the dots from the line). For this reason, it is sometimes referred to as the *least squares* method. We will not go into this more deeply, except to note that the line of best fit is the one which the regression method determines.

Regression involves significant number crunching, but can be easily done with a good computer spreadsheet program. This is illustrated in Exhibit 3.9. Exhibit 3.9 shows the regression estimate of the cost equation in the standard form:

$$Y \text{ (total cost)} = \text{constant (fixed cost)} + \text{unit variable cost}$$
$$\times X \text{ (number of units)}$$

In Exhibit 3.9, these results are: $Y = 408.95 + 1.69X$. Therefore the regression line has found that fixed costs are \$408.95 million, and variable costs are \$1.69 million per one thousand units (or \$1,690 per unit).

The regression output in Exhibit 3.9 also contains some further information. Some of this is highly technical, and we will not go into it in depth here, but we briefly discuss a few main features. First, however, it is helpful to look at the chart showing the regression line, which is displayed in Exhibit 3.10.

Interpreting the Regression Output

From Exhibit 3.10, note that the regression line seems to fit the dots very closely, and is quite similar to the eyeball line (this will not always be the case). While the fit of the regression line is good, it is not perfect, and there is some variation between the dots and the line itself. So, if we use the line to make an estimate of the costs at any given level of volume, there is likely to be some error between this regression estimate and whatever the actual cost at that volume may be. For instance, at a volume of 2,198 units the actual operating costs were \$4,523 million (see Exhibit 3.9). But the regression line estimate would be lower and appears to be just over \$4,100 from Exhibit 3.10. This is an error of about \$400 million. Of course, at other volumes, the error seems lower.

To provide a measure of the average error, the regression output tells us that the standard error of estimated cost (Y) is \$228.64 million. The statistical meaning of standard error is that the error between the regression estimate and

EXHIBIT 3.9   Banana Computer Corporation.

	Sales ($ million)	Unit Sales (,000)	Operating Costs ($ million)	Average Selling Price Per Unit ($,000)	Average Cost Per Unit ($,000)	Average Profit Per Unit ($,000)	Average Profit % Per Unit	Regression Estimate of Operating Costs ($ million)	Regression Error (Actual Less Est. Cost) ($ million)	Percent Error
1981	335	92	260	3,639	2,828	812	22.30%	564	(304)	−116.97%
1982	583	163	464	3,577	2,848	730	20.40%	684	(220)	−47.46%
1983	983	301	830	3,265	2,759	506	15.50%	918	(87)	−10.50%
1984	1,516	509	1,387	2,978	2,725	253	8.50%	1,269	118	8.50%
1985	1,918	681	1,728	2,817	2,538	279	9.90%	1,560	169	9.75%
1986	1,902	699	1,577	2,721	2,256	465	17.10%	1,590	(14)	−0.86%
1987	2,661	1,008	2,219	2,640	2,202	438	16.60%	2,112	107	4.82%
1988	4,071	1,619	3,375	2,515	2,085	430	17.10%	3,145	230	6.82%
1989	5,284	2,198	4,523	2,404	2,058	346	14.40%	4,124	400	8.83%
1990	5,558	2,503	4,641	2,221	1,854	366	16.50%	4,639	2	0.05%
1991	6,600	3,138	5,544	2,103	1,767	337	16.00%	5,712	(168)	−3.03%
1992	7,500	3,654	6,302	2,053	1,725	328	15.97%	6,584	(282)	−4.48%

Regression of Operating Costs (Y) on Unit Sales (X)

Constant 408.95

Std Err of Y Est   228.64

R Squared 0.99

No. of Observations   12.00

Degrees of Freedom   10.00

X Coefficient(s)   1.69

Std Err of Coef.   0.06

Cost equation: $Y = 408.95 + 1.69X$

EXHIBIT 3.10   Banana Computer Corporation, cost-volume chart.

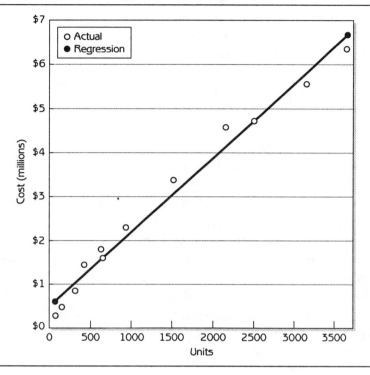

the actual cost will be less than $228.64 (either way: under or over) about two times in every three. This tells us to take the estimated cost from the regression with a grain of salt, and the size of this grain of salt will be less than $228.64 million about two-thirds of the time.

The other use of a standard error is in the estimate of X, the unit variable cost. The regression output shows that the unit variable cost of $1.69 is subject to an error (over or under) of less than $0.06 two-thirds of the time. This is a very small error (less than 4%) and indicates a high level of precision in the estimate of unit variable cost. Therefore, this unit variable cost number may be taken with a very small grain of salt.

Getting back to the variation between the regression line and the dots, there is a helpful statistical indicator of how well the regression line fits the dots, or (as statisticians term it) how well the line explains the variation (scatter) in the dots. This is known as *R Squared* on the regression output, and in Exhibit 3.9 it is .99, indicating that the line accounts for 99% of the variation. Clearly this is a very excellent fit. In fact, it is rare (and almost suspiciously fortunate) to encounter such an extremely high R Squared in practice. Experienced practitioners would probably double-check their work if that were to occur.

In order to display the size of the regression errors, they are shown in the two last columns of Exhibit 3.9. The second-to-last column shows the errors in total cost in dollars, and the last column shows the errors as percentages. The errors in percentage terms are quite large in the first two years, but after that they fall to 10% or less for the remaining 10 years, which is relatively small.

These regression results appear to be excellent, and the cost estimates based on the regression would seem to be extremely precise. This raises a very important point to take into consideration. Is this regression the last word, or are there further issues in this cost estimation study for us to examine?

Beyond the Regression

When a regression is so excellent, it is tempting to consider our work complete. But there is more information to be taken into account. Exhibit 3.9 shows average cost per unit, and this continuously decreases as volume grows. This is evidence of economies of scale. Clearly it should come as no surprise to observe these economies of scale, because we have already noted the presence of fixed costs, and we know that fixed costs give rise to economies of scale. In passing, we may point out that average selling prices also exhibit a steady decline. This indicates that the economies of scale are not being retained by Banana Computer, but are being passed on to customers (probably because of competition and its downward pressure on prices).

EXHIBIT 3.11   Banana Computer Corporation, cost-volume chart.

This is consistent with the average profit per unit, which is steady in percentage terms at about 16% since 1986. Hence, the competition appears sufficient to induce the pass through of cost savings (from economies of scale) to customers, but the competition has not been so fierce as to cause erosion of profit margins.

The cost numbers are plotted in Exhibit 3.11, which shows the regression line, and also a new line fitted to the dots. The new line is curved, not straight. It reveals some useful information. It shows that at unit volumes between 1,000 and 2,500, the regression systematically tends to undershoot the actual costs. But at volumes above 2,500, the regression line systematically tends to overestimate the costs. The value of this information is to make us aware that the regression, as excellent as it is, does not tell the whole story. It does not capture the fact that costs are not following a straight line pattern, but rather a curved line. In other words, the unit variable cost is not constant at $1,690 per computer, but is falling as volume increases. In yet other words, the economies of scale are not only due to fixed costs, but there are further economies of scale in the variable costs, too.

We should be cautious in this assessment, because there has been considerable technological change in personal computers during recent years. This change has certainly had favorable effects on costs. But, with this caution, the pattern still shows falling rather than constant variable cost. This fact can be of great strategic importance in marketing, pricing policies, plant expansion plans, and product design, as well as in other important areas of management.

Exhibit 3.12 displays the average variable cost per unit. This was derived by subtracting estimated fixed costs of $408.95 million from operating costs, to

EXHIBIT 3.12   Banana Computer Corporation.

	Sales ($ million)	Unit Sales (000s)	Operating Costs ($ million)	Total Variable Costs° ($ million)	Average Variable Cost Per Unit ($)
1991	335	92	260	(149)	(1,618)
1992	583	163	464	55	339
1993	983	301	830	422	1,400
1994	1,516	509	1,387	978	1,922
1995	1,918	681	1,728	1,319	1,938
1996	1,902	699	1,577	1,168	1,671
1997	2,661	1,008	2,219	1,810	1,796
1998	4,071	1,619	3,375	2,966	1,832
1999	5,284	2,198	4,523	4,114	1,872
2000	5,558	2,503	4,641	4,232	1,691
2001	6,600	3,138	5,544	5,135	1,636
2002	7,500	3,654	6,302	5,893	1,613

° Operating costs less estimated fixed costs of $408.95 million.

obtain total variable costs, and then dividing by the unit volume. The resulting unit variable costs are not meaningful for 1991 to 1993, probably due to some instability in the fixed cost estimates for those early years. But from 1995 through 2002, there is a definite trend for unit variable cost to decline from a level above $1,900 down to the area of about $1,600. This important trend was masked by the regression, which estimated variable cost at a constant $1,690 per unit. We therefore conclude that regression is a most valuable technique, but it can never be the last word in analysis. Nothing can substitute for common sense, close observation, and good judgment.

SUMMARY OF COST ESTIMATES

The three approaches used to estimate costs have produced the following results:

	Fixed Costs ($ million)	**Unit Variable Cost**
High-Low	$91	$1.70
Eyeball	$438	$1.70
Regression	$409	$1.69

Unit variable cost is virtually identical under all three of the methods. Fixed costs are in the same ballpark for the eyeball and the regression approaches, but are very different for the high-low method. This indicates how deceptive and unreliable the high-low method can be.

The disadvantages of using unreliable information are major. For example, consider the breakeven calculation for the three methods:

	High-Low	**Eyeball**	**Regression**
Average 2002 unit selling price	$2,053	$2,053	$2,053
Unit variable cost	1,613	1,613	1,613
Contribution	440	440	440
Fixed costs ($ million)	91	438	409
Breakeven point	91/440	438/440	409/440
Breakeven volume	206,818	995,455	929,545

There is an enormous difference in the breakeven point under the high-low method versus the other two methods. Clearly it would be dangerous to make any important business decisions based on a breakeven point of 206,818 units, when the actual breakeven is more than four times higher. These results underscore the necessity of using reliable information for making business decisions.

EXHIBIT 3.13   Business decisions: Obtaining valid information.

CONCLUSION

This chapter has explored some powerful and practical methods to assist in making business decisions. These methods make use of the contribution approach, and include CPV analysis and breakeven analysis. In order to put the contribution approach into effect, there must be reliable information on fixed and variable costs. The cost information may be found by the high-low method (when there is no better alternative), or, preferably, by means of applying the eyeball technique or regression analysis. This is summarized in Exhibit 3.13.

No matter which method is used, careful judgment is always needed. Not even the most scientific analytical methods can take the place of skilled human judgment. Neither can human intuition substitute for rigorous analytical techniques. But when the most powerful analytical methods are used together with good judgment, then the blending of objective scientific analysis and subjective human intuition becomes an unbeatable combination.

FOR FURTHER READING

Anthony, Robert N., James S. Reece, and Julie H. Hertenstein, *Accounting: Text and Cases,* 9th ed. (Homewood, IL: Richard D. Irwin, Inc., 1995).

Collins, Eliza G. C. and Mary Anne Devanna, eds. *The New Portable MBA* (New York: John Wiley & Sons, Inc., 1994).

Ferris, Kenneth R. and John Leslie Livingstone, eds. *Management Planning and Control* (Columbus, OH: Century VII Publishing Company, 1989).

Helfert, Erich A., *Techniques of Financial Analysis*, 6th ed. (Homewood, IL: Richard D. Irwin, Inc., 1987).

Horngren, Charles T. and George Foster, *Cost Accounting: A Managerial Emphasis*, 6th ed. (Englewood Cliffs, NJ: Prentice-Hall, Inc., 1987).

Kaplan, Robert S. and Anthony Atkinson, *Advanced Management Accounting*, 2d ed. (Englewood Cliffs, NJ: Prentice-Hall, Inc., 1989).

Rotch, William, Brandt Allen, and C. Ray Smith, *The Executive Guide to Management Accounting*, 4th ed. (Houston, TX: Dame Publishing Company, Inc., 1991).

4 ACTIVITY-BASED COSTING

William C. Lawler

Dan ("Doc") Webster sat staring out the window. Not even coffee-break time yet, and already three major battles had been waged. Wednesday was the worst day of the week—the most chaotic of all. It was the day that the promises made at the end of last week came home to roost and also the day when the idyllic promises for next week were to be made. To make matters worse, his accountant had informed him that it appeared the record was intact: For the seventh consecutive quarter, revenues had increased while profits had fallen.

The day started with a 7:15 call from the marketing manager, Jane Conole. She informed Doc that once again customer orders had to be backlogged due to production inefficiencies. These orders were for the new Elmos that were "guaranteed delivered" no later than last Friday. She also informed him that she was through dealing with Jim Thompson, the production manager. And since Thompson reported directly to Doc, Doc could handle it.

A subsequent call to Thompson revealed that production was not to blame. Procurement had not purchased the correct subcomponents. The line had been tooled and set up, but the misspecified subcomponents had jammed the hoppers. Thompson's workers had tried valiantly to retool, but the components were just not compatible with the process. They had wasted the better part of two days on this order.

By 8:00, Doc was on the phone to Mike Green, head of procurement. That the phone had not melted amazed Doc. Green, in very few words, made his position quite clear. Conole had made a habit of selling products that were not yet part of the product line. Since Thompson's production line was very inflexible,

Green had to ensure that any new product was sourced such that the subcomponents were compatible with the existing production technology. That meant the product engineer working with Green had to draw up the specifications on the promised product, source it, and test it before any suppliers could be qualified. Many times this process was relatively easy since most new products were similar to existing products, thus avoiding the need to qualify a new supplier. It was not uncommon for this process to take less than two weeks. In the case of the Elmo line, however, a new supplier had to be qualified, and problems were to be expected. The product had not been misspecified; the supplier misconstrued the specifications. Green assured Doc that the mix-up had been corrected and the order would soon be running.

As Doc reached for the Bushmill's to fortify his coffee, he could not help but remember that the bottle had been a gift commemorating the one-million-dollar mark in sales. He wondered how a business that once was so promising could go so sour so quickly.

BACKGROUND

The founding of The Smiling Feline, Ltd. had been pure serendipity. Five years ago, while driving to a golf outing, Doc and three friends had an inane discussion on what could possibly motivate people to put bumper stickers on their cars. One friend argued that the signs were quite practical and offered as evidence the most common one: Baby on Board. He compared this to the red stickers that local fire departments give out in the case of fire, to note rooms in a house where children are located. This argument held sway until another car went by with a plastic hand protruding from its trunk pointing to another popular bumper sticker: Mother-in-Law in the Trunk.

At the golf course, one of Doc's friends paid $25 for an animal headcover to put on his driver. When Doc asked him why on earth he would pay that amount for one novelty headcover when he could have bought a complete set of regular headcovers for the same amount, the friend answered: "For the same reason a person would buy a 'Mother-in-Law in the Trunk' bumper sticker."

The idea for The Smiling Feline was born. If people would put bumper stickers on their cars by the millions, wouldn't they stick crazy animals to their windows by the thousands, at the least?

Doc was a design engineer for a medical instruments company and had worked on a few systems that had ancillary parts which could be attached to standard systems with suction cups. Through contacts, he soon had an obsolete injection molding machine in his basement for which he had paid only scrap value plus transportation. Within two weeks, he had fashioned a crude mold that would attach four suction cups to a variety of stuffed toys that his daughter had outgrown. A number of novelty stores in local malls were interested in the concept but wanted an item with more sales appeal.

By the winter of that year, just in time for the Christmas season, Doc had four machines crammed into his basement turning out stick-on cats similar to a popular cartoon character. He had negotiated a rather exorbitant (in his mind) royalty agreement of 2.5% of the targeted retail price for the cat likeness (approximately $.50, 2.5% × $19.95) and sourced the animal body at a price of $2.50 per unit with a guaranteed minimum quantity of 5,000. His four children were paid a piece-work rate of $1 per good unit to attach the four suction cups, and each child managed to turn out four good units an hour—while also ruining approximately two per hour due to the primitive equipment and conditions in the basement.

Initially, Doc spent most of his time convincing retailers that they should buy his product for $8 since they could undoubtedly resell it for $19.95. Within a month, he spent most of his time trying to manage the many retailers that were clamoring for his product. By the time the first Christmas season ended, he was convinced that he had a viable economic venture: He had made $10,000 on sales of 12,000 units (see Exhibit 4.1).

The next year was spent turning a potentially viable economic venture into a solid business enterprise. Many wrong turns were made but by the end of the year, The Smiling Feline, Ltd. occupied 6,000 square feet of an old textile mill at a leased cost of $35,000 per year. Sales continued strong across all four quarters and reached 60,000 units by year-end, yielding almost one-half million dollars in revenues. The CPA brought in to prepare the financial statements and the tax return, after lecturing Doc on the importance of record keeping, revealed that the before-tax profit was $67,000. Doc quit his job and devoted full time to his new venture.

Vast changes took place in the following year. Jim Thompson was hired as head of production. He immediately upgraded the injection-molding machines. Automatic feeders (called hoppers) and other enhancements were added, thereby cutting the labor cost by two-thirds and the scrap by an estimated 50%. Although the machinery was secondhand, it was not cheap; but the net result still was a decrease in per-unit cost of approximately 50 cents (see Exhibit 4.1).

EXHIBIT 4.1   Automation cost savings.

	Prior to Enhancements	After Enhancements	Savings
Labor	$1.50	$ .50	$1.00
Scrap	.50	.27	.23
Machine depreciation	.50	1.25	(.75)
Total	$2.50	$2.02	$ .48

Thompson's first decision not only paid for his annual salary but also assured Doc that his greatest headache, production, was now in able hands.

Next, recognizing that if sales were to continue to grow he needed to expand his markets, Doc hired a sales representative, Jane Conole. Her job was to expand their market beyond the local area. By the end of the year, she earned the title of sales manager by negotiating a national sales contract with one of the biggest novelty store chains.

During the year, competition had pushed the wholesale price down to $7 on average, but sales again more than doubled and the before-tax profit exceeded $100,000. Workers had presented Doc with the Bushmill's when the Christmas season pushed the total sales figure over the million dollar mark. Doc was then convinced that he had made the correct decision.

The cracks began to show two years ago. Conole had managed to negotiate two additional national contracts, but competitive pressures had forced the wholesale price down to $6.75 and, by the second quarter, sales of The Smiling Feline, their only product, had leveled. To spur sales, Conole drafted a memo suggesting that the product line be expanded. A number of midwest universities had approached her. Each home football game brought close to 100,000 fans to the campus, and a reasonable portion of them probably would be willing to drive home with the team mascot firmly stuck to their windows. On a test basis, two such schools were willing to sign contracts for 25,000 units at a price of $7.75 and also waive the customary royalty ($.50)—an equivalent price of $8.25 when compared to their standard product. A novelty chain also suggested reindeer for the Christmas season, another item that would have no royalty cost. After the three special orders were accepted, The Smiling Feline was deluged with additional orders, from Cupids for the Valentine season to a mascot called the "Fighting Sandcrab" which was rejected outright due to having more than four limbs.

Thompson put his foot down. He did not have enough time to spec out each order and still run the production operation. Soon thereafter, Mike Green, a retired purchasing curmudgeon, was hired part-time to work with Thompson in drawing up the specifications, sourcing prototypes for a test run, and qualifying a supplier if the order was accepted. Green quickly found himself working 40-hour weeks.

Last year was utter chaos. Rising production costs together with increased competition threatened the profitability of their main product, the Smiling Feline. In fact, the accounting numbers for the year revealed that it cost approximately $6.61 to produce and ship a product to the customer (see Exhibits 4.2*a* and 4.2*b*) and competition had pushed the price down to only $6.60. Since rising costs could not be passed on to the consumer for this product line, more and more of the higher revenue specialty product orders were accepted and run. It seemed that Thompson and Webster were constantly nose-to-nose over the rising production costs or "inefficiencies," as the accountant called them. Webster

EXHIBIT 4.2a   The Smiling Feline, Ltd.: Comparative income statements.

	QTR 4 20X0	FY 20X1	FY 20X2	FY 20X3	FY 20X4
Sales (units)	12,000	60,000	150,000	300,000	550,000
Sales ($)	$96,000	$480,000	$1,050,000	$2,100,000	$3,850,000
Cost of goods sold:					
Rubber	3,000	15,000	37,500	75,000	137,500
Bodies	36,000	150,000	337,500	675,000	1,375,000
Labor	12,000	90,000	75,000	150,000	311,500
Overhead	34,000	146,000	447,000	895,500	1,646,000
Subtotal	$85,000	$401,000	$ 897,000	$1,795,500	$3,470,000
Gross profit	$11,000	$ 79,000	$ 153,000	$ 304,500	$ 380,000
Operating expenses:					
Freight-out	1,000	7,000	20,000	30,000	58,500
Professional fees		5,000	5,000	8,000	10,000
Conole			27,000	45,000	65,000
Other costs				29,000	30,000
Subtotal	$ 1,000	$ 12,000	$ 52,000	$ 112,000	$ 163,500
Pretax profit	$10,000	$ 67,000	$ 101,000	$ 192,500	$ 216,500
Cost of goods sold/unit	$ 7.08	$ 6.68	$ 5.98	$ 5.99	$ 6.31
Operating costs/unit	$ 0.08	$ 0.20	$ 0.35	$ 0.37	$ 0.30
Total cost/unit	$ 7.16	$ 6.88	$ 6.33	$ 6.36	$ 6.61

EXHIBIT 4.2b   The Smiling Feline, Ltd.: Comparative overhead expense accounts.

	QTR 4, 20X0	FY 20X1	FY 20X2	FY 20X3	FY 20X4
Mold depreciation	$ 6,000	$ 15,000	$ 37,500	$ 75,000	$ 137,500
Machinery depreciation	6,000	30,000	187,500	375,000	687,500
Royalty	6,000	30,000	75,000	112,500	100,000
Utilities	4,000	12,000	21,000	36,000	66,000
Scrap	12,000	30,000	40,000	78,000	185,000
Lease		29,000	36,000	75,000	100,000
Thompson			50,000	55,000	70,000
Green & assistant				35,000	95,000
Other production:					
Setup				24,000	108,000
Warehouse				20,000	30,000
Material handling				1,500	9,000
EDP system				5,500	40,000
Quality control				3,000	18,000
Total overhead	$34,000	$146,000	$447,000	$895,500	$1,646,000
Overhead/unit	$ 2.83	$ 2.43	$ 2.98	$ 2.99	$ 2.99

had faith in Thompson, yet accounting numbers don't lie—the costs per unit were increasing. Conole also was unhappy. To get this specialty business, she had to promise service, and Thompson was not delivering. A late shipment was the quickest way to lose customers, and this had happened all too often. To make matters worse, Green, having proved himself more than capable, was reminding everyone that he was supposed to be part-time. Sixty-hour weeks were not his idea of part-time, and an additional engineer had to be hired. This quarreling and infighting escalated throughout the year and led to this miserable day Doc Webster was having at the end of the first quarter. It was becoming more like rounds in a boxing match than years in a business.

THE RETREAT

At wits' end, Doc suggested a three-day top-management meeting—a corporate retreat, so to speak. Although Thompson, Conole, Green, and the outside accountant expressed varying degrees of reluctance, they all did agree that operations could not continue the way they were going. The retreat was set for the beginning of June.

The first morning began as usual, with each accusing the other of being the root cause of the problem. Conole repeated once again that potential customers were beating down the doors trying to get their specialty products. She seemed to have the specialty market to herself and, in fact, was spending the majority of her time placating customers whose orders were backlogged. Sales and income would have increased had Thompson delivered, she assured all present. Thompson and Green again emphasized that the lead time necessary to bring a new product to market was expensive. Many activities had to take place before a product could be produced, and they also reiterated their commitment to quality. They both refused to rush a product only to ruin the reputation of the company. Conole retorted that there was probably little reputation left to ruin since a key facet of quality was meeting delivery deadlines.

The Light at the End of the Tunnel

The one positive aspect of the morning session was that the outside accountant had been present to explain any of the financial numbers if the need arose. Toward the end of the morning when the combatants had exhausted themselves, he managed to gain the floor. He made a startling statement: "It seems that the services I have been providing are not what you need." He went on to note that to date he had only "recorded history." His focus had been on the collation of past transactions for IRS tax reports and not on the preparation of information for management decision making. "For example," he stated, "it seems that marketing and production have different views of the business. Jane is pushing the heck out of the specialty side because of its higher revenue potential, and Jim and Mike are suffering due to the confusion this business is causing in their respective areas. There may be a cost of this confusion that is not now being recognized."

He had their attention. The accountant continued on to explain that the production costs per unit of $5.98, $5.99, and $6.34 reported for the past three years were average costs. The conversation he was hearing indicated that the product lines were not homogeneous. That is, there are few "average" products and, hence, average costs might not be appropriate. It was clear that all felt the specialty business was more complex and, therefore, maybe more costly.

He summarized by stating, "Products do not cause costs to be incurred; rather, it is the underlying activities that bring the product from an 'idea' stage through development, through production, and on to a satisfied customer that cause the costs to be incurred. This overall horizontal view of your business is called a Value Chain. Simply stated, it represents from a customer's viewpoint the processes (for example, development, manufacturing, customer service) that add value and for which, therefore, they would be willing to pay. Processes are but groups of activities. If The Smiling Feline is to properly judge the profitability of its individual products, or at a minimum, its two business segments—standard and specialty items—it needs to look to the underlying activities that supported the segments, process by process, and cost each segment according to these activities."

The group unanimously agreed with what they had just heard and asked the accountant to prepare a report on this "activity" basis. He smiled and just shook his head.

"You people still do not understand. This type of accounting is not governed by IRS tax code or GAAP (Generally Accepted Accounting Principles). I do not know the activities that cause your costs to be incurred. Only you know these cost drivers. I suggest that you envision the flow of a product through your business—your value chain. Map out in your minds each process: What happens when a customer approaches you with a valid proposal? What happens when that valid proposal is converted to a production order and goes through your factory? and finally, What happens when that order finishes production and has to be delivered and supported? Once you do that, we, as a group, should be able to attribute costs to the activities and get a reasonable idea of, at the least, what each side of your business costs."

It was agreed that the last 45 minutes' discussion was probably the most promising one management had had in the past two years. For the afternoon, the group decided that the idea of process mapping should be discussed among The Smiling Feline people, and the accountant should return to his office and gather as much financial data as possible. They would reconvene in the morning.

The Light Grows Brighter

The second morning began with an air of anticipation and confusion. The group thought they now had a somewhat different view of their business. What they were not sure of was how this tied to the accountant's numbers or how they were going to generate better information for decision making. The accountant, who managed to find all the income statements and some supporting detail for The Smiling Feline, Ltd., told them to be patient and to take it one step at a time.

The discussion began with Conole and Green mapping the steps from a customer inquiry to a production order (see Exhibit 4.3). Conole stated that she routed all reasonable inquiries to Green. Green then talked with the potential customer to ascertain all product specifications. Next, he brought these specifications to their minidesign shop where a prototype would be constructed. The prototype had to meet both customer specifications and Thompson's ability to manufacture, given the somewhat inflexible manufacturing process. Green and Conole next brought the model to the customer for approval. If acceptable, Conole would work out price and quantity numbers. Once a contract was signed, Green would then source the body by bringing the prototype to the supplier(s) most apt to take the order and negotiate a price. Green had instituted a dominant source strategy where he dealt with a limited number of suppliers, but, on occasion, usually due to a unique product design, a new supplier would have to be qualified. Concurrently, Thompson would double-check the prototype to ensure manufacturability and a production run would be scheduled.

Green then noted that, "It is now obvious that I was hired as a direct result of the specialty line. In my first year I did spend some time organizing the procurement process for the standard line which was in a bit of disarray. Since then almost all of my time, and that of my assistant, has been spent on specialty orders. My log book for last year shows that Conole brought 45 potential specialty customers in, and, of those, 18 signed contracts. Only 6 of the 18 needed new suppliers. It looks like it takes about one week to develop the prototype and gain customer acceptance, a week to talk to suppliers to negotiate the supply contract, and two additional weeks if I have to qualify a new supplier."

He then passed around a chart showing how he assessed the 75 weeks he and his assistant worked (see Exhibit 4.4). Conole asked him if this meant that the Elmo order was more costly to bring to market since he had had to qualify a new supplier. Green was not sure he could answer that since, once the supplier was qualified, it could be used again in the future. Since the additional two weeks spent qualifying the supplier would benefit more than just the Elmo order, he was not comfortable attributing this activity, and cost, solely to this order. Green was sure, though, that it was chargeable to the specialty line. In fact, the costs of his area, procurement, were not at all chargeable to the standard line since they spent virtually no time on it.

EXHIBIT 4.3   Steps of a production order.

CUSTOMER DESIGN AND NEGOTIATION PROCESS MAP

SUPPLIER NEGOTIATION PROCESS MAP

The accountant smiled at Green's final comment and said, "Mike, let me repeat what you just said, but in accounting terminology. The process map analysis revealed to you that the activity in your functional area, we will call it *product design and procurement,* is dependent on the uniqueness of the potential product. A unique product takes one week of design and one week to negotiate a supplier contract. An extra-unique product takes one week of design, and three weeks to qualify and negotiate a supplier contract. A very crude initial model might take the total costs of your function—we would call this the *cost pool* for design and procurement—and divide it by the 75 weeks you worked. This rate could then be used to directly charge your costs to the individual products. A unique product would be charged two weeks' worth of cost and an extra-unique product, four weeks' worth.

"Since design and supplier negotiation are vastly different activities, we may want to design the accounting system to recognize these two activities sep-

EXHIBIT 4.4   Procurement activity.

Activity	Time (weeks of work)
45 design orders	45
18 supplier negotiations	18
6 supplier qualifications	12
	75

arately. That is, we probably should pool the design costs and the supplier nego-tiation costs separately, thereby developing rates for each activity. Since only 18 of the 45 designs resulted in orders, you would have to figure how to handle this factor when computing the design rate. You will find that as you study your operations, the real activities or cost drivers will eventually reveal themselves. It is sufficient to say, though, at this time we are all comfortable with the fact that your analysis clearly reveals the costs of your function should be directly charged to the specialty line and not spread like peanut butter over all units produced."

The production process was next. It had been studied in detail a year-and-a-half ago, when the proposal to double the production capacity had been inves-tigated and accepted, so Thompson was relatively confident of his information (see Exhibit 4.5).

"First," he stated, "each production order requires molds to 'shoot' the heated rubber onto the limbs of the animal and grates for the hoppers which automatically feed the molding machines. For instance, the reindeer run last Christmas season was 20,000 units. The five machines running that year were producing at a rate of 30 good units an hour each. To fill the order we needed to run all five machines for close to a month—the second week of September through the first week of October (5 machines × 8 hours per day × 30 units/hour × 17 working days is approximately 20,000 units). Five molds, one for each machine, that would hold the four legs of the reindeer were ordered at a local casting shop at $1,000 per mold. A mold lasts only about 4,000 shots (injec-tions), 5,000 if we are very lucky, so there was little waste for this order. Histor-ically, given the size of our orders, we can usually avoid only partially utilizing a mold. Therefore, 25 cents a good unit is an approximate cost for the mold "activity" ($1,000/4,000 units). Likewise, the hoppers and injection-molding machines are really nothing more than a bundle of potential units of output. A standard versus a specialty item makes no difference to them. For what we paid for the injection-molding machines and enhancements, the depreciation cost is approximately $1.25 per good unit of output.

EXHIBIT 4.5   Production process map.

"The grates for the hoppers are somewhat different. They cost approximately $1,400 per grate per machine and would last for many more than 4,000 or 5,000 units. But, since each animal body is relatively unique, we have a policy of throwing these out after the production run. Saving them in hopes of a similar body in the future would result in a shop piled to the ceiling with grates. This cost can easily be traced to an order, but might not make sense to trace it to the individual units produced in the order since the order quantities vary to a wide degree."

Thompson went on to say that to set up a run took two people about a half day and cost about $100. Likewise, there was a material handling cost to be incurred. These again were order costs, not really per unit costs. Interestingly, the group reminded Thompson that after each specialty run, the process would have to be set up once again to return to the standard line. It was agreed that the cause of this second setup was the specialty run and, thus, the cost of the setup activity was doubled to $200 a machine.

Thompson also noted that the warehouse and EDP system costs should be analyzed with respect to what activities drove these costs. With limited knowledge of these functional areas, he had no ability to map their activities but was fairly certain that the majority of these costs were a direct result of the specialty items.

The costs that he had had the most trouble with were the lease, utilities, and his own salary. He stated that these had to do with running the total production facility and could not be traced in any direct manner to either a unit-produced activity, an order-run activity, or even a product line–supported activity.

The accountant was pleased with Thompson's presentation. "It is always easier to understand the concept of an activity-based cost system when dealing with tangible production of units rather than such intangibles as design and procurement. Let's summarize what Jim just said. First, since the molds and the injection-molding machinery can be viewed as nothing more than a bundle of potential units of output, you, as a group, agreed to trace these costs to the products on a units-of-production method. As long as there is little risk of obsolescence, your method of tracing these costs to the units makes sense. Fine.

"Next, the setup and the grates caused Jim some discomfort since the cost per unit of an order would depend on the run size. A $1,400 grate for a 20,000-unit order results in a cost of 7 cents per unit; but, for a 10,000-unit order, it would double. None of you offered any advice to Jim on this problem."

The accountant then turned to Jane and asked her, "Jane, do you really need the cost per unit to negotiate with your potential customers?"

Jane thought for a few minutes and then lit up. "Of course not. In fact, I am usually asked to quote a price for the order rather than a price per unit. If Jim can tell me the cost of the order, this would be fine."

"Exactly. You are now beginning to realize that the purpose of a costing system is not to push all costs down to the unit level. Costs can be driven only to certain levels and to push them any further using somewhat arbitrary methods might not make any sense. The key is to design your cost information system such that you can trace costs by activity to the level necessitated for managerial decision making. The setup and grate costs are a perfect example of this; there is no need to trace these costs to the unit level. With further work, Jim can probably trace a good portion of the warehouse and EDP costs to the order level. Jane will have the information she needs to effectively negotiate prices with her customers.

"Sadly, I have to say that I do not have all the answers. The facility costs that Jim mentioned, the lease, utilities, and his salary, cannot be traced to a unit, order, or even the product-line activity level. As Jim stated, they have to do with running the total production process. For now, let's arbitrarily allocate them on a units-of-production basis. Simply total these costs and divide them by the total units of output to arrive at a cost per unit."

The group was not satisfied with this. Happy with this reaction, the accountant gave the group a further assignment, "OK, by now you realize that activities are the key to an effective cost-information system. I challenge you to rip these facility costs apart and in six months report back to me what degree of traceability makes sense regarding these facility costs. After all, you are the ones performing the activities!"

Next, Conole led the discussion on outbound logistics. After the units were produced, they went to a distribution area. The standard products went to an established customer base and were shipped in reusable containers. Since the production workers were familiar with the process, they did their own quality inspection, and the units went directly from shop floor to shipping container to carrier. The cost per container resulted in a shipping cost of only 9 cents per unit. Most of the specialty orders, however, had to go through an inspection station. In addition, they often were shipped in odd lots and used various carriers. Their costs were substantially greater. Although data to trace these costs were not available, Conole did vow to track these on an order basis in the future. She was, however, comfortable in charging these costs to the product-line level. All shipping in excess of the 9 cents a unit times the standard volume, and all quality costs, were charged to the specialty line. Likewise, although data were not available, the "other" costs in the operating expense area were most assuredly chargeable to unique requirements of specialty orders.

The cost that caused the most controversy was Conole's salary. Her job description indicated that the majority of her time should be spent on finding new business and only a small part on managing existing customers. At first the group thought that they should charge her salary ratably to the units sold, as they did with Thompson. Conole was not sure. She noted that last year she spent the majority of her time on the specialty orders. "Then charge her salary to the specialty line," the group voiced. But she then argued that what she had been hearing over the past two days gives her reason to believe she should have been spending more time on the standard units. After discussion cycled through many ways to charge her salary, the group finally agreed that if the method of charging her salary was that arbitrary, then maybe they should not charge it at all. A like conclusion was reached with the professional fees costs.

By then it was close to the end of the second day, and the group was exhausted but also anxious to see how this better understanding of their cost structure would impact the income statements. They agreed that this would be an interesting exercise for the third day.

The Light

The accountant entered the room on day three with a laptop computer under his arm. Using a spreadsheet package, he had loaded the total costs taken from the general ledger for the past two years. His challenge to the group was to use the operational information they had developed yesterday to trace the total costs down to the two product lines in as objective a manner as possible.

Throughout the morning the discussion of the prior day was rehashed, but this time cost dollars were included. By lunch the accountant's spreadsheet revealed the group consensus on how the overhead costs should be traced for the prior two years. There was so much discussion that the group agreed an additional column, traceability, should be included to indicate just how far down they felt they could trace these costs (see Exhibits 4.6 and 4.7).

Given the discussion that had taken place one day earlier, the results did not surprise anyone. In fact, most had expected what they saw—it was much more expensive to produce a specialty item than originally thought. Of the $1.65 million in the overhead account that had been charged to products on a volume basis last year, only 56% ([$137,500 + 687,500 + 100,000]/$1,646,000 = 56%) could be directly attributed to the unit-of-output measure. More important, almost 30% of the cost was activity-related rather than volume-related (the total of the line and order costs divided by the $1.65 million). Approximately one-half million dollars had been incorrectly allocated.

At lunch, Thompson stated how much more sense this allocation of costs made than the pure averaging they had been used to. The accountant was quick to point out that what they just had done was not "allocation." In accounting, one only allocates costs if a direct method of attaching the cost is not available. What they had done over these past two days was to use the process flows to trace the costs directly to the product lines. The only costs that were allocated were the facility costs which could not be directly attributed to either line. Conole then stated that she was interested in tracing some of those "other" costs down to the customer-order level to see just how profitable some of the specialty orders were when all the costs were taken into account. She feared that the more sales she

EXHIBIT 4.6   The Smiling Feline, Ltd.: Cost detail by segment for year ended 20X3.

	Total	Standard Line	Specialty Line	Traceability
Overhead:				
Mold depreciation	$ 75,000	$ 56,250	$ 18,750	Unit
Machinery depreciation	375,000	281,250	93,750	Unit
Royalty	112,500	112,500	—	Unit
Utilities	36,000	27,000	9,000	Facility
Scrap	78,000	35,000	43,000	Line
Lease	75,000	56,250	18,750	Facility
Thompson	55,000	41,250	13,750	Facility
Green & assistant	35,000		35,000	Line
Other production:				
Setup	24,000		24,000	Order
Warehouse	20,000	5,000	15,000	Line
Material handling	1,500		1,500	Order
EDP system	5,500		5,500	Line
Quality control	3,000		3,000	Order
Total overhead	$895,500	$614,500	$281,000	
Overhead/unit	$ 2.99	$ 2.73	$ 3.75	
Operating expenses:				
Freight-out	30,000	20,250	9,750	Order
Professional fees	8,000	N/A	N/A	
Conole	45,000	N/A	N/A	
Other costs	29,000		29,000	Order
	$112,000	$ 20,250	$ 38,750	
Operating expense/unit	$ 0.37	$ 0.09	$ 0.52	
Traceable cost/unit	$ 3.36	$ 2.82	$ 4.27	

made, the more money she lost. The accountant again noted that a future meeting should address refinements to this crude costing system. "Good cost information systems evolve over time. They are not born overnight."

Now that the group was somewhat comfortable with the tracing of the costs, the afternoon was spent developing profitability by line. Revenues were broken out by product line, and material and labor costs were reviewed. This analysis immediately brought two new pieces of information to light. First, the specialty bodies were actually more expensive than the standard ones, and, second, the specialty labor cost was also higher last year. Neither Green nor Thompson had explanations for this, but both agreed that it did make some sense due to the small lot sizes they sometimes were dealing with.

After the analysis from the morning session was added to the spreadsheet, a quiet fell over the group (see Exhibits 4.8 and 4.9). By last year, specialty items were only one quarter as profitable as the standard line and The Smiling Feline,

EXHIBIT 4.7 The Smiling Feline, Ltd.: Cost detail by segment for year ended 20X4.

	Total	Standard Line	Specialty Line	Traceability
Overhead:				
Mold depreciation	$ 137,500	$ 50,000	$ 87,500	Unit
Machinery depreciation	687,500	250,000	437,500	Unit
Royalty	100,000	100,000	—	Unit
Utilities	66,000	24,000	42,000	Facility
Scrap	185,000	30,000	155,000	Line
Lease	100,000	37,000	63,000	Facility
Thompson	70,000	25,000	45,000	Facility
Green & assistant	95,000		95,000	Line
Other production:				
Setup	108,000		108,000	Order
Warehouse	30,000	5,000	25,000	Line
Material handling	9,000		9,000	Order
EDP system	40,000		40,000	Line
Quality control	18,000		18,000	Order
Total overhead	$1,646,000	$521,000	$1,125,000	
Overhead/unit	$ 2.99	$ 2.61	$ 3.21	
Operating expenses:				
Freight-out	58,500	18,000	40,500	Order
Professional fees	10,000	N/A	N/A	
Conole	65,000	N/A	N/A	
Other costs	30,000		30,000	Order
	$ 163,500	$ 18,000	$ 70,500	
Operating expense/unit	$ 0.30	$ 0.09	$ 0.20	
Traceable cost/unit	$ 3.29	$ 2.70	$ 3.41	

Ltd. had done everything in its power to move away from this line. They all agreed that they now knew why their product was smiling!

Conole was the first to speak. "I now know why my customers were virtually beating down the door. I obviously had this segment of the market to myself due to my pricing. My God, I'm barely pricing them above cost."

Green and Thompson came quickly to her defense. They were the ones that should have known something was amiss. After all, it was their operations that caused the inequity in the costs. They should have known to challenge the accounting numbers.

They then turned to the accountant. He just shrugged and noted that Doc Webster had hired him to do the taxes, no more. "Doc should have known that one cannot run a business in today's world without a top-notch management accounting information system. Global competition has made management accounting information a strategic weapon. Without it you are outgunned."

EXHIBIT 4.8   The Smiling Feline, Ltd.: Segmented income statement for year ended 20X3.

	Total	Standard Line	Per Unit	Specialty Line	Per Unit
Sales (units)	300,000	225,000		75,000	
Sales ($)	$2,100,000	$1,518,750	$6.75	$581,250	$7.75
Cost of goods sold:					
Rubber	75,000	56,250	0.25	$ 18,750	0.25
Bodies	675,000	483,750	2.15	$191,250	2.55
Labor	150,000	112,500	0.50	$ 37,500	0.50
Overhead	895,500	614,500	2.73	$281,000	3.75
Subtotal	$1,795,500	$1,267,000	$5.63	$528,500	$7.05
Gross profit	$ 304,500	$ 251,750	$1.12	$ 52,750	$0.70
Operating expenses:					
Freight-out	30,000	20,250	0.09	$ 9,750	0.13
Other costs	29,000	0	—	29,000	0.39
Subtotal	$ 59,000	$ 20,250	$0.09	$ 38,750	$0.52
Traceable profit	$ 245,500	$ 231,500	$1.03	$ 14,000	$0.19
Nontraceable costs:					
Conole	45,000				
Professional fees	8,000				
Pretax profit	$ 192,500				

Doc was a bit embarrassed but quite happy. In three short days, his management team had traveled a great distance. They were now tripping over themselves trying to take the blame for something that was probably his fault. He knew his main task now was to hire the accountant, but the negotiations were going to be difficult. He knew what he was worth.

At the end of the next week, the accountant, Jack Hughes, was hired as Chief Financial Officer and as Chief Information Officer. The only stipulation in his contract was that he "allocate" less than 10% of his time to tax matters.

SIX MONTHS LATER

Doc could not believe the difference. Six months ago when the first retreat convened, this group entered the room with boxing gloves laced up. They attended with only one common purpose—to blame each other for their problems. Today, they were actually smiling and congratulating each other!

Jim Thompson began the meeting by reading a "regrets" letter from Mike Green. It seemed that since Green was now actually working only 20-hour weeks

EXHIBIT 4.9   The Smiling Feline, Ltd.: Segmented income statement for year ended 20X4.

	Total	Standard Line	Per Unit	Specialty Line	Per Unit
Sales (units)	550,000	200,000		350,000	
Sales ($)	$3,850,000	$1,320,000	$6.60	$2,530,000	$7.23
Cost of goods sold:					
Rubber	137,500	50,000	0.25	$ 87,500	0.25
Bodies	1,375,000	430,000	2.15	$ 945,000	2.70
Labor	311,500	100,000	0.50	$ 211,500	0.60
Overhead	1,646,000	521,000	2.61	$1,125,000	3.21
Subtotal	$3,470,000	$1,101,000	$5.51	$2,369,000	$6.77
Gross profit	$ 380,000	$ 219,000	$1.10	$ 161,000	$0.46
Operating expenses:					
Freight-out	58,500	18,000	0.09	$ 40,500	0.12
Other costs	30,000	0	—	30,000	0.09
Subtotal	$ 88,500	$ 18,000	$0.09	$ 70,500	$0.20
Traceable profit	$ 291,500	$ 201,000	$1.01	$ 90,500	$0.26
Nontraceable costs:					
Conole	65,000				
Professional fees	10,000				
Pretax profit	$ 216,500				

and that on this particular day he had scheduled a round of golf, he could be with them only in spirit.

The meeting quickly turned serious. Thompson began. "The Cost Detail by Segment Report we produced six months ago really opened my eyes (see Exhibit 4.7). By simply going down that column of numbers it was obvious that certain activities were killing our profitability—namely the $155,000 of scrap, the $108,000 of setup, and the $95,000 cost of Mike's operation. These were all traceable to the specialty line and were caused by the uniqueness of the specialty products that we were running. The setup costs proved somewhat easy to fix. I simply dedicated to specialty items half of the 10 machines that we are now running. This cut the setup costs in half since we avoided having to reset the line for the Smiling Feline—we now go from one specialty item to another on these five machines.

"This quickly led to a more focused design of our factory. We are moving toward a minifactory within our facility totally dedicated to the standard line. Since demand is relatively consistent over the year, we are now trying to bring inbound bodies straight to the production area. These units are immediately run, containerized, and shipped. We plan to eliminate all warehousing for this product line and are far along in implementing this plan. These changes should now make it easier to trace the lease and utility costs directly using the square footage occupied by the two product lines.

"We have also made great strides in attacking the costs of the specialty line. Unique products were killing us. Jane, Mike, and I sat down and went through the scrap and procurement costs on a line-item-by-line-item basis. It became obvious that only the "very" unique products were really hurting us. Thus, we have moved to a "standard" specialty line. Jane now has a sample case of 10 specialty items that we are prepared to run and she has found that this satisfies the majority of our potential customers. Rather than letting them totally design their products, we start them with a basic body type—for example, fat body, thin body, long legs, short legs, and so forth—and let them pick their options. By doing this I now reuse grates, my scrap is down almost 50%, and Mike is playing golf rather than running around qualifying suppliers for some one-of-a-kind body styles. We are all satisfied with this new strategy for the specialty line and it seems to be working. The three items I mentioned should be reduced by 60% by the end of the year. It seems so obvious now, but I just never realized this before we started thinking about activities driving costs."

The meeting lasted only a half day rather than the three of the previous retreat. It focused on how easy and rewarding it was to manage the operations once the activities revealed the "real" sources of resource consumption.

ACTIVITY-BASED COST SYSTEMS

In the early 1950s, the United States had close to 80% of the world's GNP. Faulty information systems did little damage since competition was not intense. In the subsequent 40 years, this has certainly changed.

To sustain a competitive advantage in the global marketplace of today, firms typically follow one of two strategies. If they find themselves in a commodity marketplace, they should push themselves to be the low-cost producer. If they decide to differentiate their products, thereby exiting the commodity arena, the value added to the product in the eyes of the consumer should be greater than the incremental costs to differentiate. Good cost information is a crucial part of either of these strategies. Firms that spread their overhead costs across their product lines simply cannot compete. Global competition has brought the need for state-of-the-art management accounting information systems. As previously stated, information has become a strategic weapon.

In today's world, The Smiling Feline, Ltd. could easily be competing with an Asian or a European Community firm. If you were Conole looking at an income statement, which showed that the cost to produce and deliver your major product was at $6.33 and competition coming into your market was forcing the price down—it basically was becoming a commodity—what would you have done? Add one more piece of information to the decision: A number of customers were clamoring for specialty units and were willing to pay a premium. Within a year, competition had pushed the price down even further and specialty items were obviously almost $2 more profitable (the premium price plus the avoidance of the royalty). At least this is what the accounting information system said. Ultimately, the cost per unit on a subsequent accounting statement showed that the standard items were now "losing money"—price of $6.60 versus total cost of $6.61. Would you fault Conole for handing over the standard line, a market that she essentially developed herself, to her Asian or European competition?

Recent research has shown that many American firms have abandoned lucrative markets due to poor accounting information rather than an inability to compete. Like the management of The Smiling Feline, intense competition has forced American firms to look not only at their production and distribution systems, but also at their costing system.

Cost accounting systems were initially developed in this country in the early 1800s with the rise of the textile industry. Since the product was relatively homogeneous, costs were charged to production on a unit-of-output basis. As production processes became a bit more complicated, costs were attached to products based on the factor that caused them to be incurred, labor. Envision the many pictures you have seen of early American industry. Invariably the pictures showed a multitude of workers tending machines. The overhead costs were incurred to enhance the efficiency of this labor input, and early accountants rightfully attached this pool of support costs using labor as the basis. Overhead costs would be accumulated in a pool and divided by the labor hours to arrive at a charge rate per hour, often only a small percentage of the labor cost.

Now envision a manufacturing environment in today's world. Rather than a multitude of workers, you would probably see mainly technology. Lights-out factories, as automated factories with no workers are called, are a reality. Manufacturing processes have changed dramatically. The majority of American firms today produce a multitude of products using technology as the main production input. Overhead is no longer incurred to augment the labor input; it now replaces it. Cost accounting systems, however, have changed little over these same 175 years.

It has been estimated that three-quarters of American companies still allocate their overhead costs using direct labor as a basis. On average, direct labor in these firms now amounts to less than 10% of the product cost. Overhead rates greater than 1,000% of direct labor cost are not uncommon.

The system that was developed in the preceding story could be termed a crude activity-based cost system (ABCS). Better-managed firms today are recognizing that the costs they incur are the direct result of the activities they undertake to design, produce, and support their products. If they can identify those activities through process-flow mapping, they can better understand and better manage their resource consumption.

Across all industries, manufacturing, service, and health care, early ABCS implementations have yielded consistent results. High-volume items have been subsidizing low-volume business. High-volume items generated more labor hours and, thus, were burdened with more of the overhead pool. Only after the overhead pool is broken down by activity and traced accordingly, do the "real" costs of complexity often brought on by low-volume items begin to be approximated. Again and again, volume has proven to be a poor basis on which to charge overhead costs.

One additional benefit of these systems is that they are transparent and, therefore, make sense. In most firms, managers pay little heed to the internal accounting reports since they do not make sense. Accounting is a "black box" where costs are fed in and magically allocated to end-units. The result is that line management often ignores the cost information or else develops their own "guerrilla" cost systems that they think better matches the situation. Activity systems are based upon the process knowledge of management. Grouping costs by activities is both intuitive and logical—one can now "see" how the cost system reflects the business process. It becomes transparent.

In early implementations, it has been found that management has shown much more confidence with these new accounting systems. Many companies have begun to colocate their management accounting staff with their operational management to promote better communication and, as a result, better cost information systems.

Although first developed as "cost accounting systems," ABCS are quickly becoming decision-support systems. For instance, Jim Thompson, in the preceding story, once he had the activity costs, quickly dedicated a number of machines to the specialty line since he knew, and the accounting system now concurred, that there was a double setup cost. In addition, the standard line machines would now run continually, thereby pushing the cost of this commodity item as low as possible. Jane Conole would now negotiate price on the specialty orders according to any special accommodations the customer requests.

Many ABCS projects have quickly turned into activity-based management (ABM) projects. It makes little sense to design a cost information system based upon an inefficient process. It would make more sense to first reengineer the process (ABM). When the accounting system gives managers better and more transparent information on the cost ramifications of their decisions, they should better manage these decisions. Doc Webster's management team will run a much more competitive business.

STEPS IN THE DESIGN OF AN ABCS

1. Initial feedback usually comes from your marketing function—"We cannot compete given our high costs." This can be caused by three factors: Your technology is not up-to-snuff, your operations are inefficient, or your cost accounting information system is obsolete. Ensure through benchmarking that the first two factors are not the culprit.

2. Envision your value chain—the set of processes that begins at the design stage and ends with customer support. Develop process flow maps for each stage—for example, design, production, distribution, support, and so on—to identify activities that are the root cause of resource consumption.

3. Trace the functional costs as reported in the General Ledger to the activities identified by the process maps. Do not be surprised that activities will load from many different functional areas. For example, an activity such as "product support" may draw costs from both the industrial engineering and customer support functions or "setup" may draw from material handling, indirect labor, and tooling. Think of a grid. You are used to thinking of costs in a vertical, stovepiped functional format (column totals); try to think of them in a more horizontal, activity-based format (row totals).

Activities	Functions				Activity Totals
.	xxx	xxx	xxx	xxx	XXX
.	xxx	xxx	xxx	xxx	XXX
.	xxx	xxx	xxx	xxx	XXX
.	xxx	xxx	xxx	xxx	XXX
Functional totals	XXX	XXX	XXX	XXX	XXX

4. Develop a costing rate by dividing the total cost for each activity by an appropriate measure of that activity. An *appropriate measure* is defined as a measure that is constant over the activity. For instance, if all setups were relatively the same, the appropriate measure would be simply the number of setups. If they vary, however, say due to complexity, one might use a measure of time—for example, cost per minute of setup, or of complexity—for example, simple, average, and difficult.

5. Be extremely careful in your choice of appropriate measure if your cost pool is predominately fixed in nature. For instance, if your setup cost pool was mainly salaried people costs, the appropriate measure would be some estimate of the setup capacity that pool of people could perform. To illustrate, assume that you employed four people on a salaried basis to perform the various aspects of setup for a monthly total cost of $25,000. If this group

performed 25 setups last month (assume all setups are basically the same), would this mean that a setup costs $1,000? The answer is "No." If they could perform 50 setups in a month but happened to be idle half their time last month, from a customer value chain perspective, this does not mean the idle cost should automatically be charged to the product. The cost of a setup is theoretically $500 ($25,000/50 setups per month) and the role of management is to ensure that that pool is used efficiently. If only 25 are performed, then more useful information would be to charge $12,500 to the production process (25 sets × $500 per setup) and the other $12,500 to idle time. Once this idle charge is identified, management, in an ABM mindset, should be able to find a better solution to their setup inefficiencies than to simply pass the cost on to the customer. This could lead to a disadvantage in a competitive marketplace.

6. Using these costing rates, trace the costs of your operation to the appropriate level—unit, batch/order, product line, facility, market segment, channel, or customer. Note, as The Smiling Feline management team discovered, not all costs can be traced to the unit level. But also remember that it is not always necessary to trace the costs to this level. The Smiling Feline, Ltd. found the order level was more than sufficient for decision making.

7. Facility costs will undoubtedly cause the most problems. Some accountants feel that a quasi-CVP (cost-versus-price) model is sufficient and argue that one can price the products such that the margin (price less direct costs) covers the facility costs plus the desired profit. If you feel that total costs must be calculated, then allocate the facility cost to the units. But do this carefully. For instance, what if the financial accounting system depreciates equipment using a declining balance method for tax reasons, but the operational flow indicates that a units of production method would be more appropriate? The inflated depreciation charge may prove to be a major disadvantage when developing cost information for competitive pricing. You may want to adjust this cost using the units of production depreciation method. Likewise, you may want to give thought to using future replacement estimates rather than past historical costs to value the asset being depreciated.

Above all, remember that you are making a major change in the way your organization processes information. Do not attempt to institute too major a change. Be happy to start the ball rolling. Experience to date has indicated that activity-based systems are well received under certain circumstances. Operations people readily accept the concepts integral to this information system. Unlike the black box accounting system they now deal with, this new system is both transparent and logical. Operations people understand that activities consume resources. They see this every working day. Once you start the ball rolling, it will gain its own momentum. Most companies have found that once the initial system is implemented, refinements and extensions naturally flow upward from the people performing the activities that cause the costs to be incurred.

Many ABC systems have failed, however. It is very difficult to install an ABC software system with an outside consulting firm. You might be replacing one black box with another. If an outside firm is brought in to install an ABC system, it is important that a team of managers play a lead role in the design of the system for two reasons. You need buy-in from your operational managers. First, like the situation described in the preceding story, only the managers understand the activities. And, equally as important, when the consulting firms leave, your managers must feel that they "own" the system—only then will it be maintained and updated as processes change.

FOR FURTHER READING

Brimson, James, *Activity Accounting: An Activity-Based Costing Approach* (New York: John Wiley & Sons, 1991).

Cokins, et al., *An ABC Manager's Primer* (Montvale, NJ: IMA, 1993).

KPMG Peat Marwick, et al., *Implementing Activity-Based Cost Management: Moving from Analysis to Action* (Montvale, NJ: IMA, 1992).

Pryor, Tom, *Activity Dictionary* (Arlington, Texas: ICMS, 1992).

Romano, Patrick L., ed., *Activity-Based Management in Action* (Montvale, NJ: IMA, 1994).

Shank, John K. and Vijay Govindarajan, *Strategic Cost Management* (New York: Free Press, 1993).

Turney, Peter and Alan Stratton, *Common Cents: The ABC Performance Breakthrough* (Hillsboro, OR: Cost Technology, 1992).

5 INFORMATION TECHNOLOGY AND YOU

Theodore Grossman

INTRODUCTION

While personal computers have been around for quite some time, many people are just starting to become comfortable with the technology. The range of acceptance and knowledge spans a continuum, on which the technical novice lies at one end and the "techie" at the other end. Where you fall on the continuum will dictate what you gain from this chapter. If you are fortunate to fall near the techie side, skim this chapter for ideas which you might find interesting. All the rest of you, read on.

Technology has changed the way people conduct business. Computers have replaced pencil and paper in contemporary business life. In prior times, when a new employee was hired, he or she was shown to a desk and given pen, pencil, paper, and a telephone. Today, the new hire is given a computer, usually attached to a network; a cellular phone; a beeper; and, possibly, a laptop computer for portable use. Peoples' lives have been turned upside down as they learn to manage the latest technology. E-mail is replacing U.S. Mail. Secretaries are being replaced by personal productivity technology such as voice mail. People question how much more productive they—as workers—can be. Technology will allow managers' and workers' productivity to reach the next plateau and enable them to find better and alternative modes for working and succeeding.

The 1990s have changed not only the way people work, but also, in some cases, the venue from which they perform their work. No longer are workers chained to their desks. The number of *telecommuters*—people who work from home via computer and telephone communications—is increasing dramatically. Business people who travel with their portable computers have become so prevalent that hotels have installed special hardware on their hotel room telephones that allows guests to plug their computers into the telephone system and communicate with their home offices. Sometimes people even connect their laptop computer modems to the airline telephones at their seats!

How much do you need to understand about the technology to become technologically enabled? Even though it is not necessary to understand how the watch works in order to tell time, it is nonetheless important to understand how to tell time and the importance of knowing the time of day.

HARDWARE

Computer hardware comes in several shapes and sizes. This chapter concentrates on personal computers (PCs). Over the past 10 years, Microsoft and Intel have set the standard for PC hardware and software. It is referred to as the *Wintel standard,* which is short for Microsoft Windows and the Intel CPU chip. More than 90% of all personal computers use the Wintel standard, affecting both the hardware marketplace and the applications software that is developed. Currently, Compaq is the largest producer of personal computers, with IBM following closely behind.

Personal computers come in two basic shapes, desktop and laptop. Regardless of their shape, all PCs have the same basic components. Users can choose some of these components, whereas others, they cannot. The basic components with which users must concern themselves are the CPU, RAM, hard disk, CD ROM, modem, and display.

CPU

All basic computers have a *central processing unit* (CPU). As mentioned earlier, it is usually provided by Intel Corporation or one of the clone-chip manufacturers. The Intel Pentium chip is currently the processor of choice. This computer on a chip consists of several million components. It was originally introduced in the mid-1990s, and the current version is available in several different speeds. CPUs such as the Pentium, or its future successor, the Pentium Pro, come in different speeds, expressed in megahertz (millions of cycles per second). Speed represents how fast the CPU is capable of performing its various calculations and data manipulations.

RAM

Random access memory (RAM) is the space that the computer uses to execute programs. The amount of RAM required is dictated by the number of applications that the computer is asked to run simultaneously; for most average users, 16 to 32 megabytes of RAM is an appropriate amount. You can never have too much RAM, though, so the more, the better.

Hard Disk

All programs and data are stored on the *hard disk*. Disk technology has advanced greatly in the past five years. Recording density has enabled disk capacity to approach numbers unheard of, except in large mainframe, commercial systems. In 1992, the typical disk stored 80 megabytes (millions of bytes of data). Today, disks store between 1 and 3 gigabytes (billions of bytes of data). Although it seems unimaginable to fill up an entire 1 gigabyte disk, it happens faster than one might think. Typical office applications require 100 megabytes of storage for the application alone, not including any associated data. Again, the more storage the better. However, the greater a computer's capacity, the more it tends to accumulate unnecessary information.

Reminder: Hard disk failures do occur. Always back up your data onto a removable disk or tape!

CD ROM

Today, an increasing amount of data and applications are being supplied on digital, compact disk technology. Using this technology, large amounts of data can be stored inexpensively. *CD ROMs,* which have the storage capacity for approximately 800 megabytes of data, are usually sold as read only. Inexpensive read/writable CD ROMs are starting to become available and will be more prevalent in the coming years. Other than the speed at which they access and transfer data, CD ROMs are very similar. Speed is expressed as a multiple of the speed of the original CD ROMs, which were produced in the early 1990s. Today, the standard is either 6X or 8X. Again, the faster, the better.

There are numerous information databases available on CD that would be of interest to the accountant or finance executive. For example, most census data is available on CD. Also, historical data on stock and bond prices, copies of most trade articles, IRS regulations, state tax regulations, tax forms, recent court decisions, tax services, accounting standards (GAAP and GAAS), continuing education courses, and many other topics are available on CD.

Modems

Modems are devices that allow computers to communicate with each other using standard telephone lines. In the past few years, modem technology has increased the speed of data communications over standard telephone line to speeds seven times higher than in 1990. However, there is a practical limit to how fast computers can transmit data over ordinary telephone lines, and that limit has been reached at approximately 33 KB (kilobaud—thousands of bits per second).

Because of the limitations of telephone lines, alternatives have been and are being developed, including ISDN and other leased lines available from the telephone companies. Cable will also change the paradigm of communications. Once cable companies modify their infrastructures, the speed of computer-computer and computer-Internet communications could increase by a factor of 1,000.

Multimedia

In the latter half of the 1990s, most new personal computers came equipped for *multimedia,* the ability to seamlessly display text, audio, and full-motion video. To be capable of multimedia, a computer must be equipped with a high-resolution monitor and a compact disk, and have audio capabilities. In the more recent releases of the Pentium chip, Intel has included some electronics to help speed up video processing. Because of the amount of storage that video requires, full-motion video is somewhat difficult to accomplish on a personal computer. For it to look smooth, it requires a speed of 30 frames per second, and each frame, or one computer screen's worth of information, requires about 500,000 characters of information. In other words, one minute of smooth video could require as much as 900,000,000 characters of storage. In order to manage the large amount of storage that video processing requires, the video data is compressed. Data compression examines the data and, using an algorithm or formula, reduces the amount of necessary storage space by eliminating redundancies in the data. Then, before the data is displayed, it is inflated back to its original form with little or no loss of picture quality.

Printers

Printer technology has stabilized in recent years, with two standards having emerged, *laser printers* and *inkjet printers.* Laser printers offer the best quality and speed. They are, for the most part, black and white and offer high print resolution. There are several speed and memory options, and models range in price from $400 for the individual user to several thousand dollars for a fast unit that offers printer sharing and color. Inkjet printers offer the lowest price. Models cost around $200. The print quality is excellent, though the resolution is not as good as that of a laser printer; inkjets can also print in black and white or color.

Laser printers are the clear choice for network sharing, while inkjets have become the mainstay of the individual user. In either case, Hewlett-Packard is the market leader in the development of printers.

Device Drivers

Not all hardware products are the same. Rather, some require different software in order to interface with the computer. Windows comes equipped to interface to many of the hardware products, but it requires special software drivers to act as an interpreter for both Windows and the hardware device. These device drivers accompany the hardware product, are usually supplied on a floppy disk, and must be installed when first using the new hardware product.

In its Windows95 operating system, Microsoft introduced plug and play, a feature that, for years, has been part of Apple's software. When a new device is connected to the computer for the first time, Windows will sense the presence of the product and prompt the user through the installation of the appropriate device drivers.

Desktop Computers

Underneath their covers, most desktop computers are the same. Many of the various manufacturers of desktop machines use parts from the same suppliers, as there are only a handful of companies that manufacture hard disk drives and many other desktop components. Before buying a machine, compare the attributes and capabilities of many different machines. Also, check the warranty offered by the different manufacturers. One-year warranties are standard; however, many computers come with three-year warranties. Beware of hype advertising and read the fine print. Most advertising specials do not include the monitor. The monitor could cost as much as an additional $250 to $450, depending upon its size.

Laptop Computers

The laptop has become a mainstay for the traveling worker. It provides all the functionality and most of the power of most desktop units, in a package that weighs approximately six pounds. Laptops are powered by standard electricity or, for about two hours, by their self-contained batteries. Unlike desktop units, under the covers, all laptops are not the same. While they all utilize either an Intel or Intel clone chip, the majority of the electronics is frequently custom designed. Consequently, servicing laptops is more complicated, and laptop parts are not necessarily interchangeable.

The display screen is one of the most important features of the laptop computer. Display quality and size are rapidly approaching that of desktop machines. Some laptop machines use active matrix technology, while others utilize passive matrix technology. Active matrix provides the best view of the screen, a clearer picture, and better colors. Passive matrix technology is of lesser quality, but it is also less costly to the consumer.

Although laptops provide the luxury of portability, that is their *only* advantage over desktop machines. Desktops offer better displays, more memory, and higher speed—higher performance for far less money.

OPERATING SYSTEMS

The *operating system* is the basic software that makes the computer run. *Applications software* is the software that runs a particular user function. Some say that the operating system is the software closest to the machine, while the applications software is the software closest to the user.

Microsoft Windows is the predominant software for the personal computer. In the past five years, Microsoft has become the acknowledged leader in the development of both operating system and office automation software. The Windows operating system provides a graphical format for communicating between the computer and the user, while a pointing device, such as a mouse, is used to point to the icon of the folder or application that the user wishes to open.

APPLICATIONS SOFTWARE

Applications software is the personal computer's raison d'être. Although there are a multitude of applications available for the PC, this chapter focuses on the following personal productivity types of programs:

- Word processing
- Spreadsheets
- Presentation graphics
- Databases
- Personal finance

Most of the popular packages are available as application suites, which include word processing, spreadsheets, graphics, and sometimes database management systems. Microsoft Office is one of the most widely used suites; it includes Word for Windows (word processing), Excel (spreadsheet), PowerPoint (presentation graphics), and Access (database).

The original spreadsheet application was developed at the very beginning of the PC revolution and was called VisiCalc. It was later replaced by Lotus 1-2-3, which became the standard until the tremendous success of Microsoft Office and Excel.

Word Processing

Of the two most popular applications, word processing and spreadsheets, word processing has increased people's ability to communicate more effectively. With word processing software, the user can create, edit, and produce a high-quality document that appears as professional as that of any large organization. Thus, word processing has become the great business equalizer, making it difficult to decipher a small company or single practitioner from the large, Fortune 500 company with the dedicated media department.

Today's word processing is as powerful as most desktop publishing software, and it is so simple to use that any novice equipped with simple instructions can master the software. Not only can documents include text, but they can also contain spreadsheet tables, drawings, and pictures; be specially formatted; and be in black and white or color. Most word processing applications come with clip art, which consists of drawings, cartoons, symbols, or caricatures that can be incorporated into the document for emphasis.

Spreadsheet Software

For the accounting and finance executive, spreadsheet software has had the greatest impact on productivity. Imagine the controller of a prespreadsheet software company who has been asked to prepare the budget for the coming year. The company manufactures in excess of 1,000 products with special pricing, depending on volume. The controller not only has to make assumptions about material costs, which might change over time, but also has a prior history of expense levels that must be factored into the analysis. Using pencil and paper (usually a columnar pad), the controller calculates and prepares all of the schedules necessary to produce the final page of the report, which contains the income statement and cash flow. Thinking that all the figuring has been done, the controller presents the findings to management, only to be asked to modify some of the underlying assumptions to reflect an unexpected change in the business. As a result, the controller must go back over all of the sheets, erasing and recalculating, then erasing and recalculating some more.

The creation of spreadsheets rendered this painful process unnecessary. Spreadsheets allow the user to create the equivalent of those columnar sheets, but with embedded formulas. Consequently, any financial executive can create a financial simulation of a business. Thus, merely by changing any of a multitude of assumptions, one can immediately see the ramifications of those changes. Spreadsheets allow for quick and easy *what if* analyses. What if the bank changes the interest rate on my loan by 1%? What impact will that have on my cash flow and income? In addition, most of the packages provide utilities for graphing results, which can be used independently or integrated into either a word processing report or a graphics presentation.

A spreadsheet is composed of a series of columns and rows. The intersection of a row and column is referred to as a *cell.* Columns have alphabetic letters, while rows have numbers. Cell reference B23 indicates the cell in column B and row 23.

Exhibit 5.1 provides an example of a simple spreadsheet application. A sample company's pro forma income statement, the spreadsheet is a plan for what the company expects its performance to reflect. In this example, the company expects to earn $188,936 (cell B20) after tax on $774,000 (cell B3) of sales revenues. At the bottom of the exhibit, there is a series of assumptions that govern the way the calculations are performed in this spreadsheet. For example, cost of goods sold is always equal to 32.75% of sales, and freight is always equal to 4.5% of sales. Likewise, the income tax rate for this company is set at 25%.

Looking behind the cells (Exhibit 5.2), you can see the spreadsheet's formula infrastructure. For example, cell C4, which calculates the cost of goods sold for the month of January, contains the formula that requires the spreadsheet to multiply the cost of goods sold percentage that is shown in cell B23 by the sales shown in cell C3; the formula in cell C5, which calculates the gross profit, subtracts the cost of goods sold in cell C4 from the sales in cell C3; and cell B5, which calculates the total gross profit for the six months of January through June, contains the formula that adds the contents of cells C5 through H5.

The spreadsheet is set up so that, should the user wish to change any of the assumptions, such as the cost of goods sold percentage, the contents of cell B23 would be changed to a new desired value, and the change would be instantaneously displayed. As mentioned earlier, most spreadsheet packages provide excellent facilities for displaying data in a graphical format. Exhibit 5.3 presents a graph of the information in our demonstration spreadsheet. It contrasts sales and net profit over the six months.

Presentation Graphics Software

Presentation graphics software is used to create slide presentations. These presentations can include a variety of media through which information can be presented to an audience, such as text, graphs, pictures, and sound. Special effects are also available, meaning animation can be incorporated as the system transitions from one slide to the next. Slides can be printed, in both black and white

EXHIBIT 5.1 Pro forma income statement.

	A	B	C	D	E	F	G	H
					Pro Forma Income Statement			
1								
2		Year to date	January	February	March	April	May	June
3	Sales	$ 774,000	$ 100,000	$ 125,000	$ 135,000	$ 127,000	$ 132,000	$ 155,000
4	Cost of goods sold	$ 253,485	$ 32,750	$ 40,938	$ 44,213	$ 41,595	$ 43,230	$ 50,763
5	Gross profit	$ 520,515	$ 67,250	$ 84,063	$ 90,788	$ 85,408	$ 88,770	$ 104,238
6								
7	Operating expenses							
8	Salaries	$ 86,688	$ 11,200	$ 14,000	$ 15,120	$ 14,224	$ 14,784	$ 17,360
9	Benefits	$ 19,765	$ 2,554	$ 3,192	$ 3,447	$ 3,243	$ 3,371	$ 3,958
10	Rent	$ 19,200	$ 3,200	$ 3,200	$ 3,200	$ 3,200	$ 3,200	$ 3,200
11	Utilities	$ 22,840	$ 4,300	$ 4,750	$ 3,790	$ 4,100	$ 3,100	$ 2,800
12	Depreciation	$ 7,200	$ 1,200	$ 1,200	$ 1,200	$ 1,200	$ 1,200	$ 1,200
13	Freight	$ 11,407	$ 1,474	$ 1,842	$ 1,990	$ 1,872	$ 1,945	$ 2,284
14	Advertising	$ 92,880	$ 12,000	$ 15,000	$ 16,200	$ 15,240	$ 15,840	$ 18,600
15	Supplies	$ 8,620	$ 1,300	$ 1,400	$ 1,270	$ 1,500	$ 1,550	$ 1,600
16	Total operating expenses	$ 268,600	$ 37,227	$ 44,584	$ 46,217	$ 44,579	$ 44,990	$ 51,002
17								
18	Net profit before taxes	$ 268,600	$ 30,023	$ 39,478	$ 44,571	$ 40,829	$ 43,780	$ 53,235
19	Income taxes	$ 62,979	$ 7,506	$ 9,870	$ 11,143	$ 10,207	$ 10,945	$ 13,309
20	Net profit after taxes	$ 188,936	$ 22,517	$ 29,609	$ 33,428	$ 30,622	$ 32,835	$ 39,926
21								
22	Assumptions							
23	Cost of goods sold %	32.75%						
24	Salaries (% sales)	11.20%						
25	Benefits (% salaries)	22.80%						
26	Advertising (% sales)	12.00%						
27	Income taxes %	25.00%						
28	Freight (% cost of goods)	4.50%						

EXHIBIT 5.2 Spreadsheet formula infrastructure.

	A	B	C	D	E	F	G	H
1					Pro Forma Income Statement			
2		Year to date	January	February	March	April	May	June
3	Sales	=SUM(C3:H3)	100000	125000	135000	127000	132000	155000
4	Cost of goods sold	=SUM(C4:H4)	=$B23*C3	=$B23*D3	=$B23*E3	=$B23*F3	=$B23*G3	=$B23*H3
5	Gross profit	=SUM(C5:H5)	=C3-C4	=D3-D4	=E3-E4	=F5-F4	=G3-G4	=H3-H4
6								
7	Operating expenses							
8	Salaries	=SUM(C8:H8)	=$B24*C3	=$B24*D3	=$B24*E3	=$B24*F3	=$B24*G3	=$B24*H3
9	Benefits	=SUM(C9:H9)	=$B25*C8	=$B25*D8	=$B25*E8	=$B25*F8	=$B25*G8	=$B25*H8
10	Rent	=SUM(C10:H10)	3200	3200	3200	3200	3200	3200
11	Utilities	=SUM(C11:H11)	4300	4750	3790	4100	3100	2800
12	Depreciation	=SUM(C12:H12)	1200	1200	1200	1200	1200	1200
13	Freight	=SUM(C13:H13)	=$B28*C4	=$B28*D4	=$B28*E4	=$B28*F4	=$B28*G4	=$B28*H4
14	Advertising	=SUM(C14:H14)	=$B26*C3	=$B26*D3	=$B26*E3	=$B26*F3	=$B26*G3	=$B26*H3
15	Supplies	=SUM(C15:H15)	1300	1400	1270	1500	1550	1600
16	Total operating expenses	=SUM(C16:H16)	=SUM(C8:C15)	=SUM(D8:D15)	=SUM(E8:E15)	=SUM(F8:F15)	=SUM(G8:G15)	=SUM(H8:H1)
17								
18	Net profit before taxes	=SUM(B16)	=C5-C16	=D5-D16	=E5-E16	=F5-F16	=G5-G16	=H5-H16
19	Income taxes	=SUM(C19:H19)	=$B27*C18	=$B27*D18	=$B27*E18	=$B27*F18	=$B27*G18	=$B27*H18
20	Net profit after taxes	=SUM(C20:H20)	=C18-C19	=D18-D19	=E18-E19	=F18-F19	=G18-G19	=H18-H19
21								
22	Assumptions							
23	Cost of goods sold %	0.3275						
24	Salaries (% sales)	0.112						
25	Benefits (% salaries)	0.228						
26	Advertising (% sales)	0.12						
27	Income taxes %	0.25						
28	Freight (% cost of goods)	0.045						

EXHIBIT 5.3   Pro forma sales and income.

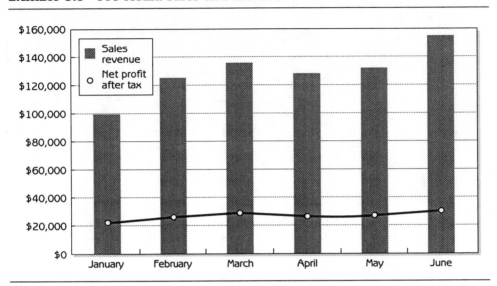

and color, for use on overhead projectors. Alternatively, the computer can be directly connected to a projection system for projection onto a screen or a television monitor, allowing the presenter to utilize the software's animation and sound features. Most of the software comes equipped with various, predeveloped background formats and clip art to help simplify the process of creating the presentation. Also, these software packages allow for the import of both graphs and text from other software packages, such as word processing and spreadsheets.

Database Software

A *database* is a collection of data stored in such a way that the user may create and identify relationships between data. For example, a mailing list of one's customers might contain information about each customer's purchases and everything about the sales transactions, including the prices they paid, who sold it to them, how they paid, and so forth. This information can be retrieved in a variety of ways, usually specified by the user at the time of execution. The user might want a list of all customers that purchased a specific product between January and May or, possibly, a list of all products a customer has purchased, in aggregate, that were ordered from a particular salesperson. The number of possible combinations and permutations and ways in which one views the data is limited only by the collection of the data and the imagination of the user. Databases are discussed in more detail in Chapter 16, Information Technology and the Firm.

Personal Finance Software

There are several software packages that allow individuals or small businesses to manage finances, such as paying bills, either electronically or by check, and monitor investments. The packages are fairly sophisticated, in that they provide for both communication with electronic payment services and the importing of current stock market quotes. The most widely used package is Quicken and, for small businesses, Quickbooks.

Exhibit 5.4 displays a sample screen that is used to enter bills to be paid. As you can see, the user input metaphor is that of a check, the very same document the user would use if he or she were preparing to pay the bill manually. The difference is that, by using this method, data is collected for a host of other purposes:

- Paying bills
- Tracking paid bills by category for budgeting purposes
- Tracking payments for tax purposes
- Reconciling the checking account

The system has the capability to keep track of more than one account and to allow for interaccount transfers.

EXHIBIT 5.4   Sample screen: Paying bills.

NETWORKING

One of the advents of the 1990s was the *networking,* or interconnecting, of computers, which has facilitated the sharing and exchanging of information. The interconnecting may be through direct wires within a building or, using modems, via the telephone system. In a computer network, a host or *file server* acts as the traffic policeman, storing common data and directing the network traffic. The user terminal is frequently referred to as the *client* in the network. A picture of a typical network appears in Exhibit 5.5.

As mentioned earlier, the file server is the centerpiece of the network, and the software that makes the network operate is called the *network operating system.* Novell's NetWare and Microsoft's Windows NT are the most popular of the network operating systems. Within a business, the typical network is called a *local area network,* or LAN. Clients are connected to the server, using wires or fiber-optic cabling. Transmission speeds are generally about 10 megabytes per second. Usually, there is a device called a *hub,* which acts as a concentrator for all of the cabling. Each PC on the network must have a network interface card if it is connected to a LAN, or a modem, if it is connected through telephone lines. When a series of LANs in different cities are interconnected, they form a *wide area network,* or WAN. Large businesses, with facilities around the country or world, network their users' personal computers together in a series of LANs, which are further interconnected into a large WAN. The largest WAN, the Internet, connects together the computers of commercial companies, government agencies, schools, colleges and universities, and not-for-profit agencies.

Preventing unauthorized people from accessing confidential information is one of the biggest challenges posed by networks. To do so, people and organizations use special security software. One technique, a *fire wall,* allows outside users to obtain only that data which is outside the "fire wall" of the file server; subsequently, only people inside of the company may access information inside the "fire wall."

EXHIBIT 5.5   A typical network.

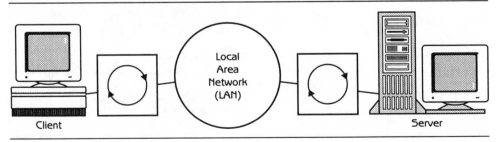

Electronic Mail (E-mail)

E-mail is the most popular network application, as it has become the method of choice for communicating over both short distances (interoffice) and long distances. It allows you to send communications to any other person on your local network, as well as to any other network within your WAN, including the Internet. E-mail has become so popular that U.S. Mail and overnight delivery services such as FedEx are being rendered obsolete for some types of communication.

Most e-mail software packages include a basic word processing application with which you can generate your letters. In addition, these packages allow you to keep mailing lists and to send a document to numerous people simultaneously. A document, once sent, can be received within minutes by people thousands of miles away. One of the more advantageous features of e-mail is that it allows you to attach another document—a spreadsheet, graphic presentation, another word processing report, or even a database—to your letter, much as you would do with a paper clip.

Imagine that you have used a spreadsheet package to prepare a budget for your division in Boston. You print out your letter and spreadsheet and mail or ship it overnight to the main office in Chicago. You may even include an electronic copy of your spreadsheet on a floppy disk, in case the individual in Chicago needs to further modify the numbers. Sometime within the next day or two, the recipient will receive the package. He or she will then read the information, and may even use the floppy disk for additional reporting. Alternatively, using e-mail, you draft your letter, electronically attach the spreadsheet file, and send it, via e-mail, to your recipient in Chicago. Within a couple of minutes, he or she will receive the electronic package and read your letter, and if necessary, extract your attachment and load it directly into a spreadsheet software package for any necessary additional processing.

Since most colleges and universities are on the Internet, many college students use e-mail regularly to keep in contact with their friends, both in the United States and around the world. Likewise, parents of college students have picked up the e-mail bug and use it to correspond with their children.

The Internet

The Internet is the worldwide WAN that has become the major growth area in technology and the business community. The network was originally developed in the 1970s by a consortium of research colleges and universities and the federal government, to find a way to share research data and provide a secure way of communicating and backing up defense facilities. The original network was called ARPANET. In the 1980s, it was replaced by the current network, which was originally not very user-friendly and used mostly by techies. The Internet's popularity exploded with the development of the World Wide Web and the necessary software programs that made the "Web" very user-friendly to explore.

Accessing the Internet requires that the user connect to it. This connection is referred to as a *node.* Large organizations have a dedicated data link to the Internet using very fast data telephone lines. Individual users access the Internet using third-party companies, called Internet providers. They allow users to dial into their computers, which are connected directly to the Internet.

World Wide Web

Though the terms Internet, World Wide Web, the Web, and the Net have become synonymous, the Web is actually a subsystem of the Internet. Every site that appears on the Internet has an address composed of a user name, a company or organization name, called a domain name, and a domain type. For example, Smith@GenRad.com refers to a user named Smith, at a commercial company named GenRad. These addresses are referred to as *universal resource locators* or URLs. The domain types are as follows:

.com	commercial organization
.org	not-for-profit organization
.mil	military group
.edu	educational institution

Each Web site displays its information using a series of Web pages. A Web page may contain text, drawings, pictures, even audio and video, as well as blue text called hypertext. Position your mouse pointer over one of these words, and the arrow changes to a drawing of a hand. Click the mouse, and the computer will automatically move to a new Web page. This move is called a *hypertext link.* Using these hypertext links, a user can move around the Internet, from page to page, company to company, state to state, country to country.

Many companies have put much of their literature on the Web, thereby using the Web as an electronic catalogue. Home pages are the first page of information that you encounter when you reach a company's information. Companies use their Web sites as a marketing tool and as a means of distributing information about their products. Instead of waiting on a telephone line for customer service, the user can go on line to get expert help about frequently asked questions (FAQs), at any time of day, unattended. For example, the AICPA has a Web site at aicpa.org. Available at that Web site are many of the AICPA services, including information on their membership, conferences, continuing education, publications, and IRS forms. The home page for The Financial Management Association, located at www.fma.org, is another interesting site for financial executives. This site provides information on all of their services with links to other pages.

Computer hardware and software companies use the Web as a device for distributing software to users. As software device drivers change, users can download the new software over the Net. The Net also provides a venue for people with common interests to "chat" electronically in "chat rooms."

Internet Search Engines

The Web has become so extensive, with so much information available to the user, that often one literally does not know where to look. Consequently, search engines were created to help users navigate the Web. Search engines like Yahoo, Alta Vista, Lycos, and Magellan constantly explore the Web, categorizing each site. When presented with key words or a topic to be searched, they will provide the user with a list and description of each site that contains the information requested in the search. The results display also includes hypertext links, enabling the user to click on and link to any of the sites presented in the search results.

Privacy on the Internet

When using the Internet for e-mail or other applications, it is essential to remember that, like the radio spectrum, it is a public network. With the right skill, anyone who is on the Internet has the ability to "listen in" on your electronic transaction. While the transaction will not be sidelined, its confidentiality might be compromised. Beware! Never send across the Net any confidential information that you would not want any other person or company to know. While there is available encryption technology to protect data from prying eyes, it is not generally used. However, because electronic commerce and the transmission of credit card data are becoming more common, encryption and other methods of security are being used more and more.

Electronic Commerce

Electronic commerce, the ability to purchase goods and services over the Net, has largely been unsuccessful to date but, nonetheless, has great potential. There have been numerous failed experiments where retailers and manufacturers have sold their products directly to consumers on the Net. There are many reasons for the lack of success. First, as previously mentioned, security for protecting credit card and other confidential data concerning sales transactions is only currently becoming available. Second, shopping in cyberspace is different from shopping in the physical space. When shopping in the physical space, consumers are buying physical products. In cyberspace, though, the metaphors by which consumers shop on the Net are only two-dimensional representations of what they see when shopping in stores. Essentially, cyberspace consumers are only being supplied information about products.

Consequently, for electronic commerce to be successful, the mode and the metaphor for the cyberspace shopping experience must be improved. New mechanisms for Internet shopping will be developed, many of which will include experiments in virtual reality and the appearance of three-dimensional venues. Also, the shopping experience will be custom-tailored to you, the individual consumer. Internet sites will learn to keep a profile on you when you visit their site. These profiles will include information on what products you buy and what products you tend to look at, allowing the Internet sites to create shopping experiences specific to your needs.

As electronic shopping becomes more effective, virtual malls, or groupings of stores that share the same electronic Internet address, will spring up on the Internet, creating the feel of a physical mall. Both consumers and retailers will be able to benefit from one-stop shopping in cyberspace.

Still, one of the most significant stumbling blocks affecting electronic shopping is the fact that the majority of Internet users are male, yet, the majority of shoppers are female. Once this gender imbalance is resolved, and more women are accustomed to using the Internet, electronic shopping will occur much more regularly.

Audio

Audio is another of the "objects" available for viewing on the Internet. There are several sites on the Net where one can obtain audio clips, listen to music, or listen to radio shows. For example, NFL football games and commentaries are available on the National Football League's or National Public Radio's respective Web pages. In addition, music companies are experimenting with allowing consumers to listen to music in the comfort of their homes before buying the albums.

THE FUTURE—TODAY, TOMORROW, AND NEXT WEEK

Although the industrial revolution occurred toward the beginning of the nineteenth century, yet today we are still feeling its effects. Consider for a moment how our everyday lives have changed as a result of those innovations. The computer revolution began about 1950, and the microprocessor—the heart of the PC revolution—has been exploited only for the last 15 years. Now think about how our everyday lives have changed as a result of these innovations. Remember, the microprocessor is part of so many of our appliances, computers, automobiles, watches, and so forth. The impact of the computer revolution is just as large, if not larger, than its precursor, the industrial revolution, and over far less time. Moreover, the acceleration of change in our lives that results from the use of computer technology has been rapidly increasing. Technologists speak about the rapid changes in the development of the Internet and its allied products. They even joke that things are happening so fast that three months is equivalent to an "Internet year." Funny, but true.

The Internet and the way we transact business from home is limited by the speed of our communications technology. As mentioned earlier in this chapter, the telephone system's transmission speed has a practical limitation of about 33 kilobytes per second, which is insufficient to support the growing communications demands. People will need to simultaneously utilize this network for data, voice, and video, a load that will require transmission bandwidths of at least 10 times the limit of normal telephone lines. The U.S. Congress passed legislation in early 1996 changing the telecommunications industry. No longer are telephone companies and long-distance companies prohibited from competing. Ultimately, there will be one fiber cable, of some sort, that will supply each home with very high-speed data access, providing voice, data, cable television, and video communications.

This section is aptly named "The Future—Today, Tomorrow, and Next Week," because the horizon for change in the world of technology is very short. Each year, major enhancements to both hardware and technology are released, rendering previous technology obsolete. Some people are paralyzed from buying computers, because they are concerned that the technology will change very soon. How right they are! The promise of technology is that it is constantly changing. Today's worker must recognize that and learn to adapt to the changing methods. Those who are technologically comfortable will be the first to gain strategic advantage in the work environment and succeed. A word to the wise: Hold on to your hat, and enjoy the ride. Adapt and go with it.

FOR FURTHER READING

There are many excellent books on the personal use of computer systems. Topics run the spectrum, ranging from books about individual software packages, with detailed "how to" examples to help the user become acclimated to the software package, to books that explain how to program a computer. Many of these books come equipped with either a floppy disk or CD and include step-by-step examples and exercises. There are several popular series of these books. The following are the names of but some of the series:

- SYBEX has a series of books on Microsoft's Office software, including *Mastering Microsoft Office Professional for Windows95* by Mosely and Boodey.
- QUE has published many books on various software applications, including *Using Microsoft Office for Windows95* and *Using the Internet.*
- IDG Books has a series of books that are very noticeable. They are all titled *"something" for Dummies,* where the "something" would be the name of the software package (e.g., Excel: *Excel for Dummies*).
- Microsoft Books also publishes numerous titles for users, including *Running Microsoft Office for Windows95* by Halverson and Young.

6 FORECASTS AND BUDGETS

Les Heitger

THE CONCEPT OF BUDGETING

Few accounting terms are used more often in everyday conversation than the term *budget* or *budgeting*. Television newscasters talk of city or state budget problems. The federal government budget deficit grows ever larger. Employees are told that attending a professional conference is, "Just not in the budget this year." A wife tells her husband, "Our spending seems to be out of hand; we need a family budget." Budgeting is mentioned regularly in the news, in our business experiences, and in our personal lives. Unfortunately, budgets do not mean the same thing to everyone. The concept of budgeting is simple enough, but the experiences that people have with budgets vary significantly from person to person.

There are many budgeting definitions, but most are similar to the following definition: A *budget* is a comprehensive, formal plan, expressed in quantitative terms, describing the expected operations of an organization over some future time period. As you can see, the characteristics of a budget are that it deals with a specific entity, covers a specific future time period, and is expressed in quantitative terms.

Virtually all organizations prepare some form of budget. City, state, and federal government organizations, for example, are required by law to prepare budgets. Businesses, although not required by law to prepare budgets, find that they just cannot operate effectively and efficiently without budgets. Even many individuals find that budgets are useful, if not essential, in many aspects of their personal lives. Below is a simple illustration of a budget for a specific activity two people are planning.

A Simple Budget Illustration

Dave and Karen are engaged to be married in five months. They are trying to decide where to go on their honeymoon. Both would like to go to the Hawaiian Islands for two weeks if they can afford the trip. In order to make their decision, Dave and Karen need to determine what the trip would cost and also how much money they will have available for the trip. In order to estimate the cost of the trip, Dave and Karen must make many decisions about the trip. How many islands should they visit? Where will they stay? How often will they eat in restaurants and what type will they be? Will they rent a car? What kinds of entertainment and special sight-seeing trips do they want? The more precise Dave and Karen's plans are, the more accurate they can make their cost estimate for the trip. Below is the result of their cost estimates for the trip:

Airfare to and from the islands	$1,500
Inter-island airfares	300
Hotel rooms	1,960
Meals	1,400
Tours and boat trips	350
Car rental	450
Souvenirs	200
Camera film, miscellaneous	200
Budgeted cost for the trip	$6,360

This cost estimate is a *cost budget* for the trip. The numbers are based on Dave and Karen's plan to visit three islands and spend a total of two weeks in the Hawaiian Islands. The couple is somewhat surprised by the total cost for the two-week trip. This is not uncommon. Often people find that plans, once converted to detailed cost estimates, are more costly than they first imagined. A major value of budgeting is its ability to provide a basis for cost comparisons between various alternative plans.

The cost budget just presented is only part of the trip budget. The other part is the *revenue budget*. In other words, how much money will Dave and Karen have available for the trip and what are the sources of the funds?

Dave and Karen have a total of $9,000 in their savings accounts. In addition, they expect to receive about $1,500 in cash as wedding gifts. Both Dave and Karen have jobs earning a combined total of $3,000 per month. Their total resources are $9,000 of savings, $1,500 of expected wedding gifts, and $15,000 ($3,000 per month times 5 months) of earnings. The total of $26,500, however, is not all available for their honeymoon expenses. Dave and Karen know that virtually all of their earnings over the next five months will be needed to meet their daily living expenses. In addition, they want to have at least $5,000 of savings in their account after they are married. They will need this amount to cover expenses of setting up their new apartment and to cover any unexpected expenses such as car repairs or medical expenses. Therefore, the revenue budget for the honeymoon trip is as follows:

Savings ($9,000 – $5,000)	$4,000
Expected cash wedding presents	1,500
Earnings during the next five months	0
Budgeted revenue for the trip	$5,500

The budgeted revenues are not large enough to cover the budgeted costs. Dave and Karen must make some decisions about how to eliminate the difference. Perhaps they can change their plans somewhat and reduce the budgeted costs of the trip. Alternatively, they may be able to find some additional revenue for the trip. Of course, they may make some adjustments to both budgets.

In this case, Dave and Karen decided they could use $500 more of their savings for the trip. This increased their total revenue budget to $6,000. On the cost side, they decided to visit only two islands, saving some inter-island airfare. In addition, they found a cheaper round-trip airfare to the islands and cut their food budget somewhat. The final budgets for the trip were as follows:

Budgeted Costs

Airfare to and from the islands	$1,400
Inter-island airfares	150
Hotel rooms	1,960
Meals	1,290
Tours and boat trips	350
Car rental	450
Souvenirs	200
Camera film, miscellaneous	200
Budgeted cost for the trip	$6,000

Budgeted Revenues

Savings ($9,000 – $4,500)	$4,500
Expected cash wedding presents	1,500
Earnings during the next five months	0
Budgeted revenue for the trip	$6,000

The process of changing budgets to reflect new information and changing plans is called *budget revision*. In businesses, budget revision occurs as managers from many different functional areas of the business bring together their plans for the upcoming budget period. As management attempts to coordinate the resource needs of many different business activities, it is necessary to make many revisions of individual budgets.

Another important concept illustrated by the simple budget presented previously is the *entity concept*. This concept simply stated says that we must always know precisely what activity or business segment we are dealing with in measuring costs and revenues. The previous illustration presents a budget for a trip to Hawaii for Dave and Karen. The costs included in the budget must relate only to the trip to Hawaii. Cost for any other trip, or costs of furnishing a new apartment are not a part of this budget. Similarly, the revenue budget includes only resources available for the trip. Savings required for other items or activities are not included. Likewise, Dave and Karen's earnings are needed for daily living costs and therefore are excluded from the travel budget. The entity concept is essential in the creation of any budget.

FUNCTIONS OF BUDGETING

The two basic functions of budgeting are planning and control. *Planning* encompasses the entire process of preparing the budget, from the initial ideas through the development of the budget. Planning is the process that most people think of when the term budgeting is mentioned. The majority of the time and effort devoted to budgeting is expended in the planning stage. Careful planning provides the framework for the second function of budgeting.

Control is the comparison of actual results with budgeted data, evaluation of the differences, and taking corrective actions to adjust for differences when necessary. The comparison of budget and actual data can occur only after the period is over and actual accounting data are available. For example, April manufacturing cost data are necessary to compare with the April production budget to measure the difference between plans and actual results for the month of April. The comparison of actual results with budget expectations is called *performance reporting*. The budget acts as a gauge against which managers compare actual costs and revenues.

Exhibit 6.1 is a budget-performance report for manufacturing overhead for the first quarter of 20X1. The difference between budgeted cost and actual cost is called a *budget variance*. Budget variances are reported for each cost so that favorable and unfavorable variances do not net out, thus hiding potential problems.

EXHIBIT 6.1   Jamestown Corporation manufacturing overhead performance report: First quarter 20X1.

Manufacturing Overhead	Budget	Actual	Variance (Favorable) (Unfavorable)	
Variable costs:				
Indirect materials	$ 13,725	$ 15,225	$ 1,500	U
Indirect labor	27,450	24,500	(2,950)	F
Employee fringe benefits	54,900	67,800	12,900	U
Payroll taxes	13,725	17,100	3,375	U
Utilities	16,470	20,250	3,780	U
Maintenance	10,980	10,650	(330)	F
Total variable costs	$137,250	$155,525	$18,275	U
Fixed costs:				
Supervision	$ 27,000	$ 27,000	$ 0	
Depreciation	36,000	36,000	0	
Maintenance	13,500	14,250	750	U
Property taxes	7,368	7,800	432	U
Insurance	4,500	4,950	450	U
Total fixed costs	$ 88,368	$ 90,000	$ 1,632	U
Total manufacturing overhead costs	$225,618	$245,525	$19,907	U

REASONS FOR BUDGETING

Budgeting is a time-consuming and costly process. Managers and employees are asked to contribute information and time in preparing the budget and in responding to performance reports and other control-phase budgeting activities. Is it all worth it? Do firms get their money's worth from their budgeting systems?

The answer to those questions cannot be stated, in general, for all firms. Some firms receive far more value than other firms for the dollars they spend on budgeting. Budgets do, however, provide a wealth of value for many firms who effectively operate their budgeting systems. We now discuss some of the reasons for investing in formal budgeting systems. In the next section of this chapter we discuss issues that contribute to effective budgeting.

Budgets offer a variety of benefits to organizations. Some common benefits of budgeting include the following:

1. Requires periodic planning.
2. Fosters coordination, cooperation, and communication.
3. Forces quantification of proposals.
4. Provides a framework for performance evaluation.
5. Creates an awareness of business costs.

6. Satisfies legal and contractual requirements.
7. Orients a firm's activities toward organizational goals.

Periodic Planning

Virtually all organizations require some planning to ensure efficient and effective use of scarce resources. Some people are compulsive planners who continuously update plans that have already been made and plan for new activities and functions. At the other extreme are people who do not like to plan at all and therefore find little or no time to get involved in the planning process. The budgeting process closes the gap between these two extremes by creating a formal planning framework that provides specific, uniform periodic deadlines for each phase of the planning process. People who are not attuned to the planning process must still meet budget deadlines. Of course, planning does not guarantee success: People must execute the plans, but budgeting is an important prerequisite to the accomplishment of many activities.

Coordination, Cooperation, and Communication

Planning by individual managers does not ensure an optimum plan for the entire organization. The budgeting process, however, provides a vehicle for the exchange of ideas and objectives among people in the various organizational segments. The budget review process and other budget communication networks should minimize redundant and counterproductive programs by the time the final budget is approved.

Quantification

Because we live in a world of limited resources, virtually all individuals and organizations must ration their resources. The rationing process is easier for some than for others. Each person and each organization must compare the costs and benefits of each potential project or activity and choose those that result in the most appropriate resource-allocation decisions.

Measuring costs and benefits requires some degree of quantification. Profit-oriented firms make dollar measurements for both costs and benefits. This is not always an easy task. For example, the benefits of an advertising campaign are increased sales and a better company image, but it is difficult to estimate precisely the additional sales revenue caused by a particular advertising campaign, and it is even more difficult to quantify the improvements in the company image. In not-for-profit organizations, such as government agencies, quantification of benefits can be even more difficult. For example, how does one quantify the benefits of better police protection, more music programs at the city park, or better fire protection, and how should the benefits be evaluated in allocating resources to each activity? Despite the difficulties, resource-allocation decisions necessitate some reasonable quantification of the costs and benefits of the various projects under consideration.

Performance Evaluation

Budgets are estimates of future events, and as such they serve as estimates of acceptable performance. Managerial performance in each budgeting entity is appraised by comparing actual performance with budgeted projections. Most managers want to know what is expected of them so that they may monitor their own performance. Budgets help to provide that type of information. Of course, managers can also be evaluated on other criteria, but it is valuable to have some quantifiable measure of performance.

Cost Awareness

Accountants and financial managers are concerned daily about the cost implications of decisions and activities, but many other managers are not. Production supervisors focus on output, marketing managers on sales, and so forth. It is easy for people to overlook costs and cost-benefit relationships. At budgeting time, however, all managers with budget responsibility must convert their plans for projects and activities to costs and benefits. This cost awareness provides a common ground for communication among the various functional areas of the organization.

Legal and Contractual Requirements

Some organizations are required to budget. Local police departments, for example, cannot ignore budgeting even if it seems too much trouble, and the National Park Service would soon be out of funds if its management decided not to submit a budget this year. Some firms commit themselves to budgeting requirements when signing loan agreements or other operating agreements. For example, a bank may require a firm to submit an annual operating budget and monthly cash budgets throughout the life of a bank loan.

Goal Orientation

Resources should be allocated to projects and activities in accordance with organizational goals and objectives. Logical as this may sound, it is sometimes difficult to relate general organizational goals to specific projects or activities. Many general goals are not operational—meaning that it is difficult to determine the impact of specific projects on the achievement of the general goals of the organization. For example, organizational goals may be stated as follows:

1. Earn a satisfactory profit.
2. Maintain sufficient funds for liquidity.
3. Provide good quality products for customers.

These goals—which use terms such as *satisfactory, sufficient,* and *good quality*—are not operational goals. The goals stated here may be interpreted differently by each manager. To be effective, goals must be more specific and provide clear direction for managers. For example, these goals can be made operational as follows:

1. Provide a minimum return on gross assets invested of 18%.
2. Maintain a minimum current ratio of 2 to 1 and a minimum quick ratio of 1.2 to 1.
3. Products must receive at least an 80% approval rating on customer satisfaction surveys.

EFFECTIVE BUDGETING

We have already noted that almost all organizations and many individuals do some budgeting. In this country huge amounts of time and money are spent on budgeting activities. Unfortunately, everyone does not achieve the same return for the time and money invested in budgeting. There are many reasons why some firms use budgeting more effectively than others. Many of the reasons are discussed as follows:

1. Budgets should be goal-oriented so that they help a firm accomplish its goals and objectives.
2. Budgets must be realistic plans of action rather than wishful thinking.
3. The control phase of budgeting must be used effectively to provide a framework for evaluating performance and improving the budget-planning-stage activities.
4. Participative budgeting should be utilized to instill a sense of cooperation and team play.
5. Budgets should not be used as an excuse for denying appropriate employee resource requests.
6. The budgeting process should be used by management as an excellent vehicle for modifying the behavior of employees to achieve company goals.

Goal Orientation

Virtually all organizations operate with limited resources. Clearly, some firms have more resources than others, but no firm seems to have all of the resources it needs to accomplish all of its goals. Consequently, budgets should provide a means by which resources are utilized for projects, activities, and business units in accordance with the goals and objectives of the organization. As logical as this may sound, it is sometimes difficult to relate general, organizational goals to specific projects or activities. Many general goals are not operational—meaning that it is difficult to determine the impact of specific projects on the achievement of the general goals of the organization.

A prerequisite to goal-oriented budgeting is the development of a formal set of operational goals. Some organizations have no formally defined goals, and even those that do, often have only general goals for the entire organization. Major operating units may function without written or clearly defined goals or objectives. A logical first step toward effective budgeting is to formalize the goals of the organization. Starting at the top, general organizational goals should be as specific as possible, carefully established, and written. Next, each major unit of the organization should develop more specific operational goals. The process should continue down the organizational structure to the lowest level of budget responsibility. This goal-development process requires management at all levels to resolve difficult issues, but it results in a budgeting framework that is much more likely to be effective. Even individuals need to understand their goals and objectives as they prepare budgets for their own activities.

Realistic Plan

Budgeting is not wishful thinking; instead it is a process designed to optimize the use of scarce resources in accordance with the goals of the company or individual in question. Unfortunately, some managers view the planning process as a welcome respite from the daily rigors of dealing with business activities that just are not going as well as expected. Some managers view budget planning as an opportunity to dream of better times in the future when business may be better. Any improvement in the current situation must be based on solid executable plans, not just wishful thinking. Many firms have budget plans that call for sales growth, higher profits, and improved market share, but to be effective such plans must be based on specific executable plans. Such plans must be based on available resources and management talent that the company can bring to bear in accomplishing the budget plan. If the management of a firm wants to move from one level of operations to another, there must be a clearly defined path between the two points that the firm is able to travel.

The Control Phase of Budgeting

The first and most time-consuming phase of budgeting is the planning process. The control phase of budgeting, however, may be when firms get the most value from their budgeting activities. Comparing actual results with the budget, adjusting plans when necessary, and evaluating the performance of managers are essential elements of budget control. Many people, however, find the control phase difficult. When business results are less than expected it may be painful to evaluate the results. For some it is much easier to look ahead to future time periods when things hopefully will be better. But, frequently, plans for future success can only be made realistically when management learns from its past mistakes. The control phase of budgeting provides much of that learning process. Firms must be willing to evaluate performance carefully, adjusting plans and performance to stay on track toward achieving goals and objectives.

Many companies have intricate budget performance reporting systems in place, but the firms achieve little control from their use. In order to provide effective control, a business must use the system as an integral part of the reward system of the company. That is, employees must understand that budget performance reports are a component of their performance evaluation. There is a relationship between budget performance and rewards such as pay raises, bonuses, and promotions.

Generally it is easy to determine if a company's budget performance reporting system is working effectively. If discussions with managers yield comments such as, "If we fail to achieve the budget, we just add more to it next period," it is likely that the budget-control process is not effective. If, on the other hand, employees state, "If we are over our budget by more than 2%, we will be called on the carpet and forced to explain the problem," then one knows the control process is having an effect.

Participative Budgeting

Most behavioral experts believe that individuals work harder to achieve objectives that they have had a part in creating. Applied to budgeting, this concept states that employees will strive harder to achieve performance levels defined by budgets if the employee has had a part in creating the budget. On the other hand, budgets imposed by top-level management may get little support from employees. The concept of building budgets up from the bottom with the input from all employees and managers affected by the budget is called *participative budgeting*.

Improper Use of Budgets

Sometimes managers use budgets as scapegoats for unpopular decisions. For example, rather than telling a department head that his or her budget request for three additional employees was not convincing when compared with all of the other budget requests, the vice president says, "The budget just would not allow any new employees this year." In another case, the director of the marketing department requested travel funds to send all of his staff to an overseas education program. The vice president believes the program is a waste of money. Instead of telling the marketing director his opinion, the vice president says, "We would really like to send your staff to the program, but the budget is just too tight this year." Of course, the truth in this situation is that the trip is not a good use of business resources, regardless of the condition of the budget. The marketing director is left with the impression that the real problem is the state of the budget, when in fact his travel proposal was not sound business. Management should be careful not to undermine the budgeting process by assigning to it adverse characteristics. The author recalls a conversation with the chief engineer of a company who, when asked his definition of budgeting, responded, "Budgeting is the formal process whereby my department is denied those things that we want and deserve, to effectively carry on our engineering function within the company."

Behavioral Issues in Budgeting

Many of the internal accounting reports prepared in business are intended to influence managers and employees to behave in a particular way. For example, many manufacturing cost reports are designed to make employees aware of costs with the intent of controlling costs or keeping costs at some desired or acceptable level. Similarly, reports that compare the performance of one division with the performance of other divisions are used to evaluate the performance of division managers and encourage better results for each division.

Budgets and budget performance reports are among the more useful internal accounting reports used by businesses to influence employee performance in a positive manner. Budget control is based on the concept that managers are held responsible for activities they manage. Performance reports reflect the degree of achievement of plans as embodied in the budget. To minimize adverse behavioral problems, care should be taken to develop and administer budgets appropriately. Budgets should not be used as a hammer to demand unattainable performance from employees. The best safeguard against unrealistic budgets is participative budgeting.

DEVELOPING A BUDGET

The Structure of Budgets

Budgets are useful, and in most cases essential, to the success of virtually all organizations whether they are profit-seeking or not-for-profit organizations. Of course, the larger and more complex the organization, the more time, energy, and resources that must be used in preparing and using the budget. Regardless of the size or type of organization, however, most budgets can be divided into two categories: the operating budget and the financial budget. The *operating budget* consists of plans for all of those activities that make up the normal operations of the firm. For a manufacturing business, the operating budget includes plans for sales, production, marketing, distribution, administration, and any other activities that the firm carries on in its normal course of business. For a merchandising firm, the operating budget includes plans for sales, merchandise purchases, marketing, distribution, advertising, personnel, administration, and any other normal activities of the merchandising firm. The *financial budget* includes all of the plans for financing the activities described in the operating budget plus any plans for major new projects such as a new production plant or plant expansions. Both the operating and financial budgets are later described in more detail.

The Master Budget

The *master budget* is the total budget package for an organization; it is the end product of the budget preparation process. The master budget consists of all the individual budgets for each part of the organization combined into one overall budget for the entire organization. The exact composition of the master budget depends somewhat on the type and size of the business. However, all master budgets represent the organization's overall plan for a specific budget period. Exhibit 6.2 lists the common components of a master budget for a manufacturing business.

    The components of the master budget form the firm's detailed operating plan for the coming year. As noted earlier, the master budget is divided into the operating budget and the financial budget. The operating budget includes revenues, product costs, operating expenses, and other components of the income statement. The financial budget includes the budgeted balance sheet, cash budget, capital expenditure budget, and other budgets used in financial management. A large part of the financial budget is determined by the operating budget and the beginning balance sheet.

Operating Budget Components

Sales Budget

The *sales budget* or *revenue budget* is the first budget to be prepared. It is usually the most important budget because so many other budgets are directly related to sales and are therefore largely derived from the sales budget. Inventory budgets, production budgets, personnel budgets, marketing budgets, administrative budgets, and other budget areas are all affected significantly by the amount of revenue that is expected from sales.

**EXHIBIT 6.2   A manufacturing firm's
master budget.**

Operating budget

Sales budget
Budget of ending inventories
Production budget
    Materials budget
    Direct labor budget
    Manufacturing overhead budget
Budgeted cost of goods sold
Administrative expense budget
Marketing expense budget
Budgeted net income from operations
Budgeted nonoperating items
Budgeted net income

Financial budget

Capital expenditure budget
Cash budget
Budgeted statement of financial position (balance sheet)
Budgeted statement of cash flows

Sales budgets are influenced by a wide variety of factors, including general economic conditions, pricing decisions, competitor actions, industry conditions, and marketing programs. For example, the invasion of Kuwait by Iraq in August of 1990 had a significant negative impact on the American economy, in general, and, in particular, on related industries such as oil. The outbreak of war with Operation Desert Storm in January of 1991 had an even bigger impact on the economy. Stock prices rose with news of military successes and crude oil prices fell. On the other hand, travel, particularly overseas travel, plummeted, causing a severe recession in travel and travel-related industries. Although many managers in the industries that were most affected by the war and prewar situations were able to predict much of the impact of these events, most had trouble predicting the severity and length of the economic impacts. In particular, it was difficult to predict the positive economic impacts of the war. Even in complex times, it is essential that firms attempt to make very precise sales budgets.

Often the sales budget starts with individual sales representatives or sales managers predicting sales in their particular areas. The basic sales data are aggregated to arrive at a raw sales forecast that is then modified to reflect many of the variables mentioned previously. The resulting sales budget is expressed in dollars and must include sufficient detail on product mix and sales patterns to provide the information necessary for making decisions about changes in inventory levels and production quantities.

Budget of Ending Inventories

Inventories comprise a major portion of the current assets of many manufacturing firms. Separate decisions about inventory levels must be made for raw materials, work in process, and finished goods. Raw material scarcities, management's attitude about inventory levels, inventory carrying costs, inventory ordering costs, and other variables may all affect inventory-level decisions.

Production Budget

The first step in making a production budget is to determine production quantity. The materials budget, direct labor budget, and manufacturing overhead budget are all derived from the production quantity budget. Together these budgets are called the production budget. Managers incorporate current and expected inventory levels and sales estimates into the materials budget. Monthly materials budgets reflect sales patterns and the time required between ordering and receiving materials.

In the last few years, many manufacturing businesses have implemented *just-in-time* (JIT) *inventory systems.* Just-in-time inventory systems are based on the premise that the only value of inventories is to facilitate efficient manufacturing and to provide finished inventory for sales. In a JIT system, sales "pull" inventories through the production process; production inventories are delivered or produced only as they are needed for production activities. The implementation of JIT inventory systems requires careful planning, major changes in most firms' production philosophies, and a great emphasis on quality. Although JIT inventory significantly reduces the level of production inventories, it actually increases the amount of planning and budgeting that firms must do for materials inventory.

Budgeted Cost of Goods Sold

For a manufacturing firm, cost of goods sold is the production cost of products that are sold. Consequently, the cost of goods sold budget follows directly from the production budget. The cost of goods sold figure is different from the production budget figure because it is affected by beginning and ending inventories.

Administrative Expense Budget

The expected administrative costs for an organization are presented in the administrative expense budget. The administrative expense budget may contain many fixed costs, some of which may be avoidable if subsequent operations indicate some cost cuts are necessary. These avoidable costs, sometimes called *discretionary fixed costs,* include such items as research and development, employee education and training programs, and portions of the personnel budget. Fixed costs that cannot be avoided during the period are called *committed fixed costs.* Mortgage payments, bond interest payments, and property taxes are classified as committed costs. Variable administrative costs may include some personnel costs, a portion of the utility costs, computer service bureau costs, and supplies costs.

Marketing Expense Budget

Sales volume is determined, to some degree, by the marketing effort. Consequently, the marketing expense budget is prepared, at least in part, early in the budgeting process when the sales budget is being prepared. Some marketing costs, such as marketing management salaries and machinery and building depreciation for marketing, do not vary directly with sales volume. Other marketing costs, such as sales commissions and product distribution costs, may vary with the level of sales volume. Marketing costs for some consumer products, such as toothpaste, are very high and in some cases even may exceed the cost of producing the product. In such cases, the marketing budget is obviously a very important budget.

Budgeted Income Statement

The budgeted income statement is the combination of all of the preceding budgets. This budget shows the expected revenues and expenses from operations during the budget period. Budgeted income is a key figure in the firm's profit plan and reflects a majority of the firm's commitment of talent, time, and resources for the period.

A firm may have budgeted nonoperating items such as interest on investments or gains or losses on the sale of fixed assets. Usually they are relatively small, although in large firms the dollar amounts can be sizable. If nonoperating items are expected, they should be included in the firm's budgeted income statement. Income taxes are levied on actual, not budgeted, net income, but the budget plan should include expected taxes; therefore, the last figure in the budgeted income statement is budgeted after-tax net income.

The Financial Budget

The financial budget presents the plans for financing the operating activities of the firm. The financial budget is made up of a number of different budgets each providing essential financial information.

Capital Expenditure Budget

The capital expenditure budget is one of the budget components that makes up the financial budget. Each of the budget components has its own unique contribution to make toward the effective planning and control of business operations. Some budget components, however, are particularly crucial in the effective management of businesses. The cash budget and the capital expenditure budget are two of the most important.

Capital budgeting is the process of identifying, evaluating, planning, and financing major investment projects of an organization. Decisions to expand production facilities, acquire new production machinery, buy a new computer, or remodel the office building are all examples of capital-expenditure decisions. Capital-budgeting decisions made now determine to a large degree how successful an organization will be in achieving its goals and objectives in the years ahead. Capital budgeting plays an important role in the long-range success of many organizations because of several characteristics that differentiate it from most other elements of the master budget.

First, most capital budgeting projects require relatively large commitments of resources. Major projects, such as plant expansion or equipment replacement, may involve resource outlays in excess of annual net income. Relatively insignificant purchases are not treated as capital budgeting projects even if the items purchased have long lives. For example, the purchase of 100 calculators at $15 each, for use in the office, would be treated as a period expense by most firms, even though the calculators may have a useful life of several years.

Second, most capital expenditure decisions are long-term commitments. The projects last more than 1 year, with many extending over 5, 10, or even 20 years. The longer the life of the project, the more difficult it is to predict revenues, expenses, and cost savings. Capital-budgeting decisions are long-term policy decisions and should reflect clearly an organization's policies on growth, marketing, industry share, social responsibility, and other goals.

Cash Budget

Of all the components of the master budget, none is more important than the *cash budget*. Of the two major goals of most profit-seeking firms—to earn a satisfactory profit and to remain liquid—liquidity is the more important. Many companies lose money for many years, but with adequate financing they are able to remain in business until they can become profitable. On the other hand, firms that cannot remain liquid are unable to pay their bills as they come due. In such cases, creditors can, and often do, force firms out of business. Even government and not-for-profit organizations such as churches and charities must pay their bills and other obligations on time.

Meeting cash obligations as they come due is not as simple as it may appear. Profitability and liquidity do not necessarily go hand in hand. Some firms experience their most critical liquidity problems when they go from a break-even position to profitability. At that time growing receivables, increased inventories, and growing capacity requirements may create cash shortages.

The cash budget is a very useful tool in cash management. Managers estimate all expected cash flows for the budget period. The typical starting point is cash from operations, which is net income adjusted for noncash items, such as depreciation. All nonoperating cash items are also included. Purchase of land and equipment, sales of bonds and common stock, and the acquisition of treasury stock are a few examples of nonoperating items affecting the cash budget. The net income figure for an accounting period usually is very different from the cash flow for the period because of nonoperating cash flow items or changes in working capital.

Often, cash budgets are prepared much more frequently than other budgets. For example, a company may prepare quarterly budgets for all of its operating budget components such as sales and production, and also for its other financial budget components such as capital expenditures. For its cash budget, however, the firm prepares weekly budgets to ensure that it has cash available to meet its obligations each week and that any excess cash is properly invested. In companies with very critical cash problems, even daily cash budgets may be necessary to meet management's information requirements. The frequency of cash budgets depends on management's planning needs and the potential for cash management problems.

Cash budgeting in general has become more and more essential to effectively managing businesses. Tight money and high interest rates make cash budgeting even more important. This author has known a number of small business owners and managers who have been ineffective and sometimes uninterested in budgeting in general, but they have been very good "seat-of-the-pants" cash budgeters. I have seen people prepare pretty effective weekly cash budgets on a paper napkin at lunch or on the edge of a newspaper. Such individuals recognize that cash budgeting often is the difference between being in business and being forced into bankruptcy. The essential issue is not how pretty or professional the cash budget is, but rather how accurately it reflects the expected cash receipts and required disbursements during the budget period.

Cash management is intended to *optimize* cash balances; this means having enough cash to meet liquidity needs and not having so much cash that profitability is sacrificed. Excess cash should be invested in earning assets and should not be allowed to lie idly in the cash account. Cash budgeting is useful in dealing with both types of cash problems.

Budgeted Balance Sheet

The *budgeted balance sheet,* sometimes called the budgeted *statement of financial position,* is derived from the budgeted balance sheet at the beginning of the budget period and the expected changes in the account balances reflected in the operating budget, capital expenditure budget, and cash budget. It is necessary to use a budgeted balance sheet for the beginning of the period because the new budget is prepared before the previous accounting period has ended. When the budgeted balance sheet for the coming accounting period is prepared, there may be several months left in the current accounting period.

The budgeted balance sheet is more than a collection of residual balances resulting from other budget estimates. Undesirable projected balances and account relationships may cause management to change the operating plan. For instance, if a lending institution requires a firm to maintain a certain relationship between current assets and current liabilities, the budget must reflect these requirements. If it does not, the operating plan must be changed until the agreed requirements are met.

Budgeted Statement of Cash Flows

The final element of the master budget package is the *statement of cash flows.* The increased emphasis by management in recent years on cash and the sources and uses of cash have made this an ever more useful management tool. This statement is usually prepared from data in the budgeted income statement and changes between the estimated balance sheet at the beginning of the budget period and the budgeted balance sheet at the end of the budget period.

FIXED BUDGETS VERSUS FLEXIBLE BUDGETS

Many organizations operate in an environment where they can predict with great accuracy the volume of business they will experience during the upcoming budget period. In such cases, budgets prepared for a single level of activity typically are very useful in planning and controlling business activities. Budgets prepared for a single level of activity are called fixed budgets.

Organizations that have trouble predicting accurately the volume of activity they will experience during the budget period often find that a budget prepared for only one level of activity is not very helpful in planning and controlling their business activities. These organizations can operate better with a budget prepared for several levels of activity covering a range of possible levels of activity. This type of budget is called a flexible budget.

Fixed Budgets

A *fixed budget,* sometimes called a *static budget,* contains budget data for only one specific volume of activity. Because fixed budgets use only one volume of activity in determining all budgeted data, the fact that some costs are fixed and some costs are variable has no impact on the budgeted figures. The budget data used in preparing the budget for the planning phase of the process are also used in budget performance reports during the control phase of the budget process regardless of whether the volume of activity is actually achieved.

The planning and control framework provided by a budgeting system is an essential element of effective management. In many organizations, fixed budgets are tools that offer managers the ability to plan and control operations and to evaluate performance. If, however, the actual volume of activity achieved by a firm is significantly different from the volume of activity planned in the fixed budget, the fixed budget may be a very poor measure on which to base the performance measurement of employees.

Flexible Budgets

A *flexible budget,* also called a *dynamic budget,* is prepared for more than one level of activity. For example, a firm may prepare budgets for 10,000, 11,000, and 12,000 units of production. The purpose of preparing budgets for multiple activity levels is to provide managers with information about a range of activity in case the actual volume of activity differs from the expected level. Managers continue to rely heavily on the budget based on the expected level of activity for planning material acquisitions, labor needs, and other resource requirements, but the flexible budget provides additional information useful in modifying plans if operating data indicate that some other level of activity will occur. When performance reports are prepared, actual results are compared with a budget based specifically on the level of activity actually achieved.

Actual activity may differ significantly from budgeted activity because of an unexpected strike, cancellation of a large order, an unexpected new contract, or other factors. In a business that frequently experiences variations in its volume of activity, a flexible budget may be more useful than a fixed budget. Flexible budgets provide managers with more useful information for planning and a better basis for comparing performance when activity levels fluctuate than is available from a fixed budget. Flexible budgets are discussed in more detail in Chapter 7.

The Profit Plan

The term *profit plan* is sometimes used to refer to a master budget. Profit plan probably best describes the operating part of the master budget of a profit-oriented firm. However, it can be argued that the entire master budget of profit-oriented firms is the total profit plan for the firm. The operating budget shows details of budgeted net income, but the financial budgets, such as cash and capital expenditure budgets, are also an integral part of the overall profit planning of the firm.

Naturally, the term profit plan is not suitable for public-sector firms. Organizations such as a fire department do not generate a net income. For public-sector organizations, master budget is the more logical term for the total budget package. Because we are concerned with both public- and private-sector organizations, we use master budget predominantly. However, be aware of profit plan because it is used occasionally in practice.

THE BUDGET REVIEW PROCESS

The budget plan determines the allocation of resources within the organization. Typically the resources available are less than the demand for the resources. Consequently, there should be some systematic process for evaluating all proposals relating to the budget. The process of systematically evaluating budget proposals is referred to as the *budget review process.*

In the early planning stages, budget review may not be a formal process. Sometimes a few people (or even a single individual) make the budgeting decisions. For example, production-line supervisors may determine resource allocations within their department. Next, a plant budget committee may evaluate budget proposals for all production supervisors. The budget proposals for the entire plant go to a division budget committee, and the final budget review is made by a budget committee of the controller and corporate vice presidents.

The budget review process varies among organizations. Even within a single firm, different budget review processes may be used in various segments of the firm and at various levels of responsibility. However, the basic review process is fairly standard. Exhibit 6.3 shows the general flow in the budget review process.

Accountants and financial managers participate in the preparation and implementation of the budget, but all business managers, including marketing managers, production supervisors, purchasing officers, and other nonfinancial managers are interested in developing budgets for their particular part of the business. In addition, each functional manager must be keenly interested in selling his or her budget to higher-level management. Selling the budget means

EXHIBIT 6.3   Budget review process.

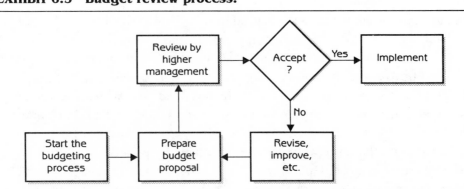

convincing the budget review committee that a particular budget proposal should be accepted. For some managers selling the budget is the single most important activity in their entire job, because if they fail at this task, even a tremendous management effort cannot obtain desired results.

With such an awesome description of the importance of selling the budget, one might conclude that it is an exceedingly difficult process. Not so! Actually the process requires a mixture of logic and diligence. There is no precise formula for success, but some common suggestions are:

1. Know your audience.
2. Make a professional presentation.
3. Quantify the material.
4. Avoid surprises.
5. Set priorities.

Know Your Audience

A large part of the budget selling strategy may be determined by the nature of the budget review audience, whether it is one person or a group of people. Information that may prove essential to the successful budget approval effort includes:

1. Strategies that have succeeded or failed in the past.
2. Pet peeves or special likes of review members.
3. A variety of other committee characteristics.

Make a Professional Presentation

Not all managers approach the budgeting process with the same level of enthusiasm. By the time budget review arrives, some managers just want to get it over with. Such an attitude can easily show during the budget review process. Review committees may interpret such attitudes as disdain for their job and their management function in general. Often the result is unfavorable action on the budget proposals under review.

A professional presentation includes:

- An enthusiastic and polished presentation
- A neat, concise, and understandable budget proposal
- Ample supporting documentation
- A willingness and ability to answer relevant questions

Quantify the Material

Because most resource allocation decisions are in some way affected by their cost-benefit relationships, it is necessary to quantify both the costs and benefits of virtually all budget proposals. Cost estimation is seldom easy, but it is usually far easier than the measurement of benefits. Even in the private sector, benefits are not always easy to measure in terms of the corporate goals of profitability and liquidity. In the not-for-profit sector, benefit measurement is even more difficult. For example, how does one measure the benefits of 20 new park rangers, 10 new police cars, or a decorative fountain in the city park? Obviously the quantification process would be different for each of these, and direct comparisons could be inconclusive. Yet, such comparisons may be necessary in arriving at final budget allocations.

It is easy to dismiss the value of quantification when the resulting numbers are hard to compare with other budget proposals, or the numbers are hard to verify. Nevertheless, some quantitative support typically is better than just general statements about the desirability of the budget proposal. Budget salesmanship should be approached with the same ingenuity that is found in the external marketing effort. If certain budget proposals have benefits that are difficult to quantify directly, various types of statistics might support the projects in an indirect way. For example, if a police department wants to justify 10 new police officers, it might offer supporting statistics on rising population in the community, rising crime rates, or relatively low per-capita police cost ratios. Although none of the suggested statistics measures direct benefits, they may be more useful in swaying a budget review committee than some vague statement about the value of more officers. Statistics that are not direct measures of benefits can be used widely in both the public and private sectors when supporting budget proposals.

Avoid Surprises

Avoid surprises to the review committee as well as surprises to those who present the budget. Brand new proposals and information are hard to sell to a budget review committee. Anything startlingly new should be introduced and developed long before the final review process.

Surprises to managers presenting the budgets most often occur during the questioning process or when a budget proposal is more detailed than prior budgets. To minimize this problem, budget presentations should be carefully rehearsed in great detail. The rehearsal might include a realistic or even pessimistic mock review committee. The mock review should ask pointed and difficult questions. Sometimes knowing the answer to a relatively immaterial question is enough to secure a favorable opinion.

Set Priorities

Few managers receive a totally favorable response to all budget requests. In a world of limited resources, wants exceed available resources, and managers should be prepared for a budget allocation that is somewhat different from the initial request. Typically all proposed budget items are not equally desirable. Some projects and activities are essential; others are highly desirable. Some would be nice, but are really not essential.

Priority systems, established by the managers of each budgeting entity before the review process starts, aid in structuring the budget proposal so that important items are funded first. Setting priorities avoids embarrassing questions and last-minute decision crises that affect the quality of a professional presentation.

FOR FURTHER READING

Carruth, Paul J. and Thurrel O. McClendon, "How Supervisors React to Meeting the Budget Pressure," Management Accounting (November 1984), p. 50.

Chandler, John S. and Thomas N. Trone, "Bottom Up Budgeting and Control," *Management Accounting* (February 1982), p. 37.

Collins, Frank, Paul Munter, and Don W. Finn, "The Budgeting Games People Play," *The Accounting Review* (January 1987), p. 29.

Geurts, Michael D. and Thomas A. Buchman, "Accounting for Shocks in Forecasts," *Management Accounting* (April 1981), p. 21.

Leitch, Robert A., John B. Barrack, and Sue H. McKinley, "Controlling Your Cash Resources," *Management Accounting* (October 1980), p. 58.

Merchant, Kenneth A., "The Design of the Corporate Budgeting System: Influences on Managerial Behavior and Performance," *The Accounting Review* (October 1981), p. 813.

Merewitz, Leonard and Stephen H. Sosnick, *The Budget's New Clothes* (Chicago: Markham Publishing Company, 1973).

Trapani, Cosmo S., "Six Critical Areas in the Budgeting Process," *Management Accounting* (November 1982), p. 52.

Wildavsky, Aaron, *The Politics of the Budgetary Process,* 2d ed. (Boston: Little, Brown and Company, Inc., 1974).

7 MEASURING PRODUCTIVITY
Michael F. van Breda

"Control is what we need. Cost control. And urgently," said owner-manager Trina Page with great emphasis to her management team. "Just a glance at these reports tells me that our costs are going up faster than our revenues. We won't survive much longer on that basis."

"Well, we could try using cheaper inks and lower quality paper," said Ken Hutchison, production manager of Page Printing.

"That's not the answer," exclaimed marketing manager Adrian du Plessis. "We're having a hard enough time as it is selling in this depressed market. If we start to produce an inferior product, our sales will tumble even further. Nobody is going to pay our prices and take cheaper quality."

"Adrian's right," said Trina. "Our aim should not be to reduce costs so much as to control them. Remember that we have a goal to meet in this organization—to produce the best quality products that we can. If we don't keep our eye on that goal, we won't be effective as an organization.

"What I am really after is efficiency. I want to see us produce quality products as cheaply as possible, but I don't want us to produce cheap products. We must improve productivity.

"To get the ball rolling, I want Ken to draw up a set of standards for production. Then we'll have an idea whether the production staff is working efficiently. If we have those standards in hand, then we can check how much our product should be costing us. And, we'll be able to compare that with what the product actually cost. Checking the difference between actual and standard will tell us where our big variances are. With that information in hand, we should be able to make some significant inroads into getting our costs under control and improving our productivity."

"Agreed," responded Adrian. "People will pay for a quality product provided it is competitively priced. We've just got to make sure that we're working as efficiently as our competition, and we'll be fine. That means, when we draw up a price quote, we need to be able to come in at or below their quote."

"That's all very well for you to say," said Ken, feeling a little aggrieved. "You're not the one who has to draw up these productivity standards. I've tried doing this before, and it's not easy—let me tell you. For starters everyone seems to want perfection."

With that the meeting broke up. Ken went back to his office, realizing that he was not quite sure where to begin. For one thing, he hadn't shared the fact that he had not succeeded in his last attempt to install a standard cost system. What chance did he have this time? A call to a friend of his, Jenny Ryan, who had just completed her MBA seemed in order.

"Jenny, I need your help badly. My boss is after a set of production standards, and I don't know what to do or where to begin!"

BUDGETARY CONTROL

Defining Standards

That evening Ken went over to Jenny's home where she produced her cost accounting text. "Tell me everything you think I need to know about standard costs."

"OK! First, Ken, let's get straight what we mean by a standard and why we're calculating it. A *standard* is a basis of comparison; it's a norm if you will, or a yardstick. Some like to compare it to a gauge—a gauge to measure efficiency.

"But a standard is more than that really because it is also the basis for control. Standards enable management to keep score. The difference between standards and actuals directs management's attention to areas requiring their efforts. In that sense, standards are attention getters. They form the heart of what is known as management by exception: That's the concept that one does not watch everything all the time; instead one focuses one's attention on the exceptions, the events that are unexpected."

Ken smiled knowingly. "I've experienced this, and it's terrible. My boss at my last job never noticed the good job that I did every day. But, when something went wrong, he was down like a shot to bawl me out!"

"That is one of the traps of managing by exception," said Jenny. "But you're smart enough as a manager to know that people need to be rewarded for their regular jobs. You also know that the exceptions are highlighted so that you can help them remedy things—not shout at them."

Types of Standards

"Then you have to realize," Jenny went on, "that there are different kinds of standards. First, you have your *basic* standards: They are unchanging over long periods of time. Many of these are captured in policy statements and may reflect things like the percentage of waste that is permitted or the amount of time one might be away from a work station. Basic standards are not much use in forming costs, though, because the work environment tends to change too much.

"At the other extreme there are *theoretical* or *ideal* standards. These get set by engineers and are the ideals to which one is expected to strive. These are the standards that I think you feel are unrealistic."

"Hear! Hear!" broke in Ken. "My guys would never take that—that's the perfection mentality I was telling you about."

"But," asked Jenny, "aren't the Japanese always striving towards ideal standards?"

"True, but the difference between them and us is that their system of lifetime employment provides a more supportive atmosphere in which they can strive for perfection and not feel they are going to get fired if they don't quite make it this time around. It's not enough to look at standards in isolation. One must view them in the context of total management."

"Right!" said Jenny approvingly. "And that means that your best norms to develop are probably what are called *currently attainable* standards. These are standards that can be met, but still represent a challenging goal. Let me read you a quote:

> Such standards provide definite goals which employees can usually be expected to reach and they also appear to be fair bases from which to measure deviations for which the employees are held responsible. A standard set at a level which is high yet still attainable with reasonably diligent effort and attention to the correct methods of doing the job may also be effective for stimulating efficiency.[1]

I think that's the kind of standard you are after."

"You're right. And, I tell you there are real advantages to standards set at this level. My guys find them very motivating. Also, when it comes time to costing jobs out for pricing purposes, we have a reasonable shot at making those standards. Of course, that wouldn't stop us from trying for perfection. It's just that we wouldn't have management breathing down our necks when we didn't make it."

Budgets

"Tell me one more thing though. Why do we have to go to all this bother to develop standards? Why can't top management just use last year's numbers? That will give them a base for comparison."

"True," said Jenny. "But you've got to remember that last year's actuals reflect last year's circumstances. Things may have changed this year so much that last year is not a fair comparison. How would you like it if they didn't adjust your materials budget for inflation but expected you to produce as much this year as you did last?"

"OK, you've made your point. But, why can't they just get our controller to draw up a budget at the start of the year? Why do I have to get involved?"

"Two reasons. One is that the controller can't draw up a budget without standards. Standard costs are the unit costs that go into a budget. The budget contains your standards multiplied by the expected volume of sales provided by the marketing department.

"The other reason you need to get involved is that the budget needs to be adjusted for volume. You want them to evaluate you on the basis of a flexible budget, as opposed to a static budget. The only way to be fair to people is to use a flexible budget. Look at these numbers for instance." She jotted down the numbers appearing in Exhibit 7.1.

"Notice how the budget is drawn up in the first column: You estimate the volume for the year and multiply it by the estimated unit selling price or the estimated unit cost, the standard cost. Fixed costs are fixed in relation to volume, of course, and are just inserted into the budget. The last column shows the actual revenues and actual costs: To get them, you multiply the actual selling or the actual unit cost by the actual volume. The middle column shows the estimated selling price and the estimated unit costs multiplied by the actual volume.

"Note that the only difference between the flexible budget in Column 2 and the static budget in Column 1 lies in the volume being used. The static budget uses the expected volume while the flexible budget uses the actual volume. In other words, the difference between flexible and static may be attributed to changing activity levels. It is, therefore, dubbed an *activity variance.*

"The unit price and cost terms for the actual revenues and costs in Column 3 differ from the corresponding price and cost terms for the flexible budget in Column 2; however, the activity level is the same: Both use the actual level of sales. In other words, the difference between actual and flexible may be attributed to changing selling and cost prices. These differences are dubbed the *price variances.* Let's summarize the definitions of these terms."

EXHIBIT 7.1   Static versus flexible budgets.

	Budget (Static)	Budget (Flexible)	Actual
Volume in units	1,000	1,200	1,200
Revenues	$10,000	$12,000	$11,400
	@$10/unit	@$10/unit	$9.50/unit
Variable costs	5,000	6,000	5,400
	@$5.00/unit	@$5.00/unit	@$4.50/unit
Fixed costs	4,000	4,000	4,680
Net Income	$1,000	$2,000	$1,320

$$\text{Activity variance} = \text{static budget} - \text{flexible budget}$$
$$\text{Price variance} = \text{actual results} - \text{flexible budget}$$
$$\text{Activity index} = \text{static budget/flexible budget}$$
$$\text{Price index} = \text{actual results/flexible budget}$$

"Now look what happens if all you have is the budget from the beginning of the year. The variable costs, for which you are responsible, are $400 above budget. You could reasonably expect to have your boss down here chewing you out for not controlling your costs. But, if you know your unit costs, you can adjust the budget for volume, and give him the number in the second column of Exhibit 7.1. That shows that you actually got your costs down by $600, namely $6,000 less $5,400. Let me show you what I mean in more depth."

With that, Jenny started to prepare Exhibit 7.2. First she compared the actual results with the original budget, the static budget. She derived the percentage change by dividing the actual by the budget, subtracting one from the result, and multiplying the remainder by 100. For instance, in the case of revenue:

Step 1: $11,400/10,000 = 1.14$
Step 2: $1.14 - 1$ $= 0.14$
Step 3: $.14 \times 100$ $= 14$ percent

Price Indices

"If you examine Panel A of Exhibit 7.2," Jenny said, "it seems that the reason for the sharp 40% increase in profit lies in the relatively sharp increase of 14% in revenue. This happened despite the increase in variable and fixed costs. The increase in profits might be interpreted as showing the superior ability of the sales staff.

"The fallacy of this interpretation is apparent when you look at Panel B, which compares the flexible budget with the actual results. Now you can see that, after adjusting for sales activity, variable costs actually showed a steep decline rather than the increase shown in Panel A. In other words, with a volume of only 1,200 units as opposed to 1,000, you should budget more for variable costs than at first expected. The $6,000 is the more appropriate budget figure. But when you compare the actual cost of $5,400 against the flexible budget, you find a decrease of 10%. With the activity effect eliminated, all of this rise must be attributed to a rise in variable costs. More precisely, budgeted unit variable costs equal $5.00, and actual unit variable costs equal $4.50. Dividing the actual cost of $4.50 by the budgeted variable cost of $5.00 yields an index of 0.90, or a percentage decrease of 10%.

"The apparent rise in revenues shown in Panel A melts away in Panel B; the apparent rise in variable costs shown in Panel A also melts away in Panel B. The result is a whole new story. Volume rose, perhaps due to the efforts of the sales

EXHIBIT 7.2   Comparing the budgets.

Panel A
Actual versus Static Budget

	Static Budget	Actual	Indices	Percentage Change
Revenue	$10,000	$11,400	1.14	14
Variable costs	5,000	5,400	1.08	8
Contribution	$ 5,000	6,000	1.12	12
Fixed costs	4,000	4,680	1.17	17
Net income	$ 1,000	$ 1,320	1.32	32

Panel B
Actual versus Flexible Budget

	Flexible Budget	Actual	Indices	Percentage Change
Revenue	$12,000	$11,400	0.95	(5)
Variable costs	6,000	5,400	0.90	(10)
Contribution	$ 6,000	6,000	1.00	0
Fixed costs	4,000	4,680	1.17	17
Net income	$ 2,000	$ 1,320	0.66	(34)

Panel C
Static versus Flexible Budget

	Static Budget	Flexible Budget	Indices	Percentage Change
Revenue	$10,000	$12,000	1.20	20
Variable costs	5,000	6,000	1.20	20
Contribution	$ 5,000	6,000	1.20	20
Fixed costs	4,000	4,000	1.00	0
Net income	$ 1,000	$ 2,000	2.00	100

staff, but probably due to the fall in the selling price. Fortunately," she said with a broad grin on her face, "this was offset by the heroic efforts of the production staff in getting their costs on a per-unit basis down by 10%."

"I like that heroic part," said Ken, approvingly.

Activity Indices

"Now look at Panel C. This compares the static budget with the flexible budget. Now the only factor to change is sales activity so the percentages measure the change in the number of units sold. As there is only one measure of activity, it is not surprising that all the activity-based indices show an increase of 20%, that is, 200 units over 1,000. Fixed costs, though, are independent of activity levels. Net income, which is a combination of activity-related and activity-independent numbers, shows a decline that reflects its mixed nature."

Market Effects

"The rise in volume may, or may not, be attributable to good management. One possibility is that it was driven by an increase in the total market. For instance, one can imagine the larger market to have an expected 8,000 units in sales. The company was expecting to get 12.5% of the market. If one now assumes that the market grew to 12,000 units, then the company's sales of 1,200 units actually represents a decrease in market share. Writing this out more formally:

$$\text{Sales activity index} = 1,200/1,000$$
$$= (10\% \times 12,000)/(12.5\% \times 8,000)$$
$$= 0.80 \times 1.50$$

In other words, given this scenario, the sales staff should be queried on why they had a decrease of 20% in market share in a market that increased 50%."

Summary

"Finally, let's try to summarize what we have learned to this point. First, note that Panel B confirms that the price index in any variance computation can be derived by dividing the actual figure by the static budget figure. Panel C demonstrates that the usage index can be derived by dividing the static figure by the flexible figure. In short, the relationship between the overall index of the change from budget to actual is given by:

$$\text{Overall index} = \text{actual/static}$$
$$= (\text{actual/flexible}) \times (\text{flexible/static})$$
$$= \text{price index} \times \text{activity index}$$

To summarize then, in the example shown in Exhibits 7.1 and 7.2, one has the following relationships:

Overall index   = Price index × Activity index
Revenue: $1.14 = 0.95 \times 1.20$
Variable cost: $1.08 = 0.90 \times 1.20$
Fixed cost: $1.17 = 1.17 \times 1.000$

So, as you can see, the pieces fit together quite logically. The points underlying these pieces can be summarized quite briefly."

1. First, we saw the need to distinguish between basic, ideal, and currently attainable standards.
2. Second, we saw the wisdom of distinguishing flexible from static budgets.
3. Third, we noted that our standards are the foundation on which these budgets are based.

4. We noted that all cost variances follow one simple formula: Actual cost less budgeted cost equals standard cost variance.

5. Activity variances = static budget − flexible budget.

   Price variances = actual results − flexible budget.

   Activity indices = static budget/flexible budget.

   Price indices = actual results/flexible budget.

6. Flexible budgets adjust variable costs and their variances for volume.

7. Volume has no effect on fixed costs or the variances derived from fixed costs.

VARIABLE COST BUDGETS

"That's fine, but what am I going to do with these variances?" Ken asked a little impatiently. "Everything that I've seen so far may help top management, but it's not much help to me."

"Good point, Ken. That's why we need to examine productivity, which is the relationship between inputs and outputs. We'll enhance your productivity and your control over costs if we can focus on the elements that go into making up your costs."

Jenny began to explain how in a typical cost-accounting system, the variable cost of a product or service is a function of:

1. The hours of labor (both direct and indirect) that go into it.
2. The units of material that are used.
3. The other components of overhead.
4. The unit cost of each of these items.

"Let's call the amount of input that goes into one unit of output the *productivity rate*. For instance, one might need 500 sheets of paper and 16 minutes of labor to produce a ream of letterhead. The material productivity rate is 500 sheets per ream; the labor productivity rate is 18 minutes per ream. When the expected cost of the inputs is attached to the expected productivity rates, then a *standard cost* is said to result. The productivity rates themselves are also known as standards. They are typically established by engineers."

As before, Jenny began sketching out a numerical illustration of the points that she was making. Her sketches appear in Exhibit 7.3. "These are the standards," she said, "that determine the variable portion of the budget for production. Note the assumption here that variable overhead is a function of direct labor hours. Other assumptions are possible, but we will stick with this one in our example.

"Fixed overhead is a little different because it does not really have a productivity rate. Let's just put down the unit fixed overhead on a budgeted and an

EXHIBIT 7.3   Standards for letterhead paper.

Material:
Budgeted productivity rate	= 500 sheets/ream
Budgeted cost per unit of input	= $0.04/sheet
Actual productivity rate	= 500 sheets/ream
Actual cost per unit of input	= $0.035/sheet

Labor:
Budgeted productivity rate	= 0.30 hr/ream
Budgeted wage per hour	= $5.00/hr
Actual productivity rate	= 0.25 hr/ream
Actual wage per hour	= $6.00/hr

Variable overhead:
Budgeted productivity rate	= 0.30 hr/ream
Budgeted cost per unit of input	= $5.00/hr
Actual productivity rate	= 0.25 hr/ream
Actual cost per unit of input	= $5.00/hr

Fixed overhead:
Budgeted fixed cost	= $4.00/ream
Actual fixed cost	= $3.90/ream

actual basis, and we can come back and discuss the details later." With that, she inserted $4.00 per ream based on $4,000 divided by 1,000 units for the budget and $3.90 for the actual figure based on $4,680 divided by 1,200 units.

From these standards she began to derive both the standard and actual costs of the product.

Standard cost = Material cost + labor cost + variable overhead cost + fixed overhead cost

$$= (1,000 \times \$0.02) + (0.30 \times \$5.00) + (0.30 \times \$5.00) + \$4.00$$
$$= \$2.00 + \$1.50 + \$1.50 + \$4.00$$
$$= \$9.00$$

Actual cost = Material cost + labor cost + variable overhead cost + fixed overhead cost

$$= (1,000 \times \$0.175) + (0.25 \times \$6.00) + (0.25 \times \$5.00) + \$3.90$$
$$= \$1.75 + \$1.50 + \$1.25 + \$3.90$$
$$= \$8.40$$

She then used these numbers to show how the budgeted and actual variable costs in Exhibit 7.1 were derived.

For the static budget:

Material costs = $2.00 × 1,000 = $2,000
Labor costs   = $1.50 × 1,000 = $1,500
Variable O/H = $1.50 × 1,000 = $1,500
Total variable costs   = $5,000

For the flexible budget:

Material costs = $2.00 × 1,200 = $2,400
Labor costs   = $1.50 × 1,200 = $1,800
Variable O/H = $1.50 × 1,200 = $1,800
Total variable costs   = $6,000

For the actual costs:

Material costs = $1.75 × 1,200 = $2,100
Labor costs   = $1.50 × 1,200 = $1,800
Variable O/H = $1.25 × 1,200 = $1,500
Total variable costs   = $5,400

Material Indices

Jenny also used the standards in Exhibit 7.3 to show Ken how indices for each of the variable components could be determined. Consider first the material costs:

$$
\begin{aligned}
\text{Material index} &= \text{Actual costs/flexible budget} \\
&= \$2,100/\$2,400 \\
&= (\$0.0175 \times 1,000 \times 1,200)/(\$0.02 \times 1,000 \times 1,200) \\
&= (0.0175/0.02) \times (1,000/1,000) \\
&= 0.875 \times 1.00 \\
&= 0.875
\end{aligned}
$$

$$
\begin{aligned}
\text{Usage index} &= \text{Actual productivity rate/budgeted productivity rate} \\
&= 1,000/1,000 \\
&= 1.0000
\end{aligned}
$$

$$
\begin{aligned}
\text{Cost index} &= \text{Actual unit cost/budgeted cost} \\
&= \$0.0175/0.02 \\
&= 0.875
\end{aligned}
$$

The material portion of the variable cost dropped $2.00 per unit to $1.75 because of a decline in the unit cost of paper, that is, there was a 12.5% reduction in the cost of paper. No efficiencies were either gained or lost in the use of the paper.

Labor Indices

Jenny performed an identical analysis for labor costs:

Labor index = Actual costs/flexible budget
$$= \$1,800/\$1,800$$
$$= (\$6.00 \times 0.25 \times 1,200)/(\$5.00 \times 0.30 \times 1,200)$$
$$= (\$6.00/\$5.00) \times (0.25/0.30)$$
$$= 1.20 \times 0.833$$
$$= 1.00$$

Efficiency index = Actual productivity rate/budgeted productivity rate
$$= 0.25/0.30$$
$$= 0.8333$$

Wage index = Actual unit cost/budgeted cost
$$= \$6.00/\$5.00$$
$$= 1.20$$

The labor portion of the variable cost remained static at $1.50 because of a 16.67% increase in efficiency in the use of labor offset by a 20% increase in hourly wages.

"You'll realize that what we have here," said Jenny, "is a great way to measure increases in productivity. The president keeps on talking about how our productivity is falling. One way to counteract that is to check how efficiently people are working. Before one measures physical productivity, though, one has to eliminate the wage effect, which is just what we have done here."

Variable Overhead Indices

Finally, Jenny repeated the analysis for variable overhead costs where she showed that:

Variable OH index = Actual costs/flexible budget
$$= \$1,500/\$1,800$$
$$= (\$5.00 \times 0.25 \times 1,200)/(\$5.00 \times 0.30 \times 1,200)$$
$$= (\$5.00/\$5.00) \times (0.25/0.30)$$
$$= 1.00 \times 0.833$$
$$= 0.833$$

Efficiency index = Actual productivity rate/budgeted productivity rate
$$= 0.25/0.30$$
$$= 0.8333$$

Rate index = Actual unit cost/budgeted cost

= $5.00/$5.00

= 1.00

The overhead portion of the variable cost fell from $1.50 to $1.25 because of the 16.67% increase in efficiency in the use of labor. Unlike direct labor, this was not offset or assisted by a change in the variable overhead rate.

Review

By now it was apparent that Ken was beginning to grow weary, so Jenny suggested that they do a quick review and then take a break.

"One last question, Jenny—where do these variable overhead rates come from?"

"That's another subject," said Jenny. "Do you want a cup of coffee? I'm bushed. But before we break, let's summarize what we've learned."

1. The cost of a product consists of material, labor, plus overhead.
2. Each of these components is made up of a productivity rate multiplied by a unit cost for that component.
3. Standard costs equal standard productivity rates times standard unit costs.
4. Actual costs equal actual productivity rates times actual unit costs.
5. The price indices equal actual unit costs divided by standard unit costs.
6. The activity indices equal actual productivity rates divided by standard productivity rates.

COLLECTING STANDARDS

After their coffee break, Jenny and Ken discussed how to develop these standard costs. Jenny reminded Ken that standard costs are made up of two parts: a standard cost per unit and a standard usage or quantity of units of input; these two are multiplied together. She pointed out that it was his responsibility to define the amount of material and labor that should go into the product. It was the responsibility of the purchasing department to determine the amount that should be paid for materials, and it was up to the personnel department to determine wages. She explained that there are several ways to determine the appropriate usage.

Engineering Studies

"First, you can do an engineering study. In other words, one can look at the specifications of the product. Many products that are designed by engineers have quite detailed and explicit instructions on what materials should go into them. These standards often include an allowance for waste, although this is not necessary. Where they do not include such an allowance, they border on the ideal.

"To take an obvious example, most automobiles have one battery and an engineering statement would state this. A perfection standard would call for one battery per automobile. On the other hand, it would not be unusual for one or more batteries to be damaged during installation. On average, then, it might appear as if automobiles actually had 1.1 batteries. One might, therefore, want to set as one's standard a currently attainable goal of 1.05 batteries on average, thus providing a 5% allowance for waste."

Time and Motion Studies

"Time and motion studies are the usual way in which engineering standards are set for the labor component. An engineer watches over the labor force as they work and determines how much time it should take for each part of the production process. When doing this, it is vital to gain labor's cooperation. If not, disastrous results can occur. I love the following quotation."

> . . . You got to use your noodle while you're working and think your work out ahead as you go along! You got to add in movements you know you ain't going to make when you're running the job! Remember, if you don't screw them, they're going to screw you! . . . Every moment counts!
>
> . . . When the time-study man came around, I set the speed at 180. I knew damn well he would ask me to push it up, so I started low enough. He finally pushed me up to 445, and I ran the job later at 610. If I'd started out at 445, they'd have timed it at 610. Then I got him on the reaming, too. I ran the reamer for him at 130 speed and .025 feed. He asked me if I couldn't run the reamer any faster than that, and I told him I had to run the reamer slow to keep the hole size. I showed him two pieces with oversize holes that the day man ran. I picked them out for the occasion! But later on I ran the reamer at 610 speed and .018 feed, same as the drill. So I didn't have to change gears.[2]

Ken smiled appreciatively at the story. As an old floor hand, he understood the sentiments completely.

Motivation

"This raises a broader question, you know," said Ken. "Should we invite people to participate in setting the standards? Will it make them more motivated? I've pondered on this from a variety of different angles. What's so interesting about it is that participation doesn't always work.

"What I have discovered from my reading around the topic is that many people prefer to be told what to do. This seems to be particularly true for people who find their jobs boring and for those with a more authoritarian personality. So one has to be really careful when inviting people to participate."

"You know more about this than I do," responded Jenny. "How do you handle feedback then. That's a sort of after-the-fact participation isn't it?"

"Well, everything that I have read—and my own experience for that matter—indicates that timely feedback is essential and a good motivator. People really need to know and to know as soon as possible how they have done. That's especially true when they have done a good job, because it really builds their self-esteem. And in some cases, it makes them want to participate more before the fact.

"Of course, I must not lead you to think that a little participation and a lot of feedback is all one needs. These are what the psychologists call *intrinsic motivators.* People need these, but they also need *extrinsic motivators* like better pay for doing a better job.

"The other problem that one encounters is that the more you focus people's attention on one goal, the more they tend to ignore other goals. It's only human nature: Ask salespeople to increase their volume and they will sell goods at a loss.

"That's one of the reasons I have had misgivings about calling in a bunch of engineers to set standards. It is much easier to time how long a job should take and reward people for quantity than to measure and to reward quality. I really rely upon the innate good sense of my staff to provide quality products. Too much emphasis on measurement can make my task of maintaining quality much more difficult."

Past Data

"In that case," Jenny said, "an easier way to get the data you need for your business is to go back over your past records to see how much time various jobs have taken and how much material was used in the past. Some of that will have to be adjusted for changes in machines, changes in personnel, different kinds of material, and so on. But you know all that better than I do.

"But enough for now. Come on over tomorrow night, and we can talk some more. We do need to discuss fixed overheads."

FIXED-COST BUDGETS

"Fixed costs," Jenny said, after they had gathered together again, "are both easier and more difficult to control than variable costs. They are easier because there are no components into which to break them. Their variance is simply actual fixed costs minus budgeted fixed costs. Their index is simply actual fixed costs divided by budgeted fixed costs. In our case, the budgeted fixed costs were

$4,000 and the actual fixed costs were $4,680. The variance was simply $680, which means a percentage increase of 17%."

"Fixed costs are more difficult to control than variable costs because one cannot create an illusion of control through the elaborate computation of price, mix, and usage variances or indices."

"How then does one control fixed costs?" asked Ken.

"First, one must recognize that if costs are truly fixed, there is no reason to control them. Consider depreciation costs as an example. Once one has purchased an item, the total depreciation costs are set—unless one disposes of the machinery, in which case a disposal cost will substitute for the depreciation cost. No control is possible here. The control in this case has to be exerted when the machinery is purchased. Thereafter, it is a sunk cost which cannot be controlled. In other words, controlling fixed costs is in the first place a matter of timing.

"It is also a matter of scale. Consider the machine again. Assume it has a capacity of 1,000 boxes of greeting cards per day. Its cost is certainly fixed within this range. However, if the analysis is being done in terms of tens of thousands of boxes, and if the corporation has a hundred of these machines, then it is possible to think of this as a variable cost. One can ask, in other words, what the cost would be to produce an additional "unit" of 1,000 boxes.

"This last example highlights the fact that most fixed costs are usually fixed only within the context of a particular analysis. Consider, for instance, the ink you use in production. Assume its price is reset by a cartel every three months. Assume also that its planned usage is reset at the same time. A budgetary control system that computed variances every month and set the budgeted price and quantity to that of the latest quarter might show a variance of zero each month. This might lead everyone to believe that they were dealing with a fixed cost. However, were the same analysis to be done on an annual basis, with prices and quantities set at the start of the year, a substantial variance could arise. The example points up the old truism that all costs are variable in the long run.

"The example also points up the need to set your net large enough to catch the fish you want to catch. Many fixed costs cannot be controlled by a monthly or even an annual budget system because they change too slowly. One needs a coarser net, that is, an annual, or a triennial, or an even longer, budgetary system to capture their change. The reverse is also true. A net that is too fine can capture a great deal of random noise. Consider, for instance, a product whose price fluctuates randomly around a fixed mean. If all you want is to see the true exceptions, then you should set the net to capture only those fluctuations that are greater than a certain number of standard deviations away from the mean.

"In short, fixed costs are best controlled in the long run and at a more aggregate level. In other words, it is important in the budgetary control of fixed costs to establish appropriate time and space horizons for one's analysis."

"Most of that's pretty obvious," said Ken. "What you haven't yet told me is where the $4 overhead rate that you had in Exhibit 7.3 fits into the whole picture."

"Well, it does and it doesn't," responded Jenny. "The rate itself comes from knowing the total fixed overhead and dividing it by the volume, that is, $4,000 divided by 1,000 units. In that sense, fixed overhead rates are residuals—unlike variable overhead rates which are primary: Variable overhead is computed by multiplying the variable overhead rate by the volume.

"Variable overhead rates are used in computing variances and indices. Fixed overhead rates are completely ignored in this context. Their main purpose is to give you an estimate of the total product cost. So they fit in when calculating unit costs; they don't fit into budgetary control systems. But let's talk about standard cost systems and all this might become clearer."

STANDARD COST ACCOUNTING SYSTEMS

"Companies rarely enter their budgets into their ledgers," Jenny said. "Usually budgetary control takes place outside of a company's books. In other words, the budget is typically drawn up using spreadsheets outside of the general ledger system. At the end of the period under investigation, the actual results are drawn out of the ledger and transferred to the spreadsheet where the comparisons are done. Two exceptions to this general rule occur."

Government Accounting

"The first does not affect private companies, but does affect state and local governments. It is common practice in their accounting systems to enter budgeted numbers into the ledgers in reverse order to an actual number. For instance, city governments will enter budgeted revenues as follows:

dr Revenue (with budgeted sales)
    cr Accounts Receivable (with budgeted sales)

As sales are made, they are entered into the books in their usual order.

dr Accounts Receivable (with actual sales)
    cr Revenue (with actual sales)

The effect is that at the end of the year, only variances are left in accounts. For instance, sales greater than expected would leave a credit variance."

Standard Variable Costs

"The second exception involves so-called standard cost systems. In a typical implementation, the standard cost of a product is entered into the work-in-process account, although an actual cost is incurred. The difference between the two creates a *variance*. For example, in the case of variable production costs, the journal entry for a single unit of product would read:

dr WIP	$5.00
cr Sundry asset and liability accounts	$4.50
Variance	0.50

The existence of a credit variance indicates that the budgeted unit cost exceeds the actual unit cost, that is, there is a favorable variance. Were the variance a debit, one would have an unfavorable variance.

"Over the course of a year, the entry to work-in-process would be:

dr WIP	$6,000
cr Sundry asset and liability accounts	$5,400
Variance	600

Note that the entry to work in process is the flexible budget amount. The difference between the charge to work in process and the actual cost credited to sundry asset and liability accounts is the same $600 we saw in Exhibit 7.1. These variable costs may be traced back to material, labor, and variable overhead effects. In fact, the journal entries would probably have read:

dr WIP	$2,100
Material variance	300
cr Direct material	$2,400
dr WIP	$1,800
cr Direct labor	$1,800
dr WIP	$1,800
cr Overhead	$1,500
O/H variance	300

Each of these variances is identical to the variances computed above; each can be stated in percentage terms to indicate their relative size: Material costs are down 12.5%, labor costs are even, and variable overhead costs are up 16.67%. The key point to realize is that variances generated by a standard cost system are identical to those generated by a budgetary control system, once one removes the volume effect."

Standard Fixed Costs

"Unfortunately," Jenny continued, "the parallels between standard cost systems and those of budgetary control systems do not extend to fixed costs. The reason for this lies in the way in which fixed costs are applied to products. In a standard cost system, a predetermined fixed overhead rate is established at the start of a period by dividing the budgeted fixed overhead by the budgeted volume. In our case, the predetermined fixed overhead rate was $4,000 divided by 1,000 units, which was the $4.00 per unit found in Exhibit 7.3. Given that each product takes an estimated 0.30 hours, one can write this as $13.33 per hour.

"Fixed overhead is then applied to goods as they are produced, by multiplying the predetermined overhead rate per hour by the number of standard hours in each product. In our example, one simply charges $4.00 of fixed overhead to each product. The total amount of fixed overhead charged this way can be computed by multiplying the predetermined overhead rate on a per-product basis by the actual number of products produced. In our case, the result is $4,800. This is known as the *applied overhead*. The journal entry would be:

dr WIP $4,800
    cr Overhead $4,680
    O/H variance   120

The net overhead variance in the ledger is:

Actual overhead − applied overhead = $4,680 − $4,800

But the only variance one is interested in is:

Actual overhead − budgeted overhead = $4,680 − $4,000

The difference between the variance produced by a standard cost system and the variance we want for budgetary control purposes is:

Budgeted overhead − applied overhead = $4,000 − $4,800
$$= (\$4 \times 1,000) - (\$4 \times 1,200)$$

In short, the error in the fixed overhead variance appearing in a standard cost system is due to volume changing from 1,000 units to 1,200 units. Stated otherwise, the standard cost system should have used an overhead rate of $3.33 ($4,000/1,200). It did not, and the result is a variance in the standard cost system that is useless for control purposes.

"The budgeted overhead will be equal only to the applied overhead when the actual volume equals the budgeted volume. Since this rarely happens, the fixed cost variance found in the ledger is of little interest for budgetary control. Instead, you should compute the spending variance directly and simply ignore the net overhead variance derived in the books."

"Now, I see why you ignored the fixed overhead when doing the variances originally," said Ken. "Let's hope that my management understands this as well as you seem to."

BUDGETARY CONTROL REVISITED

Budgetary control, as we noted at the outset, consists of comparing actual results with budget estimates. When doing this, one is advised to distinguish between revenues and costs that vary with volume and those that are fixed with respect to volume changes. A revised budget, adjusted for the actual volumes rather than the predicted volumes, yields a flexible budget as opposed to the original or static budget.

Since the static and the flexible budgets for fixed costs are identical, the fixed-cost spending variance is simply the difference between the actual and the original budget. The fixed-cost spending index is their quotient.

In the case of variable costs and revenues, a few simple rules emerge. The ratio between the flexible and the static budgets indicates the difference in the quantities expected and the quantities actually experienced. The ratio between the actual results and the flexible budget indicates the change in costs or revenues that can be attributed to changes in unit cost or selling prices.

In the case of multiple outputs or multiple inputs, the quantity indices can be further refined. They break into at least two indices: The first reveals the effect of changing mixes of either outputs or inputs; the second reveals the effect of changing the overall volume. The mix variance may be computed directly or simply by dividing the quantity index by the volume index. In the case of variable costs, it is usually possible to draw out another index indicating the total yield, that is, the amount of input required to produce a given amount of output.

All these indices can be computed using an accounting system that collects only actual costs and compares these in a spreadsheet with the budgeted costs. Alternatively, they may be derived by keeping a standard cost system. The variances that emerge as one enters standard costs into work in process and credits the corresponding asset or liability account at actual are identical to those derived from a flexible budgeting control system. The one exception to this is fixed costs, but the difference here is easily reconciled.

In short, budgetary control analysis provides one with a vehicle for controlling one's business. The budget represents, ideally, one's strategies and objectives. As actual results emerge, they are compared with the budget to see to what extent the enterprise has met its goals and productivity targets. Any differences encountered can be broken down into components to determine whether it was due to a change in usage or a change in price. Where inputs or outputs are substitutable, one can also examine the changing mix for further insight into how one achieved one's goals.

In each case, the index derived is neither good nor bad. It simply indicates a change. As noted earlier, the same rise in sales may be a matter for congratulation when markets are declining and a matter for concern when markets are expanding faster than one's sales. All that the index does is to point one to where still more information must be gathered.

FOR FURTHER READING

Anthony, Robert N., James S. Reece, and Julie H. Hertenstein, *Accounting: Text and Cases,* 9th ed. (Homewood, IL: Richard D. Irwin, 1995), esp. Chapters 19 and 20.

Davidson, Sidney and Roman L. Weil, *Handbook of Cost Accounting* (New York: McGraw-Hill Book Co., 1978), esp. Chapters 15 and 16.

Ferris, Kenneth R. and J. Leslie Livingstone, eds., *Management Planning and Control: The Behavioral Foundations* (Columbus, OH: Century VII Publishing Company, 1989), esp. Chapters 3, 8, and 9.

Horngren, Charles T. and Gary L. Sundem, *Introduction to Management Accounting,* 8th ed. (Englewood Cliffs, NJ: Prentice-Hall, 1990), esp. Chapter 7.

Kaplan, Robert S., *Advanced Management Accounting* (Englewood Cliffs, NJ: Prentice-Hall, 1982), esp. Chapters 9 and 10.

Maher, Michael W., Clyde Stickney, Roman L. Weil, and Sidney Davidson, *Management Accounting* (San Diego: Harcourt Brace Jovanovich, 1991), esp. Chapters 13 and 14.

Shank, J. K. and N. C. Churchill, "Variance Analysis: A Management-Oriented Approach," *The Accounting Review* (October 1977), pp. 950–957.

Welsch, Glenn A., Ronald W. Hilton, and Paul N. Gordon, *Budgeting: Profit Planning and Control,* 5th ed. (Englewood Cliffs, NJ: Prentice-Hall, 1989), esp. Chapter 16.

NOTES

1. National Association of Accountants, *Standard Costs and Variance Analysis* (New York: NAA, 1974), p. 9.

2. Whyte, W. F., ed. *Money and Motivation: An Analysis of Incentives in Industry* (New York: Harper & Row, 1955).

PART II
Planning and Forecasting

8 CHOOSING A BUSINESS FORM
Richard P. Mandel

The Consulting Firm

Jennifer, Jean, and George had earned their graduate business degrees together and had paid their dues in middle management positions in various large corporations. Despite their different employers, the three had maintained their friendship and were now ready to realize their dream of starting a consulting practice. Their projections showed modest consulting revenue in the short term, offset by expenditures for supplies, a secretary, a small library, personal computers, and similar necessities. Although each expected to clear no more than perhaps $25,000 for his or her efforts in their first year in business, they shared high hopes for future growth and success. Besides, it would be a great pleasure to run their own company and have sole charge of their respective fates.

The Software Entrepreneur

At approximately the same time that Jennifer, Jean, and George were hatching their plans for entrepreneurial independence, Phil was cashing a seven figure check for his share of the proceeds from the sale of the computer software firm he had founded seven years ago with four of his friends. Rather than rest on his laurels, however, Phil saw this as an opportunity to capitalize on a complex piece of software he had developed in college. Although Phil was convinced that there would be an extensive market for his software, there was much work to be done before it could be brought to market. The software had to be converted from a mainframe operating system to the various popular microcomputer systems. In

addition, there was much marketing to be done prior to its release. Phil anticipated that he would probably spend over $300,000 on programmers and sales-
people before the first dollar of royalties would appear. But he was prepared to
make that investment himself, in anticipation of retaining all the eventual profit.

The Hotel Venture

Bruce and Erika were not nearly as interested in high technology. Directly following their graduation from business school, they were planning to construct
and operate a resort hotel near a popular ski area. They had chosen as their location a beautiful parcel of land in Colorado, owned by their third partner,
Michael. Rich with ideas and enthusiasm, the three were lacking in funds. They
were certain, however, that they could attract investors to their enterprise. The
location, they were sure, would virtually sell itself.

The Purpose of This Chapter

Each of these three groups of entrepreneurs would soon be faced with what
might well be the most important decision of the initial years of their businesses:
which of the various legal business forms to choose for the operation of their
enterprises. It is the purpose of this chapter to describe, compare, and contrast
the most popular of these forms, in the hope that the reader will then be able to
make such choices intelligently and effectively. After discussing the various business forms, we will revisit our entrepreneurs and analyze their choices.

BUSINESS FORMS

Two of the most popular business forms could be described as the default forms
because the law will deem a business to be operating under one of these forms
unless it takes affirmative action otherwise. The first of these forms is the *sole proprietorship*. Unless he or she has actively chosen another form, the individual operating his own business is considered to be a sole proprietor. Two or more persons
operating a business together are considered a *partnership* (or general partnership), unless they have actively elected otherwise. Both of these forms share the
characteristic that, for all intents and purposes, are not entities separate from their
owners. Every act taken or obligation assumed as a sole proprietorship or partnership is an act taken or obligation assumed by the business owners as individuals.

Many of the rules applicable to the operation of partnerships are set forth
in the Uniform Partnership Act, which has been adopted in one form or another
by 49 states. That Act defines a partnership as "an association of two or more
persons to carry on as co-owners a business for profit." Notice that the definition

does not require that the individuals agree to be partners. Although most partnerships can point to an agreement between the partners (whether written or oral), the Act applies the rules of partnership to any group of two or more persons whose actions fulfill the definition. Thus, the U.S. Circuit Court of Appeals for the District of Columbia, in a rather extreme case, held, over the defendant's strenuous objections, that she was a partner in her husband's burglary "business" (for which she kept the books and upon whose proceeds she lived), even though she denied knowing what her husband was doing at nights. As a result of this status, she was held personally liable for damages to the wife of a burglary victim her husband had murdered during a botched theft.

In contrast, a *corporation* is a legal entity separate from the legal identities of its owners, the shareholders. In the words used by James Thurber to describe a unicorn, the corporation "is a mythical beast," created by the state at the request of one or more business promoters, upon the filing of a form and the payment of the requisite modest fee. Thereupon, in the eyes of the law, the corporation becomes for most purposes, a living breathing "person" with its own federal identification number! Of course, one cannot see, hear, or touch a corporation, so it must interact with the rest of the world through its agents, the corporation's officers and employees.

Corporations come in different varieties. The so-called professional corporation is available in most states for persons conducting professional practices, such as doctors, lawyers, architects, psychiatric social workers, and the like. A subchapter S corporation is a corporation that is the same as a regular business corporation in all respects other than taxation. These variations are discussed later.

A fourth common form of business organization is the *limited partnership,* which may best be described as a hybrid of the corporation and the general partnership. The limited partnership consists of one or more general partners, who manage the business, much in the same way as do the partners in a general partnership, and one or more limited partners, who are essentially silent investors. Like the general partnership, limited partnerships are governed in part by a statute, the Uniform Limited Partnership Act (or its successor, the Revised Uniform Limited Partnership Act), which have also been adopted in one form or another by 49 states.

Over the last decade or so, a new form of business entity, the *limited liability company* (LLC), has been made available to entrepreneurs in all but one of the United States. The LLC is a separate legal entity owned by "members" who may, but need not, appoint one or more "managers" (who may, but need not, be members) to operate the business. It is formed by filing a form with the state government and paying the prescribed fee. The members then enter into an operating agreement setting forth their respective rights and obligations with respect to the business. Most states which have adopted the LLC have also authorized the limited liability partnership which allows general partnerships to obtain limited liability for their partners by filing their intention to do so with the state. This form of business entity is normally used by professional associations which previously operated as general partnerships, such as law and accounting firms.

COMPARISON FACTORS

The usefulness of the five basic business forms could be compared on a myriad number of measures, but the most effective comparisons will most likely result from employing the following eight measures:

1. *Complexity and cost of formation.*   What steps must be taken before your business can exist in each of these forms?
2. *Barriers to operation across state lines.*   What steps must be taken to move your business out of state? What additional cost may be involved?
3. *Recognition as a legal entity.*   Who does the law recognize as the operative entity? Who owns the business's assets? Who can sue and be sued?
4. *Continuity of life.*   Does the legal entity outlive the owner? This may be especially important if the business wishes to attract investors, or if the goal is an eventual sale of the business.
5. *Transferability of interest.*   How does one go about selling or otherwise transferring one's ownership of the business?
6. *Control.*   Who makes the decisions regarding the operation, financing, and eventual disposition of the business?
7. *Liability.*   Who is responsible for the business's debts? If the company cannot pay its creditors, must the owners satisfy these debts from their personal assets?
8. *Taxation.*   How does the choice of business form determine the tax payable on the profits of the business and the income of its owners?

FORMATION

Sole Proprietorships

Reflecting its status as the default form for the individual entrepreneur, the sole proprietorship requires no affirmative act for its formation. One operates a sole proprietorship because one has not chosen to operate in any of the other forms. The only exception to this rule arises in certain states, when the owner chooses to use a name other than his own as the name of his business. In such event, he may be required to file a so-called D/B/A certificate with the local authorities, stating that he is "doing business as" someone other than himself. This allows creditors and those otherwise injured by the operation of the business to determine who is legally responsible for the business's acts.

Partnerships

Similarly, a general partnership requires no special act for its formation other than a D/B/A certificate, if a name other than that of the partners will be used. If two or more people act in a way which fits the definition set forth in the Uniform Act, they will find themselves involved in a partnership. However, it is strongly recommended that prospective partners consciously enter an agreement (preferably in writing) setting forth their understandings on the many issues which will arise in such an arrangement. Principal among these are the investments each will make in the business, the allocation and distribution of profits (and losses), the method of decision making (majority or unanimous vote), any obligations to perform services for the business, the relative compensation of the partners, and so on. Regardless of the agreements that may exist among the partners, the partnership will be bound by the actions and agreements of each partner: as long as these actions are reasonably related to the partnership business, and even if they were not properly authorized by the other partners pursuant to the agreement. After all, third parties have no idea what the partners' internal agreement says, and are in no way bound by it.

Corporations

On the other hand, in order to form a corporation, one must pay the appropriate fee and must complete and file with the state a corporate charter (otherwise known as a Certificate of Incorporation, Articles of Incorporation, or similar names in the various states). The fee is payable both at the outset and annually thereafter (often approximately $200). A promoter may form a corporation under the laws of whichever state he wishes; one is not required to form the corporation under the laws of the state in which one intends to conduct most of one's business. This partially explains the popularity of the Delaware corporation. Delaware has spent most of the last century competing with other states for corporation filing fees, by repeatedly amending its corporate law to make it increasingly favorable to management. By now, the Delaware corporation has taken on an aura of sophistication, so that many promoters form their companies in Delaware just to appear to know what they are doing! However, the statutory advantages of Delaware apply mostly to corporations with many stockholders (such as those which are publicly traded) and will rarely be significant to a small business, such as those described at the beginning of this chapter. Also, formation in Delaware (or any state other than the site of the corporation's principal place of business) will subject the corporation to additional, unnecessary expense. It is, thus, usually advisable to incorporate in the company's home state.

The charter sets forth the corporation's name (which cannot be confusingly similar to the name of any other corporation operating in the state) as well as its principal address. The names of the initial directors and officers of the corporation are often listed. Most states also require a statement of corporate purpose. Years ago this purpose defined the permitted scope of the corporation's activities. A corporation which ventured beyond its purposes risked operating "ultra vires," resulting in liability of its directors and officers to its stockholders and creditors. Today, virtually all states allow a corporation to define its purposes extremely broadly (e.g., "any activities which may be lawfully undertaken by a corporation in this state"), so that operation ultra vires is generally impossible. Still directors are occasionally plagued by lawsuits brought by stockholders asserting that the diversion of corporate profits to charitable or community activities runs afoul of the dominant corporate purpose, which is to generate profits for its stockholders. The debate over the responsibility of directors to so-called corporate "stakeholders" (employees, suppliers, customers, neighbors, and so forth) currently rages in many forms, but is normally not a concern of the beginning entrepreneur.

Corporate charters also normally set forth the number and classes of equity securities that the corporation is authorized to issue. Here an analysis of a bit of jargon may be appropriate. The number of shares set forth in the charter is the number of shares *authorized,* that is, the number of shares that the directors may issue to stockholders at the directors' discretion. The number of shares *issued* is the number that the directors have, in fact, issued and is obviously either the same or smaller than the number authorized. In some cases, a corporation may have repurchased some of the shares previously issued by the directors. In that case, only the shares which remain in the hands of shareholders are *outstanding* (a number obviously either the same or lower than the number issued). Only the shares outstanding have voting rights, rights to receive dividends, and rights to receive distributions upon full or partial liquidation of the corporation. Normally, we would expect an entrepreneur to authorize the maximum number of shares allowable under the state's minimum incorporation fee (e.g., 200,000 shares for $200 in Massachusetts), who would then issue only 10,000 or so, leaving the rest *on the shelf* for future financings, employee incentives, and so forth.

The charter also sets forth the *par value* of the authorized shares, another antiquated concept, of interest mainly to accountants. The law requires only that the corporation not issue shares for less than the par value, but it can, and usually does, issue the shares for more. Thus, typical par values are $0.01 per share or even "no par value." Shares issued for less than par are *watered stock,* subjecting both the directors and holders of such stock to liability to other stockholders and creditors of the corporation.

Corporations also adopt bylaws which are not filed with the state, but are available for inspection by stockholders. These are usually fairly standard documents, describing the internal governance of the corporation and setting forth such items as the officers' powers and notice periods for stockholders' meetings.

Limited Partnerships

As you might expect, given the limited partnership's hybrid nature, the law requires both a written agreement among the various general and limited partners and a Certificate of Limited Partnership to be filed with the state, along with the appropriate initial and annual fees. The agreement sets forth the partners' understanding of the items discussed earlier, in the context of a general partnership. The certificate sets forth the name and address of the partnership, its purposes, and the names and addresses of its general partners. In states where recent amendments to the Revised Uniform Limited Partnership Act have been adopted, it is no longer necessary to reveal the names of the limited partners, just as the names of corporate stockholders do not appear on the company's incorporation documents.

Limited Liability Companies

The LLC is formed by filing a charter (e.g., a Certificate of Organization) with the state government and paying a fee (usually similar to that charged for the formation of a corporation). The charter normally sets forth the entity's name and address, its business purpose, and the names and addresses of its managers (or persons authorized to act for the entity vis-à-vis the state if no managers are appointed). The same broad description of the entity's business which is allowable for modern corporations is acceptable for LLCs. The members of the LLC are also required to enter into an operating agreement which sets forth their rights and obligations with regard to the business. These agreements are generally modeled after the agreements signed by the partners in a general or limited partnership.

OPERATION OUT OF STATE

Sole Proprietorships and Partnerships

Partly as a result of both the Commerce and Privileges and Immunities clauses of the United States Constitution, states may not place limits or restrictions on the operations of out-of-state sole proprietors or general partnerships that are different from those placed on domestic businesses. Thus, a state cannot force registration of a general partnership simply because its principal office is located elsewhere, but it can require an out-of-state doctor to undergo the same licensing procedures it requires of its own residents.

Corporations, Limited Partnerships, and Limited Liability Companies

Things are different, however, with corporations, limited partnerships, and LLCs. As creations of the individual states, they are not automatically entitled to recognition elsewhere. All states require (and routinely grant) qualification as a foreign corporation, limited partnership, or LLC to nondomestic entities doing business within their borders. This procedure normally requires the completion of a form very similar to a corporate charter, limited partnership certificate, or LLC charter, and the payment of an initial and annual fee, similar in amount to the fees paid by domestic entities. This, incidentally, is one reason not to form a corporation in Delaware, if it will operate principally in New York or elsewhere. Much litigation has occurred over what constitutes "doing business" within a state for the purpose of requiring qualification. Similar issues arise over the obligation to pay income tax, collect sales tax, or accept personal jurisdiction in the courts of a state. Generally these cases turn on the individualized facts of the particular situation, but courts generally look for offices or warehouses, company employees, widespread advertising, or negotiation and execution of contracts within the state.

Perhaps more interesting may be the penalty for failure to qualify. Most states will impose liability for back fees, taxes, interest, and penalties. More important, many states will bar a nonqualified foreign entity from access to its courts and, thus, from the ability to enforce obligations against its residents. In most of these cases, the entity can regain access to the courts merely by paying the state the back fees and penalties it owes, but in a few states access will then be granted only to enforce obligations incurred after qualification was achieved, leaving all prior obligations unenforceable.

RECOGNITION AS A LEGAL ENTITY

Sole Proprietorships

By now it probably goes without saying that the law does not recognize a sole proprietorship as a legal entity, separate from its owner. If Phil, our computer entrepreneur, were to choose this form, he would own all the company's assets: He would be the plaintiff in any suits it brought, and the defendant in any suits brought against it. There would be no difference between Phil, the individual, and Phil, the business.

Partnerships

A general partnership raises somewhat more difficult issues. Although most states allow partnerships to bring suit, be sued, and own property in the partnership name, this does not mean that the partnership exists, for most purposes, separately from its partners. As will be seen, especially in the areas of liability and taxation, partnerships are very much collections of individuals, not separate entities.

Ownership of partnership property is a particularly problematic area. All partners own an interest in the partnership, which entitles them to distributions of profit, much like stock in a corporation. This interest is the separate property of each partner, and is attachable by the individual creditors of a partner, in the form of a so-called *charging order.* However, each partner also owns the assets of the partnership jointly with his other partners. This form of ownership (similar to joint ownership of a family home by two spouses) is called *tenancy in partnership.* Each partner may use partnership assets only for the benefit of the partnership's business; such assets are exempt from attachment by the creditors of an individual partner, although not from the creditors of the partnership. Tenancy in partnership also implies that, in most cases of dissolution of a partnership, the ownership of partnership assets devolves to the remaining partners, to the exclusion of the partner who leaves in violation of the partnership agreement or dies. The former partner is left only with the right to a dissolution distribution, with respect to his partnership interest.

Corporations and Limited Liability Companies

The corporation and LLC are our first full-fledged separate legal entities. Ownership of the business's assets is vested solely in the corporation or LLC, as separate legal entities. The corporation or LLC itself is plaintiff and defendant in suits and is the legally contracting party in all its transactions. Stockholders and members own only their stock or membership interests and have no direct ownership rights in the business's assets.

Limited Partnerships

The limited partnership, continuing in its role as a hybrid, is a little of both. The general partners own the partnership's property as tenants in partnership, operating in the same manner as partners in a general partnership. The limited partners, however, have only their partnership interests and no direct ownership of the partnership's property. This is logically consistent with their roles as silent investors. If they directly owned partnership property, they would have to be consulted with regard to its use.

CONTINUITY OF LIFE

Sole Proprietorships

The issue of continuity of life is one which should concern most entrepreneurs because it can affect their ability to sell the business as a unit, when it comes time to cash in on their efforts as founders and promoters. The survival of the business as a whole, in the form of a separate entity, must be distinguished from the survival of the business's individual assets and liabilities. Although a sole proprietorship does not survive the death of its owner, its individual assets and liabilities do. In Phil's case, for example, to the extent that these assets consist of the computer program, filing cabinets, and the like, they would all be inherited by Phil's heirs, who could then choose to continue the business or liquidate the assets as they pleased. Should they decide to continue the business, they would then have the same choices of business form which confront any entrepreneur. However, if Phil's major asset were a government license, qualification as an approved government supplier, or a contract with a software publisher, the ability of the heirs to carry on the business might be entirely dependent upon the assignability of these items. If the publishing contract is not assignable, Phil's death may terminate the business's major asset. If the business had operated as a corporation, Phil's death would likely have been irrelevant; the corporation, not Phil, would have been party to the contract.

Partnerships

Consistent with the general partnership's status as a collection of individuals, not an entity separate from its owners, a partnership is deemed dissolved upon the death, incapacity, bankruptcy, resignation, or expulsion of a partner. This is true even if a partner's resignation violates the express terms of the partnership agreement. Those assets of the partnership that may be assigned devolve to those partners who are entitled to ownership, pursuant to the rules of tenancy in partnership. These rules favor the remaining partners if the ex-partner has died, become incapacitated or bankrupt, been expelled, or resigned in violation of the partnership agreement. If the ex-partner resigned without violating the underlying agreement, he or she retains ownership rights under tenancy in partnership. Those who thus retain ownership may continue the business as a new partnership, corporation, or LLC with the same or new partners and investors or may liquidate the assets at their discretion. The sole right of any partner who has forfeited direct ownership rights is to be paid a dissolution distribution, after the partnership's liabilities have been paid or provided for.

Corporations

Corporations, on the other hand, normally enjoy perpetual life. Unless the charter contains a stated dissolution date (extremely rare), and as long as the corporation pays its annual fees to the state, it will go on until and unless it is voted out of existence by its stockholders. The death, incapacity, bankruptcy, resignation, or expulsion of any stockholder is entirely irrelevant to the corporation's existence. Such a stockholder's stock continues to be held by the stockholder, is inherited by his heirs, or is auctioned by creditors as the circumstances demand, with no direct effect on the corporation.

Limited Partnerships

As you may have guessed, the hybrid nature of the limited partnership dictates that the death, incapacity, bankruptcy, resignation, or explusion of a limited partner will have no effect on the existence of the limited partnership. The limited partner's partnership interest is passed in the same way as that of a stockholder's. However, the death, incapacity, bankruptcy, resignation, or expulsion of a general partner does automatically dissolve the partnership, in the same way as it would in the case of a general partnership. This can be extremely inconvenient if the limited partnership is conducting a far-flung enterprise with many limited partners. Thus, in most cases, the partners agree in their limited partnership agreement, that upon such a dissolution, the limited partnership will continue under the management of a substitute general partner, chosen by those general partners who remain. In such a case, the entity continues until it is voted out of existence by its partners, in accordance with their agreement, or until the arrival of a termination date, specified in its certificate.

Limited Liability Companies

The laws of the several states generally do not impose dissolution on an LLC upon the happening of any particular events. Under such laws, the LLC may have perpetual life, in the same manner as corporations. However, for reasons having to do with the tax effects normally desired by the members (which are discussed later in this chapter), the operating agreement of an LLC will normally require the vote of at least a majority of its members or managers to avoid dissolution upon any event which results in a change of ownership of a member's interest in the LLC.

TRANSFERABILITY OF INTEREST

Sole Proprietorships

To a large extent, transferability of an owner's interest in the business is similar to the continuity of life issue. A sole proprietor has no interest to transfer because he or she and the business are one and the same, and thus must be content to transfer each of the assets of the business individually—an administrative nightmare at best and possibly impractical in the case of nonassignable contracts, licenses, and government approvals.

Partnerships

To discuss transferability in the context of a general partnership, it is necessary to keep in mind the difference between ownership of partnership assets as tenants in partnership, and ownership of an individual partnership interest. A partner has no right to transfer partnership assets, except as may be authorized by vote, in accordance with the partnership agreement and in furtherance of the partnership business. However, a partner may transfer his or her partnership interest, and it may be attached by individual creditors pursuant to a charging order. This does not make the transferee a partner in the business because partnerships can be created only by agreement of all parties. Rather, it sets up the rather awkward situation in which the original partner remains, but his or her economic interest is, at least temporarily, in the hands of another. In such cases, the Uniform Partnership Act gives the remaining partners the right to dissolve the partnership by expelling the transferor partner.

Corporations

No such complications attend the transfer of one's interest in a corporation. Stockholders simply sell or transfer their shares. Since stockholders have no day-to-day involvement in the operation of the business, the transferee becomes a full-fledged stockholder upon the transfer. This means that if Bruce, Erika, and Michael decide to operate as a corporation, each risks waking up one day to find that he or she has a new "partner" if one of the three has sold his or her shares. To protect themselves against this eventuality, most closely held corporations include restrictions on stock transfer in their charter, their bylaws, or in stockholder agreements. The restriction sets forth some variation of a right of first refusal, either for the corporation or the other stockholders, whenever a transfer is proposed. In addition, corporate stock, as well as most partnership interests (general and most especially limited), are securities under the federal and state securities laws, and because the securities of these entities will not initially be registered under any of these laws, their transfer is closely restricted.

Limited Partnerships

Just as with general partnerships, the partners of limited partnerships may transfer their partnership interests. The rules regarding the transfer of the interests of the general partners are similar to those governing general partnerships described earlier. Limited partners may usually transfer their interests (subject to securities laws restrictions) without fear of dissolution, but transferees normally do not become substituted limited partners without the consent of the general partners.

Limited Liability Companies

As previously mentioned, although a membership interest in an LLC may be freely transferable under applicable state law, most LLCs, as a result of tax considerations discussed later, require the affirmative vote of at least a majority of the members or managers before a member's interest may be transferred. Furthermore, membership interests in an LLC will usually qualify as securities under relevant securities laws and will therefore be subject to the restrictions on transfer imposed by such laws.

CONTROL

Sole Proprietorships

Simply put, control in the context of a business entity means the power to make decisions regarding all aspects of its operations. But the implications of control extend to many levels. These include control of the "equity" or value of the business, control over distribution of profits, control over day-to-day and long-term policy making, and control over distribution of cash flow. Each of these is different from the others, and control over each can be allocated differently among the owners and other principals of the entity. This can be seen either as complexity or flexibility, depending upon one's perspective, but no such debate exists over the sole proprietorship. In that business form, control over all these factors belongs exclusively to the sole proprietor. Nothing could be simpler or more straightforward.

Partnerships

Things are not so simple in the context of general partnerships. It is essential to appreciate the difference between the partners' relationships with each other (internal relationships) and the partnership's relations with third parties (external relationships).

Internally, the partnership agreement governs the decision-making process and sets forth the agreed division of equity, profits, and cash flows. Decisions made in the ordinary course of business are normally made by a majority vote of the partners, while major decisions, such as changing the character of the partnership's business may require a unanimous vote. Some partnerships may weight the voting in proportion to each partner's partnership interest, while others delegate much of the decision-making power to an executive committee or a managing partner. In the absence of an agreement, the Uniform Partnership Act prescribes a vote of the majority of partners for most issues and unanimity for certain major decisions.

External relationships are largely governed by the law of agency; that is, each partner is treated as an agent of the partnership and derivatively, of the other partners. Any action that a partner appears to have authority to take will be binding upon the partnership and the other partners, regardless of whether such action has been internally authorized (Exhibit 8.1).

Thus, if Jennifer purchases a subscription to the Harvard Business Review for the partnership, and such an action is perceived to be within the ordinary course of the partnership's business, that obligation can be enforced against the partnership, even if Jean and George had voted against it. Such would not be the case, however, if Jennifer had signed a purchase and sale agreement for an office building in the name of the partnership, because reasonable third parties would be expected to know that such a purchase was not in the ordinary course of business.

These rules extend to tort liability, as well. If Jean were to wrongfully induce a potential client to breach its consulting contract with a competitor, the partnership would be liable for interference with contractual relations, even if the other two partners were not aware of Jean's actions. Such would not be the case, however, if Jean decided to dynamite the competition's offices because such an act would be judged to be outside the normal scope of her duties as a partner.

These obligations to third parties can even extend past the dissolution of the partnership, if an individual partner has not given adequate notice that he or she is no longer associated with the others. Thus, an ex-partner can be held liable for legal fees incurred by former partners, if he or she has not notified the partnership's counsel about leaving the firm.

It should also be noted that agency law reaches into the internal relationships of partners. The law imposes upon partners the same obligations of fiduciary loyalty, noncompetition, and accountability as it does upon agents with respect to their principals.

EXHIBIT 8.1   Principal and agent.

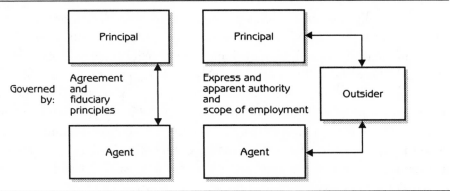

Corporations

Although there can be much flexibility in the allocation of control in the partnership form, it is in the corporate form that the opportunities for flexibility and complexity probably reach their height. Many aspects of the corporate form have been designed specifically for the purpose of splitting off individual aspects of control and allocating them differently.

Stockholders

At its simplest, a corporation is controlled by its stockholders. Yet, except in those states which have specific close corporation statutes (which are relatively rarely used), the decision-making function of stockholders is exercised only derivatively. Under most corporate statutes, a stockholders vote is required only with respect to four basic types of decisions: an amendment to the charter; a sale of the company; dissolution of the company; and election of the board of directors.

    Charter amendments may sound significant, until one remembers what information is normally included in the charter. A name change, a change in purpose (given the broad purpose clauses now generally employed), and an increase in authorized shares (given the large amounts of stock normally left on the shelf) are neither frequent nor usually significant decisions. Certainly, a sale of the company is significant, but it normally can occur only after the recommendation of the board and will happen only once, if at all. The same can be said of the decision to dissolve. It is the board of directors that makes all the long-term policy decisions for the corporation. Thus the right to elect the board is significant, but indirectly so. Day-to-day operation of the corporation's business is accomplished by its officers who are normally elected by the board, not the stockholders.

    Even given the relative unimportance of voting power for stockholders, the corporation provides many opportunities to differentiate voting power from other aspects of control and allocate it differently. Assume Bruce and Erika (our hotel developers) were willing to give Michael a larger piece of the equity of their operation to reflect his contribution of the land, but wished to divide their voting rights equally. They could authorize a class of nonvoting common stock and issue, for example, 1,000 shares of voting stock to each of themselves and an additional 1,000 shares of nonvoting stock to Michael. As a result, each would have one third of the voting control, but Michael would have one half of the equity interest.

    Alternatively, Michael could be issued a block of preferred stock representing the value of the land. This would guarantee him a fair return on his investment, before any dividends could be declared to the three of them as holders of the common stock. As a holder of preferred stock, Michael would also receive a liquidation preference upon dissolution or sale of the business, in the amount of the value of his investment, but any additional value created by the efforts of the group would be reflected in the increasing value of the common shares.

The previous information illustrates how one can separate and allocate decision-making control differently from that of the equity in the business, as well as from the distribution of profits. Distribution of cash flow can, of course, be accomplished totally separately from the ownership of securities, through salaries based upon the relative efforts of the parties, rent payments for assets leased to the entity by the principals, or interest on loans to the corporation.

Stockholders exercise what voting power they have at meetings of the stockholders, held at least annually, but more frequently if necessary. Each stockholder of record, on a future date chosen by the party calling the meeting, is given a notice of the meeting containing the date, time, and purpose of the meeting. Such notice must be sent at least 7 to 10 days prior to the date of the meeting depending upon the individual state's corporate law, although the Securities and Exchange Commission requires 30 days' notice for publicly traded corporations. No action may be taken at a meeting unless a majority of voting shares is represented (known as a *quorum*). This results in the aggressive solicitation of proxy votes in most corporations with widespread stock ownership. Unless otherwise provided (as with the two-thirds vote of all shares required in most states for a sale or dissolution of the company), a resolution is carried by a majority vote of those shares represented at the meeting.

The preceding rules require the conclusion that the board of directors will be elected by the holders of a majority of the voting shares. Thus, in the earlier scenario, even though Bruce and Erika may have given Michael one third of the voting shares of common stock, as long as they continue to vote together, Bruce and Erika will be able to elect the entire board. To prevent this result, prior to investing Michael could insist upon a cumulative voting provision in the charter (under those states' corporate laws which allow it). Under this system, each share of stock is entitled to a number of votes equal to the number of directors to be elected. By using all one's votes to support a single candidate, individuals with a significant minority interest can guarantee themselves representation on the board (e.g., ownership of more than one fifth if the board consists of five or more directors, more than one fourth if it consists of four or more, more than one third if it consists of three or more, and so forth).

More directly (and in states which do not allow cumulative voting), Michael could insist upon two different classes of voting stock, differing only in voting rights. Bruce and Erika would each own 1,000 shares of Class A and elect two directors. Michael, the sole owner of the 1,000 outstanding shares of Class B stock, would elect a third director. Of course, the board also acts by majority, so Bruce and Erika's directors could dominate board decisions in any case, but at least Michael would have access to the deliberations.

In the absence of a meeting, stockholders may vote by unanimous written consent, where each stockholder indicates his approval of a written resolution by signing it. This eliminates the need for a meeting and is very effective in corporations with only a few stockholders (such as our hotel operation). Unlike the rules governing stockholders' meetings, however, in most states unanimity is required to adopt resolutions by written consent. This apparently reflects the belief that a minority stockholder is owed an opportunity to sway the majority with his arguments. A few states, notably Delaware, permit written consents of a majority, apparently reacting to the dominance of proxy voting at most meetings of large corporations, where the most eloquent of minority arguments would fall upon deaf ears (or proxy cards).

Directors

At the directors' level, absent a special provision in the corporation's certificate, all decisions are made by majority vote. Typically, directors concentrate on long-term and significant decisions, leaving day-to-day management to the officers of the corporation. Decisions are made at regularly scheduled directors meetings; or at a special meeting, if there is need to react to a specific situation. Under most corporate laws, no notice need be given for regular meetings, and only very short notice need be given for special meetings (24 to 48 hours). The notice must be sent to all directors and must contain the date, time, and place of the meeting, but, unlike stockholders' notices, need not contain the purpose of the meeting. It is assumed that directors are much more involved in the business of the corporation and do not need to be warned about possible agenda items or given long notice periods.

At the meeting itself, no business can be conducted in the absence of a quorum, which, unless increased by a charter or bylaw provision, is a majority of the directors then in office. Reflecting recent advances in technology, many corporate statutes allow directors to attend meetings by conference call or teleconference, as long as all directors are able to hear and speak to each other at all times during the meeting. Individual telephone calls to each director will not suffice. Unlike stockholders, directors cannot vote by proxy, because each director owes to the corporation his or her individual judgment on items coming before the board. The board of directors can also act by written consent, but, even in Delaware, such consent must be unanimous, in recognition that the board is fundamentally a deliberative body.

Boards of directors, especially in publicly held corporations with larger boards, frequently delegate some of their powers to executive committees, or other committees formed for defined purposes. However, most corporate statutes prohibit boards from delegating certain fundamental powers, such as the declaration of dividends, the recommendation of charter amendments, or sale of the company. The executive committee can, however, be a powerful organizational tool to streamline board operations and increase efficiency and responsiveness.

Although directors are not agents of the corporation—in that they cannot bind the corporation to contract or tort liability through their individual actions—they are subject to many of the obligations of agents discussed in the context of partnerships, such as fiduciary loyalty. Directors are bound by the so-called "corporate opportunity doctrine," which prohibits them from taking personal advantage of any business opportunity that may come their way, if the opportunity is such as would reasonably be expected to interest the corporation. In such an event, the director must disclose the opportunity to the corporation, which normally must consider it and vote not to take advantage before the director may act on his or her own behalf.

Unlike stockholders who, under most circumstances, can vote their shares totally in their own self-interest, directors must use their best business judgment and act in the corporation's best interest when making decisions for the corporation. At the very least, the director must keep informed regarding the corporation's operations, although he or she may in most circumstances rely on the input of experts hired by the corporation, such as its attorneys and accountants. Thus, when the widow of a corporation's founder accepted a seat on the board as a symbolic gesture of respect to her late husband, she found herself liable to minority stockholders for the misbehavior of her fellow board members. Non-participation in the misdeeds was not enough to exempt her from liability; she had failed to keep herself informed and exercise independent judgment.

Directors may also find themselves sued personally by minority stockholders or creditors of the corporation, for declaration of dividends or other distributions to stockholders which render the corporation insolvent, or for other decisions of the board that have injured the corporation. Notwithstanding such lawsuits, however, directors are not guarantors of the success of the corporation's endeavors; they are required only to have used their best independent "business judgment" in making their decisions. When individual directors cannot be totally disinterested (such as the corporate opportunity issue or when the corporation is being asked to contract with a director or an entity in which a director has an interest), the interested director is required to disclose his or her interest and is disqualified from voting. In many states, the director's presence will not even count for the maintenance of a quorum.

Apart from the question of the interested director, much of the modern debate on the role of the corporate director has focused around which constituencies a director may take into account when exercising his or her best "business judgment." The traditional view has been that the director's only concern is to maximize return on the investment of the stockholders. More recently, especially in the context of hostile takeovers, directors have been allowed to take into account the effect of their decision on other constituencies, such as suppliers, neighboring communities, customers, and employees.

In an early case on this subject, the board of directors of the corporation which owned Wrigley Field and the Chicago Cubs baseball team was judged to have appropriately considered the effect on its neighbors and on the game of baseball, in voting to forgo the extra revenue that it would probably have earned if it had installed lights for night games.

When the stockholders believe the directors have not been exercising their best independent business judgment in a particular instance, the normal procedure is to make a demand on the directors to correct the decision, either by reversing it or by reimbursing the corporation from their personal funds. Should the board refuse (as it most likely will), the stockholders then bring a derivative suit against the board on behalf of the corporation. They are, in effect, taking over the board's authority to decide whether such a suit should be brought in the corporation's name. The board's vote not to institute the suit is not likely to be upheld on the basis of the business judgment rule, since the board members are clearly "interested" in the outcome of the vote. As a result, the well-informed board will delegate the power to make such a decision to an independent litigation committee, usually composed of directors who were not involved in the original decision. The decision of such a committee is much more likely to be upheld in a court of law, although the decision is not immune from judicial review.

A more detailed discussion on the board of directors is contained in Chapter 15, "The Board of Directors."

Officers

The third level of decision making in the normal corporation is that of the officers, who take on the day-to-day operational responsibilities. Officers are elected by the board and consist, at a minimum, of a president, a treasurer, and a secretary or clerk (keeper of the corporate records). Many corporations elect additional officers such as vice presidents, assistant treasurers, CEOs, and the like.

Thus, the decision-making control of the corporation is exercised on three very different levels. Where each decision properly belongs may not be entirely obvious in every situation. Thus, the decision to go into a new line of business would normally be thought of as a board decision. Yet, if by some chance, the decision requires an amendment of the corporate charter, a vote of stockholders may be necessary. On the contrary, if the decision is merely to add a twelfth variety of relish to the corporation's already varied line of condiments, the decision may be properly left to a vice president of marketing.

Often persons who have been exposed to the preceding analysis of the corporate-control function conclude that the corporate form is too complex for any but the largest and most complicated publicly held companies. This is a gross overreaction. For example, if Phil, our software entrepreneur, should decide that the corporate form is appropriate for his business, it is very likely that he will be the corporation's 100% stockholder. As such, he will elect himself the sole director and his board will then elect him as the president, treasurer, and secretary of the corporation. Joint meetings of the stockholders and directors of the corporation may be held in the shower on alternate Monday mornings.

Limited Partnerships

As you might expect, the allocation of control in a limited partnership is reflective of its origin as a hybrid of the general partnership and the corporation. Simply put, virtually all management authority is vested in the general partners. The limited partners normally have little or no authority, analogous to outside stockholders in a corporation. Third parties cannot rely on any apparent authority of a limited partner because a limited partner's name will not appear, as a general partner's name will, on the limited partnership's certificate on the public record.

General partners exercise their authority in the same way as they do in a general partnership. Voting control is allocated internally as set forth in the partnership agreement, but each general partner has the apparent authority to bind the partnership to unauthorized contracts and torts to the same extent as the partners in a general partnership.

Limited partners will normally have voting power over a very small list of fundamental business events, such as amending the partnership agreement and certificate, admitting new general partners, changes in the basic business purposes of the partnership, or dissolution. These are similar to the decisions that must be put to a stockholders' vote in a corporation. A recent amendment to the Revised Uniform Limited Partnership Act, now accepted by many states, has widened the range of decisions in which a limited partner may participate, without losing his or her status as a limited partner. However, this range is still determined by the language of the agreement and certificate for each individual partnership.

Limited Liability Companies

An LLC which chooses not to appoint managers is operated much like a general partnership. The operating agreement sets forth the percentages of membership interests required to authorize various types of actions on the LLC's behalf, with the percentage normally varying according to the importance of the act. Although the LLC is a relatively new phenomenon, it can be expected that the members will be deemed to have apparent authority to bind the entity to contracts (regardless of whether they have been approved internally) and to expose the entity to tort liability for acts occurring within the scope of the entity's business.

An LLC which appoints managers is operated much like a limited partnership. The managers make most of the decisions on behalf of the entity, as do the general partners of a limited partnership. The remaining members are treated much like limited partners and have voting rights only in rare circumstances involving very significant events. It can be expected that apparent authority to act for the entity will be reserved to the managers, as only their names will appear on the Certificate of Organization.

LIABILITY

Possibly, the factor that most concerns the entrepreneur is personal liability. If the company encounters catastrophic tort liability, finds itself in breach of a significant contract, or just plain can't pay its bills, must the owner reach into his or her own personal assets to pay the remaining liability, after the company's assets have been exhausted? If so, potential entrepreneurs may well believe that the risk of losing everything is not worth the possibility of success, resulting in diminished innovation throughout society. On the other hand, most entrepreneurs are willing to take significant risk, if the amount of that risk can be limited to the amount they have chosen to invest in the venture.

Sole Proprietorships

With the sole proprietorship, the owner has essentially traded off limitation of risk in favor of simplicity of operation. Since there is no difference between the entity and its owner, all the liabilities and obligations of the business are also liabilities and obligations of its owner. Thus, all the owner's personal assets are at risk. Failure of the business may well mean personal bankruptcy for the owner.

Partnerships

If possible, the result may be even worse within a general partnership. There, each owner is liable not only for personal mistakes, but also for those of his or her partners. Each partner is jointly and severally liable for the debts of the partnership remaining after the partnership's assets have been exhausted. This means that a creditor may choose to sue any individual partner for 100% of any liability. The partner may have a right to sue the other partners for their share of the debt, as set forth in the partnership agreement, but that is of no concern to a third party. If the other partners are bankrupt or have fled the jurisdiction, the partner left may end up holding the entire bag.

If our three consultants operate as a partnership, Jennifer is not only 100% personally liable for any contracts she may enter into, but she is also 100% personally liable for any contracts entered into by either Jean or George. What's more, she is liable for those contracts, even if they were entered into in violation of the partnership agreement, because, as was demonstrated earlier, each partner has the apparent authority to bind the partnership to contracts in the ordinary course of the partnership's business, regardless of the partners' internal agreement. Worse, Jennifer is also 100% individually liable for any torts committed by either of her partners, as long as they were committed within the scope of the partnership's business. The only good news in all this is that neither the partnership nor Jennifer is liable for any debts or obligations of Jean or

George incurred in their personal affairs. If George has incurred heavy gambling debts in Las Vegas, his creditors can affect the partnership only by obtaining a charging order against George's partnership interest.

Corporations

Thus we have the historical reason for the invention of the corporation. Unlike the sole proprietorship and partnership, the corporation is recognized as a legal entity, separate from its owners. Its owners are thus not personally liable for its debts; they are granted limited liability. If the corporation's debts exhaust its assets, the stockholders have lost their investment, but they are not responsible for any further amounts. In practice, this may not be as attractive as it sounds, because sophisticated creditors such as the corporation's bank, will likely demand personal guarantees from major stockholders. But the stockholders will normally escape personal liability for trade debt and, most important, for torts.

This major benefit of incorporation does not come without some cost. Creditors may, on occasion, be able to "pierce the corporate veil" and assert personal liability against stockholders, using any one of three major arguments. First, to claim limited liability behind the corporate shield, stockholders must have adequately capitalized the corporation at or near its inception. There is no magic formula with which to calculate the amount necessary to achieve adequate capitalization, but the stockholders normally will be expected to invest enough money or property and obtain enough liability insurance to offset the kinds and amounts of liabilities normally encountered by a business in their industry. Thus, the owner of a fleet of taxicabs did not escape liability by cancelling the liability insurance and forming a separate corporation for each cab. The court deemed each such corporation inadequately capitalized, and, in a novel decision, pierced the corporate veil laterally, by combining all the corporations into one for purposes of liability.

It is necessary to capitalize only for those liabilities normally encountered by corporations in the industry. The word *normally* is key because it is obviously not necessary to have resources adequate to handle any circumstance, no matter how unforeseeable; adequate capitalization is necessary only at the outset. A corporation does not expose its stockholders to personal liability by incurring substantial losses and ultimately dissipating its initial capitalization.

A second argument used by creditors to reach stockholders for personal liability is failure to respect the corporate form. This may occur in many ways. The stockholders may fail to indicate that they are doing business in the corporate form by leaving the words "Inc." or "Corp." off their business cards and stationery, thus giving the impression that they are operating as a partnership. They may mingle the corporate assets in personal bank accounts, or routinely use corporate assets for personal business. They may fail to respect corporate niceties, such as holding annual meetings and filing the annual reports required by the state. After all, if the stockholders don't take the corporate form seriously, why should its creditors? They are entitled to adequate notice that they may not rely on the personal assets of the stockholders. Even Phil, the software entrepreneur, would be well advised to record the minutes of his damp stockholder's and director's meetings in a corporate record book.

A third argument arises from a common mistake made by entrepreneurs. Fearful of the expense involved in forming a corporation, they wait until they are sure that the business will get off the ground before they spring for the attorneys' and filing fees. In the meantime, they may enter into contracts on behalf of the corporation and perhaps even commit a tort or two. Once the corporation is formed, they may even remember to have it expressly accept all liabilities incurred by the promoters on its behalf. However, under simple agency law, one cannot act as an agent of a nonexistent principal. And a later assignment of one's liabilities to a newly formed corporation does not act to release the original obligor without the consent of the obligee. The best advice here is to form the corporation before incurring any liability on its behalf. Most entrepreneurs are surprised at how little it actually costs to get started.

Limited Partnerships

In the tradition of its hybrid nature, a limited partnership borrows some of its aspects from the corporation and some from the general partnership. In summary, each general partner has unlimited, joint and several, liability for the debts and obligations of the limited partnership after exhaustion of the partnership's assets. In this respect, the rules are identical to those governing the partners in a general partnership. Limited partners are treated as stockholders in a corporation. They have risked their investment, but their personal assets are exempt from the creditors of the partnership.

However, as you might expect, things aren't quite as simple as they may initially appear. In limited partnerships, it is rather common for limited partners to make their investments in the form of a cash down payment and a promissory note for the rest. This occurs partially for reasons of cash flow and partially for purposes of tax planning. This arrangement is much less common in corporations because many corporate statutes do not permit it, and because the tax advantages associated with this arrangement are generally not available in the corporate form. Should the limited partnership's business fail, limited partners will be expected to honor their commitments to make future contributions to capital, despite limited liability.

In addition, it is fundamental to the status of limited partners that they have acquired limited liability in exchange for foregoing virtually all management authority over the business. The corollary to that rule is that a limited partner who excessively involves him- or herself in management may forfeit limited liability and be treated, for the purposes of creditors, as a general partner, with unlimited personal liability. In mitigation of this somewhat harsh rule, the Revised Uniform Limited Partnership Act was recently amended to increase the categories of activities in which a limited partner may participate without crossing the line. Furthermore, and perhaps more fundamentally, in states that have adopted this amendment, the transgressing limited partner is now only personally liable to those creditors who were aware of the limited partner's activities and detrimentally relied upon his or her apparent status as a general partner.

Limited Liability Companies

One of the major benefits of employing the LLC form of business entity is that it shields all members and managers from personal liability for the business's debts. However, even though the LLC is relatively new on the legal scene, it is expected that most of the same doctrines which can result in piercing the corporate veil may be applied to the veil of the LLC as well. Furthermore, it can be expected that the managers of an LLC will be held to the same fiduciary standards as corporate directors and general partners of limited partnerships, resulting in potential personal liability to the members.

TAXATION

It is remarkable how many significant business decisions are made without first taking into account the tax consequences of the various options. Tax consequences should almost never be allowed to force an entrepreneur to take actions he or she otherwise would not have considered. But often tax considerations lead one to do what one wants in a different manner and to reap substantial savings as a consequence. Such is often the case in the organization of a business. The following discussion will be confined to the federal income tax, the tax with the largest and most direct effect upon organizational issues. Each entrepreneur would be well advised to consult a tax adviser regarding this tax as well as state income, estate, payroll, and other taxes and find out how they might impact upon the specific business.

Sole Proprietorships

Not surprisingly, given the factors already discussed, a sole proprietorship is not a separate taxable entity for federal income tax purposes. The taxable income and deductible expenses of the business are set forth on Schedule C of the entrepreneur's Form 1040 and the net profit (loss) is carried back to page one, where it is added to (or subtracted from) all the taxpayer's other income. The net effect of this is that the sole proprietor will pay tax on the income from this business at his highest marginal rate, possibly as high as 39.69%, depending upon the amount of income received from this and other sources (Exhibit 8.2).

In Phil's case, for example, if his software business netted $100,000 in a particular year, that amount would be added to the substantial interest and dividend income from his other investments, so that he would likely owe the IRS $39,600 on this income. If Phil's business were run as a separate taxable corporation, the income generated from it would be taxed at the lowest levels of the tax-rate structure, because it would not be added to any other income. For example, the first $50,000 of income would be taxed at only 15% and the next $25,000 at only 25% (Exhibit 8.3).

This argument is turned on its head, however, if a business anticipates losses in the short term. Using Phil as an example, if his business operated at a $100,000 loss and as a separate taxable entity, the business would pay no tax in its first year and would only be able to net its early losses against profits in future years and only if it ever realized such profits. At best, the value of this tax benefit is reduced by the time value of money, and, at worst, the loss may never yield a tax benefit, if the business never turns itself around. On the other hand, if Phil operated the business as a sole proprietorship, the loss calculated on his Schedule C would be netted against the dividend and interest income generated by his investments, thus effectively rendering $100,000 of that income tax free. Thus, one can strongly argue that the form in which one should operate one's business

EXHIBIT 8.2   Individual federal income tax rates.

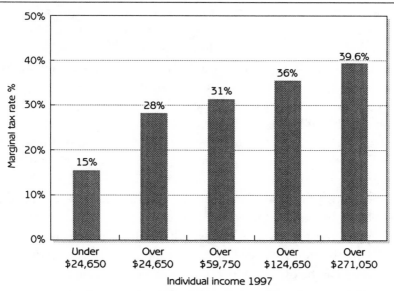

EXHIBIT 8.3   Corporate federal income tax rates.

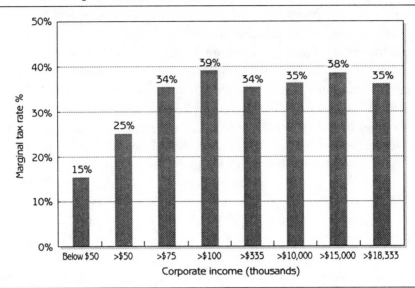

is dictated, in part, by the likelihood of its short-term success and the presence or absence of other income flowing to its owner.

Partnerships

Partnerships are also not separate taxable entities for the purposes of the federal income tax, although, in most cases, they are required to file informational tax returns with the IRS. Any profits generated by a partnership appear on the federal income tax returns of the partners, generally in proportions indicated by the underlying partnership agreement. Thus, as with sole proprietorships, this profit is taxed at the individual partner's highest marginal tax rate, and the lower rates for the initial income of a separate taxable entity are forgone. In addition, each partner is taxed upon his or her proportion of the income of the partnership, regardless of whether that income was actually distributed.

As an example, if Bruce and Erika, our hotel magnates, were to take $25,000 of a year's profits to purchase a courtesy van for the business, this expenditure would not lower the business's profits by that amount. As a capital expense it may be deducted over time only in the form of depreciation. Thus, assuming they were equal partners, even if Michael had objected to this expenditure, each of the three, including Michael, would be forced to pay a tax on $8,333 (minus that year's depreciation) despite having received no funds with which to make such a payment. The result would be the same in a sole proprietorship, but this is considered less of a problem since it can be expected that the owner would manage cash flow in a way which would minimize this negative effect upon him- or herself.

As with a sole proprietorship, this negative result becomes a positive one if the partnership is losing money. The losses appear on the partners' individual tax returns in the proportions set forth in the partnership agreement and render an equal amount of otherwise taxable income tax free. However, not all losses suffered by businesses result from the dreaded negative cash flow. As illustrated earlier in the case of the courtesy van, the next year, the hotel business might well break even or show a small profit on a cash-flow basis, but the depreciation generated by the earlier purchase of the van might well result in a loss for tax purposes. Thus, with enough depreciation, a partner might have the double benefit of a tax sheltering loss on his tax return and ownership of a growing, profitable business. This is especially true regarding real estate, such as the hotel itself. While generating a substantial depreciation loss each year, the value of the building may well be increasing, yielding the partners a current tax-sheltering loss while at the same time generating a long-term capital gain for a few years hence.

Corporations

Corporations are treated as separate entities for federal income tax purposes, consistent with their treatment as separate entities for most other purposes. They have their own set of progressive tax rates, moving from 15% for the first $50,000 of income, through 25% for the next $25,000 and 34 and 35% for amounts above that. There are also 5 and 3% additional taxes at higher levels of income, to compensate for the lower rates on lower amounts of profit made by the more profitable corporations. In addition, so-called "professional service corporations" have only a flat 35% rate at all levels of income. Also, losses generated by a corporation may be carried back as many as three years to generate a tax refund or carried forward as many as 15 years to shelter future income.

Although corporate rates may be attractive at lower levels of income, the common fear of using the corporate form is the potential for *double taxation.* Simply put, the corporation pays tax upon its profits and then distributes the remaining profit to its stockholders as nondeductible dividends. The stockholders then pay tax on the receipt of the dividends, thus amounting to two taxes on the same money. For a corporation in the 34% bracket with stockholders in the 28% bracket, the net effect is a combined tax rate of approximately 52.5%. Yet double taxation is rarely a concern for the small business. Such businesses generally manage compensation to their employees, who are usually their shareholders, in such a way that there is rarely much, if any, corporate profit remaining at the end of the year. Since compensation (as opposed to dividends) is deductible, the only level of taxation incurred by such businesses is at the stockholder level. Other opportunities for legitimate deductible payments to stockholders, which have the effect of eliminating corporate profit, include rental payments on assets leased by a stockholder to the corporation and interest on that portion of a stockholder's investment made in the form of debt.

Thus, the existence of the separate corporate entity with its own set of tax rates presents more of an opportunity for tax planning than a threat of double taxation. If the corporation intends to distribute all of its excess cash to its owners, it should manage compensation and other payments so as to show little profit and incur taxation only upon the stockholder level. If the corporation intends to retain some of its earnings in the form of capital acquisitions (thus resulting in an unavoidable profit for tax purposes), it can take advantage of the lower corporate rates without subjecting its stockholders to taxation at their level. Contrast this to a partnership where the partners would be required to pay tax at their highest marginal rates upon profits that they never received.

There are limits to the usefulness of these strategies. To begin with, one cannot pay salaries and bonuses to nonemployee stockholders who are not performing services for the corporation. In their cases, dividends may be the only way to give them a return on their investment. In addition, the Internal Revenue Service will not allow deductions for what it considers to be unreasonable compensation (measured by compensation paid to comparable employees in the same industry). Thus, a highly profitable corporation might find some of its excessive salaries to employee-stockholders recharacterized as nondeductible dividends.

However, for most start-up businesses, this corporate tax planning strategy will be useful, at least in the short term. In addition, entrepreneurs will find certain employee benefits are better offered in the corporate form because they are deductible to employers, but excluded from income only for employees. Since a sole proprietor or partner is not considered an employee, the value of benefits such as group medical insurance, group life insurance, and disability insurance policies would be taxable income to them, but tax-free to the officers of a corporation.

Professional Corporations

There are two common variations of the corporate form. The first of these is the *professional corporation*. Taxation played a major part in its invention. Originally, limitations on the amounts of money that could be deducted as a contribution to a qualified retirement plan varied greatly, depending upon whether the business maintaining the plan was a corporation, a partnership, or a sole proprietorship. The rules greatly favored the corporation. Partnerships and sole proprietorships were required to adopt Keogh or HR-10 plans with their substantially lower limits on deductibility. However, doctors, lawyers, architects, and other professionals who often could afford large contributions to retirement plans, were not allowed to incorporate under applicable state laws. The states were offended by the notion that such professionals could be granted limited liability for the harms caused by their businesses.

Eventually, a compromise was struck and the so-called "professional corporation" was formed. Using that form, professionals could incorporate their businesses, thus qualifying for the higher retirement plan deductions, but they gave up any claim to limited liability. As time went by, however, the Internal Revenue Code was amended to eliminate most of the differences between the deductions available to Keogh plans and those available to corporate pension and profit-sharing plans. Today, professional corporations are subject to virtually all the same rules as other corporations, with the exception that most are classified as professional service corporations and therefore taxed at a flat 35% rate on undistributed profit.

As the tax incentive for forming professional corporations has decreased, many states, perhaps with an eye toward maintaining the flow of fees from these corporations, have greatly liberalized the availability of limited liability for these corporations. Today, in many states, professional corporations now afford their stockholders protection from normal trade credit as well as tort liability arising from the actions of their employees or other stockholders. Even under the normal business corporation form, a stockholder is personally liable for torts arising from his or her own actions.

Subchapter S Corporations

The second common variation is the *subchapter S corporation,* named for the sections of the Internal Revenue Code that govern it. Although indistinguishable from the normal (or subchapter C) corporation in all other ways, including limited liability for its stockholders, the subchapter S corporation has affirmatively elected to be taxed as if it were a partnership. Thus, like the partnership, it is not a separate taxable entity and files only an informational return. Profits appear on the tax returns of its stockholders in proportion to shares of stock owned, regardless of whether those profits were distributed to the stockholders or retained for operations. Losses appear on the returns of the stockholders and may potentially be used to shelter other income.

Although the subchapter S corporation is often referred to as a "small business corporation," the size of the business has no bearing on whether this election is available. Any corporation that meets the following tests may, but need not, elect to be taxed as a subchapter S corporation:

1. It must have 75 or fewer stockholders.
2. It may have only one class of stock (although variations in voting rights are acceptable).
3. All stockholders must be individuals (or certain trusts).
4. No stockholder may be a nonresident alien.

The subchapter S corporation is particularly suited to resolving the problems presented by certain discrete situations. For example, if a corporation is concerned that its profits are likely to be too high to eliminate double taxation through compensation to its stockholders, the subchapter S election eliminates the worry over unreasonable compensation. Since there is no tax at the corporate level, it is not necessary to establish the right to a compensation deduction. Similarly, if a corporation has nonemployee stockholders who insist upon current distributions of profit, the subchapter S election would allow declaration of dividends without the worry of double taxation. This would undoubtedly be attractive to most publicly traded corporations were it not for the 75-stockholders limitation mentioned earlier.

Many entrepreneurs have turned to the subchapter S election in order to eliminate the two layers of tax otherwise payable upon sale or dissolution of a corporation. The corporate tax otherwise payable upon the gain realized on the sale of corporate assets is eliminated by the use of the subchapter S election, as long as the election has been in effect for 10 years or, if less, since the corporation's inception. Finally, many entrepreneurs elect subchapter S status for their corporations if they expect to show losses in the short term. These losses can then be passed through to their individual tax returns to act as a shelter for other income. When the corporation begins to show a profit, the election can be reversed.

Limited Partnerships

The tax treatment of limited partnerships is much the same as general partnerships and subchapter S corporations. The profits and losses of the business are passed through to the partners in the proportions set forth in the partnership agreement. It must be emphasized that these profits and losses are passed through to all partners, including limited partners, even though one could argue that those profits and losses are derived entirely from the efforts of the general partners. It is this aspect of the limited partnership which made it the form of choice for tax-sheltered investments. The loss incurred formerly by the business (much of which was created on paper through depreciation and the like), could be passed through to the limited partners who, typically, had a considerable amount of other investment and compensation income to be sheltered.

The IRS, in its quest to eliminate perceived abuses of these tax shelters, has taken the position that it is not bound by the taxpayer's characterization of the form of an entity. Thus, the IRS has often recharacterized an entity formed under the limited partnership law of a state as an association taxable as a corporation, thus trapping its losses at the corporate level. The IRS looks at four factors common to corporations to determine whether a limited partnership is a candidate for recharacterization:

1. *Centralized management.*   Corporations with numerous stockholders are nonetheless operated by a relatively small board of directors. Partnerships with many limited partners may be run by one or two general partners.
2. *Perpetual life.*   Corporations last forever, barring dissolution. A limited partnership which has provided in its agreement that the partners will accept a substitute general partner if an original general dies or otherwise withdraws, may also last forever.
3. *Free transferability of interests.*   Stockholders can sell their shares relatively easily. Unless otherwise provided in the agreement, limited partners may similarly transfer their partnership interests.
4. *Limited liability.*   In a corporation, no individual is personally liable for its losses. If a limited partnership is established with a corporate general partner, the same result may be achieved.

The IRS will recharacterize the partnership if it finds three of the above four factors present. Although one cannot do much about centralized management, one could establish an outside date when the partnership will automatically dissolve in order to avoid perpetual life. One might also require all transfers of limited partnership interests to be approved, at the discretion of the general partners, to avoid free transferability. And, if one insists upon a corporate general partner, be sure it is well capitalized, in accordance with IRS regulations, so that it has something substantial at risk (Exhibit 8.4).

Although the tax treatments of limited partnerships and subchapter S corporations are essentially the same, there are some differences that drove the operators of tax shelters to use partnerships over the corporate form, even at the

EXHIBIT 8.4   Association taxable as a corporation.

PROBLEM	LIMITED PARTNERSHIP SOLUTION	LLC SOLUTION
Centralized management	—	NE managers appointed
Perpetual life	Include dissolution date in agreement	Require consent of members for substitute members or managers
Transferable interests	Require consent of general partners	Require consent of managers or members
Limited liability	Adequate capitalization of corporate general partner	—

risk of some unlimited liability. For one, although profits and losses must be allocated according to stock ownership in the subchapter S corporation, they are allocated by agreement in the limited partnership. Thus, in order to give the investors the high proportion of losses they demand, promoters did not necessarily have to give them an identically high proportion of the equity. The IRS has been attacking economically unrealistic allocations in recent years, but some of these opportunities may still exist. In addition, while the amount of loss the investor can use to shelter other income is limited to the tax basis in both types of entities, the tax basis in subchapter S stock is essentially limited to direct investment in the corporation, while in a limited partnership, it is augmented by certain types of debt incurred by the entity itself.

Both types of entities have recently been afflicted by the operation of the passive loss rules, added by the Tax Reform Act of 1986, in the hope of eliminating the tax shelter. Thus, unless one materially participates in the operations of the entity (virtually impossible, by definition, for a limited partner), losses generated by those operations can normally be applied only against so-called passive income and not against active (salaries and bonuses) or portfolio (interest and dividend) income.

Limited Liability Companies

LLCs are taxed in a manner substantially identical to limited partnerships. This combination of limited liability for all members (without the necessity to construct the unwieldy, double-entity, limited partnership with a corporate general partner) and a pass-through of all tax effects to the members' personal returns, makes the LLC the ideal vehicle for whatever tax shelter activity may remain after the imposition of the passive activity rules.

However, since the LLC is an unincorporated entity, along with these positive effects comes the need to be attentive to the IRS' four-point test for associations taxable as corporations. This is especially important since LLCs automatically fail the limited liability test, and many LLCs will fail the centralized management test if they appoint managers to operate the business for the members. Thus, the operating agreements of most LLCs are careful to require at least majority approval of the members or managers for substitution of members or managers upon their death, disability, or resignation from the business and upon any proposed sale or transfer of a membership interest.

Recognizing the technical nature of these rules, in early 1996, the IRS proposed regulations which, if they are adopted, would automatically tax any unincorporated business entity as a partnership unless the entity affirmatively chose to be taxed as a corporation. If these regulations become effective, all uncertainties with regard to the tax classification of limited partnerships and LLCs would be removed. Corporations have already achieved that level of comfort through the availability of the subchapter S election.

CHOICE OF ENTITY

The sole proprietorship, partnership, corporation (including the professional corporation and subchapter S corporation), the limited partnership, and the LLC are the most commonly used business forms. Other forms exist, such as the so-called Massachusetts business trust, in which the business is operated by trustees for the benefit of beneficiaries who hold transferable shares. But these are generally used for limited, specialized purposes. Armed with this knowledge and the comparative factors discussed previously, how should our budding entrepreneurs operate their businesses?

Consulting Firm

It will be obvious to Jennifer, Jean, and George that they can immediately eliminate the sole proprietorship and limited partnership as choices for their consulting business. The sole proprietorship, by definition, allows for only one owner and there does not seem to be any need for the passive, silent investors who would serve as limited partners. Certainly, no one of the three would be willing to sacrifice the control and participation necessary to achieve limited partnership status.

The corporation gives the consultants the benefit of limited liability, not for their own mistakes, but for the mistakes of each other and their employees. It also protects them from personal liability for trade debt. This protection, however, comes at the cost of additional complexity and expense, such as additional tax returns, annual reports to the state, and annual fees. Ease of transferability and enhanced continuity do not appear to be deciding factors because a small consulting firm is often intensely personal and not likely to be transferable apart from its principals. Also, fear of double taxation does not appear to be a legitimate concern, since it is likely that the stockholders will be able to distribute any corporate profit to themselves in the form of compensation. In fact, to the extent that they may need to make some capital expenditures for word processing equipment and office furniture, the corporate form would afford them access to the lower corporate tax brackets for small amounts of income (unless they fell victim to characterization as a personal service corporation). Furthermore, if the consultants earn enough money to purchase various employee benefits, such as group medical insurance and group life and disability, they will qualify as employees of the corporation and can exclude the value of such benefits from their taxable income, while the corporation deducts these amounts.

These positive aspects of choosing the corporate form argue strongly against making the subchapter S election. That election would eliminate the benefit of the low-end corporate tax bracket and put our consultants in the position of paying individual income tax on the capital purchases made. The election would also eliminate the opportunity to exclude the value of employee benefits from their personal income tax. The same problems argue against the choice of an LLC for this business.

The other possibility would be the general partnership. In essence, by choosing the partnership, the consultants would be trading away limited liability for less complexity. The partnership would not be a separate taxable entity and would not be required to file annual reports and pay annual fees. From a tax point of view, the partnership presents the same disadvantages as the subchapter S corporation and LLC.

In summary, it appears that our consultants will be choosing between the so-called C corporation and the partnership. The corporation adds complexity, but grants limited liability. And it certainly is not necessary for a business to be large in order to be incorporated. One might question, however, how much liability exposure a consulting firm is likely to face. In addition, although the corporation affords them the tax benefits associated with employee benefits and capital expenditures, it is not likely that our consultants will be able to afford much in the way of employee benefits and capital expenditures in the short term. Further, it is not likely that these consultants will have personal incomes placing them in tax brackets considerably higher than the corporation's. A strong case can be made for either the C corporation or the partnership in this situation. One can always incorporate the partnership in the future if the business grows to the point that some of the tax benefits become important.

It may also be interesting to speculate on the choice that would be made if our three consultants were lawyers or doctors. Then, the choice would be between the partnership and the professional corporation. The comparisons would be the same with the exception that, as a personal service corporation, the professional corporation does not have the benefit of the low-end corporate tax brackets.

Software Entrepreneur

In Phil's case, he can easily eliminate the partnership and the limited partnership. Phil is clearly the sole owner of his enterprise and will not brook any other controlling persons. In addition, his plan to finance the enterprise with earnings from his last business eliminates the need for limited partner investors. Almost as easily, Phil can eliminate the sole proprietorship, since it would seem highly undesirable to assume personal liability for whatever damage may be done by a product manufactured and distributed to thousands of potential plaintiffs. The corporation, therefore, appears to be Phil's obvious choice. It gives the benefit of limited liability, as well as the transferability and continuity essential to a business that seems likely to be an acquisition candidate in the future. Again, the lack of size is not a factor in this choice. Phil will likely act as sole director, president, treasurer, and secretary.

There remains, however, the choice between subchapters C and S. As may well be obvious by now, Phil's corporation fits the most common profile of the subchapter S candidate. For the first year or more, the corporation will suffer serious losses as Phil pays programmers and marketers to develop and presell his product. Subchapter S allows Phil to show these losses on his personal tax return, where they will shelter his considerable investment income. The passive loss limitations will not affect Phil's use of these losses, since he is clearly a material participant in his venture.

Phil could achieve much the same results by choosing an LLC, rather than a subchapter S corporation. Unfortunately, however, many states require that an LLC have two or more members, making Phil's business ineligible. In states which allow single member LLCs, there would be little to recommend one choice over the other. Phil might feel more comfortable with an S corporation, however, if he fears that suppliers, customers, and potential employees might be put off by the relative novelty of the form. This might especially be true if he has any plans to eventually go public, as the LLC may not gain wide acceptance in the public markets. An S corporation can usually revoke its S election without undue negative tax effect.

Hotel Venture

The hotel venture contemplated by Bruce, Erika, and Michael presents the opportunity for some creative planning. One problem they may encounter in making their decision is the inherent conflict presented by Michael's insistence upon recognition and reasonable return for his contribution of the land. Also, Bruce and Erika fear being unduly diluted by Michael's share, in the face of their more than equal contribution to the ongoing work.

One might break this logjam by looking to one of the ways of separating cash flow from equity. Michael need not contribute the real estate to the business entity at all. Instead, the business could lease the land from Michael on a long-term (99-year) basis. This would give Michael his return, in the form of rent, without distorting the equity split among the three entrepreneurs. From a tax point of view, this plan also changes a nondepreciable asset (land) into deductible rent payments for the business. As their next move, the three may decide to form an entity to construct and own the hotel building, separate from the entity that manages the ongoing hotel business.

This plan would convert a rather confusing real estate/operating venture into a pure real estate investment opportunity for potential investors. The real estate entity would receive enough revenue from the management entity to cover its cash flow and would generate tax losses through depreciation, interest, and real estate taxes. These short-term losses will eventually yield long-term capital gains when the hotel is sold, so this entity will attract investors looking for short-term losses and long-term capital appreciation. For the short-term losses to be attractive, however, they must be usable by the investors on their personal returns and not trapped at the business entity level.

All these factors point inevitably to the use of either the limited partnership, LLC, or subchapter S corporation for the hotel building entity. All three entities allow the tax losses to pass through to the owners, for use on their personal returns. Among these three choices, the limited partnership and LLC allow more flexibility in allocating losses to the investors, and away from Bruce, Erika, and Michael (who most likely do not need them), and they provide higher limits on the amounts of losses each investor may use.

In past years, our entrepreneurs would thus face the unenviable choice between losing the tax advantages of the limited partnership to preserve the limited liability offered by the subchapter S corporation, or preserving the tax advantages (and the ability to attract investors) by either accepting personal liability as general partners or attempting to adequately capitalize a corporate general partner. This choice is no longer necessary with the advent of the LLC, which solves the problem by offering the tax advantages of the limited partnership and the liability protection of the subchapter S corporation. However, the passive loss limitations will still impact upon the usefulness of the losses for the members who do not have significant passive income, making this project (as is the case with most real estate investments in today's climate) more difficult to sell.

This leaves the entity which will operate the hotel business itself. The presence of our three principals immediately eliminates the sole proprietorship as a possibility. Because all the investment capital has already been raised for the real estate entity, there does not seem to be a need for further investors, thus eliminating the limited partnership as a possibility. The partnership seems inapplicable, since it is unlikely that any of the principals would wish to expose himself or herself to unlimited liability in such a consumer-oriented business.

Thus, the corporation and LLC with their limited liability, continuity, and transferability, seem to be the obvious choices for this potentially growing and successful business. As with Phil, it becomes necessary to decide whether to make the subchapter S election or choose an LLC to achieve tax pass-through. This decision will be made on the basis of the parties' projections. Are there likely to be serious losses in the short-term, which might be usable on their personal tax returns? Will there be a need for significant capital expenditures, thus indicating a need for the low-end corporate tax rates? Will the company offer a variety of employee benefits, which our principals would wish to exclude from their taxable income? Is the company likely to generate more profit than can be distributed in the form of "reasonable" compensation, thus calling for the elimination of the corporate-level tax. If these factors seem to favor a tax pass-through entity, the principals will likely analyze the choice between subchapter S and LLC in a manner similar to Phil mentioned earlier. In addition, they may find the LLC's lack of eligibility rules attractive should they ever consider the possibility of corporate or foreign investors, or creative divisions of equity.

CONCLUSION

These and the many other factors described in this chapter deserve careful consideration by the thousands of entrepreneurs forming businesses every month. After the basic decision to start a new business itself, the choice of the appropriate form for the business may well be the most significant decision facing the entrepreneur in the short run.

FOR FURTHER READING

Burstiner, Irving, *The Small Business Handbook: A Comprehensive Guide to Starting and Running Your Own Business* (New York: Prentice-Hall Press, 1989).

Harper, Stephen C., *The McGraw-Hill Guide to Starting Your Own Business* (New York: McGraw-Hill, 1991).

Pollan, Stephen M. and Mark Levine, *The Field Guide to Starting a Business* (New York: Simon & Schuster, 1990).

Siegel, Joel G. and Jae K. Shim, *Keys to Starting a Small Business* (New York: Barrons, 1991).

Tetreault, Wilfred F. and Robert W. Clements, *Starting Right in Your New Business* (Reading, MA: Addison-Wesley, 1987).

9 THE BUSINESS PLAN
Jeffry A. Timmons

PLANNING AND THE BUSINESS PLAN

The What

Planning is a way of thinking about the future of a venture; that is, of deciding where a firm needs to go and how fast, how to get there, and what to do along the way to reduce the uncertainty and to manage risk and change.

Effective planning is a process of setting goals and deciding how to attain them. Planning occurs in start-up situations, in growing enterprises, and in very large firms.

In some sense, most successful ventures plan. One author writing in the *Harvard Business Review* observed that:

> The smaller companies weathering the current difficult economic times seem to be those following an idea—call it a no-frills, down-to-earth, but clear plan—of how to take advantage of the environment and how to allocate resources.[1]

A business plan is one type of planning document which results from the process of planning. A business plan is a written document that (1) summarizes a business opportunity (i.e., why the opportunity exists and why the management team has what it takes to execute the plan) and (2) defines and articulates how the management team expects to seize and execute the opportunity identified.[2]

A complete business plan usually is of considerable length. In recent years, however—particularly in business based on certain technologies, products, or services, where there is turbulence, greater-than-usual unpredictability, and rapid change—an alternative to a complete full-blown business plan has become acceptable. This can be called a "dehydrated" business plan. Dehydrated business plans serve most often as trial balloons for prospective investors and are launched before a decision is made to undertake a complete business plan.

In any case, creating a business plan is more a process than simply a product, and the resulting plan is not immutable. By the same token, the business plan for a business is not "the business." A business plan is analogous to a pilot's cross-country flight plan in that it defines the most desired, most timely, and least-hazardous route to a given destination. Yet, innumerable factors, such as unexpected weather and traffic, can significantly alter the course of the actual flight. Similarly, for new companies, it is common for the actual course of the business to diverge from that originally developed in a business plan. For as was said in the first century, B.C., "It is a bad plan that admits of no modification."[3]

The Why

Business plans are used primarily (1) for raising capital and (2) as a means of guiding growth.

The decision whether to plan, and ultimately to write a business plan, then involves the following:

- Whether the venture needs to raise capital, and whether a business plan is valuable for this purpose.
- Whether the planning process itself will be valuable enough in terms of defining and anticipating potential risks, problems, and trade-offs in a venture to justify the time spent.

For ventures seeking to raise venture capital or other equity in today's highly competitive environment, a quality business plan is a must. As William Egan, founding partner of one of the nation's largest and most successful venture capital funds, Burr, Egan & Deleage, put it:

> Ten to fifteen years ago, a high-quality business plan really stood out and gave the entrepreneur a competitive edge in getting our attention. Today, you have to have a high-quality plan as a given—without it you're dead—but since everyone coming to us for money has a highly professional plan, the plan won't give you much of an edge by itself.

As a vehicle for raising capital, a business plan convinces investors that the new venture has identified an opportunity, has the entrepreneurial and management talent to exploit that opportunity, and has a rational, coherent, and believable program for achieving revenue and expense targets on time. If the business plan passes the initial screening, the plan will be given a more detailed evaluation, and it will become a prime measure of the abilities of those involved to define and analyze opportunities and problems and to identify and plan actions to deal with them.

A business plan can be particularly helpful after start-up as a tool to understand and as a means of guiding growth. One can think of developing a business plan as using a flight simulator. The consequences of different strategies and tactics and the human and financial requirements for launching and building the venture can be determined and worked through without the risk and cost of working these out in real time. The learning necessary to start a company can thus be accelerated. As Nolan Bushnell, founder of Atari, responded when asked by a student if he should prepare a business plan:

> That's exactly what you have to do. There is no way around it; you're doing the best thing. Every time you prepare a business plan, you become a better entrepreneur—I really believe that.[4]

And, as the founder and president of one venture that grew to sales of $14 million in seven years put it:

> Once you are in the business, you realize that everyone, including the founders, is learning his or her job. If you have a thoughtful and complete business plan, you have a lot more confidence in your decisions. You have a reference already there to say, "Well I have already run the numbers on inventory, or cost of goods, and this is what will happen."

For example, a business plan can be valuable in areas such as product pricing. The initial strategy of one of the founders of a new venture was to price products below the competition, even though the venture's products were based on a superior product innovation and could compete in a growing market. In the process of writing a business plan, the founders were persuaded, as a result of vigorously arguing about the pricing strategy with their venture investors, to set prices 10 percent above those of the competition. By its second year, the new company enjoyed pretax profits of $850,000, based on about $9 million in sales. Through the detailed analysis of the industry and competition of the marketing section of the business plan, the wisdom of a different pricing strategy became evident.

A business plan also can help in refining strategy and in making difficult decisions. An entrepreneur in Nova Scotia, who built commercial fishing boats, decided to raise his prices by more than 40 percent, based on an outside analysis and a critique of his business plan. Of five original orders, he knew he would lose two orders, but he also knew he would make more profit on the remaining three orders than he did on all five at the old price. His delivery time would be cut in half as well, and the shortened delivery time would lead to additional sales at the higher margins. He also decided to require progress payments. These payments would eliminate the need to raise outside equity capital.

The process also can clarify the venture's financial requirements. For example, an entrepreneur in Kentucky, with a $1 million-plus business erecting coal-loading sites, which was three years old, believed he needed $350,000 in expansion capital. After reflecting on a detailed critique of his presentation of his business plan, he concluded:

> The worst thing I could do right now is put more money into the business. The first thing I should do is get my own backyard more in order. But I will be back in two or three years.

True to his prediction, he returned two and a half years later. His company then approached $3 million in sales and had a business plan for expansion that resulted in a $400,000 debt capital investment without relinquishing any ownership.

The Whether

Philip Thurston of the Harvard Business School identified dimensions that are unique to each venture and management team. Understanding where a venture sits along these dimensions can help it decide whether to plan:[5]

- *Administrative style and ability.*   Whether to plan depends on the ability of the lead entrepreneur or chief executive officer to grasp multiple and interrelated aspects of the business, keep all that is necessary in his or her head, and retrieve it in an orderly fashion. Further, whether to plan depends on the lead entrepreneur's management style.
- *Wishes of the management team.*   Whether (and how) to plan depend on the wishes of the management team. Some management teams want to participate in the planning process, and others do not.
- *Complexity of the business.*   The complexity of a business will determine whether to plan.
- *Strength of competition.*   Strength of the competition is a factor. Some ventures compete in highly competitive environments where there is a need to be lean and tightly disciplined to survive, while others are more insulated and have a larger margin for error.
- *Level of uncertainty.*   Whether to plan depends also on the level of uncertainty the venture faces. Some ventures face a quite volatile, rapidly changing environment and must be prepared for contingencies, while some enter stable, fairly predictable industries where precipitous actions are not warranted.

In addition, ventures have to face different constituencies, both external and internal, including creditors, shareholders, regulators, customers, community groups, employee groups, and the like. The more of these a firm has to contend with and respond to, the greater the potential payoff in some form of organized and disciplined planning.

Among existing firms, especially those backed by venture capital, the harvest issue is especially important. A business plan for an ongoing business can significantly enhance its harvest potential. Such a document can focus and articulate why there is a major opportunity for a prospective buyer in much the same way a business plan does for a venture that is starting up and seeking investors. For firms not backed by professional investors, planning is important, because they do not have such a backer as the prime motivator and a driving force to realize a harvest or easy access to the skills, know-how, and networks of such a backer.

In addition, an existing firm contemplating launching a venture opportunity internally needs to consider a business plan and may already have formal planning processes in place. Take, for instance, one of the founders of a firm that had grown to $20 million in sales in about a dozen years. He used a business plan to present to his partners and to his board a statement of an opportunity for internal expansion—essentially a new business from within.

Other reasons commonly cited for planning are:[6]

- *Working smarter.*   Planning helps a management team to work "smarter" (i.e., come up with a "better way" by considering alternatives), rather than simply "harder." Planning enables a management team to understand and clarify the risks and, in turn, to devise ways to manage those risks and reduce them.

- *Future orientation.*   Planning necessitates an orientation to the future. Thinking ahead helps a team anticipate and, thus, be more alert for and responsive to problems, opportunities, and changes.

- *Testing ideas.*   Planning helps management to develop and then to update strategy by testing the sensibility of its ideas and approaches.

- *Results orientation.*   Goal setting also gives a team a "results orientation" (i.e., a concern for accomplishment and progress).[7] Developing and stating a specific goal, which is measurable and phased over time, enables performance to be evaluated.

- *Stress management.*   Establishing realistic goals can help in managing and coping with what is by nature a stressful situation.

- *Motivation.*   A more subtle consequence of planning is the effect that setting realistic goals has on motivation. Inherent in any goal is some level of effort required to attain it, and this level of effort, once made clear, can be judged in terms of its ease of attainment. Research has shown that individuals pursuing challenging but attainable goals are more motivated to work toward that goal than are individuals pursuing goals that are either too easy or too difficult.

Problems with Planning

Planning is not for everyone. Commonly cited problems, which often result in decisions not to plan, are the following:

- *Currency.*   A plan, such as a business plan, can be out of date as soon as, or even before, it is written. For example, in highly volatile and turbulent technologies and rapidly changing market niches, planning tends to be ad hoc and spontaneous and any plans are often obsolete before they get printed.

- *Inflexibility.*   It sometimes is undesirable to commit under uncertainty since the future cannot be predicted. Planning requires setting goals, making choices, and setting priorities. Inherent in this process is the possibility that future or yet unknown options, which actually might be more attractive than the one chosen, may be lost or excluded.

- *Inability to plan.*   Invariably, an event entirely beyond the control of a management team, such as the Arab oil crisis in the 1970s, may boost or sink its best-laid plans. No planning process can foresee such developments.

- *Time problems.*   During the demanding early survival stages of a new company, whose life expectancy at times may be estimated in weeks or months, major allocations of time and effort to planning for next year may not make sense.[8]

- *Sales jeopardy.*   A potentially fatal problem for entrepreneurs occurs when planning is substituted for action in getting orders.

While these are usually rationalizations, there may be times when they are valid. An example would be when the window of an attractive opportunity is closing faster than a business plan can be developed.

PITFALLS OF EFFECTIVE PLANNING

What Can Go Wrong

Finally, there are pitfalls in planning. Most important, the process of planning can be carried to extreme. One author warns of the excesses of "planning systems."[9] Excessive detail, analysis, and bureaucratic tendencies toward red tape and "checkups" can detract from the purpose of planning, which needs to be the accomplishment of goals and implementation.

This is one reason why large companies have a difficult time developing new, entrepreneurial business from within. Take, for example, an entrepreneur who headed up a new business venture for a Fortune 500 company. At a conference at the Harvard Business School in early 1989, she described how the "financial overseers" had insisted on 13 very detailed budget reviews, and defenses, during the start-up's first year. The entrepreneurs in attendance, and the author, were astounded at such a mentality and were even more delighted to discover how the competition was approaching the start-up process!

Perhaps there is no greater frustration for entrepreneurs and managers than to experience failure with plans seemingly well prepared and well intended. Not only is it frustrating and consumes precious hours, it is downright demoralizing when a plan does not work initially. The planning process goes awry for some of the following reasons:

- *Wrong emphasis.*   Planning is ineffective if the process itself is overlooked and planning is viewed as an end in itself. If a plan does not seem to work immediately, the lead entrepreneur and his or her team often retreat to the familiar and fall back on an activity-oriented routine or crisis management, which lacks or confuses priorities, has no longer-term purpose, and is not aimed at the attainment of particular objectives.

- *Rigidity.*   Planning fails when the process becomes too rigid and is performed in a lock-step, immutable order. Entrepreneurs need to be very certain that, if their strategies and plans define directions which have irreversible consequences, they are certain they wind up where they want to be and can live with the consequences.

- *Misunderstanding of the function of a business plan.*   Marketability, for example, generally outweighs technical elegance in the success equation, and it usually is necessary to plan to achieve a good fit. Yet some entrepreneurs place more faith, often unwarranted, in a product or invention, especially if it is patented. Readers will recognize the better mousetrap fallacy in this attitude. Even those who understand the value of marketing and business acumen, and who have done a great deal of thinking about how to execute an opportunity, ignore the function of planning in identifying problems, testing the soundness of their ideas internally and with knowledgeable outside sources, and so forth.

- *Misunderstanding of the process of raising capital.*   There is a misconception that a business plan is solely a selling and negotiating tool for raising money. Indeed, more than one entrepreneur has been heard to comment that the plan is "destined for the circular file" once the funds are in the bank. Such a view is wrong for several reasons. First, to prospective partners, investors, or suppliers, such an attitude communicates a shallow understanding of the requirements for creating a successful business. It also can signal to these people a promotional attitude—a search for fast money and a hope for an early sellout—and can create mistrust. In addition, entrepreneurs do not understand that business plans are used, in addition to being the basis of investment decisions, to screen investments. Thus, relying on raising money as an indication that an idea is sound is a cart-before-the-horse approach, which usually results in rejection.

Exhibit 9.1 summarizes some of the ailments of effective planning listed below, which, if not cured, can cause the death of the planning for an organization:

- *Undefined goals.*   Admirable missions, such as "improving performance," "pursuing growth," or "increasing business" are not concrete goals, and plans centered around these undefined goals are unlikely to work. Specific, measurable, time-phased, and realistic goals are necessary. New competition, loss of key personnel, overly ambitious timetables, and a host of other uncertainties rear their ugly heads as planning proceeds and as plans are implemented. Goals, therefore, need to be reviewed and revised periodically.

- *Inability to anticipate obstacles.*   Excessive optimism and overcommitment can seriously impede efforts to anticipate obstacles. Overcommitment can lead to ignoring reality and pressing ahead on a course that may be unduly risky and costly. Every plan, no matter how carefully prepared, has limitations and built-in conflicts over priorities and resources. And, every firm faces obstacles, planned and unplanned. Effective planners know that planning is not an exercise in identifying the impossible so as to rationalize failure, but rather, so as what is perceived to be impossible can be broken down into small hurdles. Concrete action steps are then established to overcome these. Further, an effective plan contains flexibility to deal with unknown and unexpected problems. Experience obtained during the planning process is used to advantage.

- *Lack of progress milestones and review.*   Plans that fail often have no concrete milestones, such as revenue, cost, and cash flow targets, and no progress review dates (or they are allowed to slip by). The rationale usually is expressed by such statements as, "It can wait," "I can remember that," or "I know how I'm doing!" Milestones and planning reviews are necessary to check on progress relative to goals. Further, in the setting of goals and establishment of milestones, interdependencies need to be recognized. For example, goals for sales and for production are related. While some deviation of progress from goals is normal in start-up situations, the falling behind in revenue targets or cost overruns can result in a firm being more than four to six months behind at the end of the year. In addition, milestones, when they are achieved, provide an important sense of accomplishment and, thus, motivation to succeed further.

- *Lack of commitment.*   It is quite easy to obtain only a "lip-service" commitment and not a commitment to and ownership of a plan. Commitment is critical to the success of any plan, because it provides the motivation for critical people to see a plan through to completion. Commitment seems to stem from involving critical people in the process of planning and develop-

EXHIBIT 9.1   Planning: Its ailments, symptoms, and cures.

Planning	Symptoms	Cure
1. No real goals	Goals are vague, general. Goals not specific, measurable, or time-phased. No subgoals or action steps. Activity oriented, not goal-oriented.	Set specific, time-phased, measurable goals, subgoals, and action steps. Keep the overall aim in mind. Be opportunistic in pursuing goals.
2. Failure to anticipate obstacles	Excessive optimism. No alternative strategies. No conflicts recognized. "Don't worry, I had thought of that." Missed meeting delivery date. Missed lead-time forecasts. Didn't get support when needed. Crises prevail.	Be flexible in planning and anticipating as far as possible obstacles and how to overcome them Face unanticipated obstacles with confidence—there'll always be some. Ask someone else to brainstorm with you, "What could go wrong or get in our way?" Realism is key.
3. Lack of milestones and progress reviews	"It can wait"; "I can remember that." "I'll know how we're doing when we get there—let's play it by ear." Don't really know how you are doing. Short-term orientation. Can't recall when we last reviewed how we are doing. No recent revisions of plan.	Set specific task milestones and progress review dates; stick to them and revise when needed. Ask each day, "What did I accomplish today toward reaching my goal?" Ask each day, "What have I learned that will help me to make more rapid progress?"
4. Lack of commitment	"I told you it wouldn't work—it wasn't *my* plan!" Procrastination. Focus on routine, daily activities. Failure to meet goals, milestones. Failure to develop specific action steps to meet goals. Lack of priorities. Missed meetings, appointments.	Set goals mutually; utilize *joint* review, negotiation, compromise, and data sharing. Meet periodically, and track progress. Encourage informal discussion with team members, both to test and to renew commitment. Keep team members informed about results obtained. Recognize and reward performance that meets your high standards.
5. Failure to revise goals	Plan never changes, lacks resiliency. Inflexible or stubborn in face of feedback dictating change. Goals not met or exceeded greatly. Unresponsive to changing situation.	Meet periodically to review goals and progress and to assess the situation. Change emphasis and approach as appropriate. Create a climate that is tolerant of bad news and invites constructive critiques and feedback.

EXHIBIT 9.1   (*Continued*).

Planning	Symptoms	Cure
	Help not sought when needed. Wasted time on unproductive tasks or activities. Activities don't match goal priorities.	
6. Failure to learn from experience	Lost sight of goals. Mistake is repeated. Feedback is ignored or denied. Same routine—same crises as previously. Unwillingness to change way of doing things. Not asking: "What do we learn from this experience?"	Set improvement and learning objectives. Use milestones, and reassess periodically. Collaborate more frequently in tracking progress and learning. Document at end of one project/ plan lessons, benchmarks, guidelines have emerged. What was learned? Be adaptive, flexible, and responsive to unfolding events. A new venture start-up is full of surprises. Concentrate on producing results, not on reports for their own sake.

ing goals from the outset, since this involvement generates their interest, inputs, and, more important, ownership in the plan.

- *Failure to revise goals.*   Effective reviews and feedback simply test the velocity, direction, and reality of the plan at any point in time. Failure to reassess and reset goals and revise plans as dictated by the realities that unfold is another reason planning fails. Failure, thus, is programmed into a plan. Progress reviews are wasted if a new situation is not met with a change in emphasis or approach. Failure to learn from current and past experience either because of unwillingness to change or denial of reality is another reason planning fails.

- *Performance expectations.*   It is easy to overlook clarity in expectations. Performance expectations need to be made clear and a win/win situation created for critical people.

Important Do's and Don'ts

Before getting into the details of what needs to be in a business plan, it is worth noting some important general do's and don'ts for preparing such plans. Exhibit 9.2 shows these do's and don'ts. These do's and don'ts have come from the experience of those writing business plans as a result of observations of the reactions of venture capitalists to a great many business plans, as well as from publications dealing with the foibles, pet hates, and preferences of venture capitalists.[10]

A CLOSER LOOK AT THE WHAT

The Relationship between Goals and Actions

Consider a team that is enthusiastic about an idea for a new business and has done a considerable amount of thinking and initial work evaluating the opportunity. Team members believe the business they are considering has excellent

EXHIBIT 9.2   Do's and don'ts.

DO

DO involve all of the management team in the preparation of the business plan.

DO make the plan logical, comprehensive, and *readable*—and as short as possible.

DO demonstrate commitment to the venture by investing a significant amount of time and some money in preparing the plan.

DO articulate what the critical risks of assumptions are and how and why these are tolerable.

DO disclose and discuss any current or potential problems in the venture.

DO identify several alternative sources of financing.

DO spell out the proposed deal—how much for what ownership share—and how investors will win.

DO be creative in gaining the attention and interest of potential investors.

DO remember that the plan is not the business and that an ounce of "can do" implementation is worth two pounds of planning.

DO accept orders and customers that will generate a positive cash flow, even if it means you have to postpone writing the plan.

DO know your targeted investor group (e.g., venture capitalist, angel, bank, or leasing company) and what they really want and what they dislike, and tailor your plan accordingly.

DO let realistic market and sales projections drive the assumptions underlying the financial spreadsheets, rather than the reverse.

DON'T

DON'T have unnamed, mysterious people on the management team (e.g., a "Mr. G" who is currently a financial vice president with another firm and who will join you later).

DON'T make ambiguous, vague, or unsubstantiated statements, such as estimating sales on the basis of what the team would like to produce.

DON'T describe technical products or manufacturing processes using jargon or in a way that only an expert can understand, because this limits the usefulness of the plan. For example, a venture capitalist will not invest in what he or she does not understand—or what he or she thinks the team does not understand, because it cannot explain these to such a smart person as he or she is.

DON'T spend money on developing fancy brochures, elaborate slide show presentations, and other "sizzle"—instead, show the "steak."

DON'T waste time writing a plan when you could be closing sales and collecting cash.

DON'T assume you have a done deal when you have a "handshake" or verbal commitment but no money in the bank. (The deal is done when the check clears!)

market prospects and fits well with the skills, experience, personal goals and values, and aspirations of its lead entrepreneur and the management team. They now need to ask questions about what the most significant risks and problems involved in launching the enterprise are; what its long-term profit prospects are; what its future financing and cash flow requirements will be; what the demands of operating lead times, seasonality, and facility location will be; what the marketing and pricing strategy needs to be; and so forth, so they can take action.

These questions now need to be answered convincingly and the evidence for them shown in writing. The planning and the development of such a business plan is neither quick nor easy. In fact, effective planning is a difficult and demanding process and demands time, discipline, commitment and dedication, and practice. However, it also can be stimulating and fun as innovative solutions and strategies to solve nagging problems are found.

The skills to write a business plan are not necessarily the ones that are needed to make a venture successful (although some of these skills are certainly useful). The best single point of departure for and an anchor during the planning process is the motto on a small plaque in the office of Paul J. Tobin, president of Cellular One, a company that was a pioneer in the cellular car phone business in America. The motto says, "CAN DO," and is an apt one for planning and for making sure that a plan serves the very practical purpose for which it is intended.

Before proceeding, however, it is essential to reiterate that effective planning is goal-oriented, rather than activity-oriented. *It is through effective goal setting that action steps are devised.*

Goals are not dreams, fantasies, or the product of wishful thinking; nor are they mere predictions or guesses about future outcomes. A *goal* is a decision or choice about future outcomes. Once set, goals should not become static targets. Goal setting is not a task but a process, a way of dealing with the world that is repeated over and over as conditions change.

There are numerous ways of actually going about goal setting and planning. Most of these approaches have in common a balanced emphasis on both the process by which goals are set and the results they seek. Research and practical experience have shown that certain ingredients are common to almost all successful planning efforts:

- Establishment of goals that are:
  —Specific and concrete
  —Measurable
  —Related to time (i.e., specific about what will be accomplished over a certain time period)
  —Realistic and attainable

—Capable of being modified and adapted

—Certain to make a significant difference

- Establishment of priorities and identification of conflicts and how to resolve them
- Identification of problems and obstacles
- Specification of necessary tasks and actions steps
- Indication of how results will be measured
- Establishment of progress milestones, especially revenue, expense, and cash targets, deadlines, and dates
- Identification of risks involved and alternatives for coping with possible contingencies
- Identification of outside help and resources that need to be marshalled and controlled
- Periodic review of progress and revision of goals as factors such as the changing competitive situation require

In the process of establishing goals and priorities, a planner needs a sense of perspective. The general wisdom is that 80% of a task usually is accomplished using the first 20% of the effort. Therefore, one needs to focus first on what will result in 80% of the accomplishments. Often, there will not be time to do otherwise.

Who Develops the Business Plan

Consideration often is given to hiring an outside professional to prepare the business plan, so the management team can use its time to obtain financing and start the business.

There are two good reasons why it is not a good idea to hire outside professionals. First, in the process of planning and of writing the business plan, the consequences of different strategies and tactics and the human and financial requirements for launching and building the venture can be examined, before it is too late. For example, one entrepreneur discovered, while preparing his business plan, that the major market for his biomedical product was in nursing homes, rather than in hospital emergency rooms, as he and his physician partner had previously assumed. This realization changed the focus of the entire marketing effort. Had he left the preparation to an outsider, this might not have been discovered, or, at the very least, it is unlikely he would have had the same sense of confidence and commitment to the new strategy.

Further, if a venture intends to use the business plan to raise capital, it is important for the team to do the planning and write the plan itself. Investors attach great importance to the quality of the management team *and* to their complete understanding of the business they are preparing to enter. Thus, investors want to be sure that what they see is what they get—that is, the team's analysis and understanding of the venture opportunity and its commitment to it. They are going to invest in a team and a leader, not in a consultant. Nothing less will do, and anything less is usually obvious.

Segmenting and Integrating Information

In the task of planning and writing a business plan, it is necessary to organize information in a way that it can be managed and that is useful.

An effective way to organize information with the idea of developing a business plan is to segment the information into "sections," such as a section about the target market, a section about the industry, one about competition, one about the financial plan, etc., and then integrate the information into a business plan.

This process works best if sections are discreet and the information within them digestible. Then the order in which sections are developed can vary, and different sections can be developed simultaneously. For example, since the heart and soul of a plan lies in the analysis of the market opportunity, of the competition, and of a resultant competitive strategy that can win, it is a good idea to start with these sections and integrate information along the way. Since the financial and operations aspects of the venture will be driven by the rate of growth and the magnitude and specific substance of the market revenue plans, these can be developed later.

The information is then further integrated into the business plan. For example, the Executive Summary is prepared last.

Establishing Action Steps

The following steps, centered around actions to be taken, outline the process by which a business plan is written.

- *Segmenting information.* An overall plan for the project, by section, needs to be devised and needs to include priorities, who is responsible for each section, the due date of a first draft, and the due date of a final draft.

- *Creating an overall schedule.* A list of specific tasks, their priorities, who is responsible for them, when they will be started, and when they will be completed needs to be made. This list needs to be as specific and detailed as possible. Tasks need to be broken down into the smallest possible components (e.g., a series of phone calls may be necessary before a trip). The list then needs to be examined for conflicts and lack of reality in time estimates. Peers and business associates can be asked to review the list of realism, timing, and priorities.

- *Creating an action calendar.*   Tasks on the "do" list then need to be placed on a calendar. When the calendar is complete, the calendar needs again to be examined for conflicts or lack of realism.
- *Doing the work and writing the plan.*   The necessary work needs to be done and the plan written. Adjustments need to be made to the "do" list and the calendar, as necessary. As part of this process, it is important to have a plan reviewed by an attorney to make sure that it contains no misleading statements and unnecessary information and caveats, and also reviewed by an objective outsider, such as an entrepreneurially minded executive who has significant profit and loss responsibility, or a venture capitalist who would not be a potential investor. No matter how good the lead entrepreneur and his or her team are in planning, there will be issues that they will overlook and certain aspects of the presentation that are inadequate or less than clear. Few entrepreneurs are good at both planning and communication. A good reviewer also can act as a sounding board in the process of developing alternative solutions to problems and answers to questions investors are likely to ask.

The remainder of this chapter is a sample business plan for the company Rapidrill.

CASE—RAPIDRILL BUSINESS PLAN

RAPIDRILL CORPORATION[*]
BUSINESS PLAN

Confidential Plan Number _____
Delivered to _____

BUSINESS PLAN
RAPIDRILL CORPORATION
15 MAIN STREET
NASHVILLE, TENNESSEE
615-365-5749
DECEMBER 10, 19X1

SECURITIES OFFERED:
240,000 SHARES OF COMMON STOCK AT $1 PER SHARE

---

[*] The name of the company and other details have been disguised.

This business plan has been submitted on a confidential basis solely for the benefit of selected, highly qualified investors in connection with the private placement of the above securities and is not for use by any other persons, nor may it be reproduced. By accepting delivery of this plan, the recipient agrees to return this copy to the Corporation at the address just listed if the recipient does not undertake to invest in the Corporation.

Table of Contents

Summary

Exhibits

SUMMARY

Rapidrill was formed in April 19X1 and incorporated in the state of Delaware in August 19X1 by a highly knowledgeable and experienced team of five executives in response to what they believed to be an attractive business opportunity created by the following conditions:

1. The market for their product, rotary drills, is substantial ($74 million in 19X0); has demonstrated a 10 percent annual growth for the past six years; and has strong indicators of accelerated future growth.

2. Prices and margins are attractive (earnings after taxes average 9% in the industry) and have been firm.

3. The major existing competitive manufacturers have high costs and high fixed investments, in both manufacturing facilities and distribution organizations. They are also producing drills at near capacity.

4. Rapidrill believes it can achieve cost savings over competitors of from 9 to 12% in total manufacturing and selling expenses.

5. Rapidrill's ability to accomplish its program is significantly related to the know-how and track record of its management team: their past team efforts increased the market share of the present industry leader from 9 to 22% of the market in the past five years. The improbability of duplicating this "team" asset by others precludes, for all practical purposes, the effective near-term entry to the market of additional competitors.

As a result of these conditions, Rapidrill believes that it has a unique opportunity to provide superior quality drills at attractive prices, and capture 7.5% of the rotary drill market in three years. This market share would produce for Rapidrill forecast sales in 19X4 of $7,585,000 and after-tax earnings of $733,000.

Rapidrill is seeking an equity investment of $240,000 to implement the plans described herein. The common stock sold for the $240,000 investment will represent about 35% of Rapidrill's outstanding common stock after the offering is completed.

1. THE INDUSTRY, THE COMPANY, AND THE PRODUCT

The Industry

Virtually all mining and medium-to-large-scale construction activities require the penetration and/or removal of significant amounts of rock. Typical applications are as follows:

- Surface mining, both coal and metals
- Quarrying

- Water-well drilling
- Highway construction
- Pipeline construction
- Foundation excavations
- Mineral explorations
- Gas- and oil-well drilling

In the various mining, quarrying, and construction applications that require removal of rock, "blast holes" are drilled into the rock so that it may be blasted into small pieces to facilitate its removal. Similar, though generally much deeper, penetration is required in the drilling of wells or exploration holes.

Over the past 15 years, the "rotary drill" has emerged as the preeminent tool for rock-drilling requirements in the above applications. Its ease of operation and superior productivity have developed in parallel with the larger capacities of complementary equipment, such as loaders, shovels, trucks, and breakers; and have created a market that has expanded from less than $10 million in 19X3 to $74 million in 19X0.

The principals of Rapidrill have collectively accumulated in excess of 70 years of marketing, engineering, manufacturing, and general management experience with rotary drills and have formed a new company to design and produce rotary drills based on their assessment of conditions in the industry, which they believe create a viable business opportunity favorable to their planned program.

There are 11 manufacturers of rotary drills that presently have a significant share of the market. Only four of these manufacturers produce a line of drills applicable to a broad range of drilling applications and attempt national market coverage. These four manufacturers command about 50% of the total market, and all market their drills through equipment distributors (Ingersoll-Rand utilizes "company owned" stores).

The four manufacturers are:

- Indiana Tool, Inc.
- Ingersoll-Rand
- Davey
- Joy Manufacturing (Robbins)

They all manufacture a full line of products (gear drives, pumps, etc.) for mining, construction, and industrial markets and share the common characteristic that all gravitated to the manufacture of drills based on their prior experience with the manufacture and packaging of air compressors. This packaging experience coupled with their existing channels of sales to the mining and construction industries created what seemed to be a natural product opportunity.

In the manufacture and packaging of compressors, however, these manufacturers commonly added between 50 and 80% of the manufacturing cost content. In a rotary drill, the compressor accounts for less than 10% of the total costs, and the total value added by the packager is about 25%, including the compressor, with the remainder in purchased material. Nevertheless, the manufacture of drills by these companies is accomplished in existing compressor manufacturing facilities with production control systems and overhead structures geared to machine shop operations. These facilities are generally very complex, with high fixed investments, rigidly unionized, and located in high-cost labor areas, all of which leads to rotary drill manufacturing costs that are unnecessarily inflated.

In addition, the product design of rotary drills by these manufacturers has generally been prejudiced by the type and size of compressors in their product line and by their ability to use their own components for mechanical drive systems, instead of basing their designs on the optimum utilization of all available components.

While these manufacturing and design decisions use as a rationale higher facility utilization and increased value added, they, in fact, force rotary drill designs that do not provide the best solution to market application requirements. And the high-cost labor content adds materially to unnecessarily inflated costs.

Rotary drills can be produced more economically in a simple assembly shop operation, located in a low-rent area, and utilizing the most cost-effective components available (there are 27 manufacturers of compressors in the United States alone).

In combination, the above considerations create a situation whereby a product line of rotary drills may be designed that better satisfies market requirements and that can be produced and distributed at costs significantly below those of the present manufacturers. An opportunity exists for the right new venture to get into the rotary drill business with significant competitive advantages.

The Company

The opportunity for a new manufacturer to enter the rotary drill industry was perceived by April 19X1 by a group of five key executives employed by the present industry leader. These executives collectively had more than 70 years of marketing, engineering, manufacturing, and general management experience in the rotary drill business. Their analysis and assessment of conditions in the industry convinced them that there was a viable growth opportunity for a new rotary drill company and that the equity capital requirements for such a new venture were very reasonable (i.e., less than $400,000).

Accordingly, these five executives formed a new company—Rapidrill—to design, manufacture, and sell rotary drills. Rapidrill was formally incorporated in the state of Delaware in August 19X1 and the principals invested $128,000 of their funds in it. Rapidrill plans to produce modern, state-of-the-art rotary drills that will be marketed through independent mining and construction equipment distributors.

The Product

The rotary drill that Rapidrill proposes to make and sell and that is discussed in this plan is a mobile system, either truck- or crawler-mounted, for drilling relatively large holes (generally 6″ to 12″ diameter) in rock formations. The drill is driven at its top by a hydraulic motor. Basically, a rotary drill provides a large downthrust and torque force to a drill stem so that a drill bit or hammer can fragment rock at the bottom of the hole being drilled. In addition, compressed air is provided to remove rock cuttings from the hole during the drilling.

Rather than being a simple manufactured product, the rotary drill is in fact a complex technical system design consisting of hydraulic, pneumatic, electrical, and mechanical components integrated into a complete drill-rig assembly having a typical value of $100,000. It is significant that for *all* present manufacturers the cost of purchased components for assembled drills is from 60 to 70% of manufacturing costs. It is also pertinent that no present manufacturer has a sufficient market share to enjoy a "most favored" position with the suppliers of such components.

The strip mining, open-pit mining, construction, quarrying, and water-well drilling industries utilize rotary drills in their operations. In the various mining, quarrying, and construction operations, blast holes are drilled into the rock overlying the coal or ore, or into the rock structures to be moved. Blasting this waste rock into small pieces enables its removal. An infinite number of different rock structures are encountered in these operations, and a wide range of hole diameters and hole depths are required. In the last 15 years, the demand for increased productivity has forced a trend toward faster production of larger, deeper holes, which has best been provided by rotary drills.

While the rotary drills used for drilling blast holes are increasing in size and productivity, the water-well drilling contractor must cope with problems of mobility. His rotary drill must have the same fast drilling capability, but it must be small enough in size to travel over the public highways and be set up to drill in small, tight areas—often between buildings.

Product Line

Design studies have been conducted by Rapidrill to determine how to best configure Rapidrill's rotary drills so that they will meet most present drilling requirements and use available components (e.g., trucks, compressors, and diesel engine frames). As a result of these studies, Rapidrill has decided on three basic drill frame sizes:

- D-30K for 6″ diameter and smaller holes
- D-40K for 6″ to 8″ diameter holes
- D-70K for 9″ to 12″ diameter holes

All of these will be hydraulic top-drive drills that are now standard in the drilling industry.

An analysis has also been conducted to determine the suitability of truck- and crawler-mounted versions of each of the preceding basic drill models for blast hole and well-drilling applications in the principal market segments.

Results of this study are shown in Exhibit 9.3. Examination of these data shows that good application coverage can be obtained with only six basic rotary drill models: a truck-mounted D-30K and D-40K for well drilling; a truck-mounted D-30K and D-40K for blast hole drilling; and a crawler-mounted D-40K and D-70K for blast hole drilling. The crawler-mounted version of D-30K and the truck-mounted version of the D-70K provide insufficient market coverage to warrant their design and manufacture by Rapidrill during its early operations. The data in Exhibit 9.3 also indicate that the most desirable order of drill development, to achieve the earliest coverage of the maximum number of market segments would be: first the D-40K, then the D-30K, and last the D-70K.

Exhibit 9.4 shows the selected Rapidrill product lines and the relationships among them. Note the high degree of component commonality that can be achieved in the different versions of the basic drill models. The prices shown are list prices to the end user (distributor prices will be about 25% lower). Sufficient detail design and component selection have been accomplished to permit accurate cost estimates to be made and to assure that the 25% discount to distributors can be achieved.

EXHIBIT 9.3   Percentage of total rock-drilling applications met by Rapidrill's possible product lines (by market segment).

| | Rotary Drill Model | | | | | |
| | D-30K | | D-40K | | D-70K | |
Market Segment	Truck	Crawler	Truck	Crawler	Truck	Crawler
Wells	70%		90%			
Blast hole drilling:						
Coal mining	20%	20%	80%	50%	30%	30%
Quarrying	30	30	30	30	10	5
Construction	10	5	35	5		
Copper mining			20	30	20	50
Iron mining				20		50

Note: Some overlap exists in the applications for each drill size. For example, 90% of all water wells drilled provide water for residential use. These wells are generally 6″ in diameter, and both the D-30K model and the D-40K model can be used to drill them.

EXHIBIT 9.4   Proposed Rapidrill models.

Parameters	Model		
	D-30K	**D-40K**	**D-70K**
Truck-mounted drills			
Well drills:			
Hole diameter (inches)	6	6–8	
Rated depth (feet)	1,000–2,000	1,000–2,000	
Bit pressure (pounds)	30,000	40,000	
Bit RPM	0–200	0–200	
Stem length (feet)	20	25	
Compressor	450 CFM-250 psi	750 CFM-250 psi	
Mounting (truck)	T-800 Ford	Crane Carrier	
Estimated weight			
(pounds)	40,000	56,000	
Selling price	$95,000	$125,000	
Blast hole drills:			
Hole diameter (inches)	6	6–8	
Rated depth (feet)	1,000	1,000	
Bit pressure (pounds)	30,000	40,000	
Bit RPM	0–200	0–200	
Stem length (feet)	20	25	
Compressor	450 CFM-250 psi	750 CFM-100 psi	
		750 CFM-250 psi	
		900 CFM-50 psi	
Mounting (truck)	T-800 Ford	Crane Carrier	
Estimated weight			
(pounds)	40,000	56,000	
Selling price	$90,000	$120,000	
Crawler-mounted drills			
Blast hole:			
Hole diameter (inches)		6–8	9–12
Rated depth (feet)		1,000	1,000
Bit pressure (pounds)		40,000	70,000
Bit RPM		0–200	0–100
Stem length (feet)		25	30–50
Compressor		750 CFM-250 psi	1050 CFM-100 psi
Estimated weight			
(pounds)		60,000	100,000
Selling price		$135,000	$225,000

2. THE MANAGEMENT TEAM

Rapidrill believes that the most important element supporting the feasibility of its proposed program is the strength and proven ability of its management team. Every key functional position in which rotary drill experience would enhance the performance of the company is filled with an individual unquestionably preeminent in the industry.

Perhaps more important than the individual competence of team members is their demonstrated ability to work effectively as a team. Over the last five years, their efforts—and significant effort was required of each of them—increased the market share of their former employer from 9 to 22% of the total rotary drill market. This 22% market share was twice the share of the nearest competitor, and it was accomplished with handicaps in capacity, delivery, and costs at least as great as those of any of their competitors.

Consideration of this performance and review of the qualifications of team members are important in judging the validity of Rapidrill's knowledge of the industry and the feasibility of its proposed marketing, product, and manufacturing plans.

The Team

The following tabulation shows the organization of Rapidrill management and the responsibility of each member prior to association with Rapidrill.

Rapidrill Organization	Former positions with Indiana Tool, Inc., Machinery Division
S. A. Price, President	Division President
M. F. Einman, VP Marketing	Product Manager, Rotary Drills
F. T. Samuels, VP Engineering	Manager of Engineering
G. A. Miller, VP Finance	Controller
W. D. MacMillan, Manager Manufacturing	Production Superintendent

Qualifications

The following summaries describe the individual qualifications of team members.

Samuel A. Price, President

Mr. Price, age 42, has both BS and MS degrees in engineering from Michigan State University. His experience includes 15 years of increasing responsibilities in engineering and marketing management and over five years of general management responsibilities in the design, manufacture, and sale of equipment for the mining, construction, and utility markets. This experience was accumulated with General Electric, Dresser Industries, and Indiana Tool, Inc.

In 19X3, as general manager of the then new Gas Turbine Division of Dresser Industries, Mr. Price staffed the division (predominantly from outside sources) and supervised the design, fabrication, and installation in customer facilities of over $5 million worth of gas-turbine-powered pipeline booster compressors within 15 months of division start-up. This program was accomplished well within original cost and time objectives.

During the four-year period from 19X5 through 19X0, under his management as president of the Machinery Division of Indiana Tool, Inc., division sales to the mining and construction markets rose from $17 million per year to $32 million per year and were profitable. This represented the most significant sales and profit growth rate of any of Indiana Tool's divisions and substantial market share improvement in all product lines. The rotary drill product lines accounted for $14 million of those 19X0 sales.

Marshal F. Einman, Vice President, Marketing and Sales

Mr. Einman, age 49, attended the Illinois State Teachers College and has prior experience of three years as president of a small privately held company. His 27 years' total experience includes 19 years in marketing and sales of rotary drills with both Hamilton Manufacturing Company and the Machinery Division of Indiana Tool, Inc.

From 19X0 to 19X1, he was product manager for rotary drills, responsible for domestic and foreign sales, sales forecasting, production requirements, product definition, product pricing, advertising, sales training, and definition of product support programs.

Under his marketing management, Indiana Tool's sales of rotary drills rose from $2.5 million in 19X0 to $14.4 million in 19X9. Much of this sales increase was directly attributable to his personal expertise in drill applications work. He has extensively traveled the United States, and, in fact, the entire free world, solving difficult drilling problems and promoting drill sales. Recent foreign trips to Australia, Vietnam, the Philippines, Morocco, Spain, Zambia, Rhodesia, and South Africa attest to the worldwide acceptance of his applications and market knowledge.

Mr. Einman is a member of the American Institute of Mining Engineers.

Frank T. Samuels, Vice President, Engineering

Mr. Samuels, age 45, holds degrees in civil engineering from Michigan State College, mechanical engineering from Worcester Polytechnic Institute, and has done graduate work in mechanical engineering at Illinois Institute of Technology. His 24 years of engineering experience includes high-pressure hydraulic research with Standard Oil Company of Indiana and 20 years of design responsibility for rotary drills commencing in 19X1, when he joined the Hamilton Manufacturing Company as chief engineer. Hamilton Manufacturing, under Mr. Samuels's engineering leadership, pioneered and developed the highly successful hydraulic top-drive rotary drill that has become the standard of the industry.

During this period, and after acquisition of Hamilton Manufacturing by Indiana Tool, Inc., in 19X7, in the capacity of chief engineer for Indiana Tool's

Machinery Division, he supervised the engineering of over 1,200 rotary drills, ranging in size and application from 5,000-pound high-speed diamond core drills to 200,000-pound crawler-mounted machines, used to bore 15″ blast holes in taconite on the Mesabi Range. He has become accepted as the technical leader and innovator in the field. In 19X0, he had engineering responsibility for over $32 million worth of mining and construction machinery sales that included $14 million worth of rotary drills.

He is a member of the Society of Automotive Engineers and is a registered professional engineer in Indiana, Pennsylvania, and New York.

George A. Miller, Vice President, Finance, Secretary, Treasurer

Mr. Miller, age 32, has a degree in accounting from Michigan State College and graduate work toward an MBA at Wayne State College.

His initial experience was with Federal-Mogul Corporation, culminating in the position of controller for its Bearings Division plant, where he designed and installed a standard cost system specifically suited for job-shop operations.

In 19X6, he joined the Vare Corporation (now Microdot, $170 million annual sales, NYSE) as group controller of its Plastics Division. Promoted to assistant corporate controller, he assisted in the $37 million loan negotiated for the acquisition of Microdot, Inc., by Vare Corporation.

Mr. Miller joined Indiana Tool, Inc., in 19X9. As division controller of the $32 million-per-year Machinery Division, he revised and modernized the division's accounting and management reporting systems and worked extensively on financial analysis of new product and manufacturing opportunities.

William D. MacMillan, Manager of Manufacturing

Mr. MacMillan, age 45, has 25 years' experience in directing the operation of machining, welding, and assembly plants. Starting in job shops, he joined Hamilton Manufacturing Company in 19X6 as its first employee and assisted in its growth to 100 employees. He was responsible for all manufacturing operations when the company was acquired by Indiana Tool, Inc., in 19X7.

With Indiana Tool's Machinery Division, he was superintendent of rotary drill production until 19X8, when he was made responsible for the production of all Machinery Division products, and in 19X0 accomplished $32 million in shipments. In this capacity he was responsible for directing the scheduling and operations of the rotary drill assembly, portable compressor assembly, and welding and fabricating departments. He initiated many cost reduction programs; most notable was modernizing the welding and fabricating departments and realizing a 30% reduction in direct labor cost.

In his total experience, Mr. MacMillan directed the assembly and test of over 1,200 rotary drill rigs, an accumulated experience unmatched in the industry.

Compensation and Ownership

Exhibit 9.5 lists the ownership, the cash investment, and the previous salary of each of Rapidrill's team members. These data demonstrate the dedication, commitment, and belief of the principals in Rapidrill and their recognition of the relative responsibility and authority of their functional positions.

Future Team Members

In addition to these five principals, three other key personnel are presently committed to Rapidrill's program. These men are district sales managers who collectively account for annual drill sales of $9 million for their present employer and are scheduled to join Rapidrill on March 1, 19X2.

Other functional skills will be required in future operations (purchasing, inventory control, etc.) and will be added when operations volume warrants their addition. However, specific rotary drill experience is not felt to be critical in these functional areas.

Board of Directors

Rapidrill's bylaws call for a board of directors of from four to six members. The present directors are Messrs. Price, Einman, Samuels, and Miller, with two directorships reserved for representation of equity investors.

Supporting Professional Services

Rapidrill is presently represented by Walter I. Bobbin of Taylor, Dolan, and Bobbin of Nashville, Tennessee, as general counsel.

EXHIBIT 9.5   Compensation and ownership of Rapidrill principals.

Principals	Shares Owned	Direct Investment	Annual Salary	Previous Salary	Salary Reduction
S. A. Price	136,000	$ 20,400	$38,000	$62,000°	40%
M. F. Einman	78,000	20,280	25,000	32,000	22
F. T. Samuels	78,000	20,280	25,000	30,000	17
G. A. Miller	42,000	12,600	25,000	27,000	8
W. D. MacMillan	36,000	14,400	18,000	20,000	10
Three district sales managers (each)	27,000	13,500	24,000	32,000	
Investment total		$128,460			

° Does not include stock options for 4,000 shares of Indiana Tool, Inc.

The firm of Tanner, Foster, and Company, CPAs, has been retained as independent auditor.

3. MARKET RESEARCH AND ANALYSIS

Market Description

The rotary drill has enjoyed a steady market growth, with an annual growth rate of 10% achieved for the last six years and sales of $74 million in 19X0. This market is shown graphically in Exhibit 9.6, which illustrates the total size of the market, the noncyclic nature of its growth since 19X4, and a projection of sales

EXHIBIT 9.6   Market size and trends of rotary drill sales.

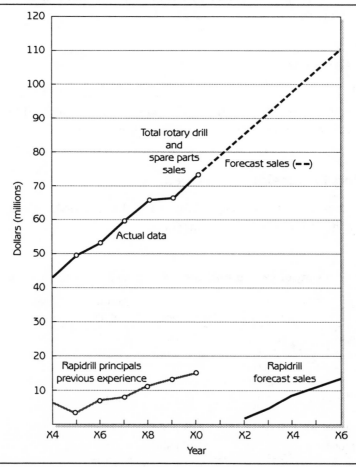

SOURCES: U.S. Bureau of Mines, Compressed Air and Gas Institute (CAGI), and *Survey of Rotary Drill Manufacturers and Suppliers,* by P. J. Lang.

through 19X5. The 19X6 sales forecast of $114 million is based on the past seven-year trend.

Market Segmentation

The noncyclic growth performance may be explained principally by the lack of a dominating market segment in the sale of drills. The five principal market segments contributed the following market shares in 19X0:

Market Segment	Market Share
Well drills	35%
Quarrying	18
Coal mining	26
Metal mining	10
Construction	11

Historically, soft performance in any of these segments has been favorably offset by stronger sales to other segments or by favorable response in those other segments to governmental economic stimulus. For example, highway and dam programs increase construction and quarrying sales, housing starts stimulated by the lowering of interest rates increase water-well drilling, and an interest in alternative energy sources stimulates the surface mining of coal.

Market Trends

The projected future energy shortage and the attendant growth in coal surface-mining production, which requires rock drilling, represent a very significant market opportunity for rotary drill sales over the next 5 to 10 years.

Exhibit 9.7 shows the growth of coal tonnage production over the last 10 years. As shown, virtually the entire growth in production has been accomplished in surface mining. A recent Bureau of Mines forecast, also shown on this curve, projects substantial increases in total coal tonnage production and an increasing trend to surface mining. In 19X6, it is estimated that 57% of the total production of coal will be mined by surface methods. The bureau further predicts a *tripling* of total coal production by 19X5 to meet the nation's energy needs.

The following considerations provide a basis that supports this forecast growth, confirms continuation of the trend to surface-mining operations, and delineates some of the rotary drill market implications:

1. Of the energy reserves in the United States, 88% are in coal, while at present only 18% of the energy consumed is provided by coal. Proven coal reserves are estimated to be sufficient to satisfy all the energy needs of the nation for over 200 years.

2. The Federal Coal Mine Health and Safety Act of 1969 has significantly lowered the productivity of underground coal-mining operations. In the 1960s,

EXHIBIT 9.7   U.S. coal production.

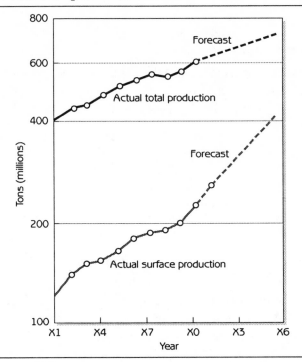

SOURCE: U.S. Bureau of Mines.

a typical miner produced 15 tons of coal per day; today this figure has dropped to 10 tons, with two thirds of the decline laid to safety legislation.

3. Recent reverses to environmentalist efforts have decimated organized opposition to surface mining.

4. Present pending legislation is directed at regulation, rather than curtailment, of surface-mining activities.

5. Achievement of the above 19X6 forecast coal production would require approximately 4,000 drills to be in operation compared to the present 1,000 working drills.

Exhibit 9.8 shows how market segment sales of rotary drills will change in response to this forecast increase in coal production and illustrates the magnitude of the opportunity that this rapidly growing segment will offer in sales growth.

Rapidrill believes this coal surface-mining market for rotary drills to be an important opportunity for concentration of its initial efforts. Those elements, in addition to this projected segment sales growth, that support this decision will be discussed in the following sections of this plan.

EXHIBIT 9.8   Market segment comparison (19X0 versus forecast 19X4; total unit sales, number of drills).

Market Segment	19X0		19X4	
	Sales	Percent of Market	Sales Forecast	Percent of Market
Water well	250	35	329	31
Quarrying	125	18	159	15
Coal mining	175	26	371	35
Metal mining	70	10	95	9
Construction	80	11	106	10
	700		1,060	

SOURCE: Compressed Air and Gas Institute (CAGI), Bureau of Census, Bureau of Mines, and Drilltech Forecast.

Competition

Exhibit 9.9 lists all present competitive manufacturers of rotary drills, indicates the range of their product lines, the market segments in which they actively participate, and their approximate present share of the total rotary drill market.

As shown, the 11 manufacturers break down into three general categories that are discussed below.

Large-Drill Manufacturer

Bucyrus-Erie (B-E) manufactures and sells only large drills as a complement to its large-shovel and dragline equipment. It presently has the market for large drills to itself and its 60 units per year produce sales of over $14 million. It sells direct, as it sells its shovels, and has made several abortive excursions into other market segments. These attempts to enter the other drill market segments were unsuccessful primarily because of its unfamiliarity with distributor marketing—the predominant method of selling drills in all but the large rotary drill market.

Gardner-Denver has initiated a program to enter the large-drill market. This program was initiated by recruitment of six of B-E's principal engineering personnel and as yet has produced no significant results. Rapidrill considers this program to be premature and believes that marketing as well as technical know-how will be required in such a program.

Successful quantity gasification or liquid conversion of coal, estimated to be practicable by the late 1970s (pilot plants are presently operating), will provide a new and large market for low-sulfur western coal. This new application will require "large" drills and will offer a significant new market opportunity for drill sales and penetration of B-E's dominance of the large-drill market.

EXHIBIT 9.9 Rotary drill competition.

	Product Line°	Market	19X0 Share of Total $ Market
Large-drill manufacturers:			
Bucyrus-Erie (B-E)	I, L	Coal, metal mining	20%
Broad-line manufacturers:			
Indiana Tool, Inc.	S, M, I	All	22
Ingersoll-Rand	S, M	All	11
Davey	S+	All	9
Joy (Robbins)	M, I	All, except water well	7
			49%
Water-well drill manufacturers:			
Gardner-Denver	S, L	Mixed, no iron mining	6
Failing	S	Water well	5
Koehring Speedstar	S	Water well	5
Schramm	S	Water well	5
Sanderson-Cyclone	S	Water well	5
Winter-Weiss	S	Water well	5
			31%
Rapidrill	S, M, I (L in future)	All	
			100%

° Hole Capability	List Price
S = 6″ or less	$ 60,000–90,000
M = 6–8″	$110,000–150,000
I = 6–12″	$200,000–250,000
L = 15–17″ or larger	$350,000 up

Note: Both product line and market classifications for the above-listed manufacturers are limited to products that are competitive and markets where efforts are effective. There are some overlaps of both product and market that are not listed; but these are of limited significance.

Broad-Line Manufacturers

Only four present manufacturers offer a product line applicable to a broad range of market segment applications: Indiana Tool, Inc. (the market leader), Ingersoll-Rand, Davey, and Joy Manufacturing.

These manufacturers share several common characteristics:

1. All are compressor manufacturers attracted to drills by their use of compressors.
2. All manufacture an extensive line of mining and construction equipment products in addition to rotary drills.
3. All sell through local equipment distributors. (Ingersoll-Rand utilizes "company owned" stores for distribution.)

4. All offer relatively modern machines (5- to 14-year-old designs) with good performance and high productivity. This is more important than price in these markets. However, all would benefit in both cost and performance by major update of designs.

The drills of these manufacturers are suitable to applications in all market segments, and as a group they account for 49% of all drill sales. Most pertinently, this 49% includes virtually all of the coal surface-mining drills: the market segment most likely to enjoy significant near-term sales growth. These manufacturers in general have had difficulty in providing sufficient productive capacity to match sales growth, so that their pricing and discounting have been firm over the last seven years. Recent increases in forecast demands will further exacerbate their capacity problem. Accordingly, Rapidrill believes that a new manufacturer can achieve significant drill sales without the disruption of drill pricing structures and that the market segments served by the broad-line drill manufacturers represent the best opportunity for market entry by a new manufacturer.

These manufacturers share one further common characteristic favorable to a new drill manufacturer—they unanimously have a well-deserved reputation for poor service and product support.

Water-Well Drill Manufacturers

Failing, Koehring Speedstar, Schramm, Sanderson-Cyclone, and Winter-Weiss all manufacture only small drills aimed primarily at the low-price portion of the water-well drill market. In general, they distribute and sell most effectively on a regional basis. Of the well drill manufacturers, only Gardner-Denver attempts national distribution and has a broad range of product lines.

The average drill offered by these manufacturers utilizes mechanical drive systems, reciprocating compressors, and other components consistent with a 30- to 40-year-old technology, and most of these manufacturers would have difficulty in developing a modern rotary drill design. While the obsolete design and generally poor productivity of these machines is apparent to knowledgeable operators, price remains an important consideration in this market and the low-price drills capture 70 to 80% of water-well drill sales.

Conversion of the market from cable tool drills to high-quality, hydraulic top-drive rotary drills has been pervasive over the last five years and will continue at a steady rate as operators become familiar with the increase in productivity available through their use of hydraulic drills. Rapidrill plans to achieve its share of water-well drill sales in the high-quality end of the market. However, attempts by Rapidrill to accelerate this conversion and capture an early dominating share of the entire market segment could be met by severe price competition in the price-conscious segment of the market.

Exhibit 9.10 presents and compares Rapidrill's primary specifications, list prices, and distributor net prices with those of the competition in each of the three hole-capability ranges. In the case of the 6″ or less hole capability, only those competitors that produce high-quality rotary drills and market them nationally are shown and considered. As noted above, Rapidrill does not intend to compete in the low-price, low-quality portion of the well market.

The data in Exhibit 9.10 show that Rapidrill's proposed drill designs have equal or better specifications than those of its competition and are competitively priced with sufficient margins to provide significantly lower distributor net prices, if required.

As noted earlier, the model D-40K rotary drill will be the first product that Rapidrill will produce and market. The design of the D-40K is sufficiently accomplished that reasonably firm detail specifications have been developed for it. Exhibit 9.11 compares a full range of the features of the D-40K with the best of its present competition with 6″ to 8″ hole capability. As can be seen, the D-40K will have significant superiority in specifications to the machines of either of its competitors and about a 10% lower price to the distributor (Exhibit 9.10).

EXHIBIT 9.10   Comparison of competing drills.

Manufacturer	Model	Drill Bit Pressure (Pounds)	Air Compressor Vol./Pres.	List Price	Distrib- utor Net
6″ or less hole capability:					
Rapidrill	D-30K Truck	30,000	450/250	$ 90,000	$ 68,400
Indiana Tool, Inc.	T-650	30,000	450/150	101,120	85,952
Ingersoll-Rand	T-3	30,000	600/125	92,080	78,268
Davey	M-8A-HP	30,000	490/250	92,195	78,366
Gardner-Denver	15W	30,000	640/150	102,855	87,427
6″ to 8″ hole capability:					
Rapidrill	D-40K Truck	40,000	750/250	120,000	91,200
Indiana Tool, Inc.	T-670	30,000	600/250	120,551	102,468
Ingersoll-Rand	T-4	32,000	600/250	120,510	102,433
Rapidrill	D-40K Crawler	40,000	750/250	135,000	102,600
Ingersoll-Rand	DM-4	32,000	600/250	139,610	118,668
9″ to 12″ hole capability:					
Rapidrill	D-70K Crawler	70,000	900/250	225,000	171,000
Bucyrus-Erie (B-E)	45-R	70,000	900/240	246,977	209,930
Robbins (Joy)	RR-12	70,000	875/250	227,962°	206,518

° Includes new D-9 Caterpillar tractor at $85,000 list.

EXHIBIT 9.11   Rotary drills: Detailed comparison of competing products.

| | Manufacturer and Model | | |
	Rapidrill D-40K	Ingersol-Rand T-4	Indiana Tool, Inc. T-670
Hole diameter (inches)	6–8	6–8	6–8
Bit pressure (pounds)	40,000	32,500	30,000
Machine weight (pounds)	56,000	42,000	43,500
Bit speed (RPM range)	0–100 0–150 0–195	0–10	0–86
Bit torque (pounds per inch)	54,000	50,000	36,000
Compressor type	Screw (domestic)	Vane	Screw (imported)
Air volume and pressure	750 @100 750 @250 900 @50	750 @150 750 @250	600 @250
Engine power	Caterpillar 4-cycle diesel	GM 2-cycle diesel	Caterpillar 4-cycle diesel
Horsepower	325	260	300
Drill stem break-out in mast	Yes	Yes	No
Automatic drill stem loader	Yes	Yes	No
Stem loader inside mast	Yes	No	No
Feed rate (FPM):			
Standard	12	12	5.5
Rapid	62	64	40
Retract	110	100	75
Leveling capacity (inches)	48	48	24
Drill stem threads	Low torque (2 thread/inch)	High torque (4 thread/inch)	High torque (4 thread/inch)
Number of best features	17	6	2

Rapidrill is able to achieve this lower price without sacrificing profitability through cost savings in purchased components, manufacturing (see Section 6), and selling expenses (see Section 4).

Estimated Market Share and Sales

Rapidrill's sales forecasts for each of its planned rotary drill models for the next five years are shown in Exhibit 9.12. Sales for truck-mounted D-30K and D-40K drills have been separately estimated for the well-drilling and blast hole-drilling applications of these units. Sales are estimated to rise from $781,000 for the second half of 19X2 to $13,680,000 in 19X6.

Exhibit 9.13 shows the total rotary drill market for the next five years; Rapidrill's total sales in each year, and the share of the total rotary drill market

EXHIBIT 9.12 Rapidrill Corporation sales forecast (in $000).

	19X2		19X3		19X4		19X5		19X6	
	Units	$	Units	$	Units	$	Units	$	Units	$
Models:										
D-40K truck-mounted (blast hole)	8	$730	16	$1,460	22	$2,006	29	$ 2,645	36	$ 3,283
D-40K truck-mounted (well)			10	950	14	1,330	20	1,900	24	2,280
D-40K crawler-mounted			7	718	8	821	9	923	12	1,231
D-30K truck-mounted (blast hole)			6	410	8	547	9	616	12	821
D-30K truck-mounted (well)			4	289	12	866	20	1,444	24	1,733
D-70K crawler-mounted					6	1,026	9	1,539	12	2,052
Spares		51		383		989		1,813		2,280
Total	8	$781	43	$4,210	70	$7,585	96	$10,880	120	$13,680

EXHIBIT 9.13   Rapidrill market share forecast (sales in $000).

	19X2 1st Year		19X3 2nd Year	19X4 3rd Year	19X5 4th Year	19X6 5th Year
	3rd Qtr.	4th Qtr.				
Total market°	$22,000	$23,000	$94,000	$100,500	$108,000	$114,000
Rapidrill share	1.3%	2.1%	4.4%	7.5%	10.1%	12.0%
Rapidrill sales°	$293	$488	$4,210	$7,585	$10,880	$13,680

° Both total market figures and Rapidrill sales include spare parts.

that the sales represent. Achievement of Rapidrill's sales forecasts would require its share of the market to rise from 2% at the end of the first year to 11.9% in the fifth year of operation.

The sales and market share forecasts shown in Exhibits 9.12 and 9.13 are believed to be reasonable—if not conservative—and attainable by the Rapidrill team. There are five principal reasons why Rapidrill believes this to be so:

1. While working for their former employer (Indiana Tool, Inc.), Rapidrill's management team increased that company's share of the total rotary drill market from 9 to 22% in the five-year period from 19X5 to 19X0. Drill sales during that time went from $4 million to $15 million. Rapidrill's management believes that it should be able to duplicate that kind of performance and capture 11.9% of the rotary drill market and $13,680,000 of profitable sales in the first five years of Rapidrill's operation.

2. Rapidrill's marketing team will include three distributor representatives who, as district sales managers, collectively produced annual rotary drill sales of $9 million for their previous employer. They should be able to obtain a large portion of this business for Rapidrill.

3. Rapidrill's distributors (see Section 4) will include three that are among the most effective in the industry. Together these three distributors could absorb all of Rapidrill's projected production in its first two or three operating years.

4. Rapidrill's rotary drills will have performance equal to or better than that of competing units and a lower price to the distributor. The superior drill performance will be achieved by upgrading the design of Rapidrill's machines and using the best and most cost-effective components that are available. Regarding engineering, F. T. Samuels, Rapidrill's vice president of engineering, is recognized as a technical leader in the industry. The selection of components as well as overhead and labor costs (see Section 6) that are less than those of other manufacturers will enable Rapidrill to offer its units to distributors at a price below that of its competition.

5. Rapidrill will offer service, warranty, and application engineering that is superior to that provided by its competition.

4. MARKETING PLAN

Distributor Plan

Rapidrill plans to sell drills through well-established equipment distributors in the mining, construction, and well-drilling industries. Close to 100% of all the drills in Rapidrill's proposed model sizes are sold through this channel of sale.

Users, rather than the manufacturers, have created this dominant channel (very favorable to a small independent manufacturer), based on their experience with the present manufacturers' failure to provide service and spare-parts support on a sufficiently localized basis. Distributors, conversely, recognize that their success will ultimately be determined by their ability to support equipment in the field and are continuously searching for more reliable and maintenance-free product lines adequately supported by a manufacturer's service and spare-parts programs.

Sufficient dissatisfaction with the product lines and support programs of present competitive manufacturers exists to create a high probability of success for Rapidrill's efforts to establish an effective distributor network.

It will be important during Rapidrill's introduction to the market to have exceptionally strong, well-established distributors. In order to attract such distributors, Rapidrill plans to offer significantly larger than standard industry discounts during an introductory period. Cost estimates have established sufficient manufacturing margins to provide discounts of 24 to 26% to distributors, compared to a firm industry standard of 15%. Such discounts would provide up to 60% greater margin to distributors, that, on a national average, achieve earnings of 2.5% on sales.

In order to minimize Rapidrill's working capital requirements during early periods, these larger discounts will be identified with prompt cash payments for drills (i.e., 7% discount for 15-day payment). Such strategy will further ensure well-financed dealers and will allow a future rationale for decreases in discounts if higher net prices are competitively available.

Over the last three months, Rapidrill has discussed its proposed drill models with three strong, well-established distributors and has tentative agreements with them for the distribution of Rapidrill's drills. These distributors are:

- Mining Supplies, Inc.
  Gadsen, Alabama

- Pierce Mining Equipment Company
  Cincinnati, Ohio

- Pennsylvania Machinery Company
  Scranton, Pennsylvania

These distributors, in the opinion of Rapidrill's principals, are among the most effective drill distributors in the industry. They adequately cover a large part of the coal-mining market for rotary drills, and they could, by themselves, absorb Rapidrill's total forecast production in its first two or three years.

The sales forecast for the next five years (Exhibit 9.12) projects sales reaching $13,680,000 by 19X6. Support of this sales forecast will require only 2 or 3 additional major distributors and a total network of 12 to 14 distributors to achieve adequate national coverage of the total drill market.

Sales Plan

Rapidrill will sell to and support the direct selling efforts of distributors with a team of distributor representatives. It plans to have at least one distributor representative for every major distributor. Representatives to cover the three above-listed distributors have already committed themselves to join Rapidrill early in 19X2. These three men are experienced rotary drill sales managers who presently are collectively responsible for annual drill sales of over $9 million.

Rapidrill believes that its single-product selling requirements and, in particular, the large "ticket" price of rotary drills offer an additional cost advantage to Rapidrill in comparison to its competitors, which sell several products (rotary drills, compressors, diesel engines) to the same distributor. Rapidrill believes that its selling expenses for rotary drills may be maintained at 9% of sales (after a sufficient production base is achieved), compared to the 12 to 13% common to competitive manufacturers. The simplistic explanation for this reduction is that a $100,000 rotary drill is about as easily sold as a $5,000 compressor or a $500 air tool. Rapidrill plans to achieve about $1 million in sales per distributor representative. The industry average for competitors is from $350,000 to $500,000.

Applications Support

An additional strong influence in rotary drill sales is provided by applications support: The ability to determine for a user the most economic equipment requirements to satisfy his drilling needs. Rapidrill's principals have marketwide recognition and extensively proven records in providing effective applications services directly to users.

Advertising and Promotion

Rapidrill's advertising and promotional efforts will be concentrated in those areas shown by experience to be the most effective. These are primarily the exhibition of equipment at trade association shows, particularly regional "buying" shows where immediate sales may be obtained, and demonstration programs where the productivity of drills can be demonstrated on a user's particular job.

Rapidrill will maintain at least one rig in inventory for demonstration purposes at all times and plans to offer additional discount incentives to distributors on demonstrator machines. Demonstrator machines are customarily sold by distributors after 100 to 200 hours of operation at about a $1,500 price markdown.

Warranty and Service

Most of the problems that have earned present manufacturers their poor reputations may be attributed to the multiplicity and complexity of the various product lines (compressors, rotary drills, diesel engines, etc.) they manufacture and to plain poor management attention.

Rapidrill believes that proper attention to service, product support, and a competitive warranty posture will enhance market penetration to a degree that pricing in these productivity-conscious market segments would never accomplish alone. Rapidrill's ability to provide such services and support for its drills is definitely aided by the single-product nature of its planned operations.

An initial step in providing good product support is Rapidrill's recently completed study of inventory stocking requirements. This study identified the minimum parts inventory that is required to have a satisfactory response time to predicted customer demands for spare parts.

5. DESIGN AND DEVELOPMENT PLANS

Rapidrill's planned product line will not require extension of any state-of-the-art technologies. The designs of all competitors are from 5 to 14 years old. The task and the opportunity consist of knowledgeable application of the latest component technology and performance available and an optimum balanced utilization of those components. The result should be significant improvements in product performance at competitive price levels.

Status

The model D-40K series of drills (e.g., truck-mounted well or blast hole and crawler-mounted units) have been selected, for reasons previously discussed, for initial design, development, and market introduction. The development of the D-40K drills will be followed by the design and development of the D-30K truck-mounted well drill and the D-70K crawler-mounted drill, in that order.

It should be emphasized that development and test work on the finished D-40K, D-30K, and D-70K designs should be minimal. The reason for this is that all the components of these drills will be used well within their operating ranges, and testing efforts are principally required to check out control feedback, valve suitability, and other minor design details. After the prototype drills have been tested and their design proven, they will be sold at a slight markdown. This is common practice in the rotary drill industry.

The product design schedule is shown on the master schedule in Section 7.

Parts Grouping

One additional Rapidrill design criterion merits discussion. In the detail design of Rapidrill's product line, "parts grouping" will be utilized. The parts grouping concept defines all optional features, such as compressor size, as a complete and interchangeable group of parts. The parts grouping requirements of the D-40K are shown graphically in Exhibit 9.14. The assembly of different versions of a drill model is facilitated by using interchangeable parts groups. Moreover, decisions made by parts groups (on a forecast, lead-time, and max-min basis) permit maximum production feasibility with minimum inventory and simplified production control requirements.

Future Products

The technology of rock drilling and the history of the rotary drill suggest that evolution of drilling equipment will be continuous. Rapidrill believes that in five to ten years the development of western coal will require "large" drills with higher capacity than that of those presently planned in its product line and that this will present a new, additional (not replacement) market for drills.

EXHIBIT 9.14   Parts grouping—model D-40K.

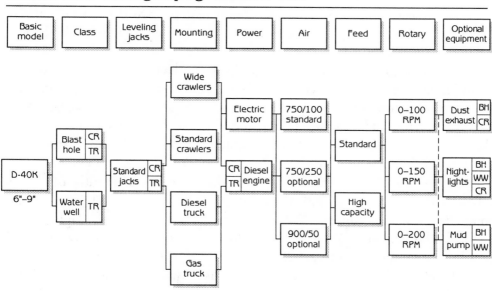

Constant desire for improved productivity will eventually create a market for automated operation of drills. Rapidrill plans to be the innovator of such systems and has already discussed a possible joint development program with a hydraulic component manufacturer.

Finally, new methods for mineral exploration and sampling may offer opportunities for innovative drill equipment design. Rapidrill plans to keep abreast of such developments and be an industry leader in the development of any new drill equipment that might be required.

6. MANUFACTURING PLAN

As previously discussed, Rapidrill's rotary drill will be essentially an engineered package with a high content of purchased components. The nature of the manufacturing efforts consists primarily of fabricating welded mounting and mast structures and assembly of all components into a final drill. Other than minor welding and painting of equipment, virtually no high-cost machine tool or other fixed investments are required. Assembly can be accomplished in simple warehouse-type structures with a modest overhead crane capacity. Such structures are available for lease or purchase in virtually every industrial area of the United States.

While most of the value added by the packager consists of this assembly labor, unit production volume is not sufficient to warrant the high fixed cost of a modern assembly line facility (and no present manufacturer has such a facility). Minimizing manufacturing costs makes low hourly labor rates, worker productivity, efficiency, and flexibility paramount considerations. Such characteristics are not typical of the operations of present competitive drill manufacturers whose plants are rigidly unionized and located in highly industrialized, high labor-rate locations.

A study by Rapidrill's principals has been conducted to identify the effects of different plant locations on the manufacturing costs of rotary drills. In its evaluation of alternative plant locations, this study considered: labor rates, labor law, labor availability and attitudes, freight and transportation costs, centers of markets, taxes, travel access, facility costs, utility costs, suitability for professional staff, and other pertinent considerations. It concluded that the manufacturing requirements for Rapidrill's operation would best be met in a southeastern city of modest size, in a state with right-to-work laws. After evaluation of several potential locations and detailed analysis of final candidates, Rapidrill has selected the Nashville, Tennessee, area for its plant location. Nashville is well located with respect to rotary drill markets.

Exhibit 9.15 illustrates some of the results of this evaluation study. It shows the net cost of typical operations in Nashville and compares these to the costs of

EXHIBIT 9.15 Comparison of Rapidrill's operation at Nashville, Tennessee, with major competitors' locations (base = $10 million annual Rapidrill sales to distributors: 86,000 productive hours).

Location	BLS Index	Direct Labor Cost ($/hr.)	Production Hour Cost L and OH	Total Cost L and OH (000)	Freight In and Out (000)	Total Value-added Cost (000)	Nashville Advantage $ (000)	Percent Rapidrill Sales
Nashville	74.2	$2.70	$12.45	$1,071	$196	$1,267	Base	Base
Competitors:								
Dallas (G-D)	90.6	3.30	14.70	1,264	191	1,455	$188	2.3%
Franklin, Pa. (ITI)	105.6	3.85	16.70	1,436	150	1,586	319	4.0
Birmingham (Joy)	87.3	3.18	14.25	1,226	157	1,383	116	1.4
West Virginia (I-R)	94.0	3.42	15.26	1,312	139	1,451	184	2.3
Milwaukee (B-E)	104.3	3.79	16.70	1,436	144	1,580	313	3.9
New Jersey (I-R)	98.6	3.59	15.82	1,360	163	1,523	256	3.2
Average							$229	2.8%

Legend:
G-D = Gardner-Denver   B-E = Bucyrus-Erie
ITI = Indiana Tool, Inc.   BLS = Bureau of Labor Statistics
Joy = Joy Manufacturing   L = Labor
I-R = Ingersoll-Rand   OH = Factory overhead (rent, heat, light, etc.)

equivalent operations at the locations of present major drill manufacturers. For the comparisons in Exhibit 9.15, which shows an average cost advantage of close to 3% for Rapidrill operations in Nashville, an equal number of productive hours and equal labor productivity and efficiency were assumed for all locations.

Improvements in efficiency and productivity are, in fact, of equal importance and represent a higher potential for cost savings than do the lower labor rates themselves. Estimates of improvements of 20 to 25% in productivity for a well-managed, open-shop fabrication and assembly operation in Nashville are considered conservative. With typical value added of about 16% of manufacturing cost for present rotary drill manufacturers, such productivity improvements would result in an additional 3 to 4% decrease in total manufacturing cost. For subsequent financial analysis these productivity improvements were assumed to be achieved by Rapidrill over a three-year period, utilizing a 90% "learning curve" on assembly operations.

Rapidrill's manufacturing operations will also seek further efficiencies through the use of modern production, inventory control, and purchasing systems that will be focused on reducing the costs of buying, storing, and handling the large content of purchased components used in rotary drills. The implementation of these systems will be significantly aided by employing "parts grouping" techniques (see Section 5) in the product line design. Parts grouping will allow flexibility in assembly scheduling and will minimize inventory requirements.

The total result of such manufacturing operations will be minimum capital equipment and inventory investment and manufacturing costs (after sufficient "learning curve" improvement) from 6 to 8% below those of present competition. This manufacturing cost reduction, together with the anticipated 3 to 4% reduction in Rapidrill's selling expenses, as compared to those of its competitors, means that Rapidrill's manufacturing and selling costs should be from 9 to 12% less than those of its competitors. Cost advantages of this order in products with a high purchased content could give Rapidrill a strong competitive advantage.

7. SCHEDULE

Exhibit 9.16 shows the master schedule for Rapidrill.

8. RISKS

As with any new venture, there are risks in Rapidrill's plans. Recognition of these risks, evaluation of their severity, and proper contingency planning for their possible occurrences have been considered in Rapidrill's planning.

EXHIBIT 9.16   The master schedule for Rapidrill.

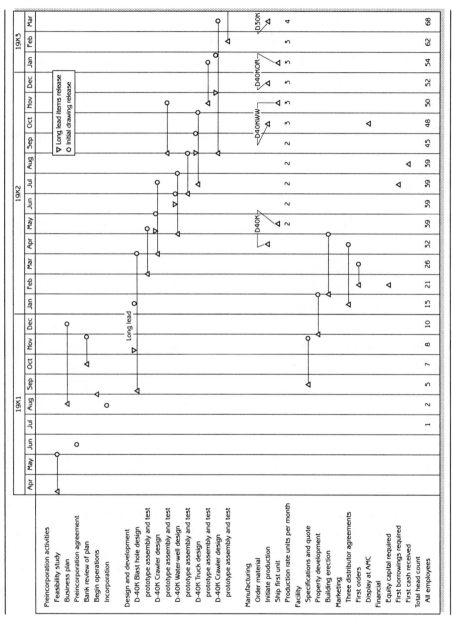

While the following discussion of specific risks is not intended to be all-inclusive, it is felt to cover those of significant possible impact. Risks are *not* listed in order of probability of occurrence or of degree of possible impact.

1. *Risk:* Legal action by Indiana Tool, Inc. (ITI).

   Evaluation: While the departure of its key team members has jeopardized ITI's rotary drill market dominance, it is the opinion of Rapidrill's counsel that no cause for action by ITI has been created. Letters between legal counsel for ITI and Rapidrill have been exchanged, and the prognosis is that the likelihood for further action by ITI is slim.

   Contingency: Rapidrill has had policy guidelines prepared by counsel and plans no actions that could be construed as unfair competition or breach of ITI's legal rights.

2. *Risk:* Price cutting by competitors.

   Evaluation: Market will absorb everyone's capacity for the next few years. At that time Rapidrill will have sufficient volume to be price competitive with any of its competitors. Historically, existing manufacturers have not responded to new competition with price cuts.

   Contingency: Financial planning included generous contingencies in unit costs. If costs are close to present estimates, Rapidrill has immediate ability to reduce its prices and remain profitable.

3. *Risk:* Cost estimates exceeded by engineering and/or manufacturing.

   Evaluation: Design has progressed sufficiently so 60% of purchased components are firmly priced. Rapidrill's principals have extensive experience with design and manufacturing start-up phases, so estimates should be accurate.

   Contingency: In financials, 10% was added to material cost estimates and 100% excess assembly time was added to Year 1 estimates, and 80% to Year 2, giving Rapidrill leeway on meeting actual costs.

4. *Risk:* Machine doesn't meet specification performance.

   Evaluation: This is considered a low-risk item. Engineering track record of F. T. Samuels is excellent; however, rapid acceptance of Rapidrill units will depend on immediate support of unit in the field.

   Contingency: In addition to $25,000 allocated to development testing (2.5 times normal), financial planning includes expenditure of $10,000 per unit in field support of first eight units (about five times past experience levels), then progressively less but allowance for significant warranty expenditures. Additional $20,000 allocated for a demonstration program could be directed to development.

5. *Risk:* Sales forecasts not achieved.

   Evaluation: Analysis shows a low breakeven level (less than 50% of Year 2 forecasts), and some fixed costs can be delayed to reduce further the breakeven if sales are falling well below forecasts.

Contingency: Procurements will be committed for lower-level production than forecast but at forecast rate, allowing time for additional procurements within lead time if sales trend to forecast levels or higher.

6. *Risk:* Delays in design and/or manufacturing.

   Evaluation: Delays in design unlikely for first unit since most design work now complete. Delays in either can be minimized to about $20,000 additional cash requirement per month delay. Financial plan shows cash balance of $64,000 for first year-end, allowing, in worst case, a two- to three-month delay.

   Contingency: Watch design and manufacturing schedule closely, and expedite procurements closely. An additional $60,000 borrowing is available to Rapidrill in Year 2 within debt-equity guidelines; so another three-month contingency could be available.

7. *Risk:* Long lead-time procurements encountered.

   Evaluation: Trucks, diesel engines, compressors, and hydraulic components are on order, with satisfactory shipments promised. Rapidrill's early requirements, two per month, can be met with minor disturbance even if vendors have major problems. Vendors have confirmed this.

   Contingency: Closely follow procurements—some purchased components have four- to five-month lead times—and we cannot afford to order backup from other vendors.

8. *Risk:* Economy downturn or fuel shortage affecting sales.

   Evaluation: Energy shortages should enhance the sale of drills to mining markets and accelerate, rather than deter, Rapidrill's growth.

   Contingency: Watch signals closely; trend should be apparent before manufacturing is started.

9. *Risk:* Tight money affecting Rapidrill's ability to obtain the required line of credit.

   Evaluation: Plan has been reviewed by three largest banks in Nashville, which supported financial assumptions regarding borrowing. Money supply has eased somewhat since those commitments.

   Contingency: Secure committed lines of credit in excess of forecast requirements to the limit of reasonable debt-equity ratios.

10. *Risk:* Legislation to curtail strip mining.

    Evaluation: In light of the forecast energy shortage and the fact that 10% of the nation's energy presently comes from surface-mined coal, this eventuality is considered small.

    Contingency: Diversion of initial selling efforts to other market segments. Planned sales of first two years could be achieved in several other market segments.

9. FINANCIAL PLAN

Introduction

Using the sales levels and rotary drill prices developed by the marketing forecast; detailed estimates of material, labor, and burden generated by engineering and manufacturing; and estimates of design, development, and general sales and administrative expenses, detailed financial statements were drawn up depicting the forecast results of Rapidrill's operations for the five years from 19X2 to 19X6, inclusive. The following assumptions were used in arriving at the results:

1. All operations are performed in a leased facility in Nashville, Tennessee. Labor rates, shipping costs, lease rates, etc., used are consistent with the area.
2. All projections are in 19X1 dollars.
3. Interest payments are computed at 15% on borrowings. Borrowings will be provided by bank lines of credit.
4. Balance sheet assumptions are:
   a. Accounts receivable: 30-day collection through mid-19X5; 45 days thereafter.
   b. Notes receivable: Average 36-month repayment schedule at 10% simple interest. Financing by Rapidrill will commence in the fourth quarter of 19X5. Earlier financing to be accomplished utilizing an independent financial institution. Cavanagh Leasing Corporation has expressed interest.
   c. Inventories: Four turns per year.
   d. Accounts payable: 60-day average through 19X5; 36–40 days thereafter.
5. Income taxes include state and federal.
6. Loss for 19X2 carried forward and deducted from 19X2 income in accordance with IRS Code Section 172.
7. Organizational expenses and initial design cost, estimated to be $14,000 and $240,000, respectively, have been expensed.

Pro forma financial statements are presented as Exhibits 9.17 through 9.25, and Exhibit 9.26 is a breakeven chart.

Financial Performance

1. *Sales and earnings forecasts* (see Exhibits 9.17 through 9.19): Sales of Rapidrill are projected to increase from $730,000 in 19X2 to $13,680,000 in 19X6. After a projected loss of $229,000 in the first year, after-tax profits are expected to increase from $326,000 in 19X3 to $1,484,000 in 19X6 (see

EXHIBIT 9.17   Rapidrill Corporation: Sales and earnings forecasts, Fiscal years ended September 30, 19X2–19X6 (000s omitted).

	19X2	19X3	19X4	19X5	19X6
Sales:					
Units	$730	$3,827	$6,596	$9,067	$11,400
Spares	51	383	989	1,813	2,280
Total sales	781	4,210	7,585	10,880	13,680
Cost of sales:					
Material	434	2,204	3,722	5,269	6,620
Labor	16	98	201	258	323
Burden	98	387	500	589	631
Total cost of sales	548	2,689	4,423	6,116	7,574
Gross Margin	233	1,521	3,162	4,764	6,106
In percent	29.8	36.1	41.7	43.8	44.6
Overhead expenses:					
Selling and marketing	84	430	648	991	1,246
Engineering	77	134	273	425	534
Administration and general	296	483	705	1,103	1,387
Total overhead expenses	457	1,047	1,626	2,519	3,167
Earnings before interest and taxes	(224)	474	1,536	2,245	2,939
Interest expense (income)	5	48	52	(3)	(64)
Earning before federal and state taxes	(229)	426	1,484	2,248	3,003
Federal and state taxes		214	751	1,137	1,519
Net earnings before extraordinary item	(229)	212	733	1,111	1,484

Extraordinary item—reduction in
  federal income taxes resulting
  from carryover of prior year's
  operating losses
		114			

Net earnings	$(229)	$326	$733	$1,111	$1,484
Percent sales before extraordinary item		5.0	9.7	10.2	10.8
Percent sales after extraordinary item		7.7	9.7	10.2	10.8

Exhibit 9.17). After-tax profit as a percentage of sales is 7.7% in the second year of Rapidrill's operation and increases to 10.8% in the fifth year. Even if actual sales are one-half of those forecast, Rapidrill will be profitable in its second year of operation (see breakeven chart, Exhibit 9.26, and Exhibit 9.17).

2. *Cash flow* (see Exhibits 9.20 through 9.22):   The equity capital raised in this offering, together with the investment of the principals and lines of

EXHIBIT 9.18 Rapidrill Corporation: Monthly sales and earnings forecasts, Fiscal year ended September 30, 19X2 (000s omitted).

	Oct.	Nov.	Dec.	Jan.	Feb.	Mar.	Apr.	May	June	July	Aug.	Sept.	Total
Sales:													
Units								$ 92	$ 182	$ 92	$ 182	$ 182	$ 730
Spares								6	13	6	13	13	51
Total sales								98	195	98	195	195	781
Cost of sales:													
Material								54	109	54	109	108	434
Labor								2	4	2	4	4	16
Burden								12	24	12	25	25	98
Total cost of sales								68	137	68	138	137	548
Gross margin								30	58	30	57	58	233
In percent								30.6	29.7	30.6	29.2	29.7	29.8
Overhead expenses:													
Selling and marketing						$ 2	$ 13	13	13	14	14	15	84
Engineering	$ 5	$ 2	$ 3	$ 6	$ 4	7	7	7	8	9	9	10	77
Administration and general	45°	15	14	16	16	17	28	39	29	29	29	29	296
	50	17	17	22	20	26	48	59	50	52	52	54	457
Earnings before interest and taxes	(50)	(17)	(17)	(22)	(20)	(26)	(48)	(20)	8	(22)	5	5	(224)
Interest expense (income)										1	2	2	5
Earnings before federal and state taxes	(50)	(17)	(17)	(22)	(20)	(26)	(48)	(20)	8	(23)	3	3	(229)
Federal and state taxes													
Net earnings	$(50)	$(17)	$(17)	$(22)	$(20)	$(26)	$(48)	$ (20)	$ 8	$ (23)	$ 3	$ 3	$ (229)

° *Note*: Includes expenses during five months prior to incorporation.

EXHIBIT 9.19a   Rapidrill Corporation: Quarterly sales and earnings forecasts, Fiscal year ended September 30, 19X3 (000s omitted).

	19X3				
	1Q	**2Q**	**3Q**	**4Q**	**Total**
Sales:					
Units	$ 764	$ 874	$1,126	$1,063	$3,827
Spares	76	88	113	106	383
Total sales	840	962	1,239	1,169	4,210
Cost of sales:					
Material	464	516	641	583	2,204
Labor	13	20	32	33	98
Burden	83	88	113	103	387
Total cost of sales	560	624	786	719	2,689
Gross margin	280	338	453	450	1,521
In percent	33.3	35.1	36.6	38.5	36.1
Overhead expenses:					
Selling and					
marketing	97	98	127	108	430
Engineering	33	33	33	35	134
Administration					
and general	115	117	124	127	483
Total	245	248	284	270	1,047
Earnings before interest					
and taxes	35	90	169	180	474
Interest expense (income)	11	13	13	11	48
Earnings before federal					
and state taxes	24	77	156	169	426
Federal and state taxes	12	39	78	85	214
Net earnings before					
extraordinary item	12	38	78	84	212
Extraordinary item—					
reduction in federal income					
taxes resulting from					
carryover of prior year's					
operating losses	6	21	42	45	114
Net earnings	$ 18	$ 59	$ 120	$ 129	$ 326
Percent sales before					
extraordinary item	1.4	4.0	6.3	7.2	5.0
Percent sales after					
extraordinary item	2.1	6.1	9.7	11.0	7.7

EXHIBIT 9.19b **Rapidrill Corporation: Quarterly sales and earnings forecasts, Fiscal years ended September 30, 19X4 (000s omitted).**

| | 19X4 | | | | |
	1Q	2Q	3Q	4Q	Total
Sales:					
Units	$1,382	$1,657	$2,086	$1,471	$6,596
Spares	207	249	313	220	989
Total sales	1,589	1,906	2,399	1,691	7,585
Cost of sales:					
Material	776	937	1,175	834	3,722
Labor	42	51	61	47	201
Burden	103	126	152	119	500
Total cost of sales	921	1,114	1,388	1,000	4,423
Gross margin	668	792	1,011	691	3,162
In percent	42.0	41.6	42.1	40.9	41.7
Overhead expenses:					
Selling and marketing	136	163	205	144	648
Engineering	68	68	69	68	273
Administration and general	176	177	176	176	705
Total	380	408	450	388	1,626
Earnings before interest and taxes	288	384	561	303	1,536
Interest expense (income)	13	18	14	7	52
Earnings before federal and state taxes	275	366	547	296	1,484
Federal and state taxes	139	185	277	150	751
Net earnings before extraordinary item	136	181	270	146	733
Extraordinary item— reduction in federal income taxes resulting from carryover of prior year's operating losses					
Net earnings	$ 136	$ 181	$ 270	$ 146	$ 733
Percent sales before extraordinary item	8.6	9.5	11.2	8.6	9.7
Percent sales after extraordinary item	8.6	9.5	11.2	8.6	9.7

EXHIBIT 9.20 Rapidrill Corporation: Pro forma cash flows, Fiscal years ended September 30, 19X2–19X6 (000s omitted).

	19X2	19X3	19X4	19X5	19X6
Cash receipts					
Accounts receivable	$ 586	$3,824	$7,320	$10,379	$13,330
Notes receivable					200
Interest				5	64
Total cash receipts	586	3,824	7,320	10,384	13,594
Cash disbursements:					
Purchase of materials	504	2,178	4,015	5,587	6,698
Manufacturing labor	56	224	418	552	617
Manufacturing overhead	74	183	185	222	225
Warranty expense	20	60	100	100	100
Administration, general, selling, and engineering	453	1,044	1,624	2,518	3,166
Equipment	28	12	12	10	10
Federal and state taxes		100	751	1,137	1,519
Interest	5	48	52	2	
Total cash disbursements	1,140	3,849	7,157	10,128	12,335
Cash provided (drained) by operations	(554)	(25)	163	256	1,259
Investment in long-term notes receivable				163	1,275
Bank borrowing (repayment)	250	(25)	(150)	(75)	
Sale of common stock	280				
Net increase (decrease) in cash balance	$ (24)	$ (50)	$ 13	$ 18	$ (16)

credit of $250,000 in 19X2, $350,000 in 19X3, and $475,000 in 19X4, should be enough to finance Rapidrill's operations. Ideally, a slightly larger line of credit should be sought to increase Rapidrill's cash in the third and fourth quarters of 19X3. Note that the cash flow provided by operations becomes positive in the third year. In the first two years, cash is being used to finance Rapidrill's start-up and working capital. Because bank borrowings are used principally to finance working capital, sales volumes less than forecast will require that less of the line of credit be drawn down.

3. *Balance sheets* (see Exhibits 9.23 through 9.25): Rapidrill's proposed financial plan provides financial strength and liquidity. The lowest ratio of current assets to current liabilities plus bank loans payable is not projected to be less than about 1:2. And much of Rapidrill's inventory consists of standard components and materials that should be readily salable. After the investment of this offering (assumed to be in February 19X2), Rapidrill's working capital is estimated not to fall below about $140,000.

EXHIBIT 9.21   Rapidrill Corporation: Pro forma monthly cash flows, Fiscal year ended September 30, 19X2 (000s omitted).

	Oct.	Nov.	Dec.	Jan.	Feb.	Mar.	Apr.	May	June	July	Aug.	Sept.	Total
Cash receipts:													
Accounts and notes received									$ 98	$195	$ 98	$195	$ 586
Interest													
Total cash receipts									98	195	98	195	586
Cash disbursements:													
Purchases of materials							$ 52		113	115	113	111	504
Manufacturing labor					$ 1	$ 4	8	$ 8	8	9	9	9	56
Manufacturing overhead					11	13	9	9	9	9	7	7	74
Warranty expense							2	3	4	3	4	4	20
Administration, general, selling, and engineering	$ 44	$ 22	$ 17	$ 22	19	26	48	49	48	55	50	53	453
Equipment	2			1		10	10			5			28
Federal and state taxes										1	2	2	5
Interest													
Total cash disbursements	46	22	17	23	31	53	129	69	182	197	185	186	1,140
Cash provided (drained) by operations	(46)	(22)	(17)	(23)	(31)	(53)	(129)	(69)	(84)	(2)	(87)	9	(554)
Investment in long-term notes receivable													
Bank borrowing (repayment)								50	100		100		250
Sale of common stock		40			240								280
Net increase (decrease) in cash balance	$(46)	$ 18	$(17)	$(23)	$209	$(53)	$(129)	$(19)	$ 16	$ (2)	$ 13	$ 9	$ (24)
Opening cash balance	88°	42	60	43	20	229	176	47	28	44	42	55	
Closing cash balance	42	60	43	20	229	176	47	28	44	42	55	64	

° Initial cash balance from investments of principals made prior to October 1, 19X1. No corporate expenditures prior to October 1, 19X1.

EXHIBIT 9.22 Rapidrill Corporation: Pro forma quarterly cash flows, Fiscal years ended September 30, 19X3–19X4 (000s omitted).

	19X3					19X4				
	IQ	2Q	3Q	4Q	Total	1Q	2Q	3Q	4Q	Total
Cash receipts:										
Accounts and notes received	$719	$890	$1,008	$1,207	$3,824	$1,375	$1,848	$2,052	$2,045	$7,320
Interest										
Total cash receipts	719	890	1,008	1,207	3,824	1,375	1,848	2,052	2,045	7,320
Cash disbursements:										
Purchases of materials	453	531	561	633	2,178	852	1,034	1,028	1,101	4,015
Manufacturing labor	31	45	74	74	224	82	111	112	113	418
Manufacturing overhead	38	52	50	43	183	45	45	48	47	185
Warranty expense	12	14	17	17	60	22	25	26	27	100
Administration, general, selling, and engineering	243	248	283	270	1,044	379	408	449	388	1,624
Equipment	5	3	2	2	12	5	2	5		12
Federal and state taxes	25	25	25	25	100	191	191	191	178	751
Interest	11	13	13	11	48	13	18	14	7	52
Total cash disbursements	818	931	1,025	1,075	3,849	1,589	1,834	1,873	1,861	7,157
Cash provided (drained) by operations	(99)	(41)	(17)	132	(25)	(214)	14	179	184	163
Investment in long-term notes receivable										
Bank borrowing (repayment)	100			(125)	(25)	250		(200)	(200)	(150)
Sale of common stock										
Net increase (decrease) in cash balance	$ 1	$ (41)	$ (17)	$ 7	$ (50)	$ 36	$ 14	$ (21)	$ (16)	$ 13
Opening cash balance	$ 64	$ 65	$ 24	$ 7		$ 14	$ 50	$ 64	$ 43	
Closing cash balance	65	24	7	14		50	64	43	27	

EXHIBIT 9.23   Rapidrill Corporation: Pro forma balance sheets, Fiscal years ended September 30, 19X1–19X6 (000s omitted).

	19X1	19X2	19X3	19X4	19X5	19X6
Current assets:						
Cash	$88	$ 64	$ 14	$ 27	$ 45	$ 29
Accounts receivable		195	581	846	1,360	1,710
Notes receivable					150	1,225
Inventory		393	563	824	1,315	1,502
Total current assets		652	1,158	1,697	2,870	4,466
Property, plant, and equipment		28	40	52	62	72
Less: Depreciation		5	13	23	33	43
		23	27	29	29	29
Total assets	$88	$ 675	$1,185	$1,726	$2,899	$4,495
Current liabilities:						
Accounts payable and accrued expenses		$ 286	$ 495	$ 453	$ 590	$ 702
Bank loans payable		250	225	75		
Total liabilities		536	720	528	590	702
Equity:						
Capital stock— common 10¢ par value, 720,000 authorized shares	$37	69	69	69	69	69
Paid-in surplus	51	299	299	299	299	299
Retained earnings		(229)	97	830	1,941	3,425
Total equity	88	139	465	1,198	2,309	3,793
Total liabilities and equity	$88	$ 675	$1,185	$1,726	$2,899	$4,495

Rapidrill's liquidity should hold up reasonably well if sales are somewhat less than forecast. This is because Rapidrill has little invested in fixed assets and bank borrowings are primarily used for working capital. If sales fall from forecasts, current assets, current liabilities, and bank borrowings should tend to drop proportionately and the effect of the sales drop on liquidity or the ratio of current assets to current liabilities plus bank debt should tend to be small.

4. *Breakeven analysis* (see Exhibit 9.26):   At its currently proposed sales prices and costs, Rapidrill's breakeven sales are about 19 units and $1,900,000. Rapidrill recognizes that this may be somewhat high. It is also apparent that a 10% increase in Rapidrill's prices would lower the breakeven to 12 units and $1,300,000 in sales. Accordingly, Rapidrill will closely watch its competitors' pricing behavior and, if appropriate, consider the

EXHIBIT 9.24   Rapidrill Corporation: Pro forma monthly balance sheets, Fiscal year ended September 30, 19X2 (000s omitted).

	Oct.	Nov.	Dec.	Jan.	Feb.	Mar.	Apr.	May	June	July	Aug.	Sept.
Current assets:												
Cash	$ 40	$ 18	$ 43	$ 20	$229	$176	$ 47	$ 28	$ 44	$ 42	$ 55	$ 64
Accounts receivable								98	195	98	195	195
Notes receivable												
Inventory					13	83	216	283	282	347	337	393
Total current assets	40	18	43	20	242	259	263	409	521	487	587	652
Property, plant, and equipment—at cost	2	2	2	3	3	13	23	23	23	28	28	28
Less: Depreciation						1	2	2	3	4	4	5
	2	2	2	3	3	12	21	21	20	24	24	23
Total assets	$ 42	$ 20	$ 45	$ 23	$245	$271	$284	$430	$541	$511	$611	$675
Current liabilities:												
Accounts payable and accrued expenses	$ 4	$ 1	$ 1	$ 1	$ 3	$ 55	$116	$232	$235	$228	$225	$286
Bank loans payable								50	150	150	250	250
Total liabilities	4	1	1	1	3	55	116	282	385	378	475	536
Equity:												
Capital stock—common 10¢ par value, 720,000 shares authorized	37	45	45	45	69	69	69	69	69	69	69	69
Paid-in surplus	51	83	83	83	299	299	299	299	299	299	299	299
Retained earnings	(50)	(67)	(84)	(106)	(126)	(152)	(200)	(220)	(212)	(235)	(232)	(229)
Total equity	36	19	44	22	242	216	168	148	156	133	136	139
Total liabilities and equity	$ 42	$ 20	$ 45	$ 23	$245	$271	$284	$430	$541	$511	$611	$675

EXHIBIT 9.25 Rapidrill Corporation: Pro forma quarterly balance sheets, Fiscal years ended September 30, 19X3–19X4 (000s omitted).

	19X3				19X4			
	1Q	2Q	3Q	4Q	1Q	2Q	3Q	4Q
Current assets:								
Cash	$ 65	$ 24	$ 7	$ 14	$ 50	$ 64	$ 43	$ 27
Accounts receivable	316	388	619	581	795	853	1,200	846
Notes receivable								
Inventory	439	477	424	563	651	630	538	824
Total current assets	820	889	1,050	1,158	1,496	1,547	1,781	1,697
Property, plant, and equipment— at cost	33	36	38	40	45	47	52	52
Less: Depreciation	7	9	11	13	15	18	20	23
	26	27	27	27	30	29	32	29
Total assets	$846	$916	$1,077	$1,185	$1,526	$1,576	$1,813	$1,726
Current liabilities:								
Accounts payable and accrued expenses	$339	$350	$ 391	$ 495	$ 450	$ 319	$ 486	$ 453
Bank loans payable	350	350	350	225	475	475	275	75
Total liabilities	689	700	741	720	925	794	761	528
Equity:								
Capital stock—common 10¢ par value, 720,000 shares authorized	69	69	69	69	69	69	69	69
Paid-in surplus	299	299	299	299	299	299	299	299
Retained earnings	(211)	(152)	(32)	97	233	414	684	830
Total equity	157	216	336	465	601	782	1,052	1,198
Total liabilities and equity	$846	$916	$1,077	$1,185	$1,526	$1,576	$1,813	$1,726

EXHIBIT 9.26   Rapidrill Corporation: 19X2–19X3 breakeven analysis.

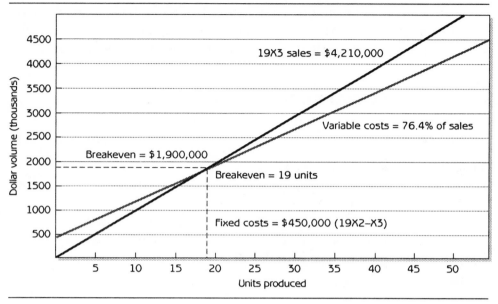

possibility of increasing its prices. In any case, if sales volume should drop, it should be possible to lower Rapidrill's fixed cost by cutting back on some of its general and administrative expenses.

Cost Control

Achievement of the financial plan delineated above will depend in significant measure on Rapidrill's ability to control its costs. To do this, Rapidrill's principals will draw on their experience in designing and implementing systems to control the costs of design, development, and manufacturing programs.

Design and development programs will use a job cost reporting system. Each equipment development project will be broken down into subtasks, and labor, overhead, purchased materials, and subcontracting costs will be separately reported for each subtask. Cost reports will be issued every two weeks and the cost and progress to date monitored and compared to budgets. These reports will be monitored by Messrs. Miller, Price, and MacMillan, and weekly meetings will be held to discuss and determine solutions to actual or potential cost problems.

When a drill model (e.g., D-40K) is released for production, a set of standard costs for assembly labor, purchased components, overhead, and so forth, will be established. Actual costs will be accumulated by subtask and cost category and compared to the standards. Significant differences between actual and standard costs will be evaluated to see if these are due to inefficiencies or are real cost increases. If the former, corrective actions will be identified and taken; if the latter, the standards may need revision. Warranty and field service costs will also be carefully monitored to ensure that Rapidrill's allowance for these is adequate.

Finally, ratio analysis of costs to sale price will be used to identify any cost element that may be deviating significantly from the norms and be cause for concern.

10. PROPOSED RAPIDRILL OFFERING

Financing

Rapidrill Corporation is incorporated in the state of Delaware and currently has 720,000 shares of 10 cents par value common voting stock authorized, with 451,000 shares issued as of November 30, 19X1.

Rapidrill now intends to raise $240,000 through the sale of 240,000 shares of its common voting stock at $1 per share. The common stock sold in this financing will represent about 35% of Rapidrill's outstanding common stock after the offering is completed.

Capitalization

Exhibit 9.27 shows the capitalization of Rapidrill before and after the proposed offering.

Use and Sources of Funds

The money raised in this offering ($240,000), together with the money raised ($128,460) earlier from the sale of stock to Rapidrill's principals and key employees, will be used primarily to design, fabricate, and test the first D-40K truck-mounted rotary drill and to set up a marketing and distribution system. These $368,000 of equity funds will be supplemented by bank borrowings that will be used to finance inventories and receivables. The bank borrowings reach maximums of $250,000 in 19X2, $350,000 in 19X3, and $475,000 in 19X4 (see Pro Forma Cash Flows and Balance Sheets). Rapidrill expects to have a $600,000 to $700,000 revolving line of credit with Nashville banks and has obtained preliminary approval of such a line of credit. Final approval will be contingent on raising the $240,000 of this offering.

NOTES TO BALANCE SHEET

Accounts Receivable

Thirty days. Considered to be 100% collectible due to financial strength of customers. These customers have demonstrated prompt and consistent payment of

EXHIBIT 9.27 Rapidrill Corporation—Present and proposed capitalization.

Stockholders	Shares Owned		Percent Ownership Postoffering	Investment	Cost per Share
	Preoffering	Postoffering			
S. A. Price	135,000	135,000	19.6%	$20,400	$0.15
M. F. Einman	78,000	78,000	11.3	20,280	0.26
F. T. Samuels	78,000	78,000	11.3	20,280	0.26
G. A. Miller	42,000	42,000	6.1	12,600	0.30
W. D. MacMillan	36,000	36,000	5.2	14,400	0.40
J. Jones°	27,000	27,000	3.9	13,500	0.50
D. Mead°	27,000	27,000	3.9	13,500	0.50
S. Ross°	27,000	27,000	3.9	13,500	0.50
Investors of this offering		240,000	34.8	240,000	1.00
	450,000	690,000	100.0%	$368,460	

° These are the three distributor representatives mentioned in Section 2.

invoices in past associations with Rapidrill's principals. The few drills that have been repossessed have repeatedly been sold in the used market for up to 90% of their original selling price, thus limiting the loss from an uncollected receivable. Experience of Rapidrill's principals indicates that with proper credit control, industrywide losses are insignificant.

Notes Receivable

Range from 12 to 60 months in duration. Usually secured by the equipment. Loss expectancy extremely low.

Inventory

Approximately 80% value in off-the-shelf, standard, stock items easily returnable; therefore, more liquid than custom-specified items.

Accounts Payable

Sixty days, 19X2 through second quarter of 19X3. Vendors have indicated a willingness to work on these terms during Rapidrill's start-up period.

Loans

Currently negotiating with local banks for a $600,000–$700,000 revolving line of credit. Already have had preliminary approvals of loans and now preparing a package to be presented to the credit committees. Final approval contingent on raising $240,000 of this offering.

Retained Earnings

No dividend payments are planned during program.

Rapidrill has 29,000 shares of common stock authorized but unissued. These shares will be used to attract additional management personnel or reserved for future use as stock options to key employees.

FOR FURTHER READING

Baty, Gordon, *Entrepreneurship for the Nineties* (Englewood Cliffs, NJ: Prentice-Hall, 1990).

Bygrave, William D. and Jeffry A. Timmons, *Venture Capital at the Crossroads* (Boston: Harvard Business School Press, 1992).

Cohen, Herb, *You Can Negotiate Anything* (Toronto: Bantam, 1980).

Fisher, Roger and William Ury, *Getting to Yes* (Boston: Houghton-Mifflin, 1981).

Gladstone, William, *Venture Capital Investing* (Englewood Cliffs, NJ: Prentice-Hall, 1988).

Gumpert, David E. and Stanley R. Rich, *Business Plans That Win $* (New York: Harper & Row Publishers, 1985).

Hornaday, J. A. (Ed.), J. A. Timmons, F. Tarpley and K. H. Vesper, *Frontiers of Entrepreneurship Research* (Babson Park, MA: Babson College, 1991).

Kao, John, *Entrepreneurship, Creativity and Organization* (Homewood, IL: Richard D. Irwin, 1989).

Timmons, Jeffry A., *The Entrepreneurial Mind* (Acton, MA: Brick House Publishing, 1989).

————, *New Business Opportunities* (Acton, MA: Brick House Publishing, 1989).

————, *New Venture Creation* 2nd ed. (Homewood, IL: Richard D. Irwin, 1989).

————, *Planning and Financing a New Business* (Acton, MA: Brick House Publishing, 1989).

Weinrauch, Donald J. and Nancy Croft Baker, *The Frugal Marketer* (New York: AMACON, 1989).

Wilson, John W., *The New Venturers* (Reading, MA: Addison-Wesley, 1985).

NOTES

1. Philip Thurston, "Should Smaller Companies Make Formal Plans?" *Harvard Business Review* (September–October 1983), p. 184.

2. See an article by J. A. Timmons, "A Business Plan Is More Than a Financing Device," *Harvard Business Review* (March–April 1980).

3. Publilius Syrus.

4. Taken from comments of Nolan Bushnell, founder of Atari, Pizza Time Theaters, and a venture capital firm, made at a seminar during his induction in 1983 into the Babson College Academy of Distinguished Entrepreneurs.

5. Thurston, "Should Smaller Companies Make Formal Plans?" pp. 162–88.

6. Ibid., pp. 162–88.

7. Peter R. Drucker, *Managing for Results* (New York: Harper & Row, 1964).

8. For a discussion of some approaches to this dilemma, see George A. Steiner, "Approaches to Long Range Planning for Small Business," *California Management Review* (Fall 1967), pp. 3–16.

9. Thurston, "Should Smaller Companies Make Formal Plans?" pp. 162–88.

10. See, for example, Charles P. Waite, "The Presentation and Other Key Elements," in *Pratt's Guide to Venture Capital Sources,* 13th ed. (Needham, MA: Venture Economics, 1989), pp. 36–38.

10 MANAGING LONG-TERM INVESTMENTS

Kenneth S. Most

Les Samuels was the chief financial officer (CFO) of Super Terrific Industries Incorporated. He sat in his corner office on the 99th floor and looked over the corporation's "wish list" for long-term projects. The list was certainly impressive. Included in the many items listed was the following sample of capital-spending proposals:

- A new semiconductor plant to be built in Austin, Texas (1.1 billion)
- Installation of antipollution equipment at the Orange, New Jersey plant ($651 million)
- Acquisition of a competitor ($500 million)
- Replacement of the central computer system at head office ($167 million)
- Addition of two executive jets to the existing fleet of corporate aircraft ($49 million)
- Purchase of laptop computers for every member of the sales force ($4 million)
- Installation of a daycare facility at the divisional office in San Diego ($0.3 million)

The wish list added up to $2.9 billion. Available funds were only $1.7 billion. So, the first problem was how to cut the capital expenditure proposals down from $2.9 billion to $1.7 billion. How could the projects be put into a prioritized order? Which projects were essential in order to sustain or advance the company's competitive edge? Which projects offered the best "bang for the buck"? Which projects were the most risky, and which the most safe? Which projects were best able to attract new financing on desirable terms from the investment community?

These are the kind of vital questions involved in selecting long-term investments. This chapter addresses these key issues.

The financial manager is responsible for acquiring funds at the lowest cost, to meet planned requirements, in accordance with the decisions of the board of directors. These financial requirements are specified in two types of budget, the operating budget and the capital budget. Chapter 8 discussed the preparation of the operating budget. This chapter reviews the capital budgeting process. Terms used in capital budgeting are defined, and techniques used in making capital budgeting decisions are demonstrated.

THE TIME VALUE OF MONEY

Capital budgeting decisions are long-term decisions, extending over periods that may amount to decades. Because of this, it is essential to take into consideration the time value of money. This concept refers to the fact that a dollar received or paid today has a different value from a dollar received or paid a year ago, or a year from now. Let's consider a simple example. If a firm receives $100 on January 1, 20X1 and deposits it in an interest-bearing account, it will have earned interest of (say) $5 by December 31, 20X1. The value of this sum is therefore $100 on January 1, but $105 on *December 31.* If a firm is owed $100 on January 1, 20X1 and this amount is not paid until December 31, 20X1, the value of the expected receipt is less than $100 on *January 1,* because of the interest forgone during the waiting period. (The calculation of how much less is demonstrated later in this chapter.)

Money receipts and payments are equated at a given point in time through the concept of *present value.* Time is viewed as linear, and the observation point is characterized as the present, or *time zero.* This device permits us to adjust the amount of any cash receipt or payment by the interest factor that must be considered when calculating its present value, or value at time zero.

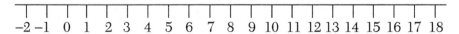

In this diagrammatic representation, 0 represents the present, the time at which it is desired to observe the value of money to be received or paid in the future. The intervals may be days, weeks, months, or years; in long-term capital budgeting decisions, it is customary to use the year as the unit of time. The negative numbers designate periods, prior to time zero, when money will be received or paid. For example, a firm that wants to build a new factory may acquire land two years before development starts; the payment for the land involves interest paid or forgone, which is part of the cost of developing. Similarly, if an airline orders an aircraft from Boeing and pays money in advance of delivery, the interest cost associated with this advance represents part of the cost of acquiring the aircraft, over and above its invoice price.

THE CAPITAL BUDGETING DECISION MODEL

The basic equations of capital budgeting are:

$$\text{Finance} = \text{Investment}$$
$$\text{Investment} = \text{Fixed assets} + \text{Working capital.}$$

Investment is the allocation of scarce resources to future production (as contrasted with consumption). Such allocation is rational only if the present value of the future production is greater than the value of the resources sacrificed. *Return on investment* (ROI) is a measure of the excess value and is conventionally expressed as a percentage ratio. For example, if $100 is invested in an inventory of goods for one year, which are sold for $130 at the end of the year, then the profit of $30 can be expressed as a rate of 30% per year.

$$\frac{\$30 \times 100}{\$100} = 30\%$$

This ratio is the ROI.

The funds must be acquired from their owner(s) and this necessitates a payment for the use of money, also expressed by means of a ratio, and called the *cost of capital.* If the $100 required to purchase the inventory is borrowed from a bank that requires a repayment of $115 at the end of the year, the cost of capital as a rate is 15% [($115 − $100 × 100)/$100].

One capital-budgeting decision model is shown in Exhibit 10.1. Investment opportunities are plotted in order of decreasing expected returns, assuming that a rational investor would seek to maximize profits. Financing costs are plotted on the assumption that the cost of capital eventually begins to increase as the total amount of financing increases beyond some specific limit. The model graphs ROI and cost of capital on the y axis, and dollar amount of investment on the x axis. The point at which ROI equals cost of capital determines the size of the capital budget I_0 because no other amount can be more profitable. Below I_0 profits will be made (returns exceed costs) and above I_0 losses will be incurred (costs exceed returns).

This model may also be used for screening, to identify projects that meet a specified criterion (ROI exceeds cost of capital) or as a preference model, to rank projects in order of their ROI. However, the model has limitations in both of these uses, which are examined in later examples.

EXHIBIT 10.1   The capital-budgeting decision model.

FINANCIAL LEVERAGE

Leverage means the use of fixed-income securities, such as debt and preferred stock, to increase returns on common stockholders' equity. The illustrations in this section utilize debt. The case of preferred stock is similar, except that preferred dividends may not be tax deductible in whole or in part.

The use of financial leverage is one of the most important aspects of financial structure. Equity capital is more costly than debt capital because (1) equity capital providers expect a premium for the higher degree of risk they run, and (2) interest on debt is tax deductible, while dividends on equity capital are not. Therefore the after-tax cost of debt is less than that of equity. As a result, a debt-financed firm that has a higher ROI than the cost of capital receives a benefit equal to the tax on the debt-interest expense. The debt is deducted from revenues when calculating taxable income.

If assets producing a given rate of return are financed in part by low-cost debt and in part by high-cost equity, the excess of the return over the cost of the debt is "levered up" to increase return on equity, as shown in Exhibit 10.2.

This diagram shows a firm that earns a 12% (income before interest but after taxes × 100/total assets) of $120, on total assets of $1,000. Assets are financed by common stock (70%) and debt (30%). The debt pays interest of 10% which, at a 40% tax rate, represents a 6% after-tax cost. The net interest cost of $18 is represented by the unshaded area under the 12% line. Because the firm earned 12% on $300 of debt capital, or $36, and the after-tax cost of

EXHIBIT 10.2   Financial leverage.

debt was only $18, the difference is profit that accrues to the equity. The diagram shows this $18 (the horizontally shaded area) being levered up on top of the equity, increasing return on equity (ROE) from 12 to 14.57% [($84 + $18 × 100)/700].

If the after-tax interest cost of debt is greater than ROI, the effect is the opposite; this is known as *negative leverage*. In this case, the ROE is reduced by leverage, not increased. In addition, debt represents a constant threat to the survival of the firm. Should the firm be unable to pay interest, or any part of the principal that falls due, the debt holders can sue for recovery, and eventually force the firm into liquidation. For these reasons, many entrepreneurs attempt to keep their financial structure debt-free, and even some large corporations strive after a similar policy.

There are several ways of measuring the effect of the leverage factor. One common approach is to calculate the ratio of return on equity with and without leverage. In this illustration, the ratio is 14.57/12.00, or 1.21.

FINANCIAL STRUCTURE AND THE COST OF CAPITAL

In financial investment theory, the cost of capital is defined in terms of maintaining the market value of the firm's securities. These, however, are affected by many factors outside the control of the firm: political events, income tax rates, interest and foreign currency exchange movements, and the price of energy, to name a few. For this reason the financial manager looks inward to the firm's cost structure and balance sheet, rather than outward to the stock and bond markets, to find the cost of capital. Because the cost of capital is *prospective* (what it will cost to finance planned investment), estimates have to be made of the future state of the stock and bond markets and other important factors, such as in income tax rates.

For this purpose we use the concept of *financial structure,* sometimes referred to as capital structure. Viewed through a firm's financial statements, the basic equation of finance is reflected in the basic equation of accounting: Assets equal liabilities plus owners' equity. Financial structure refers to the right-hand side of this equation. A firm's cost of capital is the expense necessary to raise and maintain that capital, treating dividends as expenses. Both interest and dividends must be considered, but it must be remembered that interest is tax deductible and dividends are not. For a profitable company, the cost of debt is the after-tax cost, found by multiplying the interest rate by $1 - t$ (t = the tax rate). The following example assumes that the company is profitable and does not plan to change its financial structure during the decision period.

Example

A corporation has a capital structure consisting of 100,000 shares of common stock, par value and issue price $5 each, paying an annual dividend of $1; 5,000 shares of preferred stock, par value and issue price $100, dividend rate 10% yearly; $200,000 long-term notes issued at par and bearing interest of 8% a year; and a mortgage loan of $100,000 on which the interest is 13% yearly. The tax rate is 50%. The following calculation shows the weighted average cost of capital.

	Amount	Weight %	Annual Payment	Annual After-Tax Cost
Common stock	$ 500,000	38.5	$100,000	$100,000
Preferred stock	500,000	38.5	50,000	50,000
Notes payable	200,000	15.4	16,000	8,000
Mortgage loan	100,000	7.6	13,000	6,500
Totals	$1,300,000	100.0	$179,000	$164,500

The after-tax weighted average cost of capital is $164,500 × 100/$1,300,000 = 12.65%.

Note that the firm's entire financial structure is looked at in calculating cost of capital. Suppose the firm is about to buy a building and can borrow the full amount at an after-tax interest cost of 10%. The problem with regarding the cost of capital for this decision as 10% is that such debt can be obtained only if there is an equity margin of security. Borrowing involves the use of some of the firm's equity, which would otherwise support other borrowings. If the firm is unable to sell debt securities because its ratio of debt to equity is too high, acceptance of other projects will necessitate issuance of additional equity. This is why the average cost of capital is used in capital budgeting decisions.

Component Cost

We have stated that the cost of debt capital is found on an after-tax basis. One complication arises when the stated interest rate differs from the effective interest rate, or yield to maturity. In extreme cases, such as zero-coupon bonds, there is no stated interest rate; the firm borrows say $600,000 now and must repay $1,000,000 10 years from now. The difference of $400,000 is tax-deductible interest, and the interest rate and tax-deductible amounts are found using the present-value method explained later in this chapter.

Cost of Stockholders' Equity

Three subcomponents of stockholders' equity have to be considered separately: retained earnings, common stock, and preferred stock. The cost of retained earnings is the rate of return that stockholders require for them to remain invested. In principle, this should be known from the stockholders themselves, but in practice it can be estimated from the present value of expected future dividends. In a growth situation, this can be found using the equation:

$$K_c = \frac{D}{P} + g$$

where K_c represents cost of capital

D is the current dividend

P is the current price of a share of common

g is the expected rate of dividend growth

Example

A firm's stock sells for $22.80 per share; it pays a dividend of $1.60, which is expected to grow at the rate of 7%. $K_c = (\$1.60/\$22.80 \times 100) + 7\% = 14\%$. If the firm earns a return of less than 14%, the price of its stock may be expected to fall, other factors remaining unchanged.

For new issues of common stock it is necessary to deduct issuance costs from the price of a share P in the preceding equation. Thus, if a new issue could be made at the current price of $22.80, which would net $20.00 to the firm, the cost of capital would be ($1.60/$20.00 × 100) + 7%, or 15%.

Preferred stock is similar to debt, except for the nondeductibility of the dividend. However, if a corporation holds shares in another corporation, upstream dividends may be shielded from income tax in the hands of the recipient, so that preferred stock may be sold to yield a lower rate of dividend than the rate of interest on equivalent debt.

ALTERNATIVE APPROACHES TO COST OF CAPITAL

There are several practical problems associated with the weighted average cost of capital, the principal one being the impossibility of determining an optimal financial structure. If the existing proportions of debt and equity are suboptimal, and are used in the calculation, the resulting cost of capital is inaccurate, and there is no way of projecting a financial structure that will be optimal in the light of current and future investments.

Example

On December 31, 20X0, a firm has a financial structure consisting of 50% debt (cost 8%) and 50% equity (cost 16%). The weighted average cost of capital is 12%. If the ratios had been 25% debt and 75% equity, the weighted average cost of capital would have been 14%. If projects returning 13% are accepted and the firm strengthens its capital structure by paying off debt, these projects will yield less than the cost of capital, because a lower debt ratio will raise the average cost of capital.

To avoid such problems, some firms arrive at the screening (or hurdle) rate by a process similar to that resulting from the use of the capital asset pricing model (CAPM). In the CAPM approach, the firm starts with the riskless interest rate, either the U.S. Treasury bond or 30-day Treasury bill rate, and adds risk points. Risk points are found by:

1. Estimating the firm's beta coefficient, β. The beta coefficient indicates how volatile the firm's stock price is compared to the stock market as a whole. Betas can be found for specific companies in financial reference works such as *Value Line*.

   If a stock has a beta of 1.0, this means that it fluctuates up and down in line with the stock market as a whole. If the stock market rises 9%, this stock will go up 9%; if the market drops 15%, so will this stock. A stock with a beta of 1.5 is one and a half times as volatile as the market; and if the market rises 20%, this stock tends to increase 30% (1.5 times 20). If the market declines 18%, this stock is likely to decline 27% (1.5 times 18). Stocks with betas well above 1.0 are high flyers and fall hard. On the other hand, some stocks are stable and have betas below 1.0. A stock with a beta of 0.75 will go down only 15% when the market drops 20% (20 times 0.75), and it will increase only 9% when the market goes up 12%.

2. Estimating the rate of return on the stock market as a whole, K_m.

3. Estimating the rate of return $K_s = R_f + \beta(K_m - R_f)$. In this equation R_f is the risk-free rate of return. Assume that the risk-free rate (represented by the return on U.S. Treasury bills) is 8%, the marker rate of return as a whole is 12%, and the firm's beta is 1.25. Then the firm's cost of equity is:

$$8\% + 1.25\,(12\% - 8\%)$$
$$= 8\% + 5\%$$
$$= 13\%$$

With a beta larger than 1.0, the firm is riskier than the market average. Logically, therefore, it has a cost of common equity (13%) which is higher than the 12% equity cost of the market as a whole. If the firm's beta had been 1.5, its cost of equity would have been 14% [$8\% + 1.5\,(12\% - 8\%)$]. Thus, the higher the risk, the higher the beta, and the higher the cost of equity.

Yet another approach is for the firm to identify the risks that it runs and attempt to add an estimate of the rates at which it might be insured against such risks. Such a calculation might look like this (risks are presented in summary form):

Risk-free rate	8%
Premium for demand risks	8%
Premium for supply risks	6%
Premium for financing risks	2%
Screening (hurdle, cut-off) rate	24%

Note that this is a pretax rate.

Yet another approach proceeds from the argument that investment risks attach to assets, not liabilities or equity, and should be calculated accordingly. This necessitates identifying an optimal asset structure, which is made easier because firms in particular industries can be seen to hold different types of assets in similar proportions.

In the following illustration, the firm's asset structure is normal, that is, it does not hold excessive cash balances or significant amounts of idle equipment. Cost represents *opportunity cost,* that is, what the firm would receive if it did not hold the asset. Cash is assumed to be able to earn 8%, accounts receivable could be factored at 10%, inventory could be purchased as needed at a premium of 30% (annualized), and equipment rental has an implicit cost of 20%.

Asset	Amount	Rate %	Cost
Cash	$ 1,000	8	$ 80
Receivables	20,000	10	2,000
Inventory	15,000	30	4,500
Equipment	30,000	20	6,000
Totals	$66,000		$12,580

In order to "earn its keep," an investment calling for a similar distribution of assets must earn a minimum of $12,580 before beginning to show a profit. That is, the project would break even at about 19% ($12,580/$66,000 × 100) which becomes the screening or hurdle rate. Projects with different asset structures could have different screening rates, and the capital budget would be determined by finding the amount of total investment that produces the highest rate of profit; this is a linear programming problem.

THE INFLATION PROBLEM

Inflation presents us with many problems in calculating both cost of capital and estimated future receipts, but it should be considered explicitly in all aspects of ROI evaluation. The impact of inflation is also felt in two other important aspects of the investment decision. The ROI and present value calculations are based on cash flows that do not reflect the fact that replacement value is rising, so that income taxes have a sharper effect on profits than the tax rate indicates. The depreciation tax shield, which is explained later in this chapter, is a historical-cost deduction and is not adjusted for the effect of inflation. Further, the ranking of projects according to their discounted cash flow returns (explained later) does not incorporate other important data relevant to the capital budgeting decision. For example, are the inflows and outflows of cash primarily fixed, and therefore subject to inflation effects, or are they variable, and capable of being changed to avoid those effects?

Various simple ways to adjust the capital budgeting model for inflation have been proposed. These include: using a higher discount rate (cost of capital plus expected rate of inflation), shortening the time period used to calculate present value of expected future receipts; and modifying the expected cash inflows and outflows using the expected inflation. None of these is satisfactory, and the methods described in the following pages must be substantially modified in order to give explicit effect to inflation expectations. The various ways of doing so remain the subject of considerable debate at the present time, and in the case of highly inflationary economies, call for major changes in the way of doing business.

RATE OF RETURN ON INVESTMENT (ROI)

An ROI concept is in general use. This ROI is found by dividing some measure of return, notably net income, by some measure of investment, notably total capital employed (total assets minus total liabilities). This ROI measure is sometimes called the *accounting rate of return* or the unadjusted rate of return.

Unadjusted means that it does not recognize, or adjust for, the time value of money, by means of an algorithm based on compound arithmetic. The accounting rate of return is useful for evaluating performance, but a defective measure for investment decisions.

Example

Consider the case of a machine that is to be bought for $1,000 and will produce net income of $100 annually for five years. It will then be scrapped without a residual value. Assuming straight-line depreciation, the following accounting ROIs can be calculated:

Year	Beginning Investment	Profit before Depreciation	Depreciation	Net Income	ROI on Average Investment
1	$1,000	$300	$200	$100	11.1% (a)
2	800	300	200	100	14.3% (b)
3	600	300	200	100	20.0% (c)
4	400	300	200	100	33.3% (d)
5	200	300	200	100	100.0% (e)

(a) $100/.5($1,000 + $800)
(b) $100/.5($800 + $600)
(c) $100/.5($600 + $400)
(d) $100/.5($400 + $200)
(e) $100/.5($200 + $0)

Which ROI number shall we use for the investment decision? Note that this problem becomes infinitely more complex if we (1) admit accelerated or production-based depreciation methods, (2) confront fluctuating profit from year to year, (3) consider the effect of income taxes on each year, and (4) expect to incur additional capital expenditure on the machine during its useful life.

One possible way out is to use the average return, found by summing the ROIs and dividing by n, the number of periods. In the previous example, this is 35.7% (178.7/5). This indicator is also defective, because, like the others, it ignores the time value of money. Reverse the order of the ROIs and the average remains the same, even though it is intuitively obvious that a series of returns starting with 100% in Year 1 and ending with 11.1% in Year 5 is preferable to a series of returns in the reverse order.

In this example, the accounting returns were constant from year to year; consider the following comparison.

Example

Two projects are being evaluated; both require an investment of $100, which is not recoverable until the end of the project's three-year life. Project 1 will produce returns of $60, $50, and $40 during the period; Project 2 will produce returns of $40, $50, and $60. The average return for each is 50% per annum (yearly).

$$\frac{(\$150/3) \times 100}{\$100}$$

Which would you choose?

In summary, accounting ROI is not suitable for use in investment decisions, whether to screen or rank in preference order. For screening decisions—those that involve determining whether a project meets a specified ROI criterion—it fails to provide an unequivocal answer. For preference decisions—selecting from several valid alternatives—it fails to give effect to the time value of money.

USING THE TABLES TO CALCULATE PRESENT VALUES

Before proceeding to a consideration of investment decision making, we next examine the use of Exhibits 10.3 and 10.4.

Example

I own a house that I wish to rent for two years while I am working abroad. Two prospective tenants appear, John Doe and Steve Smith. Doe offers me $1,000 on the signing of the lease, and $3,000 at the end of each year. Smith offers me $4,000 at the end of Year 1 and $3,500 at the end of Year 2. My time value of money is 10% per annum. Which deal do I prefer, assuming that the tenants are equally desirable in other respects. (The exhibits are based on receipt or payment at the end of the year; other tables must be used for a different timing.)

To find the present value of Doe's offer: The first expected receipt takes place at time t_0 and is therefore not discounted (the present value is the amount received). It can be expressed as $1,000 multiplied by a factor of 1 (not found in the exhibits). Exhibit 10.3 shows the present value of $1 at different rates of discount, for various periods other than the present. The present value of the first $3,000 is found by multiplying the amount by the factor in Exhibit 10.3 found in the column labeled 10%, in the row for Year 1. The present value of the second $3,000 is found by multiplying the factor in the same column, in the row for Year 2.

Present value of Doe's offer: ($1,000 × 1) + ($3,000 × .909)
+ ($3,000 × .826) = $6,205

To find the present value of Smith's offer: The first expected receipt takes place at the end of Year 1, and the second at the end of Year 2. Using the same present value factors from the column for 10%:

Present value of Smith's offer: ($4,000 × .909) + ($3,500 × .826)
= $6,527

EXHIBIT 10.3   The present value of one dollar discounted annually for N years.

Year	1%	2%	3%	4%	5%	6%	7%	8%	9%	10%
1	.990	.980	.971	.962	.952	.943	.935	.926	.917	.909
2	.980	.961	.943	.925	.907	.890	.873	.857	.842	.826
3	.971	.942	.915	.889	.864	.840	.816	.794	.772	.751
4	.961	.924	.888	.855	.823	.792	.763	.735	.708	.683
5	.951	.906	.863	.822	.784	.747	.713	.681	.650	.621
6	.942	.888	.837	.790	.746	.705	.666	.630	.596	.564
7	.933	.871	.813	.760	.711	.665	.623	.583	.547	.513
8	.923	.853	.789	.731	.677	.627	.582	.540	.502	.467
9	.914	.837	.766	.703	.645	.592	.544	.500	.460	.424
10	.905	.820	.744	.676	.614	.558	.508	.463	.422	.386
11	.896	.804	.722	.650	.585	.527	.475	.429	.388	.350
12	.887	.789	.701	.625	.557	.497	.444	.397	.356	.319
13	.879	.773	.681	.601	.530	.469	.415	.368	.326	.290
14	.870	.758	.661	.577	.505	.442	.388	.340	.299	.263
15	.861	.743	.642	.555	.481	.417	.362	.315	.275	.239
16	.853	.726	.623	.534	.458	.394	.339	.292	.252	.218
17	.844	.714	.605	.513	.436	.371	.317	.270	.231	.198
18	.836	.700	.587	.494	.416	.350	.296	.250	.212	.180
19	.828	.686	.570	.475	.396	.331	.277	.232	.194	.164
20	.820	.673	.554	.456	.377	.312	.258	.215	.178	.149
21	.811	.660	.538	.439	.359	.294	.242	.199	.164	.135
22	.803	.647	.522	.422	.342	.278	.226	.184	.150	.123
23	.795	.634	.507	.406	.326	.262	.211	.170	.138	.112
24	.788	.622	.492	.390	.310	.247	.197	.158	.126	.102
25	.780	.610	.478	.375	.295	.233	.184	.146	.116	.092
30	.742	.552	.412	.308	.231	.174	.131	.099	.075	.057
35	.706	.500	.355	.253	.181	.130	.094	.068	.049	.036
40	.672	.453	.307	.208	.142	.097	.067	.046	.032	.022
45	.639	.410	.264	.171	.111	.073	.048	.031	.021	.014
50	.608	.372	.228	.141	.087	.054	.034	.021	.013	.009

Thus, no matter how tempted I might be to take Doe's $1,000 right away, the present value of Smith's offer is higher, and a rational individual would prefer it, given the assumptions stated.

Note, however, that the amounts of $6,205, $6,527, and the difference between them, $322, are not money in the form of purchasing power. In that unit of measure, Doe offers $7,000 and Smith, $7,500. The other measures are in *present values* at the same point in time (the beginning of the lease), expressed as sums of money.

Example

A wealthy aunt would like to help you through school and into your first job. She offers you the choice of two annuities (a regular periodic receipt or payment is

EXHIBIT 10.3 *(Continued)*.

Year	11%	12%	13%	14%	15%	16%	17%	18%	19%	20%
1	.901	.893	.885	.877	.870	.862	.855	.847	.840	.833
2	.812	.797	.783	.769	.756	.743	.731	.718	.706	.694
3	.731	.712	.693	.675	.658	.641	.624	.609	.593	.579
4	.659	.636	.613	.592	.572	.552	.534	.516	.499	.482
5	.593	.567	.543	.519	.497	.476	.456	.437	.419	.402
6	.535	.507	.480	.456	.432	.410	.390	.370	.352	.335
7	.482	.452	.425	.400	.376	.354	.333	.314	.296	.279
8	.434	.404	.376	.351	.327	.305	.285	.266	.249	.233
9	.391	.361	.333	.308	.284	.263	.243	.225	.209	.194
10	.352	.322	.295	.270	.247	.227	.208	.191	.176	.162
11	.317	.287	.261	.237	.215	.195	.178	.162	.148	.135
12	.286	.257	.231	.208	.187	.168	.152	.137	.124	.112
13	.258	.229	.204	.182	.163	.145	.130	.116	.104	.093
14	.232	.205	.181	.160	.141	.125	.111	.099	.088	.078
15	.209	.183	.160	.140	.123	.108	.095	.064	.074	.065
16	.188	.163	.141	.123	.107	.093	.081	.071	.062	.054
17	.170	.146	.125	.108	.093	.080	.069	.060	.052	.045
18	.153	.130	.111	.095	.081	.069	.059	.051	.044	.038
19	.138	.116	.093	.083	.070	.060	.051	.043	.037	.031
20	.124	.104	.087	.073	.061	.051	.043	.037	.031	.026
21	.112	.093	.077	.064	.053	.044	.037	.031	.026	.022
22	.101	.083	.068	.056	.046	.038	.032	.026	.022	.018
23	.091	.074	.060	.049	.040	.033	.027	.022	.018	.015
24	.082	.066	.053	.043	.035	.028	.023	.019	.015	.013
25	.074	.059	.047	.038	.030	.024	.020	.016	.013	.010
30	.044	.033	.026	.020	.015	.012	.009	.007	.005	.004
35	.026	.019	.014	.010	.008	.006	.004	.003	.002	.002
40	.015	.011	.008	.005	.004	.003	.002	.001	.001	.001
45	.009	.006	.004	.003	.002	.001	.001	.001	.000	.000
50	.005	.003	.002	.001	.001	.001	.000	.000	.000	.000

called an *annuity*). The Provident Benefit Annuity pays $5,000 at the end of each year, for five years. The Southeastern Mutual Annuity pays $6,250 at the end of each year, for four years. The present values of annuities of $1 are shown in Exhibit 10.4, for different time values of money and various years. Your time value of money is 20% per annum. Using Exhibit 10.4, under the column 20%, we find the factors for five and four years respectively.

Present values:

Provident Benefit proposal:	$5,000 × 2.991 = $14,955
Southeastern Mutual proposal:	$6,250 × 2.589 = 16,181
Advantage to the Southeastern Mutual proposal:	$1,226.

Note that if your time value of money had been 10%, the advantage would have been smaller.

$5000 × 3.791 = 18,955$

$6250 × 3.170 = 19,812$

857

EXHIBIT 10.4   The present value of an annuity of one dollar discounted annually for *N* years.

Year	1%	2%	3%	4%	5%	6%	7%	8%	9%	10%
1	.990	.980	.971	.962	.952	.943	.935	.926	.917	.909
2	1.970	1.942	1.913	1.886	1.859	1.833	1.808	1.783	1.759	1.736
3	2.941	2.884	2.829	2.775	2.723	2.673	2.624	2.577	2.531	2.487
4	3.902	3.808	3.717	3.630	3.546	3.465	3.387	3.312	3.240	3.170
5	4.853	4.713	4.580	4.452	4.329	4.212	4.100	3.993	3.890	3.791
6	5.795	5.601	5.417	5.242	5.076	4.917	4.767	4.623	4.486	4.355
7	6.728	6.472	6.230	6.002	5.786	5.582	5.389	5.206	5.033	4.868
8	7.652	7.326	7.020	6.733	6.463	6.210	5.971	5.747	5.535	5.335
9	8.566	8.162	7.786	7.435	7.108	6.802	6.566	6.247	5.995	5.759
10	9.471	8.983	8.530	8.111	7.722	7.360	7.024	6.710	6.418	6.145
11	10.368	9.787	9.253	8.760	8.306	7.887	7.499	7.139	6.805	6.495
12	11.255	10.575	9.954	9.385	8.863	8.384	7.943	7.536	7.161	6.814
13	12.134	11.348	10.635	9.986	9.394	8.853	8.358	7.904	7.487	7.103
14	13.004	12.106	11.296	10.563	9.899	9.295	8.746	8.244	7.786	7.367
15	13.865	12.849	11.938	11.118	10.380	9.712	9.108	8.560	8.061	7.606
16	14.718	13.578	12.561	11.652	10.838	10.106	9.447	8.851	8.313	7.824
17	15.562	14.292	13.166	12.166	11.274	10.477	9.763	9.122	8.544	8.022
18	16.398	14.992	13.754	12.659	11.690	10.828	10.059	9.372	8.756	8.201
19	17.226	15.679	14.324	13.134	12.085	11.158	10.336	9.604	8.950	8.365
20	18.046	16.352	14.878	13.590	12.462	11.470	10.594	9.818	9.129	8.514
21	18.857	17.011	15.415	14.029	12.821	11.764	10.836	10.017	9.292	8.649
22	19.661	17.658	15.937	14.451	13.163	12.042	11.061	10.201	9.442	8.772
23	20.456	18.292	16.444	14.857	13.489	12.303	11.272	10.371	9.580	8.883
24	21.244	18.914	16.936	15.247	13.799	12.550	11.469	10.529	9.707	8.985
25	22.023	19.524	17.413	15.622	14.094	12.783	11.654	10.675	9.823	9.077
30	25.808	22.397	19.601	17.292	15.373	13.765	12.409	11.258	10.274	9.427
35	29.409	24.999	21.487	18.665	16.374	14.498	12.948	11.655	10.567	9.644
40	32.835	27.356	23.115	19.793	17.159	15.046	13.332	11.925	10.757	9.779
45	36.095	29.490	24.519	20.720	17.774	15.456	13.606	12.108	10.881	9.863
50	39.197	31.424	25.730	21.482	18.256	15.762	13.801	12.234	10.962	9.915

Present values:

Provident Benefit proposal: $5,000 × 3.791 = $18,955

Southeastern Mutual proposal: $6,250 × 3.170 =   19.812

Advantage to the Southeastern Mutual proposal: $857

The higher the discount rate and/or the longer the waiting period, the smaller the present value. This is simply the mathematical consequence of assuming that money has a positive time value.

DISCOUNTED FUTURE CASH FLOWS AND NET PRESENT VALUE

If the amount of an investment, the expected future cash flows arising, and the time value of money are known, the present value of the returns can be found

EXHIBIT 10.4 *(Continued).*

Year	11%	12%	13%	14%	15%	16%	17%	18%	19%	20%
1	.901	.893	.885	.877	.870	.862	.855	.847	.840	.833
2	1.713	1.690	1.668	1.647	1.626	1.605	1.585	1.566	1.547	1.528
3	2.444	2.402	2.361	2.322	2.283	2.246	2.210	2.174	2.140	2.106
4	3.102	3.037	2.974	2.914	2.855	2.798	2.743	2.690	2.639	2.589
5	3.696	3.605	3.517	3.433	3.352	3.274	3.199	3.127	3.058	2.991
6	4.231	4.111	3.998	3.889	3.784	3.685	3.589	3.498	3.410	3.326
7	4.712	4.564	4.423	4.288	4.160	4.039	3.922	3.812	3.706	3.605
8	5.146	4.968	4.799	4.639	4.487	4.344	4.207	4.078	3.954	3.837
9	5.537	5.328	5.132	4.946	4.772	4.607	4.451	4.303	4.163	4.031
10	5.889	5.650	5.426	5.216	5.019	4.833	4.659	4.494	4.339	4.192
11	6.207	5.938	5.687	5.453	5.234	5.029	4.836	4.656	4.487	4.327
12	6.492	6.194	5.918	5.660	5.421	5.197	4.988	4.793	4.611	4.439
13	6.750	6.424	6.122	5.842	5.583	5.342	5.118	4.910	4.715	4.533
14	6.982	6.628	6.303	6.002	5.724	5.468	5.229	5.008	4.802	4.611
15	7.191	6.811	6.462	6.142	5.847	5.575	5.324	5.902	4.876	4.675
16	7.379	6.974	6.604	6.265	5.954	5.669	5.405	5.162	4.938	4.730
17	7.549	7.120	6.729	6.373	6.047	5.749	5.475	5.222	4.990	4.775
18	7.702	7.250	6.840	6.467	6.128	5.818	5.534	5.273	5.033	4.812
19	7.839	7.366	6.938	6.550	6.198	5.877	5.585	5.316	5.070	4.843
20	7.963	7.469	7.025	6.623	6.259	5.929	5.628	5.353	5.101	4.870
21	8.075	7.562	7.102	6.687	6.312	5.973	5.665	5.384	5.127	4.891
22	8.176	7.645	7.170	6.743	6.359	6.011	5.696	5.410	5.149	4.909
23	8.266	7.718	7.230	6.792	6.399	6.044	5.723	5.432	5.167	4.925
24	8.348	7.784	7.283	6.835	6.434	6.073	5.747	5.451	5.182	4.937
25	8.422	7.843	7.330	6.873	6.464	6.097	5.766	5.467	5.195	4.948
30	8.694	8.055	7.496	7.003	6.566	6.177	5.829	5.517	5.235	4.979
35	8.855	8.176	7.586	7.070	6.617	6.215	5.858	5.539	5.251	4.992
40	8.951	8.244	7.634	7.105	6.642	6.233	5.871	5.548	5.258	4.997
45	9.008	8.283	7.661	7.123	6.654	6.242	5.877	5.552	5.261	4.999
50	9.042	8.305	7.675	7.133	6.661	6.246	5.880	5.554	5.262	4.999

(see Exhibit 10.5). This information can be used in a decision rule: Invest if the present value of the expected returns is greater than the amount of the investment. The difference between the present value of the returns, PV, and the amount of the investment, I, is called the *net present value,* or NPV. Thus, the decision rule can be restated as: Invest if NPV is positive.

Example

A firm is contemplating opening a new sales office, expected to produce net cash flows (receipts from sales less out-of-pocket purchase and expense costs) of $80,000 a year. It will cost $200,000 to equip this office, which will also require working capital of $300,000. The life of the investment will be 10 years, after which it will be expanded significantly or closed down. The investment cutoff rate (the time value of money) is 15%. Ignore income tax for the time being. The format shows how to compare the present value of the investment with the present value of the returns.

EXHIBIT 10.5   Diagram showing relationship between present value and future value.

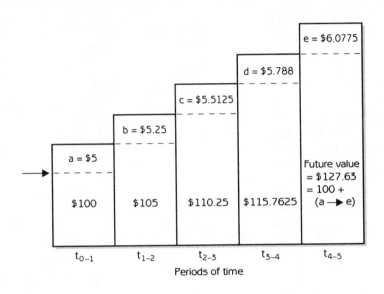

	Amount	Time	Factor	PV
Investment at t_0				
Equipment	$200,000	0	1.000	$200,000
Working capital	300,000	0	1.000	300,000
Present value of investment, I				500,000
Returns				
Net cash flows	80,000	1–10	5.019[1]	401,520
Working capital liquidation	300,000	10	0.247[2]	74,100
Present value of returns, PV				475,620
Net present value (PV − I)				$−24,380

1. From Exhibit 10.4.
2. From Exhibit 10.3.

It can be seen that although the absolute value of the returns ($1,100,000) exceeds the absolute value of the investment ($500,000), the effect of taking into consideration the time value of money produces the opposite result for their present values.

In cases such as this, where the estimates for the future are clearly subject to great uncertainty, a decision of this kind may be subjected to sensitivity analysis. A number of scenarios can be analyzed using different estimates of net cash flows. Probabilities can be introduced by asking several managers to state their subjective probability estimates for each of a number of possible results.

Example

To the previous example, three managers are now added: Bob Jones, Bill Coe, and Jim Marks. They are asked to state their beliefs about the potential outcome of opening the new sales office and to attach probabilities to each of them. For example, Mr. Jones reports "a one-in-five chance of cash flows of $50,000." Their individual responses are then converted to percentages, thus, Mr. Jones' estimate is expressed as a 20% chance.

The three managers each provide estimates of possible net cash flows and the probability of each (see Exhibit 10.6). Each manager's total probabilities must add up to 100%, because the new sales office will surely produce some net cash flow, positive or negative.

This series of calculations draws attention to the critical significance of the assumptions about future net cash flows. If Bob Jones is regarded as more reliable, the project will not be accepted, but if the other managers have better track records as predictors, it probably will. A similar sensitivity analysis may also be undertaken using different cost of capital rates, to see the effect of these assumptions.

To summarize: One capital budgeting decision tool involves the calculation of NPV, which can serve both to screen and rank potential investment decisions. To calculate NPV we must know the time value of money (the cutoff or cost of capital rate), the total cash investment and its timing, and the estimated future net cash flows and their timing. We then calculate the present value of the investment and the present values of the returns. If the sum of the present val-

EXHIBIT 10.6   Project sensitivity analysis.

Cash Flows	Bob Jones		Bill Coe		Jim Marks	
	Prob.	Value	Prob.	Value	Prob.	Value
$ 30,000 ×	0.1 =	$ 3,000	0.0	$ 0	0.0	$ 0
50,000 ×	0.2 =	10,000	0.1	5,000	0.0	0
80,000 ×	0.4 =	32,000	0.2	16,000	0.1	8,000
100,000 ×	0.2 =	20,000	0.4	40,000	0.3	30,000
150,000 ×	0.1 =	15,000	0.2	30,000	0.5	75,000
200,000 ×	0.0 =	0	0.1	20,000	0.1	20,000
Expected values		$ 80,000		$111,000		$133,000
Present values at 15% (× 5.019)		$401,520		$557,109		$667,527
Present value of recovery of working capital		74,100		74,100		74,100
Total		$475,620		$631,209		$741,627
Net present values		$ (24,380)		$131,209		$241,627

ues of the returns exceeds the present value of the investment outlays, NPV is positive and the project may be accepted.

Note that the calculation of NPV is performed entirely by modifying expected cash flows. There is no place in this decision model for any accounting data other than cash receipts and payments and discounting factors.

INCORPORATION OF INCOME TAX EFFECTS

In the real world, investors must pay income taxes on their profits. The preparation of an investment decision, therefore, involves the identification of after-tax cash inflows and outflows. This complicates the calculations, and care must be taken in adapting the model for this purpose.

Example

Suppose in the sales office example the estimated net cash flows are $100,000 per annum for 10 years; the profit on the investment is subject to income tax at the rate of 50%; equipment purchased for $100,000 includes office machinery for which old equipment will be given in part exchange, $10,000; the balance of equipment is a nondeductible building remodeling; and the firm will use straight-line depreciation on the new equipment for both book and tax purposes. Exhibit 10.7 shows how the net present value is calculated in a somewhat expanded format to accommodate tax effects. If we had used the pretax figures, NPV would have been positive:

$$PV = \$501,900 + \$74,100 = \$576,000$$
$$I = \$490,000$$
$$NPV = \$86,000$$

The example illustrates the effect of income taxes on investment decisions and the business argument that high income taxes are bad for the economy. Many projects that appear viable before the income tax effect is factored in prove unacceptable on an after-tax basis. This reduces the volume of investment, and with it the amount of employment and the future income taxes to be collected by the government. Inflation and the accompanying high interest rates aggravate this situation by raising the cost of capital. High income taxation coupled with high inflation is a recipe for economic disaster.

The situation is only partly relieved by the ability of firms to use accelerated depreciation methods for computing taxable income. In the preceding example, if we had used double-declining balance depreciation of 20%, the present value of the depreciation tax shield would have been only $4,280

EXHIBIT 10.7   Calculating the net present value.

	Amount	Tax Effect	After-Tax Amount	Time	Factor @ 15%	Present Value
Investment:						
Sale of old equipment	$ (10,000)			0	1.00	$ (10,000)
Purchase equipment	100,000		$100,000	0	1.00	100,000
Remodel building	100,000		100,000	0	1.00	100,000
Working capital	300,000		300,000	0	1.00	300,000
I =						$ 490,000
Returns:						
Annual net cash flow	100,000	50,000[1]	50,000	1–10	5.019	250,950
Depreci. effect	10,000	5,000[2]	5,000	1–10	5.019	25,095
Working capital	300,000	—	300,000	10	0.247	74,100
PV =						$ 350,145
Net present value (PV – I)						$(139,855)

[1] This is the amount of income tax that would be payable on the incremental annual cash flows if there were no depreciation "tax shield," given the income tax rate of 50%.
[2] Depreciation of $10,000 is an annual tax deduction, giving rise to a tax saving of 50% × $10,000 = $5,000 each year for 10 years.

higher. The project would still have had a negative NPV of $135,556. (The factors are from Exhibit 10.3.)

Year			
1	$ 20,000 × 50% × 0.870 =	$ 8,700
2	16,000 × 50% × 0.756 =	6,048
3	12,800 × 50% × 0.658 =	4,211
4	10,240 × 50% × 0.572 =	2,929
5	8,192 × 50% × 0.497 =	2,036
6	6,554 × 50% × 0.432 =	1,416
7[1]	6,554 × 50% × 0.376 =	1,232
8	6,554 × 50% × 0.327 =	1,072
9	6,554 × 50% × 0.284 =	931
10	6,552 × 50% × 0,247 =	809
Totals	$100,000	$29,384

1. Switch to straight-line here to maximize deductions.

INTERNAL RATE OF RETURN

In the examples in this chapter we have used the concept of ROI. If the time value of money adjusted ROI is known, the investment decision model can be stated in the form: Invest in any project with an ROI greater than the cost of capital (or the hurdle rate). This ROI is known by many names: Discounted cash flow (DCF) rate of return, time adjusted rate of return, true rate of return, internal rate of return, and more. Because it best expresses how this ROI is calculated, we shall refer to it as the *internal rate of return* (IRR).

Example

Consider an investment that produces an after-tax net cash flow of $2,000 annually for ten years, the amount of investment (I) being $10,000. At a discount rate of 6%, the present value of the receipts is $2,000 × 7.36 or $14,720. At a discount rate of 8%, PV is $2,000 × 6.71 = $13,420. Note that the higher the discount rate, the lower the PV. Clearly, there must be a discount rate at which PV = I = $10,000. That discount rate is the IRR. In this example it is slightly more than 15%; the PV of the cash flows discounted at 15% is $10,038 ($2,000 × 5.019).

The IRR is defined as that rate of discount at which the sum of the present values of a series of expected future cash flows is equal to the amount required to produce them. Given a known I (investment) and a known R (series of expected future receipts), we can solve the equation for i (IRR):

$$I = \frac{R_1}{(1+i)} + \frac{R_2}{(1+i)^2} + \cdots + \frac{R_n}{(1+i)^n}$$

With a computer program the IRR is easy to find. Without a computer or programmed calculator, two possible methods may be used. If the future cash flows are unequal in amount, then trial and error is required. A "high-low" approach will help in finding the IRR, as in the following example.

Example

An investment of $10,000 will produce the following expected future cash flows:

End of year 1	$7,000
End of year 2	3,000
End of year 3	2,000
End of year 4	1,000

Present Value at 5%		**Present Value at 20%**	
$7,000 × 0.952 = $ 6,664		$7,000 × 0.833 = $5,831	
3,000 × 0.907 = 2,721		3,000 × 0.694 = 2,082	
2,000 × 0.864 = 1,728		2,000 × 0.579 = 1,158	
1,000 × 0.823 = 823		1,000 × 0.482 = 482	
Total	$11,936	Total	$9,553

The internal rate of return is slightly less than 20%. Try 18% and 16%.

Present Value at 18%		**Present Value at 16%**	
$7,000 × 0.847 = $ 5,928		$7,000 × 0.862 = $ 6,034	
3,000 × 0.718 = 2,148		3,000 × 0.743 = 2,229	
2,000 × 0.609 = 1,218		2,000 × 0.641 = 1,282	
1,000 × 0.516 = 516		1,000 × 0.552 = 552	
Total	$ 9,810	Total	$10,097

The IRR is between 16 and 18%, and a better result can be obtained by interpolation.

$$16\% + \frac{97}{97 + 190}\,(2\%) = 16.7\%$$

If the future cash flows represent an annuity, the payback number can be used. *Payback* is defined as the period (in years) over which net cash flows liquidate the investment, and is calculated by the formula, I/R, where I is the amount of the investment and R is the periodical annual receipt.

An approximation to the IRR in this case can be found by inspecting the line on Exhibit 10.4 for the life of the project, to obtain the column in which appears a number as close as possible to the payback number. This is an approximation of the IRR, and interpolation can be used to provide a more exact result.

Example

Consider the investment of $10,000 that produces $2,000 annually for 10 years. The payback number is 5 (10,000/2000). In row 10 of Exhibit 10.4, the number 5 appears in the column for 15% (the factor is actually 5.019). Thus, the IRR must be more than 15% but less than 16% (factor 4.833). Interpolation allows the approximate IRR to be determined.

Factors from Exhibit 10.4

15%	5.019	5.019
Payback		5.000
16%	4.833	
Differences	0.186	0.019

$$15\% + \frac{.019}{.186}\,(1\%) = 15.1\%$$

Payback is sometimes used as an investment decision tool. The payback of several possible investments is calculated, and the project with the shortest payback (the lowest payback number) is preferred. This decision model avoids the calculation of ROI and ignores the time value of money, and for these reasons is not highly regarded as a tool for investment. It may be a useful indicator, however, because it expresses the period over which the investment is expected to be at risk.

IRR AND NPV COMPARED

The IRR would appear to be more useful for capital budgeting decisions than the NPV in straightforward comparisons between rate of return and cost of capital. The IRR can be interpreted as the maximum rate of interest that could be paid for the capital employed over the life of the investment in order for it to break even. A positive difference between IRR and cost of capital, therefore, means that the investment will be profitable. A project with a positive NPV must have an IRR higher than the cut-off rate.

The IRR is capable of giving clearer indications than the NPV in preference decisions. Consider these cases:

I	NPV	IRR
$20,000	$1,234	15%
10,000	544	30%

Most investors would prefer an investment producing a 30% annual return to one producing a 15% annual return, yet the first project has the higher NPV. It would be preferred in a system that ranked projects by NPV.

Further, the IRR can be used for comparisons with other investments, and thus fulfill a control function as well as a planning function.

The two decision models share the same basic assumptions and methods, as the following amortization tables demonstrate. In this example, an investment of $1,000 produces net cash flows of $250 annually for five years.

Calculation of net present value at 6%.

Year	Amount at Beginning	Interest for 1 Year at 6%	Principal Plus Interest	Return	Amount at End
1	$1,000.00	$60.00	$1,060.00	$250.00	$810.00
2	810.00	48.60	858.60	250.00	608.60
3	608.60	36.50	645.10	250.00	395.10
4	395.10	23.70	418.80	250.00	168.80
5	168.80	10.10	178.90	250.00	(71.10)

NPV of the project at 6% cost of capital is $71.10, the excess of returns over principal plus interest.

Calculation of net present value at 7.9%.

Year	Amount at Beginning	Interest for 1 Year at 7.9%	Principal Plus Interest	Return	Amount at End
1	$1,000.00	$79.00	$1,079.00	$250.00	$829.00
2	829.00	65.50	894.50	250.00	644.50
3	644.50	50.90	695.40	250.00	445.40
4	445.40	35.20	480.60	250.00	230.60
5	230.60	18.20	248.80	250.00	(1.20)

IRR of the project is fractionally above 7.9%, approximation being responsible for the residual NPV of $1.20. The true IRR would result in an NPV of $0.

CAPITAL BUDGETING

This chapter is concerned with investment decisions for making capital expenditures. Capital expenditures represent the acquisition of additional or replacement capacity. They provide the firm with equipment and working capital that will permit it to produce more goods or services, or to produce the same amount at a lower total cost. By definition, they have effects on more than one year, and can be called *long-term expenditures*. Simply stated, a capital investment decision involves incurring a current cost in the expectation of future benefits, extending for more than one year.

There are two theories of financial investment: (1) Each capital expenditure stands on its own. Evaluation of the project involves identification of the source of the finance to be used, and explicit inclusion of the cost of that capital in the calculation of ROI. (2) The firm has a common fund of capital and does not raise it for specific projects. Thus, there is a cost of capital to the firm as a whole. The decision model calculates ROI without including cost of capital, so that it may be compared with the latter.

It should be clear from this chapter that the second of these theories prevails at the present time, perhaps because of the dominant position occupied by very large corporations in our modern economy, and their practice of raising capital by the issue of shares or bonds for a variety of projects, often without reference to planned investments but because conditions on financial markets are favorable. The methods of capital budgeting are adaptable to both situations. But why capital *budgeting?*

Example

A firm has a number of capital expenditure projects under review. These projects add up to a total of $1,430,000. In order not to frighten the firm's existing creditors, the chief executive has decided that the maximum amount that can be borrowed is $1 million. The company's principal shareholder is at this time opposed to the issue of any amount of additional equity. The problem is, which capital expenditures to make, sometimes referred to as *capital rationing*. Once the decisions about what to include and what to leave out are made, the firm can prepare a capital budget. This will show the $1 million to be borrowed and how it will be spent. Additional working capital requirements may be included in the amount allocated to each project, or specified as a separate amount.

Assume that ROI has been calculated for each project. The projects can now be ranked and the decision process can begin. Note that the limit resulted in the rejection of projects with ROIs above the cost of capital. The cut-off point in this example is expressed as a sum of money, rather than as a hurdle rate—accept no project with an ROI below 12%.

Project ranking example.

Project Rank No.	Description of Project	Investment Amount	ROI %
1	New lathes	$ 100,000	30
2	Conveyor system	200,000	21
3	Modernize sales offices	400,000	19
4	Develop new product	300,000	15
	Subtotal	1,000,000 ◄——— limit	
5	Replace truck	50,000	14
6	Research new market	100,000	13
	Subtotal (cost of capital) ——►	1,150,000	12
7	New drilling machine	200,000	9
8	Replace air conditioners	80,000	7
	Total all projects	$1,430,000	

We have explained in detail two decision rules:

1. Invest in a project with a positive net present value; do not invest in a project with a negative NPV.

2. Invest in a project with an internal rate of return greater than the cost of capital; do not invest in a project if the cost of capital is greater than the IRR.

Unfortunately, these two rules do not always produce the identical project rankings. Exhibit 10.8 demonstrates graphically the different results that NPV and IRR may give.

Projects could be ranked differently as follows:

EXHIBIT 10.8   The difference between NPV and IRR.

1. Investment A, IRR 49%.   NPV of $7,370, ranks 4th.
2. Investment B, IRR 32%.   NPV of $107,700, ranks 2nd.
3. Investment C, IRR 21%.   NPV of $248,000, ranks 1st.
4. Investment D, IRR 15%.   NPV of $22,000, ranks 3rd.

The ranking problem in capital rationing situations is very difficult to handle, and volumes have been written to analyze the possible outcomes. In the finance literature, the NPV method, or some adaptation of it, is stated to be preferable, because it invariably produces a unique mathematical result. The calculation of IRR is complicated, not only because of the trial-and-error method by which it is found (a computer or programmed calculator takes care of that), but because, in certain situations, multiple IRRs are found. In particular, projects that require net outflows in any year after t_0 produce more than one IRR solution, difficult to interpret.

An additional problem with using the IRR is the concealed reinvestment assumption of the discounting (DCF) model. This can be seen most readily if we consider projects having lives of uneven length. Suppose that we are facing two mutually exclusive projects, A and B. A has an IRR of 30% over its four-year life; B has an IRR of 20% over five years. If we choose A because of its higher IRR, we are implicitly assuming that we can reinvest the capital portion of the return at an IRR greater than 20%.

Unequal project lives can be taken care of in capital budgeting by making them equal. Two methods allow projects with unequal life spans to be compared. In the first, the shortest project life is the time horizon, and projects having longer lives are treated as terminating at this point. This means finding salvage values for them at the time horizon.

In the second method, the longest project life is considered the time horizon, and projects with shorter lives are extended to that point by assuming replacement at the earlier termination date. For example, if a three-year vehicle lease is being compared with its purchase, and the vehicle has a six-year life, the longer period can be used if it is assumed that a new three-year lease is executed at the end of the first three years.

BOOK VALUE OF EQUIPMENT—EXCLUDING TAX EFFECTS

Many investment decisions involve equipment replacement or renovation. We recognize three situations: emergency, replacement, and improvement. An *emergency* is where the expenditure is essential if the business is to function, as when a factory building is destroyed by fire. *Replacement* is the acquisition of a new or used piece of equipment to substitute for an identical or similar piece that will be scrapped or sold for salvage value. An *improvement* is the acquisition of a larger, or more productive, or more economical, piece of equipment in place of one that will be scrapped or sold.

The equipment to be scrapped or sold is referred to as "old equipment," the replacement or improvement as "new equipment." A capital budgeting decision is involved whenever new is being substituted for old equipment. In general, where there are no income tax effects, because the subject is a not-for-profit entity, or a business not expected to be in a tax-paying situation in the foreseeable future, book value of old equipment is irrelevant and should be ignored.

Example

A machine capable of producing net cash flows of $12,000 annually can be replaced with a similar machine capable of producing net cash flows of $18,000. (This could be in the form of cost savings.) Both machines have useful lives of five years. The old machine has a book value of $12,000 (cost $20,000 less accumulated depreciation, $8,000) and can be sold for $5,000. The new machine costs $40,000. The firm uses a cut-off rate of 12% for investment decisions.

The old equipment should be kept because, over the five-year period, it produces $5,000 more than the new equipment. Note that the advantage to the old equipment becomes more pronounced at any positive discount rate, because the present value of the excess inflows from the new equipment ($6,000 for five years) cannot exceed the present value of the investment ($40,000 less $5,000). $6,000 multiplied by any discount factor for five years (Exhibit 10.4) is always less than $35,000. This result can be demonstrated by preparing comparative operating statements for the five years.

	Keep Old Equipment	**Buy New Equipment**	**Difference**
Operating income before depreciation	$60,000	$90,000	
Loss on sale of old equipment		(7,000)	
Depreciation on old equipment	(12,000)		
Depreciation on new equipment		(40,000)	
Net operating income	$48,000	$43,000	$5,000

BOOK VALUE OF EQUIPMENT—INCLUDING TAX EFFECTS

To demonstrate the effect of income taxes on the computation, assume in the preceding example (a) that income tax is payable at the rate of 40 percent of net income, and (b) tax deductibility of straight-line depreciation and of the loss on the sale of the old equipment. In this case, although the book value itself of the old equipment remains irrelevant, the tax effect of selling it below book value is relevant. Using the recommended format:

	Amount	Tax Effect	After-tax Amount	Time	Factor @ 12%	Present Value
Investment:						
Purchase	$40,000		$40,000	0	1.00	$ 40,000
Sale old equipment[1]	(5,000)	(2,800)	(7,800)	0	1.00	(7,800)
Total (I)						32,200
Returns:						
Differential net cash flow[2]	6,000	(2,400)	3,600	1–5	3.605[3]	12,978
Depreciation— new machine	(8,000)	3,200	3,200[4]	1–5	3.605	11,536
Depreciation— old machine	2,400	960	(960)[5]	1–5	3.605	(3,461)
Total (PV)						21,053
NPV (PV – I)						$(11,147)

1. Tax deduction for loss, $7,000 × 40%.
2. Tax liability, $6,000 × 40%.
3. Exhibit 10.4, factor for 12% for 5 years.
4. Tax saving, 40% × straight-line depreciation, annually.
5. Lost tax saving, through not being able to deduct $2,400 annual depreciation, $2,400 × 40%.

The effect of taxes in this case is to make the investment even less attractive, in spite of the deductibility of the tax loss on the old equipment.

Note that income tax effects may be included in the calculation only if the investor expects to be in a tax-paying situation. They would not apply to a not-for-profit organization, nor would there be tax effects if the firm had sustained losses that could be carried forward to offset taxable income on the new investment.

WORKING CAPITAL AND THE BUSINESS PLAN

The planning requirements of a capital budget include fixed capital, generally referred to as equipment, and working capital. Equipment is found from such sources as priced blueprints, manufacturers' catalogs, and costed specifications. Working capital presents a different kind of measurement problem.

To an accountant, working capital is the excess of current assets over current liabilities. Current assets are those that will be sold, used, or otherwise turned into cash within one year or within the firm's operating cycle, whichever is longer. Current liabilities are those obligations that must be met from current assets, typically liabilities payable within one year. Current assets consist of cash, short-term investments, accounts receivable and other debts owed to the firm, inventories, and prepaid expenses. Current liabilities include accounts payable, accrued expenses (such as insurance, payroll, and taxes), deferred revenues, and short-term notes payable.

A company's actual working capital usually differs from its working capital requirements, that is, the current assets and liabilities necessarily arising from the firm's operations. Let us call these *transaction needs*. Current assets will also include precautionary needs and speculative needs. Current liabilities will include additional debts over and above those arising from operations, such as accounts payable for equipment.

Precautionary Needs

If demand is likely to fluctuate, a company may have to maintain cash balances in excess of those dictated by operations. Suppose that a restaurant normally serves 100 meals on a Saturday night, but is occasionally called upon to cater for a large party on short notice. To do this additional business it may have to send out for food and drink, and to hire additional waiters and kitchen staff, both requiring payment in cash. A firm that buys from a major supplier prone to strikes will stock up on inventory as a necessary precaution.

Speculative Needs

Sales of some products cannot be expanded through growth; it takes too long, and the risk does not justify the cost. Firms in such industries must be prepared to buy other companies in order to grow, and they accumulate war chests for this purpose. The amounts of cash and short-term investments in their balance sheets will include such war chests. A company in the land development business may expect occasionally to be offered property at a very attractive price, which does not fit its current program, but can be held for resale at a higher price. The property will be included in inventory.

Current Liabilities

Two types of obligation are frequently included in current liabilities that do not arise out of the operations of the firm: current portion of long-term debt and amounts due for purchase of equipment. All or part of a long-term loan will be reclassified as a current liability if it is within one year of repayment, unless refunding has been arranged. Even though funding for the purchase of equipment may have been obtained from long-term sources (debt or equity), the liability is classified when it is purchased as a current one, if payable within one year.

For these reasons, the actual amounts of working capital at any point in time, and the relationship between individual current asset and liability amounts and balance sheet totals, are not the point of departure for calculating working capital requirements. These are derived from the operating budget, a plan for operating the capacity acquired with the capital budget.

A business plan is a detailed explanation of the assumptions on which the capital budget is based. It reports the research that was carried out to obtain these assumptions, and gives a detailed account of how the investment decision based on these assumptions will be executed, and the expected results. A business plan will include sections on:

- Marketing, including credit terms
- Production, including factory layout and product design
- Purchasing, including capital equipment
- Personnel
- Financial requirements

It will also provide a full set of projected financial statements for at least the first five years of planned operations. Chapter 9 contains a detailed example of a business plan.

The amount of working capital required is found during the preparation of the projected financial statements, because each of the periods planned will result in a balance sheet, showing the amounts of current assets and current liabilities at the end of the period. For example, if a shoe store is to be established that plans to sell $1 million of shoes during its first year, the inventory to be carried can be found if the gross margin and turnover period are known.

Example

A shoe store operates with a gross margin of 40% of selling price, and normally turns over its inventory about four times a year; the inventory holding period is 90 days. (Inventory turnover is calculated as cost of sales/inventory, and expressed as a number of sales days by dividing this ratio into 365.) The planned sales for the year have a cost of $600,000, and an inventory turnover of 4 dictates that an inventory of $150,000 be carried at all times. If the same rate of sales is forecast for the first quarter of the second year, this will be the inventory amount at the end of the first. A higher projected sales level for Year 2 will dictate a higher inventory.

If the marketing plan calls for sales of $85,000 monthly, the store will need to purchase shoes for $51,000 in order to replenish its inventory. If purchase terms are net 30 days, this will be the accounts payable component of current liabilities. Other components are found the same way.

One of the biggest problems is to plan the cash requirement. It seems intuitively advisable to carry a cash balance, and this may well be necessary for the firm as a whole, for precautionary or speculative reasons. In calculating working capital requirements, however, the need to carry cash must be demonstrated in the same way as the other working capital items. If a department store has 50 cash registers, each with a $50 float, then $2,500 in cash must be on hand at all times. Cash requirements are found in a part of the planned operating budget called the *cash forecast*.

CONCLUSION

Capital budgeting decisions are among the most important made. Upon them rest the firm's long-term profitability, and even its survival. It has been remarked that firms compete today principally by means of their investments, which determine the quality of their products, their operating costs, and their operating efficiency. The world's materials, labor, and finance are available to all, but not the ability to make good investment decisions.

The consequences of capital budgeting decisions cannot be changed in the short run because they are strategic, and often permanent. Finally, capital budgeting decisions are usually made at top management level, although relatively minor amounts may be allocated by operating management.

The capital budgeting process involves careful long-term planning. Prospective investments must be identified and scarce resources allocated in the most efficient manner possible. Developing an optimal plan for each project ensures the highest probability of an optimal ROI or NPV for the investment. The ROIs may be evaluated using sensitivity analysis, Monte Carlo simulations, and other methods, before projects are prioritized. Risk and inflation must be considered during the process, so that the firm attempts to maximize expected future returns for a given degree of risk. The end result is a capital budget, one of the essential elements of any firm's overall budget package.

Although DCF methods of calculating ROI have become widely used since the 1960s, they are not the only way in which investments are evaluated. Two alternatives, frequently used in conjunction with DCF methods, are:

1. Calculation of cash flow per share on an annual basis. This calculation indicates how much will be available for dividends to the company's stockholders, during the life of the investment.
2. Preparation of pro forma financial statements to show the effect of the investment on future earnings per share. Since the advent of the computer, such financial simulations have become commonplace.

Other calculations, such as the unadjusted accounting ROI and payback, are not recommended, though no doubt better than no evaluation at all. Because of the importance of the capital budgeting decision, many firms compute a variety of values for each proposed investment: IRR, NPV, accounting rate of return, payback, effect on projected earnings and cash flow per share. They prepare pro forma income statements and balance sheets for five or more years into the future. Although they know that these numbers may well yield conflicting signals, they believe that experienced investors and managers can weigh the tradeoffs between them, to come up with the best possible decisions.

One reason why financial managers don't rely exclusively on DCF methods is the inherently difficult task of predicting future cash flows. These may be accurately predicted for apartments rented under multiyear leases, or gas wells whose future production is to be delivered under contract at fixed prices. But most businesses find it extremely difficult to predict net cash flows: The outflows are relatively straightforward, but the inflows depend on too many exogenous variables. A pop group that records an album may not sell one copy (except to relatives and friends) but it may also go platinum. In between these extremes are historical results from previous investments that may prove to be a useful guide to the future. DCF methods are best suited to situations in which cash inflows and outflows can be predicted with reasonable assurance, and in which cost of capital can be reliably estimated. Financial managers know how rare such predictable situations really are.

FOR FURTHER READING

Barfield, Jesse T., Cecily A. Raiborn, and Michael A. Dalton, *Cost Accounting* (St. Paul, MN: West Publishing Co., 1991).

Bennett, Robert E. and James A. Hendricks, "Justifying the Acquisition of Automated Equipment," *Management Accounting* (July 1987).

Bierman, Harold Jr. and Seymour Smidt, *The Capital Budgeting Decision: Economic Analysis of Investment Projects* (New York: Macmillan, 1989).

Brealey, Richard and Stewart C. Myers, *Principles of Corporate Finance* (New York: McGraw-Hill, 1988).

Brigham, Eugene F., *Financial Management: Theory and Practice* (New York: The Dryden Press, 1982).

Fremgen, James M., "Capital Budgeting Practices: A Survey," *Management Accounting* (May 1973).

Gitman, Lawrence J. and John R. Forrester, "A Survey of Capital Budgeting Techniques Used by Major U.S. Firms," *Financial Management* (Fall 1977).

Harrison, Jan W., *Capital Investment Appraisal* (London: McGraw-Hill, 1973).

National Association of Accountants, "Management Accounting Terminology," *Statement on Management Accounting, Number 2* (Montvale, NJ: National Association of Accountants, June 1, 1983).

Polimeni, Ralph S., Frank J. Fabozzi, Arthur H. Adelberg, and Michael A. Kole, *Cost Accounting* (New York: McGraw-Hill, 1991).

Solomon, Ezra and John J. Pringle, *An Introduction to Financial Management* (Santa Monica, CA: Goodyear Publishing, 1977).

11 TAXES AND BUSINESS DECISIONS

Richard P. Mandel

It is not possible, of course, to fully describe the federal taxation system in the space of one book chapter. It may not even be realistic to attempt to describe federal taxation in a full volume. After all, a purchaser of the Internal Revenue Code (the "Code") can expect to carry home at least two volumes consisting of more than 6,000 pages, ranging from Section 1 through Section 9,602, if one includes the estate and gift tax and administrative provisions. And this does not even begin to address the myriad of Regulations, Revenue Rulings, Revenue Procedures, Technical Advice Memoranda, private letter rulings, court decisions, and other sources of federal tax law, which have proliferated over the better part of this century.

Fortunately, most people who enroll in a federal tax course during their progression toward an M.B.A. have no intention of becoming professional tax advisers. An effective tax course, therefore, rather than attempting to impart encyclopedic knowledge of the Code, instead presents taxation as another strategic management tool, available to the manager or entrepreneur in his or her quest to reach goals in a more efficient and cost-effective manner. After completing such a course, the businessperson should always be conscious that failure to consider tax consequences when structuring a transaction may result in needless tax expense.

It is thus the purpose of this chapter to illustrate the necessity of taking taxation into account when structuring most business transactions, and the need to consult tax professionals early in the process, not just when it is time to file the return. This will be attempted by describing various problems and opportunities encountered by a fictitious business owner, as he progresses from early successes, through the acquisition of a related business, to intergenerational succession problems.

THE BUSINESS

We first encounter our sample business when it has been turning a reasonable profit for the last few years under the wise stewardship of its founder and sole stockholder, Morris. The success of his wholesale horticultural supply business (Plant Supply, Inc.) has been a source of great satisfaction to Morris, as has the recent entry into the business of his daughter, Lisa. Morris paid Lisa's business school tuition, hoping to groom her to take over the family business, and his investment seems to be paying off as Lisa has become more and more valuable to her father. Morris (rightly or wrongly) does not feel the same way about his only other offspring, his son, Victor, the violinist, who appears to have no interest whatsoever in the business, except for its potential to subsidize his attempts to break into the concert world.

At this time, Morris was about to score another coup: Plant Supply purchased a plastics molding business so it could fabricate its own trays, pots, and other planting containers instead of purchasing such items from others. Morris considered himself fortunate to secure the services of Brad (the plant manager of the molding company) because neither he nor Lisa knew very much about the molding business. He was confident that negotiations then underway would bring Brad aboard with a satisfactory compensation package. Thus, Morris could afford to turn his attention to the pleasant problem of distributing the wealth generated by his successful business.

UNREASONABLE COMPENSATION

Most entrepreneurs long for the day when their most pressing problem is figuring out what to do with all the money their business is generating. Yet this very condition was now occupying Morris's mind. Brad did not present any problems in this context. His compensation package would be dealt with through ongoing negotiations and, of course, he was not family. But Morris was responsible for supporting his wife and two children. Despite what Morris perceived as the unproductive nature of Victor's pursuits, Morris was determined to maintain a standard of living for Victor befitting the son of a captain of industry. Of course, Lisa was also entitled to an affluent lifestyle, but surely she was additionally entitled to extra compensation for her long hours at work.

The simple and natural reaction to this set of circumstances would be to pay Lisa and Morris a reasonable salary for their work, and have the corporation pay the remaining distributable profit (after retaining whatever was necessary for operations) to Morris. Morris could then take care of his wife and Victor as he saw fit. Yet such a natural reaction would ignore serious tax complications.

The distribution to Morris beyond his reasonable salary would likely be characterized by the IRS as a dividend to the corporation's sole stockholder. Since dividends cannot be deducted by the corporation as an expense, both the corporation and Morris would pay tax on these monies (the well-known bugaboo of corporate double taxation). A dollar of profit could easily be reduced to a mere 46 cents of after-tax money in Morris's pocket (Exhibit 11.1).

Knowing this, one might argue that the distribution to Morris should be characterized as a year-end bonus. Since compensation is tax deductible to the corporation, the corporate level of taxation would be removed. Unfortunately, Congress has long since limited the compensation deduction to a "reasonable" amount. The IRS judges the reasonableness of a payment by comparing it to the salaries paid to other employees performing similar services in similar businesses. It also examines whether such amount is paid as regular salary or as a year-end lump sum when profit levels are known. The scooping up by Morris of whatever money was not nailed down at the end of the year would surely come under attack by an IRS auditor. Why not then put Victor on the payroll directly, thus reducing the amount that Morris must take out of the company for his family? Again, such a payment would run afoul of the "reasonableness" standard. If Morris would come under attack despite his significant efforts for the company, imagine attempting to defend payments made to an "employee" who expends no such efforts.

Subchapter S

The solution to the unreasonable compensation problem may lie in a relatively well-known tax strategy known as the subchapter S election. A corporation making this election remains a standard business corporation for all purposes other than taxation (retaining its ability to grant limited liability to its stockholders, for example). The corporation elects to forgo taxation at the corporate level and to be taxed as if it were a partnership. This means that a corporation that has

EXHIBIT 11.1   Double taxation.

$1.00	Earned
− .34	Corporate tax at 34%
.66	Dividend
− .20	Individual tax at 31%
.46	Remains

elected subchapter S status will escape any taxation on the corporate level, but its stockholders will be taxed on their pro rata share of the corporation's profits, regardless of whether these profits are distributed to them. Under this election, Morris's corporation would pay no corporate tax, but Morris would pay income tax on all the corporation's profits, even those retained for operations.

This election is recommended in a number of circumstances. One example is the corporation which expects to incur losses, at least in its start-up phase. In the absence of a subchapter S election, such losses would simply collect at the corporate level, awaiting a time in the future when they could be "carried forward" to offset future profits (should there ever be any). If the election is made, the losses would pass through to the stockholders in the current year, and might offset other income of these stockholders such as interest, dividends from investments, and salaries.

Another such circumstance is when a corporation expects to sell substantially all its assets, sometime in the future, in an acquisition transaction. Since the repeal of the so-called General Utilities doctrine, such a corporation would incur a substantial capital gain tax on the growth in the value of its assets from their acquisition to the time of sale, in addition to the capital gain tax incurred by its stockholders when the proceeds of such sale are distributed to them. The subchapter S election (if made early enough), again eliminates tax at the corporate level, leaving only the tax on the stockholders.

The circumstance most relevant to Morris is the corporation with too much profit to distribute as reasonable salary and bonuses. Instead of fighting the battle of reasonableness with the IRS, Morris could elect subchapter S status, thus rendering the controversy moot. It will not matter that the amount paid to him is too large to be anything but a nondeductible dividend, because it is no longer necessary to be concerned about the corporation's ability to deduct the expense. Not all corporations are eligible to elect subchapter S status. However, contrary to common misconception, eligibility has nothing to do with being a "small" business. In simplified form, to qualify for a subchapter S election, the corporation must have 75 or fewer stockholders, holding only one class of stock, all of whom must be individuals who are either U.S. citizens or resident aliens. Plant Supply qualifies on all these counts.

Alternatively, many companies have accomplished the same tax results, while avoiding the eligibility limitations of subchapter S, by operating as limited liability companies (LLCs). Unfortunately for Morris, however, most states require LLCs to have more than one owner.

Under subchapter S, Morris can pay himself and Lisa a reasonable salary and then take the rest of the money either as salary or dividend without fear of challenge. He can then distribute that additional money between Lisa and Victor, to support their individual lifestyles. Thus, it appears that the effective use of a strategic taxation tool has solved an otherwise costly problem.

Gift Tax

Unfortunately, like most tax strategies, the preceding solution may not be cost free. It is always necessary to consider whether the solution of one tax problem may create others, sometimes emanating from taxes other than the income tax. To begin with, Morris needs to be aware that under any strategy he adopts, the gifts of surplus cash he makes to his children may subject him to a federal gift tax. This gift tax supplements the federal estate tax, which imposes a tax on the transfer of assets from one generation to the next. Lifetime gifts to the next generation would, in the absence of a gift tax, frustrate estate tax policy. Fortunately, in order to accommodate the tendency of individuals to make gifts for reasons unrelated to estate planning, the gift tax exempts gifts by a donor of up to $10,000 per year to each of his or her donees. That amount is doubled if the donor's spouse consents to the use of his/her $10,000 allotment to cover the excess. Thus, Morris could distribute up to $20,000 in excess cash each year, to each of his two children, if his wife consented.

In addition, the federal gift/estate tax does not take hold until the combined total of taxable lifetime gifts in excess of the annual exclusion amount plus taxable bequests at death exceeds $600,000. Thus, Morris can exceed the annual $20,000 amount by quite a bit before the government will get its share.

These rules may suggest an alternate strategy to Morris, under which he may transfer some portion of his stock to each of his children, and then have the corporation distribute dividends to him and to them directly each year. The gift tax would be implicated to the extent of the value of the stock in the year it is given, but, from then on, no gifts would be necessary. Such strategy, in fact, describes a fourth circumstance in which the subchapter S election is recommended: when the company wishes to distribute profits to nonemployee stockholders, for whom salary or bonus in any amount would be considered excessive. In such a case, like that of Victor, a company can choose a subchapter S status, a gift to the nonemployee of stock, and a policy of distributing annual dividends from profits, thus avoiding any challenge to a corporate deduction based on unreasonable compensation.

MAKING THE SUBCHAPTER S ELECTION

Before Morris rushes off to make his election, however, he should be aware of a few additional complications. Congress has historically been aware of the potential for corporations to avoid corporate-level taxation on profits and capital gains earned prior to the subchapter S election, but not realized until afterward. Thus, for example, if Morris's corporation has been accounting for its inventory on a last in, first out (LIFO) basis, in an inflationary era (such as virtually any time during the last 50 years), taxable profits have been depressed by the use of higher cost inventory as the basis for calculation. Earlier lower-cost inventory has been left on the shelf (from an accounting point of view), waiting for later sales. However, if those later sales will now come during a time when the corporation is avoiding tax under subchapter S, those higher taxable profits will never be taxed at the corporate level. Thus, for the year just preceding the election, the Code requires recalculation of the corporation's profits on a first in, first out (FIFO) inventory basis to capture the amount which was postponed. If Morris has been using the LIFO method, his subchapter S election will carry some cost.

Similarly, if Morris's corporation has been reporting to the IRS on a cash-accounting basis, it has been recognizing income only when collected, regardless of when a sale was actually made. The subchapter S election, therefore, affords the possibility that many sales made near the end of the final year of corporate taxation will never be taxed at the corporate level, because these receivables will not be collected until after the election is in effect. As a result, the IRS requires all accounts receivable of a cash-basis taxpayer to be taxed as if collected in the last year of corporate taxation, thus adding to the cost of Morris's subchapter S conversion.

Of course, the greatest source of untapped corporate tax potential lies in corporate assets that have appreciated in value while the corporation was subject to corporate tax, but are not sold by the corporation until after the subchapter S election is in place. In the worst nightmares of the IRS, corporations which are about to sell all their assets in a corporate acquisition, first elect subchapter S treatment and then, immediately sell out, avoiding millions of dollars of tax liability.

Fortunately for the IRS, Congress addressed this problem in 1986, by revamping an older provision of the Code to provide for taxation on the corporate level of all so-called "built-in gain," realized by a converted S corporation within the first 10 years after its conversion. *Built-in gain* is the untaxed appreciation that existed at the time of the subchapter S election. It is taxed not only upon a sale of all the corporation's assets, but any time the corporation disposes of an asset it owned at the time of its election. This makes it advisable to have an appraisal done for all the corporation's assets as of the first day of subchapter S status, so that there is some objective basis for the calculation of built-in gain upon sale somewhere down the line. This appraisal will further deplete Morris's coffers, if he adopts the subchapter S strategy. Despite these complications, it is still likely that Morris will find the subchapter S election to be an attractive solution to his family and compensation problems.

Pass-Through Entity

Consider how a subchapter S corporation might operate were the corporation to experience a period during which it was not so successful. Subchapter S corporations (such as LLCs, partnerships, and limited partnerships) are known as *pass-through entities,* because they pass through their tax attributes to their owners. This not only operates to pass through profits to the tax returns of the owners (whether accompanied by cash), but also results in the pass-through of losses. As discussed earlier, these losses can then be used by the owners to offset income from other sources, rather than having the losses frozen on the corporate level, waiting for future profit.

The Code, not surprisingly, places limits upon the amount of loss which can be passed through to an owner's tax return. In a subchapter S corporation, the amount of loss is limited by a stockholder's basis in his investment in the corporation. Basis includes the amount invested as equity plus any amount the stockholder has advanced to the corporation as loans. As the corporation operates, the basis is raised by the stockholder's pro rata share of any profit made by the corporation and lowered by his pro rata share of loss and any cash distributions received by him.

These rules might turn Morris's traditional financing strategy on its head, the next time he sits down with the corporation's bank loan officer to negotiate an extension of the corporation's financing. In the past, Morris has always attempted to induce the loan officer to lend directly to the corporation. This way Morris hoped to escape personal liability for the loan (although, in the beginning he was forced to give the bank a personal guarantee). In addition, the corporation could pay back the bank directly, getting a tax deduction for the interest. If the loan were made to Morris, he would have to turn the money over to the corporation, and then depend upon the corporation to generate enough profit so it could distribute monies to him to cover his personal debt service. He might try to characterize those distributions to him as repayment of a loan he made to the corporation, but given the amount he had already advanced to the corporation in its earlier years, the IRS would probably object to the debt/equity ratio and recharacterize the payment as a nondeductible dividend, fully taxable to Morris. We have already discussed why Morris would prefer to avoid characterizing the payment as additional compensation: His level of compensation was already at the outer edge of reasonableness.

However, under the subchapter S election, Morris no longer has to be concerned about characterizing cash flow from the corporation to himself, in a manner which would be deductible by the corporation. Moreover, if the loan is made to the corporation, it does not increase Morris's basis in his investment (even if he has given a personal guarantee). This limits his ability to pass losses through to his return. Thus, the subchapter S election may result in the unseemly spectacle of Morris begging his banker to lend the corporation's money directly to him, so that he may in turn advance the money to the corporation and increase his basis. This would not be necessary in an LLC, since most loans advanced to the business entity increase the basis of its owners.

Passive Losses

No discussion of pass-through entities should proceed without at least touching on what may have been the most creative set of changes made to the Code in the 1986 revision. At that time, an entire industry had arisen to create and market business enterprises whose main purpose was to generate losses to pass through to their wealthy investor/owners. These losses, it was hoped, would normally be generated by depreciation, amortization, and depletion. These would be mere paper losses, incurred while the business itself was breaking even or possibly generating positive cash flow. They would be followed some years in the future by a healthy long-term capital gain. Thus, an investor with high taxable income could be offered short-term pass-through tax losses, with a nice long-term gain waiting in the wings. In those days, long-term capital gain was taxed at only 40% of the rate of ordinary income, so the tax was not only deferred, it was substantially reduced. These businesses were known as *tax shelters.*

The 1986 Act substantially reduced the effectiveness of the tax shelter, by classifying taxable income and loss into three major categories: active, portfolio, and passive. *Active income* consists mainly of wages, salaries, and bonuses; *portfolio income* is mainly income and dividends; while *passive income* and loss consist of distributions from the so-called "pass-through" entities, such as LLCs, limited partnerships, and subchapter S corporations. In their most simple terms, the passive activity loss rules add to the limits set by the above described basis limitations (and the similar so-called "at-risk rules"), making it impossible to use passive losses to offset active or portfolio income. Thus, tax shelter losses can no longer be used to shelter salaries or investment proceeds; they must wait for the taxpayer's passive activities to generate the anticipated end-of-the-line gains, or be used when the taxpayer disposes of a passive activity in a taxable transaction (see Exhibit 11.2).

Fortunately for Morris, the passive activity loss rules are unlikely to affect his thinking for at least two reasons. First, the Code defines a passive activity as the conduct of any trade or business "in which the taxpayer does not materially participate." Material participation is further defined in a series of Code sections and Temporary Regulations—which mock the concept of tax simplification, but let Morris off the hook—to include any taxpayer who participates in the business for more than 500 hours per year. Morris is clearly materially participating in his business, despite his status as a stockholder of a subchapter S corporation, and thus, the passive loss rules do not apply to him. The second reason Morris is not concerned is that he does not anticipate any losses from this business: Historically, it is very profitable. Therefore, let us depart from this detour into unprofitability and consider Morris's acquisition of the plastics plant.

EXHIBIT 11.2   Passive activity disposal.

ACQUISITION

Morris might well believe that the hard part of accomplishing a successful acquisition is locating an appropriate target and integrating it into his existing operation. Yet, once again, he would be well advised to pay some attention to the various tax strategies and results available to him, when structuring the acquisition transaction.

To begin with, Morris has a number of choices available to him in acquiring the target business. Simply put, these choices boil down to a choice among acquiring the stock of the owners of the business, merging the target corporation into Plant Supply, or purchasing the assets and liabilities of the target. The choice of method will depend upon a number of factors, many of which are not tax-related. For example, acquisition by merger will force Plant Supply to acquire all the liabilities of the target, even those of which neither it nor the target may be aware. Acquisition of the stock of the target by Plant Supply will also result in acquisition of all liabilities, but isolates them in a separate corporation, which becomes a subsidiary. (The same result would be achieved by merging the target into a newly formed subsidiary of Plant Supply—the so-called *triangular merger.*) Acquisition of the assets and liabilities normally results only in exposure to the liabilities Morris chooses to acquire and is thus an attractive choice to the acquirer (Exhibit 11.3).

Yet tax factors do normally play a large part in structuring an acquisition. For example, if the target corporation has a history of losses and thus boasts a tax-loss carryforward, Morris may wish to apply such losses to its future profitable operations. This would be impossible if he acquired the assets and liabilities of the target for cash, since the target corporation would still exist after the transaction, keeping its tax characteristics to itself. If the acquirer obtains the

EXHIBIT 11.3   Acquisition strategies.

BEFORE	AFTER

Merger

Target — Acquirer

Owned by T's stockholders

A

T

Owned by T's stockholders

Acquisition of stock

T — A

Owned by T's stockholders

T

Owned by

A

Owned by T's stockholders

Purchase of assets

T — T's assets — A

Owned by T's stockholders

T — A — T's assets

Owned by T's stockholders

---

stock, or merges the two entities, the acquirer has taken control of the taxable entity itself, thus obtaining its tax characteristics for future use. This result inspired a lively traffic in tax-loss carryforwards in years past, where failed corporations were marketed to profitable corporations seeking tax relief.

Congress has put a damper on such activity in recent years by limiting the use of a tax-loss carryforward, in each of the years following an ownership change of more than 50% of a company's stock. The amount of that limit is the product of the value of the business at acquisition (normally its selling price) times an interest rate linked to the market for federal treasury obligations. This amount of tax-loss carryforward is available each year, until the losses expire (15 years after they were incurred). Since a corporation with significant losses would normally be valued at a relatively low amount, the yearly available loss is likely to be relatively trivial.

Acquisition of the corporation's assets and liabilities for cash eliminates any use by the acquirer of the target's tax-loss carryforward, leaving it available for use by the target's shell. This may be quite useful to the target, because, as discussed earlier, if it has not elected subchapter S status for the last 10 years (or for the full term of its existence, if shorter), it is likely to have incurred a significant gain upon the sale of its assets. This gain would be taxable at the corporate level before the remaining portion of the purchase price could be distributed to the target's shareholders (where it will be taxed again).

The acquirer of assets may have lost any carryforwards otherwise available, but it does obtain the right to carry the acquired assets on its books at the price paid (rather than the amount carried on the target's books). This is an attractive proposition because the owner of assets used in business may deduct an annual amount corresponding to the depreciation of those assets, subject only to the requirement that it lower the basis of those assets by an equal amount. The amount of depreciation available corresponds to the purchase price of the asset. This is even more attractive because Congress has adopted available depreciation schedules that normally exceed the rate at which assets actually depreciate. Thus, these assets likely have a low basis in the hands of the target (resulting in even more taxable gain to the target upon sale). If the acquirer were forced to begin its depreciation at the point at which the target left off (as in a merger or purchase of stock), little depreciation would likely result. All things being equal (and especially if the target has enough tax-loss carryforward to absorb any conceivable gain), Morris would likely wish to structure his acquisition as an asset purchase and allocate all the purchase price among the depreciable assets acquired.

This last point is significant because Congress does not recognize all assets as depreciable. Generally speaking, an asset will be depreciable only if it has a demonstrable "useful life." Assets which will last forever, or whose lifetime is not predictable, are not depreciable, and the price paid for them will not result in future tax deductions. The most obvious example of this type of asset is land. Unlike buildings, land has an unlimited useful life and is not depreciable. This has spawned some very creative theories, including one enterprising individual who purchased a plot of land containing a deep depression, which he intended to use as a garbage dump. The taxpayer allocated a significant amount of his purchase price to the depression and took depreciation deductions as the hole filled up.

Congress has recognized that the above rules give acquirers incentive to allocate most of their purchase price to depreciable assets like buildings and equipment and very little of the price to nondepreciable assets such as land. Additional opportunities for this include allocating high prices to acquired inventory, so that it generates little taxable profit when sold. This practice has been limited by legislation requiring the acquirer to allocate the purchase price in accordance with the fair market value of the individual assets, applying the rest to goodwill (which may now be depreciated over 15 years).

Although this legislation will limit Morris's options significantly, if he chooses to proceed with an asset purchase, he should not overlook the opportunity to divert some of the purchase price to consulting contracts for the previous owners. Such payments will be deductible by Plant Supply over the life of the agreements and are, therefore, just as useful as depreciation. However, the taxability of such payments to the previous owners cannot be absorbed by the target's tax-loss carryforward. And, the amount of such deductions will be limited by the now familiar "unreasonable compensation" doctrine.

EXECUTIVE COMPENSATION

Brad's compensation package raises a number of interesting tax issues, which may not be readily apparent, but which deserve careful consideration in crafting an offer to him. Any offer of compensation to an executive of his caliber will include, at the very least, a significant salary and bonus package. These will not normally raise any sophisticated tax problems; the corporation will deduct these payments, and Brad will be required to include them in his taxable income. The IRS is not likely to challenge the deductibility of even a very generous salary, since Brad is not a stockholder or family member and, thus, there is little likelihood of an attempt to disguise a dividend.

Business Expenses

However, even in the area of salary, there are opportunities for the use of tax strategies. For example, Brad's duties may include the entertainment of clients or travel to suppliers and other business destinations. It is conceivable that Brad could be expected to fund these activities out of his own pocket, on the theory that such amounts have been figured into his salary. Such a procedure avoids the need for the bookkeeping associated with expense accounts. If his salary reflects these expectations, Brad may not mind declaring the extra amount as taxable income, since he will be entitled to an offsetting deduction for these business expenses.

Unfortunately, however, Brad would be in for an unpleasant surprise under these circumstances. First of all, these expenses may not all be deductible in full. Meals and entertainment expenses are deductible, if at all, only to the extent they are not "lavish and extravagant" and even then, they are deductible only for 50% of the amount expended. In addition, Brad's business expenses as an employee are considered "miscellaneous deductions"; they are deductible only to the extent that they, and other similarly classified deductions, exceed 2% of Brad's adjusted gross income. Thus, if Brad's gross taxable income is $150,000, the first $3,000 of miscellaneous deductions will not be deductible.

Moreover, as itemized deductions, these deductions are valuable only to the extent that they, along with all other itemized deductions available to Brad, exceed the "standard deduction," an amount Congress allows each taxpayer to deduct, if all itemized deductions are foregone. Furthermore, under tax legislation passed in late 1990, itemized deductions that survive the above cuts are further limited for taxpayers whose incomes are over $121,200 (the 1997 inflation-adjusted amount). The deductibility of Brad's business expenses is, therefore, greatly in doubt.

Knowing all this, Brad would be well advised to request that Morris revise his compensation package. Brad should request a cut in pay by the amount of his anticipated business expenses, along with a commitment that the corporation will reimburse him for such expenses or pay them directly. In that case, Brad will be in the same economic position, since his salary is lowered only by the amount he would have spent anyway. In fact, his economic position is enhanced, since he pays no taxes on the salary he does not receive, as well as escaping from the 50% ceiling and 2% floor described above.

The corporation pays out no more money this way than it would have if the entire amount were salary. Taxwise, the corporation is only slightly worse off, since the amount it would have previously deducted as salary can now still be deducted as ordinary and necessary business expenses (with the sole exception of the 50% ceiling on meals and entertainment). In fact, were Brad's salary below the Social Security contribution limit (FICA), both Brad and the corporation would be better off, because what was formerly salary (and thus subject to additional 7.65% contributions to FICA by both employer and employee) would now be merely expense reimbursements and exempt from FICA.

Before Brad and Morris adopt this strategy, however, they should be aware that in recent years, Congress has turned a sympathetic ear to the frustration the IRS has expressed about expense accounts. Legislation has conditioned the exclusion of amounts paid to an employee, as expense reimbursements, upon the submission by the employee to the employer of reliable documentation of such expenses. Brad should get into the habit of keeping a diary of such expenses for tax purposes.

Deferred Compensation

Often, a high-level executive will negotiate a salary and bonus which far exceed his or her current needs. In such a case, the executive might consider deferring some of that compensation until future years. Brad may feel, for example, that he would be well advised to provide for a steady income during his retirement years, derived from his earnings while an executive of Plant Supply. He may be concerned that he would simply waste the excess compensation and consider a deferred package as a form of forced savings. Or, he may wish to defer receipt of the excess money to a time (such as retirement) when he believes he will be in a lower tax bracket. This latter consideration was more common when the federal income tax law encompassed a large number of tax brackets and the highest rates were as high as 70%.

Whatever Brad's reasons for considering a deferral of some of his salary, he should be aware that deferred compensation packages are generally classified as one of two varieties for federal income tax purposes. The first such category is the qualified deferred compensation plan, such as the pension, profit-sharing, or stock bonus plan. All these plans share a number of characteristics. First and foremost, they afford taxpayers the best of all possible worlds, by granting the employer a deduction for monies contributed to the plan each year, allowing those contributions to be invested and to earn additional monies without the payment of current taxes, and finally, taxing the employee only upon withdrawal of funds, as needed in the future. However, in order to qualify for such favorable treatment, these plans must conform to a bewildering array of conditions imposed by both the Code and the Employee Retirement Income Security Act (ERISA). Among these requirements is the necessity to treat all employees of the corporation on a nondiscriminatory basis with respect to the plan, thus rendering qualified plans a poor technique for supplementing a compensation package for a highly paid executive.

The second category is nonqualified plans. These come in as many varieties as there are employees with imaginations, but they all share the same disfavored tax treatment. The employer is entitled to its deduction only when the employee pays tax on the money, and if money is contributed to such a plan, the earnings are taxed currently. Thus, if Morris were to design a plan under which the corporation receives a current deduction for its contributions, Brad will pay tax now on money he will not receive until the future. Since this is the exact opposite of what Brad (and most employees) have in mind, Brad will most likely have to settle for his employer's unfunded promise to pay him the deferred amount in the future.

Assuming Brad is interested in deferring some of his compensation, he and Morris might well devise a plan which gives them as much flexibility as possible. For example, Morris might agree that the day before the end of each pay period, Brad could notify the corporation of the amount of salary, if any, he wished to defer for that period. Any amount thus deferred would be carried on the books of the corporation as a liability to be paid, per their agreement, with interest, after Brad's retirement. Unfortunately, such an arrangement would be frustrated by the "constructive receipt" doctrine. Using this potent weapon, the IRS will impose tax (allowing a corresponding employer deduction) upon any compensation which the employee has earned and might have chosen to receive, regardless of whether he so chooses. The taxpayer may not turn his back upon income otherwise unconditionally available to him.

Taking this theory to its logical conclusion, one might argue that deferred compensation is taxable to the employee because he might have received it if he had simply negotiated a different compensation package. After all, the impetus for deferral in this case comes exclusively from Brad; Morris would have been happy to pay the full amount when earned. But the constructive receipt doctrine does not have that extensive a reach. The IRS can tax only monies the taxpayer was legally entitled to receive, not monies he might have received if he had negotiated differently. In fact, the IRS will even recognize elective deferrals if the taxpayer must make the deferral election sufficiently long before the monies are legally earned. Brad might, therefore, be allowed to choose deferral of a portion of his salary if the choice must be made at least six months before the pay period involved.

Frankly, however, if Brad is convinced of the advisability of deferring a portion of his compensation, he is less likely to be concerned about the irrevocability of such election as about ensuring that the money will be available to him when it is eventually due. Thus, a mere unfunded promise to pay in the future may result in years of nightmares over a possible declaration of bankruptcy by his employer. Again, left to their own devices, Brad and Morris might well devise a plan under which Morris contributes the deferred compensation to a trust for Brad's benefit, payable to its beneficiary upon his retirement. Yet such an arrangement would be disastrous to Brad, since the IRS would assess income tax to Brad upon such arrangement, using the much criticized "economic benefit" doctrine. Under this theory, monies irrevocably set aside for Brad grant him an economic benefit (presumably by improving his net worth or otherwise improving his creditworthiness), upon which he must pay tax.

If Brad were aware of this risk, he might choose another method to protect his eventual payout, by requiring the corporation to secure its promise to pay with such devices as a letter of credit or a mortgage or security interest in its assets. All of these devices, however, have been successfully taxed by the IRS under the self-same economic benefit doctrine. Very few devices have survived this attack. However, the personal guarantee of Morris himself (merely another unsecured promise) would not be considered an economic benefit by the IRS.

Another successful strategy is the so-called "rabbi trust," a device first used by a rabbi who feared his deferred compensation might be revoked by a future hostile congregation. This device works similarly to the trust described earlier, except that Brad would not be the only beneficiary of the money contributed. Under the terms of the trust, were the corporation to experience financial reverses, the trust property would be available to the corporation's creditors.

Since the monies are thus not irrevocably committed to Brad, the economic benefit doctrine is not invoked. Of course, this device does not protect Brad from the scenario of his nightmares, but it does protect him from a corporate change of heart regarding his eventual payout. From Morris's point of view, he may not object to contributing to a rabbi trust, since he was willing to pay all the money to Brad as salary, but he should be aware that since Brad escapes current taxation, the corporation will not receive a deduction for these expenses until the money is paid out of the trust in the future.

Interest-Free Loans

As a further enticement to agree to work for the new ownership of the plant, Morris might additionally offer to lend Brad a significant amount of money, to be used, for example, to purchase a new home or acquire an investment portfolio. Significant up-front money is often part of an executive compensation package. While this money could be paid as a bonus, Morris might well want some future repayment (perhaps, as a way to encourage Brad to stay in his new position). Brad might wish to avoid the income tax bite on such a bonus so he can retain the full amount of the payment for his preferred use. Morris and Brad might well agree to an interest rate well below the market, or even no interest at all, to further entice Brad to his new position. Economically, this would give Brad free use of the money for a period of time, during which it could earn him additional income with no offsetting expense. In a sense, he would be receiving his salary in advance while not paying any income tax until he earned it. Morris might well formalize the arrangement by reserving a right to offset loan repayments against future salary. The term of the loan might even be accelerated should Brad leave the corporation's employ.

This remarkable arrangement was fairly common until recently. Under current tax law, however, despite the fact that little or no interest passes between Brad and the corporation, the IRS deems full market interest payments to have been made and further deems that said amount is returned to Brad by his employer. Thus, each year, Brad is deemed to have made an interest payment to the corporation, for which he is entitled to no deduction. Then, when the corporation is deemed to have returned the money to him, he realizes additional compensation upon which he must pay tax. The corporation realizes additional interest income, but gets a compensating deduction for additional compensation paid (assuming it is not excessive when added to Brad's other compensation).

Moreover, the IRS has not reserved this treatment for employers and employees only. The same treatment is given to loans between corporations and their shareholders and loans between family members. In the latter situation, although there is no interest deduction for the donee, the deemed return of the interest is a gift and is thus excluded from income. The donor receives interest income, and has no compensating deduction for the return gift. In fact, if the interest amount is large enough, he may have incurred an additional gift tax on the "returned" interest. The amount of income created for the donor, however, is limited to the donee's investment income, except in very large loans. In the corporation/stockholder situation, the lender incurs interest income and has no compensating deduction as its deemed return of the interest is characterized as a dividend. Thus the IRS gets increased tax from both parties unless the corporation has selected subchapter S (see Exhibit 11.4).

All may not be lost in this situation, however. Brad's additional income tax arises from the fact that there is no longer any deduction allowable for interest paid on unsecured personal loans. However, interest remains deductible in limited amounts on loans secured by a mortgage on either of the taxpayer's principal or secondary residence. If Brad grants Plant Supply a mortgage on his home to secure the repayment of his no- or low-interest loan, his deemed payment of market interest may become deductible and may thus offset his additional deemed compensation from the imaginary return of this interest. Before jumping into this transaction, however, Brad will have to consider the limited utility of itemized deductions described earlier.

SHARING THE EQUITY

If Brad is as sophisticated and valuable an executive employee as Morris believes he is, Brad is likely to ask for more than just a compensation package, deferred or otherwise. Such a prospective employee often demands a "piece of the action" or a share in the equity of the business, so that he may directly share in the growth and success he expects to create. Morris may even welcome such a demand because an equity share (if not so large as to threaten Morris's control)

EXHIBIT 11.4   Taxable interest.

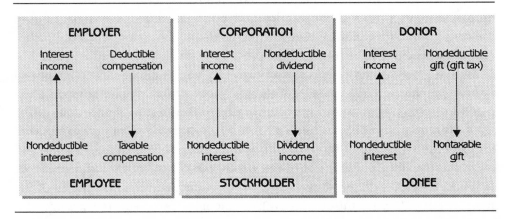

may serve as a form of golden handcuffs, giving Brad additional reason to stay with the company for the long term.

Assuming Morris is receptive to the idea, there are a number of different ways to grant Brad a share of the business. The most direct way would be to grant him shares of the corporation's stock. These could be given to Brad without charge, for a discount from fair market value or for their full value, depending upon the type of incentive Morris wishes to design. In addition, given the privately held nature of Morris's corporation, the shares will probably carry restrictions, designed to keep the shares from ending up in the hands of persons who are not associated with the company. Thus, the corporation will retain the right to repurchase the shares should Brad ever leave the corporation's employ or wish to sell or transfer the shares to a third party. Finally, in order to encourage Brad to stay with the company, the corporation will probably reserve the right to repurchase the shares from Brad at cost should Brad's employment end before a specified time. As an example, *all* the shares (called *restricted stock*) would be subject to forfeiture at cost (regardless of their then actual value) should Brad leave before one year; two thirds would be forfeited if he left before two years; and one third if he left before three years. The shares not forfeited (called *vested* shares) would be purchased by the corporation at their full value at the time periods described above.

One step back from restricted stock is the stock option. This is a right granted to the employee to purchase a particular number of shares for a fixed price over a defined period of time. Because the price of the stock does not change, the employee has effectively been given the ability to share in whatever growth the company experiences during the life of the option, without paying for the privilege. If the stock increases in value, the employee will exercise the option near the end of the option term. If the stock value does not grow, the employee will allow the option to expire, having lost nothing. The stock option is a handy device when the employee objects to paying for his piece of the action (after all, he is expecting compensation, not expense), but the employer objects to giving the employee stock whose current value represents growth from the period before the employee's arrival. Again, the exercise price can be more than, equal to, or less than the fair market value of the stock at the time of the grant, depending upon the extent of the incentive the employer wishes to give. Also, the exercisability of the option will likely "vest" in stages over time.

Often, however, the founding entrepreneur cannot bring himself to give an employee a current or potential portion of the corporation's stock. Although he has been assured that the block of stock going to the employee is too small to have any effect on his control over the company, the objection may be psychological and impossible to overcome. The founder seeks a device which can grant the employee a growth potential similar to that granted by stock ownership, but without the stock. Such devices are often referred to as *phantom stock* or *stock appreciation rights* (SARs). In a phantom stock plan, the employee is promised that he may, at any time during a defined period, so long as he remains employed by the corporation, demand payment equal to the then value of a certain number of shares of the corporation's stock. As the corporation grows, so does the amount available to the employee, just as would be the case if he actually owned some stock. SARs are very similar, except that the amount available to the employee is limited to the growth, if any, that the given number of shares has experienced since the date of grant.

Tax Effects of Phantom Stock and SARs

Having described these devices to Morris and Brad, it is, of course, important to discuss their varying tax impacts upon employer and employee. If Brad has been paying attention, he might immediately object to the phantom stock and SARs as vulnerable to the constructive receipt rule. After all, if he may claim the current value of these devices at any time he chooses, might not the IRS insist that he include each year's growth in his taxable income, as if he had claimed it? Although the corporation's accountants will require that these devices be accounted for in that way on the corporation's financial statements, the IRS has failed in its attempts to require inclusion of these amounts in taxable income, because the monies are not unconditionally available to the taxpayer. In order to receive the money, one must give up any right to continue to share in the growth represented by one's phantom stock or SAR. If the right is not exercisable without cost, the income is not constructively received.

However, there is good reason for Brad to object to phantom stock and SARs from a tax point of view. Unlike stock and stock options, both of which represent a recognized form of intangible capital asset, phantom stock and SARs are really no different from a mere promise by the corporation to pay a bonus based upon a certain formula. Since these devices are not recognized as capital assets, they are not eligible to be taxed as long-term capital gains when redeemed. This difference was quite meaningful when the maximum ordinary income tax rate was 50% and the maximum long-term capital gain rate was 20%. It is significant again today when the maximum rates have once again diverged to 39.6% and 28%, respectively. Thus, Brad may have good reason to reject phantom stock and SARs, and insist upon the real thing.

Taxability of Stock Options

If Morris and Brad resolve their negotiations through the use of stock options, careful tax analysis is again necessary. The Code treats stock options in three different ways, depending upon the circumstances, and some of these circumstances are well within the control of the parties (Exhibit 11.5).

If a stock option has a "readily ascertainable value," the IRS will expect the employee to include in his taxable income the difference between the value of the option and the amount paid for it (this amount is normally zero). Measured in that way, the value of an option might be quite small, especially if the exercise price is close or equal to the then fair market value of the underlying stock. After all, the value of a right to buy $10 of stock for $10 is only the speculative value of having that right when the underlying value has increased. That amount is then taxed as ordinary compensation income, and the employer receives a compensating deduction for compensation paid. When the employee exercises the option, the Code imposes no tax, nor does the employer receive any further deduction. Finally, should the employee sell the stock, the difference between the price received and the total of the previously taxed income and the amounts paid for the option and the stock is included in his income as capital gain. No deduction is then granted to the employer as the employee's decision to sell his stock is not deemed to be related to the employer's compensation policy.

This taxation scenario is normally quite attractive to the employee, because he is taxed upon a rather small amount at first, escapes tax entirely upon exercise, and then pays tax on the growth at a time when he has realized cash with which to pay the tax, at a lower long-term capital gain rate. Although the employer receives little benefit, it has cost the employer nothing in hard assets, so any benefit would have been a windfall.

Because this tax scenario is seen as very favorable to the employee, the IRS has been loathe to allow it in most cases. Generally, the IRS will not recognize an option as having a "readily ascertainable value" unless the option is traded on a recognized exchange. Short of that, a case has occasionally been made when the underlying stock is publicly traded, such that *its* value is readily ascertainable. But the IRS has drawn the line at options on privately held stock and at all

EXHIBIT 11.5   The taxation of stock options.

		GRANT	EXERCISE	SALE
READILY ASCERTAINABLE VALUE	Employee	Tax on value	No tax	Capital gain
	Employer	Deduction	No deduction	No deduction
NO READILY ASCERTAINABLE VALUE	Employee	No tax	Tax on spread	Capital gain
	Employer	No deduction	Deduction	No deduction
ISOP	Employee	No tax	No tax	Capital gain
	Employer	No deduction	No deduction	No deduction

options that are not themselves transferable. Since Morris's corporation is privately held and since he will not tolerate Brad's reserving the right to transfer the option to a third party, there is no chance of Brad's taking advantage of this beneficial tax treatment.

The second tax scenario attaches to stock options which do not have a readily ascertainable value. Since, by definition, one cannot include their value in income on the date of grant (it is unknown), the Code allows the grant to escape taxation. However, upon exercise, the taxpayer must include in income the difference between the then fair market value of the stock purchased and the total paid for the option and stock. When the purchased stock is later sold, the further growth is taxed at the applicable rate for capital gain. The employer receives a compensation deduction at the time of exercise, and no deduction at the time of sale. Although the employee receives a deferral of taxation from grant to exercise in this scenario, this method of taxation is generally seen as less advantageous to the employee, since a larger amount of income is exposed to ordinary income rates, and this taxation occurs at a time when the taxpayer has still not received any cash from the transaction with which to pay the tax.

Recognizing the harshness of this result, Congress invented a third taxation scenario which attaches to "incentive stock options." The recipient of such an option escapes tax upon grant of the option and again upon exercise. Upon sale of the underlying stock, the employee includes in taxable income the difference between the price received and the total paid for the stock and option, and pays tax upon that amount at long-term capital gain rates. This scenario is extremely attractive to the employee who defers all tax until the last moment and pays at a lower rate. Under this scenario, the employer receives no deduction at all, but since the transaction costs him nothing, that is normally not a major concern.

However, the Code imposes many conditions upon the grant of an incentive stock option. Among these are that the options must be granted pursuant to a written plan, setting forth the maximum number of shares available and the class of employees eligible; only employees are eligible recipients; the options cannot be transferable; no more than $100,000 of underlying stock may be initially exercisable in any one year by any one employee; the exercise price of the options must be the fair market value of the stock upon the date of grant; and the options must expire substantially simultaneously with the termination of the employee's employment. Perhaps most important, the underlying stock may not be sold by the employee prior to the expiration of two years from the option grant date or one year from the exercise date, whichever is later.

This latter requirement has led to what was probably an unexpected consequence. Assume that Plant Supply has granted an incentive stock option to Brad. Assume further that Brad has recently exercised the option, and has plans to sell the stock he received. It may occur to Brad that by waiting a year to resell, he will be risking the vagaries of the market for a tax savings which cannot exceed 11.6%

(the difference between the maximum income tax rate of 39.6% and the maximum capital gain rate of 28%. By selling early, Brad will lose the chance to treat the option as an incentive stock option, but will pay, at worst, only a marginally higher amount at a time when he does have the money to pay it. Furthermore, by disqualifying the options, he will be giving his employer a tax deduction at the time of exercise. An enterprising employee might go so far as to offer to sell early in exchange for a split of the employer's tax savings.

Tax Impact on Restricted Stock

The taxation of restricted stock is not markedly different from the taxation of nonqualified stock options without a readily ascertainable value (Exhibit 11.6). *Restricted stock* is defined as stock that is subject to a condition that affects its value to the holder and which will lapse upon the happening of an event or the passage of time. Since the value of the stock to the employee is initially speculative, the receipt of the stock is not considered a taxable event. In other words, since Brad may have to forfeit whatever increased value his stock may acquire, if he leaves the employ of the corporation prior to the agreed time, Congress has allowed him not to pay the tax until he knows for certain whether he will be able to retain that value. When the stock is no longer restricted (when it "vests"), the tax is payable. Of course, Congress is not being entirely altruistic in this case; the amount taxed when the stock vests is not the difference between what the employee pays for it and its value when first received by the employee, but the difference between the employee's cost and its value at the vesting date. If the value of the stock has increased, as everyone involved has hoped, the IRS receives a windfall. Of course, the employer receives a compensating deduction at the time of taxation, and further growth between the vesting date and the date of sale is taxed upon sale at appropriate capital gain rates. No deduction is then available to the employer.

Recognizing that allowing the employee to pay a higher tax at a later time is not an unmixed blessing, Congress has provided that an employee who receives restricted stock may, nonetheless, elect to pay ordinary income tax on the difference between its value at grant and the amount paid for it, if the employee files notice of that election within 30 days of the grant date. Thus, the employee can choose for himself which gamble to accept.

This scenario can result in disaster for the unaware employee. Assume that Morris and Brad resolve their differences by allowing Brad to have an equity stake in the corporation, if he is willing to pay for it. Thus, Brad purchases 5% of the corporation for its full value on the date he joins the corporation, for example, $5.00 per share. Since this arrangement still provides incentive in the form of a share of growth, Morris insists that Brad sell the stock back to the corporation for $5.00 per share should he leave the corporation before he has been

EXHIBIT 11.6   Restricted stock tax impact.

		GRANT	RESTRICTION REMOVED	SALE
RESTRICTED STOCK	Employee	No tax	Tax based on current value	Capital gain
	Employer	No deduction	Deduction	No deduction
RESTRICTED STOCK 83(b) ELECTION	Employee	Tax based on value without restriction	No tax	Capital gain
	Employer	Deduction	No deduction	No deduction

employed for 3 years. Brad correctly believes that since he has bought $5.00 shares for $5.00, he has no taxable income, and reports nothing on his income tax return that year.

Brad has failed to realize that despite his paying full price, he has received restricted stock. As a result, Congress has done him the favor of imposing no tax until the restrictions lapse. Three years from now, when the shares may have tripled in value and have finally vested, Brad will discover to his horror that he must include $10.00 per share in his taxable income for that year. Despite the fact that he had no income to declare in the year of grant, Brad must elect to include that nullity in his taxable income for that year by filing such an election with the IRS within 30 days of his purchase of the stock.

VACATION HOME

Morris had much reason to congratulate himself on successfully acquiring the plastics molding operation as well as securing the services of Brad, through an effective executive compensation package. In fact, the only real disappointment for Morris was that the closing of the deal was scheduled to take place during the week in which he normally took his annual vacation.

Some years ago, Morris had purchased a country home for use by himself and his wife as a weekend getaway and vacation spot. With the press of business, however, Morris and his wife had been able to use the home only on occasional weekends and for his two-week summer vacation each year. Morris always took the same two weeks for his vacation so he could indulge his love of golf. Each year, during that two weeks, the professional golfers would come to town for their annual tournament. Hotels were always booked far in advance, and Morris felt lucky to be able to walk from his home to the first tee and enjoy his favorite sport, played by some of the world's best.

Some of Morris's friends had suggested that Morris rent his place during the weeks that he and his wife didn't use it. Even if such rentals would not generate much cash during these off-season periods, it might allow Morris to deduct some of the expenses of keeping the home, such as real estate taxes, mortgage payments, maintenance, and depreciation. Morris could see the benefit in that, since the latter two expenses were deductible only in a business context, and although taxes and mortgage interest were deductible as personal expenses (assuming, in the case of mortgage interest, that Morris was deducting such payments only with respect to this and his principal residence and no other home), the previously mentioned limits on the use of itemized deductions made the usefulness of these deductions questionable.

However, in addition to the inconvenience of renting one's vacation home, Morris had discovered a few unfortunate tax rules which had dissuaded him from following his friends' advice. First of all, the rental of a home is treated by the Code in a fashion similar to the conduct of a business. Thus, Morris would generate deductions only to the extent that his expenses exceeded his rental income. In addition, to the extent he could generate such a loss, the rental of real estate is deemed to be a passive activity under the Code, regardless of how much effort one puts into the process. Thus, in the absence of any relief provision, these losses would be deductible only against other passive income, and would not be usable against salary, bonus, or investment income.

Such a relief provision does exist, however, for rental activities in which the taxpayer is "actively" involved. In such a case, the taxpayer may deduct up to $25,000 of losses against active or portfolio income, unless his total income (before any such deduction) exceeds $100,000. The amount of loss which may be used by such taxpayer, free of the passive activity limitations, is then lowered by $1 for every $2 of additional income, disappearing entirely at $150,000. Given his success in business, the usefulness of rental losses, in the absence of passive income, seemed problematic to Morris, at best.

Another tax rule appeared to Morris to limit the usefulness of losses even further. Under the Code, a parcel of real estate falls into one of three categories: personal use, rental use, or mixed use. A personal use property is one which is rented 14 days or less in a year and otherwise used by the taxpayer and his family. No expenses are deductible for such a facility except taxes and mortgage interest. A rental use property is used by the taxpayer and his family for less than 15 days (or 10% of the number of rental days) and otherwise offered for rental. All the expenses of such an activity are deductible, subject to the passive loss limitations. A mixed use facility is one that falls within neither of the other two categories.

If Morris were to engage in a serious rental effort of his property, his occasional weekend use, combined with his two-week stay around the golf tournament, would surely result in his home falling into the mixed-use category. This would negatively impact him in two ways. The expenses, which are deductible only for a rental facility (such as maintenance and depreciation), would be deductible only on a pro rata basis for the total number of rental days. Worse yet, the expenses of the rental business would be deductible only to the extent of the income, and not beyond. Expenses which would be deductible anyway (taxes and mortgage interest) are counted first in this calculation and only then are the remaining expenses allowed. The result of all this is that it would be impossible for Morris to generate a deductible loss, even were it possible to use such a loss in the face of the passive loss limitations.

Naturally, therefore, Morris had long since decided not to bother with attempting to rent his country getaway when he was unable to use it. However, the scheduling of the closing this year presents a unique tax opportunity of which he may be unaware. In a rare stroke of fairness, the Code, while denying any deduction of not otherwise deductible expenses in connection with a home rented for 14 days or less, reciprocates by allowing taxpayers to exclude any rental income should they take advantage of the 14-day rental window. Normally, such an opportunity is of limited utility, but with the tournament coming to town and the hotels full, Morris is in a position to make a killing, by renting his home to a golfer or spectator during this time at inflated rental rates. All that rental income would be entirely tax-free. Just be sure the tenants don't stay beyond two weeks.

LIKE-KIND EXCHANGES

Having acquired the desired new business and secured the services of the individual he needed to run it, Morris turned his attention to consolidating his two operations, so that they might function more efficiently. After some time, he realized that the factory building acquired with the plastics business was not contributing to increased efficiency because of its age and, more important, because of its distance from Morris's home office. Morris located a more modern facility near his main location, which could accommodate both operations and allow him to eliminate some amount of duplicative management.

Naturally, Morris put the molding facility on the market and planned to purchase the new facility with the proceeds of the old, plus some additional capital. Such a strategy will result in a tax upon the sale of the older facility, equal to the difference between the sale price and Plant Supply's basis in the building. If Morris purchased the molding company by purchasing its assets for cash, then the capital gain to be taxed here may be minimal, because it would consist only of the growth in value since this purchase, plus any amount depreciated after the acquisition. If, however, Morris acquired the molding company through a merger or purchase of stock, his basis will be the old company's preacquisition basis, and the capital gain may be considerable. Either way, it would surely be desirable to avoid taxation on this capital gain.

The Code affords Morris the opportunity to avoid this taxation, if, instead of selling his old facility and buying a new one, he can arrange a trade of the old for the new, so that no cash falls into his hands. Under Section 1031 of the Code, if properties of "like-kind" used in a trade or business are exchanged, no taxable event has occurred. The gain on the disposition of the older facility is merely deferred until the eventual disposition of the newer facility. This is accomplished by calculating the basis in the newer facility, starting with its fair market value on the date of acquisition and subtracting from that amount, the gain not recognized upon the sale of the older facility. That process builds the unrecognized gain into the basis of the newer building, so that it will be recognized (along with any future gain) upon its later sale. There has been considerable confusion and debate over what constitutes like-kind property outside of real estate, but there is no doubt that a trade of real estate used in business for other real estate to be used in business will qualify under Section 1031.

Although undoubtedly attracted by this possibility, Morris would quickly point out that such an exchange would be extremely rare, since it is highly unlikely that he would be able to find a new facility which is worth exactly the same amount as his old facility, and thus any such exchange will have to involve a payment of cash as well as an exchange of buildings. Fortunately, however, Section 1031 recognizes that reality by providing that the exchange is still nontaxable to Morris so long as he does not receive any non-like-kind property (i.e., cash). Such non-like-kind property received is known as *boot,* and will include, besides cash, any liability (such as a mortgage debt) assumed by the exchange partner. The facility he is purchasing is more expensive than the one he is selling, so Morris will have to add some cash, not receive it. Thus, the transaction does not involve the receipt of boot and still qualifies for tax deferral. Moreover, even if Morris did receive boot in the transaction, he would recognize gain only to the extent of the boot received, so he might still be in a position to defer a portion of the gain involved. Of course, if he received more boot than the gain in the transaction, he would recognize only the amount of the gain, not the full amount of the boot.

But Morris has an even more compelling, practical objection to this plan. How often will the person who wants to purchase your facility own the exact facility you wish to purchase? Not very often, he would surmise. In point of fact, the proposed buyer of his old facility is totally unrelated to the current owner of the facility Morris wishes to buy. How then can one structure serve as an exchange of the two parcels of real estate? It would seem, therefore, that a taxable sale of the one, followed by a purchase of the other, will be necessary in almost every case.

Practitioners have, however, devised a technique to overcome this problem, known as the *three-corner exchange.* In a nutshell, the transaction is structured by having the proposed buyer of Morris's old facility use his purchase money (plus some additional money contributed by Morris) to acquire the facility Morris wants to buy, instead of giving that money to Morris. Having thus acquired the new facility, he then trades it to Morris for Morris's old facility. When the dust settles, everyone is in the same position they would have occupied in the absence of an exchange. The former owner of the new facility has his cash; the proposed buyer of Morris's old facility now owns that facility and has spent only the amount he had proposed to spend; and Morris has traded the old facility plus some cash for the new one. The only party adversely affected is the IRS, which now must wait to tax the gain in Morris's old facility until he sells the new one.

This technique appears so attractive that when practitioners first began to use it, they attempted to employ the technique, even when the seller of the old facility had not yet found a new facility to buy. They merely had the buyer of the old facility place the purchase price in escrow and promise to use it to buy a new facility for the old owner as soon as he picked one out. Congress has since limited the use of these so-called "delayed" like-kind exchanges, by requiring the seller of the old facility to identify the new facility to be purchased within 45 days of the transfer of the old one, and further requiring that the exchange be completed within six months of the first transfer.

DIVIDENDS

Some time after Morris had engineered the acquisition of the molding facility, the hiring of Brad to run it, and the consolidation of his company's operations through the like-kind exchange, Plant Supply was running smoothly and profitably enough for Morris's thoughts to turn to retirement. Morris intended to have a comfortable retirement funded by the fruits of his lifelong efforts on behalf of the company, so it was not unreasonable for him to consider funding his retirement through dividends, on what would still be his considerable holdings of the company's stock. Although Brad already held some stock, and Morris expected that Lisa and Victor would hold some at that time, he still expected to have a majority position and thus sufficient control of the board of directors to ensure such distributions.

However, Morris also knew enough about tax law to understand that such distributions would cause considerable havoc from a tax point of view. We have already discussed how characterizing such distributions as salary or bonus would avoid double taxation, but with Morris no longer working for the company, such characterization would be unreasonable. These payments would be deemed dividends on his stock. They would be nondeductible to the corporation (if it were not a subchapter S corporation at the time) and would be fully taxable to him.

However, Morris had another idea. He would embark upon a strategy of turning in small amounts of his stock on a regular basis, in exchange for the stock's value. Although not a perfect solution, the distributions to him would no longer be dividends, but payments in redemption of stock. Thus, they would be taxable only to the extent they exceeded his basis in the stock, and even then, only at long-term capital gain rates (not as ordinary income). Best of all, if such redemptions were small enough, he would retain his control over the company for as long as he retained over 50% of its outstanding stock.

However, the benefits of this type of plan have attracted the attention of Congress and the IRS over the years. If an individual can draw monies out of a corporation, without affecting the control he asserts through the ownership of his stock, is he really redeeming his stock, or simply engaging in a disguised dividend? Congress has answered this question with a series of Code sections purporting to define a redemption.

Substantially Disproportionate Distributions

Most relevant to Morris is Section 302(b)(2), which provides that a distribution in respect of stock is a *redemption* (and thus taxable at preferential rates after subtraction of basis), only if it is substantially disproportionate. This is further defined by requiring that the stockholder hold, after the distribution, less than half of the total combined voting power of all classes of stock, and less than 80% of the percentage of the company's total stock that he owned prior to the distribution.

Thus, if Morris intended to redeem 5 shares of the company's stock at a time when he owned 85 of the company's outstanding 100 shares, he would be required to report the entire distribution as a dividend. His percentage of ownership would still be 50% or more (80 of 95 or 84%), which in itself dooms the transaction. In addition, his percentage of ownership will still be 80% or more than his percentage before the distribution (dropping from 85% to 84% or 99%).

To qualify, Morris would have to redeem 71 shares, since only that amount would drop his control percentage below 50% (14 of 29 or 48%). And since his percentage of control would have dropped from 85% to 48%, he would retain only 56% of the percentage he previously had (less than 80%).

Yet, even such a draconian sell-off as thus described would not be sufficient for the Code. Congress has taken the position that the stock ownership of persons other than oneself must be taken into account in determining one's control of a corporation. Under these so-called "attribution rules," a stockholder is deemed to control stock owned not only by himself, but also by his spouse, children, grandchildren, and parents. Furthermore, stock owned by partnerships, estates, trusts, and corporations affiliated with the stockholder may also be attributed to him. Thus, assuming that Lisa and Victor owned 10 of the remaining 15 shares of stock (with Brad owning the rest), Morris begins with 95% of the control and can qualify for a stock redemption only by selling all his shares to the corporation.

Complete Termination of Interest

Carried to its logical conclusion, even a complete redemption would not qualify for favorable tax treatment, since Lisa and Victor's stock would still be attributed to Morris, leaving him in control of 67 percent of the corporation's stock. Fortunately, however, Code Section 302(b)(3) provides for a distribution to be treated as a redemption if the stockholder's interest in the corporation is completely terminated. The attribution rules still apply under this section, but they may be waived if the stockholder files a written agreement with the IRS requesting such a waiver. In such agreement, Morris would be required to divest himself of any relationship with the corporation other than as a creditor and agree not to acquire any interest in the corporation for a period of 10 years.

In addition to the two safe harbors described in Sections 302(b)(2) and (3), the Code, in Section 302(b)(1), grants redemption treatment to distributions which are "not essentially equivalent to a dividend." Unlike the previous two sections, however, the Code does not spell out a mechanical test for this concept, leaving it to the facts and circumstances of the case. Given the obvious purpose of this transaction to transfer corporate assets to a stockholder on favorable terms, it is unlikely that the IRS would recognize any explanation, under this section, other than that of a dividend.

Thus, Morris's plan to turn in his stock and receive a tax-favored distribution for his retirement will not work out as planned, unless he allows the redemption of all his stock, resigns as a director, officer, employee, consultant, and so forth, and agrees to stay away for a period of 10 years. He may, however, accept a promissory note for all or part of the redemption proceeds and thereby become a creditor of the corporation. Worse yet, if Lisa obtained her shares from Morris within the 10 years preceding his retirement, even this plan will not work, unless the IRS can be persuaded that her acquisition of the shares was for reasons other than tax avoidance. It may be advisable to be sure she acquires her shares from the corporation rather than from Morris, although one can expect, given the extent of Morris's control over the corporation, that the IRS would fail to appreciate the difference.

Employee Stock Ownership Plans

Although Morris should be relatively happy with the knowledge that he may be able to arrange a complete redemption of his stock to fund his retirement and avoid being taxed as if he had received a dividend, he may still believe that the tax and economic effects of such a redemption are not ideal. Following such a plan to its logical conclusion, the corporation would borrow the money to pay for Morris's stock. Its repayments would be deductible only to the extent of the interest. At the same time, Morris would be paying a substantial capital gain tax to the government. Before settling for this result, Morris might well wish to explore ways to increase the corporation's deduction and decrease his own tax liability.

Such a result can be achieved through the use of an *Employee Stock Ownership Plan* (ESOP), a form of qualified deferred compensation plan as discussed earlier in the context of Brad's compensation package. Such a plan consists of a trust to which the corporation makes deductible contributions, either of shares of its own stock, or cash to be used to purchase such stock. Contributions are divided among the accounts of the corporation's employees (normally in proportion to their compensation for that year), and distributions are made to the employees at their retirement or earlier separation from the company (if the plan so allows). ESOPs have been seen as a relatively noncontroversial way for American employees to gain more control over their employers, and they have been granted a number of tax advantages not available to other qualified plans, such as pension or profit-sharing plans. One advantage is illustrated by the fact that a corporation can manufacture a deduction out of thin air by issuing new stock to a plan (at no cost to the corporation) and deducting the fair market value of the shares.

A number of attractive tax benefits would flow from Morris's willingness to sell his shares to an ESOP, established by his corporation, rather than to the corporation itself. Yet, before he could appreciate those benefits, Morris would have to be satisfied that some obvious objections would not make such a transaction inadvisable.

To begin with, the ESOP will have to borrow the money from a bank in the same way the corporation would; yet the ESOP has no credit record or assets to pledge as collateral. This is normally overcome, however, by the corporation's giving the bank a secured guarantee of the ESOP's obligation. Thus, the corporation ends up in the same economic position it would have enjoyed under a direct redemption.

Morris might also object to the level of control an ESOP might give to lower-level employees of Plant Supply. After all, his intent is to leave the corporation under the control of Lisa and Brad, but qualified plans must be operated on a nondiscriminatory basis. This objection can be addressed in a number of ways. First, the allocation of shares in proportion to compensation, along with standard vesting and forfeiture provisions, will tilt these allocations toward highly compensated, long-term employees, such as Lisa and Brad. Second, the shares are not allocated to the employees' accounts until they are paid for. While the bank is still being paid, an amount proportional to the remaining balance of the loan would be controlled by the plan trustees (chosen by management). Third, even after shares are allocated to employee accounts, in a closely held company, employees are allowed to vote those shares only on questions which require a two-thirds vote of the stockholders, such as a sale or merger of the corporation. On all other more routine questions (such as election of the board) the trustees still vote the shares. Fourth, upon an employee's retirement and before distribution of his shares, a closely held corporation must offer to buy back the distributed shares at fair market value. As a practical matter, most employees will accept such an offer, rather than moving into retirement with illiquid, closely held company stock.

If Morris accepts these arguments and opts for an ESOP buyout, the following benefits accrue. Rather than being able to deduct only the interest portion of its payments to the bank, the corporation may now contribute the amount of such payment to the plan as a fully deductible contribution to a qualified plan. The plan then forwards it to the bank as a payment of its obligation.

Furthermore, the Code allows an individual who sells stock of a corporation to the corporation's ESOP to defer paying any tax on the proceeds of such sale, if the proceeds are rolled over into purchases of securities. No tax is then paid until the purchased securities are ultimately resold. Thus, if Morris takes the money received from the ESOP and invests it in the stock market, he pays no tax until and unless he sells any of these securities, and then, only on those sold. In fact, if Morris purchases such securities and holds them until his death, his estate will receive a step-up in basis for such securities and thus avoid income tax on the proceeds of his company stock entirely (Exhibit 11.7).

ESTATE PLANNING

Contemplating the complete divorce from the Company—which will be necessary for Morris to achieve his tax-favored retirement—his thoughts may naturally turn to the tax consequences of his remaining employed by the company in some capacity until his death. Morris's lifelong efforts have made him a rather

EXHIBIT 11.7 Corporate redemption versus ESOP purchase.

CORPORATE REDEMPTION	ESOP PURCHASE
Only interest deductible	Principal and interest deductible
Capital gain	Gain deferred if proceeds rolled over

wealthy man, and he knows that the government will be looking to reap a rather large harvest from those efforts upon his death. He would no doubt be rather disheartened to learn that after a $600,000 exemption, the federal government will receive from 37 to 55% of the excess upon his death. Proper estate planning can double the amount of that grace amount by using the exemptions of both Morris and his wife, but the amount above $1,200,000 appears to be at significant risk.

Redemptions to Pay Death Taxes and Administrative Expenses

Since much of the money to fund this estate tax liability would come from redemption of company stock, if Morris had not previously cashed it in, Morris might well fear the combined effect of dividend treatment and estate taxation. Of course, if Morris's estate turned in all his stock for redemption at death, redemption treatment under Section 302(b)(3) would appear to be available, since death would appear to have cut off Morris's relationship with the company rather convincingly. However, if the effect of Morris's death on the company, or other circumstances, made a wholesale redemption inadvisable or impossible, Morris's estate could be faced with paying both income and estate tax on the full amount of the proceeds.

Fortunately for those faced with this problem, Code Section 303 allows capital gain treatment for a stock redemption, if the proceeds of the redemption do not exceed the amount necessary to pay the estate's taxes and those further expenses allowable as administrative expenses on the estate's tax return. To qualify for this treatment, the company's stock must equal or exceed 35% of the value of the estate's total assets. Since Morris's holdings of company stock will most likely exceed 35% of his total assets, if his estate finds itself in this uncomfortable position, it will at least be able to account for this distribution as a stock redemption instead of a dividend. This is much more important than it may first appear, and much more important than it would have been were Morris still alive. The effect, of course, is to allow payment at long-term capital gain rates (rather than ordinary income tax rates), for only the amount received in excess of the taxpayer's basis in the stock (rather than the entire amount of the distribution). Given that the death of the taxpayer increases his basis to the value at date of death, the effect of Section 303 is to eliminate all but that amount of gain occurring after death, thus eliminating virtually all income tax on the distribution.

Of course, assuring sufficient liquidity to pay taxes due upon death is one thing; controlling the amount of tax actually due is another. Valuation of a majority interest in a closely held corporation is far from an exact science, and the last thing an entrepreneur wishes is to have his or her spouse and other heirs engage in a valuation controversy with the IRS after his or her death. As a result, a number of techniques have evolved over the years which may have the effect of lowering the value of the stock to be included in the estate, or, at least, making such value more certain for planning purposes.

Estate Freezes

One technique that attained great popularity before attracting the attention of Congress is the "estate freeze." In its simplest form, the *estate freeze* involves a recapitalization of the corporation, through declaration of a stock dividend to all holders of common stock, in the form of a preferred stock issue. The preferred stock is structured with par value, liquidation, and dividend preferences, such that virtually all of the present value of the corporation resides in the preferred stock, upon its issuance. In our case, Morris would arrange this recapitalization while he owns virtually all the common stock. Thus, when the recapitalization is completed, virtually all of the corporation's value would be represented by the preferred stock Morris would then own.

Although the preferences and par value of the preferred stock have absorbed virtually all of the value of the corporation, the nature of the preferred stock is such that its value will not typically increase substantially, no matter how well the corporation may be doing. Although this recapitalization has taken virtually all the value out of the common stock, all increase in value due to future growth will nonetheless reside there.

This presents Morris with the opportunity and mechanism to make gifts of large amounts of the common stock without much gift tax impact. Because the value of the corporation has been absorbed by the preferred stock, Morris will be able to dispose of much of the common stock (to his daughter, for example) without exceeding the $10,000 per donee gift tax exemption ($20,000 if his wife agrees to have the gift count against her annual quota as well). How much of the stock he gives away depends only upon the amount of control he wishes to retain. Most likely he will wish to retain at least a majority interest in the corporation, while he is still actively involved in it. In any case, whatever portion of the common stock he gives away removes that portion of the corporation's future growth from his estate, "freezing" his estate's value at its current level. As growth accumulates in the common stock, it belongs to Lisa without ever having passed through Morris's estate.

The enormous potential for tax avoidance inherent in this technique caused Congress to enact Code Section 2036(c), the *antifreeze* provision. This provision purported to include in the estate of the donor, any portion of an enterprise given away by the donor, if the portion did not give a measure of control over the enterprise proportionate to its value. This section and the regulations proposed thereunder were both immensely complex and arguably overinclusive. Congress repealed this section shortly after its enactment. Replacing it is a series of Code sections, designed to ensure that the valuation of the common and preferred stock is based upon valid economic realities.

The corporation's postestate freeze common stock, for example, cannot be assigned less than 10% of the value of the corporation. Another example of this approach deals with the valuation of the preferred stock on the basis of its dividend preference. In earlier times, the dividend preference was calculated to enhance the value of the preferred stock, but it was commonly understood that the preference would not be paid. Each year, the directors (with the founder's tacit approval) would vote to skip that year's dividend, which in extreme circumstances was not even cumulative. Under the new rules, the preference must be cumulative, and, for all practical purposes, the dividend must be paid. This should not concern Morris, however, since he is already the recipient of a significant cash flow from the corporation and can adjust his compensation to accommodate this new imperative. It may even be a welcome supplement to his retirement income later on. However, Morris would be forced to forgo the benefits of subchapter S, since the corporation would now have more than one class of stock.

Preferred Stock Bailouts

The last step in the estate freeze scenario is the redemption of the preferred and common stock held by Morris, upon his eventual death. This ensures that there will be adequate liquid assets to pay the amount of estate tax which is assessed upon his estate, even with the lower valuation achieved. At this point, the wary taxpayer is presented with another trap that he must be careful to avoid.

If a corporation has significant earnings and profits, accumulated during a period of time when it was not treated as a subchapter S corporation, a dividend to its stockholders would not be deductible to the corporation and would be taxable income to its stockholders. If, instead of declaring a cash dividend, the corporation declared a stock dividend and distributed preferred stock, whose value approximated the accumulated earnings and profits of the corporation, the stockholders would then be presented with two alternative opportunities. They could sell the preferred stock to a third party and declare the difference between the sale price and the basis allocated to that stock as capital gain, or they could cause the corporation to redeem the preferred stock, again at capital gain rates. Both options convert ordinary dividend income to capital gain.

This apparent abuse was curbed by the enactment of Section 306 of the Code. This provision, as applied to the scenario just described, puts a "taint" on stock issued as a dividend on other stock (except for common on common), if the corporation making such distribution has earnings and profits at the time. Upon a sale of the tainted stock to a third party, the proceeds are taxed to the selling stockholder as receipt of a dividend, to the extent of the pro rata earnings and profits existing at the time of the stock's issuance. Thus, Section 306 does not impose a tax at the time of the stock dividend, but recovers tax on the forgone cash dividend at the time of the preferred stock "bailout." If the preferred stock is eventually redeemed by the corporation instead of being sold to a third party, the Code imposes an even more disfavored treatment. It taxes the proceeds as a dividend to the extent of the corporation's earnings and profits at the time of the redemption, not at the time of issuance.

Morris's corporation did not have much in the way of accumulated earnings and profits in its early years, because it distributed most of its earnings in the form of compensation. After the subchapter S election, all earnings and profits were immediately taxed to the stockholders, so Section 306 would not apply. Thus, Morris may not be overly concerned that the eventual redemption of his preferred stock would be taxed as a dividend. Fortunately for him, however, even if some untaxed earnings and profits remain, the Code specifically exempts a redemption from the operation of Section 306, if the redemption acts as a complete termination of the stockholder's interest in the corporation. Thus, the same analysis which freed Morris from dividend treatment upon a redemption, in the absence of an estate freeze, will free him from such treatment after a freeze, if both his preferred and any remaining common are redeemed together.

Buy-Sell Agreements

Having been assured that his stock would not be "tainted," if he were to attempt an estate freeze, Morris would likely be interested in an arrangement requiring the corporation or its stockholders to purchase whatever stock he may still hold at his death. Such an arrangement can be helpful with regard to both of Morris's estate-planning goals: setting a value for his stock that would not be challenged by the IRS and assuring sufficient liquidity to pay whatever estate taxes may ultimately be owed.

There are two basic variations of these agreements. Under the most common, Morris would agree with the corporation that it would redeem his shares upon his death, for a price derived from an agreed formula. The second variation would require one or more of the other stockholders of the corporation (e.g., Lisa) to make such a purchase. In both cases, in order for the IRS to respect the valuation placed upon the shares, it will be necessary for Morris to agree that he will not dispose of the shares during his lifetime without first offering them to the other party to his agreement at the formula price. Under such an arrangement, the shares will never be worth more to Morris than the formula price, so it can be argued that whatever higher price the IRS may calculate is irrelevant to him and his estate.

This argument had led some stockholders in the past to agree to formulas that artificially depressed the value of their shares, when the parties succeeding to power in the corporation were also the main beneficiaries of the stockholders' estates. Since any value forgone would end up in the hands of the intended beneficiary anyway, only the tax collector would be hurt. Although the IRS had long challenged this practice, this strategy was put to a formal end at the same time as the repeal of 2036(c), by requiring that the formula used result in a close approximation to fair market value.

Which of the two variations of the buy-sell agreement should Morris choose? If we assume for the moment that Morris owns 80 of the 100 outstanding shares and Lisa and Brad each own 10, a corporate redemption agreement leaves Lisa and Brad each owning half of the 20 outstanding shares remaining. If, however, Morris chooses a cross-purchase agreement with Lisa and Brad, each would purchase 40 of his shares upon his death, leaving them as owners of 50 shares each. Both agreements leave the corporation owned by Lisa and Brad in equal shares, so there does not appear to be any difference between them.

Once again, however, significant differences lie slightly below the surface. To begin with, many such agreements are funded by the purchase of a life insurance policy upon the life of the stockholder involved. If the corporation were to purchase this policy, the premiums would be nondeductible, resulting in additional taxable profit for the corporation. In a subchapter S corporation, such profit would pass through to the stockholders in proportion to their shares of stock in the corporation. In a C corporation, the additional profit would result in additional corporate tax. If, instead, Lisa and Brad bought policies covering their halves of the obligation to Morris's estate, they would be paying the premiums with after-tax dollars. Thus, a redemption agreement will cause Morris to share in the cost of the arrangement, while a cross-purchase agreement puts the entire onus on Lisa and Brad. This can, of course, be rationalized by arguing that they will ultimately reap the benefit of the arrangement by succeeding to the ownership of the corporation. Or, their compensation could be adjusted to cover the additional cost.

If the corporation is not an S corporation, however, there is an additional consideration that must not be overlooked. Upon Morris's death, the receipt of the insurance proceeds by the beneficiary of the life insurance will be excluded from taxable income. However, a C corporation is also subject to the corporate alternative minimum tax. Simply described, that tax guards against profitable corporations paying little or no tax by "overuse" of certain deductions and tax credits otherwise available. To calculate the tax, the corporation adds to its otherwise taxable income, certain "tax preferences" and then subtracts from that amount a $40,000 exemption for most corporations. The result is taxed at 20%. If that tax amount exceeds the corporate tax otherwise payable, the higher amount is paid. The result of this is additional tax for those corporations with substantial tax preferences.

Among those tax preferences is a concept known as *adjusted current earnings*. This concept adds as a tax preference, three quarters of the difference between the corporation's earnings for financial reporting purposes and the earnings otherwise reportable for tax purposes. A major source of such a difference would be the receipt of nontaxable income. And the receipt of life insurance proceeds is just such an event. Therefore, the receipt of a life insurance payout of sufficient size will ultimately be taxed, at least in part, to a C corporation, while it would be completely tax free to an S corporation or the remaining stockholders.

An additional factor pointing to the stockholder cross-purchase agreement rather than a corporate redemption is the effect this choice would have upon the taxability of a later sale of the corporation after Morris's death. If the corporation were to redeem Morris's stock, Lisa and Brad would each own one half of the corporation through their ownership of 10 shares each. If they then sold the company, they would be subject to tax on capital gain measured by the difference between the proceeds of the sale and their original basis in their shares. However, if Lisa and Brad purchased Morris's stock at his death, they would each own one half of the corporation through their ownership of 50 shares each. Upon a later sale of the company, their capital gain will be measured by the difference between the sale proceeds and their original basis in their shares plus the amount paid for Morris's shares. Every dollar paid to Morris lowers the taxable income received upon later sale. In a redemption agreement, these dollars are lost (Exhibit 11.8).

Pointing in the other direction, however, is the Section 306 taint, if Morris dies after attempting an estate freeze, at a time when the corporation had

EXHIBIT 11.8   Corporate redemption versus a cross-purchase agreement.

untaxed accumulated earnings and profits from its existence as a C corporation. Even though Morris contemplates a sale, which would completely terminate his interest in the corporation after his death, a cross-purchase would involve a purchase by a person (Lisa) whose ownership would be attributable to Morris under the attribution rules discussed previously. Although such attribution may be waived and a complete termination of interest achieved, for the purpose of removing the 306 taint in a redemption by the corporation, the Code does not allow such a waiver for 306 purposes, when the tainted stock is sold to Lisa. Thus, redemption is indicated after an estate freeze, if a C corporation's earnings and profits existed at the time of the freeze.

SPIN-OFFS AND SPLIT-UPS

Morris's pleasant reverie caused by thoughts of well-funded retirement strategies and clever estate plans was brought to a sudden halt, a mere two years after the acquisition of the molding operation, when it became clear that the internecine jealousies between Brad and Lisa were becoming unmanageable. Ruefully, Morris conceded that it was not unforeseeable that the manager of a significant part of his business would resent the presence of a rival who would be perceived as having attained her present position simply by dint of her relationship to the owner. This jealousy was, of course, inflamed by the thought that Lisa might succeed to Morris's stock upon his death and become Brad's boss.

After some months of attempting to mediate the many disputes between Lisa and Brad, which were merely symptoms of this underlying disease, Morris came to the conclusion that the corporation could not survive with both of them vying for power and influence. He determined that the only workable solution would be to break the two businesses apart once again, leaving the two rivals in charge of their individual empires, with no future binding ties.

Experienced in corporate transactions by this time, Morris gave the problem some significant thought and devised two alternate scenarios to accomplish his goal. Both scenarios began with the establishment of a subsidiary corporation, wholly owned by the currently existing company. The assets, liabilities, and all other attributes of the molding operation would then be transferred to this new subsidiary in exchange for its stock. At that point in the first scenario (known as a *spin-off*), the parent corporation would declare a dividend of all such stock to its current stockholders. Thus, Morris, Lisa, and Brad would own the former subsidiary in the same proportions in which they owned the parent. Morris, as the majority owner of the new corporation, could then give further shares to Brad, enter into a buy-sell agreement with him, or sell him some shares. In any case, upon Morris's death, Brad would succeed to unquestioned leadership in this corporation. Lisa would stay as a minority stockholder, or sell her shares to

Morris while he was alive, if she wished. Lisa would gain control of the former parent corporation upon Morris's death.

In the second scenario (known as a *split-off*), after the formation of the subsidiary, Brad would sell his shares of Plant Supply to that parent corporation in exchange for stock affording him control of the subsidiary. Lisa would remain the only minority stockholder of the parent corporation (Brad's interest having been removed) and would succeed to full ownership upon Morris's death through one of the mechanisms discussed earlier.

Unfortunately, when Morris brought his ideas to his professional advisers, he was faced with a serious tax objection. In both scenarios, he was told, the IRS would likely take the position that the issuance of the subsidiary's stock to its eventual holder (Morris in the spin-off and Brad in the split-off) was a taxable transaction, characterized as a dividend. After all, this plan could be used as another device to cash out the earnings and profits of a corporation, at favorable rates and terms. Instead of declaring a dividend of these profits, a corporation could spin off assets, with the fair market value of these profits, to a subsidiary. The shares of the subsidiary could then be distributed to its stockholders as a nontaxable stock dividend, and the stockholders could sell these shares and treat their profits as capital gain. The second scenario allows Brad to receive the subsidiary's shares and then make a similar sale of these shares, at favorable rates and terms.

As a result, the Code characterizes the distribution of the subsidiary's shares to the parent's stockholders as a dividend, taxable to the extent of the parent's earnings and profits at the time of the distribution. This would certainly inhibit Morris, if he was the owner of a profitable C corporation. It would be less of a concern if his corporation were operating as an S corporation, although even then, he would have to be concerned about undistributed earnings and profits dating from before the S election.

Recognizing that not all transactions of this type are entered into to disguise the declaration of a dividend, the Code does allow spin-offs and split-offs to take place tax-free, under the limited circumstances described in Section 355. These circumstances track the scenarios concocted by Morris, but are limited to circumstances in which both the parent and subsidiary will be conducting an active trade or business after the transaction. Moreover, each trade or business must have been conducted for a period exceeding five years prior to the distribution and cannot have been acquired in a taxable transaction during such time. Since Morris's corporation acquired the molding business only two years previously, and such transaction was not tax-free, the benefits of Section 355 are not available now. Short of another solution, it would appear that Morris will have to live with the bickering of Brad and Lisa for another three years.

SALE OF THE CORPORATION

Fortunately for Morris, another solution was not long in coming. Within months of the failure of his proposal to split up the company, Morris was approached by the president of a company in a related field, interested in purchasing Plant Supply. Such a transaction was very intriguing to Morris. He had worked very hard for many years and would not be adverse to an early retirement. A purchase such as this would relieve him of all his concerns over adequate liquidity for his estate and strategies for funding his retirement. He could take care of both Lisa and Victor with the cash he would receive, and both Lisa and Brad would be free to deal with the acquirer, regarding future employment and to collect on their equity.

However, Morris knew better than to get too excited over this prospect before consulting with his tax advisers. And his hesitance turned out to be justified. Unless a deal was appropriately structured, Morris was staring at a significant tax bite, both on the corporate and the stockholder levels.

Morris knew from his experience with the molding plant that a corporate acquisition can be structured in three basic ways: a merger, a sale of stock, and a purchase of assets. In a *merger,* the target corporation disappears into the acquirer by operation of law, and the former stockholders of the target receive consideration from the acquirer. In the *sale of stock,* the stockholders sell their shares directly to the acquiring corporation. In a *sale of assets,* the target sells its assets (and most of its liabilities) to the acquirer, and the proceeds of the sale are then distributed to the target's stockholders, through the liquidation of the target. The major theme of all three of these scenarios involves the acquirer forming a subsidiary corporation to act as the acquirer in the transaction.

In each case, the difference between the proceeds received by the target's stockholders and their basis in the target's stock would be taxable as capital gain. Morris was further informed that this tax at the stockholder level could be avoided, if these transactions qualified under the complex rules that define tax-free reorganizations. In each case, one of the requirements would be that the target stockholders receive stock of the acquirer rather than cash. As the acquirer in this case was closely held, and there was no market for its stock, Morris was determined to insist upon cash. He thus accepted the idea of paying tax on the stockholder level.

Morris was quite surprised, however, to learn that he might also be exposed to corporate tax on the growth in the corporation's assets over its basis in them, if they were deemed to have been sold as a result of the acquisition transaction. For one thing, he had been under the impression that a corporation was exempt from such tax, if it sold its assets as part of the liquidation process. He was disappointed to learn that this exemption was another victim of the repeal of the

General Utilities doctrine. He was further disappointed, when reminded that even subchapter S corporations recognize all "built-in gain" that existed at the time of their subchapter S election, if their assets are sold within 10 years after their change of tax status.

As a result of the previous considerations, Morris was determined to avoid structuring the sale of his corporation as a sale of its assets and liabilities, in order to avoid any tax on the corporate level. He was already determined not to structure it as a sale of stock by the target stockholders, because he was not entirely sure Brad could be trusted to sell his shares. If he could structure the transaction at the corporate level, he would not need Brad's minority vote to accomplish it. Thus, after intensive negotiations, he was pleased that the acquiring corporation had agreed to structure the acquisition as a merger between Plant Supply and a subsidiary of the acquirer (to be formed for the purpose of the transaction). All stockholders of Plant Supply would receive a cash down payment and a five-year promissory note from the parent acquirer in exchange for their stock.

Yet even this careful preparation and negotiation leaves Morris, Lisa, and Brad in jeopardy of unexpected tax exposure. To begin with, if the transaction remains as negotiated, the IRS will likely take the position that the assets of the target corporation have been sold to the acquirer, thus triggering tax at the corporate level. In addition, the target's stockholders will have to recognize, as proceeds of the sale of their stock, both the cash and the fair market value of the promissory notes, in the year of the transaction, even though they will receive payments on the notes over a period of five years.

Under the General Utilities doctrine, it was necessary for a corporation that was selling substantially all its assets, to adopt a "plan of liquidation" prior to entering into the sale agreement, in order to avoid taxation at the corporate level. The repeal of the doctrine may have left the impression that the adoption of such a liquidation plan is unnecessary, because the sale will be taxed at the corporate level in any event. Yet, the Code still requires such a liquidation plan, if the stockholders wish to recognize notes, received upon the dissolution of the target corporation, on the installment basis. Moreover, the liquidation of the corporation must be completed within 12 months of adoption of the liquidation plan.

Thus, Morris's best efforts may still have led to disaster. Fortunately, a small adjustment to the negotiated transaction can cure most of these problems. Through an example of corporate magic known as the *reverse triangular merger*, the newly formed subsidiary of the acquirer may disappear into Morris's target corporation, but the target's stockholders can still be jettisoned for cash, leaving the acquirer as the parent. In such a transaction, the assets of the target have not been sold; they remain owned by the original corporation. Only the target's stockholders have changed. In effect, the parties have sold stock without the necessity of getting Brad's approval. Because the assets have not changed hands, there is no tax at the corporate level. In addition, since the target corporation has not liqui-

EXHIBIT 11.9   A reverse triangular merger.

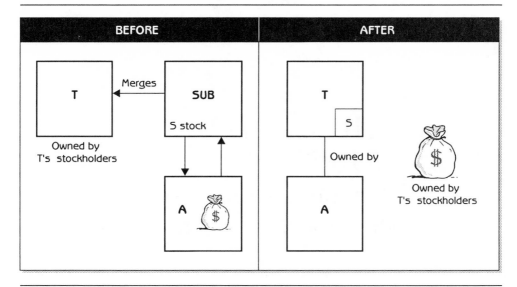

dated, no plan of liquidation is required, and the target stockholders may elect installment treatment, as if they had sold their shares directly (Exhibit 11.9).

CONCLUSION

Perhaps no taxpayers will encounter quite as many cataclysmic tax decisions, in as short a time, as did Morris and Plant Supply. Yet, Morris's experience serves to illustrate that tax issues lurk in almost every major business decision made by a corporation's management. Many transactions can be structured to avoid unnecessary tax expense, if proper attention is paid to tax implications. To be unaware of these issues is to play the game without knowing the rules.

FOR FURTHER READING

Herwitz, David R., *Business Planning*, temporary 2d ed. (Mineola, NY: The Foundation Press, 1984).

Painter, William H., *Business Planning*, 2d ed. (St. Paul, MN: West Publishing Co., 1984).

Scholes, Myron S. and Mark A. Wolfson, *Taxes and Business Strategy* (Englewood Cliffs, NJ: Prentice-Hall, 1992).

Sommerfeld, Ray M. and Sally M. Jones, *Federal Taxes and Management Decisions* (Homewood, IL: Richard D. Irwin, Inc., 1991).

12 THE GLOBAL BUSINESS

Eugene E. Comiskey
Charles W. Mulford

EMERGENCE OF MANAGERIAL AND FINANCIAL REPORTING ISSUES AT SUCCESSIVE STAGES IN THE FIRM'S LIFE CYCLE

Fashionhouse Furniture started as a small Southern retailer of furniture acquired mainly in bordering southeastern states. With a growing level of both competition and affluence in its major market areas, Fashionhouse decided that its future lay in a niche strategy involving specialization in a high-quality line of Scandinavian furniture. Its suppliers were located mainly in Denmark, and they followed the practice of billing Fashionhouse in the Danish krone. Title would typically pass to Fashionhouse when the goods were delivered to the dock in Copenhagen. Payment for the goods would normally be required within periods ranging from 30 to 90 days. As its business expanded and prospered, Fashionhouse became convinced that it needed to exercise greater control over its furniture supply. This was accomplished through the purchase of its principal Danish supplier. As this supplier also had a network of retail units in Denmark, the manufacturing operations in Denmark supplied both the local Danish market as well as the U.S. requirements of Fashionhouse.

More recently, Fashionhouse has been searching for ways to increase manufacturing efficiency and to lower product costs. It is contemplating relocation of part of its manufacturing activity to a country with an ample and low-cost supply of labor. However, it has noted that most such countries experience very high levels of inflation. Moreover, Fashionhouse has also become aware that, in some of the countries being considered, business practices are occasionally employed that are a source of concern to Fashionhouse management. In some cases, the practices raise issues that extend beyond simple ethical considerations. Fashionhouse management is still attempting to determine how to evaluate and deal with some of the identified managerial and financial issues associated with this contemplated move.

Each of the new stages in the evolution of the Fashionhouse strategy creates new issues that have important implications for both management and financial reporting. The evolution from a strictly domestic operation to one involving the foreign purchase of goods thrusts Fashionhouse into the global marketplace, with all of the attendant risks and rewards. The major issues implicit in the Fashionhouse scenario outlined earlier are identified here and are discussed and illustrated in the balance of this chapter.

1. Fashionhouse incurs a foreign-currency obligation when it begins to acquire furniture from Danish suppliers. A decrease in the value of the dollar between purchase and payment date increases the dollars required to discharge the Danish krone obligation and results in a foreign currency transaction loss.

    Financial reporting issue: How are the foreign currency obligations recorded in the Fashionhouse books, which are maintained in U.S. dollars?

    Management issue: Are there methods available to avoid the currency risk associated with foreign sourcing and should they be employed?

2. Purchase of the Danish supplier requires that it henceforth be consolidated into the financial statements of Fashionhouse and its U.S. operations.

    Financial reporting issues: (a) How are the Danish statements converted from the krone in order to consolidate them with the U.S. dollar statements of Fashionhouse? (b) What differences in accounting practices, if any, exist between Denmark and the United States and what must be done about such differences.

    Management issues: (a) Is there currency risk associated with the Danish subsidiary comparable to that previously described with the foreign purchase transactions? Are there methods available to avoid the currency risk–associated ownership of a foreign subsidiary and should they be employed? (b) How will the financial aspects of the management of the Danish subsidiary be evaluated in view of (1) the availability of two different sets of financial statements, that is, those expressed in krone and those in U.S. dollars, and (2) the fact that most of its sales are to its U.S. parent, that is, Fashionhouse.

3. Relocation of manufacturing to a high inflation and low labor-cost country.

    Financial reporting issues: How will inflation impact upon the local country financial statements and their usefulness in evaluating the performance of the company and its management?

Management issues: (a) Are their special risks associated with locating in a highly inflationary country and how can they be managed? (b) What are the restrictions on U.S. business practices related to dealing with business and governmental entities in other countries?

For clarification, and to indicate their order in the subsequent discussion, the issues just raised are enumerated again, without distinction this time, between those that are mainly financial reporting and those that are essentially managerial issues:

1. Financial reporting of foreign-currency denominated transactions.
2. Risk-management alternatives for foreign-currency denominated transactions.
3. Translation of the statements of foreign subsidiaries.
4. Managing the currency risk of foreign subsidiaries.
5. Differences in U.S. and foreign accounting policies.
6. Evaluation of the performance of foreign subsidiaries and their management.
7. Impact of inflation on the financial performance of foreign subsidiaries.
8. U.S. government restrictions on business practices associated with foreign subsidiaries and governments.

Financial Reporting of Foreign-Currency Denominated Transactions

When a U.S. company buys from or sells to a foreign firm, a key issue is the currency in which the transaction is to be denominated. In the case of Fashionhouse, its purchases from Danish suppliers were invoiced to Fashionhouse in the Danish krone. This creates the risk of a *foreign exchange transaction loss* should the dollar fall in value, or a gain should the dollar increase, between the time that furniture is dropped on the dock in Copenhagen and the required payment date. That is, the Fashionhouse *dollar* cost for the furniture will be more than the dollar obligation originally recorded. Fashionhouse would be said to have *liability exposure* in the Danish krone. If, instead, Fashionhouse had been invoiced in the U.S. dollar, then it would have had no currency risk. Rather, its Danish supplier would bear the currency risk associated with having a claim to U.S. dollars, in the form of an account receivable. If the dollar were to decrease in value, the Danish supplier would incur a foreign exchange transaction loss, or a gain should the dollar increase in value. A summary of foreign exchange gains and losses, by type of exposure, due to exchange rate movements is shown in Exhibit 12.1.

To illustrate the computational aspects of the earlier discussion, and the nature of exchange rates, assume that Fashionhouse recorded a 100,000 krone

EXHIBIT 12.1   Type of foreign currency exposure.

Movement of Foreign Currency	Exposure	
	Asset	**Liability**
Appreciates	Gain	Loss
Depreciates	Loss	Gain

purchase when the exchange rate for the krone was $.178.[1] That is, it takes 17.8 cents to purchase one krone.

The exchange rate is $.182 when the account payable from the purchase is paid.

Dollar amount of obligation at payment date, 100,000 × .182	$18,200
Dollar amount of obligation at purchase date, 100,000 × .178	17,800
Foreign exchange transaction loss	$ 400

The dollar depreciated against the krone over the period of time when Fashionhouse had an obligation in the krone. As a result, it took $400 more to discharge the obligation than the amount at which it was originally recorded by Fashionhouse.

If the foreign exchange losses incurred were significant, it might prove difficult to pass on this increased cost to Fashionhouse customers, and it could cause its furniture to be somewhat less competitive than that offered by other U.S. retailers with domestic suppliers. Fashionhouse might attempt to avoid the currency risk by convincing its Danish suppliers to invoice it in the dollar. However, this means that the Danish suppliers would bear the currency risk. Experience indicates that such suppliers would expect to be compensated for bearing this risk, and would charge more for their products.[2] An alternative approach, the use of hedging transactions, is the more common method employed to manage the risk of foreign currency exposure.

RISK MANAGEMENT ALTERNATIVES FOR FOREIGN-CURRENCY DENOMINATED TRANSACTIONS[3]

Hedging is designed to protect the dollar value of a foreign-currency asset position, or to hold constant the dollar burden of a foreign-currency liability. At the same time, the volatility of a firm's earnings stream is also reduced. This is accomplished by maintaining an offsetting position that produces gains when the asset or liability position is incurring losses, and vice versa. Such offsetting positions may be created as a result of arrangements involving internal offsetting balances, created through operational activities, or they may entail specialized external transactions with financial firms or markets.

Hedging with Internal Offsetting Balances

UAL Corporation (the parent company of United Airlines) disclosed its efforts to limit exposure to exchange-rate fluctuations in its 1993 Annual Report (p. 23). United's principal source of exposure was from unhedged debt denominated in the Japanese yen. The aggregate amount of these yen-denominated liabilities exceeded its yen-denominated assets. "During 1993, United increased the amount of its yen-denominated assets to minimize the impact of foreign exchange rate changes on reported financial results." Thus, UAL reduced its exchange risk with internal offsetting balances.

California First Bank (now Union Bank) provides an example of hedging with offsetting balances created through internal operational activities. In its 1987 Annual Report (p. 20), California First reported that it had incurred a 20 million Swiss franc obligation. The dollar valuation of the obligation—the number of dollars required to buy the francs to pay off the debt—increased to $15,494,000 at the end of 1987 from $12,281,000 at the end of 1986. However, the transaction loss that this liability growth produced was offset by a gain on an offsetting (that is, hedge) transaction. As the 1987 Annual Report disclosed (p. 20): "A transaction has been entered into for the same foreign currency, with a similar term and principal amount which eliminates any significant earnings impact. . . ." California First booked a Swiss franc loan (an asset balance), an operational activity for the Bank, to hedge its liability exposure in the Swiss franc. If the franc appreciates against the dollar, then the asset balance produces a gain that offsets a loss, due to expansion in the dollar valuation of the Swiss franc liability.

Like California First, Federal Express created a debt hedge, the debt denominated in their case in the Japanese yen, through a creative structuring of business transactions with its own customers. Its 1989 Annual Report disclosed (p. 35): "To minimize foreign exchange risk on the term loan, the Company has commitments from certain Japanese customers to purchase a minimum level of freight services through 1993." As the yen appreciates, that is, the dollar devalues against the yen, the dollar burden of the Federal Express yen debt increases and a transaction loss results. However, this loss is offset by the increased dollar value of the stream of yen receipts from the freight-service contracts.[4] If the yen depreciates, a gain on the debt will be offset by losses on the service contracts. A summary of the operation of this hedge is provided in Exhibit 12.2.

California First and Federal Express both employed arrangements with their customers in order to create hedges. On occasion, a *natural* hedge will exist due to offsetting balances that result from ordinary business transactions with no special arrangements being required. For example, Lyle Shipping, a Scottish firm, had

EXHIBIT 12.2   Offsetting gains and losses produced by Federal Express hedge.

Movement of Foreign Currency	Change in Dollar Value of the Loan (Liability)	Change in Dollar Value of the Revenue (Asset)
Appreciates	Increases (loss)	Increases (gain)
Depreciates	Decreases (gain)	Decreases (loss)

borrowings in the U.S. dollar. An increase in the value of the dollar would increase the pounds required to repay Lyle's dollar debt and result in a transaction loss. However, because Lyle's ships were chartered out at fixed rates in U.S. dollars, there would be an offsetting increase in the pound value of future lease receipts— a gain.[5] A similar natural hedge was generally held to exist for Australian mining companies that produce products priced in U.S. dollars. Should the U.S. dollar depreciate, the exposure to shrinkage in the Australian dollar value of receipts (U.S. dollar asset exposure) was offset by similar shrinkage in the Australian dollar value of U.S. dollar debt (U.S. dollar liability exposure).[6]

Fashionhouse would probably find it difficult to duplicate the hedging techniques used by California First and Federal Express. Circumstances giving rise to a natural hedge, as in the case of Lyle Shipping, may or may not exist. It might have some capacity to hedge by applying the method of *leading and lagging*. This method involves matching the cash flows associated with foreign currency payables and receivables by speeding up or slowing down their payment or receipt. It is more likely that a specialized external transaction, such as an exchange-traded or privately negotiated hedging instrument would be used to hedge currency risks.

Hedging with Specialized External Transactions

The range of possibilities here includes forward contracts to buy or sell currencies in the future at fixed exchange rates, foreign currency swaps, foreign currency futures, options, and options on futures. The forwards, swaps, and over-the-counter options have the advantage of making it possible to tailor the hedge to meet individual requirements in terms of amounts and dates. The exchange-traded futures and options have liquidity and a ready market, but a limited number of dates and contract sizes. Examples of the use of both classes of instruments, privately negotiated and exchange traded, are discussed next.

Forward Exchange Contracts

AMR Corporation issued $82.4 million of 9.2% foreign-currency debt in 1982. Through forward exchange contracts, AMR contracted, at a fixed price, to buy the foreign currency required to pay off its foreign currency debt in the future.

Initially, $26.2 million of the amount was hedged with a privately negotiated forward exchange contract. In 1988, the remainder of the debt was hedged. AMR reported in its 1989 Annual Report (p. 51) that "The overall effective interest rate for all the notes during the term of the hedge contracts was 13.5%."

Prior to 1988, when all of the debt became hedged, AMR was still exposed to significant currency risk. AMR's 1987 income statement included $32 million of foreign currency exchange losses; an undisclosed portion of the loss no doubt resulted from the unhedged portion of the 9.2% notes. Notice that, as a result of the hedging, the effective interest cost goes from 9.2 to 13.5%. This cost increase results from the premium over the spot value of the foreign currency that AMR agreed to pay in order to fix the future cost of acquiring the foreign currency to repay the debt.[7] Through fully hedging its foreign-currency debt, AMR incurs a significant increase in overall borrowing cost, that is, from 9.2 to 13.5%. However, it also avoids any future transaction losses should the dollar depreciate against the foreign currencies in which its debt is denominated.

Ingersoll-Rand also reports the use of forward contracts for hedging purposes in its 1995 Annual Report (p. 43). Related to the earlier discussion on hedging with internal offsetting balances, the Company considers hedging after it ". . . first attempts to hedge transaction exposures through natural offsets. To the extent this is not practicable, major exposure areas which are considered for hedging include foreign-currency denominated receivables and payables, intercompany loans, firm committed transactions, anticipated sales and purchases and dividends related to foreign subsidiaries." As part of its required financial instrument's disclosures, Ingersoll-Rand detailed in U.S. dollars the forward contracts to buy and sell foreign currencies as shown in Exhibit 12.3.

Ingersoll-Rand also notes the following about its use of forward contracts:

1. The contracts do not create risk for the company due to exchange-rate movement because the gains and losses on the forward contracts are offset by losses and gains on the assets, liabilities, or other transactions being hedged.

2. The counterparties to the forward contracts are major international financial institutions with strong credit ratings and, as a result, there is no significant credit risk to the Company. That is, there is every reason to expect that the counterparties will perform in accordance with the terms of the forward contracts.

Option Contracts

AMR, the parent of American Airlines, uses option contracts in a portion of its currency-hedging activities. American entered into put option agreements dur-

**EXHIBIT 12.3   Forward contracts outstanding by currency:
Ingersoll-Rand (in millions).**

	1995		1994	
	Buy	**Sell**	**Buy**	**Sell**
Austrian schilling	$ 9.6	$ 1.6	$ 3.5	$ .3
Belgian franc	3.2	8.3	.3	1.4
Canadian dollar	10.4	6.6	2.4	13.3
Deutsche mark	10.2	135.6	8.4	81.8
Dutch guilder	20.2	7.8	—	1.3
French franc	24.1	38.5	3.3	10.6
Italian lira	41.1	6.9	34.9	2.3
Japanese yen	19.0	2.0	3.4	19.2
Pound sterling	25.1	128.8	59.1	55.5
South African rand	3.5	12.8	6.6	14.4
Other	6.5	7.6	8.5	13.4
Total	$172.9	$365.5	$130.4	$213.5

SOURCE: Ingersoll-Rand Company, annual report, December 1995, p. 43.

ing 1995 in a number of different currencies. The option agreements are denominated in the same foreign currencies in which projected foreign cash flows are expected to be denominated. The agreements extend out to 1998 and protect American against a reduction in the dollar value of these cash flows.

American's put options give it the right to sell the foreign currencies at a fixed price, termed the *strike* price. Should the foreign currencies in which the cash flows are denominated fall in value, then the dollar value of the expected cash inflows will be reduced and a loss will result. However, the put option will produce an offsetting gain. This results from the fact that the right to sell a foreign currency at a fixed price becomes more valuable when the market value of that currency is falling. For example, holding a common stock put option to sell IBM shares at $150 clearly becomes more valuable if IBM drops to $100. The same holds true for currency options.

If American had obligations denominated in foreign currencies, instead of assets, then creating a hedge with an option contract would call for investing in a *call* option. The call option gives the holder the right to purchase the needed foreign currency at a fixed strike price. If the foreign currency increases in price, then the option increases in value. A hedge is created because the gain on the option contract would be offset by a loss on the increase in the dollar valuation of the obligation, resulting from the decline in the value of the dollar.

Analog Devices provides a further example of the use of options for hedging purposes. Its 1995 Annual Report (p. 31) indicates that currency options are used to hedge "certain probable anticipated, but not firmly committed, foreign currency transactions related to the sale of product during the ensuing nine months." Because the sales will produce cash inflows denominated in a foreign currency, Analog Devices would invest in put options. This provides the Company with the right to sell foreign currency at an agreed strike price. If the dollar strengthens, that is, the foreign currency depreciates, then the dollar value of the cash inflow from the eventual sale would decline. However, this loss would be offset by the gain in value of the option. If instead the dollar weakens, that is, the foreign currency appreciates, then the option may expire without value. In this latter case, Analog Devices notes the following: "Conversely, when the dollar weakens, the increase in value of the future currency cash flows is reduced only by the premium paid to acquire the options."

With options, the offsetting gain and loss characteristic of a hedge results only when the foreign currency moves either up with a call or down with a put. In the Analog Devices example, asset exposure is hedged with a put option. Only when the foreign currency depreciates, is a loss—a decline in dollar value of the foreign-currency cash inflow—offset by a gain on the option contract.

A summary of the hedging performance of puts and calls is provided in Exhibit 12.4.

Futures Contracts

Southmark Corporation's 1987 Annual Report (p. 40) reported the existence of notes payable denominated in the Swiss franc. Across 1987, the Swiss franc appreciated against the dollar, and the dollar valuation of the notes went up sharply. However, Southmark reported (p. 41) that "Southmark uses Swiss franc futures contracts to hedge its exposure to foreign currency fluctuations with respect to its Swiss franc-denominated debt. The gains or losses from this activity are recognized concurrently with, and offset, the gains or losses from fluctuations in the Swiss franc debt liability."

EXHIBIT 12.4   Hedging performance of currency options.

	Movement of Foreign Currency			
	Appreciates		Depreciates	
	Asset Exposure			
Option Position	**Option**	**Asset**	**Option**	**Asset**
Put	Loss°	Gain	Gain	Loss
	Liability Exposure			
	Option	**Liability**	**Option**	**Liability**
Call	Gain	Loss	Loss°	Gain

° Loss or expense of the option is limited to the option premium paid.

The currency-futures contracts used by Southmark are an exchange-traded instrument (International Monetary Market at the Chicago Mercantile Exchange in the United States). The standard Swiss franc futures contract is for 125,000 francs. A margin deposit is required for each contract and a round-trip commission is charged. A futures contract can either be bought, a long position, or sold, a short position. A gain results if a futures contract is bought and the Swiss franc appreciates; a loss is incurred if the Swiss franc depreciates. If, initially, a contract is sold, then a loss results from appreciation of the franc. A loss is incurred because the position must be closed out by subsequently buying a contract to cover the short position at a now increased value for the franc. A gain is created, when the franc falls in value, by covering the short position at a reduced cost.

Southmark incurs a transaction loss on its Swiss franc notes if the franc appreciates against the dollar. To hedge its liability, Southmark needs an offsetting asset position in the Swiss franc futures contract. This position will produce an offsetting gain in the event of appreciation in the franc. If, instead of notes payable, Southmark had notes receivable in the Swiss franc, then a short position would be taken in the futures market. A falling franc means that the short position can be closed out at a price that is less than the price at which the contract was originally sold, when the short position was established.[8] A summary of the offsetting gains and losses of hedges of both asset and liability exposure with futures positions is summarized in Exhibit 12.5.

The hedging positions, long versus short, are determined by whether an asset or liability position exists in the foreign currency. Where an asset position exists, then currency futures are sold; that is, a short position is established. The opposite position, long, is established when a hedge of a liability position is to be established. Consider the short position designed to hedge asset exposure. When the foreign currency appreciates, a gain results because an asset is held in an appreciating currency. The asset is worth more in dollars. However, a loss results on the short position. The short position must be closed out by buying a futures

EXHIBIT 12.5   Hedging performance of currency futures.

	Movement of Foreign Currency			
	Appreciates		Depreciates	
	Asset Exposure			
Futures Position	**Futures**	**Asset**	**Futures**	**Asset**
Short	Loss	Gain	Gain	Loss
	Liability Exposure			
	Futures	**Liability**	**Futures**	**Liability**
Long	Gain	Loss	Loss	Gain

contract. Since the price of the futures contract goes up with the increase in the value of the foreign currency, it costs more to close the short position than the value of the futures contract sale when the hedge was established.

A summary of the appropriate hedge positions based upon the type of exposure, that is, asset or liability, and the instrument being used, is provided in Exhibit 12.6.

The information in Exhibit 12.6 indicates how a number of different instruments can be used to hedge currency risk. However, management must decide whether, and to what extent, to hedge such risk. All combinations are observed in practice, from the full hedging of all exposure to leaving all exposure unhedged. An informative disclosure, by Armstrong World Industries, of the amount of currency exposure hedged and unhedged, is provided in Exhibit 12.7. Armstrong prefaces the schedule with the statement: "The company normally hedges cash flow exposures up to one year" (1995 annual report, p. 31).

Some firms (Southmark was such an example) create foreign-currency exposure as a means of taking a position on the movement of exchange rates.[9] The decision to hedge or not will be influenced, at least in part, by the attitude of management towards the risk associated with foreign-currency exposure. Other things equal, a highly risk-averse management will be more inclined to hedge all currency-related risk. If hedging is instituted, the choice of instruments will depend on such matters as flexibility and the capacity to tailor the instruments to hedging needs, the liquidity of the instruments, documentation requirements, tax considerations, cost, and so forth. An extensive technical consideration of these issues is beyond the scope of this chapter.[10] However, the following section provides examples from recent annual reports of factors that influenced and shaped hedging policies.

INFLUENCES ON THE HEDGING DECISION

A number of factors that influence hedging policy and its implementation are listed here. Although not listed as a separate category, the hedging instruments

EXHIBIT 12.6   Foreign currency exposure and hedging decisions: Forwards, options, and futures.

Hedging Instrument	Exposure	
	Asset	Liability
Forward contract	Sell foreign currency	Buy foreign currency
Option	Buy put options	Buy call options
Futures	Sell futures contract	Buy futures contracts

EXHIBIT 12.7   Hedged versus unhedged currency exposure: Armstrong World Industries.

Foreign Currency Exposure (Millions)	Gross	Net Hedge	Unhedged
Canadian dollar	$ 30.0	$15.3	$14.7
Italian lira to French franc	23.0	10.2	12.8
French franc	22.4	22.4	—
German mark	15.0	7.9	7.1
Irish pound to British pound	8.9	—	8.9
Spanish peseta to French franc	8.0	4.0	4.0
Other	24.0	2.5	21.5
Total	$131.3	$62.3	$69.0

SOURCE: Armstrong World Industries, annual report, December 1995, p. 31.

used are disclosed in many of the examples. The focus here is on policies that guide the hedging of *transaction* exposure. Hedging policies dealing with the *translation* exposure associated with foreign subsidiaries are discussed later in the chapter.

Purpose

Ralston Purina Company 1995 Annual Report (p. 43)

The Company enters into foreign exchange contracts and options to mitigate the *economic exposure* to changes in exchange rates. The Company views these exposures as arising from three major areas: (a) non-U.S. dollar *cash flows* to the U.S. from subsidiaries expected within a year or less, (b) *cash flows* to a foreign country in a currency other than the subsidiary's functional currency, and (c) future *cash flows* at the operating margin level (all italics were added).

Armstrong World Industries 1995 Annual Report (p. 31)

The Company selectively uses foreign currency forward and option contracts to offset the effects of exchange rate changes on *cash flow exposures* (italics added) in foreign currencies. These exposures include firm or anticipated intercompany trade accounts, royalties, service fees, dividends, intercompany loans, and third party sales or payments.

The Procter & Gamble Company 1996 Annual Report (p. 36)

The primary purpose of the Company's foreign currency hedging activities is to protect against the volatility associated with local currency purchase transactions.

Amoco Corporation (p. 52)

The Corporation has entered into foreign currency forward contracts to manage its foreign currency exposure associated with the construction of a joint-venture plant in Singapore.

Fluor Corporation 1995 Annual Report (p. 40)

The company enters into forward exchange contracts to hedge foreign currency transactions and not to engage in currency speculation.

Hedging Cost

Apple Computer, Inc. 1995 Annual Report (p. 26)

To reduce the costs associated with these ongoing foreign exchange hedging programs, the Company also regularly sells foreign exchange option contracts and enters into certain other foreign exchange transactions.

Baxter International 1995 Annual Report (p. 39)

The company routinely assesses the costs and benefits of various hedging strategies and implements those strategies that are considered appropriate and cost effective.

Compaq Computer Corporation 1995 10-K Report (p. 15)

For certain of its markets, particularly Latin America, the company has determined that ongoing hedging of its U.S. dollar net monetary assets is not cost effective and instead attempts to minimize currency exposure risk through working capital management.

Hedge Duration

Amgen 1995 Annual Report (p. 34)

. . . it has purchased foreign currency option and forward contracts to hedge possible reductions in values of anticipated foreign currency cash flows over the next 12 months.

Amoco Corporation 1995 Annual Report (p. 52)

The hedge contracts generally have the same maturities as the related debt and commitments.

BMC Software, Inc. 1996 Annual Report (p. 36)

The term of the forward contracts is generally 30 days. . . . The term of the option contracts is rarely more than one year.

TRANSLATION OF THE STATEMENTS OF FOREIGN SUBSIDIARIES

A number of new financial and managerial issues were added to the Fashionhouse agenda when it purchased its former Danish supplier. *Transactional* issues continue to the extent that (1) some of its purchases continue to be made from foreign suppliers and (2) the foreign suppliers continue to invoice Fashionhouse in the foreign currency. In addition, Fashionhouse's Danish subsidiary may also have its own transactional exposure. Since the Danish company is a wholly owned subsidiary, U.S. GAAP requires consolidation. However, the financial statements of the Danish subsidiary are in the Danish krone. This introduces a *translational* issue; the Danish subsidiary statements must be restated into dollars before their consolidation with Fashionhouse, the parent, can take place. To the extent that the accounting practices used in preparing a subsidiary's statements differ from those of their parent, then the subsidiary's statements would need to be restated to conform to the accounting practices of the parent.[11] This would, of course, be the case with Fashionhouse and its Danish subsidiary. The issue of international GAAP differences is discussed in a subsequent section of this chapter.

All-Current Translation Procedure

The basic formula used to translate the statements of a foreign subsidiary is quite simple:

Foreign currency balance × exchange rate = translated balance.

In the typical case, under U.S. GAAP, balance-sheet and income-statement accounts are translated as follows:

1. All assets and liabilities in the balance sheet are translated at the exchange rate at the balance-sheet date.
2. Paid-in-capital is translated at the exchange rate existing at the date of the share issue.
3. Income-statement accounts are translated at the average exchange rate for the reporting period, unless revenues or expenses are distributed across the reporting period in a distinctly uneven manner.

The above procedure is normally referred to as the *all-current* method. The all-current procedure is illustrated in Exhibit 12.8:

1. Foreign Sub is formed on January 1, 20X1 with an initial funding from a stock issue that netted FC1,000 (FC = foreign current units).
2. Selected exchange rates were:

	($ per FC)
At January 1, 20X1	$.58
Average for 20X1	$.62
At December 31, 20X1	$.66

EXHIBIT 12.8   Trial balance in FC and translated US$ at December 31, 20X1.

Accounts	FC	Rate	US$
Cash	200	.66	132
Accounts receivable	100	.66	66
Inventory	300	.66	198
Property and equipment	2,000	.66	1,320
Cost of sales	600	.62	372
SG&A expense	100	.62	62
Tax provision	120	.62	74
Totals	3,420		2,224
Accounts payable	400	.66	264
Notes payable	1,020	.66	673
Common stock	1,000	.58	580
Retained earnings	0		0
Translation adjustment	0		87
Sales	1,000	.62	620
Totals	3,420		2,224

The above rates indicate the amount of U.S. currency required to equal (buy) a single unit of the foreign currency. The increase in the rate across the year means that the dollar has lost value and that the foreign currency has appreciated.

3. The trial balance of Foreign Sub, both in FC and in U.S. dollars and translated following the all-current rule, is given in Exhibit 12.8. Those accounts that would have debit balances, assets and expenses, are grouped first, and those with credit balances, liabilities, equities, and revenues, are grouped second.

The two collections of account balances must balance. Notice that this is achieved only in the U.S. dollar trial balance through introduction of a translation adjustment account with a balance just sufficient to recreate this equality. Without the addition of the $87 translation adjustment account balance, the total of the *translated* assets and expenses, $2,224, exceeds the total of the *translated* liabilities, shareholders' equity, and sales accounts by $87. The translation adjustment can also be directly calculated as shown next:

Beginning net assets (assets minus liabilities) times change in exchange rate from 1/1/X1 to 12/31/X1 (.66 − .58)	FC1,000 .08	$80
Net income times difference between end of year and average exchange rates (.66 − .62)	FC180 .04	7
Translation adjustment		$87

The $80 component represents the growth in the beginning net assets due to appreciation in the value of Sub's foreign currency. The $7 component is the additional net assets due to the translation of the income statement balances at the average rate for the year of $.62 and balance-sheet amounts at the end-of-year rate of $.66. There is no retained earnings balance in the previous trial balance because 20X1 is the first year of operation, and the net income for the year is added to retained earnings through the later process of closing the books.

The translated income statement and balance sheet are presented in Exhibits 12.9 and 12.10, respectively. They can be constructed from the translated data presented earlier. The translation of the FC data is presented again in these statements simply to reinforce understanding of the translation process.

In the absence of dividends, the retained earnings in the balance sheet (Exhibit 12.10) are simply the net income for the year. The translation adjustment of $87 will be included in the consolidated shareholders' equity of Foreign Sub's parent upon consolidation. The net assets of Foreign Sub are in a currency that appreciated across the year. This growth in net assets is captured in the process of translation and represented, again, by the translation adjustment balance. If, instead, the FC had depreciated, then the translation adjustment would reduce shareholders' equity and appear as a deduction in Exhibit 12.10. With the translation completed, the preceding statements would now be ready for consolidation with their U.S. parent—as long as they had initially been prepared in accordance with U.S. GAAP.

In addition to the all-current translation procedure illustrated previously, an alternative procedure, referred to as *remeasurement,* must be employed under certain conditions. Briefly summarized, this alternative procedure is applied when (1) the foreign subsidiary does not conduct its business in the local currency of its country of domicile or (2) the local country is a highly inflationary economy, that is, cumulative inflation of approximately 100% over the most recent three-year period.[12] In both of these cases, the local currency is not considered to be the firm's

EXHIBIT 12.9   Translated income statement.

Income Statement	FC	Rate	US$
Sales	1,000	.62	620
Less cost of sales	600	.62	372
Gross margin	400		248
Less SG&A	100	.62	62
Pretax profit	300		186
Less tax provision	120	.62	74
Net income	180		112

EXHIBIT 12.10 Translated balance sheet.

Balance Sheet	FC	Rate	US$
Cash	200	.66	132
Accounts receivable	100	.66	66
Inventory	300	.66	198
Property & equipment	2,000	.66	1,320
Total assets	2,600		1,716
Accounts payable	400	.66	264
Notes payable	1,020	.66	673
Common stock	1,000	.58	580
Translation adjustment			87
Retained earnings	180	(income statement)	112
Total liabilities & equity	2,600		1,716

"functional" currency. The functional currency is ". . . the currency of the primary economic environment in which the entity operates . . . in which an entity primarily generates and expends cash."[13]

Cases in which the functional currency is not the local currency of the country in which the subsidiary operates are common. For example, Storage Technology Corporation discloses in its 1995 Annual Report (pp. 31–32) the following: "The functional currency of StorageTek's foreign subsidiaries is the U.S. dollar, reflecting the significant volume of intercompany transactions and associated cash flows which result from the fact that the majority of the Company's products sold worldwide are manufactured in the United States." In addition to an alternative translation rule, under this approach any translation gain or loss that emerges is included in computing net earnings for the year, and not added or subtracted directly to or from shareholders' equity.[14]

Temporal (Remeasurement) Translation Procedure

The process of remeasurement employs a translation rule that has traditionally been referred to as the *temporal* method. The method is summarized as follows:

1. All monetary assets (cash, accounts receivable, etc.) and monetary liabilities (accounts payable, accrued liabilities, notes payable, etc.) are translated at the current exchange rate.

2. All nonmonetary assets (inventory, plant and equipment, etc.) and liabilities (deferred income) are translated at historical exchange rates, that is, rates existing at the transaction date when the asset or liability was recorded.

3. Shareholders' equity is translated just as under the all-current method.

4. Revenues and expenses are generally translated at the average exchange rate for the reporting period. Exceptions are expenses, such as cost of sales

and depreciation, which are derived from assets translated at historic rates and, therefore, are translated at these same historical rates.

The previously mentioned trial balance, income statement, and balance sheet are retranslated to illustrate the impact of this alternative method and shown in Exhibit 12.11. Two new assumptions are necessary: (1) Property and equipment was acquired when the exchange rate was $.58 and depreciation of FC60 was included in SG&A expense, and (2) ending inventory was acquired at the average exchange rate of $.62.

Notice how this different translation rule dramatically changes net income. Net income was $112 under the all-current method but only $27 under the temporal method. This difference of $85 can be explained as follows:

All-current method net income	$112
Reduction in SG&A, including depreciation, under temporal method (.62 − .60)	.02
Translation loss under temporal method	(87)
Temporal method net income	$ 27

The explanation for the emergence of the *translation loss* is that it results from the change in balance-sheet exposure in going from the all-current to temporal method. In the all-current example, all assets and liabilities are translated using the current rate. Asset exposure existed under the all-current method because assets exceeded liabilities. As a result, the appreciation of the foreign currency resulted in a growth (gain) in net assets. This gain of $87 was reported as a direct addition to shareholders' equity. Under the temporal method, balance-sheet exposure is the net of monetary assets and liabilities, that is, those balance-sheet accounts translated at the ever changing current rate. None of the other nonmonetary balance-sheet accounts creates exposure because their dollar value is frozen at fixed, historical exchange rates—for example, $.58 in the case of property and equipment. In the preceding example, monetary liabilities are well in excess of monetary assets and liability exposure results. Appreciation of the foreign currency increases the dollar valuation of this net liability exposure and produces a translation loss of $87. This loss must be included in computing net income. Beyond these separately reported income-statement effects of translation gains and losses, the income statement is affected in some other less obvious ways. These are discussed next.

Further Effects of Statement Translation

Rather obvious effects of translation are the appearance of translation gains or losses in the income statement, under the temporal method, and translation adjustments within shareholders' equity, under the all-current translation method. However, translation under both the all-current and temporal methods can also

EXHIBIT 12.11   Financial statements in FC and translated US$ at December 31, 20X1, trial balance.

Accounts	FC	Rate	US$
Cash	200	.66	132
Accounts receivable	100	.66	66
Inventory	300	.62	186
Property and equipment	2,000	.58	1,160
Cost of sales	600	.62	372
SG&A expense	40	.62	25
Depreciation	60	.58	35
Tax provision	120	.62	74
Translation loss			87
Totals	3,420		2,137
Accounts payable	400	.66	264
Notes payable	1,020	.66	673
Common stock	1,000	.58	580
Retained earnings	0		0
Sales	1,000	.62	620
Totals	3,420		2,137

Income Statement	FC	Rate	US$
Sales	1,000	.62	620
Less cost of sales	600	.62	372
Gross margin	400		248
Less: SG&A	40	.62	25
Depreciation	60	.58	35
Translation loss		(above)	87
Pretax profit	300		107
Less tax provision	120	.62	74
Net income	180		27

Balance Sheet	FC	Rate	US$
Cash	200	.66	132
Accounts receivable	100	.66	66
Inventory	300	.62	186
Property & equipment	2,000	.58	1,160
Total assets	2,600		1,544
Accounts payable	400	.66	264
Notes payable	1,020	.66	673
Common stock	1,000	.58	580
Retained earnings	180	(income statement)	27
Total liabilities & equity	2,600		1,544

increase or decrease earnings, and as a result shareholders' equity, in other less obvious ways.

In its 1995 Annual Report (p. 22), Illinois Tool Works reported: "The weakening of the U.S. dollar against foreign currencies in 1995 (primarily European currencies) resulted in increased operating revenues of $116 million and increased net income per share of approximately 10 cents." Compaq Computer also explained how results can be affected by translation (1995 Compaq Annual Report, p. 15):

> When the U.S. dollar strengthens against other currencies, sales made in those currencies translate into lower sales in U.S. dollars, and when the U.S. dollar weakens, sales made in local currencies translate into higher sales in U.S. dollars. Correspondingly, costs and expenses incurred in non-U.S. dollar currencies increase when the U.S. dollar weakens and decline when the U.S. dollar strengthens.

In an effort to clarify the impact of changes in exchange rates on results, it is common for companies to identify the contribution of rate fluctuations to changes in revenues. For example, Black & Decker Corporation provides detailed analyses of the contribution made by changes in exchange rates to its 1995 sales growth. The 13% growth in 1995 revenues achieved by the European region of its Consumer and Home Improvement Products segment was broken down as shown in Exhibit 12.12 (1995 Annual Report, p. 23).

The information in Exhibit 12.12 is important in evaluating the performance of firms such as Black & Decker, as well as that of its management. This topic is discussed further in a later section. However, in anticipation of this discussion, growth produced mainly from increases in volume or price adjustments should be preferred to growth resulting from favorable exchange-rate movements. Revenue growth driven by changes in exchange rates may prove to be only temporary. Sustained revenue growth would require comparable exchange rate changes in subsequent periods—not a likely prospect.

Just as with transaction exposure, management must decide whether to actively manage translation exposure. Central to this decision is whether these translation gains and losses are included in computing net income, under the

EXHIBIT 12.12 Factors explaining revenue growth in Black & Decker's sales.

Sources of Growth	Growth in Revenue
Unit volume	4%
Price	—
Currency	9%
Total	13%

SOURCE: Black & Decker annual report, December 1995, p. 23.

temporal method, or reported as direct additions to or deductions from shareholders' equity, under the all-current method. This matter is discussed next.

MANAGING THE CURRENCY RISK OF FOREIGN SUBSIDIARIES

Many view the currency risk associated with the statements of foreign subsidiaries, *translational exposure,* to be significantly different from that associated with foreign-denominated transaction balances, that is, *transactional exposure.* Transactional exposure has the clear potential to expand or contract the cash flows associated with foreign currency asset and liability balances. However, in the case of translation exposure, there are no identifiable cash inflows or outflows associated with the translation gains or losses. A recent study of both U.S. and U.K. multinationals by Collier, Davis, Coates, and Longden found that ". . . it was generally agreed that translation exposure management was a lesser concern" (than transaction exposure management).[15]

The absence of the same cash-flow risk in the case of translation causes some companies not to apply currency risk management methods to translation exposure. Others do attempt to manage translation risk to avoid the potential negative impact on (1) earnings, in the case of subsidiaries whose statements are subject to remeasurement, that is, temporal-method translation, and on (2) shareholders' equity, in the case of application of the all-current method. A common view is that hedging activities are more likely to be applied if the temporal method is being used because the translation gains and losses are included in the income statement. The translation exposure of subsidiaries, translated using the all-current method, creates gains and losses that go directly to shareholders' equity. The absence of an impact on earnings makes it less likely that such exposure will be hedged.

Prior to the issuance of Statement Financial Accounting Standards Board (FASB) *Statement No. 52: Foreign Currency Translation,* all firms were required to use the temporal method and include all translation gains and losses in the computation of net income.[16] As a result, one would expect the hedging of translation exposure to decline after the issuance of Statement No. 52. Available evidence supports this view. For example, Houston and Mueller note, "In particular, firms which must no longer include all translation gains or losses arising from their foreign operations in their income statements are more likely to have stopped or reduced hedging translation exposure."[17]

Where management decides to hedge *translation* exposure, all of the hedging vehicles discussed for use in hedging *transaction* exposure could also be used. Moreover, where the translation gains or losses are reported in shareholders' equity, the offsetting gains or losses on the hedging instrument are also included in shareholders' equity. For example, the 1995 Annual Report of Analog Devices, Inc. notes the following (p. 31): "The Company uses currency swap agreements to hedge the value of its net investment in certain of its foreign subsidiaries. Realized and unrealized gains and losses on such agreements . . . are recognized in the cumulative translation adjustment component of stockholders' equity. . . ."

In addition to the use of hedging instruments such as forwards, futures, options, and swaps, hedging of translation exposure can involve transactions structured by the firm itself. Recall that California First hedged its liability exposure in the Swiss franc by denominating one of its loans, an asset, in the Swiss franc. These techniques are also used by some firms in hedging translation exposure. For example, DeKalb Genetics, with subsidiaries in Argentina, reported that "Significant interest expense was incurred in Argentina on a hedge loan. . . . In anticipation of continued hyperinflation and significant devaluation of the austral (now the peso), a portion of the austral-based receivables was hedged . . ." (1990 Annual Report, p. 21). Notice in Exhibit 12.13 how the hedge was designed to function.

As sometimes happens with the best laid plans, the hedge did not work quite as planned. DeKalb reported that "unexpected Argentine government action resulted in the austral strengthening against the dollar, while at the same time interest rates soared. Interest expense incurred because of this transaction was $4.1 million" (1990 Annual Report, p. 21). Offsetting gains and losses still would result from revaluation of both the asset and liability at the current rate for the austral. However, the cost of achieving the hedge was increased by unexpected movement in interest rates.

Bear in mind that because Argentina was a highly inflationary country per Statement of Financial Accounting Standard No. 52, DeKalb's translation exposure is determined by the relation between its monetary assets and liabilities. These are the balances that create currency exposure because they must be translated at the current rate. If accounts receivable were the major monetary balance on the statements of the Argentine subsidiaries, then appreciation or depreciation of the austral could produce significant translation (remeasurement) gains or losses. These gains and losses would be included in DeKalb's con-

EXHIBIT 12.13   Operation of the DeKalb Genetics translation hedge.

Value of the Austral	Austral Receivables (Asset)	Austral Loan (Liability)
Appreciates	Gain	Loss
Depreciates	Loss	Gain

SOURCE: DeKalb Genetics annual report, December 1990, p. 21.

solidated earnings. Again, protection of earnings from a translation loss on the austral receivables was achieved by the hedge, but at the cost of more interest expense than DeKalb apparently anticipated.

Practice obviously varies regarding whether to hedge either transaction or translation exposure and, if so, how to accomplish such hedging. Practice would seem to suggest the following ordering of management demand for hedging, from high to low:

1. To protect cash flow and earnings, both level and stability.
2. To protect earnings, both level and stability.
3. To protect shareholders' equity, both level and stability.

In continuing to observe hedging motivated by the second and third points just cited, it is well to consider the significance of earnings and equity amounts without regard to the issue of cash flows. Two examples: (1) Management compensation is frequently based, at least in part, upon reported earnings. (2) Covenants in debt and loan agreements often call for maintenance of specified amounts of shareholders' equity or ratios of debt to shareholders' equity. Differences in hedging practices are explained in part by different attitudes towards bearing currency risk as well as the cost and capacity to hedge exposures in different countries. In addition, firms will differ in their capacity to minimize currency exposure through various operational, organizational, and business arrangements.

A small sampling of company policies on the hedging of translation exposure is provided in Exhibit 12.14.

DIFFERENCES IN U.S. AND FOREIGN ACCOUNTING POLICIES

A variety of new financial, accounting, tax, and managerial issues faced Fashionhouse when it acquired its Danish subsidiary. The issues of statement translation and currency risk-management were discussed earlier. Recall that the requirement to consolidate the Danish subsidiary into the dollar-based statements of Fashionhouse, the parent, necessitates translation. In addition, to the extent that Danish accounting practices differ from those in the United States, adjustments must be made so that the subsidiary's statements conform to U.S. GAAP.

International GAAP Differences and the IASC

A review of the statements of companies located in different countries would reveal many financial reporting examples that are in agreement and many that are in disagreement. In order to address the high level of disagreement found in

EXHIBIT 12.14   Hedging translation exposure: Selected company policies.

Company	Hedging Policy
Becton Dickinson and Company (1995 Annual Report, p. 24)	The Company does not generally hedge these translation exposures since such amounts are recorded as cumulative translation adjustments, a separate component of shareholders' equity, and do not impact reported earnings or current cash flow.
Black & Decker Corporation (1995 Annual Report, p. 35)	During 1995, the Corporation decided to limit the future hedging of its net investment in foreign subsidiaries. This action may increase volatility of reported equity in the future but will result in more predictable cash flows from hedging activities.
Raychem Corporation (1995 Annual Report, p. 35)	The company periodically enters into forward foreign exchange contracts to hedge a portion of its equity in foreign subsidiaries.

accounting practices internationally, the International Accounting Standards Committee (IASC) was formed in 1973. The IASC, which was composed initially of representatives from the leading professional accounting bodies of Australia, Canada, France, Germany, Japan, Mexico, the Netherlands, the United Kingdom and Ireland, and the United States, began working toward the harmonization of accounting standards internationally. Today, the IASC represents accounting bodies from over 70 countries. Each member body has agreed to work toward the compliance of accounting standards in its home country with the standards issued by the IASC. In fact, a number of countries, such as India, Kuwait, Malaysia, Singapore, and Zimbabwe, either adopt IASC standards as their own generally accepted accounting principles or place heavy reliance on them in developing their own accounting standards. To date, 32 international accounting standards and several exposure drafts have been issued. The IASC has also issued a document that both identifies major differences in international accounting practices and categorizes them in terms of their being (1) the required or preferred treatment, (2) the allowed alternative treatment, or (3) the treatment eliminated.[18] The immediate goal of the proposal is to eliminate most of the choices in accounting treatment now available in standards issued by the IASC. The IASC enumerated the expected benefits of this harmonization in financial reporting as follows:[19]

1. Improve the quality of financial reporting.
2. Make easier the comparison of the financial position, performance, and changes in financial position of enterprises in different countries.
3. Reduce the costs borne by multinational enterprises that presently have to comply with different national standards.

4. Facilitate the mutual recognition of prospectuses for multinational securities offerings.

A subsequent statement has reported responses to this initial document and outlined plans for implementation of some of the initial proposals and additional study for others.[20] The major approach to implementation of the IASC proposals is to incorporate those proposals on which agreement has been reached into revised International Accounting Standards.

Examples of some of the accounting treatments that would be *eliminated* under the IASC proposals follow:

1. Completed contract method for the recognition of revenue on construction contracts.
2. Deferral of exchange gains and losses on long-term monetary items.
3. Translation of statements of subsidiaries operating in hyperinflationary economies, without first applying price-level adjustments.
4. Use of the closing (end-of-period) exchange rate to translate income statement balances.
5. Maintenance of investment properties on the books without depreciation.
6. Immediate deduction of goodwill against shareholders' equity.

Examples of U.S. and international GAAP differences are provided in the next section along with an illustration of how international firms mitigate the impact of differences for U.S. statement users.[21]

U.S. and International GAAP Differences

Reviewing the accounting policies of a selection of non-U.S. firms quickly highlights many GAAP differences. Some of the more prominent of these GAAP differences are presented in Exhibit 12.15.

With the continuing globalization of financial markets, international firms have become more sensitive to the analytical burdens that result from foreign versus domestic GAAP differences. Further, the U.S. Securities and Exchange Commission requires that some foreign firms file reports that include schedules reconciling earnings under U.S. and foreign GAAP (the 20-F Report, examples of which disclosures are provided from Akzo Nobel in Exhibits 12.16 and 12.17). As is typical of these disclosures, Akzo Nobel provides reconciliations, from Netherlands to U.S. GAAP, of both net income and shareholders' equity—provided in Exhibits 12.16 and 12.17. The principal differences between U.S. and Netherlands GAAP underlying these statements are briefly summarized here:

1. Goodwill arising on the purchase of other companies is deducted immediately from shareholders' equity. U.S. GAAP requires that it be amortized over a period not to exceed 40 years.

EXHIBIT 12.15   Examples of international GAAP differences.

Accounting Policy	Country/Company	GAAP Difference
Software costs	England/Reuters Holdings	Reuters expenses all software costs; some would be capitalized under U.S. GAAP.
Tax accounting	Malaysia/United Malacca Rubber Estates, Berhad	Deferred taxes are not booked where temporary differences are deferred indefinitely; deferred taxes are booked on all temporary differences under U.S. GAAP.
Investments	Australia/BHP Limited	Equity accounting is not applied to investments in excess of 20% of voting shares; U.S. GAAP generally requires equity method.
Property	Hong Kong/Hong Kong Telecommunications	Tangible fixed assets and property may be restated on the basis of appraised values; upward revaluations not permitted under U.S. GAAP.
Sale/leaseback gains	Netherlands/PolyGram	Gains on sale/leaseback transactions are recognized in the year of sale; such gains are deferred and amortized under U.S. GAAP.
Construction interest	Sweden/Pharmacia	Interest related to the construction of assets is expensed; U.S. GAAP requires capitalization and amortization.
Foreign exchange gains and losses (on loans to acquire aircraft)	England/British Airways	Foreign exchange gains and losses are deducted from or added to the cost of aircraft; included in income as incurred under U.S. GAAP.
Unrealized foreign exchange gains and losses	Germany/Continental Aktiengesellschaft	Losses are deducted from income but gains are not recorded; U.S. GAAP recognizes both in earnings.

2. Accounting for pensions as well as other postretirement benefits (e.g., health care and life insurance) requires additional annual expense recognition to conform with U.S. GAAP.

3. The recognition of both deferred tax expenses and benefits differs between Netherlands and U.S. GAAP.

4. The addition of 391 million guilders in the shareholders' equity reconciliation results from the Netherlands practice of recognizing dividends as a reduction of retained earnings sooner than under U.S. GAAP. There is no impact on earnings.

Notice in Exhibit 12.16 that net income under U.S. GAAP is well below that under Netherlands GAAP for each of the years from 1993 to 1995, while shareholders' equity is much higher under U.S. GAAP. This is a fairly typical out-

EXHIBIT 12.16 Reconciliation from Netherlands to U.S. GAAP of 1993 to 1995 net income: Akzo Nobel, N.V. (in millions of Netherlands guilders).

	1993	1994	1995
Net income in accordance with Netherlands GAAP	549	1,178	1,314
Adjustments to reported income:			
Amortization of goodwill	(86)	(179)	(173)
Nobel restructuring and environmental provisions	—	(103)	(150)
Nobel acquisition hedging	21	37	—
Goodwill writedowns	(56)	(186)	(31)
Pensions	(35)	(4)	(7)
Postretirement benefits	(29)	(10)	(13)
Joint venture			(58)
Income taxes	17	1	(5)
Deferred taxes	(35)	(39)	(140)
Net income in accordance with U.S. GAAP before cumulative effect adjustments	346	695	737
Cumulative effect of adjustment for postretirement benefits under SFAS No. 106	(246)		
Cumulative effect adjustment for income under SFAS No. 109	35	—	—
Net income in accordance with U.S. GAAP	135	695	737

Note: Footnote references in this statement have been omitted.
SOURCE: Akzo Nobel N.V. annual report on form 20-F, December 1995, p. 95.

come when the results of foreign firms are restated in accordance with U.S. GAAP, and it has raised questions about a possible negative impact on the international competitiveness of U.S. firms; that is, U.S. firms might be viewed as fundamentally less profitable, even though such profit differences may simply be the result of differences in U.S. versus foreign GAAP.

Domestic users of foreign financial statements need to be aware of the differences in financial reporting practices, and also have some information on the effect of these differences on such key financial statistics as earnings-per-share and shareholders' equity. For example, security analysts use ratios of market price to earnings-per-share (the *price/earnings,* or *P/E ratio*) as one way to judge whether a stock might be either over- or undervalued. Akzo Nobel's P/E ratio is lower under Netherlands GAAP because its earnings per share are higher than they would be under U.S. GAAP. Under Netherlands GAAP, Akzo Nobel would appear to be more conservatively valued than under U.S. GAAP. Similarly, bankers use the relationship of total debt to stockholders' equity to judge the capacity of firms to handle their level of borrowed funds. By this statistic, Akzo Nobel might appear more highly leveraged because its stockholders' equity is far lower under Netherlands GAAP.

EXHIBIT 12.17   Reconciliation from Netherlands to U.S. GAAP of 1994 and 1995 stockholders' equity: Akzo Nobel, N.V. (in millions of Netherlands guilders).

	1994	1995
Stockholders' equity in accordance with Netherlands GAAP	6,257	6,605
Adjustments to stockholders' equity:		
Goodwill	5,693	5,206
Restructuring provisions	30	—
Pensions	(64)	(71)
Excess minimum liability over unrecognized prior service cost		(21)
Postretirement benefits	(423)	411
Joint venture	—	157
Income taxes	188	194
Deferred	211	121
Dividends	391	391
Stockholders' equity in accordance with U.S. GAAP	12,283	12,171

Note: Footnote references in this statement have been omitted.
SOURCE: Akzo Nobel N.V. annual report on form 20-F, December 1995, p. 96.

GAAP Differences and the Level Playing Field

Some argue that international competitiveness of a country can be impaired if earnings and financial position appear to be weaker under local GAAP versus that of its major competitor countries. That is, the playing field will not be level. As an example, in recent years concern about international GAAP differences have focused on acquisition (of other companies) accounting. A typical acquisition will include the payment of a premium, in some cases involving billions of dollars, for what is collectively termed *goodwill*. This amount consists of the difference between the purchase price and the current value of the net assets acquired, as in the following example:

Purchase price	$1,000
Current fair value of net assets acquired (assets – liabilities)	700
Goodwill	$ 300

It has been a common practice in other countries to deduct immediately, from shareholders' equity, the goodwill recorded in an acquisition. (This is one of the practices that the IASC hopes to see eliminated under its harmonization project discussed earlier.) U.S. GAAP requires that goodwill be amortized through the income statement. Notice in the Akzo Nobel reconciliation cited previously that U.S. GAAP earnings are lowered to adjust for the failure of Akzo Nobel, under Netherlands GAAP, to amortize goodwill.

If Akzo Nobel and a U.S. firm were both bidding for the same company, Akzo Nobel would forecast a stronger postacquisition earnings picture. This results because Akzo Nobel would deduct the goodwill directly from the balance sheet, that is, shareholders' equity, whereas the U.S. firm will take the charge through its future income statements. A further negative for a U.S. firm has been the fact that goodwill amortization has not, in the past, been deductible for tax purposes.[22]

It could be argued, the tax issue aside, that the profit differences that result from the disparity in accounting for goodwill are purely cosmetic, and that they should not cause a U.S. bidder to be at a disadvantage in the acquisitions market. That is, the impact of the acquisition on the bidder's future cash flow should be the central issue. Differences in accounting policy should not have a direct impact on future cash flow. However, it is well to remember that, cash flow aside, the reported numbers take on a significance in their own right, to the extent they are either (1) a factor in determining managerial compensation or (2) are used by lenders to monitor compliance with debt agreements.

The international competitiveness issue was raised with respect to the FASB statement on postretirement benefits accounting, SFAS No. 106. The Statement requires companies to apply accrual accounting to what are termed other postretirement benefits, mainly health and life insurance. When proposed, there was fierce lobbying against issuing the statement. Some excerpts from a statement to the FASB by the then chief financial officer of Chrysler Corporation make the key points:[23]

> . . . this higher cost recognition will depress reported profitability, and thereby ultimately discourage capital formation in job-creating enterprises in the U.S. There will be a powerful incentive to move our employment base to Canada, Europe and Third World countries. . . .
>
> Foreign-based companies will not be forced to adopt your new rules—all other things being equal, a European or Japanese company will report a billion dollars more profit doing the same business as Chrysler. In that environment, we will simply be unable to compete fairly for investor capital. Ultimately, I believe you will have added to the trend of foreign ownership of our U.S. industrial base.

One can only hope for the success of the IASC program to increase international harmony in reporting practices, if the arguments concerning the anticompetitive potential of diversity in international GAAP are meritorious.

EVALUATION OF THE PERFORMANCE OF FOREIGN SUBSIDIARIES AND THEIR MANAGEMENT

With the acquisition of its Danish subsidiary, Fashionhouse is faced with the need to report and evaluate the performance of the subsidiary as an economic entity, as well as the performance of the subsidiary's management. The discussion here will focus only on those differences that result from the foreign character of the subsidiary. Aside from this, performance evaluation should be fundamentally the same as for a domestic firm. The fact that, after the translation process, financial statements are available in both the domestic currency (krone in the case of Fashionhouse) and the U.S. dollar is an important difference. Should performance of the subsidiary and its management be judged on the basis of the krone or dollars results? Moreover, the earnings performance of the Fashionhouse subsidiary will be affected each year by (1) the movement of the krone against the dollar and (2) prices set (a transfer price) on the goods sold to Fashionhouse in the United States.

Impact of Exchange Rate Movements on Performance Evaluation

A number of years ago, an issue arose concerning the incentive compensation of the manager of a Netherlands subsidiary of a major U.S. heavy-equipment manufacturer. A strong profit performance was produced in the European currency, but the translated results were a loss. (Note: Translation followed the temporal and not the all-current method.) After lengthy consideration by senior management, a decision was made that no incentive compensation was to be awarded. Management held that failure of the Netherlands subsidiary to earn a profit in dollars resulted in its making no contribution to the parent, whose goal was to maximize the dollar earnings of the consolidated entity. The manager of the Netherlands subsidiary was not pleased.

A central precept of performance evaluation is that managers should be held responsible only for results that incorporate variables over which they exercise some significant influence. Depending upon the circumstances, this might mean that in judging the performance of a department foreman, the quantity of material used is considered controllable, but not its price. For performance evaluation purposes, the material used would be priced at some prearranged standard and not its actual cost. On the other hand, the vice president of manufacturing might well be held responsible for actual material cost on the basis that he or she has been assigned responsibility for the price of material used, as well as its quantity. Applied to evaluating the performance of the management of a foreign subsidiary, the concept of a *controllable* performance indicator would call for either (1) using the profit results from the foreign currency statements or (2) using the translated dollar earnings, after adjustments designed to remove the effects of changes in the value of the dollar, that is, the price of the dollar. As (1) involves no unique adjustments related to foreign subsidiary status, only (2) will be discussed further.

Consider the income statements in Exhibit 12.18 in foreign currency (FC) and the U.S. dollar used in the earlier all-current translation example—now designated Year 1:

EXHIBIT 12.18   Year 1 income statement.

	FC	Rate	US$
Sales	1,000	$.62	620
Less cost of sales	600	.62	372
Gross margin	400		248
Less SG&A	100	.62	62
Pretax profit	300		186
Less tax provision	120	.62	74
Net income	180		112

Assume that in the following year, domestic results are as given in Exhibit 12.19 and that the foreign currency has depreciated to an average rate of $.58 for the year (recall that income-statement amounts are translated at the average rate under the all-current method). The new translation would now be as shown in Exhibit 12.19.

Net income in Year 2, in the foreign currency, increased by 65% over Year 1. However, the income improvement on a translated dollar basis was less than half this amount, only 32%. The impact of the change in exchange rates needs to be removed if the translated income statement is to be used to evaluate performance of the subsidiary's management—on the assumption that management has no control over exchange rates. Net income can be adjusted as follows:

Foreign currency Year 2 net income	FC297
Translate at Year 1 exchange rate	× .62
Year 2 net income at constant exchange rate	$ 184

The above adjustment holds constant the value of the foreign currency in measuring net income for purposes of performance evaluation. In judging the subsidiary itself as an economic unit, translation at the depreciated value of the foreign currency would remain appropriate. The dollar value of the net income

EXHIBIT 12.19   Year 2 income statement.

	FC	Rate	US$
Sales	1,200	$.50	600
Less cost of sales	660	.50	330
Gross margin	540		270
Less SG&A	115	.50	58
Pretax profit	425		212
Less tax provision	128	.50	64
Net income	297		148

produced is indeed lower because of the currency depreciation in the subsidiary's home country.[24]

There is ample evidence in U.S. annual reports of adjustments to control for the impact of exchange movements on performance. It is standard for the Management's Discussion and Analysis of Operations section, an SEC requirement, to include commentary on the impact of exchange rate changes on revenues, though far less frequently on earnings. Two recent examples follow:

Raychem Corporation (1995 Annual Report, p. 21)

Revenues in the electronics business segment increased 17% to $611 million in 1995 from $522 million in 1994, although growth on a constant-currency basis was only 13%.

Praxair, Inc. (1995 Annual Report, p. 21)

Sales for 1995 in Europe increased 14% primarily due to volume growth (4%) and improved merchant and packaged gases pricing in Southern Europe. Currency translation effects were responsible for 7% of the sales increase.

In addition to discussions by management, security analysts often comment on the implications of exchange rate changes. They consider them both in their analysis of past results and in their forecasts of future performance. The selections below are from various issues of *The Value Line Investment Survey*.[25]

NCH Corporation (September 27, 1996 issue)

Modest domestic sales increases were offset by a decline in foreign volume. However, when measured in local currency, foreign sales were up 2%, but declined after adjustments for unfavorable translations.

AMP, Inc. (October 25, 1996 issue)

For the first half of the year, AMP reported increases in sales in every region's local currency. However, in terms of U.S. dollars, only the U.S. showed a year-to-year increase. Management believes that these factors (others, beyond the currency effects, were also identified) contributed to a decline in earnings during the third quarter and will allow for only a modest gain for all of 1996. Therefore, we have lowered our 1996 share-net estimate by $0.25 to $2.05.

Fischer & Porter Company (December 2, 1990 issue)

Reported sales increases at Fischer & Porter are not as good as they look. The company does a lot of business through its foreign subsidiaries. Because of the weakness of the dollar, these sales translate into more U.S. currency. In the third quarter, for example, reported corporate sales of $62.2 million would have been about $57 million if exchange rates had been the same as a year earlier. In other words, sales declined about 3% in real terms. The currency gains don't bolster profits because expenses also gain in the translation.

Explanatory comments: The issue of how profits are affected by strengthening foreign currencies requires some comment. Notice that sales would have declined in the absence of the currency appreciation. This highlights a weakness in sales that might otherwise be masked by the impact of the sales growth due to the exchange rate effects. This decline in real sales is even more troublesome given that, other things equal, the Fischer & Porter products are cheaper to foreign customers in view of the appreciation in the value of their currencies. Isolating the impact of exchange rate changes on sale growth helps to identify growth that is more likely to be sustainable because it is not the result of foreign-currency appreciation. The characterization of the impact of currency gains on profits (that is, "The currency gains don't bolster profits . . .") may be an overstatement. Consider the following data, which assume that sales and expenses in the foreign currency (FC) are the same in Years 1 and 2:

		Year 1		Year 2	
FC Results		**FX Rate**	**$ Results**	**FX Rate**	**$ Results**
Sales	100	$.50	$50	$.60	$60
Expenses	80	$.50	40	$.60	48
Profit	20		$10		$12

Profits, of course, do not go up by the amount of the sales increase due to FC appreciation: 100FC ($.60 − $.50) = $10. This is because the translated value of expenses will also increase due to the FC appreciation: 80FC × ($.60 − $.50) = 8. However, because sales exceed expenses, profits do increase by the percentage growth in the FC value: (.60 − .50)/.50 = 20%.

Changes in exchange rates present a clear challenge in evaluating the performance of both the economic units, for example, the foreign subsidiaries, as well as the management of these organizations. The emphasis on foreign operations is on results in the domestic and not the foreign currency. This can create obvious problems in evaluation of the management of foreign subsidiaries because their results in the foreign currency may improve or decline while their performance expressed in the domestic currency declines or improves. If foreign entity managers have little control over their results in the parent's currency, then judging their performance in that currency presents clear problems. Performance evaluation in the domestic currency should require that unit management have currency-risk management as part of their responsibilities. At least in the case of transactional exposure, Black & Decker managers have this as part of their duties (Black & Decker, 1995 Annual Report, p. 35):

Foreign currency transaction and commitment exposures generally are the responsibility of the Corporation's individual operating units to manage as an integral part of their business. Management responds to foreign exchange movements through many alternative means, such as pricing actions, changes in cost structure, and changes in hedging strategies.

The goal of the above discussion is to highlight how the evaluation of foreign subsidiaries and their management represents a special challenge because of the many ways in which exchange rate movements can affect measures of financial performance. Another factor that also affects such performance evaluation is the issue of transfer pricing. These are the prices charged when goods are transferred between related foreign and domestic firms. The issue of *transfer pricing* is briefly discussed next.

Transfer Pricing and the Multinational Firm

The prices at which goods or services are transferred between related entities, for example, parents and subsidiaries and divisions of the same firm, are referred to as *transfer prices*. Transfer prices will be a major factor in determining the profits of the Fashionhouse Danish subsidiary because much of its product is shipped to its U.S. parent. As in the preceding case, the discussion here focuses on the dimensions of transfer pricing that are influenced by the foreign status of the subsidiary. The general topic of transfer pricing has been the subject of much debate over many years. The setting of transfer prices to both encourage optimal decision making and to facilitate performance evaluation is not yet a settled matter.

Transfer prices are generally based upon cost, cost plus some markup, or some approximation of market. Firms with international operations typically disclose their method of pricing transfers of goods and services among different taxing jurisdictions—typically countries. Some recent examples of transfer pricing policies are presented here:

1. *Both cost and market-based prices*

   The Dow Chemical Company (1995 Annual Report, p. 42)

   Transfers between area and industry segments are generally valued at cost. The exception is that movements between the agricultural chemicals and consumer products businesses and the other businesses are generally valued at market-based prices.

2. *Cost plus a markup*

   The Goodyear Tire and Rubber Company (1995 Annual Report, p. 38)

   Inter-geographic sales were at cost plus a negotiated mark up.

3. *Reasonable profit*

   Black & Decker Corporation (1995 Annual Report, p. 42)

   Transfers between geographic areas are accounted for at cost plus a reasonable profit.

4. *Market value*

   Chevron Corporation (1995 Annual Report, p. 46)

   Sales from the transfer of products between segments and geographic areas are generally at estimated market prices.

5. *Arm's-length principles*

   Baxter International (1995 Annual Report, p. 69)

   Inter-area transactions are accounted for using arm's-length principles.

   The levels at which transfer prices are set are influenced by a wide range of sometimes conflicting objectives. These include maximizing worldwide profits *after taxes,* maintaining flexibility in the repatriation of profits, encouraging optimal decision making by profit center management, providing profit data that are reliable indicators of managerial performance and entity profitability, building market share, and maintaining competitiveness in foreign markets.[26]

   There is obviously great variation in the transfer pricing policies used by U.S. firms. Moreover, these policies can have a major impact on measures of financial performance of the foreign subsidiary. They become another factor, in addition to changing exchange rates, that must be considered in evaluating financial performance of a foreign subsidiary and its management.

Taxes and Transfer Pricing

A major issue surrounding transfer prices in the international arena is how they impact on the total tax burden of parent firms. Each of the preceding disclosures of transfer-pricing policy conveys a sense of its inherent reasonableness. The levels of income taxes and tariffs vary considerably across countries. For example, the corporate income tax rate is 16.5% in Hong Kong and ranges up to 50% and more in such countries as Korea, Denmark, India, and Ireland. This opens up the possibility that transfer prices may be set in part to minimize a firm's worldwide tax bill. Establishing the reasonableness of international transfer prices is the principal defense against a charge of transfer price manipulation.

   Ignoring other factors bearing on the setting of transfer prices, assume that the objective is to minimize worldwide income taxes. The income tax rate of the parent is 40% and that of the foreign subsidiary is 30%. Further, the parent is the manufacturer and transfers are made to the foreign subsidiary. The total cost of the product is $100 per unit, and it can be sold by the foreign subsidiary at insignificant additional cost for an amount equal to $150. Therefore, the total worldwide profit to be recognized is $50.

While the parent would not have unlimited flexibility in setting the transfer price, the objective of tax minimization would call for recognizing as much of the profit as possible in the earnings of the subsidiary. This is accomplished by setting a relatively low transfer price as illustrated in Exhibit 12.20.

The tax authorities of countries are well aware that multinationals have strong incentives to shift profits into low-rate countries. Recent years have seen governments increasingly willing to challenge tax computations that they believe are based upon the use of unreasonable transfer prices. Therefore, the previous example simply shows how total tax payments can be influenced by alternative transfer prices, although the degree of flexibility shown may or may not be available.

Notice, in the preceding example, that no change in policy would result if the foreign country also had an ad valorem tariff. Worldwide taxes would still be minimized by a low transfer price because this would also minimize the tariff. However, circumstances would differ if the parent's income tax rate were less than that of the subsidiary. Setting a high transfer price would cause more of the profit to be taxed at the lower income tax rate of the parent. However, this benefit is offset to some extent by the higher tariff in the subsidiary's country. The analysis would need to be extended to include tariffs in the total taxes to be minimized.

Other Influences on Transfer Pricing Policy and Potential Conflicts

Factors other than tax minimization also bear on the establishment of transfer prices. An effort to build market share or to respond to severe price competition

EXHIBIT 12.20   International transfer pricing and tax minimization.

	Low Transfer Price		High Transfer Price	
Parent revenue	$110		$140	
Cost	100		100	
Pretax profit	10		40	
Income tax (40%)	4	$ 4	16	$16
Subsidiary revenue	150		150	
Cost (transfer price)	110		140	
Pretax profit	40		10	
Income tax (30%)	12	12	3	3
Worldwide tax		$16		$19
Composite tax rate		32%		38%

might call for low transfer prices. At the same time this could be in conflict with a tax-minimization objective, if income tax rates in the country receiving the transferred goods (transferee country) had higher rates than the country from which the transfer was made (transferor country).

Restrictions on the ability to repatriate profits are sometimes circumvented by charging high transfer prices. This effectively involves taking out profits in the form of payments for the goods shipped. There are, of course, some potential offsetting disadvantages from this practice:

1. Charging higher transfer prices will increase ad valorem tariffs.
2. Charging higher transfer prices will lower profits of the transferee firm and potentially present problems in the evaluation of the profit performance of the unit and its management.
3. Charging higher transfer prices might impair the competitive position of the transferee firm.
4. Charging higher transfer prices lowers profits of the transferee firm and could reduce its apparent financial strength in the eyes of lenders and other users of its financial statements.

This enumeration of factors bearing on the setting of transfer prices is not exhaustive. However, it should be sufficient to highlight the inherent complexity of setting transfer prices. This complexity is magnified as the global reach of multinational firms extends into greater numbers of countries with wide variations in taxes, competitive conditions, business practices, types of governmental control, variability in exchange rates, and rates of inflation. This last factor, rates of inflation, is discussed next in terms of its impact on measuring the financial performance of both domestic firms as will as foreign subsidiaries.

IMPACT OF INFLATION ON THE FINANCIAL PERFORMANCE OF FOREIGN SUBSIDIARIES

As Fashionhouse continued its evolution as a global firm, it considered locating manufacturing capacity in countries with low labor costs. However, in many cases high rates of inflation were linked to low labor costs. Judging performance in highly inflationary environments presents special problems. At some point, financial statements prepared from unadjusted (historical) cost data lose their ability to provide reasonable indicators of either the financial performance or status of firms. Several different approaches have been developed to adjust historical cost financial statements. The principal methods can be classified as involving either (1) general price level or (2) current cost adjustments. These two methods are illustrated next and contrasted with historical-cost statements as the baseline. To provide some useful background, commentary on the impact of inflation on financial performance drawn from selected U.S. annual reports will first be presented.

Management Commentary on the Impact of and Response to Inflation

Management's Discussion and Analysis, a section of the annual report required by the SEC, often includes commentary on the impact of inflation on financial performance. This commentary provides useful insight into both management's assessment of the impact of inflation as well as any company circumstances or actions taken, which mitigate inflation's negative effects. A series of these comments is presented next.

1. *Pricing policy, late payment charges, and working capital management.*

   Praxair, Inc. (1995 Annual Report, p. 21)

   The Company manages its Brazilian operations with a focus on U.S. dollar results. This is achieved through a pricing policy that is consistent with local inflation, protection of accounts receivable value through charges for late payment, and effective working capital management.

2. *Use of LIFO inventory method.*

   Jefferson Smurfit Corporation (1995 Form 10-K, 21)

   The Company uses the last-in, first-out method of accounting for approximately 80% of its inventories. Under this method, the cost of products sold reported in the financial statements approximates current cost and thus reduces the distortion in reported income due to increasing costs.

3. *Selling price adjustments and cost efficiencies.*

   Ralston Purina Company (1995 Annual Report, p. 18)

   Management recognizes that inflationary pressures may have an adverse effect on the Company through higher asset replacement costs and related depreciation and higher material costs. The Company tries to minimize these effects through cost reductions and efficiency improvements as well as price increases to maintain reasonable profit margins.

4. *Use of accelerated depreciation.*

   Newport Corporation (1990 Annual Report, p. 16)

   Additionally, the Company depreciates its equipment using accelerated depreciation methods which lessen the impact of expensing historical dollars of depreciation when compared to fixed-asset replacement cost.

5. *Price escalation provisions.*

AMP Incorporated (1989 Annual Report, pp. 20–21)

Gold and plastic resins . . . are also subject to wide price fluctuations, particularly gold. Sales contracts frequently allow for price adjustments on the gold content of the Company's product.

Management concerns, revealed above, center on avoiding an erosion of profits due to inflation's impact on both costs and revenues. Techniques employed included raising prices on a timely basis, lowering costs through operating efficiencies, and, though less common, achieving some price protection through the use of escalation features in pricing arrangements. Protection from cost inflation of *commodities* is often achieved through the use of the same types of hedging vehicles employed to avoid cost increases created by exchange rate movements. An example: "Genetics has contractual commitments with seed growers for payments based on Chicago Board of Trade futures prices. These payments are hedged by using Chicago Board of Trade futures and options contracts" (DeKalb Genetics, 1990 Annual Report, p. 29). Public transit systems and airlines also seek cost protection by investing in petroleum futures. Should petroleum prices increase, the gain on futures contracts will offset the increased cost of petroleum products, used by the transit systems and airlines.

The other major concern revealed in the previous selections was that profits not be overstated in periods of significant inflation. A common method used to avoid this result is the LIFO method of inventory valuation. This ensures that the cost of inventory items deducted from revenues approximates their replacement cost. Profit overstatement was also avoided if most depreciable assets were relatively new, so that the depreciation expense deducted from revenues was much closer to replacement cost than if depreciation were composed mainly of the lower costs of older assets.

The use of LIFO and the reliance upon relatively new depreciable assets to cause expenses to approximate current (replacement) costs suffers from (1) only representing a partial adjustment for the impact of inflation and (2) not being uniformly available or applicable to all firms. That is, some firms may find it disadvantageous from a tax standpoint to use LIFO, and others may not be endowed with mainly new depreciable assets. Price-level adjusted profit calculations are applied uniformly to historical-cost statements, regardless of the accounting policies applied, for example, LIFO versus FIFO, or the vintage of fixed assets.

Price-Level Adjusted Performance Measurement[27]

Beginning in 1979, certain large U.S. firms were required to provide supplemental information on the impact of inflation on financial performance.[28] The primary new disclosures called for earnings computed on both a constant-dollar and a current-cost basis. The *constant-dollar* method retains historical cost as the basis of financial measurement. However, it does make selected restatements so that all financial statement balances are presented in units of the same purchasing power, that is, expressed in the same price index. The *current-cost* method replaces historical cost balances with current (replacement) costs as the basis for financial statement measurement. Exhibit 12.21 provides an example of disclosure of adjusted profit as provided in the 1980 Tiger International Annual Report (p. 39, excerpts).

The major message conveyed by this schedule is that a significant level of historical-cost profits is almost eliminated, when current-cost adjustments are applied, and that the profit actually turns into a loss under the constant-dollar alternative. The investment of purchasing power, as represented by the constant-dollar amount of expenses, exceeds that recovered, as represented by Tiger's constant-dollar revenues. Closer study of the data is necessary to understand the reasons behind these quite different messages.

The revenues in each of the three earnings statements are measured in the average price level for the year; the index used is the *Consumer Price Index for All Urban Consumers*. Tiger's revenues are earned fairly evenly across the year, and therefore, the revenues in the historical (as reported) income statement are already expressed in average prices for the year. Accordingly, the same revenue amount can be used in both the constant-dollar and current-cost statements. The same applies to the amounts for selling, general, and administrative; interest, net; and the income tax provision.

EXHIBIT 12.21 **Tiger International, Inc. and subsidiaries' statement of income adjusted for changing prices for the year ended December 31, 1980 (in thousands).**

	Historical Financials	Constant Dollar	Current Cost
Revenues	$1,562,270	$1,562,270	$1,562,270
Cost and Expenses			
Cost of operations	1,104,672	1,109,324	1,108,673
Selling, general, and administration	139,462	139,462	139,462
Depreciation and amortization	118,332	171,096	151,924
Interest, net	140,929	140,929	140,929
Income tax provision	16,500	16,500	16,500
	1,519,895	1,577,311	1,557,488
Net income (loss)	$ 42,375	$ (15,041)	$ 4,782

SOURCE: Tiger International annual report, December 1980, p. 39.

Modest adjustments were made to cost of operations in the historical income statement to convert them to constant dollar and current cost, respectively. The constant-dollar adjustment is made by multiplying the historical cost of operations by a ratio of price indices. The index in the numerator is the average price index for the current year, and in the denominator, it is the value of the index, at the date closest to the date on which the expense was incurred. To illustrate, assume that a $1,000 expense was recorded on January 1, 20X1 when the price index was 100; the average price index for 20X1 was 110. Adjustment to constant dollars is:

$$\$1,000 \times (110/100) = \$1,100$$

The same methodology is applied in adjusting historical cost of operations to current-cost amounts. The difference is that indices of specific replacement cost, or alternative measures of replacement cost, are used in place of a general price index.

Tiger reported that increases in inventory costs, included in cost of operations, accounted for the adjustments to historical cost of operations. In general, adjustments of historical cost of sales will be small if the LIFO inventory valuation method is used; the LIFO cost flow ensures that cost of sales already approximates current costs. Adjustments will generally be greater where the LIFO or average-cost methods are in use.

Impact of Differences in General and Specific Price Index Movements

The major Tiger cost adjustment was to depreciation and amortization. Depreciation and amortization represent the conversion to expense, of asset balances carried on the balance sheet. In many cases, these balances were recorded years earlier, when the price indices were at far lower values. Notice that the percentage increase in the constant dollar and current cost depreciation and amortization, over the historical-cost amount, is 45% and 29%, respectively. Tiger's disclosures explain the reason for the differences: "Depreciation expense . . . (is) greater when adjusted for general inflation than when adjusted for changes in specific prices. The difference reflects the Consumer Price Index (general inflation) rising faster than the increase of costs over the last several years of the type of property, plant and equipment used in the Company's various businesses . . ." (1980 Annual Report, p. 39).

Impact of Monetary Balances on Adjusted Results

In addition to the above two inflation-adjusted income presentations, Tiger provided additional income data because it did not feel that the required disclo-

EXHIBIT 12.22   Tiger International, Inc. and subsidiaries' earnings adjusted for purchasing power gains from monetary position (in thousands).

	Historical Financials	Constant Dollar	Current Cost
Net income	$42,375	$(15,041)	$ 4,782
Decrease in depreciation and interest expense . . . from decline in purchasing power of net monetary liabilities		82,195	82,195
Net income adjusted for decrease in depreciation and interest expense	$42,375	$67,154	$86,977

SOURCE: Tiger International annual report, December 1980, p. 39.

sures, adjusting mainly depreciation and cost of sales, were adequate. These adjustments added to the preceding display as shown in Exhibit 12.22.

Tiger's final adjusted net incomes tell a totally different story from the initial display. The new income element results from the impact of changes in the price level, on the purchasing power of monetary assets and liabilities. Tiger explains the impact of price changes on monetary balances as follows (1980 Annual Report, p. 40):

> A monetary asset represents money or a claim to receive money without reference to future changes in prices. Similarly a monetary liability represents an obligation to pay a sum of money which is fixed or determinable without reference to changes in future prices. Holding a monetary asset during periods of inflation results in a decline in the value of the asset since the dollar loses purchasing power when it is held. Conversely, holders of monetary liabilities benefit during inflationary periods because less purchasing power is required to satisfy future obligations when they can be paid with less valuable dollars.

Under this reasoning, Tiger earned an unrealized purchasing-power gain because its monetary liabilities exceeded its monetary assets. The impact of both inflation and deflation on purchasing-power gains, under conditions of both monetary assets exceeding monetary liabilities (net asset exposure) and monetary liabilities exceeding monetary assets (net liability exposure) are summarized in Exhibit 12.23.

Tiger treats the purchasing power gain as an adjustment to depreciation and interest expense based upon the following reasoning (1980 Annual Report, p. 40): "Because Tiger finances substantially all of its fixed assets with long-term debt, it effectively hedges against the impact of inflation on depreciation and interest expense." Tiger's liability exposure serves as a hedge because it produces a gain under inflationary conditions, to offset increases in the cost of asset replacement

EXHIBIT 12.23 Purchasing power gains and losses and net monetary position.

Price Movement	Net Monetary Position	
	Asset	Liability
Inflation	Loss	Gain
Deflation	Gain	Loss

and interest expense, which go hand in hand with inflation. The GAAP requirement followed by Tiger, FASB Statement No. 33, did call for computation and disclosure of the purchasing power gain or loss.[29] However, it did not permit its inclusion in income adjusted for changing prices.

The price-level adjusted reporting just illustrated proved to be a very controversial requirement. It was difficult to document that the data were used by creditors or investors, or that they aided analysis and decision making in any significant way. In 1986, *FASB Statement No. 89: Financial Reporting and Changing Prices,* was issued, which eliminated mandatory disclosure of price-level adjusted data.[30] The Statement did encourage continued disclosure on a voluntary basis. U.S. firms have, however, not responded to this encouragement; the price-level adjusted disclosures have not been continued.

Like the Americans, the British, who debated for years requiring price-level adjusted data, finally required current cost data to be provided. Then, in response to much the same pressure as in the U.S., they abandoned the requirement.[31] Disclosure of price-level adjusted data continues to be a requirement in some countries that have been subject to high and sustained inflation. However, deciding when and how to adjust financial data for the impact of changing prices remains a contentious and unresolved issue.

U.S. GOVERNMENT RESTRICTIONS ON BUSINESS PRACTICES ASSOCIATED WITH FOREIGN SUBSIDIARIES AND GOVERNMENT[32]

The last issue raised in the opening Fashionhouse scenario dealt with U.S. governmental restrictions on business practices associated with overseas operations. Recall that, in reviewing the possibility of relocation of manufacturing to a high inflation/low labor-cost country, Fashionhouse management became aware of potential ethical and legal issues.

In recent years, the U.S. government became concerned with the practices sometimes followed by U.S. firms, when doing business overseas. Of special concern were payments to foreign governmental officials made to obtain business.

From hearings over a number of years, which focused on such incidents, a recurring theme emerged: In addition to the fact that such payments did indeed take place, key members of management were often unaware that such payments were being made.

The U.S. Congress addressed the issue of controlling what they saw to be improper activities, by passing the *Foreign Corrupt Practices Act of 1977*. The key features of this law were:

1. The prohibition of bribery of foreign governmental or political officials in order to promote business.
2. The requirement that firms (a) keep accurate and detailed records of the company financial activities and (b) maintain a system of internal accounting controls sufficient to provide reasonable assurance that transactions are properly authorized, recorded, and accounted for.

These requirements are incorporated as amendments to Section 13(b) of the Securities Exchange Act of 1934, and apply to all publicly held companies. The recordkeeping and internal control features of the Act were a response to claims that companies had been unaware of bribery payments, because their internal control systems had failed to detect or prevent them.

In a report addressed to the SEC, the National Commission on Fraudulent Financial Reporting made the following recommendation:

> All public companies should be required by SEC rule to include in their annual reports to stockholders management reports signed by the chief executive officer and the chief accounting officer and/or the chief financial officer. The management report should acknowledge management's responsibilities for the financial statements and internal control, discuss how these responsibilities were fulfilled, and provide management's assessment of the effectiveness of the company's internal controls (p. 44).[33]

While the SEC has not adopted the Commission's recommendation, many companies have elected to provide voluntarily a report of management's responsibilities.[34] And while the precise title of the report may vary, representative titles include Report of Management Responsibility for Financial Statements and Internal Control and Financial Reporting Responsibility. Although the precise language of the report differs from company to company, the example from the 1996 Annual Report of Procter & Gamble Company is representative (p. 28) and is shown in Exhibit 12.24.

The precise meaning of the provisions of the Foreign Corrupt Practices Act continues to evolve. However, in considering expansion into a country, where improper payments have a long and durable tradition, Fashionhouse must pay special attention to the existence and requirements of the Act.

EXHIBIT 12.24   Procter & Gamble Company Statement of Responsibility for the Financial Statements.

The consolidated financial statements and the related financial information included in this report are the responsibility of Company management. This responsibility includes preparing the statements in accordance with generally accepted accounting principles and necessarily includes estimates that are based on management's best judgments.

To help insure the accuracy and integrity of Company financial data, management maintains a system of internal controls that is designed to provide reasonable assurance that transactions are executed as authorized and accurately recorded and that assets are properly safeguarded. These controls are monitored by an extensive and ongoing program of internal audits. These audits are supplemented by a self-assessment program that enables individual organizations to evaluate the effectiveness of their control structure. Careful selection of employees and appropriate divisions of responsibility also are designed to achieve our control objectives. The Company's "Worldwide Business Conduct Manual" sets forth management's commitment to conducting its business affairs in keeping with the highest ethical standards.

Deloitte & Touche LLP, independent public accountants, have audited and reported on the Company's consolidated financial statements. There audits were performed in accordance with generally accepted auditing standards.

The Board of Directors, acting through its Audit Committee composed entirely of outside directors, oversees the adequacy of the Company's control environment. The Audit Committee meets periodically with representatives of Deloitte & Touche LLP and internal financial management to review internal control, auditing, and financial reporting matters. The independent auditors and the internal auditors also have full and free access to meet privately with the Audit Committee.

Note: Signed by the Chairman and Chief Executive Officer along with the Chief Financial Officer

SUMMARY

The evolution of Fashionhouse from a purely domestic firm to a truly global entity continues to confront it with new and increasingly complex problems of accounting, finance, and management. This chapter has followed Fashionhouse through this evolution and attempted to help the reader become aware of the problems faced and how they might be addressed. The range of issues addressed is broad and increasingly complex. It has not been possible, nor would it have been appropriate in a volume such as this, to deal with all aspects of every issue raised. The reader should consult the many books and articles cited throughout the chapter and in the list of further readings for additional background.

FOR FURTHER READING

Beaver, W. and W. Landsman, *Incremental Information Content of Statement 33 Disclosures* (Stamford, CT: Financial Accounting Standards Board, 1983).

Choi, F., ed., *Handbook of International Accounting* (New York: John Wiley & Sons, 1991).

Epstein, B. and A. Mirza, *Interpretation and Application of International Accounting Standards 1997* (New York: John Wiley & Sons, 1997).

Financial Accounting Standards Board, *Proposed Statement of Financial Accounting Standards, Accounting for Derivative and Similar Financial Instruments and for Hedging Activities* (Norwalk, CT: Financial Accounting Standards Board, June, 1996).

————, *The IASC-U.S. Comparison Project: A Report on the Similarities and Differences between IASC Standards and U.S. GAAP* (Norwalk, CT: Financial Accounting Standards Board, November 1996).

————, *Financial Reporting in North America—Highlights of a Joint Study* (Norwalk, CT: Financial Accounting Standards Board, December 1994).

Flicker, S. and D. Bline, "Managing Foreign Currency Exchange Risk," *Journal of Accountancy* (August 1990).

Frishkoff, P., *Financial Reporting and Changing Prices: A Review of Empirical Research* (Stamford, CT: Financial Accounting Standards Board, 1982).

Goldberg, S. and J. Godwin, "Foreign Corrupt Practices Act: Some Pitfalls and How to Avoid Them," *The Journal of Corporate Accounting and Finance* (Winter 1995/96).

Goodwin, J., S. Goldberg, and C. Tritschler, "Understanding Foreign Currency Derivative Measurements as FASB Moves Toward Fair Value Reporting," *The Journal of Corporate Accounting and Finance* (Spring 1996).

Haskins, M., K. Ferris, and T. Selling, *International Financial Reporting and Analysis* (Chicago: Richard D. Irwin, 1996).

Kim, H., *Fundamental Analysis Worldwide* (New York: John Wiley & Sons, 1996).

Radebaugh, L. and S. Gray, *International Accounting for Multinational Enterprises,* 3d ed. (New York: John Wiley & Sons, 1993).

Shapiro, A., *Multinational Financial Management,* 5th ed. (Upper Saddle River, NJ: Prentice-Hall, 1996).

ANNUAL REPORTS TO SHAREHOLDERS REFERENCED IN THIS CHAPTER

AMP Incorporated (1989)

Akzo Nobel, N.V. (1993)

Amgen (1995)

Amoco Corporation (1995)

AMR Corporation (1989 and 1995)

Analog Devices, Inc. (1995)

Apple Computer, Inc. (1995)

Armstrong World Industries (1995)

Baxter International (1995)

Becton Dickinson & Company (1995)

Black & Decker Corporation (1995)

BMC Software, Inc. (1996)

California First Bank, now Union Bank (1987)

Chevron Corporation (1995)

Compaq Computer Corporation (1995)

DeKalb Genetics (1990)

The Dow Chemical Company (1995)

Federal Express Corporation (1989)

Fluor Corporation (1995)

The Goodyear Tire and Rubber Company (1995)

Illinois Tool Works, Inc. (1995)

Ingersoll-Rand (1995)

Jefferson Smurfit Corporation (1995)

Newport Corporation (1990)

Praxair, Inc. (1995)

The Procter & Gamble Company (1996)

Ralston Purina Company (1995)

Raychem Corporation (1995)

Southmark Corporation (1987)

Storage Technology Corporation (1995)

Tiger International (1980)

UAL Corporation (1993)

NOTES

1. Foreign currency exchange rates can be quoted in either a direct or an indirect fashion. When quoted directly, the foreign currency exchange rate is expressed in terms of the reporting currency. Quoting the exchange rate for the krone as $.178 is a direct quote, indicating the number of dollars (the reporting currency) per krone. An indirect quotation for this example would be K5.618 (1/.178), indicating the number of krone per dollar.

2. A U.S. electronics company recently attempted to eliminate currency risk by having its Japanese supplier invoice it in the U.S. dollar. The Japanese supplier agreed to do this and introduced a new, higher schedule of prices in dollars. The U.S. company deemed the increases to be so high that it decided to continue to be invoiced in the Japanese yen and to manage the associated exchange risk.

3. Each of the actual case examples discussed in this section is treated in more detail, including income tax and cash-flow issues, in Comiskey and Mulford, "Risks of Foreign Currency Transactions: A Guide for Loan Officers," *Commercial Lending Review* (Summer 1990), pp. 44–60.

4. The accounting treatment to ensure that the offsetting gains and losses are included in the income statements at the same time is a bit technical. Federal Express reports that ". . . exchange rate gains and losses on the term loan are deferred and amortized over the remaining life of the loan as an adjustment to the related hedge (service) revenue" (Federal Express 1989 Annual Report, p. 36).

5. This example is discussed in "FX Translation—Lyle Shipping's Losses" (no author), *Accountancy* (December 1984), p. 50. Lyle has an *economic* hedge of its dollar exposure but not an *accounting* hedge. Lyle's risk is controlled, in whole or in part, by the offsetting dollar flows. However, under conventional accounting practices, the gain or loss on the dollar liability is recognized in the periods in which the exchange rates change. Offsetting gains or losses are not recorded in the same periods because the future dollar charter inflows have yet to be earned and are not reflected as an asset on Lyle's books until they are actually collected.

6. See Peter J. Maloney, "Managing Currency Exposure: The Case of Western Mining," *Journal of Applied Corporate Finance* (Winter 1990), for an analysis of the effectiveness of this natural hedge during the 1980s.

7. The forward price of a foreign currency can also be at a discount to the spot price. This premium or discount relationship is determined mainly by the relative level of interest rates in the countries representing, respectively, the foreign and domestic currency.

8. Southmark's 1987 Annual Report (p. 41) reported that "Southmark also invested in additional Swiss franc futures contracts on which it recognized a gain of $16.2 million." These contracts did not serve to hedge Swiss franc debt. Rather, they represented a means of taking a position on the likely movement of the franc. Because the franc appreciated, Southmark made a gain. If the franc had depreciated, then a loss would have resulted. It is common to refer to these nonhedge positions as speculations.

9. Speculative positions in derivative instruments, of which forwards, futures, and options are examples, received much bad press in the 1990s, as the result of dramatic losses incurred by some major U.S. firms. Some firms now make it a point to declare that they do not use derivatives for speculative purposes. In its 1995 annual report (p. 36), Ford Motor Company declared that ". . . company policy specifically prohibits the use of derivatives for speculative purposes."

10. Judy C. Lewent and A. John Kearney, "Identifying, Measuring and Hedging Currency Risk at Merck," *Journal of Applied Corporate Finance* (Winter 1990), pp. 19–28, for additional technical background.

11. Information on Danish GAAP can be found in Comiskey and Mulford, "Comparing Danish Accounting and Reporting Practices with International Accounting Standards," *Advances in International Accounting* (vol. 4, JAI Press, Greenwich, CT, 1991), pp. 123–142, edited by Kenneth S. Most.

12. For further detail on all matters related to accounting for foreign-currency transactions and statement translation, consult Financial Accounting Standards Board, Statement of Financial Accounting Standards No. 52, *Foreign Currency Translation* (December 1981).

13. Ibid., paragraph 39.

14. Statement No. 52, *Foreign Currency Translation*, refers to this alternative procedure as remeasurement and not translation. However, in the vast majority of cases, the remeasurement is from the foreign currency to the U.S. dollar. Therefore, remeasurement produces statements in the U.S. dollar that are ready to be consolidated with the statements of their U.S. parent. Remeasurement is tantamount to translation.

15. P. Collier, E. W. Davis, J. B. Coates, and S. G. Longden, "The Management of Currency Risk: Case Studies of US and UK Multinationals," *Accounting and Business Research* (Summer 1990), p. 208.

16. Statement of Financial Accounting Standards Number 8, *Accounting for the Translation of Foreign Currency Transactions and Foreign Financial Statements* (October 1975).

17. Carol Olson Houston and Gerhard G. Mueller, "Foreign Exchange Rate Hedging and SFAS No. 52—Relatives or Strangers?," *Accounting Horizons* (December 1988), p. 57.

18. International Accounting Standards Committee, Exposure Draft 32, *Comparability of Financial Statements* (January 11, 1989).

19. Ibid., paragraph 6.

20. International Accounting Standards Committee, Statement of Intent, *Comparability of Financial Statements* (July 1990).

21. For a standard-by-standard analysis of the differences between current U.S. GAAP and IASC standards, see "The IASC-U.S. Comparison Project: A Report on the Similarities and Differences between IASC Standards and U.S. GAAP" (Financial Accounting Standards Board, November, 1996).

22. A 1993 change in the tax law, Internal Revenue Code, section 197, now makes it possible to amortize goodwill in the tax return for qualifying acquisitions.

23. From a statement made by R. S. Miller, Jr., executive vice president and chief financial officer of Chrysler Corporation, to the Financial Accounting Standards Board, Washington, DC, November 3, 1989, p. 3.

24. Removing the effects of exchange rate changes in cases where the subsidiary is using the temporal (remeasurement) translation method, as opposed to the all-current method, is a greater challenge and beyond the scope of this chapter.

25. *The Value Line Investment Survey: Ratings & Reports* (New York: Value Line Publishing, Inc., 1990 and 1996).

26. The following two references were of great assistance in preparing this discussion of transfer pricing: Frederick D. S. Choi and Gerhard G. Mueller, *An Introduction to Multinational Accounting* (Englewood Cliffs, NJ: Prentice-Hall, Inc., 1978), chapter 9; and Jeffrey S. Arpan and Lee H. Radebaugh, *International Accounting and Multinational Enterprises* (New York: Warren, Gorham & Lamont, 1981), chapter 10.

27. *Accounting for Changing Prices: Replacement Cost and General Price Level Adjustments* (Santa Barbara, CA: Wiley/Hamilton, 1976) by Largay and Livingstone was helpful in preparing this section.

28. Financial Accounting Standards Board, Statement of Financial Accounting Standards Number 33, *Financial Reporting and Changing Prices* (September 1979).

29. Ibid.

30. *Statement of Financial Accounting Standards No. 89: Financial Reporting and Changing Prices* (Stamford, CT: FASB, 1986).

31. Institute of Chartered Accountants in England and Wales, Accounting Standards Committee, Statement of Standard Accounting Practice No. 16, *Current Cost Accounting* (1980).

32. For further background on this topic, see K. Fred Skousen, *An Introduction to the SEC*, 4th ed. (Cincinnati: South-Western Publishing Company, 1987), pp. 32–35.

33. *Report of the National Commission on Fraudulent Financial Reporting* (Washington, DC, 1987).

34. In an article entitled, "What is Internal Control? Who Owns It?" published in *Management Accounting,* Schiff and May report the results of a Deloitte & Touche survey, which indicates that almost 60% of companies with an excess of $500 million in sales include a management report in their annual reports.

13 MANAGING FINANCIAL RISK
Steven P. Feinstein

For better or worse, the business environment is fraught with risks. Uncertainty is a fact of life. Profits are never certain, input and output prices change, competitors emerge and disappear, customers' tastes constantly evolve, technological progress creates instability, interest rates fluctuate, as do foreign currency values and asset prices. Nonetheless, managers must continue to make decisions. Businesses must cope with risk in order to operate. Managers and firms are often evaluated on overall performance, even though performance may be affected by risky factors beyond their control. The goal of risk management is to maximize the value of the firm by reducing the negative potential impact of forces beyond the control of management.

There are essentially four basic approaches to risk management: risk avoidance, risk retention, loss prevention and control, and risk transfer. Suppose after a firm has analyzed a risky business venture, and weighed both the costs and benefits of exposure to risk, management chooses not to embark on the project. They determine that the potential rewards are not worth the risks. Such a strategy would be an example of risk avoidance. *Risk avoidance* means choosing not to engage in a risky activity because of the risks. Choosing not to fly in a commercial airliner, due to the risk that the plane might crash, is an example of risk avoidance.

Risk retention is another simple strategy, in which the firm chooses to engage in the project and do nothing about the identified risks. After weighing the costs and benefits, the firm chooses to proceed. It is the "damn the torpedoes" approach to risk management. For many firms, risk retention is the optimal strategy for all risks. Investors expect the company's stock to be risky, and they do not reward managers for reducing risks. Investors cope with business risks by diversifying their holdings within their portfolios, and so they do not want business managers to devote resources to managing risks within the firm.

Loss prevention and control involves embarking on a risky project, yet taking steps to reduce the likelihood and severity of any losses potentially resulting from uncontrollable factors. In the flying example, loss prevention and control would be the response of the airline passenger who chooses to fly, but also selects the safest airline, listens to the preflight safety instructions, sits near the emergency exit, and perhaps brings his or her own parachute. The passenger in this example has no control over how many airplanes crash in a given year, but he or she takes steps to make sure not to be on one of them, and if so, to be a survivor.

Risk transfer involves shifting the negative consequences of a risky factor to another person, firm, or party. For example, buying flight insurance shifts some of the negative financial consequences of a crash to an insurance company and away from the passenger's family. Should the airplane crash, the insurance company suffers a financial loss, and the passenger's family is financially compensated. Forcing foreign customers to pay for finished goods in your home currency rather than in their local currency is another example of risk transfer, whereby you transfer the risk of currency fluctuations to your customers. If the value of the foreign currency drops, the customers must still pay you an agreed-upon number of dollars, for example, even though it costs them more to do so in terms of their home currency.

No one risk management approach is ideal for all situations. Sometimes risk avoidance is optimal; sometimes risk retention is the desired strategy. Recent developments in the financial marketplace, however, have made risk transfer much more feasible than in the past. More and more often now, especially when financial risks are involved, it is the most desirable alternative.

In recent years, there has been revolutionary change in the financial marketplace. The very same marketplace that traditionally facilitated the transfer of funds from investors to firms, has brought forth numerous derivative instruments that facilitate the transfer of risk. Just as the financial marketplace has been innovative in engineering various types of investment contracts, such as stocks, bonds, preferred stock, and convertible bonds, the financial marketplace now engineers risk transfer instruments, such as forwards, futures, options, swaps, and a multitude of variants of these derivatives.

Reading stories about derivatives in the popular press might lead one to believe that derivative instruments are dangerous and destabilizing—evil creatures that emerged from the dark recesses of the financial marketplace. The cover of the April 11, 1994 *Time Magazine* introduced derivatives with the caption "HIGH-TECH SUPERNERDS ARE PLAYING DANGEROUS GAMES WITH YOUR MONEY." The use of derivatives has been implicated in most of the financial calamities of the past decade: Barings Bank, Orange County, Procter & Gamble, Metallge-sellschaft, and Askin Capital Management, to name a few. In each of the cases, vast sums of money quickly vanished, and derivatives seemed to be to blame.

WHAT WENT WRONG: CASE STUDIES OF DERIVATIVES DEBACLES

Derivatives were not responsible for the financial calamities of the 1990s. Greed, speculation, and probably incompetence were. But just as derivatives facilitate risk management, they facilitate greed and accelerate the consequences of spec-ulation and incompetence. For example, consider the following case histories of Barings Bank, Procter & Gamble, Metallgesellschaft, Askin Capital Manage-ment, and Orange County, and then draw your own conclusions.

Barings Bank

On February 26, 1995, Baring PLC, Britain's oldest merchant bank and one of the most venerable financial institutions in the world collapsed. Did this failure follow years of poor management and bad investments? Hardly. All of the bank's $615 million of capital had been wiped out in less than four months, by one employee, halfway around the world from London. It seems that a Barings deriv-atives trader named Nicholas Leeson, stationed in Singapore, had taken huge positions in futures and options on Japanese stocks. Leeson's job was supposed to be *index arbitrage,* meaning that he was supposed to take low-risk positions exploiting discrepancies between the prices of futures contracts traded in both Singapore and Osaka. Leeson's job was to buy whichever contract was cheaper and sell the one that was more dear. The difference would be profit for Barings. When he was long in Japanese stock futures in Osaka, he was supposed to be short in Japanese stock futures in Singapore, and vice versa. Such positions are inherently hedged. If the Singapore futures lost money, the Japanese futures would make money, and so little money, if any, could be lost.

Apparently, Leeson grew impatient taking hedged positions. He began to take unhedged bets, selling both call options and put options on Japanese stocks. Such a strategy, consisting of written call options and written put options is called a *straddle.* If the underlying stock price stays the same or does not move much, the writer keeps all the option premium, and profits handsomely. If, on the other hand, the underlying stock price either rises or falls substantially, the writer is vulnerable to large losses. Leeson bet and lost. Japanese stocks plummeted, and the straddles became a huge liability. Like a panicked gambler, Leeson tried to win back his losses by going long in Japanese stock futures. This position was a stark-naked speculative bet. Leeson lost again. Japanese stocks continued to fall. Leeson lost more than $1 billion, and Barings had lost all of its capital. The bank was put into receivership.

Procter & Gamble

Procter & Gamble, the well-known manufacturer of soap and household products, had a long history of negotiating low interest rates to finance operations. Toward this end, Procter & Gamble entered an interest rate swap with Bankers Trust in November of 1993. The swap agreement was far from plain-vanilla. It most certainly fit the description of an exotic derivative. The swap's cash flows were determined by a formula that involved short-term, medium-term, and long-term interest rates. Essentially, the deal would allow Procter & Gamble to reduce its financing rate by $\frac{1}{10}$ of 1% on $200 million of debt, if interest rates remained stable until May 1994. If, on the other hand, interest rates spiked upward, or if the spread between 5-year and 30-year rates narrowed, Procter & Gamble would lose money and have to pay a higher rate on its debt.

Even in the rarefied world of derivatives, one cannot expect something for nothing. In order to achieve a cheaper financing rate, Procter & Gamble had to give up or sell something. In this case, implicit in the swap, they sold interest rate insurance. The swap contained an embedded option, sold by Procter & Gamble. If the interest rate environment remained calm, Procter & Gamble would keep a modest premium, thereby lowering its financing costs. If interest rates became turbulent, Procter & Gamble would have to make big payments. Most economists in 1993 were forecasting calm. The bet seemed safe. But it was a bet, nevertheless. This was not a hedge, this was *speculation*. And they lost.

The Federal Reserve unexpectedly raised interest rates on February 4, 1994. Procter & Gamble suddenly found itself with a $100 million loss. Instead of lowering their financing rate by $\frac{1}{10}$ of 1%, they would have to pay an additional 14%!

Rather than lick its wounds and retire from swaps, Procter & Gamble went back for more—with prodding, of course, from Bankers Trust. As losses mounted on the first deal, Procter & Gamble entered a second swap, this one tied to German interest rates. German medium-term interest rates are remarkably stable, and so this bet seemed even safer than the first one. Guess what happened. Another $50 million of losses mounted before Procter & Gamble finally liquidated its positions. Losses totaled $157 million. Procter & Gamble sued Bankers Trust, alleging deception, mispricing, and violation of fiduciary responsibilities. Procter & Gamble claimed that they did not fully understand the risks of the swap agreements, nor how to calculate their value. Bankers Trust settled with Procter & Gamble, just as they settled with Gibson Greeting Cards, Air Products and Chemicals, and other companies that lost money in similar swaps.

Metallgesellschaft

Experts are still divided over what went wrong in the case of Metallgesellschaft, one of Germany's largest industrial concerns. This much is certain: In 1993, Metallgesellschaft had assets of $10 billion, sales exceeding $16 billion, and equity capital of $50 million. By the end of the year, this industrial giant was nearly bankrupt, having lost $1.3 billion in oil futures.

What makes the Metallgesellschaft case so intriguing is that the company seemed to be using derivatives for all the right reasons. An American subsidiary of Metallgesellschaft, MG Refining and Marketing (MGRM) had embarked upon an ingenious marketing plan. The subsidiary was in the business of selling gasoline and heating oil to distributors and retailers. To promote sales, the company offered contracts that would lock in prices for a period of 10 years. A variety of different contract types was offered, and the contracts had various provisions, deferments, and contingencies built in, but the important feature was a long-term price cap. The contracts were essentially forwards. The forward contracts were very popular and MGRM was quite successful at selling them.

MGRM understood that the forward contracts subjected the company to oil price risk. MGRM now had a short position in oil. If oil prices rose, the company would experience losses, as it would have to buy oil at higher prices and sell it at the lower contracted prices to the customers. To offset this risk, MGRM went long in exchange-traded oil futures. The long position in futures should have hedged the short position in forwards. Unfortunately, things did not work out so nicely.

Oil prices fell in 1993. As oil prices fell, Metallgesellschaft lost money on its long futures, and had to make cash payments as the futures were marked to market. The forwards, however, provided little immediate cash, and their appreciation in value would not be fully realized until they matured in 10 years. Thus, Metallgesellschaft was caught in a cash crunch. Some economists argue that if Metallgesellschaft had held onto its positions and continued to make margin payments the strategy would have worked eventually. But time ran out. The parent company took control over the subsidiary and liquidated its positions, thereby realizing a loss of $1.3 billion.

Other economists argue that Metallgesellschaft was not an innocent victim of unforeseeable circumstances. They argue that MGRM had designed the entire marketing and hedging strategy, just so they could profit by speculating that historical patterns in oil prices would persist. Traditionally, oil futures prices are lower than spot prices, so the general trend in oil futures prices is upward as they near expiration. MGRM's hedging plan was to repeatedly buy short-term oil futures, holding them until just before expiration, at which point they would roll over into new short-term futures. If the historical pattern had repeated itself, MGRM would have profited many times from the rollover strategy. It has been alleged that the futures was the planned source of profits, while the forward contracts with customers was the hedge against oil prices dropping.

Regardless of what was the intent of MGRM's management, the case teaches at least two lessons. First, it is important to consider cash flow and timing when constructing a hedge position. Second, when a hedge is working effectively, it will appear to be losing money when the position it is designed to offset is showing profits. Accounting for hedges should not be independent of the position being hedged.

Askin Capital Management

Between February and April 1994, David Askin lost all $600 million that he managed on behalf of the investors in his Granite Hedge Funds. Imagine the surprise of the investors. Not only had they earned over 22% the previous year, but the fund was invested in mortgage-backed securities—instruments guaranteed by the U.S. government not to default. The lesson from the Askin experience is that in the age of derivatives, investments with innocuous names might not be as safe and secure as they sound.

The particular type of mortgage-backed securities that Askin purchased were *collateralized mortgage obligations* (CMOs), which are bonds whose cash flows to investors are determined by a formula. The formula is a function of mortgage interest rates and also of the prepayment behavior of home buyers. Since the cash flow to CMOs is a function of some other economic variable, interest rates in this case, these instruments are categorized as derivatives. Some CMOs rise in value as interest rates rise, others fall. Askin's CMOs were very sensitive to interest rates. Askin's portfolio rose in value as interest rates fell in 1993. When interest rates began to rise again in February 1994, his portfolio suffered. Interest rate increases alone, however, were not the sole cause of Askin's losses. As interest rates rose and CMO prices fell, CMO investors everywhere got scared and sold. CMO prices were doubly battered as the demand dried up. It was a classic panic. Prices fell far more than the theoretical pricing models predicted. Eventually, calm returned to the market, investors trickled back, and prices rebounded. But it was too late for Askin. He had bought on margin, and his creditors had liquidated his fund at the market's bottom.

Orange County, California

Robert Citron, treasurer of Orange County, California in 1994, fell into the same trap that snared Procter & Gamble and David Askin. He speculated that interest rates would remain low. The best economic forecasts at the time supported this outlook. Derivatives allowed speculators to bet on the most likely scenario. Small bets provided modest returns. Big bets promised sizable returns. What these speculators did was akin to selling earthquake insurance in New York City. The likelihood of an earthquake there is very small, so insurers would almost assuredly get to keep the modest premiums without having to pay out any claims. If an earthquake did hit New York, however, the losses to the insurers would be enormous.

Citron bet and lost. The earthquake that toppled his portfolio was the unexpected interest rate hikes beginning in February 1994. Citron had borrowed against the bonds Orange County owned, and he invested the proceeds in derivative bonds called *inverse-floaters,* whose cash flow formulas made them extra sensitive to interest rate increases. Citron lost about $2 billion of the $7.7 billion he managed, and Orange County filed for bankruptcy in December 1994.

Conclusions

The lesson from these case studies should now be obvious. Risk management is not the art of picking good bets. Bets no matter how good are speculation. Speculation increases risk, and subjects corporations, investors, and even municipalities to potential losses. Derivatives are powerful tools to shed risk, but they can also be used to take on risk. The root causes of the debacles described in these cases are greed, speculation, and incompetence, not derivatives. But just as derivatives facilitate risk management, they facilitate greed and speculation. Anything that can be done with derivatives, can be done slower the old-fashioned way with positions in traditional financial instruments. Speculators have always managed to lose large sums. With the aid of derivatives they now can lose larger sums faster.

Government regulation is not the answer. The benefits of regulation must be weighed against the costs. Derivatives, properly used, are too important in the modern financial marketplace to be severely restricted. Abuse by a few does not warrant constraints on all users. A better solution to prevent repetition of the past debacles is full information disclosure by firms, portfolio managers, and municipalities. Investors and citizens should demand to know how derivatives are being used when their money is at stake. Better information and oversight is the most promising approach to prevent misuse of derivatives while retaining the benefits.

The fact of the matter is that derivatives can be dangerous, but they can also be tremendously useful. Dynamite is an appropriate analogy. Misused, it is destructive; handled with care, it is a powerful and constructive tool.

Derivatives are tools that facilitate the transfer of risk. Interest rate derivatives enable managers to shed business exposure to interest rate fluctuations, for example. But when one party sheds risk, another party necessarily must take on that very exposure. And therein lies the danger of derivatives. The same instrument that serves as a hedge to one firm, might be a destabilizing speculative instrument to another. Without a proper understanding of derivatives, a manager who intends to reduce risk, might inadvertently increase it. This chapter aims to provide the reader with a basic understanding of derivatives so that they can be used appropriately to manage financial risks. This understanding should help the reader avoid the common pitfalls that have proved disastrous to less-informed managers.

WIDESPREAD USE

A *derivative* is a financial instrument whose value or contingent cash flows depend on the value of some other underlying asset. For example, the value of a stock option depends on the value of the underlying stock. Derivatives as a class comprise forwards, futures, options, and swaps. Numerous hybrid instruments, combining the features of these basic building blocks have also been engineered. The first thing the interested manager must understand about derivatives is that the business in these instruments is now huge, and their use is pervasive. Since the initiation of trading in the first stock index futures contract in December of 1992—the Standard and Poor's 500 futures contract—the daily volume of this one instrument has grown so that it now exceeds the daily volume in all trading on the New York Stock Exchange. (Note that the volume of futures is measured in terms of *notional principal,* which is a measure of exposure.) On just one day, Tuesday, January 21, 1996, the notional volume of the Standard and Poor's 500 futures contract was just shy of $40 billion. The volume on the NYSE that same day was approximately $23 billion. Just one specific futures contract is now bigger than the entire Big Board stock market in terms of daily volume.

Similarly, the swaps market, which did not exist two decades ago, has revolutionized banking and finance. The notional principal of outstanding interest rate swaps today is greater than the sum total of all assets in United States banks. Assets of domestic U.S. banks amounted to $2.9 trillion in 1993, whereas the notional principal of outstanding swaps was over $7 trillion.

The volume in the derivatives market reflects how widespread derivatives use has become in business. Almost all major corporations now use them in one form or another. Some use derivatives to hedge commodity price risks. Some use them to speculate on price movements. Some firms reduce their exposures to volatile interest rates and foreign exchange. Other firms take on exposures via derivatives in order to potentially increase profits. Some firms use derivatives to secure cheaper financing. Many corporations use derivatives to reduce the transaction costs associated with managing a pension fund, borrowing money, or budgeting cash. Some firms implement derivative strategies to reduce their tax burdens. Many companies offer stock options, a derivative, as employee compensation. Some investment funds enhance returns by replacing traditional portfolios with what are called *synthetic portfolios*—portfolios composed in part of derivatives. Some investment funds buy derivatives that act as insurance contracts, protecting portfolio value. Since their emergence in the early 1980s, derivatives have touched every aspect of corporate finance, banking, the investments industry, and, arguably, business in general.

THE INSTRUMENTS

The major derivative instruments are forwards, futures, options, and swaps. Also available today are hybrid instruments, exotics, and structured or engineered instruments. The hybrids, exotics, and engineered instruments are contracts that combine features of the basic building blocks: the options, futures, forwards, and swaps. Consequently, familiarity with the basic building blocks goes a long way toward understanding the whole mélange of derivative instruments available today. We will begin with forwards.

Forwards

Imagine the following nearly idyllic scenario. It is late summer. You are a wheat farmer in Kansas. The hard work of sowing and tending your acreage is about to pay off. You expect a bumper crop this year, and the harvest is just a few weeks away. The weather is expected to remain favorable. The crops have been sprayed to protect them from pests. In fact, you may even have purchased crop insurance to protect against crop damage.

Still, you cannot relax. One major uncertainty is keeping you awake at night. You figure that if you are expecting a bumper crop, the likelihood that your neighbors are also expecting a bumper crop is high. If the market is flooded with wheat, prices will plummet. If prices drop, you will receive little revenue for your harvest, and perhaps you will show a loss for the year. A worst-case scenario might be that prices fall so low, that you cannot make the mortgage payments on your land or for the machinery you bought. You very well might lose the farm—and through no fault of your own. You farmed well, but if prices fall, you will fail nevertheless.

Meanwhile, at the same time, another group of business people is feeling similar anxiety. A baked goods company has recently built a new cookie bakery. The company identified its market niche as a provider of inexpensive, mass-produced, medium quality, cookies. The project analysis that led to the go-ahead for the new bakery assumed that wheat prices would stay fixed at their current levels. If wheat prices should rise, it is altogether possible that the firm will not be able to sell its cookies for a profit. The new bakery will appear to be a failure.

In these scenarios, both the farmers and the bakers are exposed to wheat price risk. The farmers worry that wheat prices will fall. The bakers worry that prices will rise. A forward contract is the obvious solution for both parties.

The farmers and bakers can negotiate a deferred wheat transaction. The farmers will deliver wheat to the bakers, one month from now, for a price currently agreed upon. Such a contract for a deferred transaction is a forward contract. A *forward contract* specifies an underlying asset to be delivered, a price to be paid, and the date of delivery. The specified transaction price is called the *forward price.* The party that will be selling wheat (the farmer) is known as the "short" party; the party that will be buying wheat (baker) is known as the "long" party. In the jargon of the derivatives market, the long party is said to "buy" the forward, and the short party "sells" the forward. Note, however, that when the deal is initially struck, no money changes hands and no one has yet bought or sold anything. The "buyer" and "seller" have agreed to a deferred transaction.

Notice that the wheat forward reduces risk for both the farmers and the bakers. In this transaction, both parties are hedgers—that is, they are using the forward to reduce risk. Forward contracts are "over-the-counter" instruments, meaning that they are negotiated between two parties and custom-tailored, rather than traded on exchanges.

Suppose after one month, when the forward expires and the wheat is delivered, the current, or *spot,* price of wheat has risen dramatically. The farmer may have some regret that he entered into the contract. Had he not sold forward, he would have been able to receive more for his wheat by selling on the spot market. He may feel like a loser. The bakers, on the other hand, will feel like winners. By contracting forward they insulated themselves from the rising wheat price. When spot prices rise, the long party wins while the short party loses. A little reflection, however, will convince the farmer that although he lost some money relative to what he could have gotten on the spot market, going short in the forward was indeed a worthwhile strategy. He had peace of mind over the one month. He was guaranteed a fair price, and he did not have to fear losing the farm. Though there was an opportunity loss, he benefited by shedding risk. The farmer probably never regrets that he has never collected on his life insurance either. He similarly should not regret that the forward contract represents an opportunity loss. He would be well advised to go short again next year.

The wheat forward contract can be used by speculators as well as hedgers. An agent who anticipates a rise in wheat prices can profit from that foresight by going long in the forward contract. By going long in the contract, the speculator agrees to buy wheat at the fixed forward price. Upon expiration of the contract, the speculator takes delivery of the wheat, pays the forward price, and then sells the wheat on the spot market for the higher spot price. The profit is the difference between the spot and forward prices. Of course, if the speculator's forecast is wrong, and the wheat price falls, the speculator would suffer losses equal to the difference between the forward and spot price. For example, suppose the initial spot price is $3 per bushel, and the forward price is $3.50 per bushel. If the spot price upon expiration is $4.50 per bushel, the long speculator would earn a profit of $1 per bushel. The profit is the terminal spot of $4.50 minus the $3.50 initial forward price. If, alternatively, the terminal spot price is $3.25, the speculator would *lose* 25 cents per bushel—that is, $3.25 minus $3.50. Notice that the $3 initial spot price is irrelevant in both cases.

Speculators play important roles in the derivatives markets. For one, speculators provide liquidity. If farmers wish to short forward contracts but there are no bakers around who want to go long, speculators will step in and offer to take the long side when the forward price is bid down low enough. Similarly, they will take the short side when the forward price is bid up high enough. Speculators also bring information to the marketplace. The existence of derivatives contracts and the promise of speculative profits make it worthwhile for speculators to devote resources to forecasting weather conditions, crop yields, and other factors that impact prices. Their forecasts are made known to the public as they buy or sell futures and forwards.

Futures

Futures contracts are closely related to forward contracts. Like forwards, futures are contracts that spell out deferred transactions. The long party commits to buying some underlying asset, and the short party commits to sell. The differences between futures and forwards are mainly technical and logistical. Forward contracts are custom-tailored, over-the-counter agreements, struck between two parties via negotiation. *Futures,* alternatively, are standardized contracts that are traded on exchanges, between parties who probably do not know each other. The exact quantity, quality, and delivery location can be negotiated in a forward contract, but in a futures contract the terms are dictated by the exchange. Because of their standardization and how they are traded, futures are very liquid, and their associated transaction costs are very low.

Another feature differentiating futures from forwards is the process of marking-to-market. All day and every day, futures traders meet in trading pits at the exchanges and cry out orders to buy and sell futures on behalf of clients. The forces of supply and demand determine whether futures prices rise or fall. *Marking-to-market* is the process by which at the end of each day, losers pay winners an amount equal to the movement of the futures price that day. For example, if the wheat futures price at Monday's close is $4.00 per bushel, and the price rises to $4.10 by the close on Tuesday, the short party must pay the long party 10 cents per bushel after trading ends on Tuesday. If the price had fallen 10 cents, then long would pay short 10 cents per bushel. Both long and short parties have trading accounts at the exchange clearinghouse, and the transfer of funds is automatic. The purpose of marking-to-market is to reduce the chance of default by a party who has lost substantially on a futures position. When futures are marked to market, the greatest possible loss due to a default would be an amount equal to one day's price movement.

Futures are marked-to-market every day. When the contract expires, the last marking to market is based on the spot price. For example, suppose two days prior to expiration the futures price is $4.10 per bushel. On the second-to-last day the futures price has risen to $4.30. Short pays long 20 cents per bushel. Suppose at the end of the next day, the last day of trading, the spot price is recorded at $4.55. The last mark-to-market payment is from short to long for 25 cents per bushel, equal to the difference between the spot price upon expiration and the previous day's futures price.

Upon expiration, the futures contract might stipulate that the short party now deliver to the long party the specified quantity of wheat. The long party must now pay the short party the *spot price* for this wheat. Yes, the spot price, not the original futures price! The difference between the terminal spot price and the original futures price has already been paid via marking to market. A numerical example will make the mechanics of futures clearer and show how similar futures are to forwards.

Suppose with five days remaining until expiration, the wheat futures price is $4.00 per bushel. A baker "buys" a futures contract in order to lock in a purchase price of $4.00. Suppose the futures prices on the next four days are $4.10, $3.90, $4.00, and $4.25. The spot price on the fifth day, the expiration day, is $4.30. Given those price movements, short pays the long baker 10 cents the first day. The long baker pays short 20 cents on the second day. On the third day, short pays long 10 cents, followed by a payment from short to long of 25 cents on the fourth day, and a payment from short to long of 5 cents on the last day. On net, over those five days, short has paid long 30 cents. When long now pays the spot price of $4.30 to short for delivery of the wheat, long indeed is paying $4.00 per bushel, net of the 30 cents profit on the futures contract. Recall that $4.00 was the original futures price. Thus, the futures contract did effectively lock in a fixed purchase price for the wheat.

A contract that stipulates a spot transaction in which the underlying commodity is actually delivered at expiration, is called a *physical delivery* contract. Many futures contracts do not stipulate such a final spot transaction with actual delivery of the underlying asset. After the last marking to market, the game is over. No assets are delivered. Contracts that stipulate no terminal spot transaction are called *cash-settled*. It should make little difference to traders whether a contract is cash settled or physical delivery. A cash-settled contract can be turned into a physical delivery deal simply by choosing to make a spot transaction at the end. Likewise, a physical delivery contract can be turned into a cash-settled deal by either making an offsetting spot transaction at the end, or by exiting the futures contract just before it expires.

Examples of the Use of Forwards and Futures in Risk Management

A wide variety of underlying assets is covered by futures and forwards contracts these days. For example, exchange-traded futures contracts are available on stocks, bonds, interest rates, foreign currencies, oil, gasoline, grains, livestock, metals, cocoa, coffee, sugar, and even orange juice. Consequently, these instruments are versatile risk-management tools in a wide variety of situations. The most actively traded futures, however, are those that cover financial risks. Consider the following examples.

A foreign currency hedge

Suppose an American electronics manufacturer has just delivered a large shipment of finished products to a customer in France. The French buyer has agreed to pay 1 million French francs in exactly 30 days. The manufacturer is worried that the French franc may be devalued relative to the American dollar during that interval. If the franc is devalued, the dollar value of the promised payment will fall and the American manufacturer will suffer losses. The American manufacturer can shed this foreign currency exposure by going short in a franc forward contract or a franc future. The contract will specify a quantity of francs to be exchanged for dollars, at a fixed exchange rate, 30 days in the future. The contract locks in the terms at which the deferred franc revenue can be converted to dollars. No matter what happens to the franc-dollar exchange rate, the American manufacturer now knows exactly how many dollars he or she will receive.

A short-term interest rate hedge

Suppose a manufacturer of automotive parts has just delivered a shipment of finished products to a client. Business has been growing, and the company has approved plans to expand capacity next year. The manufacturer expects to receive payment from the customer in 60 days, but will need to use those funds for the planned capital expenditure 90 days after that. The plan is to invest the revenue in three-month Treasury bills as soon as the revenue is received. Interest rates are currently high. Managers worry that by the time the receivables are collected from the customer, however, interest rates will fall, resulting in less interest earned on the invested funds. The company can hedge against this risk by buying a Treasury bill futures contract, that essentially locks in the price and yield of Treasury bills to be purchased 60 days hence.

Longer-term interest rate hedge

A manufacturer of speed boats notices that when interest rates rise, sales fall, and the value of the firm's stock gets battered. The correlation is easy to understand. Customers buy boats on credit, and so when rates rise, the boats effectively become more expensive to buy. In order to insulate the company's fortunes from the vicissitudes of interest rates, the company could enter a contract that pays money when rates rise. A long position in a Treasury bond futures contract would pay off when rates rise and could thus be a desirable hedge. Each time the futures contract expires, the company can roll over into a new contract. The size of the position in the futures should be geared to the fluctuation in sales resulting from changes in interest rates. The Treasury bond hedge can reduce the volatility in the firm's net income, and the volatility of the firm's equity value.

Synthetic cash

A company's pension fund is invested primarily in the stocks of the Standard and Poor's 500. The pension fund manager worries that there may be a downturn in the stock market sometime over the next six months. She considers selling all of the stock and investing the funds in Treasury bills. An alternate hedge strategy that will save considerable transaction costs would be to short S&P 500 futures contracts. By establishing a short futures position, she locks in the price at which the stocks will be sold six months hence. The fund is now insulated from any fluctuations in stock prices. Since the fund is now essentially risk-free, it will earn the risk-free interest rate. Selling futures while holding the underlying spot instrument is a strategy known as *synthetic cash*. The strategy essentially turns stock into cash. The fund performs as if it were invested in Treasury bills.

Synthetic stock

A company's pension fund is invested primarily in Treasury bills. The stock market has been rising rapidly in recent weeks, and the pension fund manager wishes to participate in the boom. One strategy would be to sell the T-bills and invest the proceeds in equities. A more economical strategy would be to leave the value parked in T-bills, and gain exposure to the stock market by going long in stock futures. When the market rises, the futures will pay off. Should the market fall, the fund will suffer losses. The fund will thus behave as if it were invested in stocks. Ergo the name, *synthetic stock*.

Market timing

A manager wishes to be exposed to the stock market when he anticipates a market rise, and be out of stocks and into T-bills when he anticipates a drop. Buying and selling stocks to achieve this purpose is very expensive in terms of commissions. But entering and exiting the market via futures is very cheap. The manager should keep all his funds invested in T-bills. When he feels the market will rise, he should go long in stock index futures, such as S&P 500 futures. When he feels the market will drop, he should sell those futures, unwinding the position. If alternatively he wished to assemble a diversified portfolio such as the S&P 500 the old-fashioned way—a portfolio consisting of actual stocks and no derivatives—he would have to buy each of the 500 stock issues while selling his Treasury bills. This positioning would involve 501 separate transactions. Turning the actual stock portfolio back into T-bills would similarly require 501 transactions. Turning T-bills effectively into stocks via long futures contracts, on the other hand, involves just one futures trade. Unwinding the futures position would also be just one single trade. Market timing is much more economically executed with futures contracts than with actual equity trades.

A cross hedge

A manufacturer of plastic water pistols wishes to hedge against increases in raw plastic pellet prices. Unfortunately, there are no futures contracts covering plastic prices. There is, however, a contract on oil prices, and the price of plastic is highly correlated with the price of oil. By going long in an oil contract, the manufacturer will be paid money when oil prices rise, which will likely be also when plastic prices rise. Hedging an exposure with a contract tied to a correlated underlying instrument is called a *cross hedge*.

A Common Pitfall

The ease with which futures facilitate hedging sometimes coaxes managers to occasionally take speculative positions. A photographic film manufacturer, for example, might become experienced and comfortable hedging silver prices by going long in silver futures. Managers at the firm might come to believe that no one is better able to forecast silver prices than they are. A time may come when they wholeheartedly believe that silver prices will fall. Not only might they choose not to enter a long silver future hedge at this time, but they may choose to go short in silver futures so as to capitalize on the falling price. If silver prices fall they will not only benefit from a cheaper raw input, but the short silver futures will pay off as well. The danger here is that the manufacturer has lost sight of the fact that it is in the film manufacturing business, and not the business of speculating on commodity prices. Although silver prices might be expected to fall, there is always the possibility that they will rise instead. The probability of a rise might be small, but the consequences would be catastrophic. Not only will the firm's raw material price rise, but the firm will suffer additionally as it loses on the futures contract. The lesson here is that firms should stay clearly focused on what their business line is, and what role the use of futures plays in their business. Futures use should generally be authorized only for hedging and not for speculation. Auditing systems should be in place to oversee that futures are used appropriately.

Futures and Forwards Summary

As the previous examples illustrate, futures and forwards are useful tools for hedging a wide variety of business and financial risks. Futures and forwards contracts essentially commit the two parties to a deferred transaction. No money changes hands initially. As prices subsequently change, however, one party wins at the other's expense. Futures and forwards thus enable businesses to shed or take on exposure to changing prices. When used to offset an exposure the firm faces naturally, futures and forwards reduce risk.

Options

Options are another breed of derivatives. They share some similarities with futures and forwards, but they also differ in many important respects. Like futures and forwards, option prices are a function of the value of an underlying asset, thus they satisfy the definition of derivative. Unlike futures and forwards, however, *options* are assets that must be paid for initially. Recall that no money changes hands initially as parties enter into forwards and futures. Options, though, are an asset that has to be bought for a price at the outset.

There are two kinds of options, call and puts. A *call option* is an asset that gives the owner the right but not the obligation to buy some other underlying asset, for a set price, on or up to a set date. For example, consider a call option on Disney stock, that gives the owner the right to purchase one share of Disney stock for $70 per share, on or up to next June 15th. (Actually, options are usually sold in blocks covering 100 shares. For expository purposes, however, we will describe an option on only one single share.) The underlying asset would be one share of Disney stock. The prespecified price, known as the *strike price,* would be $70 per share. The expiration date would be June 15th. The Disney option might cost $3 initially.

If on the expiration date, June 15th, the market price of Disney stock stood at $75, the call option owner would exercise the option, allowing him to buy a share of Disney stock for $70. He could then turn around and sell the share for $75 in the marketplace, realizing a terminal payoff from the option of $5. The terminal payoff is $5, so the profit net of the $3 initial option price is $2.

Suppose alternatively that the market price of Disney stock on June 15th were $69. It would not be profitable to exercise the call option and thereby purchase for $70 what is elsewhere available for $69. In such a case, the option owner would choose not to exercise, and the call would expire worthless. It is the right not to execute the transaction that is the major difference between options and forwards. The long party in a forward contract must buy the goods upon expiration whether it is advantageous to do so or not. By contrast, a call option owner does not have to buy the underlying asset if he or she chooses not to. At expiration, a call option should be exercised if and only if the market price exceeds the strike price. When the market price is above the strike price, the call option is said to be "in the money." When the market price is less than the strike price, the call is "out of the money." When the market price equals the strike price, the option is "at the money." An option that is out of the money, or even at the money, at expiration, will expire unexercised and worthless.

An option's payoff is defined as the maximum amount of money the option owner would receive at expiration, if the owner totally liquidated his or her position. If the option expires out of the money, the payoff is zero. If the option expires in the money, the payoff is the amount of money received from exercising the call option, and then selling the stock in the open market. For example, if the strike price is $70 and the terminal stock price is $60, the payoff would be zero, since the option would be out of the money and should not be exercised. If the terminal stock price were $80, the payoff would be $10, since the option should be exercised, allowing the owner to buy the stock for $70, and then sell that stock for $80 in the open market. Mathematically, the payoff is the maximum of zero or the stock price minus the strike price.

The payoff ignores the initial price that was paid for the option. Payoff treats the initial price as a sunk cost, and measures only what the option owner might subsequently receive. The payoff minus the initial price is known as the *option profit*. The option payoff is the same for all owners of the option, regardless of what they each initially paid for it. Profit, however, depends on what was initially paid and therefore differs from one investor to another.

A payoff diagram is a valuable analytical device for understanding options. A payoff diagram graphs the payoff of an option as a function of the underlying asset's spot price at expiration. Exhibit 13.1 depicts the payoff diagram for the Disney call option with a strike price of $70.

EXHIBIT 13.1   Call option payoff diagram.

The payoff diagram is a picture of the option. It tells you when you will receive money and when you will not. It helps to visualize how the contract will perform, and whether or not the option is appropriate for any particular application.

The payoff diagram is flat and equal to zero in the entire range where the option is out of the money—that is, where the stock price is less than the strike price. This means that someone who buys an option might lose the entire investment in that option. You may pay $3 for the option, and lose 100% of that $3 by the expiration date. On the brighter side, the payoff diagram confirms that the most you can lose in an option is the initial premium, the $3 you paid for it. Unlike futures or forwards, you will never be called upon to make additional payments at a later date. Initially, you pay for the option, perhaps $3. From then on you can only receive cash inflows.

Note that the payoff diagram begins to rise at the point where the stock price equals the strike price. The payoff is dollar for dollar greater than zero for every dollar that the stock price exceeds the strike price. Thus we see that a call option rises in value as the underlying asset rises in price. For this reason, some people refer to call options as "bullish" instruments.

Hedging with a Call Option

Consider the trucking company whose rates are regulated yet costs fluctuate with market prices. The chief raw material purchased by the company is diesel fuel. If fuel prices rise, the trucking company will suffer losses, and may in fact be put out of business. As we saw above, the company can guarantee a fixed price for fuel by going long in a future or forward. Another strategy would be to buy a diesel fuel call option contract. The strike price of the call option would lock in the *highest* price that the company will have to pay for fuel. If fuel prices should drop below the strike price, the company would be under no obligation to exercise the option. It would simply buy fuel at the low market price. If, however, fuel prices rise above the strike price, the company would exercise the option and buy fuel at the relatively low strike price.

The added flexibility of the option over the futures strategy comes at a cost. When the company buys the call option it must pay a price or *premium*. The call option is essentially an oil price insurance contract for the firm, insuring that fuel prices will not exceed the strike price. If fuel prices remain low, below the strike price, the company will not collect on this insurance policy, and the initial premiums will be lost.

Pricing Options

At this point the reader may wonder how the initial price of an option is determined. Option pricing is no trivial exercise, and a thorough treatment of option pricing is beyond the scope of this chapter. Some basic principles, however, can be explained here. First, an option's *intrinsic value* prior to expiration is equal to its payoff; that is, if an option is out of the money, its intrinsic value is zero. If a call option is in the money (for example, if the strike price is $70 and the current stock price is $80), then the intrinsic value equals the stock price minus the strike price (or $10 in our example).

The value of an option, however, exceeds its intrinsic value. An out-of-the-money option is worth more than zero, and the in-the-money option described earlier is worth more than $10. This extra value is due to the fact that the downside losses are capped off, but the upside potential is unlimited. As long as there is still time remaining in the option's life, it is possible that an out-of-the-money option can go in-the-money. An in-the-money option can go further in the money, and has more upside potential than downside.

A call option's value is a function of the underlying stock price, the strike price, the amount of time remaining to expiration, the interest rate, the stock's dividend rate, and the volatility of the underlying asset price. As the underlying stock price rises, so will the call option's value. Holding the other variables constant, a call option's value will be greater when there is a higher stock price, lower strike price, longer time to expiration, higher interest rate, lower dividend rate, and more volatility in the underlying asset. Researchers have succeeded in formalizing an equation that prices options as a function of these input variables. The formula is known as the *Black-Scholes option pricing formula.* It is widely available on programmed computer software and in many option theory textbooks.

A Written Call Option

In the case of life insurance or automobile insurance, when the insured party collects, another party must pay. It is a zero-sum game. So it is with options. The party that sells the option is liable for the future payoff. "Writing" an option and "shorting" an option are synonymous with selling an option. The payoff diagram for a written call option position is the mirror image of the long or bought call option position. As shown in Exhibit 13.2, the x-axis is the reflecting surface.

Note that once the call option writer has received the initial premium, all subsequent cash flows will be outflows. The best the writer can hope for is that the call will expire out of the money. Note that the potential liability of the written option position is unlimited. Notice as well, that the amount of money the buyer of the option might receive at expiration is the exact amount that writer will have to pay. Thus, when the media report that a particular company has lost millions of dollars in options, the reader should realize that this means some other party has made millions. The newspapers tend to focus on the losers.

Strategies Using Written Call Options

Why would anybody wish to sell a call option if doing so subjects them to the possibility of unlimited future liabilities? One answer is that speculators some-

EXHIBIT 13.2   Payoff diagram for a written call option position.

$70 = strike price

times deem the risks worthwhile in light of the expected reward. They may be confident that the underlying asset price will not rise and the option will expire worthless.

Written call options can also be used to hedge in certain circumstances. Consider oil exporting nations such as Mexico and Venezuela. When oil prices are low they are hungry for funds, funds that are much needed for national development projects. When oil prices are high, they have plenty of excess revenue. A reasonable strategy would be to sell high strike price oil call options when oil prices are low. The country thus receives premiums when funds are most needed, and incurs a liability that needs to be paid only when funds are most plentiful. The oil call options help to smooth the flow of funds into the country. (For more on the use of written call options in such a setting, please see "Covered Call Options: A Proposal to Ease Less Developed Country Debt," by Peter Abken and Steven Feinstein, *Federal Reserve Bank of Atlanta Economic Review,* March/April 1990.)

Warrants

Warrants are call options that are sold by the company whose stock is the underlying asset. If Microsoft pays its executive with Microsoft call options, those options would be called warrants. When warrants are exercised, the total outstanding supply of Microsoft stock would rise. Warrants are valuable, even if they are not yet in the money. Clearly they must be worth something, otherwise executives would not want them and would give them away! Offering warrants as compensation to executives is not free for the firm's shareholders.

Put Options

The second type of option is a put. A *put option* is a contract that gives the owner the right but not the obligation to *sell* some underlying asset for a prespecified price, on or up to a given date. Consider a put option on Microsoft stock. Suppose the strike price is $100 and the expiration date is December 15th. The put option owner has the right, but not the obligation, to sell a share of Microsoft stock for $100, on or up to December 15th. If the market price of Microsoft is above $100, say $120, the put option owner would not exercise. Why should the owner force someone to pay $100 for the stock when there is more money to be made by selling the stock in the open market. Thus, a put option is out of the money if the stock price is *above* the strike price. If the stock price is below the strike price, however, then the put option is in the money. If the market price of Microsoft is $80 on December 15th, the owner of the put can reap a $20 payoff. To realize this payoff, he or she would buy the Microsoft stock in the marketplace for $80, and then turn around and sell it for $100 by exercising the put option. Thus, a put option is in the money when the stock price is below the strike price. A put option's payoff at expiration, and its intrinsic value prior to expiration, is the strike price minus the stock price, or zero, whichever is greater.

Exhibit 13.3 presents the payoff diagram for a put option. Should the stock price fall to zero, the put option's payoff would be equal to the strike price. At that point, the put option owner would have the right to sell a worthless stock for $100. From that point, the put option payoff falls one dollar for each dollar that the stock price rises. The payoff reaches zero when the stock price equals the

EXHIBIT 13.3   Put option payoff diagram.

$100 = strike price

strike price, and then remains at zero no matter how much higher the stock price goes. As is the case with call options, the put option cannot fall in value below zero. Once the put option premium is paid, the owner is never called upon to make another payment. Any subsequent cash flow is positive. It is altogether possible, however, for the buyer of the put option to lose the entire premium, so one should not think that buying a put option is a safe investment.

Notice that the put option payoff rises as the stock price falls. For this reason, puts are thought of as "bearish" instruments—instruments that are more profitable the more the underlying asset falls in value. Because of this negative relationship with the underlying asset, puts can be good hedging instruments for someone who owns the underlying asset.

Like the call option's payoff diagram, the put's payoff diagram is *kinked*— that is, there is an elbow at the strike price. A kinked payoff diagram is the hallmark of an option. If a payoff diagram has no kink, then the instrument depicted is not an option.

The payoff diagram for a written put option position is the mirror image of the put's payoff diagram. Such a payoff diagram is shown in Exhibit 13.4. The possible payoff reaped by the buyer of the put option is exactly equal to the possible outflow paid by the writer. Put options, too, are a zero-sum game. Notice that whereas the writer of a call option has unlimited potential liability, the writer of a put option has a potential liability limited to the strike price. Furthermore, notice that a long put option payoff looks nothing like a short call option. Simi-

EXHIBIT 13.4   Payoff diagram for a written put option position.

larly, notice that a long call option payoff is not the same as a short put. Both long puts and short calls are bearish positions, just as both short puts and long calls are bullish positions, but each of these four positions is unique in the direction, size, and timing of cash flows. Long calls and long puts have to be paid for up front, and then receive a subsequent positive payoff depending on what happens to the underlying stock. Short calls and short puts receive all of their cash inflows up front and then become potential liabilities.

A Protective Put Strategy

A put option can be thought of as price insurance for someone who owns the underlying asset. For example, suppose you are a pension fund manager, and you hold hundreds of shares of Microsoft stock. You hold the stock because you believe the stock will rise in value. You worry, however, that the stock price can fall, and losses will be so great that the fund will be unable to meet the needs of the retirees. An effective hedging strategy would be to buy Microsoft put options. You would choose the strike price to be at a level that would guarantee the solvency of the fund. If Microsoft stock falls below the strike price of the put options, the put options will pay off the difference between the new lower market price and the strike price. If Microsoft stock rises, the put options would expire out of the money. The insurance would not pay off, but you would reap the high return of the rising stock. This strategy is known as buying a protective put. It is essentially portfolio insurance. The strategy allows for the upside appreciation of the portfolio, yet sets a floor below which the value of the portfolio cannot fall.

A protective put strategy can also be implemented by a producer who faces the risk of his or her product's price falling. For example, a cattle rancher can buy put options on cattle, thereby fixing the lowest price at which to be able to sell the herd.

Swaps

The third category of derivative we will examine is swaps. A *swap* is an agreement between two parties to exchange cash flows over a period of time. The size and direction of the cash flows are determined by an agreed-upon formula spelled out in the swap agreement—a formula that is contingent on the performance of other underlying instruments. Due to this contingency on other underlying assets, swaps are considered derivatives.

One easy type of swap to understand is the equity swap. Suppose Back Bay Investment Management owns a large block of Standard and Poor's 500 stocks. Suppose another firm, Capital Bank owns a large block of NASDAQ stocks. Back Bay would like to diversify into NASDAQ stocks, and simultaneously Capital Bank would like to diversify into S&P 500 stocks. The old-fashioned way of achieving the desired objectives would be for both parties to sell the stocks they do not want, and reinvest the proceeds in the stocks they do want. Such an approach is very expensive in terms of commissions. A much cheaper alternative is for both parties to keep their own portfolio intact and arrange between themselves an equity swap.

The swap agreement might dictate the following terms. For every percentage point that the NASDAQ stock index rises over the course of the year, Capital Bank will pay Back Bay Investment Management $1 million. Simultaneously, for every percentage point that the S&P 500 rises over the course of the year, Back Bay will pay Capital $1 million. Thus, if the NASDAQ index rises 15% and the S&P 500 rises 11%, there will be a net payment of $4 million from Capital to Back Bay. If in the following year the NASDAQ index rises 23% and the S&P 500 rises 29%, Back Bay will pay Capital $6 million on net. The equity swap is illustrated in Exhibit 13.5.

In this equity swap, the notional principal is $100 million—that is, the payments equal a base of $100 million times the indices' respective returns. The net effect of the swap is to essentially convert $100 million of Back Bay's Standard and Poor's stocks into $100 million of NASDAQ stocks. Simultaneously $100 million of Capital Bank's NASDAQ stocks will now perform as if they were $100 million of Standard and Poor's 500 stocks. Both sides keep their assets parked where they were, but they swap exposures on the notional principal.

Some arithmetic will prove the point that Back Bay's portfolio will now perform as if it were invested in NASDAQ stocks instead of S&P stocks. If Back Bay did in fact own $100 million of NASDAQ stocks by the end of the first year, after the 15% rise in NASDAQ stocks, this portfolio would have grown to be worth $115 million. But Back Bay owns $100 million of S&P stocks and has a position in an equity swap. The $100 million of S&P stocks grows to $111 million after the 11% S&P rise in the first year. The swap, however, pays Back Bay $4 million at the end of the first year. Thus, at the end of the first year, Back Bay does have $115 million in total portfolio value. Verify that the total value of Capital Bank's portfolio at the end of the first year will be $111 million, just as if it had invested $100 million in S&P stocks.

EXHIBIT 13.5 An equity swap.

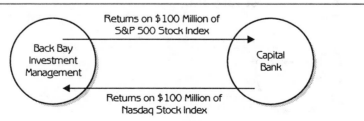

Since the notional principal remains fixed at $100 million, the swap will continue to convert $100 million of Back Bay's S&P stocks into $100 million of NASDAQ stocks, and vice versa for Capital Bank. Total portfolio performance in subsequent years depends on how the swap proceeds are reinvested by each party.

Interest Rate Swaps

The most common type of swap is an interest rate swap. The typical, or *plain-vanilla* interest rate swap, is a "fixed-for-floating swap," whereby cash flows depend on the movement of variable interest rates. For example, consider two firms Michel/Shaked Manufacturing (M) and Healing Heart Hospital (H). The swap agreement might specify that M pay H a fixed 10% per year on a notional principal of $100 million, and H pays to M the prime rate, as quoted in the *Wall Street Journal,* times $100 million. Settlement might be once per year. The prime rate quoted at the beginning of each year will determine the cash flow paid at the end. Thus, if at first the prime rate is 12%, H will pay M $2 million at the end of the first year. If by the end of the first year the prime rate has fallen to 7%, at the end of the second year M will pay H $3 million. And so the swap continues for a specified number of years. H will benefit if rates fall; M will benefit if rates rise. This interest rate swap is depicted in Exhibit 13.6.

Examples of Hedging Interest Rate Exposure with a Swap

The Keating Computer Company assembles and markets computer hardware systems. In the past several years Keating Computer has been one of the fastest growing computer hardware companies. They borrowed extensively to finance this growth. Currently on the books is a very large long-term variable rate loan. Also on the books is a sizable amount of short-term debt. The managers of Keating Computer have observed that they are dangerously exposed to interest-rate risk. If rates should rise, they will have to pay more in debt service on the variable rate loan, and they will face higher interest rates when they roll over their short-term debt. The company is currently profitable, but they worry that rising interest rates can wipe out that profit. Since the company is planning an equity offering in coming years, management is very concerned about the prospect of reporting any losses over the near term.

EXHIBIT 13.6   An interest rate swap.

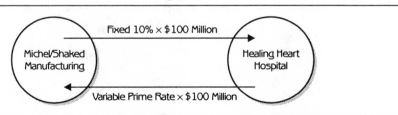

One solution to Keating Computer's problem would be to refinance at fixed interest rates. The transaction costs of refinancing, however, are sizable, and the rates currently offered on long-term debt are not favorable. Entering an interest rate swap is a better hedging strategy. The company should enter as the fixed-rate payer, which means it would be the variable rate receiver. As interest rates rise, the company will make money on the swap, offsetting the higher payments it must make on its own debt. Since swaps are over-the-counter instruments, the company can tailor the terms of the swap so that the hedge will be in force for the exact number of years it is needed. Moreover, the notional principal can be tailored so that the money received when rates rise is closely matched to the new, higher debt service obligations.

Another Example

Kayman Savings and Loan holds most of its assets in the form of long-term mortgages, mortgage-backed securities, and 30-year Treasury bonds. The liabilities of Kayman Savings are mostly short-term certificates of deposits. Kayman has also sold some short-term commercial paper of its own. Stephen Kayman, the president of Kayman Savings, suddenly realizes that they are in the same precarious predicament as that of many savings and loans (S&Ls) that went bust in the 1980s. Long-term fixed income instruments are more sensitive to interest rates than short-term instruments. When interest rates rise, both long-term and short-term instruments fall in value, but the long-term instruments fall much more. Consequently, if interest rates should rise, the market value of the S&L's assets will fall farther than the market value of its liabilities. When this happens, the S&L's equity will be wiped out. The bank will be bankrupt. Even if government auditors do not shut down the S&L, the institution will experience cash flow problems. The relatively low fixed-interest revenue from the long-term assets will not be enough to keep up with the rising interest expenses of the short-term liabilities. What can Kayman do to protect against the risk of rising interest rates?

The predicament faced by Kayman Savings is known as a *duration gap*—the duration of the assets is greater than the duration of the liabilities. As rates rise, equity vanishes. Kayman Savings needs a hedge that will pay off when rates rise. Entering an interest rate swap as the fixed payer can close the duration gap. The swap will grow in value as rates rise, offsetting the equity losses. Again, the size, timing, and other terms of the interest rate swap can be tailored to meet the particular needs of Kayman Savings.

HOW TO CHOOSE THE APPROPRIATE HEDGE

We have now examined forwards, futures, call options, put options, and swaps. We have observed how these instruments can be used to hedge in a wide variety of risky scenarios. How does one choose which of these instruments to use in a particular situation? When is a future better than a forward? When should an option be used instead of a future? Should interest rate exposure be hedged with bond futures or swaps? The following steps will provide some guidance.

The first task in implementing a hedge strategy is to identify the exposures that the firm faces. Does the firm gain or lose when interest rates rise? Does it gain or lose as the dollar appreciates? Is a falling wheat price good news or bad news for the company? What about oil prices and stock prices? How about foreign stock and bond prices? Is the company exposed, and if so, which direction causes a loss?

Clearly the answers to these questions vary from firm to firm. The bakers benefited from falling wheat prices while the farmers suffered. Rising interest rates might hurt a firm that has variable rate debt but might help a pension fund that is about to invest in bonds. A rising dollar benefits American importers but hurts American exporters. The first step in risk management is to identify the exposures.

Once the exposures are identified, one should narrow the search for an appropriate hedge to the set of derivatives that compensate the firm when the adverse scenario is realized. For example, an airline that purchases jet fuel will see higher costs when the price of oil rises. The airline should look for derivatives that pay off when oil prices rise. Thus, the airline should consider a long position in an oil future, or a long oil forward, or an oil call option. A bank that suffers losses when interest rates rise should consider a long position in a bond future, a bond forward, bond call options, or the fixed-payer side of an interest rate swap. An exporter that expects to receive Mexican pesos might wish to go short in peso futures or forwards, or buy peso puts.

The next step is to choose from among futures, forwards, options, and swaps. This is perhaps the trickiest part of the analysis. To guide the selection, it is helpful to categorize the risks and the instruments as either symmetric or asymmetric. Futures, forwards, and swaps are symmetric hedging instruments, in that they pay off money if prices move in one direction, but incur losses if prices move in the opposite direction. Options, on the other hand, are asymmetric hedging instruments. They pay off money if prices move in one direction, yet result in no cash outflows if prices should move the other way. A *symmetric risk* is one in which the firm is hurt if underlying prices move one way but benefits if prices move in the opposite direction. An *asymmetric risk* is one in which the firm is hurt if prices move in one direction, but the firm does not benefit appreciably if the price moves in the other direction. For example, a firm that exports to Japan and receives payment in yen benefits when the value of the yen rises, but is hurt when the yen falls in value. This foreign exchange risk is thus symmetric. The symmetric foreign exchange risk can be eliminated most completely with a symmetric instrument such as a future or forward, not an option.

A portfolio manager invested in stocks also faces a symmetric risk. He benefits if stock prices rise and loses money if stock prices fall. The portfolio manager, however, might wish to modify the exposure in an asymmetric way, insuring against losses on the downside while maintaining the potential for upside appreciation. An asymmetric instrument, a put option, would be the appropriate hedge instrument in this case, since an asymmetric instrument converts a symmetric risk into an asymmetric exposure.

An automobile leasing company is an example of a commercial venture that faces an asymmetric risk. If interest rates rise, the firm's interest expenses rise. If the firm tries to offset these higher costs by charging higher prices to customers, the firm would lose business. However, if interest rates fall, buying an automobile on credit becomes a more attractive substitute for leasing unless the leasing company also lowers its prices. Thus, the leasing company suffers when rates rise, but does not benefit when rates fall. An asymmetric hedge, such as a bond call option would be the best choice of instrument in this case. The bond call option will pay off when rates rise, but will not require a cash outflow when rates fall.

The key to choosing between symmetric and asymmetric instruments is to first identify the nature of the risk that is faced, and then to choose the type of instrument which will modify the risk appropriately. A symmetric risk can best be eliminated with a symmetric instrument. An asymmetric risk can best be eliminated with an asymmetric instrument. A symmetric risk can be turned into an asymmetric exposure with an asymmetric instrument.

Finally, the last step is to choose between exchange-traded and over-the-counter instruments. Forwards and swaps are over-the-counter instruments; futures are exchange-traded instruments. Options are generally exchange-traded, but they can also be bought over the counter. Exchange-traded instruments are standardized, and are thus liquid and entail low transaction costs. But since they are standardized, they may not perfectly suit the risk exposure the firm wishes to hedge. Over-the-counter instruments can be custom tailored, but they are therefore less liquid and more expensive in terms of transaction costs. The firm must weigh the costs and benefits of liquidity, differences in transaction costs, and custom fit. The correct choice depends on the particular hedging situation.

A couple of examples will illustrate the process of putting all the factors together to pick the best suited hedge. An American manufacturing firm owns a production facility in Canada. Rent and wages are paid in Canadian dollars. Consequently, if the Canadian dollar rises in value, the wages and rent translated into American dollars would become more expensive. If the Canadian dollar falls, the expenses in terms of American dollars decline. Thus, the exposure is symmetric. If the firm wishes to completely eliminate the exposure, a symmetric instrument is called for, ruling out options. The firm should go long in Canadian dollar futures or forwards, since either of these instruments will provide positive cash flows when the Canadian dollar is rising. An exchange-traded Canadian dollar futures contract is available. The commission on the forward is greater than the commission on the futures, but the futures contract covers slightly more Canadian dollars than the firm wishes to hedge, and the timing does not exactly correspond to the timing of wage and rent payments. An over-the-counter forward contract could be constructed so that cash flows are synchronized with wage and rent payments. After weighing the two alternatives, the managers decide that the benefit from lower commissions on the futures contract outweighs the disadvantage of the futures' slight mismatch in the hedge. They go long in Canadian dollar futures.

The same manufacturing firm has many customers in Venezuela. If the Venezuelan currency (the bolivar) falls in value, the American dollar value of the revenue will fall. If the Venezuelan currency rises in value, the dollar revenue will rise. Thus, the risk is symmetric, and so the list of hedging candidates is narrowed to futures and forwards. The firm benefits from a rise in the bolivar, and loses when the bolivar falls. Thus, the firm should go short in bolivar futures or forwards, so that a cash flow will be received when the bolivar falls. No bolivar futures contracts are available on exchanges, so the firm must go short in over-the-counter Venezuelan bolivar forwards.

A producer of copper wire purchases large amounts of copper as a raw material. When copper prices rise, the firm must either absorb the higher expenses or raise the price of copper wire. Raising the price of wire, however, causes customers to cut back on purchases, and so the firm is stuck with unsold inventory. When copper prices fall, alternatively, competitors lower their prices and so the firm must also lower its price in order to sell its output. Consequently, the firm's profits suffer when copper prices rise, but profits do not increase when copper prices fall. Management would like to increase production capacity, but it is difficult to forecast how much the firm can sell, given recent copper price fluctuations. With current levels of raw copper inventory, management believes that raw copper prices can rise as much as 10% without significantly impacting the firm's bottom line. What is the appropriate hedge?

Clearly, the firm faces an asymmetric risk. The firm is hurt when copper prices rise, but does not benefit when the price falls. An option will best mitigate the risk. Since the firm is hurt when copper prices rise, a call option that pays off when copper prices rise is the best choice. Since the firm can tolerate a 10% rise in copper prices without suffering significant losses, an out-of-the-money copper call option that begins to pay off only when copper prices rise more than 10% is ideal. Exchange-traded copper call options exist, and so due to their greater liquidity and low transaction costs, they would be the best choice.

A cellular communications firm has sold a six-year variable rate bond, where the interest payments are tied to LIBOR, the London Interbank Offer Rate. When LIBOR rises, so too do the company's interest payments. When LIBOR falls, the firm's interest payments fall. The company's interest payments are due twice a year, on the last days of February and August. The firm raised $160 million this way. With competition holding cellular telephone rates down, the firm worries that an increase in interest rates can wipe out all profits. What is the appropriate hedge instrument?

The interest rate exposure is symmetric, ruling out options. The firm needs an instrument that will pay it money when interest rates rise. Thus, the firm should go long in either bond futures or forwards, or the firm should be the fixed-rate payer in an interest rate swap. Since the cash flows that the firm is trying to hedge do not conform to those of any exchange-traded future, the correct choice is narrowed to the over-the-counter instruments—a forward or a swap. The firm must hedge 12 interest rate payments, two per year for six years. Forwards are generally constructed to provide one payment only. Swaps are designed to hedge multiple payments over longer terms. Thus, entering a six-year interest rate swap as the fixed payer is the ideal hedge in this situation.

SUMMARY AND FINAL RECOMMENDATIONS

This chapter has presented the basics of risk management using derivatives. By separating an asset's value from its exposure, derivatives allow firms to exchange exposures without exchanging the underlying assets. It is much more economical to transfer exposures, rather than assets, and thus derivatives have greatly facilitated risk management. Derivatives are indeed powerful risk-management tools, but in the wrong hands they can be dangerous and destructive. It is essential that managers fully understand how much and under what conditions derivatives will provide positive cash flows or require cash outflows. If it is not absolutely clear when and how much the cash flows will be, do not enter the contract. Managers should strive to identify the nature, magnitude, and size of their risk exposures. They can then match those exposures with countervailing positions in derivatives. Managers should never forget that their job is to preserve value by reducing risk. The temptation to speculate should be avoided. Don't be greedy.

FOR FURTHER READING

Bernstein, Peter, *Against the Gods* (New York: John Wiley & Sons, Inc., 1996).

Brown, Keith C. and Donald J. Smith, *Interest Rate and Currency Swaps: A Tutorial* (Charlottesville, VA: The Research Foundation of the Institute of Chartered Financial Analysts, 1995).

Chance, Don M., *An Introduction to Derivatives* (New York: Dryden Press, 1995).

Chew, Lillian, *Managing Derivative Risks: The Use and Abuse of Leverage* (New York: John Wiley and Sons, 1996).

Daigler, Robert T., *Financial Futures and Options Markets: Concepts and Strategies* (New York: Harper Collins, 1994).

Hull, John, *Options, Futures, and Other Derivative Securities* (Englewood Cliffs, NJ: Prentice-Hall, 1993).

Various authors, "Managing Risks," special report in *Business Week,* October 31, 1994, pp. 86–104.

PART III
Making Key Strategic Decisions

14 GOING PUBLIC
Paul G. Joubert

Going public refers to the process of transforming a company from a privately owned, often owner-managed concern to a publicly owned company. The decision to take a company public is usually a complex one, and the actual process of going public can be time-consuming, expensive, and take a substantial amount of key management effort away from the day-to-day operations of the company. To illustrate the decision-making process and what needs to be done to take a company public, we will follow Acme Business Software, a fictional, but not atypical, example of a company deciding to go public and working through the process.

John Hand, founder, CEO, and majority owner of Acme Business Software prepared for a critical meeting with his board of directors. He and the board would hear a presentation by Pam Burns, Acme's CFO, on the pros and cons of taking Acme Business Software public. At their last meeting, the board concluded that going public was the primary alternative source of cash left, to finance Acme's planned expansion overseas and its new product development: They asked Burns to make a presentation at the next meeting. Hand did not know much about the process of going public, but he did realize that the company he had started, just five years ago, would change dramatically if it became a public company.

John Hand was a computer jock during his college days as an engineering student at Massachusetts Institute of Technology. After graduating, he couldn't resist his father's offer to join the family's hearing-aid manufacturing business. Once at work, Hand's fascination with computers led to his work on and eventual development of a state-of-the-art MRP software for his father's company. Shortly after developing the software, Hand realized he had an excellent piece of software, which he believed could help many small to mid-size manufacturing firms. Hand convinced his father and a few of his father's friends to provide the seed money to produce, market, and sell the MRP software. With seed money and one product, Acme Business Software was born.

After a year in operation, Acme Business Software had a few sales, a lot of potential, and very little cash. To grow and compete in its market, the company needed significant funds for research and development and marketing. One of Hand's initial investors introduced Hand to a venture capital firm, specializing in start-up businesses. After extensive analysis of the management team and due diligence on the technology, the venture capital firm eventually agreed to invest in Acme. Although Hand was happy to get the needed capital, he had to give up 40% of his ownership in Acme to the venture capitalists. His deal with the venture capitalists also required that he form a board of directors and that two of the five members be selected by the venture capital firm. With a new board of directors, Hand now had to answer to someone for his business decisions, a hard pill to swallow for this founder, owner, and manager.

With the venture capital money, Acme prospered: Over the next four years, Acme grew to $10 million in sales and was extremely profitable. Hand had assembled a professional management team, at the board's urging, and the company had several new state-of-the-art products in the final design stage, which Hand believed were sure winners. Management and the board were convinced that, with a little luck and lots of hard work, Acme could grow to $50 million in sales over the next five years.

The major problem they now faced was finding the capital to bankroll Acme's overseas expansion and new product introductions. The venture capitalists wanted to spread the risk and were not interested in investing any more money. After four years, the venture capitalists were looking for a way to cash in on their Acme investment. Initial discussions with Acme's bankers also made it clear that the bank would not lend Acme the kind of money it needed, unless Acme received a substantial infusion of equity. As a software company, Acme had few tangible assets to use as collateral for additional bank lines. Acme's board felt that taking Acme public was the most promising alternative, if Acme wanted to take advantage of the tremendous growth opportunities in the software market.

THE DECISION TO GO PUBLIC

The presentation on taking Acme public was the only item on the board's agenda for the meeting. Burns brought a representative from Gold Brothers, a well-known investment bank, to assist her with the presentation. Gold Brothers had extensive experience taking companies public and came highly recommended by the venture capitalists on Acme's board. If Acme did decide to go public, Gold Brothers would certainly want to bid for the opportunity to be the lead underwriter on the public offering.

Burns began the presentation by stating that there were many advantages and disadvantages to taking Acme public, and she thought it would be helpful to put these on the table for discussion. Although the venture capitalists on the board were already well-schooled in public offerings, Hand and the other board members needed a full education.

Burns began by discussing the advantages of going public.

Advantages of Going Public

Access to Permanent, Noninterest-Bearing Capital

If Acme went public, it would be able to raise enough capital to pay for its planned overseas expansion and several new product introductions. She suggested that the company issue its common stock to the public, in what is termed an *initial public offering* (IPO). Acme would never have to pay the investors their money back and would reward the investors by paying dividends (if the board decided it was appropriate) and by growing the business under its five-year business plan. The investors would expect to receive their return primarily through stock appreciation and subsequent trading of the stock on the open market. Therefore, as long as Acme remained profitable and the stock appreciated, the investors would be happy.

Access to Subsequent Capital

Once Acme became a public company, raising additional capital would be much easier. As long as the company remained attractive to investors, Acme could finance future projects with new stock offerings or public debt offerings.

The Opportunity for Owners to Cash Out

Taking Acme public would give Hand, the venture capitalists, and the other initial investors a chance to get some of their initial investment out of the business. This could be accomplished by including a secondary offering, selling shares that are already owned by individuals, with the IPO of newly created shares, or by selling stock in the open market, after Acme had gone public. At this point in the meeting, the representative from Gold Brothers pointed out that it was important to decide how much existing stock would be included in the initial offering. He warned that if Hand or others on the senior management team were perceived by the market to be bailing out of their company, potential investors would be turned off, as would Gold Brothers and the other investment bankers who would be involved in the underwriting.

Increased Public Awareness of the Company

As a publicly traded company, Acme would have a much higher profile with the public. Business pages in newspapers across the country would print Acme's quarterly and annual financial results, and Acme and its products would receive increased attention from the business press in general. Hopefully, this additional exposure would lead to new opportunities and new customers. The representative from Gold Brothers discussed the importance of public relations in an IPO and its importance for publicly traded companies in general. He also warned of the various securities laws prohibiting inappropriate release of confidential information before, during, and after an IPO. The laws are extensive and the board agreed that a more expansive discussion was needed before an IPO was undertaken.

Enhanced Credibility with Suppliers, Banks, and Customers

Acme's credibility would also be enhanced in the eyes of its existing suppliers, banks, and customers because of the respect most in the business community give to well-capitalized public companies. This could lead to better credit terms with suppliers and banks and to more loyalty from existing customers.

Ability to Attract and Retain Key Management through Use of Stock and Options

As a public company, Acme could craft creative incentive packages for important managers, using various combinations of cash, stock, and options, to purchase stock in the future at current stock prices. With a publicly traded stock, managers could evaluate their incentive package and feel comfortable that they could cash in their shares, when and if they so chose. In addition, managers would see a tangible reward from higher stock prices and would feel that they were sharing the fruits of Acme's success. Cashing in the stock of a private company is often difficult, if not impossible, and often leads to disputes as to stock value. Free trading in the company's stock would result in an open-market determination of the company's value.

Others Can Participate in the Company's Success

All levels of employees, in addition to senior management, customers, suppliers, distributors, and others could buy into the company and share the rewards, if the company was successful. This could be an important tool to help Acme get the most out of its employees and vendors.

Equity Allows Access to More and Possibly Cheaper Debt

As the bankers told Acme several weeks ago, if the company had more equity, it could also borrow more. With a stronger equity base, the company's borrowing rate should decrease as well.

Merger or Acquisition Is Easier

Although Acme has no plans to merge or to acquire other companies, the day may arrive when a strategic alliance with another company makes sense. If Acme wanted to acquire another company, Acme could potentially offer the other owners Acme stock, instead of cash. If Acme wanted to merge with another company, a public market would make valuation of the two companies, and the transaction, much easier.

After finishing her discussion of all the advantages of taking Acme public, Burns was quick to point out that there was a long list of disadvantages to be considered, before everyone jumped on the "going public" bandwagon.

Disadvantages of Going Public

The Cost and Time of an IPO

Burns had lived through a public offering at her previous job, so she spoke from personal experience about how difficult and time-consuming the public offering process was for senior managers. No one on the senior management team would be spared, and it would be difficult if not impossible for managers to do much of anything else, once the process got rolling. In addition to the time involved, the process would be extremely expensive. Acme would spend 15 to 20% of the offering proceeds to pay the underwriters, accountants, printers, and lawyers. There would also be risk that some unforeseen trouble would arise, either in the financial markets or at Acme that would kill the offering after Acme had already spent a lot of money on it.

The Lack of Operating Confidentiality

Going public requires companies to tell all. Information about Acme's markets, margins, salaries, and plans for the future would all be public information. This would mean that Acme's competitors, customers, suppliers, and employees would all have access to information about the inner workings of the company. The potential problems that could result from this are numerous.

Possible Loss of Management Control

Already, the senior management of Acme owns only 60% of the company. A public offering of any size would dilute that holding to possibly 15%. The other large stockholders would probably want representation on the board and some input into how Acme should be run.

Possible Loss of Business Flexibility
Due to Required Board Approvals

With an expanded board and public oversight, senior management would have to install expanded systems of controls and approvals. Currently, the board runs very informally and can usually reach agreement rather quickly. It is difficult to imagine a larger, more diverse board, under public oversight, running as effectively.

Pressure on Short-Term Performance

The aspects of going public that would be most frustrating would be emphasis on short-term performance. Like all public companies, Acme would have to report earnings on a quarterly basis. The financial markets, investment bankers, and shareholders would be very unforgiving if Acme had a bad quarter. What makes this particularly frustrating is that, sometimes, lower quarterly earnings result from smart, strategic, long-term investment decisions. No matter how much management fought it, it would find itself managing with an eye toward the next earnings report. Every strategic decision would be framed by its effects on near-term performance and the resulting stock market reaction to that performance. This pressure would make management of Acme a much more difficult task.

Restrictions on Management as a Result of SEC Regulations

As a public company, Acme would be required to comply with a host of SEC regulations.

The SEC is the principal federal regulatory agency for the securities industry in the United States. Created in 1934 by an act of Congress, it functions as an independent agency, performing a vital and quasi-judicial role in the regulation of securities distribution and exchange. The Securities Act of 1933 originally came under the jurisdiction of the Federal Trade Commission. However, the Securities and Exchange Act of 1934 created the SEC and, subsequently, the administration of the Securities Act of 1933 was transferred to this new agency.

The SEC is governed by presidentially appointed commissioners. They are responsible for administering the following statutes: the Securities Act of 1933; the Securities and Exchange Act of 1934; the Public Utility Holding Company Act of 1935; the Trust Indenture Act of 1939; the Investment Company Act of 1940; and the Investment Advisors Act of 1940.

The Securities Act of 1933 was designed to protect the public from misrepresentation, manipulation, and other fraudulent practices during the purchase and sale of securities. The 1933 Act requires that securities be registered with the agency, prior to their sale to the public. Securities of the U.S. government; state, municipal, and other governmental units; and securities of certain common carriers are exempt from registration.

The objectives of the Securities Act of 1933 are to provide protection for the investor, through the full and fair disclosure of financial and other information, pertinent to new securities being offered and to the business of the issuer. With few exceptions, an issuer of registered securities falling under the 1933 Act is subject to the quarterly and annual reporting requirements of the Securities and Exchange Act of 1934.

The Securities and Exchange Act of 1934, in contrast to the 1933 Act, is concerned with the trading of outstanding (previously issued) securities. Two of its principal objectives are:

1. The dissemination of significant financial and other information related to the trading of securities.
2. The regulation of the securities market.

The Act also empowers the SEC to regulate the pledging of customers' securities by dealers and the proxy solicitation of stockholders by registered companies.

Other regulations directly affect senior management who qualify as "insiders" according to the SEC. As insiders, they have to be careful not to discuss Acme's affairs with people outside the company, who could unfairly use the insider information to make money by trading Acme stock. There are also strict rules regulating when and how insiders are able to buy and sell Acme shares as individuals. In other words, the key management team and board of directors cannot trade their stock as freely as other investors.

More Extensive Accounting and Tax Requirements

As a public company, Acme would have a host of new and more stringent reporting requirements. Acme's independent outside accountants would have to issue audit reports, expressing an opinion on whether the financial statements were prepared in accordance with GAAP, and Acme would have to comply with various SEC accounting and reporting requirements. Acme would almost certainly have to improve its accounting systems and beef up its staffing in the accounting area, to be able to meet all the new requirements. This would be expensive and would be an ongoing expense.

Ongoing Costs as a Public Company

In addition to the costs necessary to enhance Acme's accounting capabilities, there would be several other new, ongoing costs that Acme would bear as a public company. First, there would be the cost of issuing all the reports that are required of public companies. Second, the company would have to hire staff to handle shareholder relations. The new shareholders would be owners of Acme and management would have to answer their questions, address their concerns, and keep them informed about what was happening at Acme. Burns cautioned that management might be surprised at the level of attention shareholders would demand. Finally, new shareholders would eventually demand dividends. As a new public company, shareholders would understand that the cash generated probably needed to be reinvested in the business. However, there would come a time when shareholders would expect Acme to start paying dividends, particularly if the shareholders were not seeing a return on their investment through stock appreciation.

Susceptibility to Hostile Takeover

If Acme became a public company, senior management would no longer control 50% of the stock and the company would become a potential takeover target. Anyone could decide that the stock was undervalued, or that they could do a better job running the company than current management, and attempt a takeover of the company. If they were successful in accumulating enough shares, the company would become their company, and there would be little that management could do about it. As a private company, the owners have to sell only if they want to sell.

IPOs Are Typically Priced at a 10 to 15% Discount

Although the underwriters would assure Acme that it was getting a fair price for its new shares in the IPO, it is common knowledge that IPOs are generally priced at a discount, to encourage an upward movement in the stock, in the period after the offering. Basically, this discount on the initial offering represents value being transferred from the initial investors to the investors who purchase the stock in an IPO. Furthermore, the final price of the offering is not set until days before the public offering. Thus there would be no guarantee that Acme would get the price per share that its underwriters initially estimated, in their proposals to be the lead underwriter.

Burns finished her presentation on the advantages and disadvantages of taking Acme public and opened the meeting to discussion. The representative from Gold Brothers spoke up, and, not surprisingly, stated that he thought Acme was an excellent candidate to take public and believed that Acme would command a good price from the market. He concluded by stating that if Acme went public, at the price level he thought was attainable, the venture capitalists would have an opportunity to get an excellent return on their investment in Acme. He noted that John Hand would end up a very wealthy man, and the other senior managers who owned shares in the company would receive a very large payoff for all of their hard work.

After the investment banker was done speaking, Hand looked around the room. He knew that the venture capitalists on the board wanted an exit vehicle from Acme and were strongly in favor of taking the company public. He also knew that the other senior managers on the board would like the "large payoff" that the representative from Gold Brothers spoke of, but that they would ultimately follow Hand's lead in the boardroom. He was very reluctant to take Acme public. He was nervous about the loss of control, the many operating changes that would become necessary, and the fact that Acme would become a very different company from the one he had spent his entire adult life building. However, he recognized that Acme was ready to enter a new stage and badly needed the additional capital. If Acme did not go public, its growth would slow and its long-term viability would be in doubt. Furthermore, Hand liked the potential of becoming a rich man. When all of the factors were considered, Hand felt he had no choice but to support taking Acme public.

As Hand expected, the rest of the board agreed with his conclusion. The board's final act at this meeting was to instruct Burns to come to a special board meeting in four weeks, to explain the details of the process of going public to the board. In addition, Burns was charged with soliciting bids from several investment banks for the position of the lead underwriter of Acme's public offering. The board would evaluate the proposals and choose a lead underwriter at the next meeting.

CHOOSING A LEAD UNDERWRITER

Four weeks later, Burns came to the board with proposals from four investment banks. On Burns's recommendation, the board decided to evaluate the proposals using six criteria:

1. The investment bank's valuation of Acme's worth and its recommended offering price.
2. The investment bank's reputation and experience with similar IPOs.
3. The investment bank's experience in the software industry.
4. The investment bank's distribution network and its ability to sell Acme's shares.
5. The investment bank's record of postoffering support: its ability to avoid a postoffering fall in Acme's stock price.
6. The type of underwriting the bank was offering: best efforts, best efforts— all or none, or firm commitment.

The board evaluated each proposal using the criteria listed above. The board initially eliminated a proposal from a regional investment bank because of the board's desire to use a bank with the ability to sell Acme nationwide. Acme sold software throughout the country, and the board believed that a national distribution effort would make the offering more successful.

The board eliminated a second proposal because of the type of underwriting the investment bank was offering. Acme's board wanted a firm-commitment underwriting agreement, which means that the investment bank agrees to buy all of the shares being offered, and the investment bank assumes the risk of not being able to sell the shares. Much of this risk is minimized by the bank, in this case, because of its preselling effort and its ability to adjust the offering price just before the offering becomes effective. The rejected proposal suggested a best-efforts underwriting agreement, in which the investment bank agrees to make a best effort to sell as many shares as possible, but does not commit to purchasing any shares. The third type of agreement, best efforts—all or none—means that the offering is cancelled if all shares are not sold.

The two remaining proposals were from large, national investment banks with extensive public offering experience and experience in the software industry. Not surprisingly, the valuations of the two banks were very similar. The board actually chose the bank with the slightly lower valuation—Gold Brothers—based on Burns's recommendation and the positive report from the venture capitalists who had dealt with the investment bank on previous offerings. The board was impressed with the representative who had attended the earlier meeting and felt very comfortable with its choice of lead underwriter.

With a lead underwriter now chosen, the next step for the board was to assemble the rest of the underwriting team. Burns explained that the underwriting team is usually made up of the lead underwriter, the underwriter's counsel, the company's counsel, an independent accountant, and a financial printer. Each member of the team has a critical role. The lead underwriter is ultimately responsible for selling the stock to the public. The lead underwriter generally chooses the underwriter's counsel, who drafts the underwriting agreements for the underwriter. The company's counsel advises the company on the steps it must take to abide by all SEC rules and regulations. The independent accountant issues an audit opinion on the financial statements, which must be filed with the SEC, and a comfort letter to the underwriter (see Appendix 1). The contents of the comfort letter are negotiated with the company's management: The letter comments generally on the financial statements, their compliance with SEC regulations, and the changes in the company's financial position since the last audit. The financial printer prints all the various financial statements: It must be large enough to handle large, last-minute jobs and be familiar with SEC requirements.

Burns had the name of a financial printer recommended by Gold Brothers, and Acme already had corporate counsel and a "big six" independent accountant, Coopers & Lybrand. The lead underwriter would choose its own counsel: Then the team would be complete. The board suggested that the underwriting team meet the next week with Hand and Burns to review the steps Acme needs to take and initiate the offering process. As they were leaving the meeting, Hand asked Burns to set up a meeting with Acme's counsel so that the counsel could brief him and Burns on the SEC's rules and regulations.

THE SEC

Acme's counsel began the briefing meeting with Hand and Burns by explaining that there are two primary laws that guide public companies: the Securities Act of 1933 and the Securities Exchange Act of 1934.

The Securities Act of 1933 requires new issues of public securities to be registered with the SEC prior to issuance. The Act outlines the registration process, specifies exempt securities and exempt transactions, and outlines antifraud provisions, which apply to all securities, whether exempt or not. The focus of this act is the protection of the public from fraudulent activity during the process of issuing new securities.

The Securities Exchange Act of 1934 established the SEC and focuses on regulation of public companies after they have gone public. The act details who must register and report to the SEC on an ongoing basis. Basically, any company with publicly traded stock and assets of over $1 million must register and report. Typically, these companies must file 10-Qs (quarterly financial reports), 10-Ks (annual reports with financial statements audited by a qualified independent public accounting firm), and 8-Ks (reports of certain material events, filed within 15 days of the event). Although there are many different provisions in the act, the lawyer pointed out that the most important provisions for Acme's senior management are the rules regarding insiders and short-swing profits. These provisions define officers, directors, and large shareholders as *insiders*. Insiders must report their initial holdings to the SEC and report any changes by amending their initial report. Insiders are prevented from making short-term profits on the purchase and sale of company stock within a six-month period. The provision preventing short-swing profits states that no one may use inside information to make short-term profits in the stock market. Therefore, senior management has a responsibility to keep inside information inside the company.

THE PROCESS OF GOING PUBLIC

The underwriting team gathers together, several days later, to discuss the process and develop a timetable for going public. The representative from Gold Brothers took the lead in outlining the process to the other participants.

The first step in the process is preparing the initial registration statement. The registration statement is the primary document that is filed with the SEC during the process of going public. The document in this first step is called an initial statement because the SEC will review and comment on this statement. It is probable that the company will make changes to the statement after the SEC review.

There are several different types of registration statements. The appropriate form to use depends on the size of the public offering and whether any of the industry-specific forms are required. Acme will use the S-1 form, the basic form for large public offerings (see Appendix 2).

The registration statement consists of two parts: The first part usually doubles as the prospectus. It contains information about the company, financial statements, management's discussion and analysis of the business, information about the intended use of the offering proceeds, potential risks faced by the company, as well as a host of other information and documents. The second part of the registration statement contains more technical information, which will be available to the public through the SEC, but is usually not widely distributed.

The preparation of the initial registration statement for Acme's public offering will be particularly demanding on two fronts: writing the analysis of the business and presenting its financial results and activities over the past five years. Even though the senior management at Acme is very knowledgeable about its business, writing the analysis of the business is usually a very time-consuming and difficult task. The primary reason this task is so difficult is the dual nature of the registration statement. On the one hand, the SEC requires that the statement contain an accurate description of the risks that Acme faces and a discussion of everything that could go wrong. On the other hand, this part of the registration statement is going to be used by investors to evaluate whether Acme is a good investment. Therefore, the discussion of all that can go wrong with Acme's business has to serve also as a selling document. Constructing an effective selling document is critical to the success of the offering, and management needs to spend a lot of time making sure it is perfect. The lawyers will be active in the development of the document, to ensure compliance with applicable laws and to minimize potential litigation related to inadequate disclosure.

The second big task is obtaining audited financial statements for the last three years and presenting the results of operations for five years. Acme has had its financial statements reviewed by its independent public accountants for the last four years. But there is a big difference between a review of financial statements and an audit of those same statements, in compliance with SEC rules and regulations. The objectives of an audit are to obtain and evaluate evidence to corroborate management's assertions regarding its financial statements, and to express an opinion on the financial statements, taken as a whole. A review does not include evaluation of corroborating information and does not provide a basis for expressing an opinion. An audit provides reasonable assurance that the financial statements fairly present the company's financial position and the results of operations, while a review offers a much lower degree of assurance. Due to Acme's excellent financial record-keeping and the accountant's familiarity with Acme's financial statements, the underwriting team decides to have Acme's audit conducted at the same time that the financial information is put into the format required by the SEC for the registration document.

The representative from Gold Brothers thought that the initial registration statement could be done within six to eight weeks. This would require a herculean effort, but Gold Brothers felt it was important to get this process moving as quickly as possible because the market was performing well and was very receptive to software IPOs. The market could change at any time, so Acme needed to put the offering on a fast track to take advantage of current positive conditions.

When the initial registration statement is filed with the SEC, the SEC will review it, focusing on whether Acme has followed all the rules, or has omitted or misstated any material facts, and will determine whether a full and complete disclosure was made. The SEC review can take up to two months. Once the SEC completes their review, they will document their findings in a letter of comment. In all likelihood, Acme will change the registration statement to address any comments or suggestions noted by the SEC. During this review period, it is critical that corporate counsel keep in touch with the SEC. If there are major problems with the registration statement, the SEC will let Acme know during the review process, so that management can begin work on resolving the issues.

During this review period, sometimes called the *cooling off* period, management and the investment bankers will begin to market the offering. Gold Brothers will begin to distribute the preliminary prospectus, known in the trade as a *red herring* (because of the bright red letters in the cover, stating that it is preliminary), to potential investors and possible participants in the underwriting syndicate. This document is basically the same document as the initial registration statement filed for review with the SEC. The underwriting syndicate is a group of investment bankers from other firms who agree to sell a certain portion of the offering to their clients. During this cooling off period, the red herring is the only written material used to market the offering.

After distributing the preliminary prospectus, Acme's senior management and representatives from Gold Brothers will travel around the country for approximately two weeks, making presentations to investors and underwriters about the offering and Acme Business Software. This trip is called a *road show* and is very time-consuming. Several of Acme's senior managers should be present at all of these meetings.

While distributing the red herring and doing the road show, the lawyers will be filing the various forms required by the different states before securities can be sold in that state. These various state requirements are called the *Blue Sky Laws* and must be compiled for each state within which Acme plans to offer stock. Acme has chosen to market the stock nationally, so meeting all the blue-sky requirements will take a lot of work.

Toward the end of the cooling off period, a due diligence meeting will be held, where all parties will gather and go over Acme's business statements to make sure that Acme has made a full disclosure and has not omitted anything that could be considered material by the SEC.

The cooling off period ends when the company receives the SEC comments on the initial registration statement. If the SEC notes some deficiencies in the registration statement, or if some aspect of Acme's business has changed, in the period since it filed the statement originally, the registration statement will be amended.

Once Acme addresses the SEC's comments, Acme will agree to the final offering price for the stock and sign an underwriting agreement with the underwriter. Usually this is done the day before the issue is effective, so that the underwriter can adjust the price to the market conditions that exist at the time of issuance. Once the price is established and the final underwriting agreement is signed, a final amendment to the registration statement will be filed.

At this point, the registration statement will automatically become effective in 20 days. However, the SEC can accelerate the effective date of the registration statement to the date of the final amendment. The SEC will generally grant an acceleration, unless a company has not responded properly to the issues the SEC identified during its review. The accelerated effective date is very important to ensure that the price set reflects current market conditions. A lot can change in the market in 20 days.

As soon as the SEC gives its approval, selling starts. Seven days later, the closing takes place. The accountant will give the underwriters a comfort letter as part of the due-diligence process, and the company will exchange cash for shares. Except for some postoffering support work by Gold Brothers, the process of going public will be complete, and Acme will begin its life as a public company.

FIVE YEARS LATER: A LOOK BACK

Five years later, John Hand looked back on the IPO process and analyzed what had made the Acme IPO a success and what had happened at Acme in the five years since the public offering. Hand remembered that the three months from the beginning of the IPO process to the actual closing were the worst three months he had spent at Acme to that point. Instead of doing what he enjoyed, running his own software company, Hand had spent virtually all of his time doing what he hated, dealing with investment bankers, lawyers, and accountants. Ultimately, however, the effort had paid off and the public offering had been a tremendous success. Acme did not get as much per share as it had expected, but Hand knew that this was typical of IPOs.

On reflection, Hand thought that there were two major groups of factors that had led to the success of Acme's public offering. The first group of factors were characteristics of Acme as a company.

Acme Was Well-Established with a Competitive Product Line

Although Hand knew very little about the financial markets before going through the IPO process, he soon realized that it would be difficult to fool the markets. Looking back, Hand concluded that if Acme had not been a well-established company with a successful and promising product line, it would never have been able to go public.

Acme Had a Record of Profitable Performance

Acme's record of profitable performance over the several years immediately prior to the IPO had been just as important as a strong product line. During the selling process, Hand noted, investors had looked very closely at Acme's profitability over the last four to six quarters to see if there had been any bad quarters or indications of weakness. Hand believed that if Acme had experienced one or two losing quarters in the year or two prior to the offering, the offering would not have been as successful.

Acme Had a Strong Management Team

Investors were ultimately investing in Acme's future performance, not its track record of past success. Hand believed that Acme's strong and experienced management team gave investors confidence that Acme could continue to succeed in the future, even if times got tougher for the software industry.

Acme's Senior Management Was Not Bailing Out

In addition to seeing a strong management team in place, investors want to make sure the team is sticking around and not just cashing out. Hand had wanted to sell a significant block of shares in the offering. Gold Brothers had advised against it, arguing that if investors thought Hand might be leaving, the offering would suffer. Hand had taken their advice and held off selling shares until almost a year after the offering was complete. The other senior managers with stock had also refrained from selling their shares, and Hand believed that this had been an important factor in the offering's success.

Acme Had a Need for Long-Term Capital

Acme had a clear, demonstrable need for more capital. Without additional capital, Acme would not have been able to introduce several new products or expand overseas. Investors looked very closely at Acme's plans for the offering proceeds. Hand concluded that if Acme had not clearly needed capital, the offering would not have been successful.

Acme Had the Potential for Long-Term Growth

Investors bought Acme's stock because they believed that Acme could continue to grow for a long time. Investors counted on a return from stock appreciation. Most investors knew that Acme would not pay any dividends in the near future. Investors also knew that the only way the stock would appreciate was if Acme continued to grow and remain profitable for several years.

In addition to the positive influence of Acme's characteristics on the IPO, Hand also felt that there had been some other important factors in Acme's success: factors which had little to do with Acme itself, and over which Acme had little control or influence.

Acme Was in a "Hot" Industry

In the mid-1980s, software companies were very attractive to investors and Acme was able to capitalize on this through its public offering. Although there were IPOs by companies in a wide variety of industries during the year Acme went public, the fact that Acme was a successful software company helped create the tremendous demand for Acme stock by investors. What's "hot" can change quickly, so an entrepreneur needs a lot of luck to hit it just right.

The Market Conditions Were Receptive to IPOs

Acme went public at a time when the market was very receptive to IPOs, but that is not always the case. The 1960s and the 1980s (up until the 1987 crash) were generally known as good times for IPOs, but the 1970s were considered very difficult years for public offerings. However, positive conditions do not last for entire decades. Market conditions can change dramatically overnight, and today's very attractive public offering can be tomorrow's cancelled IPO. The combination of market factors and company characteristics were just right to result in a successful IPO for Acme.

LIFE AS A PUBLIC COMPANY

Hand thought about the five years after the IPO with very mixed feelings. On the positive side, Acme Business Software had used the capital wisely and watched its business soar. Several of the new products had been successful, and the company had built an international reputation. The original investors were extremely pleased. They had seen Acme's stock price rise steadily for the first couple of years after the offering. Hand had reason to be most pleased of all. By following his investment banker's advice and not selling a large part of his stock holdings in the IPO, Hand had benefited from the company's success. He had seen the value of his holdings grow tremendously, as the stock price climbed after the offering: He was wealthy beyond his wildest dreams.

Despite all the positive aspects of going public, Hand also saw a negative side. Like many other successful entrepreneurs, Hand had been unprepared for the role of running a public company. Prior to going public, Hand had felt that he really had a hand in every phase of business. He had been active in new product development, he had played an important role in selling Acme's products to some of its larger customers, and he had been able to meet regularly with his senior managers to help them solve their problems. He had created a smoothly functioning team, and he was their captain.

After taking Acme public, Hand noticed that his role changed very quickly. The most difficult change for Hand was responding to all of the new constituents. Wall Street analysts and brokers always seemed to be on the phone looking for information. Shareholders called at all times and reporters nosed around, looking for good stories. Acme was forced to hire a company spokesperson to handle press inquiries and prepare regular press releases, as well as several new employees to deal with shareholder relations. In addition, the newly expanded board of directors took a much more active role in the affairs of the company. Hand felt as if there were always someone looking over his shoulder. He was constantly explaining and justifying his decisions. To make matters worse, all of his decisions began to be framed by their effect on short-term earnings. The discussions inevitably turned to what the decision would do to the quarterly earnings number.

Hand found that he had little time for new product development, and dealt with customers principally when they had a major complaint. He became increasingly disenchanted with his role as CEO of Acme. After two years of watching Acme's sales and profits grow along with his unhappiness, Hand suggested to the board of directors that maybe it was time to consider bringing in a new CEO. The board reluctantly agreed and created a new position for Hand in which he would oversee new product development.

The new position kept Hand happy for a little while. He was happy to be working with computers and other engineers, rather than with Wall Street analysts and institutional investors. But after a time, he realized that what he enjoyed doing the most was running his own company. He loved putting everything he had into his company, and he loved the thrill of living or dying with the company's success. He yearned for the early days of Acme Business Software and wished that there was some way he could turn Acme back into the company it had been before it went public.

Hand realized that this could never happen and so, almost five years after taking Acme public, John Hand left the company he had founded and began making plans to start a new software company. Ironically, because of the success of the IPO and the value of Acme stock, this time Hand would not have to worry about attracting venture capitalists or investment bankers to finance his new company. At least, not for a few years.

FOR FURTHER READING

Arkebauer, James B. and Ronald M. Schultz, *Cashing Out: The Entrepreneur's Guide to Going Public* (New York: HarperBusiness, 1991).

Dobbin, Muriel, *Going Public* (New York: Carol Publishing Group, 1991).

Malone, Michael S., *Going Public: MIPS Computer and the Entrepreneurial Dream* (New York: HarperCollins, 1991).

Roberts, Holme and Harold A. S. Bloomenthal, *Going Public Handbook,* 1991 ed. (New York: Clark Boardman, 1991).

Weiss, Martin, *Going Public* (New York: Tab Books, 1990).

Wood, Ira, *Going Public* (Zoland Books, 1991).

APPENDIX 1

Comfort Letter

(Letters for Underwriters)

The following items are covered in a typical comfort letter.

1. A statement regarding the independence of the accountants.
2. An opinion regarding whether the audited financial statements and schedules included in the registration statement comply in form, in all material respects, with the applicable accounting requirements of the Act and the related published rules and regulations.
3. Negative assurance with respect to whether the unaudited condensed interim financial statements included in the registration statement: (a) Comply in form, in all material respects, with the applicable accounting requirements of the Act and the related published rules and regulations; (b) Are in conformity with GAPP, applied on a basis substantially consistent with that of the audited financial statements included in the registration statement.
4. Negative assurance with respect to whether, during a specified period following the date of the latest financial statements in the registration statement and prospectus, there has been any change in capital stock, long-term debt, or any decrease in other specified financial statement items.

Source: AICPA Professional Standards by Commerce Clearing House, 1982.

Example of a Comfort Letter

June 30, 19X6

[Addressee]

Dear Sirs:

We have audited the consolidated balance sheets of the Blank Company, Inc. (the company) and subsidiaries as of December 31, 19X5 and 19X4 and the consolidated statements of income, retained earnings, and cash flows for each of the three years in the period ended December 31, 19X5 and the related schedules all included in the registration statement (no. 2-00000) on Form S-1 filed by the company under the Securities Act of 1933 (the Act); our reports with respect thereto are also included in that registration statement. The registration statement, as amended on June 23, 19X6, is herein referred to as the registration statement.*

In connection with the registration statement—

1. We are independent certified public accountants with respect to The Blank Company, Inc., within the meaning of the Act and the applicable published rules and regulations thereunder.

2. In our opinion [include the phrase "except as disclosed in the registration statement," if applicable], the consolidated financial statements and schedules audited by us and included in the registration statement comply in form in all material respects with the applicable accounting requirements of the Act and the related published rules and regulations.

3. We have not audited any financial statements of the company as of any date or for any period subsequent to December 31, 19X5; although we have conducted an audit for the year ended December 31, 19X5, the purpose (and therefore the scope) of the audit was to enable us to express our opinion on the consolidated financial statements as of December 31, 19X5, and for the year then ended, but not on the financial statements for any interim period within that year. Therefore, we are unable to and do not express any opinion on the unaudited consolidated condensed statements balance sheet as of March 31, 19X6, and unaudited consolidated condensed statements of income, retained earnings, and cash flows for the three-month periods ended March 31, 19X6, and 19X5, included in the registration statement, or on the financial position, results or operations, or cash flows as of any date or for any period subsequent for December 31, 19X5.

4. For purposes of this letter we have read the 19X6 minutes of meetings of the stockholders, the board of directors, and [include other appro-

priate committees, if any] of the company and its subsidiaries as set forth in the minute books at June 25, 19X6, officials of the company having advised us that the minutes of all such meetings through the date were set forth therein; and we have carried out other procedures to June 25, 19X6 (our work did not extend to the period from June 26, 19X6, to June 30, 19X6, inclusive), as follows:

a. With respect to the three-month periods ended March 31, 19X6 and 19X5, we have—

(i) Read the unaudited consolidated condensed balance sheet as of March 31, 19X6, and unaudited consolidated condensed statements of income, retained earnings, and cash flows for the three-month periods ended March 31, 19X6 and 19X5, included in the registration statement; and

(ii) Made inquiries of certain officials of the company who have responsibility for financial and accounting matters regarding (1) whether the unaudited consolidated condensed financial statements referred to in a(i) comply in form in all material respects with the applicable accounting requirements of the Act and the related published rules and regulations and (2) whether those unaudited consolidated condensed financial statements are in conformity with generally accepted accounting principles applied on a basis substantially consistent with that of the audited consolidated financial statements included in the registration statement.

b. With respect to the period from April 1, 19X6, to May 31, 19X6, we have—

(i) Read the unaudited consolidated financial statements of the company and subsidiaries for April and May of both 19X5 and 19X6 furnished us by the company, officials of the company having advised us that no such financial statements as of any date or for any period subsequent to May 31, 19X6, were available; and

(ii) Made inquiries of certain officials of the company who have responsibility for financial and accounting matters regarding whether the unaudited financial statements referred to in b(i) are stated on a basis substantially consistent with that of the audited financial statements included in the registration statement.

The foregoing procedures do not constitute an audit conducted in accordance with generally accepted auditing standards. Also, they would not necessarily reveal matters of significance with respect to the comments in the following paragraph. Accordingly, we make no representations regarding the sufficiency of the foregoing procedures for your purposes.

5. Nothing came to our attention as a result of the foregoing procedures, however, that caused us to believe that—

a. (i) The unaudited consolidated condensed financial statements described in 4a(i), included in the registration statement, do not comply in form in all material respects with the applicable accounting requirements and (ii) the unaudited consolidated condensed financial statements are not in conformity with generally accepted accounting principles applied on a basis substantially consistent with that of the audited consolidated financial statements; or

b. (i) At May 31, 19X6, there was any change in the capital stock or long-term debt of the company and subsidiaries consolidated or any decreases in consolidated net current assets or net assets as compared with amounts shown in the March 31, 19X6, unaudited consolidated condensed balance sheet included in the registration statement or (ii) for the period from April 1, 19X6, to May 31, 19X6 there were any decreases, as compared with the corresponding period in the preceding year, in consolidated net sales or in the total or per-share amounts of income before extraordinary items or of net income, except in all instances for changes or decreases that the registration statement discloses have occurred or may occur.

6. As mentioned in 4b, company officials have advised us that no consolidated financial statements as of any date or for any period subsequent to May 31, 19X6, are available; accordingly, the procedures carried out by us with respect to changes in financial statement items after May 31, 19X6, have, of necessity, been even more limited than those with respect to the periods referred to in 4. We have made inquiries of certain company officials who have responsibility for financial and accounting matters regarding whether (a) there was any change at June 25, 19X6, in the capital stock or long-term debt of the company and subsidiaries consolidated or any decreases in consolidated net current assets or net assets as compared with amounts shown on the March 31, 19X6, unaudited consolidated condensed balance sheet included in the registration statement or (b) for the period from April 1, 19X6, to June 25, 19X6, there were any decreases, as compared with the corresponding period in the preceding year, in consolidated net sales or in the total share or per-share amounts of income before extraordinary items or of net income. On the basis of these inquiries and our reading of the minutes as described in 4, nothing came to our attention that caused us to believe that there was any such change or decrease,

except in all instances for changes or decreases that the registration statement discloses have occurred or may occur.

7. This letter is solely for the information of the addressees and to assist the underwriters in conducting and documenting their investigation of the affairs of the company in connection with the offering of the securities covered by the registration statement, and it is not to be used, circulated, quoted, or otherwise referred to within or without the underwriting group for any other purpose, including but not limited to the registration, purchase, or sale of securities, nor is it to be filed with or referred to in whole or in part in the registration statement or any other document, except that reference may be made to it in the underwriting agreement or in any list of closing documents pertaining to the offering of the securities covered by the registration statement.

---

* As described in paragraph 18, the accountants may refer in the introductory paragraphs to the fact that they have issued reports on other financial information. For example, if the accountants refer to the fact that a review of interim financial information had been performed, an additional introductory paragraph, such as the following, may be added.

Also, we have made a review of the unaudited consolidated condensed financial statements for the three-month periods ended March 31, 19X6 and 19X5, as indicated in our report dated May 15, 19X6, which is included [incorporated by reference] in the registration statement.

Source: Reprinted, by permission, from *Professional Standards,* Copyright ©1991 by American Institute of Certified Public Accountants, Inc.

APPENDIX 2

Registration Statement Form

OMB APPROVAL
OMB Number: 3235-0065
Expires: May 31, 1994
Estimated average burden
hours per response . 1258.00

UNITED STATES
SECURITIES AND EXCHANGE COMMISSION
Washington, D.C. 20549

FORM S-1

REGISTRATION STATEMENT UNDER THE SECURITIES ACT OF 1933

_____
(Exact name of registrant as specified in its charter)

_____
(State or other jurisdiction of incorporation or organization)

_____
(Primary Standard Industrial Classification Code Number)

_____
(I.R.S. Employer Identification Number)

_____
(Address, including zip code, and telephone number,
including area code, of registrant's principal executive offices)

_____
(Name, address, including zip code, and telephone number,
including area code, of agent for service)

_____
(Approximate date of commencement of proposed sale to the public)

If any of the securities being registered on this Form are to be offered on a delayed or continuous basis pursuant to Rule 415 under the Securities Act of 1933, check the following box: ☐

Calculation of Registration Fee

Title of Each Class of Securities to be Registered	Amount to be Registered	Proposed Maximum Offering Price Per Unit	Proposed Maximum Aggregate Offering Price	Amount of Registration Fee

SEC 870 (8/91) 1 of 5

GENERAL INSTRUCTIONS

I.   Eligibility Requirements for Use of Form S-1

This Form shall be used for the registration under the Securities Act of 1933 ("Securities Act") of securities of all registrants for which no other form is authorized or prescribed, except that this Form shall not be used for securities of foreign governments or political subdivisions thereof.

II.   Application of General Rules and Regulations

> A. Attention is directed to the General Rules and Regulations under the Securities Act, particularly those comprising Regulation C (17 CFR 230.400 to 230.494) thereunder. That Regulation contains general requirements regarding the preparation and filing of the registration statement.

> B. Attention is directed to Regulation S-K (17 CFR Part 229) for the requirements applicable to the content of the non-financial statement portions of registration statements under the Securities Act. Where this Form directs the registrant to furnish information required by Regulation S-K and the item of Regulation S-K so provides, information need only be furnished to the extent appropriate.

III.   Exchange Offers

If any of the securities being registered are to be offered in exchange for securities of any other issuer, the prospectus shall also include the information which would be required by Item 11 if the securities of such other issuer were registered on this Form. There shall also be included the information concerning such securities of such other issuer which would be called for by Item 9 if such securities were being registered. In connection with this instruction, reference is made to Rule 409.

PART 1—INFORMATION REQUIRED IN PROSPECTUS

Item 1.   Forepart of the Registration Statement and Outside Front Cover Page of Prospectus.

> Set forth in the forepart of the registration statement and on the outside front cover page of the prospectus the information required by Item 501 of Regulation S-K (§229.501 of this chapter).

Item 2.   Inside Front and Outside Back Cover Pages of Prospectus.

> Set forth on the inside front cover page of the prospectus or, where permitted, on the outside back cover page, the information required by Item 502 of Regulation S-K (§229.502 of this chapter).

Item 3.   Summary Information, Risk Factors and Ratio of Earnings to Fixed Charges.

> Furnish the information required by Item 503 of Regulation S-K (§229.503 of this chapter).

Item 4.   Use of Proceeds.

> Furnish the information required by Item 504 of Regulation S-K (§229.504 of this chapter).

Item 5.   Determination of Offering Price.

> Furnish the information required by Item 505 of Regulation S-K (§229.505 of this chapter).

Item 6.   Dilution.

> Furnish the information required by Item 506 of Regulation S-K (§229.506 of this chapter).

Item 7.   Selling Security Holders.

> Furnish the information required by Item 507 of Regulation S-K (§229.507 of this chapter).

Item 8.   Plan of Distribution.

Furnish the information required by Item 508 of Regulation S-K (§229.508 of this chapter).

Item 9.   Description of Securities to be Registered.

Furnish the information required by Item 202 of Regulation S-K (§229.202 of this chapter).

Item 10.   Interests of Named Experts and Counsel.

Furnish the information required by Item 509 of Regulation S-K (§229.509 of this chapter).

Item 11.   Information with Respect to the Registrant.

Furnish the following information with respect to the registrant:

(a) Information required by Item 101 of Regulation S-K (§229.101 of this chapter), description of business;

(b) Information required by Item 102 of Regulation S-K (§229.102 of this chapter), description of property;

(c) Information required by Item 103 of Regulation S-K (§229.103 of this chapter), legal proceedings;

(d) Where common equity securities are being offered, information required by Item 201 of Regulation S-K (§229.201 of this chapter), market price of and dividends on the registrant's common equity and related stockholder matters;

(e) Financial statements meeting the requirements of Regulation S-X (17 CFR Part 210) (Schedules required under Regulation S-X shall be filed as "Financial Statement Schedules" pursuant to Item 15, Exhibits and Financial Statement Schedules, of this Form), as well as any financial information required by Rule 3-05 and Article 11 of Regulation S-X;

(f) Information required by Item 301 of Regulation S-K (§229.301 of this chapter), selected financial data;

(g) Information required by Item 302 of Regulation S-K (§229.302 of this chapter), supplementary financial information;

(h) Information required by Item 303 of Regulation S-K (§229.303 of this chapter), management's discussion and analysis of financial condition and results of operations;

(i) Information required by Item 304 of Regulation S-K (§229.304 of this chapter), changes in and disagreements with accountants on accounting and financial disclosure;

(j) Information required by Item 401 of Regulation S-K (§229.401 of this chapter), directors and executive officers;

(k) Information required by Item 402 of Regulation S-K (§229.402 of this chapter), executive compensation;

(l) Information required by Item 403 of Regulation S-K (§229.403 of this chapter), security ownership of certain beneficial owners and management; and

(m) Information required by Item 404 of Regulation S-K (§229.404 of this chapter), certain relationships and related transactions.

Item 12.   Disclosure of Commission Position on Indemnification for Securities Act Liabilities.

Furnish the information required by Item 510 of Regulation S-K (§229.510 of this chapter).

PART II—INFORMATION NOT REQUIRED IN PROSPECTUS

Item 13.   Other Expenses of Issuance and Distribution.

   Furnish the information required by Item 511 of Regulation S-K (§229.511 of this chapter).

Item 14.   Indemnification of Directors and Officers.

   Furnish the information required by Item 702 of Regulation S-K (§229.702 of this chapter).

Item 15.   Recent Sales of Unregistered Securities.

   Furnish the information required by Item 701 of Regulation S-K (§229.701 of this chapter).

Item 16.   Exhibits and Financial Statement Schedules.

   (a) Subject to the rules regarding incorporation by reference, furnish the exhibits as required by Item 601 of Regulation S-K (§229.601 of this chapter).

   (b) Furnish the financial statement schedules required by Regulation S-X (17 CFR Part 210) and Item 11(e) of this Form. These schedules shall be lettered or numbered in the manner described for exhibits in paragraph (a).

Item 17.   Undertakings.

   Furnish the undertakings required by Item 512 of Regulation S-K (§229.512 of this chapter).

SIGNATURES

Pursuant to the requirements of the Securities Act of 1933, the registrant has duly caused this registration statement to be signed on its behalf by the undersigned, thereunto duly authorized in the City of _____ ,

State of _____ , on _____ , 19 _____ .

_____
(Registrant)

_____
By (Signature and Title)

Pursuant to the requirements of the Securities Act of 1933, this registration statement has been signed by the following persons in the capacities and on the dates indicated.

_____
(Signature)

_____
(Title)

_____
(Date)

Instructions.

1. The registration statement shall be signed by the registrant, its principal executive officer or officers, its principal financial officer, its controller or principal accounting officer and by at least a majority of the board of directors or persons performing similar functions. If the registrant is a foreign person, the registration statement shall also be signed by its authorized representative in the United States. Where the registrant is a limited partnership, the registration statement shall be signed by a majority of the board of directors of any corporate general partner signing the registration statement.

2. The name of each person who signs the registration statement shall be typed or printed beneath his signature. Any person who occupies more than one of the specified positions shall indicate each capacity in which he signs the registration statement. Attention is directed to Rule 402 concerning manual signatures and to Item 601 of Regulation S-K concerning signatures pursuant to powers of attorney.

INSTRUCTIONS AS TO SUMMARY PROSPECTUSES

1. A summary prospectus used pursuant to Rule 431 (§230.431 of this chapter), shall at the time of its use contain such of the information specified below as is then included in the registration statement. All other information and documents contained in the registration statement may be omitted.

    (a) As to Item 1, the aggregate offering price to the public, the aggregate underwriting discounts and commissions and the offering price per unit to the public;

    (b) As to Item 4, a brief statement of the principal purposes for which the proceeds are to be used;

    (c) As to Item 7, a statement as to the amount of the offering, if any, to be made for the account of security holders;

    (d) As to Item 8, the name of the managing underwriter or underwriters and a brief statement as to the nature of the underwriter's obligation to take the securities; if any securities to be registered are to be offered otherwise than through underwriters, a brief statement as to the manner of distribution; and, if securites are to be offered otherwise than for cash, a brief statement as to the general purposes of the distribution, the basis upon which the securities are to be offered, the amount of compensation and other expenses of distribution, and by whom they are to be borne;

    (e) As to Item 9, a brief statement as to dividend rights, voting rights, conversion rights, interest, maturity;

    (f) As to Item 11, a brief statement of the general character of the business done and intended to be done, the selected financial data (Item 301 for Regulation S-K (§229.301 of this chapter)) and a brief statement of the nature and present status of any material pending legal proceedings; and

    (g) A tabular presentation of notes payable, long term debt, deferred credits, minority interests, if material, and the equity section of the latest balance sheet filed, as may be appropriate.

2. The summary prospectus shall not contain a summary or condensation of any other required financial information except as provided above.

3. Where securities being registered are to be offered in exchange for securities of any other issuer, the summary prospectus also shall contain that information as to Items 9 and 11 specified in paragraphs (e) and (f) above which would be required if the securities of such other issuer were registered on this Form.

4. The Commission may, upon the request of the registrant, and where consistent with the protection of investors, permit the omission of any of the information herein required or the furnishing in substitution therefor of appropriate information of comparable character. The Commission may also require the inclusion of other information in addition to, or in substitution for, the information herein required in any case where such information is necessary or appropriate for the protection of investors.

15 THE BOARD OF DIRECTORS

Charles A. Anderson
Robert N. Anthony

This chapter describes the nature and function of the board of directors, which has the ultimate responsibility for the governance of a corporation. It describes the board's activities in normal meetings, in strategy meetings, and in special situations. It also describes the work of three especially important board committees: the compensation committee, the audit committee, and the finance committee.[1]

The description focuses on the approximately 13,000 corporations that are subject to regulations of the Securities and Exchange Commission (SEC), but most of the description is also relevant to the boards of smaller corporations.

WHY HAVE A BOARD OF DIRECTORS?

Every corporation is required by law to have a board of directors. Its legal function is to govern the affairs of the corporation. However, in a small corporation whose chief executive officer (CEO) is also the controlling shareholder, the CEO actually governs, and the board acts primarily as an advisor.

When a corporation grows to the size in which it needs outside capital, it may go public by selling shares of stock (as explained in Chapter 14), and the board then represents the interests of these shareholders. The shareholders, who are the owners of the corporation, have a say in the way their company is run. They expect to receive regular, reliable reports on the company's operations.

If the company is profitable, they expect to receive dividends. If the company has problems, the owners need to know about them, so that they can take remedial action, if necessary.

A corporation may have many shareholders. Companies listed on the New York Stock Exchange must have at least 2,200 shareholders; General Motors Corporation has 1.6 million. Shareholders obviously are too numerous to govern the company directly; moreover, most of them are engaged in their own pursuits and will not give much, if any, time to governance. They therefore elect the board of directors to act for them.

SIZE AND COMPOSITION OF THE BOARD

A 1996 survey of large corporations found that the typical size of the board was 12, compared with 16 in the early 1980s.[2] Some boards, especially those in banks, are much larger. Large boards must delegate much of their work to an executive committee.

Most members of a typical board are "outside directors"; that is, they are not employees of the corporation. At one time, most board members were "inside directors," and in a few boards, this is still the case. The trend toward outside directors results because shareholders believe it is in their best interests for the board to have a significant degree of independence from the company's management. The board is responsible for selecting, appraising, and compensating management; if the board and management are the same people, the board can hardly perform its governance role in an objective manner.

The principal sources of outside board members are CEOs and senior officers of other corporations (but not competitors). Other outsiders are lawyers, bankers, physicians (on health care boards), scientists and engineers (on high-technology boards), retired government officials, and academics. A few people are professional board members; that is, their full-time occupation is serving on boards. The number of female and minority board members has increased substantially in recent years. The CEO and, perhaps, one or two senior members of management are typically members of the board.

Board members are compensated. In 80% of the large companies surveyed in 1989, there was an annual retainer of at least $20,000, plus a fee for each board or committee meeting attended. Two thirds of the boards had retirement plans (compared with only one-fifth in 1983).

Board members are elected at the annual meeting of shareholders. The shareholders almost always elect a slate proposed by the incumbent board; therefore, as a practical matter, the board is self-perpetuating. The process of selecting candidates for filling board vacancies is an important board function. It is becoming increasingly common to have staggered terms, that is, to elect one third of the board each year, for a three-year term. This practice is intended to discourage corporate raiders from seeking to obtain control of the company.

RELATION TO THE CEO

The board of directors "directs" and the chief executive officer "executes" the board's directions, but these terms are not an accurate description of their roles. In the majority of companies, the chief executive officer is also chairman of the board of directors and is the principal architect of policies, as well as being responsible for their execution. The CEO is indeed the "chief."

The board selects the CEO. Having selected what it believes to be the best available person for the job, the board wants to give the CEO its full support. To do less would inhibit the CEO from doing the job that the board expects. The CEO is accountable to the board and is subject to termination if the board decides that his or her performance was unsatisfactory.

The appropriate relationship is one of trust. The board must believe beyond any question that the CEO is completely trustworthy, will provide the board with all the information it wants and needs, will withhold nothing, and will not slant arguments to support a preconceived position. Conversely, the CEO must believe that he or she has the full support of the board.

Appraising the CEO

A major responsibility of the board is to appraise the CEO. If performance is below expectations, there are two possible explanations: (1) The CEO is to blame; (2) extraneous influences are responsible. In most cases, both factors are involved, and the directors have the extraordinarily difficult job of judging their relative importance. If they conclude that the CEO has made an incorrect decision, they may suggest a different course of action. More likely, however, they will say nothing and mentally file the incident away, for future reference, in evaluating the CEO. The Business Roundtable, a group of CEOs of leading companies, succinctly described the director's role vis-à-vis the CEO as "challenging, yet supportive and positive."

An important function of board meetings, of conversations, and even of social occasions, is to give the directors a basis for continuously appraising the CEO. Directors usually cannot make constructive suggestions on the details of current operations. Occasionally, they may call the CEO's attention to a certain matter. Primarily, however, they listen carefully to what the CEO says and do their best to judge whether things are going satisfactorily and, if they are not, decide where the responsibility lies.

The directors want the CEO to be frank and to give an accurate analysis of the company's status and prospects; concealing bad news is one of the worst sins a CEO can commit. Nevertheless, human nature is such that directors cannot expect the CEO to be completely objective. Incipient problems may go away, and making them known, even in the relative privacy of the boardroom, may cause unnecessary alarm. Directors are therefore on the alert for indications of significant problems that may lie ahead. In many of the well-publicized bankruptcies of public companies, the directors were significantly responsible; they did not identify or act on the problem soon enough.

Louis B. Cabot, former chairman of the board of Cabot Corporation, had a frustrating experience with the ill-fated Penn Central Corporation, one of the largest bankruptcies that had occurred up to that time. He joined the Penn Central board about a year before the company collapsed. From the outset, he was disturbed by management's unwillingness to furnish the information about performance that he felt he needed. A few months after joining the board, he wrote the CEO a letter that contains a succinct description of the director's role:

> I believe directors should not be the managers of a business, but they should ensure the excellence of its management's performance. To do this, they have to measure that performance against agreed-upon yardsticks.

The Next CEO

It is impossible to tell beforehand whether an executive will make a good CEO. The best indicator is how well a candidate performs. In most instances, therefore, the board looks to senior executives with proven track records as candidates for the CEO position. One of the most important jobs that a board assigns to a CEO, therefore, is to develop a succession plan for the company's senior managers. The purpose of such a plan is to identify potential CEO candidates, provide them with opportunities for growth, and groom them for higher level positions. The board participates actively in this process, by meeting with the CEO (usually once a year) in a meeting devoted largely to reviewing the senior management. Typical questions asked are: How is a key executive performing? What is his or her potential? Who are potential successors for the CEO—now and in the future? When this process works properly, an agreed-upon CEO candidate is available in an emergency, as well as having a CEO in place to take over from a retiring CEO, in a normal succession.

At Carborundum Company, for example, when William Wendel was chairman, such an annual meeting was referred to as the "truck meeting" because Bill always started with the question: "Suppose I am run over by a truck tomorrow; what will you do?" At Carborundum, two and sometimes three persons were identified as potential CEOs. As time went on, individuals were added to or eliminated from the list, and their relative ranking changed.

If the board fails to deal effectively with succession, it must go outside the company for a new CEO. Under most circumstances, the chances for an effective succession are much higher when the CEO position is filled by a proven executive from within the organization. If on the other hand, the board believes that the organization needs a "good shaking up," it sometimes will go outside the company for a CEO who has a fresh perspective.

NORMAL BOARD MEETINGS

Most boards meet eight, nine, or ten times a year. Some meet only quarterly, and a few meet monthly. The typical meeting lasts two or three hours, but may go considerably longer if contentious issues arise.

Premeeting Material

Prior to the meeting, board members are sent an agenda and a packet of material on topics to be discussed at the meeting. This "homework" usually requires several hours of study. Also, prior to the meeting, directors may query the CEO on matters that require clarification.

Current Situation and Outlook

The first substantive topic on the agenda usually is a discussion of current information about the company and its outlook. The CEO leads this discussion, perhaps delegating part of it to another senior officer. Much of the information is financial, that is, condensed income statements for each division, or groups of divisions and key balance-sheet items, such as inventory, receivables, and corporate expenses. There are three formats for presenting this financial information:

1. Comparison of management's current estimate of performance for the whole year with budgeted performance for the year: How do we now estimate that the company is going to perform for the whole year? This is the most important type of information. However, it is also the most sensitive, and many companies do not circulate it prior to the meeting.

2. Comparison of actual performance for the current period and for the year-to-date with budgeted performance for these periods. Because the actual numbers are firm, they provide a more objective basis for analysis than the current estimate for the year.

3. Comparison of actual performance with performance for the same periods last year. A carefully prepared budget incorporates changes in the business and the economy that have occurred since the prior year. It is, therefore, a

more meaningful basis for comparison than last year's numbers. If, however, the budgeted amounts, particularly the estimate of revenue, are highly uncertain, the numbers for last year provide a firmer foundation for a comparison.

Variances between actual and budgeted performance are discussed. Are unfavorable variances temporary? If not, what steps will be taken to eliminate them, or, if they result from unforeseen outside forces, what adjustments should be made in the company's operations?

In reviewing the company's financial performance and raising questions or making suggestions to management, directors form judgments regarding the company's affairs. In short, they are brought up to date. Moreover, preparing and presenting to the board a report on the company's performance is an important discipline for management.

Other Actions

Next, a number of proposed actions are submitted for board approval. Many of these recommendations come to the full board from committees which have discussed the topics in meetings held prior to the board meetings. These are described in a later section of this chapter. Questions may be raised about these recommendations, but these are usually requests for clarification. Board members rely on committee members to explore these matters thoroughly; there is not enough time to do so in the full board meeting. Unless new information surfaces, these recommendations are usually approved.

The board then takes up a number of routine items, each of which is listed on the agenda. These may be requests for approval for capital projects, approval of signature authority for various banking connections, approval of exceptions to pension plans, and approval of certain types of contracts. Except for large capital projects, these items are usually referred to as *boilerplate*. In most cases, they come to the board because state law, corporate bylaws, or written policy requires board action. They are approved with little discussion, sometimes in a single motion, despite the fact that the minutes may state for each of them: "After a full discussion, a motion to adopt the recommendation was duly made and seconded, and the motion was approved."

Education

A division manager assisted by senior associates may make a presentation about the activities of the division. This is a valuable educational device and an educational experience for the directors. Some board meetings may be held at company plants or other facilities.

The meeting itself, and the informal activities that usually are associated with it, are also educational. The directors have an opportunity to appraise company officials and their own colleagues. Judgments about these individuals may be invaluable, if the board is at some time required to deal with a crisis situation.

Setting Standards

Directors communicate to management the standards they believe should govern the organization's actions partly in written policy statements, but primarily in their attitudes. There are two general types of standards: They might be labeled economic standards and ethical standards, although neither term is precisely correct.

With respect to economic standards, the directors communicate the overall goals they believe the company can and should attain. They describe the relative importance of sales growth, earnings per share, and ROI, and the specific numbers they believe are attainable. They indicate the relative importance of short-run versus long-run performance. In the final analysis, the board generally relies on management's recommendations, but the enthusiasm, or lack of enthusiasm, with which they support a given recommendation conveys important information to management.

Ethical standards are nebulous. The written policy statements are always impeccably virtuous, but the actual expectations of the directors are indicated by the way they react to specific ethical problems. How does the company deal with its female and minority employees? What happens to an employee who has a drinking problem? Does the company have a policy concerning support for the communities in which it has operations? These and many other issues have ethical implications, and the manner in which the board reacts to them establishes the real policy, regardless of what is in the written statement.

It is easy to rely on counsel's answer to the question: Must we report this unpleasant development to the SEC? The answer depends on the legal interpretation of the regulations. It is much more difficult for the directors to agree, and to convey to management, that a certain course of action, although perhaps within the letter of the law, should not be tolerated. Currently, directors of many companies must wrestle with policies concerning affirmative action.

STRATEGY

A company should have a set of strategies that are well thought out, clear, and well understood by the organization. Strategies include the industry in which the company has decided to operate, its product lines within that industry, the price and quality position of these products, the targeted customers and markets (local, regional, national, international), its distribution channels (direct sales, dealers, distributors), marketing policies (advertising, sales promotion), manufacturing policies (in-house production, plant locations, outside sourcing), and financial policies (mix of debt and equity financing, retained earnings).

The board usually does not have the knowledge necessary to initiate a strategy or to choose among alternative strategies. It must rely on management to take the initiative, make the necessary analyses, and bring its recommendations to the board. What the board can and should do is described by Kenneth R. Andrews in *The Concept of Corporate Strategy*.[3] Andrews writes, as a summary:

> A responsible and effective board should require of its management a unique and durable corporate strategy, review it periodically for its validity, use it as the reference point for all other board decisions, and share with management the risks associated with its adoption.

Whereas it is unrealistic to expect directors to formulate strategies, they should satisfy themselves that management has a sound process for developing them. The strategy is probably acceptable if:

- It is based on careful analysis by people who are in the best position to evaluate it, rather than on an inspiration accepted without study.
- The reasoning seems sensible.
- No significant information has been omitted from the analysis.
- The results expected from the strategy are clearly set forth, so that actual accomplishment can be compared with them.

Strategy Meetings

As a basis for considering strategic plans, many companies arrange a meeting at which directors, together with senior managers, spend one, two, or three days discussing where the company should be headed. In order to minimize distractions and to provide an opportunity for informal discussion and reflection, these meetings are often held at a retreat, distant from the corporate offices. The frequency of these meetings varies widely from company to company, but because of the time and the preparation required they are not held often. Some companies never hold them.

The primary purpose of a strategy meeting is to explain the strategies and the foundations on which they are based. The explanations themselves provide useful information to the directors. The quality of the rationale for the strategies is an indication of the competence of senior management and of the managers of the divisions concerned. Thus the strategies provide additional insight about the CEO's abilities and about the abilities of participants who may be candidates for CEO.

Having adopted a corporate strategy, it is important that management adhere to it. Management brings many matters to the board for decision and approval that should be consistent with the company's strategy. Major capital expenditure proposals, acquisitions, divestitures, and financing proposals are just a few of these. If these proposals are not consistent with the adopted strategy, the company may drift off course and into serious trouble.

DEALING WITH MAJOR CRISES

Boards occasionally must deal with unexpected crises. These usually require special board meetings. We describe two of these: firing the CEO or dealing with takeover attempts.

Firing the CEO

There are times when a board must replace its CEO. A major criticism of some boards is that they fail to take timely action, when it becomes clear that the CEO should be replaced. Although there may be considerable justification for such criticism, one should recognize that it is much easier for an outside observer to be critical, than it is to actually be a director faced with this decision. This is especially so when the outsider's opinion is based on hindsight.

The decision to replace a CEO is subjective and usually emotional. Sometimes there are compelling reasons for taking action—for example, the CEO has become an alcoholic and has seriously embarrassed the company, or his or her corporate performance has dramatically deteriorated. In most instances, however, the justification is not so clear. Earnings may not have kept pace with those of industry leaders, because the board discouraged management from assuming additional debt, which would have enabled the company to expand. Or, perhaps, a major acquisition, which the board supported, did not work out. In such instances, it is not obvious that the primary blame belongs with the CEO.

There are, however, several important signals that can alert a board to potential trouble when it is evaluating the CEO's capabilities:

- *Loss of confidence in the CEO.*   If a significant number of directors have lost confidence in, or no longer trust, the CEO, he or she should be replaced.
- *Steady deterioration in corporate results.*   In most instances, this means that earnings seriously lag industry norms for several periods, without a defensible explanation. This problem is usually accompanied by the consistent failure to meet projections. The board must act before it is too late.
- *Organizational instability.*   A CEO who consistently has problems in retaining qualified senior executives probably should be replaced.

It is one thing for board members to begin to doubt the CEO's capabilities, but it is quite another thing for them to muster the courage and consensus needed to take action. The CEO and the outside directors have usually worked together for some time and are good, if not close, friends. For the CEO, dismissal is a catastrophic event. It is, therefore, understandable that directors have great difficulty in bringing themselves to take an action that will probably destroy the career of a business associate.

Replacing the CEO precipitates a crisis, both for the board, and also for the entire organization. Furthermore, when it happens, the board must be prepared to announce a successor and to deal with the problems inherent in the transfer of executive authority. Such action puts a major burden on the outside directors. Yet this is their responsibility to the shareholders and to the other constituencies of the corporation.

A widely reported example of the replacement of the CEO occurred in 1992 at General Motors Corporation. According to press reports, the board became increasingly dissatisfied with GM's performance under the leadership of Robert C. Stempel. Stempel resigned as chairman and CEO at the October 1992 board meeting. An outside board member, John G. Smale, was named chairman and John F. Smith, president of GM since April 1992 and formerly head of its international operations, became chief executive officer. Smale, who was the retired chairman of Procter & Gamble, continued as chairman of GM until 1995 when Smith was appointed to be both chairman and CEO.

The preceding account makes this transaction sound rather routine. Actually (although the directors were properly discreet in not making public statements), this must have been a traumatic and difficult period for the board. Over many weeks the directors were required to hold private meetings, clarifying and refining their judgments, getting legal advice, and making very certain that they were in unison on a decision that would influence the corporation for many years to come and which was bound to be highly controversial. This is perhaps the most severe test to which a board can be subjected.

Among the pressures brought to bear on the GM board was the rather newly aggressive position taken by some very large institutional shareowners. Traditionally these shareowners (large pension funds, institutional investors, and so forth) have tended to be fairly passive. In recent years, however, some of them led by the California Employees Pension Fund with assets totaling $100 billion have begun to bring pressure to bear on boards of directors to take actions which they perceive to be in the interest of the corporation. As representatives of the shareowners, boards can hardly ignore well-reasoned suggestions from these large and powerful constituencies. They can and do bring pressure on issues ranging from board memberships to board and executive compensation, corporate policies and, in the case of GM, the selection of the CEO. This practice is likely to continue.

Unfriendly Takeover Attempts

Another type of crisis event is the hostile takeover attempt. The board of the target company is in a highly stressful situation. Decisions vital to the company's future—even its continued existence—must be made in circumstances in which emotions are high, vested interests are at stake, and advice is often conflicting. The business press reports daily the dramatic developments of offers and counteroffers, tactics and strategies, as each side in the struggle seeks to gain an advantage. The increase in takeover attempts in recent years has resulted in a preoccupation, on the part of both boards and managements, in seeking ways to avoid attack or to prepare a defense. These efforts are both time-consuming and expensive, and while they may be necessary, they certainly are not productive.

One of the problems in takeover situations is that the board, as the representative of the shareholders, may have different interests from those of management. In most successful, unfriendly takeovers, the senior management of the target company becomes unemployed. A common accusation, therefore, is that in resisting a takeover, management is simply trying to entrench itself, even though the deal would result in a handsome gain for the shareholders. Directors in these situations must exercise great care to make certain that their decisions are in the interest of the shareholders and, in some cases, in the interest of the community, employees, and other stakeholders. This is not always an easy matter. What is the intrinsic value of the corporation? What is the real value of the "junk bonds" being offered to the shareholders? What consideration, if any, should the directors give to the interests of other parties? Obviously, these are complex issues for the board.

Although legally the directors are responsible *only* for protecting the interests of the shareholders, conscientious directors do consider the interests of these other parties. In doing so, they run the risk of a lawsuit, alleging that they have not discharged their legal duty.

Directors encounter special problems when the company's management attempts to acquire control through a leveraged buyout. A large and highly publicized transaction (an award-winning movie was based on it) was the 1988 buyout at RJR Nabisco.[4] In that situation, F. Ross Johnson, president and CEO, and several of his senior executives, made an offer to the board to buy the company for $75 per share (at that time the stock was selling in the forties). On the surface this looked like a good deal. The board, however, mindful of its obligation to the shareholders, sought to get the highest price possible. A special committee of outside board members was selected to "auction" the company to the highest bidder. After several offers and counteroffers from a number of parties and much negotiation, the board agreed to sell the company to Kohlberg, Kravis, Roberts & Co., an investment banking firm specializing in takeovers, for $109 per share, or a total of $24.9 billion.

One can speculate as to whether Mr. Johnson was acting properly as a director and CEO of the company. He was hired to lead and manage the company, not to enrich himself. He and his associates had available more information than anyone else as to the company's true value. Even though they offered $75 per share, while the stock market was valuing the company at much less, was it proper for him to try to buy the company, and was his offer fair to the shareholders? The board had to wrestle with these complicated, emotional issues.

In an unfriendly takeover attempt, the directors of the target company must rely on legal advice. Takeovers inevitably give rise to lawsuits. The board also must have expert advice from one or more investment banks, as to the value of their company and the value of offers to acquire it.

In practice, when a hostile takeover is initiated, the company's lawyers, investment bankers, accountants, and other advisors, together with the board and management, become involved in a hectic struggle that may last for weeks or months. It is a 24-hour day, 7-day week, effort; nearly everything else stops. There is intense preoccupation on survival or on striking the best possible deal. When the episode is over, all involved will know that they have experienced a crisis.

Boards can take steps to prepare for an unfriendly takeover attempt. Lawyers can advise on an almost endless series of defensive tactics, such as staggered terms for directors, a variety of "poison pills," and "golden parachutes." Boards are briefed and kept informed on the tactics that might be employed on both sides in a takeover battle. Arrangements are made in advance with lawyers, investment banks, proxy solicitors, and other advisors with whom the board can work, in the event that there is a surprise takeover attempt.

In the final analysis, the board itself plays the key role in dealing with a takeover attempt. This type of crisis is the ultimate test of a board's capability and durability.

DELEGATION OF BOARD WORK

Much of the work of the board is done in committees. They meet prior to the board meeting, hear reports, and prepare summaries and recommendations for full board action. There is not time in the board meetings for a thorough discussion; these take place in committees. In this section, we describe the activities of the three committees that deal with finance and accounting matters: the compensation committee, audit committee, and finance committee. Some boards have additional committees. They include a nominating committee that proposes new directors; a governance committee that appraises the board's performance and recommends changes in its practices; and a public affairs committee that judges the corporation's relationship with its constituencies.

COMPENSATION COMMITTEE

The board determines the compensation of the CEO and the other principal corporate officers. In many boards, a compensation committee, composed of outside board members, analyzes what the compensation should be and makes its recommendations to the full board.

CEO Compensation

When the board sets the CEO's compensation, it is also establishing a compensation standard for managers throughout the company. Their compensation is integrally related to the CEO's, and this is, therefore, the single most important compensation decision the board must make.

In most instances, this decision is not an easy one. A CEO is typically ambitious and competitive, and compensation is his or her report card. Since compensations of all CEOs of public companies are disclosed in proxy statements, each is able to see just where he or she stands in relation to others. Virtually every CEO would like to stand higher on that list. Thus the compensation committee deals with a sensitive issue, affecting the corporation's most important person.

The compensation committee considers three principal factors in deciding on compensation. The CEO's compensation should: (1) be related to performance, (2) be competitive, and (3) provide motivation.

Performance

The CEO's compensation should be related to performance. Superior performance should be rewarded with high compensation, while poor performance, if not warranting dismissal, should at least result in minimal compensation. Nevertheless, there is justification for the claim that in some companies, top executive compensation just keeps going up and up, without regard to performance. The problem is complex. In theory, the CEO should be rewarded for increasing the shareowners' wealth over the long term. Although this is a splendid generalization, the criterion is hard to measure, especially on a year-to-year basis.

Despite the difficulties, most compensation committees do make an effort to relate the CEO's compensation to the company's performance. They arrive at a collective, albeit subjective, judgment as to how well the company has done during the preceding year, as a basis for deciding on an appropriate raise (if any). In addition, most companies have long-term incentive arrangements, such as stock options or performance share plans, that are designed to relate the CEO's compensation to the company's performance over time. These plans, however, are far from perfect, and compensation committees constantly struggle to find new arrangements or formulas in an effort to relate compensation more closely to performance.

Competitive Range

Compensation committees look at where the CEO's compensation stands relative to the competition. What are other companies paying? They can be sure that their CEO has this information, and that if the CEO believes the compensation is not competitive or fair, he or she will become dissatisfied.

There are many sources for salary information. They include proxy statements from similar organizations, as well as published surveys. Some consulting organizations specialize in executive compensation; they can provide data as well as advice on these matters. In the end, however, and with all of the information at hand, the committee makes its judgment as to where in the competitive spectrum they want the CEO's compensation to fall.

Motivation

The third element that compensation committees consider is: How can we structure a compensation package that motivates the CEO to do what the board expects? If the company has a plan to move aggressively and take unusual risks in the near term, with the possibility of significant long-term payoff, the committee can structure a compensation plan that will reward that kind of behavior. For example, the CEO might receive a multiyear contract that will provide assurance of employment during the high-risk phase, together with a long-term stock-option plan. At the other extreme, a mature company might be interested in moderate growth, but secure dividends. In this instance, the compensation committee might structure a plan weighted heavily toward a fixed salary, reviewed annually, with only modest incentive features.

Thus, there are a wide variety of compensation arrangements, each providing a different type of motivation: base salary reviewed annually; base salary, plus annual discretionary bonus; base salary, with bonus based on a formula; stock-option plans; performance share plans; and multiyear incentive plans. Benefits play an important part in CEO compensation arrangements, retirement programs in particular. Each plan has its own motivational features, and the compensation committee attempts to structure a plan that provides the type of motivation for the CEO that the board wishes to generate.

Compensation Reviews

In addition to setting the CEO's compensation, the committee also determines compensation for the other senior executives, that is, corporate officers and others whose salary is above a given level. The review process usually takes place at a meeting of the compensation committee, with the CEO and the personnel policy staff officer.

At this review meeting, the CEO, with the assistance of the staff officer, presents the committee with a recommendation for each executive in the group.

The compensation history of each executive is made available, and the CEO gives reasons for each recommendation. There is usually some discussion about a few of the recommendations, and a few changes may be made. For the most part, however, the committee accepts the CEO's recommendations. Nevertheless, the review process is important. It enables the compensation committee to assure itself that the CEO is following sensible guidelines and consistent policies and is not playing favorites. It is also good discipline for the CEO to have to justify his or her recommendations to the committee.

Board Remuneration

Another function of the compensation committee is to recommend the compensation arrangements for the board itself. This is a delicate matter, since the board is disbursing company funds (actually shareholder funds) to itself.

Directors' compensation is disclosed in the annual proxy statement. Most companies would like to see their directors "respectably" compensated, and while compensation usually is not the compelling reason for holding a directorship, directors want to feel that they are being compensated on a competitive basis. On the other hand, most directors want to feel confident that their compensation is not excessive, and that they could never be criticized for improperly compensating themselves.

To help reach a balanced level of compensation, considerable survey information is available on corporate practices with respect to board retainer fees, board meeting fees, compensation for committee chairs, and so on. The committee evaluates this information from similar corporations, and then decides the appropriate level of compensation for its own board. This recommendation is then made to the full board.

AUDIT COMMITTEE

The audit committee is responsible for making certain that the company's published financial statements are fairly presented, that they are in conformance with generally accepted accounting principles (GAAP), and that the company's internal control system is effective. The audit committee also deals with important cases of alleged misconduct on the part of employees, including violations of the company's code of ethics. It also ratifies the selection of the company's external auditor.

Until 1960, only a few boards had audit committees. Currently, all companies listed on major stock exchanges are required to have audit committees, and most other corporations also have them.

Responsibility

Although the full board can delegate certain functions to the audit committee, this delegation does not relieve an individual board member of his or her responsibility for governance. In its 1967 decision in the BarChris case, the federal court emphasized this fact:

> Section 11 [of the Securities Act of 1933] imposes liability in the first instance upon a director, no matter how new he is. . . . He is presumed to know his responsibility when he became a director. He can escape liability only by using that reasonable care to investigate the facts which a prudent man would employ in the management of his own property.[5]

Directors have directors' and officers' (D&O) insurance, but this is only a partial protection against loss from suits claiming that they acted improperly. Courts are increasingly willing to examine the soundness of directors' decisions. For example, in a 1985 decision the Delaware Supreme Court stated that the directors of Trans Union Corporation acted too hastily, and without sufficient information, in approving the sale of the company to another group; the directors settled out of court for $23.5 million, of which only $10 million was covered by D&O insurance.

A study of the experience of nearly 2,000 companies, conducted by the Wyatt company, found that 300 of these companies had filed claims under their D&O policies. Forty percent of these claims resulted from actions initiated by shareholders, with "misleading representation" being the most prominent allegation. Payments were made in 39% of the cases, at an average cost (including both claims cost and legal defense fees) of $1.3 million.

Audit committee members walk a tightrope. On the one hand, as directors, they want to support the CEO—the person whom the board itself selected. On the other hand, they have a clear responsibility to uncover and act on management inadequacies. If they do not do so, they, along with the other board members, are subject to criticism at the very least, and, at worst, they may go to jail. Their task is neither easy nor pleasant.

Published Financial Statements

Obviously, the audit committee does not directly conduct audits; it relies on two other groups to do this. One is the outside auditor, a firm of certified public accountants. All listed companies (that is, companies whose securities are listed on stock exchanges) are required to have their financial statements examined by an outside auditor, and most other corporations do so in order to satisfy the requirements of banks and other lenders. The other group is the company's internal audit staff, a group of employees whose head reports to a senior officer, usually the CEO or chief financial officer.

Selection of Auditors

Ordinarily, management recommends that the current auditing firm be appointed for another year and that its proposed audit scope and fee schedule be adopted. After some questioning, the audit committee usually recommends that the board approve the selection. Subsequently, the recommendation is submitted to the shareholders in the annual meeting. Occasionally, the audit committee gives more than routine consideration to this topic.

There may be advantages in changing auditors, even when the relationships between the audit firm and the company have been satisfactory for a period of years. One reason for doing this is that the possibility that the board may be seeking bids from other firms may cause the current firm to think carefully about its proposed fees. However, the public may perceive a change in outside auditors as evidence that the superseded firm would not go along with a practice that the company wanted. For this reason, the SEC requires that if a new auditing firm is appointed, the reason for making the change be reported on Form 8-K. Also, a new firm's initial task of learning about the company requires management time; this is a reason why management may be reluctant to recommend a change.

Public accounting firms often perform various types of consulting engagements for the company: developing new accounting and control systems, analyzing proposed pension plans, and analyzing proposed acquisitions. The compensation for this work may exceed the compensation for audit work.

The Audit Opinion

In its opinion letter, the public accounting firm states that management, not the auditor, is responsible for the financial statements. Most companies receive a *clean opinion,* in which the auditor states that the financial statements "present fairly, in all material respects" the financial status and performance of the company in accordance with GAAP. If the auditing firm cannot make this statement, it gives a *qualified opinion,* or it states that it is unable to give any opinion. If the qualification is important, or if there is no opinion, the stock exchange immediately suspends trading in the company's stock. Note that the auditor's statement does not say that the financial statements are 100% accurate, or whether different numbers would have been even more fair. The audit committee's task is to decide whether the directors should concur with the outside auditor's opinion. Occasionally, the committee resolves differences if the auditors are unwilling to give a clean opinion on the numbers that management proposes.

Management has some latitude in deciding on the amounts to be reported, especially the amount of earnings. Since managers are human beings, it is reasonable to expect them to lean in the direction of reporting performance in a favorable light. Examples of this tendency are described next: smoothing of earnings, reporting unfavorable developments, and the "big bath."

Smoothing Earnings

There is a widespread belief (not necessarily supported by the facts) that ideal performance is a steady growth in earning, certainly from year to year, and desirably from quarter to quarter. Within the latitude permitted by GAAP, therefore, management may desire to smooth reported earnings, that is, to increase reported earnings or to move income from what otherwise would be a highly profitable period to a less profitable period.

The principal techniques for doing this are to charge the adjustments for inventory amounts, for bad debts, for returns and allowances, and for warranties. The audit committee therefore pays considerable attention to the calculations of these adjustments and allowances and to the accounts receivable, inventory, and accrued liability amounts that result from them. Changes in the reserve percentages from one year to the next are suspect. Within limits, the audit committee tolerates a certain amount of smoothing; indeed, it may not be aware that smoothing has occurred. Outside these limits, however, the committee is obligated to make sure that the reserves and accrual estimates are reasonable.

Not all attempts to smooth earnings are improper. For example, there are documented stories of managers who personally worked around the clock at year end, loading goods into United Parcel Service containers for shipment. This enabled them to count the value of the goods in the containers as revenue in the year that was about to end. Counting as revenue goods that actually were shipped is legitimate. By contrast, certain division managers at H.J. Heinz counted millions of dollars worth of items as revenues, even though the goods had not been shipped. This practice is wrong; when it was uncovered, there was unfavorable publicity, an SEC investigation, and punishment.[6]

Reporting Unfavorable Developments

The SEC requires that a report, Form 8-K, be filed promptly, whenever an unusual, material event that affects the financial statements becomes known. The principal concern is with the bottom line, that is, the amount of reported earnings. Management, understandably, may be inclined not to report events that might (but also might not) have an unfavorable impact on earnings. Potentially material events include the probable bankruptcy of an important customer, an important inventory shortage, a reported cash shortage that might (or might not) turn out to be a bookkeeping error, a possibly defective product that could lead to huge returns or to product-liability suits, possible safety or environmental violations, an allegation of misdeeds by a corporate officer, the departure of a senior manager, or a lawsuit that might be well-founded. It is human nature to hope that borderline situations will not actually have a material impact on the company's earnings.

Furthermore, publicizing some of these situations may harm the company unnecessarily. Disclosure of a significant legal filing against the company is necessary, but disclosure of the amount that the company thinks it might lose in such litigation, in a report that the plaintiff can read, would be foolish. Management and the audit committee have difficulty in deciding which items should be reported on a Form 8-K report or its equivalent.

The audit committee should be kept fully informed about all events that might eventually require filing a Form 8-K. One might think that the CEO would welcome the opportunity to inform the board of these events, because this would shift the responsibility for disclosure to the board. Nevertheless, managers, like most human beings, prefer not to talk about bad news if there are reasonable grounds for waiting awhile.

Occasionally, a manager may attempt to "cook the books," that is, to produce favorable accounting results by making entries that are not in accordance with GAAP. The Stirling Homex case is a prominent example: Management reported sales revenues for 10,000 of its modular homes, even though 9,100 of these homes were still in inventory.[7] The audit committee must rely on the auditors (or occasionally on a whistle-blower) to detect these situations.

The Big Bath

A new management may "take a big bath"; that is, it may write off or write down assets in the year in which it takes over, thereby reducing the amount of costs that remain to be charged off in future periods. This increases the reported earnings in the periods for which the new management is responsible. Because the situation that led to the replacement of the former CEO may justify some such charge-offs, and because the directors don't want to disagree with the new CEO during the honeymoon period, this tactic is sometimes tolerated. If the inflated earnings lead to extraordinarily high bonuses in future years, the board may come to regret its failure to question these proposals.

Audit Committee Activities

In probing for the possible existence of any of the situations previously described, the audit committee takes two approaches. First, it asks probing questions of management: Why has the inventory-reserve percentage or the receivables-reserve percentage changed? What is the rationale for a large write-off of assets?

Second, and much more important, the committee asks similar questions of the outside auditors. The audit committee usually meets privately with the outside auditors and tells them, in effect: "If you have any doubts about the numbers, or if you have any reason to believe that management has withheld material information, let us know. If you don't inform us, the facts will almost certainly come to light later on. When they do, you will be fired."

A more polite way of probing is to ask questions such as the following:

- Is there anything more you should tell us?
- What were your largest areas of concern?
- What were the most important matters, if any, on which you and management differed?
- Did the accounting treatment of certain events differ from general practice in the industry? If so, what was the rationale for the difference?
- How do you rate the professional competence of the finance and accounting staff?

Usually, these questions are raised orally. Because the auditors know from experience what to expect, they come prepared to answer them. Some audit committees state their questions in writing.

Although cases of inadequate disclosure make headlines, they occur in only a tiny fraction of 1% of all listed companies. Most such incidents reflect poorly on the work of the board of directors and its audit committee. Increasingly, the courts penalize such boards for their laxness. Directors ponder this fact: When serious misdeeds surface, the CEO often leaves the company, but the directors must stay with the ship and endure public criticism and the blot on their professional reputations. Their lives will be much more pleasant in the long run if they act promptly.

Quarterly Reports

In addition to the annual financial statements, the SEC requires companies to file a quarterly summary of key financial data on Form 10-Q. Because the timing of the release of this report usually does not coincide with an audit committee meeting, the audit committee ordinarily does not review it. Instead, it asks the CEO to inform the chairman of the committee, if there is an unusual situation that affects the quarterly numbers. The chairman then decides either to permit the report to be published as proposed, or, if the topic seems sufficiently important, to have the committee meet in a telephone conference call to discuss it.

Internal Control

In addition to its opinion on the financial statements, the outside auditing firm writes a *management letter,* which lists possible weaknesses in the company's control system that have come to the auditor's attention, together with recommendations for correcting the situation. In the boilerplate preceding this list, the auditor disclaims responsibility for a complete analysis of the system; the listed items are only those that the auditing firm happened to notice.

The internal auditor may write a report on aspects of the control system. The audit committee follows up on such a report by asking management to respond to the criticism. If management disagrees with the recommended course of action, its rationale is considered and is either accepted or rejected. If action is required, the committee keeps the item on its agenda until it is satisfied that the action has been taken.

If an especially serious problem is uncovered, the committee may engage its public accounting firm, or another firm, to make a special study. If the problem involves ethical or legal improprieties, an outside law firm may be engaged. As soon as a material problem is identified, it must be reported promptly to the SEC on Form 8-K.

The audit committee has a difficult problem with internal audit reports. In the course of a year, even a moderately sized staff may write 100 or more reports. Many of them are too trivial to warrant the committee's attention. (One of the authors participated in an audit committee meeting of a multibillion dollar company, in which 15 minutes were spent discussing a recommendation for an improvement in data processing that was expected to save $24,000 annually.) Drawing a line between important reports and trivial ones is difficult, however. A rule of thumb, such as "Tell us about the dozen most important matters," may be used, but it does not allow for the possibility that the thirteenth matter may also warrant committee attention.

In its private meeting with the head of internal audit, the audit committee assures itself that the CEO has given the internal audit staff complete freedom to do its work. The committee also makes it clear that the head of internal audit has direct access to the audit committee chairman if a situation that may warrant immediate board attention is uncovered. The internal auditor normally would report the matter in question to his superior first, but his primary obligation is to the audit committee. The committee, in turn, should guarantee, as well as it can, that the internal auditor will be fully protected against possible retaliation.

Internal Audit Organization

The committee also considers the adequacy of the internal audit organization. Is it large enough? Does it have the proper level of competence? (For example, does at least one member know how to audit computer systems?) In many companies, the internal audit organization is a training ground where promising accountants are groomed for controllership. The audit committee may find it useful to get acquainted with the internal audit staff, as a basis for judging future candidates for the controller organization.

When campaigns to reduce overhead are undertaken, the internal audit staff may be cut more than is healthy. The audit committee questions such cuts and asks the outside auditing firm for its opinion as to their desirability. However, because internal auditors do much of the verifying that otherwise would be done by external auditors, and at a lower cost per hour, external auditors may not have an unbiased view of the proper size of the internal audit organization.

FINANCE COMMITTEE

The board is responsible to the shareholders for monitoring the corporation's financial health and for assuring that its financial viability is maintained. The finance committee makes recommendations on these matters. (Nevertheless, as pointed out earlier, the full board cannot escape its ultimate responsibility for making sound decisions on these and other matters.)

The committee's agenda includes analyses of proposed capital and operating budgets and regular reviews of the company's financial performance as reported on the income statement. Occasionally, the committee may review the company's financial condition as reported on the balance sheet. It also reviews the estimated financial requirements over the next several years and decides how these requirements will be met. It recommends the amount of quarterly dividends. The finance committee (or a separate pension committee) reviews pension fund matters and also those of the fund for paying health care and other postemployment benefits; it reviews the policies that determine the annual contribution to the funds and the performance of the firm or firms that invest these funds.

This section descries aspects of these matters that are dealt with at the board-of-directors level. In some companies, the functions described here are divided among three committees—a budget committee, a finance committee, and a pension committee—and the names may be different. Our purpose is to describe what the committee or committees do, regardless of their titles.

Analysis of Financial Policies

Financial policies are recommended by management. Tools of analysis are increasingly sophisticated. Management, not the finance committee, is responsible for using these tools to evaluate risk and return. These tools help to quantify risk, but they are not a substitute for a definite policy on risk. An attitude toward risk is a personal matter, and the finance committee should recognize it as such. Each CEO has a personal attitude toward risk, and so does each individual director.

The committee's responsibility is to probe management's rationale for its policies and thereby assure itself that management has thought them through and that the policies are within acceptable limits.

Dividend Declaration

A financial policy that is specifically a matter for board decision is the declaration of dividends. Dividends are paid only if the company declares them; this declaration usually is made quarterly.

Some companies regularly distribute a large fraction of earnings, while others retain a large fraction within the corporation. Although generous dividends may be fine for the shareholder in the short run, they can deprive the corporation of resources needed for growth, thereby penalizing the shareholder in the long run. Conversely, if a large fraction of earning is retained, shareholders may be deprived of the opportunity to make profitable alternative investments. Thus, the finance committee must weigh the interest of the corporation against the interest of individual shareholders.

Some boards take a simplistic approach to dividends: "Always pay out X percent of earnings," or "Increase dividends each year, no matter what." Either statement has merit as a guide, but neither is more than a guide. In some industries, a certain payout ratio is regarded as normal, and a company that departs substantially from industry practice may lose favor with investors. There is good evidence that a record of increasing dividends over time, or at least a record of stable dividends, is well regarded by investors. By contrast, an erratic dividend pattern is generally undesirable; it creates uncertainty for investors.

Dividend policy warrants careful analysis. The principal factors that the board considers are:

- What are the company's financial needs? These needs depend on how fast the company wants to grow and how capable it is for growing. Or, as is the case with some companies, what is needed to preserve the company during a period of adversity?
- How does the company want to finance its requirements for funds? It can meet its needs by retaining earnings, by issuing debt, by issuing equity, or some combination of these approaches. Each source of funds has its own cost and its own degree of risk.
- What return does the company expect to earn on shareholder equity, and what degree of risk is it willing to assume in order to achieve this objective? The trade-off between risk and return will determine the appropriate type of financing and thus influence the extent to which earnings should be retained or paid out in dividends.

These are complex questions. Moreover, the factors involved in arriving at answers to them interact with one another. Hewlett-Packard is a useful example. When the company was organized in 1939, the founders decided to finance growth by reinvesting earnings. They thought that earnings would generate adequate funds to finance growth, and they believed that retaining earnings was the best investment the shareholders could make. Contributing to this decision was the fact that the company was originally a "garage-in-the-backyard" start-up, with no reputation, so the company would have had to pay dearly for outside financing of either debt or equity.

For many years, the company paid no dividends at all, and in 1996 its pay-out was less than 25% of earnings. In 1996, the market value of Hewlett-Packard stock totaled $60 billion. Another well-known high-technology, growth company, Intel, paid no dividend and had virtually no debt. Its total market value in 1996 exceeded $100 billion.

The Pacific Gas & Electric Co. had a very different dividend policy. It paid out an average of 80% of its earnings in dividends. As is the case with most pub-lic utility companies, its earnings are relatively stable from year to year, and it can rely on the capital markets for financing needs. Its long-term debt is roughly equal to its shareowners' equity. The total market value of PG&E common stock in 1996 was approximately $10 billion.

These two contrasting dividend policies reflect the differing characteristics of hi-tech growth companies and the more static or stable nature of the public utility industry. Boards of directors select a dividend policy that is suited to the needs and characteristics of their particular company and its industry.

Pension Funds

The finance committee considers two aspects of pension fund policy: the amount required to be added to the fund and the investment of the fund.

Size of the Pension Fund

Most corporate pension plans are defined-benefit plans. In deciding on the size of the fund required to make benefit payments to retirees, directors tend to rely heavily on the opinion of an actuary. Given facts about the size and demographic characteristics of the covered employees, facts about the provisions of the plan, and assumptions about the ROI of the fund and about probable wage and salary increases over time, an actuary can calculate the size of the pension fund that is currently needed to meet those requirements. (With available software, the company can make the same calculations.)

However, there is no way of measuring the reasonableness of two key assumptions: the future ROI and the future wage and salary payments on which the pensions are based. Since the actuarial calculations are no more valid than the accuracy of these assumptions, the calculations should not be taken as gospel. Both of these variables are roughly related to the future rate of inflation, and the spread between the two should remain roughly constant. That is, when one variable changes by one percentage point, so approximately should the other.

Pension Fund Investments

The most conservative practice is to invest the pension fund in annuities or in bonds whose maturities match the anticipated pension payments. Such a policy is said to "lock in" the ability to make payments. For employees who have already retired, this is so. It is not necessarily so, however, for employees who are currently working. If their compensation increases at a faster rate than is assumed in the actuarial calculations, or if the plan itself is sweetened, the fixed return will turn out to be inadequate. Under a defined-benefit plan, there is no sure way of guaranteeing that the cash will be available when it is needed. In any event, with such a conservative policy, the company gives up the opportunity of earning what is usually a greater return from an investment in equities.

Most companies hire one or more banks or investment firms to manage their pension fund. Voluminous data are available on the past performance of such managers. The catch is, however, that an excellent past record is no guarantee of excellent future performance. Any firm is a collection of individuals. Investment performance is partly a function of the individual doing the investing, and the fund's record may change when the individual leaves or loses his or her skill. For many years, when it was managed by Peter Lynch, the Magellan Fund was the most successful of all mutual funds; but after Mr. Lynch left, its performance was below the average of all stocks. Performance is also partly a matter of luck.

Some companies divide the pension fund among several managers, periodically compare their performance, and replace the one with the poorest record. This may spread the risk somewhat, but it does not guarantee optimum performance; luck and the individual who manages the fund continue to be dominant factors. Although judging performance is difficult, some managers are better than others. The finance committee watches performance carefully and is cautious about making changes based primarily on short-run performance; it will do so promptly when it is convinced that a better manager has been identified.

The finance committee also decides the broad investment policies: how much should be in equities, how much in fixed-income securities, how much in real property, how much in new ventures, how much in overseas securities, and the maximum percentage to be placed in a single company or industry.

Beginning in 1993, companies are also required to provide for the costs of health care and other benefits of employees who have not yet retired. The problems of estimating these costs are similar to those facing pension fund managers, but with the additional complication that health care costs continue to increase at an unpredictable rate.

SUMMARY

In doing its job, the board accepts certain responsibilities. It should:

- Actively support the CEO, both within the organization and to outside parties, as long as his or her performance is judged to be generally satisfactory.

- Discuss proposed major changes in the company's strategy and direction, major financing proposals, and other crucial issues, usually as proposed by the CEO.

- Formulate major policies regarding ethical or public responsibility matters and convey to the organization the fact that the board expects adherence to these policies. Assure that violations of these policies are not tolerated.

- Assure, to the extent feasible, that the CEO has identified a successor and is grooming that person for the job.

- Require that the CEO explain the rationale behind operating budgets, major capital expenditures, acquisitions, divestments, dividends, personnel matters, and similar important plans. Accept these proposals if they are consistent with the company's strategy and if the explanation is reasonable. Otherwise, require additional information.

- Analyze reports on the company's performance, raise questions to highlight areas of possible concern, and suggest possible actions to improve performance, but always with the understanding that the CEO, not the board, is responsible for performance.

- Assure that financial information furnished to shareholders and other outside parties fairly presents the financial performance and status of the company. Assure that internal controls are satisfactory.

- Replace the CEO promptly if the board concludes that his or her performance is, and will continue to be, unsatisfactory.

- Participate actively in decisions to elect or reelect directors.

- Decide on policies relating to compensation of senior management, including bonuses, incentives, and perquisites. Determine the compensation of the CEO. Review recommendations of the CEO and ratify compensation of other executives.

FOR FURTHER READING

American Bar Association, *Corporate Director's Guidebook* (Chicago, IL: ABA, 1994).

————, *The Evolving Role of Outside Directors* (Chicago, IL: ABA, 1993).

American Law Institute-American Bar Association, *Current Issues in Corporate Governance: ALI-ABA Course of Study Materials* (Philadelphia, PA: ALI-ABA, 1996).

Anderson, Charles A. and Robert N. Anthony, *The New Corporate Directors* (New York: Wiley, 1986).

Bacon, Jeremy, *Corporate Boards and Corporate Governance* (New York: Conference Board, 1993).

Berenbeim, Ronald, *Corporate Boards: Improving and Evaluating Performance: A Research Report* (New York: Conference Board, 1994).

Bowen, William G., *Inside the Boardroom: Governance by Directors and Trustees* (New York: Wiley, 1994).

Burrough, Bryan and John Helyar, *Barbarians at the Gate: The Fall of RJR Nabisco* (New York: Harper & Row, 1990).

Donaldson, Gordon and Jay W. Lorsch, *Decision Making at the Top* (New York: Basic Books, 1983).

Ernst & Young, *Compensation Committees: Fulfilling Your Responsibilities in the 1990s* (New York: Ernst & Young, 1995).

Home Box Office, *Barbarians at the Gate,* videorecording (New York: HBO Video, 1993). Based on *Barbarians at the Gate: The Fall of RJR Nabisco* (see Burrough and Helyar, op. cit.).

Knepper, William E. and Dan A. Bailey, *Liability of Corporate Officers and Directors,* 6th ed. (Charlottesville, VA: Michie Co., 1993).

Kotter, John P., *The General Managers* (New York: The Free Press, 1982).

Lorsch, Jay W., *Pawns or Potentates: The Reality of America's Corporate Boards* (Boston: Harvard Business School Press, 1989).

Mace, Myles L., *Directors: Myth and Reality,* rev. ed. (Boston: Division of Research, Harvard Business School, 1984).

National Association of Corporate Directors, *Report of the NACD Blue Ribbon Commission on Director Professionalism* (Washington, DC: NACD, 1996).

Newman, William H., E. Kirby Warren, and Andrew R. McGill, *The Process of Management: Strategy Action, Results,* 6th ed. (Englewood Cliffs, NJ: Prentice-Hall, 1987).

Stoner, James A. F., R. Edward Freeman, and Daniel R. Gilbert, Jr., *Management,* 6th ed. (London: Prentice-Hall International, 1995).

Taylor, Bernard and Bob Taylor, eds., *The Director's Manual* (Cambridge, England: Directors Bks, 1990–). Covers U.S. Directors of Corporations.

Vance, Stanley C., *Corporate Leadership, Boards, Directors, and Strategy* (New York: McGraw-Hill, 1983).

Vancil, Richard F., *Passing the Baton: Managing the Process of CEO Succession* (Boston: Harvard Business School Press, 1987).

Varallo, Gregory V. and Daniel A. Dreisbach, *The Board of Directors*, Corporate Practice series (Washington, DC: Bureau of National Affairs, 1993–).

Ward, Ralph D., *21st Century Corporate Board* (New York: Wiley, 1996).

Weidenbaum, Murray L., *The Evolving Corporate Board* (St. Louis: Center for the Study of American Business, Washington Univ., 1994).

Worthy, James C. and Robert P. Neuschel, *Emerging Issues in Corporate Governance* (Evanston, IL: Northwestern University Press, 1984).

NOTES

1. For a more complete discussion of the topics in the chapter, with many case examples, see Charles A. Anderson and Robert N. Anthony, *The New Corporate Directors* (New York: John Wiley & Sons, 1986).

2. Survey of Fortune 500 companies by Catalyst group, reported by Associated Press December 11, 1996.

3. Kenneth R. Andrews, *The Concept of Corporate Strategy* (Homewood, IL: Dow-Jones Irwin, 1980).

4. Bryan Burrough and John Helyar, *Barbarians at the Gate: The Fall of RJR Nabisco* (New York: Harper & Row, 1990).

5. *Escott v. BarChris Construction Corp.*, 283 F. Supp. 643 (S.D.N.Y. 1968).

6. *Wall Street Journal,* issues of March 18, 1980 (p. 7), April 23, 1980 (p. 38), and May 19, 1980 (p. 10).

7. SEC 1975 Release 34–115.4.

16 INFORMATION TECHNOLOGY AND THE FIRM

Theodore Grossman

INTRODUCTION

The personal use of information technology was discussed in an earlier chapter. This chapter will discuss the firm's use of information technology.

Of all the chapters in this book, the two dealing with information technology will have the shortest half-life. Because of the constant flow of new technology, what is written about today will have changed somewhat by tomorrow. This chapter presents a snapshot of how technology is used, today, in industry finance and accounting. By the time you compare your experiences with the contents of this chapter, some of the information will no longer be applicable. Change means progress. Unfortunately, many companies will not have adapted; consequently, they will have lost opportunity and threatened their own futures.

HISTORICAL PERSPECTIVE

To understand the present and future of information technology, it is important to understand its past. In the 1960s and 1970s, most companies' information systems were enclosed in the "glass house." If you entered any company that had its own computer, it was located behind a glass wall with a security system that allowed only those with access rights to enter the facility. A single computer controlled all of a company's data-processing functions. Referred to as a host-centric environment, the computer was initially used for accounting purposes—

accounts payable, accounts receivable, order entry, payroll, and so forth. In the late 1970s and 1980s, most companies purchased in-house computer systems and stopped outsourcing their data processing. Recognizing the power and potential of information technology, companies directed the use of their technology toward operations, marketing, and sales; and they created a new executive position, Chief Information Officer (CIO), to oversee this process.

In the 1980s, many companies gradually changed from host-centric to distributed computing. Instead of processing all of the information on one large, mainframe computer, companies positioned minicomputers to act as processors for departments or special applications. The minicomputers were, in many cases, networked together to share data. Databases became distributed, with data residing in different locations, yet accessible to all the machines in the network.

The personal computer had the greatest impact on the organization. It brought true distributed processing. Now everybody had his or her own computer, capable of performing feats that, until then, were available only on the company's mainframe computer. This created both opportunities and headaches for the company, some of which are addressed in the section on controls. As companies entered the 1990s, these computers were networked, forging the opportunity to share data and resources, as well as to work in cooperative groups. In the mid-1990s, these networks were further enhanced through connection to larger, wide area networks (WANs) and to the ultimate WAN, the Internet. Companies are doing what was unthinkable just a couple of years ago. They are allowing their customers and their suppliers direct connection into their own computers. New technology is being introduced every day, and new terms are creeping into our language (Internet, Intranet, Extranet, and so forth). It is from this perspective that we start by looking at computer hardware.

HARDWARE

Most of the early computers were large, mainframe computers. Usually manufactured by IBM, they were powerful batch processing machines. Large numbers of documents (e.g., invoices or orders) were entered into the computer and then processed, producing various reports and special documents, such as checks or accounts receivable statements.

Technology was an extremely unfriendly territory. In many companies, millions of lines of software were written to run on this mainframe technology. Generally speaking, these machines were programmed in a language called COBOL and used an operating system that was proprietary for that hardware. Not only was it difficult to run programs on more than one manufacturer's computer, but, because there were slight differences in the configurations and operating systems, it was difficult to run the same software on different computers, even if they were produced by the same manufacturer.

In the 1980s, technology evolved from proprietary operating systems to minicomputers with open systems. These were the first open systems, computers that functioned using the UNIX operating system. In the 1970s, although Bell Labs actually developed UNIX as an operating system for scientific applications, it later became an accepted standard for commercial applications. Platform-independent, the operating system and its associated applications could run on a variety of manufacturers' computers, creating both opportunities for users and competition within the computer industry. Users were no longer inexorably tied to one manufacturer. UNIX became the standard as companies moved into the 1990s. However, standards change rapidly in the 1990s, and UNIX has lost ground due to the development of client-server technology.

In the early 1990s, technologists predicted the demise of the mainframe. IBM's stock declined sharply as the market realized that the company's chief source of margin was headed towards extinction. However, the mainframe has reinvented itself as a superserver, and, although it has been replaced for some of the processing load, the mainframe and IBM are still positioned to occupy important roles in the future.

Server technology is heading toward a design in which processors are built around multiple, smaller processors, all operating in parallel. Referred to as *symmetrical multiprocessors* (SMPs), there are between two and eight processors in a unit. SMPs are made available by a range of manufacturers and operating systems, and they provide processor power typically not available in a uniprocessor. Faced with the demanding environment of multiple, simultaneous queries from databases that exceed hundreds of gigabytes, processors with *massively parallel processors,* or MPPs, are being utilized more and more; MPPs are processors that have hundreds of smaller processors within one unit. The goal of SMPs and MPPs is to split the processing load among the processors.

In a typical factory in the 1800s, one motor usually powered all of the machinery, to which it was connected by a series of gears, belts, and pulleys. Today, that is no longer the case, as each machine has its own motor or, in some cases, multiple, specialized motors. For example, the automobile's main motor is the engine, but there are also many other motors that perform such tasks as opening and closing windows, raising and lowering the radio antenna, and powering the windshield wipers. Computers are the firm's motors, and like motors, they, too, have evolved. Initially, firms used a host-centric mainframe, one large computer; today, they are using many computers to perform both specialized and general functions.

In the early 1990s, Xerox's prestigious Palo Alto Research Center introduced "ubiquitous computing," a model that it feels reflects the way companies and their employees will work in the future. In *ubiquitous computing,* each worker will have available differing quantities of three different size computers: 20 to 50 Post-it note–size portable computers, three or four computers the size of a writing tablet, and one computer the size of a six-foot-by-six-foot white board. All of the computers will work together by communicating to a network through, in most cases, wireless connections.

The progress of chip technology has been highly predictable. In the early 1960s, Gordon Moore, the inventor of the modern CPU at Intel, developed *Moore's Law,* which predicts that the density of the components on a computer chip will double every 18 to 24 months, thereby doubling the chip's processing power. This hypothesis has proven to be very accurate. Exhibit 16.1 shows the growth of the various Intel CPU chips that have powered the personal computer and many other machines. As can be seen, the PC's power has just about doubled every 18 to 24 months.

This growth can be seen more dramatically when the graph is plotted logarithmically, as in Exhibit 16.2.

SOFTWARE

Exhibit 16.3 represents the information systems paradigm. Operational control systems, which run the company's day-to-day operations, are typically used by the lowest level of the organization, are run on a scheduled basis, and usually contain large volumes of input data, output reports, and information. These sys-

EXHIBIT 16.1   Moore's law.

EXHIBIT 16.2   Moore's law, plotted logarithmically.

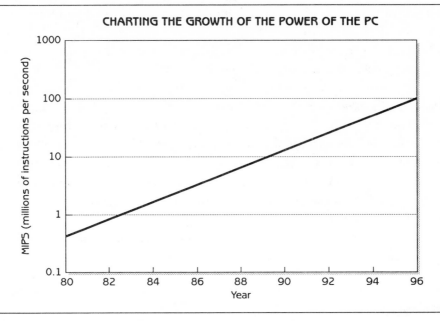

CHARTING THE GROWTH OF THE POWER OF THE PC

tems might be accounts payable, accounts receivable, payroll, order entry, or inventory control.

Decision support systems are generally used by middle-level managers to supply them with information with which they can make decisions. Usually run on an ad hoc basis and involving small amounts of data, budgets, exception reporting, cash flow forecasting, accounts receivable dunning reports, "what if" analyses, audit analysis reports, and variance analyses are examples of these deci-

EXHIBIT 16.3   Types of information systems.

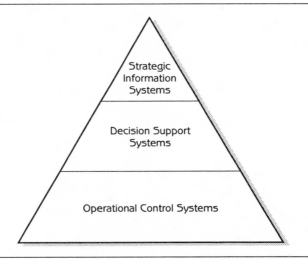

sion support systems. Many of the newer applications packages come with facilities for managers without any programming knowledge to create their own decision reports.

Strategic information systems are used by senior management to make decisions on corporate strategy. For example, a retail company might use demographic census data, along with a computerized geographical mapping system, to evaluate the most appropriate locations at which it should open new stores. A manufacturing company, given its demands for both skilled and unskilled labor, might use a similar method to determine the optimal location for a new plant.

While most older hardware has given way to newer computers, most companies use a combination of newly acquired and older, self-developed software. The latter was developed over a period of years, perhaps 20 or more, using COBOL, which, until recently, was the standard programming language in business applications. Today, many companies' mission-critical systems still run on mainframe technology, using programs written in COBOL; in fact, there are billions of lines of COBOL programming code still functional in U.S. business.

These "legacy" systems have become a major issue of concern for many companies, though. In many instances, they have grown like patchwork quilts, as they have been written and modified by programmers who are no longer with their firms. More often than not, documentation of these changes and enhancements is not available, and the guidelines for many of these software applications no longer exist. Replacing these applications is cost prohibitive, and the distraction to the organization caused by the need to retrain workers would be tremendous. While these legacy systems still function well, they present obstacles and dangers to the firm, some of which are presented later in this chapter.

Today, most programmers write in C++, C, or fourth-generation programming languages. C++ is an object-oriented programming language; object-oriented languages provide the programmer with a facility to create a programming object or module that may be reused in many applications. Fourth-generation programming languages are usually provided with sophisticated relational database systems. These database systems provide high-level tools and programming languages that allow programmers to create applications quickly, without having to concern themselves with the physical and logical structure of the data. Oracle, Informix, Sybase, and Progress are some of the more popular relational database package companies.

TODAY'S APPLICATION SYSTEMS

In the 1970s and 1980s, application software systems were stand-alone. There was little sharing of data, leading to the frequent redundancy of information. For example, in older systems, there might have been vendor data files for both inventory and accounts payable, resulting in the possibility of multiple versions of the truth. Each of the files may have contained address information, yet each of the addresses may have been different for the same vendor. Today, however, software applications are integrated across functional applications (accounts payable, accounts receivable, marketing, sales, manufacturing, and so forth). Database systems contain only one vendor data location, which all systems utilize. These changes in software architecture better reflect the integration of functions that has occurred within most companies.

Accounting systems, while used primarily for accounting data, also provide a source of data for sales and marketing. While retail stores' point-of-sale cash registers are used as a repository for cash and to account for it, they are also the source of data for inventory, sales, and customer marketing. For example, some major retailers ask their customers for their zip codes when point of sale transactions are entered, and that data is shared by all of the companies' major applications.

Accounts receivable systems serve two purposes. On one hand, they allow the company to control an important asset, their accounts receivable. Also, the availability of credit enables customers to buy items, both commercial and retail, that they otherwise would not be able to buy if they had to pay in cash. Credit card companies, which make their money from the transaction fees and the interest charges, understand this function well. Frequently, they reevaluate the spending and credit patterns of their client base and award increased credit limits to their customers. Their goal is to encourage their customers to buy more, without necessarily paying off their balance any sooner than necessary. Information systems make it possible for the companies to both control and promote their products, which, in this case, are credit card transactions.

These examples of horizontally integrated systems, as well as the understanding of the strategic and competitive uses of information technology, demonstrate where industry is headed.

ACCOUNTING INFORMATION SYSTEMS

As mentioned earlier, computer-based accounting systems were, for most companies, the first computerized applications. As the years progressed, these systems have become integrated and consist of the following modules:

- Accounts payable
- Order entry and invoicing
- Accounts receivable
- Purchase order management and replenishment
- Inventory control

- Human resource management
- Payroll
- Fixed assets
- General ledger and financial statements

Whereas, in past years, some of these modules were acquired and others were self-developed, today, most companies purchase packaged software.

In the 1980s, shrink-wrapped software was developed and introduced. Lotus Corporation, along with other companies, was a pioneer, selling software like its 1-2-3 application in shrink-wrapped packages. The software was accompanied by sufficient documentation and available telephone support, ensuring that even companies with limited technical expertise could manage their own destinies.

There are a host of software packages that will satisfy the needs of companies of all sizes. Smaller companies can find software selections that run on personal computers and networks, are integrated, and satisfy most of the companies' requirements. Quicken and Computer Associates have offerings that provide most of the necessary functional modules for small and medium-size companies, respectively. The more advanced packages, like Macola and AccPac, are equipped with interfaces to bar code scanners and scales, which, together, track inventory and work-in-process and weigh packages as they are shipped, producing not only invoices but also shipping documents for most of the popular freight companies, such as FedEx and UPS. These packages range in price from $100 for the entire suite of accounting applications for the smallest packages to approximately $800 per module for the larger packages, which, of course, have more robust features. While some of the smaller packages are available through computer stores and software retailers, the larger packages are acquired through independent software vendors (ISV), who, for a consulting fee, will sell, install, and service the software. The practice of using third-party ISVs began in the 1980s, when large hardware and software manufacturers realized that they were incapable of servicing all of the smaller companies that would be installing their products, many of whom required a lot of hand-holding. Consequently, a cottage industry of distributors and value-added dealers developed, in which companies earn profits on the sale of hardware and software and the ensuing consulting services.

Larger companies are following a trend toward large, integrated packages from companies like SAP and Oracle. These packages not only integrate the accounting functions, but also the manufacturing, warehousing, sales, marketing, and distribution functions. SAP has spawned an entire industry of consulting companies that assist large companies in implementing its software, a process that may take several years to complete. As in any software implementation, one must always factor into the timetable the process's cost and the distraction it causes the organization. In today's lean business environment, people have little extra time for new tasks. Implementing a major new system or, for that matter, any system, requires a major commitment of time and effort.

INFORMATION TECHNOLOGY IN BANKING AND FINANCE

Banking and finance is the leading industry in its use of information technology (IT). According to a survey conducted in 1996 by the accounting firm of Deloitte & Touche, in recent years, the banking and finance industry has spent 6.0% of its annual revenue on IT, more than double that of any other industry, as shown in Exhibit 16.4.

The comparison is even more eye-opening when IT expenditures per employee are compared across industry, as shown in Exhibit 16.5.

The graph in Exhibit 16.5 also illustrates how integral a role real-time information plays in the finance and banking industry, whether it be for accessing stock quotes or processing bank deposits. The financial services industry has become a transaction-processing industry that is information-dependent. Very little real money is ever touched. Rather, all transactions, from stock purchases to the direct deposit of workers' checks, are processed electronically. Information technology has paved the way for innovations like the NASDAQ trading system, in which, unlike the New York Stock Exchange (NYSE), all of the trades are conducted totally electronically.

EXHIBIT 16.4   Information technology budget by industry.

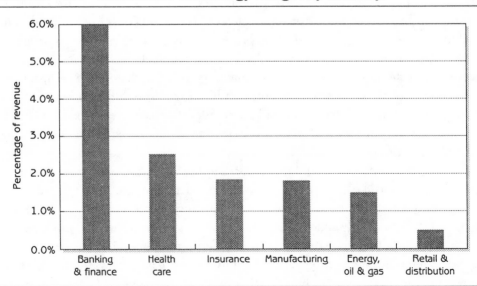

EXHIBIT 16.5   Information technology expenditures by industry per company employee.

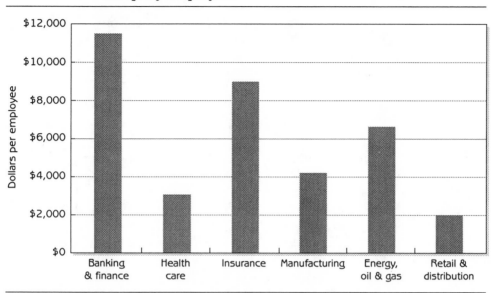

NETWORKS AND COMMUNICATIONS

It is becoming increasingly common in industry to create virtual wide area networks, using multiple, interconnected local area networks. These networks also connect the older mainframe and midrange computers that industry uses for its older legacy systems to the client terminals on the users' desks. Exhibit 16.6 is a model of a typical company's wide area network, and it demonstrates how all of the older technology interconnects with the newer local area networks and the Internet.

In the early 1990s, there were numerous, competing network operating systems and protocols. While Novell and its NetWare software holds the largest market share, Microsoft's Windows NT is becoming the network operating system of choice, and, because of the Internet's overwhelming success, Terminal Control Protocol/Internet Protocol (TCP/IP) is rapidly becoming the standard communications protocol. Remember, though, success is very fragile in the world of information technology. Today's standard can easily become yesterday's news. If you are always prepared for change, then you won't be surprised by it.

Electronic Data Interchange (EDI) allows companies to communicate and conduct electronic commerce from one computer to another. EDI is one of the industry's growing uses for data communications, and many companies are using it to send purchase orders to their suppliers, thereby lessening the time it takes for purchase orders to be mailed and then entered and processed by the suppli-

EXHIBIT 16.6   Model of wide area network.

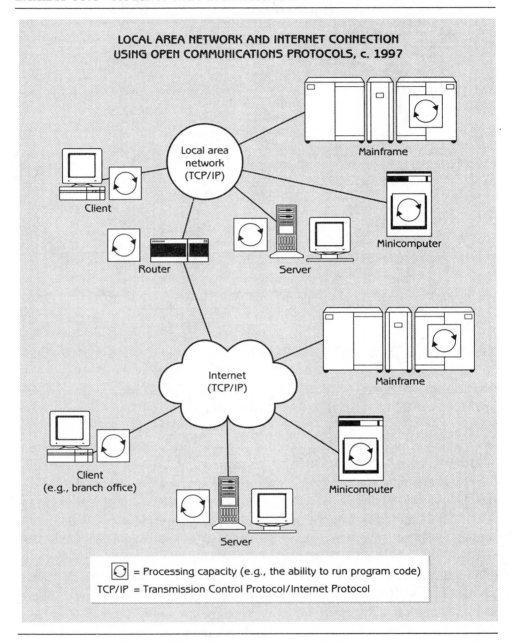

LOCAL AREA NETWORK AND INTERNET CONNECTION
USING OPEN COMMUNICATIONS PROTOCOLS, c. 1997

ers. Inventories are lowered by speeding up the turnaround time of ordering and receiving goods and materials. On the flip side, many suppliers use EDI to send their customers advance ship notifications (ASN), advising them of what has been shipped so that they can prepare their warehouses for the goods and materials. Lastly, some companies use EDI to transmit their invoices and then to receive the subsequent payments. While industries use different versions of EDI in different ways, their goals are always the same: minimize the processing time and lower inventory costs and overhead expenses. An industry organization in Washington, D.C. developed and maintains a standard format that dictates how all transactions are sent, ensuring that all companies that wish to implement EDI can be assured that all vendors' and customers' computers will understand each other's transactions, without requiring any custom programming.

The 1990s have also seen the advent of virtual organizations. Virtual organizations are formed when companies join together to create products or enterprises that, individually, they could not have. In most cases, information technology allows companies to create these partnerships and share information, as if they were one company. Using communications and groupware products like Lotus Notes, the partners can share information with each other about their individual progress, in order to ensure the best possible success. This is discussed further in the paragraph on IT strategy.

DATABASE

The following scenario depicts what information systems looked like prior to the use of database management systems. Imagine a physical office in which each person has his or her own file cabinet. The information in the file cabinets belongs to the people whose desks are closest to them. They decide what information will be in their file cabinets and how it will be organized. For example, sales might refer to gross sales in one worker's cabinet and net sales in another's. Yet, the discrepancy would be unimportant, because there was actually very little sharing of data.

Database management systems assume that information is a corporate asset to be shared by all workers in the enterprise. Database technology, therefore, allows a company to have one integrated location for the storage of all company data. These systems create a standard vocabulary, or *data dictionary*, by which all references are consistent (e.g., sales always means net sales). They also enable each user to have an individual view of the data, as if the information were still in the file cabinet next to his or her desk. Users need not concern themselves with the physical location or physical order of the data, either. Database management systems are capable of presenting the data as necessary. In fact, with distributed databases, the data does not even have to reside in the same location or computer. It can be spread around the world if necessary. Database systems are sufficiently intelligent and can find the data and process it as if it were located directly on the user's personal computer.

Most of the software that was developed in the earlier years relied on data structures called flat files. While some companies utilized database technology to store information, those database management systems were, in many cases, unwieldy and very expensive to both acquire and maintain. They were usually hierarchical or network database systems, which, alone, cost in excess of $200,000 and frequently required special database administrators just to constantly fine-tune the system.

Today's database technology is based on a relational model, and, on a very simplistic basis, it resembles a spreadsheet. In a relational database, there are a series of tables or files. Similar to a spreadsheet table, each table has columns with attributes and rows of data. The difference is that there is only one table in a spreadsheet, while there can be an almost unlimited number of tables in a database. In addition, there is a practical limit to the size of a spreadsheet, but databases can contain thousands of columns and millions of rows of data. In addition, databases also allow users to relate or connect tables that share common columns of data.

Exhibit 16.7 is an example of a very simple portion of a payroll application. There are two different tables. The "Employee" table contains data about each of the company's employees: name, address, marital status, number of dependents, and so on. The "Pay" table contains data about every time each of the employees is paid: gross payroll, social security taxes, federal withholding, state tax, and so forth.

First, notice the common column between the two tables, the employee number. This column enables the database management system to relate the two tables. It allows the system, for example, to print a payroll journal that has both the weekly payroll information from the "Pay" table and to access the employees' names from the "Employee" table. This effectively combines all the data into one table.

DATA WAREHOUSE

Data warehousing attempts to reconcile and live with past applications software, while still benefiting from today's newer technology. As mentioned earlier, industry is rife with older legacy systems that are currently cost-prohibitive to replace. Most of these older systems are mission-critical operational control systems (see Exhibit 16.3) and satisfy most of the operational needs of the company. However, they are built on technology that cannot support the kinds of decision-support tools that management requires. Many of these systems use older file structures or obsolete database management systems and are almost incapable of accessing and manipulating data.

As an alternative to replacing these systems, data warehousing provides a state-of-the-art database management system that is fed data from the older

EXHIBIT 16.7 Database example.

EMPLOYEE TABLE

Employee Number	First Name	Middle Initial	Last Name	Social Security Number	Marital Status	Number of Dependents	Date of Birth	Date of Hire	Date of Termination	Date of Last Pay Raise	Payrate	Hourly or Salary
1	Mary	E	Smith	123456789	M	4	4/1/63	7/21/91		9/1/96	8.505	H
2	Tom	T	Day	234567890	M	3	3/2/55	11/15/91		1/15/96	750.000	S
3	Harry	F	Jones	345678901	S	1	11/50/71	1/15/92	9/24/96	11/6/94	12.500	H
4	Sally	D	Kraft	456789012	S	0	10/5/65	3/6/92		3/5/96	14.755	H
5	Charlie		Malt	567890123	S	1	6/6/80	6/2/93		6/17/96	900.000	S
6	John	K	Free	678901234	M	5	8/5/49	11/1/94		12/15/95	17.500	H

PAY TABLE

Employee Number	Date	Number of Regular Hours	Number of Overtime Hours	Gross Payroll	Social Security Tax	Medicare Tax	Federal Withholding Tax	State Withholding Tax	Net Pay	Check Number
1	1/7/96	40.0	4.0	391.23	24.26	5.67	101.16425	21.52	238.62	1
2	1/7/96	40.0	0.0	750.00	46.50	10.88	193.935	41.25	457.44	2
3	1/7/96	40.0	0.0	500.00	31.00	7.25	129.29	27.50	304.96	3
4	1/7/96	40.0	4.0	678.73	42.08	9.84	175.506	37.33	413.97	4
5	1/7/96	40.0	0.0	900.00	55.80	13.05	232.722	49.50	548.93	5
6	1/7/96	40.0	2.5	765.63	47.47	11.10	197.97531	42.11	466.97	6
1	1/14/96	40.0	12.0	493.29	30.58	7.15	127.55493	27.13	300.87	7
2	1/14/96	40.0	0.0	750.00	46.50	10.88	193.935	41.25	457.44	8
3	1/14/96	40.0	8.0	650.00	40.30	9.43	168.077	35.75	396.45	9
4	1/14/96	40.0	7.9	765.05	47.43	11.09	197.82579	42.08	466.62	10
5	1/14/96	40.0	0.0	900.00	55.80	13.05	232.722	49.50	548.93	11
6	1/14/96	40.0	0.0	700.00	43.40	10.15	181.006	38.50	426.94	12
1	1/21/96	40.0	0.0	340.20	21.09	4.93	87.968916	18.71	207.49	13
2	1/21/96	40.0	0.0	750.00	46.50	10.88	193.935	41.25	457.44	14
3	1/21/96	40.0	2.4	545.00	33.79	7.90	140.9261	29.98	332.41	15
4	1/21/96	40.0	6.7	738.49	45.79	10.71	190.95816	40.62	450.42	16
5	1/21/96	40.0	0.0	900.00	55.80	13.05	232.722	49.50	548.93	17
6	1/21/96	40.0	5.0	831.25	51.54	12.05	214.94463	45.72	507.00	18

legacy systems. However, data does get duplicated, which can potentially cause a synchronization problem between the data in the warehouse and the data in the older legacy systems. Consequently, IT management must put stringent controls in place. Still, the benefits outweigh the potential problems, for the data warehouse comes with all of the high-tech tools that will enable management to create a plethora of queries and reports. Most of the newer Decision Support Tools and Executive Information Systems, which are discussed later, require a storage capability similar to the data warehouse.

CONTROLS

Because the initial software applications that were developed in the 1960s and 1970s were accounting oriented, data processing (which is what information technology was called at that time) typically reported to the Chief Financial Officer, creating a control atmosphere consistent with accounting controls. A central group of trained data entry operators was responsible for entering and verifying data. Access to the "glass house" was restricted, and, in some cases, access to the data entry and report distribution areas was also restricted. Because everything was self-contained, control was not a major issue.

In the late 1970s and early 1980s, on-line terminals began appearing on users' desks, outside of the glass house, allowing them access to data. Initially, these terminals were used for information inquiry. Yet, even this limited function was tightly controlled by strict software access control and password protection. While workers were getting additional capabilities, they were also creating opportunities for lapses in control. This was just the beginning of the Trojan Horse. Eventually, data entry moved out of the glass house to the warehouse receiving dock to be used for inventory receipts; the order entry desk to be used for new orders; the purchasing department to be used for purchase orders; and, in the case of retailing, on to the sales floor for point-of-sale processing. No longer were trained data entry operators responsible for the quality of the data; others were responsible for entering data, and it was just an ancillary part of their job, for which they were not necessarily even trained.

The control environment was breaking down, and the introduction of the personal computer only complicated the issue. No longer was control centralized. While access to data could be controlled, control over the use of data and the content of reports was lost. For example, two people could each issue a report on sales, and the numbers could easily be different. Yet, both reports could be accurate. How is this possible? Simple. One of the reports may have been about gross sales and the other about net sales, or one may have been based on data through Friday and the other on data through Saturday.

When all programming was controlled by a small professional group, control was much easier. However, because today's spreadsheet programs are user-friendly, and software does not require programming knowledge, everybody is his or her own programmer. Thus, it is difficult to control the consistency of the information that is being distributed.

The problems become only more complicated. Now companies allow their business partners, vendors, and even outsiders to access their computers, using the Internet and EDI. Data is interchanged, and moneys are exchanged electronically, often without paper backup. While technology can prevent most unauthorized access to data, as recent history has shown, even the U.S. Defense Department has not successfully prevented the best hackers from accessing its computers and wreaking havoc. What was relatively simple to control before 1990 is now a nightmare. Accountants, systems professionals, and auditors must remain forever vigilant against both inadvertent and intentional unauthorized use and abuse of company data.

YEAR 2000—VIRUS OR DEADLY DISEASE?

Over the past five years, computer viruses have grown to become an accepted reality. A few years ago, there was a lot of publicity about the Michelangelo virus that was programmed to disable personal computers on Michelangelo's birthday. Like most viruses, this problem was easy to solve. However, the Year 2000 virus is neither malicious nor easily cured. It is estimated that, worldwide, it will cost in excess of $300 to $600 billion just to fix the problem, a figure that does not include the cost of the havoc that will be created if it is not fixed.

During the 1960s, 1970s, and 1980s, programmers coded date fields in the following format: MM/DD/YY. For example, January 5, 1996 would appear as 01/05/96. Until recently, disk space was at a premium, and programmers were forced to find ways to conserve valuable computer resources. In order to save space in computer files, lessen data preparation and input time, and conserve space on computer screens and printouts, only two digits were allocated to the year entry. Since the late 1980s, most companies have been using relational databases, which automatically use four digit years. However, there are no guarantees that those programs were written correctly.

Whereas, years ago, the two-digit year was a space saver, today, it is a catastrophe. If, in 1996, a program were to calculate the length of employment for someone that began working for a company in 1985, it would subtract 85 from 96, and the result would be 11. In the year 2000, however, the program would subtract 85 from 00, and the result would be a very inaccurate −85. If you sort a list of bonds by their maturity dates, in what order would they be listed if there are bonds that will mature in or after 2000? How about an aging of receivables or payables? Will employees' time clocks function after the ball drops on this millennium? A bank in Canada is concerned that the time locks on its vaults will not open after New Year 2000. We do not have to wait until then to find out the answers to many of these questions. There are a lot of systems that will be looking forward as we approach 2000. For example, in 1989, the Social Security Administration discovered that it had a problem, because some of its software that projects 10 years ahead developed serious problems when it encountered the year 00 (2000).

Typically, the systems written in the 1960s, 1970s, and 1980s using third-generation languages like COBOL, BASIC, and RPG are susceptible to the Year 2000 virus. That is not to say that all programs written in those languages, or only programs written in those languages, are affected by this problem. Unfortunately, these "legacy" systems are usually mission-critical systems that control the everyday operations of a company. These systems use older technology, are usually, but not exclusively, mainframe- or minicomputer-based, and have been in place for a long time with little or no documentation. They work, but nobody wants to tinker with them. Eventually, they will be replaced with newer technology, but there are other priorities. The systems have been functioning well for the last two decades, and there are more important, new applications that are needed.

What about the systems that you purchased from other vendors? Are they susceptible to the problem? Do you even have the source code to be able to determine your risk? What is the vendors' responsibility to your company? Do they have any liability for their software? What were their warrantees? Will outside companies that process data, such as payroll, for other companies be prepared? What about those companies that are dependent upon other companies feeding their systems with date-sensitive data? Are they prepared?

Unlike a virus which can be removed with a viricide program, there is no simple solution to this problem, and there are no easy answers to these questions. Each and every system and program must be inspected to determine if there are date-sensitive fields and operations and how they are handled. If necessary, the fields must then be expanded to accommodate a four-digit year. This solution is not complex, just time-consuming. It is more complicated than it should be, though. Because the affected programs are written in older, third-generation languages that most companies no longer use and are accompanied by little or no documentation, there is a limited supply of programmers who are capable of handling this massive problem. It will take a lot of effort to either fix or replace the affected systems. Companies cannot afford to wait until the last minute, either. Some of those systems that look forward will malfunction as soon as they encounter years greater than 1999.

Proactive companies have created Year 2000 teams to inventory and fix their software. Programming tools have been developed to help identify date fields within programs, but these tools are not perfect. Companies will have to reserve for the cost of the Year 2000 modifications on their balance sheets, and, based upon current FASB rulings, those costs must be expensed, not capitalized.

INFORMATION TECHNOLOGY STRATEGY

How do companies decide how to invest their IT money? What projects get funded? Which projects are of higher priority? IT strategy is not created in a vacuum. Rather, like all of the other operational departments within a corporation, IT must support the direction and goals of the company. The Chief Information Officer's job is to educate the rest of senior management about IT's ability to create opportunities for the company and help it move in directions that make sense.

IT architecture is developed to support the IT and corporate strategy. If additional networks, workstations, or data warehouses are required, they are either acquired or developed.

In the late 1980s and early 1990s, Wal-Mart adopted an everyday low-pricing strategy. To accomplish this goal, Wal-Mart needed to change the manner in which it both conducted business with its suppliers and managed the inbound logistics, warehousing, and distribution of merchandise to its stores. It needed to abolish warehousing as much as possible and quicken the process by which stores ordered and received merchandise. Also, Wal-Mart needed to eliminate any unnecessary inventory in stores and allow stores to order merchandise only as needed. Lastly, lags in its distribution centers needed to be prevented, enabling goods to be received from their suppliers and immediately shipped to stores.

As a result, Wal-Mart designed a systems and technology infrastructure that, through EDI, enables the stores to order goods, as needed, from their suppliers. Moreover, Wal-Mart permits manufacturers to access computerized sales information directly from its computers, which, in turn, allows them to gauge Wal-Mart's demand and then stage production to match it. Wal-Mart effectively shifted the burden of warehousing merchandise from its own warehouses to the vendors, eliminating the costs of both warehouse maintenance and surplus inventory. The distribution centers were automated, allowing cross-docking, whereby goods being received for specific stores were immediately sent to the shipping area designated for those stores, thus putting an end to all time lags.

Wal-Mart now has the lowest cost of inbound logistics in its industry. Its selling G&A expense is 6% below its nearest competitor, enabling it to be the most aggressive retailer in its industry. Wal-Mart aligned its IT strategy and infrastructure to support the company's overall strategy. IT was the agent for change. Without the newer information technologies, none of the newer strategies and directions could have been successful.

JUSTIFYING THE COST OF INFORMATION TECHNOLOGY

Should companies take that giant leap of faith and invest millions of dollars in new machines and software? Can we measure the return on a company's investment in technology?

These are questions that, for years, have concerned professional technology managers. Today, information technology consumes an increasing share of companies' budgets. While we cannot live with the cost of technology, ultimately, we cannot live without the technology. Thus, when every new version of the personal computer chip or Windows hits the market, companies must decide whether it is a worthwhile investment. Everyone wants the latest and greatest technology, clearly assuming that, with it, workers will be more productive.

Although IT is the medium for change, its costs and soft benefits are difficult to measure. As technology gets disbursed throughout a company, it becomes increasingly difficult to track costs. As workers become their own administrative assistants, each company must determine whether its workers are more or less productive when they type their own documents and prepare their own presentations. These are many of the issues that companies are facing now and in the future as they struggle with new IT investments.

INTERNET/INTRANET/EXTRANET

The Internet, Intranet, and Extranet provide companies with a plethora of opportunities to find new ways of transacting business. An alternative to some of the older technology, the Intranet, a subsystem of the Internet, was developed in 1996 to allow employees from within a company to access data in the company's system. A *fire wall* prevents outsiders from accessing any data that a company wishes to keep confidential. The Intranet refers to those systems that are inside the fire wall. Employees have the access authority to break through the fire wall and access information, even though they might be using a computer outside of the company. Remember, the Internet is just one large party line on which everybody is sending around data.

One manufacturing company provided an Intranet facility for its employees to learn about their health, life and disability insurance, and educational benefits. The system allows them to sign up for these programs and, in the frequently asked questions (FAQs) section, to inquire about some of the most common issues specific to the programs. When on-line, employees can also access and sign up for a list of in-house training courses, read an employee newsletter, and check the current price of the company's publicly traded stock.

The Extranet is a version of the Intranet that allows external users to access data inside of the fire wall. For example, part of Wal-Mart's ordering and logistics system allowed its vendors and suppliers to access Wal-Mart's store sales data directly from Wal-Mart's computer systems. If these transactions occurred over the Internet, they would be referred to as Extranet transactions.

DECISION SUPPORT SYSTEMS/EXECUTIVE INFORMATION SYSTEMS

A class of software that is used mostly by middle level and senior executives to make decisions, this software combines many of the features of traditional exception reporting with the graphical display tools available in spreadsheets. It allows users to make their own inquiries into large volumes of data, stored in databases or data warehouses, and provides for drill-down reporting, or "slice and dice" analysis.

Typically, most data in a database or data warehouse are three-dimensional and look something like a Rubic's cube. Consider a database model for a chain of 300 retail stores. The first dimension may be the company's merchandise; the second dimension may be its store locations; and the third dimension may represent different points in time. An executive might examine the men's department sales. Not satisfied with the results, she might then probe to learn what categories of items sold better than others. After finding an underperforming category, she may check how different groups or districts of stores performed for that category. Knowing how each store performed, she might explode down, looking at individual items, and compare their performance to that of a prior week or year. This process is like taking the Rubic's cube and continually rotating the levels, looking at each of the cube's faces. Each face of each small cube represents data for a piece of merchandise for a store for a period of time. That is why this process is referred to as "slice and dice." You can slice and turn the data any way you desire. The data can also be viewed and sorted in a tabular or graphical mode. The same theory applies whether the database contains retailing data, stock market data, or accounting data. Exhibits 16.8 and 16.9 show examples of a decision support system's output. The output was created by Pilot Software's executive information system.

ADVANCED TECHNOLOGY

Many new technologies are on the horizon, two of which are database mining and intelligent agents. Both address the issue of information overload. In the 1970s, the average database was perhaps 100 megabytes (millions of bytes) in size. In the 1980s, databases were typically 20 gigabytes (billions of bytes). Now, databases are in the terabytes (trillions of bytes). With all that data, it is difficult for a user to know where to look. It is not the question that the user knows to ask

EXHIBIT 16.8   Example of options screen for a decision support system.

that is necessarily important, but, rather, the question that the user doesn't know to ask that will come back to haunt.

These new technologies examine entire databases, scanning them for any data that does not fit the business's model and identifying any data that the user needs to examine further. These data-mining techniques can be used successfully in many industries. For example, auditors might use them to scan client transaction detail to look for transactions that do not conform to company policies, and stock analysts can use them to scan data on stock prices and company earnings over a period of time in order to look for opportunities.

CONCLUSION

The world of business has changed dramatically in the past ten years. What was unimaginable then is ordinary today. Product life cycle times have decreased from years to months. New technology is being introduced every day. An Internet year is equal to three or four calendar months. The manager who is comfort-

EXHIBIT 16.9   Example of output from a decision support system.

able with and understands the practical implications of technology will be one of the first to succeed. Imagination and creativity are vital. Don't be afraid of change. Understand it, and embrace it.

FOR FURTHER READING

Frenzel, Carroll, *Management of Information Technology* (Danvers, MA: Boyd & Fraser Publishing Company, 1996).

Fried, Louis, *Managing Information Technology in Turbulent Times* (New York: Wiley: QED, 1995).

Kanter, Jerry, *Information Literacy* (Wellesley, MA: Babson Press, 1996).

Reynolds, George, *Information Systems for Managers* (St. Paul: West Publishing Company, 1995).

Turban, E., E. Mclean, and J. Wetherbe, *Information Technology for Management* (New York: John Wiley and Sons, 1996).

17 PROFITABLE GROWTH BY ACQUISITION

William W. Alberts

The subject of this chapter is growth by acquisition, the strategy of entering new product markets by purchasing the common stock or assets of a business or businesses already operating in these markets. The aim of the chapter is to outline answers to six major questions that face a typical industrial company about to undertake such a strategy:

1. What should be the rationale for our acquisition strategy?
2. What are the principal acquisition options open to us, both directional (the different kinds of markets we should consider entering) and structural (the different ways we can effect a purchase)?
3. What test must any acquisition pass to be profitable for us?
4. What are the conditions of profitable growth by acquisition (the determinants of whether a purchase in fact will pass the profitability test)?
5. Based on these profitability conditions, which criteria should be used to target acquisition candidates?
6. What must we do to ensure that the profitability potential of an acquisition is fully realized once it is made?

The company currently is organized into three business units called Red, Green, and Blue in internal planning documents. Each operates in a distinct product market. The company itself, General Products (GP), is a publicly owned corporation whose common shares trade on a stock exchange. One third of its assets are financed with long-term debt. Its percentage cost of equity capital (the minimum rate of return that is acceptable to its owners) has been averaging about 13%: This represents the sum of the risk-free rate of interest (as measured by the long-term U.S. Treasury bond rate) and a risk premium appropriate for the company.

ACQUISITION OBJECTIVE AND GOAL(S)

When a company undertakes growth by acquisition, it ordinarily has at least one *immediate* reason, or motive, and an *ultimate* one for doing so. The immediate reason for an acquisition is called a goal of the undertaking and the ultimate reason is called its objective.

Almost always a goal is formulated when a perception surfaces in management's mind that the company has or will have a "problem" or "deficiency" that can be remedied by diversification in general (defined in this chapter simply as an increase in the number of businesses a company operates) and diversification by acquisition in particular. Different companies have different problems that they want to solve by diversifying through growth and, thus, cite different goals for the strategy. Exhibit 17.1 shows the eight goals (and the problems that give rise to them) that seem to be cited most frequently.

The first two goals share the perception that the company's overall growth target cannot be achieved by internal growth alone; external, or diversifying,

---

EXHIBIT 17.1   Alternative goals of growth by acquisition.

- Goals that trigger CLASSIC diversification
  1. Countering a significant decrease in the company's overall earnings growth. ("All our major product markets are mature and a couple face decline.")
  2. Countering the effect on the company's earnings of an absolute decline in one of its major businesses. ("Our commodity chemical company is dead and we have to replace it.")
- Goals that trigger DEFENSIVE diversification
  3. Putting excess capacity to work. ("We've got three facilities operating only part time and that's hurting our cost position badly.")
  4. Coping with a vertical competitive threat. ("Rivals are buying up the companies that supply components to our industry, and we're afraid that if we don't get one ourselves, we may face control problems.")
  5. Protecting a competitive position. ("A Japanese company has beachheaded a market segment adjacent to ours, and we're afraid that if we don't get in there and cause it some trouble, we may come under attack ourselves.")
  6. Correcting inadequacies in the company's technology base. ("We need to buy somebody who can educate us in laser printing technology.")
- Goals that trigger OPPORTUNISTIC diversification
  7. Moving up in the *Fortune* size rankings. ("We want to double our present size in five years.")
  8. Putting accumulated cash holdings to work. ("We've got $5 billion and want to invest it.")

growth also is needed. The next four goals share the perception that a particular business in the company's portfolio faces a competitive threat and that this threat can be neutralized by the right acquisition. In the case of the third goal this means acquiring a business in a position to use the excess capacity; for the fourth goal it means acquiring an upstream business; for the fifth goal it means acquiring a business whose product complements or substitutes for the company's product; and for the sixth goal it means acquiring a business which is a potential or actual supplier of the technology or a product incorporating the technology. The only commonality of the last two goals is that they are neither classic nor defensive in nature.

Because GP is a typical company we can assume that at least one of the goals in the exhibit will motivate each of its own planned acquisitions. We also can assume that GP's objective in growing by acquisition is to increase its profitability, and that the company measures profitability by the magnitude of the cash flows it can generate for its owners over time, or equivalently, by the magnitude of the discounted present value—the *market value*—of these flows.

By implication, for any acquisition to meet the company's objective, it must cause this market value to be greater than it would be in the absence of the acquisition. The acquisition will fail to meet the company's objective if it causes the company's market value to be *less* than it otherwise would be. Will a "value-creating" acquisition also achieve the company's goal or goals? Ordinarily, yes. But there is no guarantee that the converse holds. The prospect that an acquisition will solve the problem or problems that triggered it tells the company nothing about the prospect that the acquisition also will be profitable, and thus create value. Whether an acquisition is profitable depends not on why it is done but on how it is done.

Many acquisition specialists would argue that the seventh goal cited in Exhibit 17.1 is a dubious one; management should not use shareholder capital to finance an advance in the Fortune 500 rankings. If an acquisition is triggered by this goal and works to destroy value, the point obviously is well-taken. But if the acquisition works not to destroy but to create value, management can argue that it doesn't really matter what the immediate motive was. A similar line of argument can be articulated about the eighth goal. If management faces a choice between distributing its cash holdings to shareholders or investing them unprofitably, it should distribute the holdings. But if the choice is between distributing the holdings and investing them in a profitable acquisition, shareholders probably will want management to go with the second option.

Finally, it should be noted that there are at least some companies for whom growth by acquisition is *not* triggered by one of the classic or defensive goals. Rather, these companies want simply to exploit value-creating acquisition opportunities which they have spotted. For them the immediate and the ultimate reasons for undertaking the acquisitions are the same; their goal is to achieve their value-creation objective.

ACQUISITIONS OPTIONS: DIRECTIONAL AND STRUCTURAL

GP begins the development of an acquisition strategy by working out for itself, first the directions in which it can look for candidates, and then the means by which it can best structure the acquisition. We shall assume that GP already has decided that it doesn't want to undertake "megadiversification": the acquisition of large, multibusiness companies and, as a result, simultaneous entry into a number of new markets. Instead, it wants to enter new markets one at a time and, accordingly, plans to acquire only single-business companies (or divisions of companies).

In recent years the number of reported acquisitions has been running between 3,000 and 4,000 a year. Most appear to have been single-business acquisitions. Price per transaction (including megaacquisitions) has averaged about $50 million.

Directional Options

As Exhibit 17.2 shows, GP can undertake entry into two broad groupings of markets, those that are related in some way to the markets which Red, Green, and Blue now serve, and those that have no relation to any of the company's served markets. Some managers use the term diversification not as a synonym for entry into new markets in general, but as a synonym for entry into unrelated markets.

There are six classes of markets that can be described as related to Red's market or markets:

1. *Regional market extensions.*   These are markets for Red's product outside the geographical region in which Red now operates. An example would be an entry into the Mexican market for the product.

2. *Technology market extensions.*   These are markets for products based on the core technology Red uses in its current product. If Red produces aluminum siding for buildings, an example would be the market for aluminum boats. If Red produces engine valves, an example would be the market for engine carburetors.

3. *Markets for substitute products.*   These are markets for products that use different technologies to meet the needs of Red's current customers. If Red produces minicomputers, an example would be the market for workstations. If Red produces glass milk containers, an example would be the market for plastic milk containers.

4. *Markets for complementary products.*   These are markets for products that Red's customers view as complementary to Red's product. If Red produces lawnmowers, an example would be the market for lawn fertilizer. If Red produces personal computers, an example would be the market for printers.

EXHIBIT 17.2   The company's directional options for diversifying growth.

5. *Upstream markets.*   These are markets for products that Red now buys (supplies, parts, components). If Red produces personal computers, an example would be the market for disc drives. If Red publishes a newspaper, an example would be the market for newsprint.

6. *Downstream markets.*   These are markets in which Red's product is now sold. If Red produces lawnmowers, an example would be the retail lawnmower market. If Red produces wool yarn and sells it to sweater manufacturers, an example would be the sweater market.

What these markets (and the markets that similarly surround Green and Blue) all have in common, from GP's perspective, is that there are key managers in the company who know at least something about them. In the case of regional extensions, it is the product itself (and knowledge about competitors); in the case of technology extensions, it is the technology itself (and knowledge of competitors); in the case of complementary and substitute products, it is the customers (and knowledge about competitors); and in the case of vertical extensions, it is the new rivals (who formerly were suppliers and customers). The markets into which defensive diversification would lead GP are all related in one or more of these senses to the company's existing markets.

What unrelated markets have in common is that no one in GP knows anything about their products, the technologies in which these products are rooted, the customers of these products, or the nature of competition between companies that sell these products. In short, every related market opportunity surrounding Red, Green, and Blue passes to some degree a "knowledgeability" test. No unrelated market opportunity does.

Structural Options

Not only are there many directions in which GP can look for acquisition candidates, there are also various ways it can effect the actual acquisition of a specific candidate. We can assume that the candidate has passed through the selection screen described later in this chapter and that negotiations with the management group empowered to make the sale are well under way. Conceivably, GP triggered the negotiations by purchasing a significant fraction of the candidate's shares in the open market or directly from the candidate's shareholders (through a "tender" mechanism). Such an approach would be unusual, though. In the last two or three decades negotiations for all but a small minority of acquisitions (and these were megaacquisitions) have begun with a face-to-face meeting between a candidate's managers and the managers who want to acquire it.

Exhibit 17.3 shows the three alternative legal means by which GP can effect the acquisition: statutory merger, affiliation, and asset purchase. If GP chooses the first or third option, it will add the acquiree's current and fixed assets to the left side of the balance sheet; if it chooses the second option, it will add its holdings of the acquiree's common shares to the left side of its balance sheet.

Note that the terminology in this exhibit is not universally used. Some people define the term "merger" generically (as a synonym for "acquisition," as that term is used here). Others define the term "acquisition" narrowly as a synonym for affiliation and asset purchase. When investment bankers say "We do mergers and acquisitions" or "We do M&A work," they are saying that they help effect mergers, affiliations, and asset purchases.

If the acquiree is a nonaffiliate of another company (and thus has no common shares of its own), GP will purchase its assets. If the acquiree *does* have its own shares, GP will find it administratively much simpler (and therefore less expensive) to purchase these shares, unless the acquiree has significant liabilities of a questionable nature that would have to be taken off its balance sheet. But will GP merge with the acquiree or set it up as an affiliate? That depends on how GP will take joint account of seven related considerations: (1) the percentage of the

EXHIBIT 17.3   Growth by acquisition: Structural options.

acquiree's shares that GP wants to purchase (100% or between 50 and 100%); (2) the percentage of this purchase that GP wants to finance by an exchange of shares (100%, between 50 and 100%, or less than 50%); (3) the tax implications shown in Exhibit 17.4 of each of these three financing options for each structural option; (4) the tax option that the acquiree prefers; (5) the weight that GP thinks should be given to this preference; (6) the weight that GP thinks should be given to *its own* tax preference; and (7) the ease or difficulty of securing shareholder approval of the merger option.

Assuming that, as is usually the case, the purchase price per share of the acquiree exceeds the tax basis of typical shareholders (that is, exceeds the average price paid originally by these shareholders), the acquiree will prefer that the transaction be designated a nontaxable reorganization. So if GP puts heavy weight on that preference (as an alternative to paying a much higher price), and wants to finance the acquisition entirely by an exchange of shares (because it does not want to leverage the acquisition, or because it thinks its shares are overpriced), the company presumably:

- Will opt for the affiliation route if it wants to limit its dollar investment in the candidate (by limiting the percent of the candidate's shares it purchases), or if it views the task of obtaining shareholder approval as onerous, and
- Will opt for the merger route if it wants to purchase all the candidate's shares and does not see the shareholder approval requirement as a problem.

EXHIBIT 17.4   The tax implications of alternative structural-financing options.

Percentage of the Purchase Price Financed by an Exchange of GP's Common and Preferred Shares	If GP Purchases the Common Shares of the Candidate Company	
	and Effects a Merger with It, the IRS Will Designate the Acquisition a:	and Establishes It as an Affiliate, the IRS Will Designate the Acquisition a:
100%	Nontaxable "type A" reorganization	Nontaxable "type A" reorganization
50–100%	Nontaxable "type A" reorganization	Taxable purchase
<50%	Taxable purchase	Taxable purchase

• Nontaxable: selling company shareholders pay no gains tax on the difference between the purchase price and the "tax basis" of their shares.

• Taxable: selling company shareholders do pay gains tax on the difference between the purchase price and the tax basis of their shares.

If GP puts heavy weight on the acquiree's preference for nontaxable status and wants to finance up to 50% of the acquisition with cash (borrowed or on hand), presumably it will choose the merger option. If GP does not put heavy weight on the acquiree's preference for nontaxable status and does not want to finance the acquisition by an exchange of shares (because it wants to leverage the acquisition significantly, or because it thinks its shares are underpriced), GP will choose between a merger and affiliation, based on the importance it places on obtaining shareholder approval, and on whether it wants to purchase less than 100% of the acquiree.

Finally, suppose the prospective purchase price is considerably greater than the acquiree's book value. Then if the acquisition was designated a taxable purchase, GP would be able to reduce its tax bills over time by writing off the part of the purchase price allocated to the acquiree's depreciable assets. This consideration will increase GP's inclination to finance and structure the acquisition in such a way as to achieve purchase status. However, this inclination may have to be balanced against an inclination to satisfy the acquiree's desire for reorganization status, and, perhaps, an inclination to finance the acquisition by an exchange of shares.

If GP does not finance the acquisition by an exchange of shares, it will be required under GAAP to both: (a) add to its balance sheet not the book value of the candidate's assets, but the price paid for them; and (b) amortize over 40 years or less any difference between the latter and the former. Even if the premium over book value paid for the acquiree—usually called *goodwill*—is large, meeting this amortization requirement will have no effect on the new unit's postacquisition cash flows over time; "amortization of goodwill" is a noncash charge. Accordingly, accounting considerations should play no significant role in GP's determination of which structural option to choose.

CANDIDATE SCREENING: THE PROFITABILITY TEST

Targeting candidates for acquisition is a two-stage process. First, screen for candidates that look as though they *might* be profitable. Then, screen the survivors for those that look as though they *will* be profitable. Both screens depend on having a specific test, or criterion, for distinguishing between profitable and unprofitable acquisitions. What should this test be?

The Positive Net Present Value (NPV) Test

Because GP's objective in growing by acquisition is to increase its overall market value, it should specify a profitable acquisition as one that is worth more to GP than it costs. Put more precisely, the test requires that the market value to GP of the new business, M, must exceed the increment of the equity capital, or equity cost, EC, that GP would have to invest in order to take control of the business. Because GP is likely to speak of the difference between M and EC as the NPV of the investment, a profitable investment also can be characterized as one that has a positive NPV.

In general, M, for any candidate, will equal the discounted value of the equity cash flows, ECF, it would generate each year as a business unit of GP. For any particular year ECF is simply another way to designate the dividend which the unit would distribute to GP. Accordingly, it will equal the difference between the unit's earnings, E, and the part of these earnings that is retained and used to finance additions to the unit's fixed and current assets; retained earnings will in turn equal the product of E and the earnings retention, or "plowback," ratio, r.

The Test Specified More Elaborately for a Zero-Growth Candidate

If the unit's earnings are not expected to grow over time, no investment will take place, r will be zero each year, and earnings will be fully distributed. In this case, M can be determined with the simple equation

$$M = \frac{E}{k_e},$$

where E designates the unit's uniform annual earnings and k_e is the percentage cost of equity capital for the unit. For example, if k_e equalled 13% (GP's own k_e), and if GP would have to invest $40 million in equity capital to acquire the unit, the profitability of this investment would depend on the size of the units earnings stream:

Scenario	EC	E	M	NPV	Evaluation
1	$40m	$7.8m	$60m	$20m	profitable
2	40	6.5	50	10	profitable
3	40	5.2	40	40	normally profitable
4	40	3.9	30	−10	unprofitable
5	40	2.6	20	−20	unprofitable

The Test Specified More Elaborately for a Growing Candidate

If the new unit's earnings are expected to grow over time, then almost certainly its assets will grow too. Thus, some mix of new equity funds and debt (borrowed) funds will have to be raised each year to finance this asset growth. Since the equity funds will come from earnings retention, r will be some positive magnitude each year. Whether it is large or small will depend on whether the asset additions are large or small, and on whether GP will finance the additions with a small amount or a large amount of debt funds.

With earnings being partly retained each year, M must be determined with the more complicated equation:

$$M = \frac{E_1[1 - r_1]}{(1 + k_e)} + \frac{E_2[1 - r_2]}{(1 + k_e)^2} + \frac{E_3[1 - r_3]}{(1 + k_e)^3} + \frac{E_4[1 - r_4]}{(1 + k_e)^4}$$

$$+ \frac{E_5[1 - r_5]}{(1 + k_e)^5} + \frac{TM_6}{(1 + k_e)^5}.$$

In this equation the planning period equals 5 years; E_3, for example, represents a forecast of the earnings the new unit would generate in Year 3, and r_3 represents a forecast of the fraction of E_3 that would be reinvested; $E_3[1 - r_3]$, therefore, represents a forecast of ECF in Year 3; and TM_6 represents a forecast of the unit's "terminal" market value at the beginning of Year 6 (and end of Year 5). The latter is the best estimate of what the unit would be worth (and thus could be sold for) at that time, and would depend on what ECF stream the unit could be expected to generate after Year 5.

How would GP actually use this equation to calculate M for a particular candidate? It first must study:

- The economics of the candidate's market (especially its future growth and the intensity of price competition).
- The candidate's probable competitive strategy as a unit of GP (especially the extent to which its product will be differentiated).

- The historical financial statements of both the candidate and the candidate's major rivals.

Then GP must forecast in the light of these studies the most likely magnitudes for each year over the planning period of the new unit's:

- Sales growth (given its sales in the current year)
- Ratio, or margin, of pretax operating earnings to sales
- Net fixed asset turnover (ratio of sales to net fixed assets)
- Current asset turnover (ratio of current assets to sales)
- Percentage of asset additions that will be financed with debt
- Percentage cost of this debt
- Effective tax rate

The debt ratio would reflect GP's opinion of the appropriate debt policy for the unit. In addition, GP must decide how much of the unit's present long-term debt it will assume.

    Next, GP must deduce from these forecasts (and a forecast of future interest charges on its assumed debt) the new unit's pro forma financial statements for the period: sales, pretax operating earnings, operating earnings, earnings, debt (assumed plus new), equity (the initial EC plus new equity investments in the form of earnings retention), and ECF. For purposes of understanding more fully the prospective profitability performance of the new unit, GP also ought to calculate the unit's ROE for each of the 5 years. For Year 3, for example, ROE would equal the ratio of E_3 to the equity capital on the pro forma balance sheets as of the beginning of Year 3.

    Finally, GP must estimate the TM as of the end of the planning period, TM_6. This would require, essentially, forecasting the new unit's earnings for Year 6, E_6, and then multiplying this forecast by the best estimate possible of the appropriate "price earnings" or "value-earnings" ratio for the unit at that point in time. Assuming k_e continues to equal 13%, this ratio will be given by the equation:

$$\frac{TM_6}{E_6} = \left[1 - \frac{g}{\Delta ROE} \right] \div [0.13 - g],$$

where g is the unit's prospective long-run earnings growth rate, ΔROE is the unit's prospective long-run incremental ROE (the average annual rate of return on *new* equity investments beyond Year 5), and the ratio of g to ΔROE gives the unit's prospective long-run retention ratio.

    So if, for example, g is forecasted to be 2% and ΔROE is forecasted to equal k_e plus 1 point, the value-earnings multiple will be:

$$\left[1 - \frac{.02}{.14} \right] \div [0.13 - .02] = 7.8.$$

But if g is forecasted to equal 6% and ΔROE is forecasted to equal k_e plus 3 points, the multiple will be:

$$\left[1 - \frac{.06}{.16}\right] \div [0.13 - .06] = 8.9.$$

What are the long-term growth rate and ΔROE likely to be for a candidate unit that GP thinks may be promising? If the unit's product market will not slip from maturity to decline, g presumably will run somewhere between zero and the average rate at which nominal GNP is expected to grow. The exact location depends on just how mature the market will be. The ΔROE probably cannot exceed k_e by more than two or three percentage points unless barriers to market entry are unusually high and durable; the best bet for most markets is that the "spread" between ΔROE and k_e will be about one percentage point. Note that the closer to zero this long-term spread is, the less sensitive the value-earnings multiple will be to the magnitude of g.

To illustrate the actual evaluation of the candidate after all the forecasts have been made, we can suppose that GP determines for the candidate that

- The present discounted value of the unit's ECF stream over the planning period equals $30 million.
- The present discounted value of TM6 equals $90 million.

Thus, if the initial EC of the candidate equalled $140 million, GP would conclude that

$$NPV = \$30m + \$90m - \$140m = -\$20m.$$

Therefore, the acquisition is prospectively unprofitable; the price is too high given the margins, turnovers, and growth rates being forecasted. But if EC equalled $100m, GP would conclude instead that

$$NPV = \$30m + \$90m - \$100m = \$20m.$$

In this case the acquisition is prospectively profitable.

Complications in Applying the Test

In applying the positive NPV test to any particular acquisition opportunity, GP's biggest problem is producing realistic forecasts. But that is not the company's only problem. It will have to judge the riskiness of the new unit and the extent to which the unit should be financially leveraged. If the unit holds cash or the acquisition offers the prospect of synergistic benefits, account must be taken of this element (or these elements, if both prevail).

Risk and the Percentage Cost of Equity Capital, k_e

For an average large company and the average business unit of this company, k_e is given by the equation

$$k_e = k_T + MRP,$$

where k_T is the long-term U.S. Treasury bond rate, and MRP is the market, or average, risk premium. In the early part of 1996, the former was running at about 6.5%. Over the last decade, the latter appears to have averaged about 4.5%. For companies and business units in general, k_e is given by the equation

$$k_e = k_T + B[MRP], \quad B \gtreqless 1,$$

where B (beta) should be thought of as a multiplier that tells the company or unit whether its own risk premium is greater or less than average, and if so, by how much. For most large companies and most business units of these companies, B is somewhere between 0.7 and 1.3. Whether B, and thus k_e, for a particular company or unit is small or large relative to the average depends primarily on whether the variability of margins over time (business risk) is small or large, and on whether the percentage of assets financed with long-term debt (financial risk) is small or large.

Financial Leverage

What percentage of the new unit's assets should be financed with long-term debt? There are two principles GP can use to answer this question.

The first is that as this percentage increases (and the ratio of pretax operating earnings to interest payments—the coverage ratio—decreases), the negative impact on earnings each year is dominated by the decrease in equity capital that GP has to invest initially and over time. As a consequence, the average ROE (calculated against an initial base of EC) generated by the acquisition also increases with the use of leverage, subject to two critical conditions. The first is that the product of the unit's asset turnover and operating earnings margin must *exceed* consistently the aftertax cost of debt funds. The asset turnover in the first year of the new unit's life is defined as the ratio of sales to the sum of EC and all of the candidate's debt that GP assumes. The second condition is that all the debt GP chooses to use in financing the new unit will be long-term, and therefore permanent (in the sense that each debt instrument will be replaced at maturity with a comparable instrument). If these conditions do *not* hold, leverage will not magnify the new unit's ROE's *consistently* over time.

The second principle is that although financial risk, and therefore k_e, increases as the average permanent coverage ratio decreases, the ROE increases faster, at least until this ratio reaches some threshold level. Unfortunately, for most companies it is unclear precisely what this threshold is: 4.0, 3.0, 2.0, or some other magnitude. There is reason to believe, however, that taking the coverage ratio down to 3.0, and perhaps even 2.5, would add only about three percentage points to k_e, and that this increment ordinarily would be significantly less than the concomitant increment in ROE (assuming the two magnification conditions are being met).

What do these two guidelines tell us about the profitability of "leveraged buyouts," acquisitions financed with a very large fraction of debt? (In some cases—for example, the Safeway and R.J. Reynolds acquisitions by Kravis, Kohlberg, and Roberts (KKR)—the debt is so large that initially the coverage ratio is *less than* 1.0.) By themselves the guidelines do not actually tell us very much. The reason is that, with few exceptions, companies that leverage acquirees heavily undertake as soon as possible to reduce debt-to-asset ratios significantly. (Returning to the R.J. Reynolds example, by early 1991 KKR already had replaced about one third of the $25 billion in debt that it had put on the company's balance sheet at the time of the acquisition two years earlier.) So for leveraged buyouts in general, if *long-run* leverage ratios are not very different from the leverage ratios that characterize acquisitions in general, the *relative* profitability of leveraged buyouts will depend on other factors. The two most important are the relative prices paid for them (do these buyouts command higher premiums?) and the relative effectiveness with which they are managed subsequent to the deals (do these buyouts show greater improvement in margins and turnovers?).

Cash

If the candidate holds, say, $15 million in nonoperating "cash" (funds that are not needed to facilitate transactions and that, accordingly, are invested in some type of securities), GP can account for the $15 million in its evaluation in one of two ways. It can treat the cash as an inflow and add it to M, or it can treat the cash as a discount from the price and subtract it from EC. Some companies in calculating an acquisition NPV do both, but that is double counting. It also would be double counting to add the cash to M and include interest returns on the cash to the forecasted ECF stream.

Synergy

GP's acquisition of a particular candidate might work because of the combination's ability to generate synergistic benefits for the new unit ("synergy-out"), for the company ("synergy-in"), or for both. Synergy-out benefits could take the form of an increase in demand for the new unit's product (because GP's brand is put on the product) or a decrease in the unit's production costs (because GP makes excess capacity available to the unit), or both. Synergy-in benefits could take the form of an increase in demand for, say, Red's product (because the new unit's brand is put on the product), a decrease in GP's costs (because the unit brings a tax-loss carry-forward with it), or both.

If the positive NPV test is applied along the lines described earlier, the impact of synergy-out benefits would be included in the forecasts GP makes of the new unit's sales, pretax operating earnings margins, and asset turnovers. The impact of synergy-in benefits would not be included in these forecasts. They would have to be factored into the NPV calculation as add-ons.

CANDIDATE SCREENING: PROFITABILITY CONDITIONS

Suppose GP has identified both a target market and a company, Brown, operating in this market that is for sale at some price. What are the conditions that must be met for the acquisition of Brown to be profitable? It is easier to deal with this question if we first look at the conditions necessary for entering the market profitably by start-up (that is, by constructing the plant and assembling the people and equipment required to conduct operations in the market at the desired scale).

Conditions of Profitable Growth by Start-up

GP would assess the profitability of a start-up the same general way it would assess the profitability of an acquisition: by comparing the M of the resulting new business unit with the initial EC of the undertaking. For M to be greater than EC, there are three major conditions that must be met.

First, the target market must represent a good "fit" for GP. *Fit* is a shorthand term for the idea that the new market is related to one or more of GP's existing markets, at least to some significant degree. Without a good fit—without knowledge of either the market's customers, its major incumbent rivals, its technology, or some combination of the three—GP would soon find itself at a disadvantage in the market. With a good fit GP at least stands a chance of being able to compete effectively. Fit alone is not sufficient for a good competitive position, but it is necessary.

Second, the economics of the market must be good. This means that there is little excess capacity in the market (and that price competition therefore is not intense), that warfare in the promotion arena is not too expensive, that barriers to entry by newcomers are on the high side, and that the market will not slide from maturity to decline. In such a market there is a strong presumption that incumbent rivals are generating ROEs that on average exceed k_e significantly.

Third, the unit must stand not just a chance, but a good chance of being able to compete effectively in the market. This is equivalent to saying that although advantage barriers around the market are high, the unit, unlike other prospective entrants, can surmount them by the development of offering and cost advantages that eliminate or reverse the advantages of incumbents.

For any particular start-up that meets the fit test, the relationship between M and EC will depend on the combined impact of the market economics that GP expects to see and the competitive position that it expects to attain. If the market economics and competitive position are strong, M will be greater than EC; if the market economics and competitive position are weak, M will be less than EC.

The Conditions of Profitable Growth by Acquisition

Returning now to the question of what it takes for an acquisition to be profitable, the answer starts the same way the answer started to the question of what it takes for a start-up to be profitable. Entry by acquisition is not likely to be profitable unless it meets the fit test. If GP doesn't know very much about the market in which Brown operates, the odds are stacked against success. The rest of the answer is different, though.

Let M(M) be Brown's *actual* preacquisition market value, M(SA) be GP's opinion of Brown's stand-alone market value (its value as an independent company), and M be, again, GP's opinion of Brown's market value as one of its own business units. In addition, note that Brown's present owners almost certainly will not accept less than M(M) for their shares. Finally, assume for the time being that GP does not think that Brown is underpriced on a stand-alone basis, that GP will not have to pay a premium over M(M) for Brown, and that GP will keep Brown's stand-alone coverage ratio unchanged (and by implication will not finance any part of the price of Brown with debt). Together, these temporary assumptions tell us that

$$M(M) = M(SA) = EC.$$

It follows that the equity cost of Brown's common stock will reflect fully the economics of the market and Brown's stand-alone competitive position in that market. For example, suppose that Brown's book equity equals $100 million and that because the market economics and competitive position are both weak, the ratio of M(M) to book is 0.7. Then we would see

$$M(M) = \$70m$$
$$M(SA) = \$70m$$
$$EC = \$70m.$$

If instead market economics and competitive position both are strong, with the result that the ratio of M(M) to book is, say, 1.4, we would see

$$M(M) = \$140m$$
$$M(SA) = \$140m$$
$$EC = \$140m.$$

The more Brown is worth as an independent company (the "better" a company it is), the more it will cost.

It also follows that for the acquisition to be profitable, M must be greater than M(M); Brown must be worth more to GP than it is worth as an independent company to Brown's present owners. Regardless of what drives M(M) and M(SA), there must be some benefit or set of benefits from acquiring Brown which are not reflected in M(SA). Brown must represent to GP one or more types of a "value bargain." Under our current assumptions, there are four such types:

1. *"Turnaround" bargain.* The prospect exists that GP can create value (that is, add an increment to M), by improving Brown's management performance.

2. *"Expansion" bargain.* The prospect exists that GP can create value by undertaking profitable investments in new related businesses which Brown could have undertaken itself but didn't.

3. *"Synergy" bargain.* The prospect exists that GP can create value by combining one or more of its own units with Brown in a way that generates favorable side effects on demand or cost in Brown, GP, or both.

4. *"Restructure" bargain.* The prospect exists that GP can create value by selling, or "divesting," Brown units for an equity price greater than their current contributions to M(SA).

In short, subject to one caveat, the Brown acquisition will be profitable if for any combination of these four reasons GP can increase Brown's ECF stream (defined broadly to include the net equity proceeds from any divestiture GP might make of a Brown operation and any "synergy-in" benefits that would be generated) relative to what the stream would be on a stand-alone basis. The caveat? Before GP can elevate Brown's ECF stream, it must be able to replicate the stand-alone stream. The base from which it improves Brown's financial performance must be the base it acquires Here is where the "fit" condition specifically enters the picture. GP cannot in fact achieve this replication unless it starts from a competitive position that is at least as good as Brown's stand-alone position. To do this it must be knowledgeable about Brown's market. The less this knowledgeability, the weaker the chance that Brown is a potential value bargain.

But won't Brown bring that knowledge with it? After all, GP would be acquiring more than Brown's assets and customer base; it also would be taking on board the people that now manage Brown. Judging from case materials reported primarily in the business press, GP at best would have a year or two after acquiring Brown before the current top management group leaves and has to be replaced by managers from GP's own cadre. If Brown is a turnaround bargain, GP would have to supply new managers immediately; the same may be true if Brown is an expansion bargain.

Are there any other reasons Brown might represent a value bargain to GP? If we introduce the possibility that M(M) is less than M(SA), and that GP would be able to decrease Brown's interest coverage ratio, there are two. Subject, again, to our fit caveat, Brown could be either or both of these bargain types:

1. *"Underpricing" bargain.* The prospect exists that GP will experience value creation if the market currently undervalues Brown, but at some point can be expected to revise upward its forecast of Brown's stand-alone ECF stream.

2. *"Leverage" bargain.* The prospect exists that GP can create value by increasing the degree to which Brown is leveraged with long-term debt.

What are the clues that tell GP it may face a turnaround, expansion, synergy (defined now for simplicity as "synergy-out"), restructure, underpricing or leverage bargain? How can GP persuade itself that these clues really do signal the potential for value creation?

Exhibit 17.5 answers these questions in a stylized way for each of the six types of bargains. Note that some of the clues in column 2 probably can be picked up from publicly available financial statements (ROE, relative use of leverage, relative margins, relative asset turnovers, relative growth), while some cannot (excess capacity, offering position relative to positions of comparable offerings in other regions, complementarity and brandability of the offering, business profitability and value, percentage cost of equity capital). Note, too, that none of the cases in column 3 can be made routinely. GP must put work into them before it can say with confidence that Brown is a potential value bargain.

The Premium Problem

History indicates that contrary to what we have been assuming, GP will not just have to pay more than M(M) for Brown, it will have to pay significantly more. For 201 acquisitions (many of which were large) undertaken over the period 1976 to 1990, premiums over M(M) ranged up to 120% and averaged around 60%; the range quartiles ran roughly as follows:

First quartile: 35%
Third quartile: 80%.

The prospect of having to pay a premium for Brown means that for the acquisition to be profitable, Brown must be not just a value bargain, but a value bargain of sufficient magnitude to permit both "recapture" of the premium and generation of GP's minimum acceptable level of value creation. For example,

EXHIBIT 17.5   Targeting value bargains.

Bargain Types	Targeting Criteria: Clues—Establishing Potential	Targeting Criteria: Establishing Realizability
Turnaround	Brown is an underperformer relative to incumbent rivals; its margin, asset turn, and growth levels all fall below theirs.	GP must make a case that it can fix the problem by reducing costs, improving the offering, and pricing for return instead of volume.
Expansion	Brown's regional offering has features and characteristics that beat the features and characteristics of similar offerings in other regions.	GP must make a case that it has the resources (management and financial) to take Brown's offering national.
Synergy	GP has excess capacity that can be used in a Brown operation; further, Brown's offering complements one of GP's product lines and may be able to take GP's stronger brand.	GP must make a case that its capacity can be put to work *efficiently,* that the Brown offering is indeed brandable, and that branding will build demand, relative to what it otherwise would be.
Restructure	One of Brown's units is unprofitable, and is therefore contributing negatively to Brown's value, M(SA); it would be very difficult to turn around.	GP must make a case that it can divest the unit for equity proceeds considerably greater than the unit's contribution to M(SA).
Underpricing	Brown's ROE is running above the company's cost of equity capital but its market-to-book ratio is significantly less than 1.0.	GP must make a case that this ROE is sustainable *and* that the stock market eventually will pick this up even if Brown becomes part of GP.
Leverage	Brown uses significantly less leverage (has a higher coverage ratio) than incumbent rivals.	GP must make a case that matching the interest coverage ratios of rivals would not increase Brown's cost of equity capital very much.

suppose that the latter is 15%, that M(M) equals $100 million, and (to keep matters from getting too complicated) that Brown is not a leverage bargain. Then GP would have to turn Brown into a business unit worth

- $145m if it pays a below-average 30% premium ($145m equals $100m times the sum of 1.30 and .15)

- $175m if it pays an average 60% premium ($100m times the sum of 1.60 and .15)

- $205m if it pays an above-average 90% premium ($100m times the sum of 1.90 and .15)

How should GP deal with this problem? To begin with, it must acknowledge to itself that fully recapturing a typical premium (to get 15% value creation) is a very challenging task. If on a stand-alone basis Brown is growing at the GNP rate and generating an ROE of 14% (calculated against an initial base of Brown's present book equity), GP in order to turn Brown into a $175 million unit would have to push its book-based ROE up *permanently* to the 19% level (unless it can add permanently a point or two of growth). This would be difficult to do in most U.S. industrial markets. Competition ordinarily is simply too fierce to allow *sustainable* increases in ROE of this magnitude. Put another way, GP must realize that unless the Brown acquisition is very unusual, it cannot expect to make a value-creating investment unless it can keep the premium under a level significantly below the average.

But how can GP achieve in practice this appealing goal of premium limitation? If Brown has hired an investment banker, it will have heard a number of times that "every acquiree gets a large premium and so should you." If GP also has hired a banker, it will have heard, first, that "a large premium is the going price for doing a deal," and then, that "there is no need to worry: As long as there's no dilution you're all right."

There are two general approaches GP can take to the problem of premium limitation. Both presuppose that the company and its candidate will use outside help (for dealing with legal, valuation, and strategic issues) only on a time-based or fixed-fee basis. Taking advice from people who charge a fee geared to the acquisition price is a questionable idea.

The first approach is rooted in the principle that openness is the best policy in growth by acquisition. If GP applied the principle to Brown (let's say that Brown appears to be a combination expansion, synergy, and leverage bargain), it would show its complete postacquisition value creation plan—its analysis of all Brown's opportunities for value creation—to Brown's managers (who GP probably wants to stay on). Then it would offer to split the sum of value increments on some mutually agreeable basis: perhaps 50:50, or perhaps 60% for the company and 40% for Brown's current shareholders. Assuming the latter, if GP can add 30% to the value of Brown, Brown would get a premium of 12%. If GP can add 40% to the value of Brown, the premium would equal 16%.

An obvious possibility here, though, is that Brown will take issue with the company's analysis: "If you exploit properly the expansion bargain opportunities we represent, Brown's value could be increased 60%; our premium ought to be 24%." In the event this is said, GP should switch to the second approach. In general, suggest that Brown share the upside risk. In particular, respond to Brown's contention with one of these two proposals: (1) Instead of cash, take our common stock in exchange for your common stock. If the price of our stock does not yet reflect the 40% value increment we foresee, you will get a part of the capital gain when the price does reflect that increment, or if you are right, when the price does reflects the value increment you foresee. If the price of our stock already reflects the 40% value increment and you are right about the 60% value increment, you will get part of the capital gain when the market comes to accept your view. (2) We'll set the deal up as an earn-out. You'll get a 16% premium today plus 40% of all equity cash flows that Brown generates over the next five years in excess of those we have projected.

The Implementation Problem

There is one final condition of profitable growth by acquisition. Not only must GP make a case that the investment in Brown will generate good pro formas, it must make these projected statements come true. GP must see to it that Brown's potential for value-creation is realized.

How successful GP's realization effort turns out to be will depend on GP's ability to develop and execute effectively the strategy called for by the nature of the acquisition. If Brown is a potential turnaround bargain, GP actually must improve its product, reduce its costs, and revise its pricing. If Brown is an expansion bargain, GP actually must carry out profitable start-up entries into the regional markets where its studies indicate that Brown's offering would have a significant advantage. If Brown is a synergy bargain, GP actually must employ the unit's excess capacity in a way that reduces the company's consolidated average costs, and actually must brand and subsequently promote Brown's offering in a way that builds demand for it.

It was stressed earlier that for GP to have this ability, the company must be knowledgeable about Brown's markets. It also must be stressed that this knowledgeability cannot be brought to bear on the task unless GP can integrate Brown into the GP management structure. Brown's management "model" must be made compatible with GP's model; Brown soon must come to embrace the same profitability objective that GP does, *measure* profitability in the same way, evaluate strategic alternatives in the same way, set and monitor the achievement of performance targets in the same way, and "incentivize" executive compensation in the same way.

Companies who come up short in their integration efforts sometimes are said to have trouble "digesting" acquirees. Not long ago, for example, Bridgestone was reported to be having a digestion problem with its Firestone acquisition, and Daimler was reported to be having a similar problem with several large acquisitions it made in the second half of the last decade. In the United States, indigestion problems are thought to be one of the major reasons for the large fraction—some estimate it at 50%—of acquisitions that have ended up as divestitures.

GROWTH BY ACQUISITION: GOOD IDEA, OR NOT SO GOOD?

Should companies undertake to diversify themselves by acquiring other companies? Is growth by acquisition likely to be a profitable strategy? It would be easier to answer these questions if we first could develop full postpurchase profitability audits of all the acquisitions made over the last 20 years. But that is not in the cards. On the one hand, we do not have the comprehensive financial data that is necessary for producing audits of the acquired units themselves; acquiring companies with few exceptions do not publish separate earnings statements and balance sheets for their acquirees. On the other hand, while we do have a lot of financial data on the acquiring companies (including the postacquisition behavior of their stock prices), these data do not tell us very much about how profitable the acquisitions turned out to be; if General Electric's ROE and stock price both increased over the two or three years after the company's acquisition of RCA, was that because of or in spite of the acquisition?

Nonetheless, we do have some data about past acquisitions: a record of acquisitions that subsequently were divested, a record of premiums paid for acquirees, and a body of brief reports on selected acquisition outcomes which various acquirors have given to the business press, security analysts, and consultants. And judging from both these data and our knowledge of ROE levels in most product market groups, there can be little doubt that profitability results have been quite mixed for companies pursuing a strategy of growth by acquisition.

It is not clear exactly what the average outcome has been (although a good guess is that the typical acquisition has been at least somewhat unprofitable). It is clear, though, that the range of outcomes has distributed around this average, whatever its magnitude has been. Those on the lower end of the distribution have done poorly (they have been significantly unprofitable and some have been spectacularly unprofitable), and those on the upper end have done much better (most, and perhaps all, have been profitable and some have been very profitable). Herein lies the moral for companies contemplating growth by acquisition: The moral has two parts.

First, the strategy should be undertaken with a keen awareness of how difficult it is to implement profitably. The road to success is strewn with landmines: picking the wrong product market in which to look for a candidate; picking the right product market but the wrong candidate; picking the right candidate but paying the wrong price for it; or paying the right price for the right candidate but executing the wrong program for realizing the potential of the acquisition. It is because of these landmines that so many acquisitions have been, and undoubtedly will continue to be, value-destroying.

Second, the strategy also should be undertaken with a keen awareness that the landmines can be dodged. Growth by acquisition has been profitable when companies carrying it out have avoided all the critical mistakes that companies in the lower end of the distribution make. In short, the question is not whether growth by acquisition can be profitable. It can. The question is what guidelines should be followed in order to raise the odds to a high level that it will be profitable.

FOR FURTHER READING

Alberts, William W., "The Profitability of Growth by Merger," in William W. Alberts and Joel E. Segall, eds., *The Corporate Merger* (Chicago, IL: University of Chicago Press, 1974).

Brealey, Richard A. and Stewart C. Myers, *Principles of Corporate Finance,* Fifth Edition (New York: McGraw-Hill, 1996).

Fortier, Diana, "Hostile Takeovers and the Market for Corporate Control," *Economic Perspectives* (Chicago, IL: Federal Reserve Bank of Chicago, January/February 1989).

Haspeslagh, Phillipe and David B. Jemison, *Managing Acquisitions: Creating Value Through Corporate Renewal* (New York: Free Press, 1991).

Porter, Michael, "From Competitive Advantage to Corporate Strategy," *Harvard Business Review* (May–June 1987).

Rappaport, Alfred, *Creating Shareholder Value* (Chicago, IL: Free Press, 1986).

Salter, Malcolm S. and Wolf A. Weinhold, *Diversification Through Acquisition* (Chicago, IL: Free Press, 1979).

Weston, J. Fred, Twang S. Chung, and Susan E. Hoag, *Mergers, Restructuring, and Corporate Control* (Englewood Cliffs, NJ: Prentice-Hall, 1990).

18 BANKRUPTCY

Ronald J. Sutter

Grant W. Newton

THE SCENE IS SET

Even as a teenager, David Brown knew that one day he would own a professional basketball team. While other kids were practicing free throws, David would rush home from school, flip through his collection of basketball cards, and choose twelve stars to play for his imaginary team.

Those memories seemed a bit distant as he rode the elevator to the executive suite of the North American Basketball League (NABL). His dream seemingly crushed, David, now 38, was going to tell the commissioner of the league that his team, the Hartford Crabs, could not pay its bills. David, who had realized his dream three years earlier, when he purchased the Hartford Crabs for $75 million, needed financial help.

Just where David went wrong, he wasn't sure. Maybe he had overestimated his ability to pay the debt service on the $35 million he had borrowed to buy the team. Had he overlooked the fact that he was buying into a highly competitive market? In nearby Boston, another NABL team had a seeming monopoly in the region.

That team drew hordes of fans to its cavernous arena and tapped the wealthiest local cable television stations for fat broadcast right fees. His team, which had never been a winner, was often relegated to the back of the newspapers' sports sections.

The Crabs had no cable television contract and attendance at its games was likely to remain at its current level. Later, David would find out that even this projection was overly optimistic.

The Crabs' other two revenue streams, a share of the league's national television contract and team-licensing pie, had risen only modestly in three years.

On the other side of the ledger, the Crabs' biggest expense was payroll. The year he had bought the team, payroll had accounted for 55% of his expenses. A year later, that number had climbed to 70%; it went to 80% during the 1990–1991 season. There were serious cost overruns when general and administrative expenses were added to the mix.

Unlike most other owners, David had nowhere to turn for help. There were no car dealerships or family money that he could use to subsidize his team. David had no choice but to file for bankruptcy.

Is Bankruptcy the End?

Does bankruptcy mean a business has irrevocably failed? Are there any alternatives? When and how does a company file a bankruptcy petition? Is there any chance of recovery? These are just a few of the terrifying questions raised, when bankruptcy looms as an imminent occurrence in a troubled company.

Such feelings are certainly justified, considering the history of bankruptcy: Debtors suffered physical punishment and imprisonment until early bankruptcy laws were reformed. In the United States, this reform started in 1787. Even today, we hear tales of woe from those exposed to our bankruptcy system.

After listening to one debtor complain about the injustice over the handling of his second bankruptcy proceeding, a chief bankruptcy judge stated very eloquently that debtors generally come before the bankruptcy court system with very high, often unrealistic expectations. They often blame everyone else, when these expectations are not reached, while at the same time overlook their own failures, which brought them before the bankruptcy court.

Unrealistically high expectations are not limited to debtors. Creditors, too, fall into this frame of mind. This is especially so for the victims of fraudulent schemes, which are perpetuated on the uninformed and vulnerable. Here, the creditors expect the bankruptcy system to completely recover their lost investments.

Bad publicity, high cost, prolonged and stressful periods of time, restraints imposed by the bankruptcy system, and the need for professionals and turnaround specialists are all viewed negatively.

So what about some positives? What of the opportunity for a fresh start, continued employment of personnel, a learning experience, and a partial or complete reorganization? These positives may be achieved if the right ingredients exist.

Early recognition of the problem or problems and their causes are essential to any successful reorganization of a troubled business. It gives one time to consult with professionals (attorneys, CPAs, and bankers) who can provide for adequate planning or opportunities for:

- Selection of alternatives to a bankruptcy petition, such as out-of-court workouts.
- Selection of the most advantageous time to file the bankruptcy petition.
- Minimization of taxes for both pre- and postpetition periods.
- Determination of the causes of the business problems and a plan for their elimination.
- Development of a reorganization plan for consideration shortly after, or in some cases even before, a bankruptcy petition is filed.

A reorganization plan is in itself a good-faith gesture to the court and creditors. It indicates that the petition was well thought out and was not used as just another delaying tactic, as is the case with many bankruptcy petitions.

All too often, the troubled business seeks specialized professional consultation only hours before a major asset is to be lost through foreclosure. Cash-flow problems may have existed over an extended period of time, without any real acknowledgment of the problems; even though default notices have been received on unpaid loans or leases. Such last-minute bankruptcy petitions are almost doomed to failure before they start.

The selection and early engagement of professional help is essential. Attorneys who specialize in insolvency matters and CPAs who hold the CIRA (Certified Insolvency and Reorganization Accountant) designations will be far more capable to access the situation and provide advice than professionals who do not specialize in this area of practice. Independence and objectivity of a professional are essential so as to provide assistance without the burden of justifying their past associations with the debtor. Often the professionals previously engaged by the debtor are a part of the problem, but more often than not, the major problem is the existing management.

Did David react quickly enough? Probably. David hired an attorney, specializing in professional sports-team management, to review his operation. The attorney soon discovered that David was somewhat lacking in managerial skills. Among other things, David didn't recognize the leverage he had over the city, when he began lease negotiations for the arena. David could have asked for and gotten a percentage of the parking and concessions, or at least bid down the $10,000 per game rental fee.

David, who served as the team's general manager, had also been wildly inconsistent in negotiating contracts with his players. One minute, he was giving an untested rookie a $1 million signing bonus. The next, he was stonewalling a veteran starting guard over a $100,000 clause in the player's contract.

The attorney picked up on these inadequacies right away. He had seen it numerous other times, when teams were pushed to the brink of bankruptcy and called on him for help.

Preparation: Become Informed

Bankruptcy services are complex, and this chapter can serve only as an introduction: It should not be used as a substitute for complete authoritative research of legal and financial issues. If this chapter heightens your interest in the subject of bankruptcy, the next steps are to:

1. Obtain and thoroughly study texts on the accounting and tax considerations in reorganization and bankruptcy proceedings (see suggestions for further reading at the end of the chapter).

2. Take seminars on accounting, tax, and legal aspects of reorganization and bankruptcy proceedings. Seminars are available through your state CPA Society, the American Institute of CPAs, the Association of Insolvency Accountants, the Practicing Law Institute, the American Bar Association, and many universities.

3. Take other seminars related to litigation support services and special-report writing.

Copies of the Bankruptcy Code and Rules are also essential tools of the trade. Like most laws, the Bankruptcy Code is often amended, thus requiring your *continued* education. This chapter deals principally with issues related to Chapter 7 (liquidation) and Chapter 11 (reorganization) of the Bankruptcy Code (Title 11 of the United States Code).

WHERE TO START

The greatest service to a troubled business is to prevent its failure. Accordingly, the best time to help is when problems first begin to develop. Action, if taken early enough, can avoid the need to file a bankruptcy petition.

David's troubles might not have mushroomed if he had hired an experienced executive from another team, when he purchased the Crabs. At the very least, he would have obtained knowledge of how other teams in the NABL handled management issues. David might also have hired a marketing executive, someone to provide his team with a new image. That executive could have probed the weaknesses of the Crabs' competitor in Boston and helped the Crabs generate revenue at the gate and interest from the media.

Now David was faced with a much more costly option. A bankruptcy proceeding, which must at all times weigh the interests of the debtor, its creditors, and other involved parties, is very expensive, and it takes considerable time to sort out the facts and determine the appropriate action. Far too often, a business facing severe financial problems will attempt to cure its ills by cutting back on the very experts that it needs: the *specialized* professionals who can determine the underlying cause of the financial difficulty and develop a plan of action, which will allow the company to recover, without filing a bankruptcy petition. The old saying, "An ounce of prevention is worth a pound of cure" also holds true for a troubled business.

A professional, diagnosing David's team and helping him avoid financial ruin, would attempt to gather information about the organization, its operating results, its financial position, competition, industry trends, and analysis ratios. The word *attempt* is used because some or much information about a troubled business may not be available. Lack of this data may be related to the causes of the business problem. What is unavailable will also be instructive. The following is the information that should be put together:

1. Samples of operating management financial reports.
2. Detailed financial reports for at least the last five years by line of business.
3. A completed internal control questionnaire.
4. Industry operating ratios and statistics.
5. The structure (both legal and operational) of the business and its operations, including: (a) organizational charts, (b) operating locations, and (c) a brief description of all its business operations (production, marketing, customer service).
6. A list of the major assets of the business and a determination of their liquidation and market values, indicating whether the assets are pledged as collateral for debts.
7. A description of the parts of the business that are responsible for most of the historical profits or losses and cash flow.
8. An aging of the receivables *and* payables.
9. The terms of all leases, loans, and contracts payable.
10. The status of deposits for taxes with the IRS and state taxing authorities.

The next step is to analyze the information obtained. Plotting trends and ratios is generally the first analytical process, and one that very often provides early fruitful results. These ratios should then be compared with industry statistics.

Often management simply does not know what negative changes have taken place. Often their *only* financial reports are the classic, summarized balance sheet, profit and loss statements, and income tax returns they receive from their bookkeeper or accountant. These are *not* adequate to manage most businesses. Detailed aging reports of receivables could have saved many businesses if they had been available and properly used.

The major cause of business failures is inadequate management, evidenced by a lack of profits and inadequate sales. Experience has shown that a significant portion of the blame for lack of profits and inadequate sales rests with management.

David's experience is typical of many business failures. Consider the following pattern: A business is started by a person who is technically competent in a particular area, but has very little, if any, capital or management experience. The business prospers, but as it grows, it fails to grow in management depth. The owner/manager is very self-confident, based upon his or her earlier success, and will not believe that the company will be unable to grow without additional specialized management in the areas of marketing, production, accounting, and finance.

Receivables and payables climb. A bank loan is obtained but, as time goes on, that is not enough. High-risk transactions are entered into for the appearance of success. Accounting records and procedures are neglected. Excessive salaries and questionable "perks" (generally personal expenses) continue, no matter what projects must be pushed aside. The owner/manager is typically an eternal optimist who believes that a big new contract or "a deal" will come in very soon and will cure everything. His or her philosophy is: "When up a tree, branch out." New facilities and equipment are obtained. Questionable "deals" are recorded, and doubtful receivables are carried without reserves. Payroll taxes go unpaid, and the bank loan goes into default. The business is then forced to file a bankruptcy petition at the very last minute. Of course, the debtor will claim: "It's all the fault of the bank or a supplier because they would not increase the amount of a loan and extend the repayment terms."

Studies have found that approximately 50% of business failures generally occur in the enterprise's first five years of operation, with the retail and services industries leading the way. (Source: *Business Failure Record,* New York: Dun & Bradstreet, Inc., 1995).

Aside from inadequate management, many other factors can contribute to a business failure. There is often a combination of factors, including:

- Credit extension policies
- Aging of notes and accounts receivable
- Collection policies and efforts
- Competition
- Inadequate sales
- Improper pricing
- Collection policies and efforts
- Outdated manufacturing facilities
- Excessive expenses
- Excessive debt often resulting from an LBO
- Insufficient working capital

- Insufficient equity capital in relation to debt and the size and composition of assets
- Purchasing policies
- Policy concerning payment of debt
- Overinvestment in fixed assets or inventories (i.e., obsolete, excessive, utilization)
- Operational inefficiencies
- Marketing and distribution methods and policies
- Inadequate cash management
- Overexpansion
- Excessive discounting

Many of these factors can be determined by simple ratio and trending techniques. Use of a good graphics program will greatly enhance these analytical methods. The use of percentages to indicate relationships is also useful.

The art of predicting a business failure or bankruptcy has been addressed by scholars for some time now. Edward I. Altman and others utilized selected key financial ratios to develop a bankruptcy probability index. If properly utilized, such methods can prove very useful for the early detection of a business that is headed for trouble.

The importance of good business plans (see Chapter 9) and forecasts (see Chapter 6) cannot be overlooked. When prepared with diligence, and used as a comparison to actual achievements, the variances between budgeted and actual financial results can provide a signal for astute managers, allowing them to head off a problem before it gets out of control (see Chapter 7).

BANKRUPTCY: AN OVERVIEW FROM BEGINNING TO END

Alternatives for the Troubled Business

The debtor's first alternatives are to locate new financing, merge with another company, or find some other basic solution to its situation, in order to avoid the necessity of discussing its problems with representatives of its creditor body. David Brown wants desperately to avoid going to the bank and admitting that he has a problem. Fortunately, he may not have to take that step. By approaching the league and the city, two entities that can least afford the Crabs' demise, David is hoping he can get financial assistance to relieve his problems. Other companies may not have these kind of options. The debtor may be required to seek a remedy from creditors, either informally (out of court) or with the help of judicial proceedings.

Out-of-Court Settlements

The informal settlement is an out-of-court agreement that usually consists of an extension of time (stretch-out), a pro rata cash payment for full settlement of claims (composition), an issue of stock for debt, or some combination of these options. The debtor, through counsel or a local credit association, calls an informal meeting of the creditors for the purpose of discussing its financial problems. In many cases, the credit association makes a significant contribution to the out-of-court settlement by arranging a meeting of creditors, providing advice, serving as secretary for the creditors' committee, and serving as a disbursing agent, under an informal arrangement with creditors.

A credit association is composed of credit managers of various businesses in a given region. Its functions are to provide credit and other business information to member companies concerning their debtors, to help make commercial credit collections, to support legislation favorable to business creditors, and to provide courses in credit management for members of the credit community.

At the creditors' meeting, the debtor will describe the causes of failure, discuss the value of assets (especially those unpledged) and its unsecured liabilities, and answer any questions the creditors may ask. The main objective of the meeting is to convince the creditors that they will receive more if the business is allowed to operate than if it is forced to liquidate, and that all parties will be better off if a settlement can be worked out.

In other cases, the debtor may elect to meet with each of the largest creditors individually, before a meeting of all creditors is arranged.

Creditors' Committee

To make it easier for the debtor to work with the creditors, a committee of creditors is often appointed during the initial meeting of the debtor and its creditors, providing, of course, that the case is judged to warrant some cooperation by the creditors. It should be realized that the creditors are often as interested in working out a settlement as is the debtor. The debtor's job, running the business while under the limited monitoring of the creditors' committee, can be made easier if the creditors selected are those most friendly to the debtor.

Duties of the Committee

The creditors' committee, where appointed, serves as the bargaining agent for the creditors, monitors the operation of the debtor during the development of a plan, and solicits acceptance of a plan once it has been approved by the committee. Generally, the creditors' committee will meet as soon as it has been appointed, for the purpose of selecting a presiding officer and counsel. The committee may also engage an independent accountant to review, audit, or analyze the books and records of the debtor, as well as its proposed reorganization plan and related forecasts or projections.

At the completion of the financial analysis, the creditors' committee will meet to discuss the results. If the study reveals that the creditors are dealing with something less than a completely forthright and honest debtor, the settlement plan will probably fail or at best, the amount of settlement that will be acceptable to the creditors will be increased significantly. It becomes very difficult for a debtor to avoid a bankruptcy court proceeding under these conditions. On the other hand, if the debtor is honest and demonstrates the ability to reverse the unprofitable operating trend and reestablish the business, some type of plan may eventually be approved.

Plan of Settlement

There is no set pattern for the form that a plan of settlement proposed by the debtor must take. It may call for 100% payment over an extended period of time; payments on a pro rata basis, in cash, for full settlement of creditors' claims; satisfaction of debt obligations with stock; or some combination of these options. A carefully developed forecast of operations, based on realistic assumptions—developed by the debtor with the aid of its accountant—can help creditors determine if the debtor can perform under the terms of the plan and operate successfully in the future.

Generally for unsecured creditors to accept a plan, the amount they will receive must be at least equal to the dividend they would receive if the estate were liquidated. This dividend, expressed as a percent of the amount owed, is equal to the sum of forced-sale values of all assets, including accounts receivable, cash, and prepaid items; less the cost of asset liquidations, priority claims, secured claims, and expenses of administration; divided by the total amount of unsecured claims.

This valuation process is illustrated in Exhibits 18.1 and 18.2. In this case, the general unsecured creditor must decide to take a small 16% return through a plan of reorganization.

In bankruptcy, a key issue is how to distribute the assets (which are usually few) to the creditors (who are usually many). Exhibit 18.1 is an analysis of the liquidation values of all of the assets of the Hartford Crabs. The total book value of the assets is $927,000, but the estimated liquidation value amounts to only $760,800, which is $166,200 less than book value. Of the $760,800 estimated liquidation value, unpledged assets amount to only $41,300 (leaving $719,500 for the pledged assets).

A secured creditor has first call against the particular asset that has been pledged against that creditor's claim. The claims of the secured creditors total $666,600 out of the estimated $719,500 liquidation value of the pledged assets,

EXHIBIT 18.1 Hartford Crabs, Inc., Analysis of free and pledged assets, December 31, 1997.

	Book Value	Estimated Liquidation Value	Other Creditors	Last National Bank	Supplier A	NABL	Finance Company A	Finance Company B	Unencumbered Assets
Cash in banks	$ 13,800	$ 13,800		$ 5,500					$ 8,300
Accounts receivable	327,500	205,000		205,000					
Allowances for bad debts	(32,000)								
Inventories:									
Stationery and supplies	19,000	7,500							7,500
Promotional materials	34,000	20,000			15,000				5,000
Uniforms and shoes	17,000	4,000		4,000					
Souvenirs and programs	47,000	22,500		22,500					
Prepaid expenses	7,500	4,500							4,500
Other assets	8,500	8,500	$ 8,500						
Franchise fee	288,500	380,000				$380,000			
Scoreboard and equipment	102,500	58,000					$ 25,000	33,000	
Automobiles	58,700	21,000						21,000	
Leasehold improvements	52,000	–0–							
Depreciation and amortization	(113,000)								
Notes receivable	75,000	15,000							15,000
Interest receivable	15,000	–0–							
Trademark	6,000	1,000							1,000
Total assets	$ 927,000	$760,800	$ 8,500	$ 237,000	$15,000	$380,000	$ 25,000	$ 54,000	$ 41,300
Less total assets		927,000							
(Loss) on liquidation		(166,200)							

	Other Creditors	Last National Bank	Supplier A	NABL	Finance Company A	Finance Company B	Total	Summary Partially Secured	Fully Secured
Collateralized debts									
Principal balance	$ 11,500	$ 250,000	$13,000	$258,400	$ 24,500	$ 73,000	$630,400	$359,000	$271,400
Accrued interest		5,200	400	25,500	900	4,200	36,200	10,300	25,900
Total collateralized debts	$ 11,500	$ 255,200	$13,400	$283,900	$ 25,400	$ 77,200	$666,600	$369,300	$297,300
Collateral excess (shortage)	$ (3,000)	$ (18,200)	$ 1,600	$ 96,100	$ (400)	$(23,200)	$ 52,900	$ (44,800)	$ (97,700)

Assets Pledged as Collateral to Creditors

EXHIBIT 18.2   Hartford Crabs, Inc., Statement of affairs as of December 31, 1997.

Assets	Net Book Values	Estimated Liquidation Values	Gain/(Loss) Upon Liquidation	Estimated Assets Available for Unsecured Creditors
1. Assets pledged to fully secured creditors:				
Inventories	$ 15,000	$ 15,000	$ –0–	
Franchise	247,500	380,000	132,500	
Total		395,000		
Less fully secured debts (contra)		297,300		
Excess available for unsecured creditors		$ 97,700		$ 97,700
2. Assets pledged to partially secured creditors:				
Cash	5,500	5,500	–0–	
Accounts receivable	295,500	205,000	(90,500)	
Inventories	64,000	26,500	(37,500)	
Other assets	8,500	8,500	–0–	
Scoreboard	71,500	58,000	(13,500)	
Autos	26,700	21,000	(5,700)	
Total deducted (contra)		$324,500		
3. Assets unencumbered:				
Cash	8,300	$ 8,300	–0–	8,300
Inventories	38,000	12,500	(25,500)	12,500
Prepaid expenses recoverable	7,500	4,500	(3,000)	4,500
Notes and interest receivable	90,000	15,000	(75,000)	15,000
Trademark	6,000	1,000	(5,000)	1,000
Leasehold improvements	43,000	–0–	(43,000)	–0–
Total		$ 41,300		139,000
Less debts having priority (contra)				107,500
4. Assets estimated to be available for unsecured creditors (approximately 16¢/$)				31,500
5. Estimated deficiency to unsecured creditors				169,300
6. Estimated gain/(loss) upon liquidation of assets (deducted contra)			$(166,200)	
Totals	$927,000			$200,800

(Continued)

EXHIBIT 18.2 *(Continued).*

Liabilities and (Deficiency) in Net Assets	Net Book Values		Amounts Unsecured
7. Liabilities fully secured:			
NABL	$283,900	$283,900	
Payable to suppliers	13,400	13,400	
Total deducted (contra)		$297,300	
8. Liabilities partially secured:			
Payable to bank on line of			
credit	255,200	$255,200	
Payable to finance			
companies	102,600	102,600	
Payable to other creditors	11,500	11,500	
Total		$369,300	
Less assets pledged (contra)		324,500	
Amount unsecured		$ 44,800	$ 44,800
9. Liabilities with priorities:			
Estimated liquidation and			
other administrative costs	85,000	$ 85,000	
Wages payable	10,000	10,000	
Payroll taxes payable	12,500	12,500	
Total deducted (contra)		$107,500	
10. Unsecured liabilities:			
Trade payables	121,000		121,000
Loans from shareholder	35,000		35,000
11. Total liabilities	$930,100		$200,800
12. Stockholders' (deficiency):			
Common stock issued	1,000	1,000	
Accumulated (deficiency) at			
December 31, 1987	(4,100)	(4,100)	
Estimated loss upon			
liquidation (contra)		(166,200)	
Total stockholders			
(deficiency)	(3,100)	$(169,300)	
Totals	$927,000		$200,800

which results in an overall surplus of $52,900 ($719,500 less $666,600) on secured claims, as shown in Exhibit 18.1.

    The fact that there is an overall surplus does not mean that each and every secured creditor can be paid in full, from the proceeds of the asset pledged to that creditor. For example, Last National Bank has a deficiency of $18,200 on its claim, and Finance Company A has a shortage of $400. On the other hand, the NABL has a surplus of $96,100. Secured creditors who have deficiencies will be treated in the same manner as unsecured creditors, with respect to the amount of their deficiencies. For secured creditors with surpluses, the amount of the surplus is added to the pool available for distribution to unsecured creditors.

Who gets what is shown in Exhibit 18.2. First, consider the left side of the exhibit, starting with section 1. Section 1 consists of assets pledged to secured creditors who have surpluses. These are (from Exhibit 18.1) the inventory of promotional materials, $15,000, pledged to Supplier A, and the $380,000 value of the franchise, which has been pledged to the NABL. As reflected in section 7, the total amount owed to these secured creditors is $297,300. After paying these two secured creditors in full, the amount of $97,700 is left over as surplus, which becomes available for unsecured claims, as shown in section 1 of Exhibit 18.2.

Section 2 of Exhibit 18.2 shows assets pledged to creditors with deficiencies. These assets are estimated to have a total liquidation value of $324,500, while as shown in section 8, the related claims total $369,300. The resulting total deficit, reflected in section 8, is $44,800.

Section 3 shows unpledged assets, estimated at a total value of $41,300. To this is added the surplus of $97,700 from section 1, for a total of $139,000. This $139,000 will be used to pay unsecured claims that have priority under the laws of bankruptcy, as shown in section 9; these total $107,500. These claims are mainly fees and expenses to be incurred by the trustee in order to liquidate the assets and pay out the proceeds to the creditors. Once these priority unsecured claims of $107,500 have been paid, there will be $31,500 left (reflected in section 4) to cover all remaining unsecured creditors.

The remaining unsecured claims consist of two components: One is the $44,800 total deficit on the secured creditors' claims (see section 8). The second component is unsecured claims of $121,000 and $35,000, as shown in section 10. The total of the unsecured claims is $200,800, as reflected in section 11.

Therefore, there are estimated funds of $31,500 available to pay claims of $200,800. These will be shared equally and the resulting payout to unsecured creditors will be about 16 cents on the dollar ($31,500/$200,800 = $0.16) as section 4 shows. The remaining unpaid 84 cents on the dollar is a loss to the unsecured creditors, as reflected in section 5, and it totals $169,300.

Finally, last in line are the shareholders. Since there was insufficient money to fully pay the creditors, there are no funds left for the shareholders. They are wiped out; section 12 shows their sad tale.

It is worth summarizing the order of payment in bankruptcy, and in many out-of-court settlements, which is as follows:

1. Secured creditors, from the proceeds of the specific assets collaterized to respective creditors. A surplus on a secured creditor's claim leaves funds which will be used to pay the next category of creditor. A deficit on any secured claim acquires the status of an unsecured creditor.

2. Unsecured claims that have priorities, such as the administrative expenses, prepetition wages and taxes, and other priority claims.
3. Unsecured creditors without priorities.
4. Stockholders.

For the sake of simplicity, the impact of income taxes has not been considered in the illustrations of Exhibits 18.1 and 18.2. Care must be taken that the income tax liability generated upon the sale of assets does not exceed the net sale proceeds. Such tax liabilities would be considered as an administrative expense priority claim.

Advantages and Disadvantages

A few of the reasons why the informal settlement is used in today's environment are summarized here:

1. The out-of-court settlement is less disruptive to a business that continues operations.
2. The debtor can receive considerable benefits from the advice of a committee, especially if some of the committee members have substantial business experience, preferably, but not necessarily, in the same line of business.
3. The informal settlement avoids invoking the provisions of the Bankruptcy Code and, as a result, more businesslike solutions can be adopted, without as much negative publicity as is associated with a formal bankruptcy.
4. Frustrations and delays are minimized because problems can be resolved informally without the need for court hearings.
5. An agreement can usually be reached much faster, informally, than in court proceedings.
6. The costs of administration are usually less in an out-of-court settlement than in a formal reorganization.

The weaknesses of informal (sometimes called *composition*) settlements are as follows:

1. A successful plan of settlement requires the approval of substantially all creditors, and it may be difficult to persuade certain creditors to accept a settlement that calls for payment of less than 100 cents on the dollar.
2. The assets of the debtor are subject to attack while a settlement is pending. (The debtor can, of course, point out to the creditor that if legal action is taken, a petition in bankruptcy court will have to be filed.)
3. The informal composition settlement does not provide a method to resolve individual disputes between the debtor and specific creditors.

4. Executory contracts, especially leases, may be difficult to avoid.

5. Certain tax law provisions make it more advantageous to file a bankruptcy court petition.

6. Priority debts owed to the United States under Rev. Stat. section 3466 must be paid in full, before other creditors can be paid.

Prepackaged Chapter 11 Plans

Before filing a Chapter 11 plan, some debtors develop and obtain approval of the plan by all impaired claims and interests. The court may accept the voting that was done prepetition provided that the solicitation of the acceptance (or rejection) was in compliance with applicable nonbankruptcy law governing the adequacy of disclosure in connection with the solicitation. If no nonbankruptcy law is applicable, then the solicitation must have occurred after or at the time the holder received adequate information as required under section 1125 of the Bankruptcy Code.

It is necessary for a Chapter 11 plan to be filed for several reasons, including:

1. Income from debt discharge is taxed in an out-of-court workout to the extent that the debtor is or becomes solvent. Some tax attributes may be reduced in a bankruptcy case, but the gain from debt discharged is not taxed.

2. The provisions of section 382(1)(5) and section 382(1)(6) of the Internal Revenue Code (I.R.C.) apply only to bankruptcy cases (see §§ 6.24 and 6.25).

3. Some bond indenture agreements provide that amendments cannot be made unless all holders of debt approve the modifications. Because it is difficult, if not impossible, to obtain 100% approval, it is necessary to file a bankruptcy plan to reduce interest or modify the principal of the bonds.

Because the professional fees and other costs, including the cost of disrupting business, of a prepackaged plan are generally much less than costs of a regular Chapter 11, a prepackaged bankruptcy may be the best alternative.

Preplanned Bankruptcies

Prepackaged bankruptcies are generally best used when the main problems of the business are financing rather than operating, or when action is taken early enough in the process to turn the business around with creditor support. Most Chapter 11s that are successful file the petition after a plan to solve operating problems has been developed, such as which products to eliminate, which stores to close, and so forth. A business plan is often prepared along with suggested terms for the plan of reorganization. After these activities have been completed, the Chapter 11 petition is filed. The voting and confirmation process is completed under supervision of the bankruptcy court. Filings of this nature are referred to as *preplanned bankruptcies.*

Assignment for Benefit of Creditors

A remedy available to a debtor in serious financial difficulties, under some state laws, is an assignment for the benefit of creditors. In this instance, the debtor voluntarily transfers title to its assets to an assignee, who then liquidates them and distributes the proceeds among the creditors. An assignment for the benefit of creditors is an extreme remedy because it results in the cessation of the business. This informal liquidation device (court-supervised in many states) requires the consent of all creditors, or at least their agreement to refrain from taking separate action. The appointment of a custodian over the assets of the debtor gives creditors the right to file an involuntary bankruptcy petition.

Bankruptcy Code Protection

Bankruptcy court proceedings are generally the last resort for the debtor whose financial condition has deteriorated to the point where it is impossible to acquire additional funds. When the debtor finally agrees that bankruptcy court proceedings are necessary, the liquidation value of the assets often represents only a small fraction of the debtor's total liabilities. If the business is liquidated, the creditors get only a small percentage of their claims. The debtor is discharged from its debts and is free to start over; however, the business is lost and so are all of its assets.

Normally, liquidation proceedings result in large losses to the debtor, to the creditor, and also to the business community in general. Chapter 7 of the Bankruptcy Code covers the proceedings related to liquidation. Another alternative under the Bankruptcy Code is to seek some type of relief, so that the debtor will have enough time to work out agreements with creditors, and with the help of the bankruptcy court, will be able to continue operations. Chapters 11, 12, and 13 of the Bankruptcy Code provide for this type of operation, referred to generally as "reorganization" cases.

A summary of bankruptcy law is given in Exhibit 18.3. This law is very comprehensive and covers liquidation (Chapter 7 of the Bankruptcy Code), reorganization (the famous "Chapter 11"), and compromise with creditors for individuals with regular income (Chapter 13 of the Code).

Chapters 1, 3, and 5 apply to all proceedings under the Code, except Chapter 9, to which only specified sections of Chapters 1, 3, and 5 apply. A case commenced under the Bankruptcy Code (Chapters 7, 9, 11, 12, or 13) is referred to as a "Title 11" case.

EXHIBIT 18.3   The bankruptcy law.

The bankruptcy law is contained in Title 11 of the U.S. Code. The code is divided into eight chapters:

Chapter 1:	General provisions
Chapter 3:	Case administration
Chapter 5:	Creditors, the debtor, and the estate
Chapter 7:	Liquidation
Chapter 9:	Adjustment of debts of a municipality
Chapter 11:	Reorganization
Chapter 12:	Adjustment of debts of a family farmer with regular income
Chapter 13:	Adjustment of debts of an individual with regular income

Included within the general provisions of Chapter 1 are the "definitions" used in the Bankruptcy Code. If you are to be involved in a bankruptcy proceeding, be sure to read, if nothing else, the relatively few pages devoted to these definitions. They contain a wealth of information upon which the balance of the Code rests.

Bankruptcy Courts

The Bankruptcy Reform Act of 1978 established a bankruptcy court in each judicial district, with jurisdiction to decide almost any matter related to bankruptcy. This jurisdiction included not only the traditional "case matters," such as objections to discharge or claims, but also affirmative actions against third parties, such as for the recovery of preferential transfers or fraudulent transfer actions.

The Bankruptcy Amendments and Federal Judgeship Act of 1984 provide that the bankruptcy judge may hear and decide all cases and all "core proceedings" arising in a case, referred to the bankruptcy court by the district court. Generally, *core proceedings* include such matters as the administration of the estate, operation of the business during reorganization, allowance of claims, objections to discharge, and confirmation of plans.

The Office of the U.S. Trustee

Within each federal judicial district, except for those in Alabama and North Carolina, there is an appointed U.S. Trustee. The Office of the U.S. Trustee is an agency operated under the U.S. Attorney General, U.S. Department of Justice.

The purpose of this office is to establish, maintain, and supervise a panel of private trustees, serve as trustee if need be, and supervise the administration of all cases under Chapters 7, 11, 12, and 13 of the Bankruptcy Code.

Such duties include monitoring applications for employment of professionals, their compensation applications, monitoring and appointing trustees, examiners, creditor, and equity holder committees, monitoring reorganization plans and disclosure statements, setting guidelines and reporting requirements (i.e., operating reports) for operating businesses during the bankruptcy proceedings and, in general, monitoring the progress of each case.

Cases filed under Chapter 11 require the quarterly payment of a fee to the Office of the U.S. Trustee. This fee is based on the amount of the disbursements made in that period by the debtor.

Cooperation by a debtor with the U.S. Trustee is essential to the smooth administration of the bankruptcy proceedings. For most purposes, the U.S. Trustee becomes a party-in-interest in each case pending. As such, it may on its own accord file motions and make appearances before the bankruptcy court.

Chapter Selection

The Bankruptcy Code consists of five Chapters, under which a petition can be filed. An *individual* may file under Chapters 7, 11, 12, or 13. (Chapter 12 deals with the special case of family farmers and is not covered in this chapter.) A *partnership* or *corporation* may file under Chapters 7, 11, or 12. A *municipality* files under Chapter 9. In the following sections, the general provisions for Chapters 7, 11, and 13 are discussed.

Chapter 7—Liquidation

Chapter 7 is concerned with the liquidation of a debtor in financial trouble and contains provisions for the automatic appointment of a trustee, liquidation of the business and its assets, distribution of the estate to the creditors, and discharge of the debtor from liability.

The person filing voluntarily need not be insolvent in either the bankruptcy or equity sense; the essential requirement is that the petitioner have debts. As soon as the order for relief has been entered, the U.S. Trustee will appoint a disinterested person, from a panel of private trustees, to serve as the interim trustee. If a person was serving as trustee, in an involuntary case, prior to the order for relief, he or she may also be appointed as interim trustee.

Unless the creditors at a meeting, called under section 341(a), elect a trustee, the interim trustee appointed by the office of the U.S. Trustee will continue as the trustee.

The trustee may, with court approval, operate the business for a short time period, if this is necessary to increase the amount that is available to creditors. After the property of the estate has been reduced to money, and the secured claims have been satisfied to the extent allowed, the property of the estate shall be distributed to the holders of claims in a specified order. Unless a claim has been subordinated under the provisions of section 510, section 726(a) provides that the balance is distributed in the following order:

1. To the holders of priority claims, as set forth in section 507.

2. To the holders of general unsecured claims who filed timely proof of claim, and those who filed late because of lack of notice or knowledge of the case.

3. To the holders of general unsecured claims, filed late.

4. In payment of an allowed secured or unsecured claim, not compensation for actual pecuniary losses, for fines, penalties, forfeitures, or damages suffered by the claim holder.

5. In payment of interest on the preceding claims, at the legal rate, from the date of filing the petition.

6. Any balance to the debtor.

Section 726(b) provides for claims within a particular classification to be paid on a pro rata basis, when there are not enough funds to satisfy all of the claims of a particular classification in full. There is one exception to this policy. If there are not enough funds to pay all administrative expenses, and part of the administrative expenses related to a Chapter 11, 12, or 13 case, prior to conversion to Chapter 7, then those administrative expenses incurred in Chapter 7, after conversion, will be paid first. Thus, professional fees in a Chapter 11 case, unpaid at the time of conversion, might not be paid in full, if there are insufficient funds for all Chapter 7 administrative expenses.

After the assets have been liquidated and the proceeds distributed in proper order, the trustee will make a final report and file a final account of the administration of the estate with the court. At this time the trustee will be discharged from further responsibility, and the case is concluded.

Chapter 11—Reorganization

The purpose of Chapter 11 is to provide the debtor with court protection, allow the debtor (or trustee) to continue the operations of the business while a plan is being developed, and minimize the substantial economic losses associated with liquidations. Chapter 11 is designed to allow the debtor to use different procedures, depending on the nature of the debtor's problems and the needs of the creditors. Agreements under this chapter can affect unsecured creditors, secured creditors, and equity holders. A voluntary or involuntary petition can be filed under Chapter 11.

Upon the filing of the *involuntary* petition, on request of an interested party, the court may appoint a trustee. The appointment is not mandatory and the debtor may, in fact, continue to operate the business as if a bankruptcy petition had not been filed, except that certain transactions may be avoided under the Bankruptcy Code. If the creditors prove the allegations set forth in the involuntary petition, an order for relief is entered, and the case will then proceed in a manner identical to a voluntary case.

The Bankruptcy Code provides that a creditors' committee will be appointed in a Chapter 11 case. Chapter 11 proceedings will determine if the business (or some part of the business) is worth saving, and whether it will be able to operate profitably in the near future. If it is determined that it is not worth saving, then the business should be liquidated without incurring further losses. The current bankruptcy law allows that if it is determined that the business should be liquidated, the debtor may propose a plan that would provide for the orderly liquidation of the business, without conversion of the proceedings to Chapter 7.

In Chapter 11, the debtor—through its own management team—will continue to operate the business, unless a party-in-interest requests that the court appoint a trustee, on certain specified grounds. Appointment of a trustee is the exception, not the rule. It is not necessary, as it was under prior law, for an order to be granted to allow the debtor to continue to operate the business. A party cannot solicit the acceptance or rejection of a plan from creditors and stockholders affected by the plan, unless they are given a written disclosure statement containing adequate information, as approved by the court. Section 1125(b) of the Bankruptcy Code requires that this disclosure statement be provided prior to, or at the time of, the solicitation. The disclosure statement must be approved by the court, after notice and hearing, as containing adequate information. A more detailed discussion of the disclosure statement follows.

In cases where the debtor is allowed to operate the business, as debtor-in-possession, the debtor has 120 days after the order for relief, to file a plan, and 180 days after the order for relief, to obtain acceptance, before others can file a plan. This is sometimes referred to as the "plan exclusivity period." These time periods may be extended by the court. After the creditors and the equity holders have approved the plan, the court will hold a hearing to confirm the plan, and the debts not provided for in the plan will be discharged.

Only a very small percentage of petitions, filed by businesses under Chapter 11, result in a successful reorganization. Most are either liquidated in Chapter 11, converted to Chapter 7 where a trustee is appointed to liquidate the estate, or dismissed outright from the protection provided by the bankruptcy system.

Chapter 13—Adjustment of Debts of an Individual with Regular Income

The objective of Chapter 13 is to provide individuals (employees as well as proprietors) with regular income, with some alternative other than liquidation, when they experience financial trouble. Chapter 13 allows the individual, with court supervision, to work out a plan that can provide for full or partial payment of debts over an extended period of time. This concept is similar to a Chapter 11 reorganization, but on a less-formalized and more practical scale.

Section 109(e) of the Bankruptcy Code provides that only an individual with regular income who, at the time the petition is filed, owes noncontingent, liquidated, unsecured debts of less than $250,000, and noncontingent, liquidated, secured debts of less than $750,000, can file a petition under Chapter 13. The definition of regular income requires that individuals filing the petition have sufficient, stable, and reliable income to enable them to make payments under the Chapter 13 plan. The limit on amount of indebtedness will prevent some wage earners from filing a petition. The purpose of this limitation is to allow some small sole proprietors to file under this chapter—because the filing of a Chapter 11 petition might be too cumbersome for them—but to still require the larger individually owned businesses to use Chapter 11.

Commencement of Case

A *voluntary* case is commenced by the filing of a bankruptcy petition under the appropriate chapter, selected by the debtor. The filing of a voluntary petition constitutes an order for relief, resulting in the debtor and the debtor's property being under the supervision of the court.

An *involuntary* petition can also be filed by creditors with aggregate unsecured claims of at least $10,000 and can be initiated only under Chapter 7 or 11. If there are 12 or more creditors with unsecured claims, at least 3 creditors must sign the petition, and if the number of unsecured creditors is less than 12, a single creditor can force the debtor into bankruptcy. Only one of two requirements must be satisfied, in order for the creditors to force the debtor into bankruptcy:

1. The debtor generally fails to pay debts that are not disputed, as they become due.
2. Within 120 days prior to the petition, a custodian was appointed, or a custodian took possession of substantially all of the debtor's property.

To discourage creditors from filing petitions that are unwarranted, section 303(i) provides that the court may require the petitioners to cover the debtor's costs and reasonable attorney's fees; compensate for any damages, resulting from the trustee's (if appointed) taking possession of debtor's property; and, if filed in bad faith, compensate for any damages caused by the filing, including punitive damages.

Automatic Stay

Section 362 of the Bankruptcy Code provides that the filing of a petition results in an automatic stay of the actions of creditors. As a result of the stay, no party, with minor exceptions, including unsecured creditors and creditors having a security or adverse interest in the debtor's property, can take any action that will interfere with the debtor or its property, regardless of where the property is located, until the stay is modified or removed. The debtor or the trustee is permitted to use, sell, or lease property (other than cash collateral), in an ordinary course of business, without notice or hearing, providing the business has been authorized to operate in a Chapter 7, 11, 12, or 13 proceeding and that the court has not restricted the powers of the debtor or trustee, in the order authorizing operation of the business.

The stay of an act against the property of the estate continues, unless modified, until the property is no longer the property of the estate. The stay of any other act continues until the case is closed or dismissed, or the debtor is granted or denied a discharge. The earliest occurrence of one of these events terminates the stay. The automatic stay provision does not operate as a stay against the commencement or continuation of a criminal action or proceeding against the debtor, the enforcement of governmental police or regulatory powers, or certain other actions.

Section 362(d) provides that for relief of the stay to be granted, it is necessary for a party to institute action with the Bankruptcy Court, requesting such relief. The court may grant relief, after notice and hearing, by terminating, annulling, modifying, or conditioning the stay. The court may grant relief for cause, including the lack of adequate protection of a secured creditor's interest. With respect to an act against property, relief may be granted under Chapter 11, if the debtor does not have an equity in the property, and the property is not necessary for an effective reorganization.

Filing Schedules and the Statement of Affairs

Schedules are a prescribed form for the listing of the assets and liabilities of the debtor, required by section 521. The assets, according to the schedule requirements, are reported at their "market value," including a brief description of the asset and its location; however, the court *may* accept "book values." Each individual liability is reported in defined classifications:

1. Creditors holding security.
2. Creditors having priority (as defined by statute).
3. Creditors having unsecured claims without priority.

In the case of secured claims, the related collateral and its market value are reported. The status of the claim is also reported and has a very important impact upon the proceeding. If a claim is reported by the debtor as "disputed," the creditor will be required to file a "proof of claim" in the proceeding. If it is not disputed, the claim is deemed to be filed for the amount shown, on behalf of the creditor, by means of the schedules filed by the debtor. Claims may also be listed as contingent, unmatured, or unliquidated.

The Statement of Financial Affairs (not to be confused with the accountant's use of the same term) is a prescribed series of questions concerning the debtor, its business, and its financial records. The statement contains information regarding the operations and actions of the debtor within the last year or so.

Schedules and the Statement of Financial Affairs are filed with the bankruptcy court at the time the petition is filed, or shortly thereafter, and are filed under penalty of perjury. The accountant for the debtor often assists in the preparation of these reports, which also serve as the basis for inquiry by creditors, a trustee, and other parties-in-interest.

Employment of Professionals

In proceedings before the bankruptcy court, all professionals must, upon application to the court, obtain an order authorizing their engagement under section 327. This order should be obtained prior to commencing services. If for some reason, work must start before obtaining such an order, it must be obtained relatively soon (within a few weeks) thereafter, and the application should explain the reason for the delay and request retroactive treatment.

Obtaining authority from the court is required for any engagement, where the bankruptcy estate will be requested to pay for such services. Without this authority, request for compensation is subject to rejection, even though the services were performed.

Engagements which must have authority from the court (excluding services as a trustee or examiner, where the order of appointment suffices) include all professional services, including those of an accountant, attorney, or expert witness for the debtor, trustee, or official creditors' committee. If a professional is engaged by a creditor or other parties-in-interest, and the creditor or interested party has agreed to pay for these services, no application to the court is required. However, if reimbursement will be sought from the bankruptcy estate, an application is necessary. The application to the court must provide disclosure of all relationships, which the professional now has, or had, with the debtor or any other parties involved.

Under section 330, fees for services may be paid only after a very detailed application is made, and upon a noticed hearing before the court. The professional should work closely with the appropriate attorneys in the preparation and filing of the fee application. Generally, the fee application is far more detailed than those in other areas of professional practice. To help in the preparation of fee applications, guidelines have been issued by the Office of the U.S. Trustee. It should include a specific description of the service performed, the date it was performed, and the time and charges involved. This is detailed for each individual working on the engagement. Descriptive and detailed time records are essential. Fee applications are subject to challenge by the court and all parties-in-interest to the case, including the U.S. Trustee, and the court may not always award compensation for the full amount requested. All compensation must be reasonable and for actual and necessary services rendered. Lack of adequate time records may be a basis to reduce or deny compensation.

Debtor-in-Possession

When the management of a Chapter 11 debtor continues to control and operate the business (as opposed to its takeover by a trustee), it is referred to as the *debtor-in-possession.* As such, under section 1107, its management has a *fiduciary responsibility,* which must be exercised with utmost care. The debtor-in-possession must place the best interest of the estate above the best interest of management, directors, and shareholders. To view the bankruptcy estate as an entity separate from the interest of equity holders becomes very difficult, when management and ownership are the same. In fact, the strong-willed owner manager is often unable to recognize this distinction and act in the required fiduciary capacity.

Many actions of a debtor-in-possession (like those of a trustee) require prior approval of the court. Such actions include the approval of wages to key management personnel; the hiring of professionals; the obtaining of additional capital by way of loans; the issue of new equity certificates; the pledging of assets; and the sale of assets (other than goods normally held for sale). The advice of counsel should be obtained in all such cases.

Creditor and Equity Security Holder Committees

In Chapter 11, a committee of unsecured creditors is appointed by the U.S. Trustee, as soon as is practical, after an order for relief is entered. Other creditor or equity security holder committees may also be appointed by the U.S. Trustee, when authorized by the court, though this usually occurs only in larger cases. The committees generally consist of the seven largest parties, in each class, who are willing to serve. Under section 1103, the committees are the "watch dogs" over the activities of the debtor, and will be the primary negotiating bodies with the debtor, for the formulation of a reorganization plan. The members of these committees must exercise care that they act in a fiduciary capacity, for the benefit of all members in their class, and not solely in their individual best interest. The official committees may apply to the court for authority to engage professional assistance. This is another opportunity for an accountant, knowledgeable of bankruptcy proceedings, to provide a unique service.

Surprisingly, the appointed committees are often completely inactive. An active committee can provide a great benefit to the debtor, when a good working relationship exists. This relationship becomes very important when seeking the acceptance of a proposed plan of reorganization. Without the committees' support, acceptance of a reorganization plan will be extremely difficult. Open, truthful, and complete communication between the debtor and the committees is generally the best policy.

The creditor and equity security holder committees also need to be active in protecting their own interests. These committees must see that adequate controls are in place, to assure that the asset base of the debtor is not dissipated.

Trustee and Examiner

Under section 1104, the bankruptcy court may, after giving notice and conducting a hearing, order the U.S. Trustee to appoint a trustee for cause, including fraud, dishonesty, incompetence, gross mismanagement of the affairs of the debtor by current management, or if such appointment is in the interest of creditors, any equity security holders, or other interests of the estate.

If the court does not order the appointment of a trustee, upon request of a party-in-interest and after notice and hearing, the court may order the U.S. Trustee to appoint an examiner, to conduct an appropriate investigation of the debtor. The examiner will investigate any allegations of fraud, dishonesty, incompetence, misconduct, mismanagement, or irregularity in the management of the affairs of the debtor, on the part of the debtor's current or former management and will report on the investigation. An examiner may be appointed upon request, if the court determines such appointment to be in the best interests of creditors, equity security holders, or other interests of the bankruptcy estate, or if the unsecured liabilities of the debtor exceed $5,000,000.

When a trustee is appointed, he or she becomes the chief executive of the business with all the associated powers. However, like a debtor-in-possession, the trustee must file operating reports and seek the approval of the court, for the sale of assets not used in the ordinary course of business. Additionally, according to section 1106, the trustee has all the duties of a debtor-in-possession *and* investigates:

> ". . . the acts, conduct assets, liabilities, and financial condition of the debtor, the operation of the debtor's business and the desirability of the continuance of such business, and any other matter relevant to the case or to the formulation of a plan [of reorganization]. . . ."

The trustee then prepares a report of his or her investigation of the affairs of the debtor and of its current and past management.

An examiner's duties are generally limited to conducting an investigation and preparing a report on the investigation. However, the court has the power to limit or expand upon the duties of an examiner. The expansion of the duties of an examiner is becoming a more frequent tool of the court.

The selection of a trustee or examiner may be made from a panel of trustees, maintained by the U.S. Trustee, who devote most or all of their time to such matters, or to parties who possess a particular expertise in business and financial management: Attorneys and CPAs often fill this role. Rather than use the trustee appointed by the U.S. Trustee in Chapters 7 and 11 cases, the creditors may elect a trustee.

A trustee is compensated based upon a percentage of monies disbursed. The percentage is set by section 326 (25% of the first $5,000 or less, 10% on the next $45,000, 5% on the next $950,000, and 3% on an amount in excess of $1,000,000). The court may award less than the percentage formula. The compensation of a trustee depends largely upon the facts of a particular case, and the trustee's ability to make the case as successful as possible.

The compensation of an examiner is handled in the same manner as other professionals, generally on an hourly rate.

Filing Operating Reports

Operating reports for Chapter 11 cases are filed monthly with the court and the U.S. Trustee, to reflect the financial activities of the operating bankruptcy estate. These reports show the cash receipts, cash disbursements, and cash position in detail, as well as other financial information, prepared in the format prescribed by the U.S. Trustee.

The operating reports are extremely important because they act as the key source of information between the debtor and the court and the court-appointed committees. The purpose of the reports is to provide the parties-in-interest with current financial information concerning the results of operations of the debtor and its financial position. Often, it is information included (or intentionally excluded) from the operating report, which, in part, forms the basis for the appointment of a trustee or examiner.

The preparation of monthly operating reports is another service that can be provided by CPAs: It is often the area in which CPAs obtain their first exposure to bankruptcy practice.

Liquidation versus Reorganization

Should the debtor liquidate or attempt a reorganization? If that question has not been thoroughly analyzed and answered before the filing of a petition for relief, it will become the first major question addressed, after the filing of a Chapter 11 petition.

As previously discussed, the assets of the debtor may be reported at their market value in the schedule of assets and liabilities filed with the court at the beginning of the case. In general, these reported market values are on the high side due to the optimism of a debtor, in hope of reorganization.

The valuation of the business as a going concern should be carefully evaluated, with regard to the possibilities of selling the business as a whole, or selling only part of its operating divisions or assets. It is entirely possible that a portion of the business is highly salable, at the same time that another portion would require liquidation. An open and imaginative mind will produce the best solution.

On the other side of the value range is the liquidation value. At what value will the assets be realized, upon sale in an orderly liquidation, net of selling expenses? The unsecured and secured creditors will compare the liquidation return with the amount that may possibly be received under the proposed reorganization plan, and with the likelihood of the debtor's success under the plan. Based on this analysis, the creditors will decide whether to advocate liquidation or to support the proposed reorganization plan.

Proofs of Claims or Interests

A proof of claim is filed by a creditor. A proof of interest is filed by an equity security holder of the corporation, or a general or limited partner, in the case of a partnership. A properly filed claim, under section 502, is deemed allowed, unless a party-in-interest files an objection. If any party objects to a claim, a court hearing is held, after notice, to determine the allowable amount.

If the debtor listed the creditor's claim or equity security holders' interest in the filed schedules (in a Chapter 11 case), as undisputed and in an amount and classification (i.e., secured versus unsecured) which that party agrees is correct, this is considered prima facie evidence of the validity and amount of such claim or interest, and the creditor or equity security holder shall not be required to file a proof of claim or interest. This illustrates the care that must be taken when the debtor prepares the schedules. Still, every creditor should protect its own interest and, in most cases, file a proof of claim. In a Chapter 7 case, it is mandatory that creditors file a proof of claim. Claims may be disallowed only for specific reasons set forth in the Bankruptcy Code.

Remember that a creditor filing a collateralized claim may have two classes of claim:

1. A secured claim, to the extent of the related equity (based upon value) in the collateral.
2. An unsecured claim, for the balance of the total claimed amount.

The administration of claims and interests is another significant task, which is undertaken by a bankruptcy estate. Depending upon the number of claims and interests involved, such tasks can be significant, and the use of a computer is essential. Such tasks may include:

1. Investigation of all or some claims and interests.
2. Comparison of proofs of claims and interests filed, to the books and records of the debtor and to the schedules filed.
3. Elimination of duplicate proofs of claims and interests.
4. Classifications, such as secured versus unsecured, different equity security interests, reorganization plan classes, or other descriptive categories.
5. Calculation of the results of voting for the acceptance or rejection of a reorganization plan.
6. Determination of amounts allowed, allowable, or disallowed.
7. Determination of amounts to be paid or securities (i.e., stock of a corporation) issued, in accordance with a reorganization plan.
8. Maintenance of the claim and interests register and the master mailing list.

In actual practice, duplicate proof of claims and interest and multiple classifications of a single proof of claim are common. Materiality and the extent and nature of investigation are matters that must be thoroughly explored with the debtor or trustee and the case attorney, before undertaking such tasks and before developing a database. Revisions at a later time are costly.

Information from these services will be used to assist in the development of a reorganization plan and to assess its feasibility. Additionally, the information collected and summarized from the claim analysis, for use in the objection to certain proofs of claim or interests, may be used by the accountant in testimony as an expert witness.

Conversion or Dismissal of Bankruptcy Petition

When a case is converted from one chapter to another, section 348(a) provides that the conversion constitutes an order for relief, under the chapter to which converted; the date of filing of the petition, the commencement of the case, and the original order for relief do not change. The conversion from one chapter to another terminates the services of any trustee or examiner who is serving, at the time of conversion.

Relief from Stay

A creditor may make a motion under section 362(d), for relief from the automatic stay, discussed earlier. After proper notice and hearing, the court will either grant relief from the stay, or deny the relief requested. Such hearings can become very controversial, with each side calling various expert witnesses to support its cause.

Consider the following example: A creditor holds a first-mortgage debt of $100,000 on real property, owned by the debtor, having a value determined by the creditor of $75,000. The creditor will seek relief from the stay on foreclosure on the property, by claiming that the debtor has no equity in the property, that the property is not essential to the reorganization of the debtor, or that reorganization is not possible or feasible.

The debtor may argue that the value of the property exceeds the $75,000 value, assigned by the creditor. What value did the debtor assign to this asset, on the schedules filed with the court? It may be difficult to argue that the asset is worth over $100,000, if the value listed on the schedules is $75,000. Once again we see the significance of the determination of value in a bankruptcy case.

Assurance that the asset will not diminish in value is another consideration, which must be addressed. Often the collateral for a loan is the inventory and accounts receivable of the debtor. The value of these receivables may be in a constant state of change, due to continued business operations. The cash generated from the sale of items in inventory, or the collection of accounts receivable, is referred to as *cash collateral*. The collateral of the creditor must be protected, and its use is subject to challenge by a "relief from stay" motion, before the court. The use of cash collateral and the related adequate protection consideration is a very complicated issue; it is often a key issue in a Chapter 11 reorganization proceeding.

Classification and Priorities of Claims and Interests

Classification

Claims and interests are classified, in accordance with section 1122, by their nature, and all claims and interests, placed into a particular class (a common group), must be substantially similar. Generally, such classifications are determined by the legal description of the claim or interest. As an example, preferred stockholders and common stockholders have different rights and, therefore, their claims require separate classifications. Creditors holding claims collateralized by different property will generally be classified separately, as will general unsecured trade creditors.

Priorities

Claims and interests are assigned a priority; this leaves their legal, equitable, and contractual rights unaltered, with certain exceptions. Generally speaking, the priority status takes the following order.

1. Collateralized claims, to the extent that they are secured, but only against the property that is collateral for that claim.
2. "Priority" claims, as defined (see following).

3. Unsecured claims, including undersecured claims.

4. Equity interests.

Section 507 in the Bankruptcy Code creates a special category of allowed expenses and claims, which have priority in the following order:

1. Administrative expenses and costs of preserving the bankruptcy estate, including compensation for services rendered to the estate, after the commencement of the bankruptcy proceeding.

2. Unsecured claims arising after the filing of an involuntary case, but before the entry of an order for relief.

3. Wages earned by an individual, written 90 days prior to the filing of the bankruptcy petition, but only to the extent of $4,000 per individual.

4. Unsecured claims for contributions to an employee benefit plan, in connection with services rendered within 180 days prior to the filing of the bankruptcy petition, but only to the extent of $4,000, multiplied by the number of employees so covered, less:

   a. The aggregate amount paid under (3), and

   b. The aggregate amount paid by the bankruptcy estate, on behalf of the employees, to any other benefit plan.

5. Certain unsecured claims of farmers and fishermen, but only to the extent of $4,000 for each individual.

6. Certain unsecured claims of individuals arising from the deposit of money, for the purchase, lease, or rental of property, or the purchase of services that were not delivered or provided, but only to the extent of $1,800 for each individual.

7. Claims for debts to a spouse, former spouse, or child of the debtor, for alimony to, maintenance for, or support of such parties, in connection with a separation agreement, divorce decree, or determination made in accordance with State law by a governmental unit, or a property settlement agreement.

8. The unsecured claims of government units, but only for:

   a. A tax, measured by income or gross receipts, for a taxable year ending on the date of or prior to the filing of the bankruptcy petition, and for which a return (if required) was last due (including extensions of time for filing), within three years prior to the filing of the bankruptcy petition.

   b. A property tax, assessed prior to the filing of the bankruptcy petitions, which was last due, without penalty, within one year prior to the filing of the bankruptcy petition.

   c. A tax, collected or withheld, in whatever capacity.

   d. An employment tax on wages or other forms of compensation, earned from the debtor prior to the filing of the bankruptcy petition (whether actually paid), for which a return was last due (including extensions of time for filing), within three years prior to the filing of the bankruptcy petition.

 e. An excise tax, relating to a transaction occurring prior to the filing of the bankruptcy petition, for which a return was last due (including extensions of time for filing), within three years prior to the filing of the bankruptcy petition.

 f. Custom duties on merchandise imported within one year prior to the filing of the bankruptcy petition.

 g. A penalty, related to claims specified above as priority claims, and as compensation for actual pecuniary loss.

9. Allowed unsecured claims based upon any commitment by the debtor to a federal depository institution's regulatory agency (such as the F.D.I.C.) to maintain the capital of an insured depository institution.

Subordination

The court, under the authority of section 510(c), may, after notice and hearing, subordinate a claim or interest. Such subordination, under principles of equity, is generally seen to apply to circumstances where the claimant, generally an "insider," is found guilty of inequitable conduct.

Preferences and Fraudulent Transfers

The detection and assertion of preferences and fraudulent transfers may require a determination of the point in time when the debtor became insolvent, and performance of a liquidation analysis of the debtor. A trustee may avoid such transactions by bringing an action before the court.

The transfer of property of the debtor can be voided, as a preference, under section 547, if it was:

1. For the benefit of a creditor.
2. For, or on account of, an antecedent debt, owed by the debtor before such transfer was made.
3. Made at a time when the debtor was insolvent.
4. Made on or within 90 days preceding the filing date of the bankruptcy petition (such time is extended to one year if that creditor, at the time of the transaction, was considered to be an insider).
5. A transaction that enabled the creditor to receive more than it would have received, if: the case had been in a Chapter 7 liquidation; the transfer had not been made; or the creditor had been paid under other provisions of the Bankruptcy Code (i.e., under the reorganization plan).

There are exceptions to a preference transfer including:

1. Contemporaneous exchange for new value.
2. A transfer made in the ordinary course of business of the debtor, according to ordinary business terms.
3. The creation of a security interest in property, acquired for new value.

An action brought to recover a preference is one that in most cases boggles the mind of the preference recipient. Take the case of Mr. A, an innocent party who unknowingly invested in a fraudulent Ponzi scheme, who within 90 days of the bankruptcy petition, got back his principal and a significant return. Given that the bankruptcy estate is grossly insolvent and that other equally innocent but unpaid investors would receive significantly less, or nothing, shouldn't Mr. A be required to return to the estate, the funds he received, and participate in a pro rata equitable distribution to all creditors? Generally speaking, this is the intent of the law, but just try to explain this, as a trustee, to a very upset Mr. A, when he is presented with this dilemma.

The transfer of an interest of the debtor, in property, or any obligation incurred by the debtor, made or incurred within one year (the one-year period may be extended, depending upon applicable state law), before the filing of the bankruptcy petition, may be avoided by the trustee, as a fraudulent transfer under section 548, if the debtor:

1. Made such transfer, or incurred such obligation, with actual intent to hinder, delay, or defraud a creditor; or,
2. Received less than fair value; and (a) was or became insolvent as a result of such transaction; (b) was left with an unreasonably small amount of capital; (c) intended or believed that it would not be able to pay the debts incurred as they matured.

The preference and fraudulent transfer avoidance provisions are very controversial and powerful tools, to a trustee or debtor-in-possession, especially in cases where the debtor acted in a fraudulent manner. A keen eye must be used when evaluating transactions of the debtor, and especially so, for those involving insiders, including those involved in leveraged buyout transactions.

Any action to recover a preference or fraudulent transfer must be taken within two years after the petition is filed or if a trustee is appointed during the second year within one year after the appointment.

Dischargeable Debts

The extent to which a debt is discharged depends on whether the debtor is an individual or corporation, the chapter under which the petition is filed, and the nature and priority of the debt.

Individual Debtors

Section 523 lists several debts that are excepted from a discharge of an individual debtor. These debts are exempted from discharge, in a filing under Chapters 7, 11, and 12; but Chapter 13 has special provisions. Among the items listed are taxes with priority under section 507(a), incurred by false pretenses, false representations, or actual fraud, including issuance of false financial statements; debts which were not scheduled in time to permit timely action by the creditors to protect their rights, unless they had notice or knowledge of the proceedings; and alimony, maintenance, or support obligations.

Chapter 7 Cases

Only an individual debtor can obtain a discharge in a Chapter 7 case. A partnership or a corporation may not obtain a discharge in a Chapter 7 case. Further, a corporation or partnership, liquidating under a plan adopted in a Chapter 11 case, would not obtain a discharge. Because a corporation effectively goes out of business as a result of the liquidation, it might appear that the actual granting of a discharge is unimportant. A corporation, however, does not have to go out of existence, and shareholders have kept these corporate shells alive, so that they could be reactivated at a later date, for tax reasons, or to avoid the costs of creating another corporation. A debtor will be reluctant to use these corporate shells, under the current bankruptcy law, because any assets owned by the corporation are subject to attachment by creditors for prebankruptcy debts.

Chapter 11 Cases

Section 1141(d) provides that in a Chapter 11 case—except to the extent that debt repayment has been agreed to in the plan—confirmation of the plan discharges the debtor from any debt that arose before the confirmation of the plan. This discharge takes place whether the proof of claim was filed or deemed filed, and whether such claim is allowed under section 502, or the holder of such claim has accepted the plan. Individuals may not discharge a debt that is of the type listed in section 523. This provision makes it very important for creditors to review thoroughly any proposed Chapter 11 reorganization plans.

Plan of Reorganization

A plan of reorganization is the blueprint that delineates how creditors and equity security holders will be satisfied under Chapter 11 of the Bankruptcy Code. It is not necessary that all creditors and equity security holders be completely satisfied, in a plan, because there may simply not be sufficient assets or earning power available to do so.

Provisions

Section 1123 promulgates certain provisions, which are mandatory for all Chapter 11 plans. A plan must designate classes for all claims and interests; specify those classes that are not impaired; specify the treatment of all classes which are impaired; provide for the same treatment for each claim or interest in a particular class (unless a particular party agrees to a less favorable treatment); and provide adequate means to implement the provisions of the plan. In addition, if the debtor, or its successor, is a corporation, the plan must provide a provision prohibiting the issuance of nonvoting equity securities and provide other provisions regarding the seniority of different equity security classes.

Other provisions *may* be included in a plan, such as to impair or leave unimpaired any class of claims or interests; provide for the assumption, rejection, or assignment of executory contracts or unexpired leases; settle, adjust, retain, and enforce any claim or interest belonging to the debtor; provide for the sale of all, or substantially all, the assets of the debtor; and distribute the resulting proceeds to holders of claims and interests of the debtor.

Impaired Claims and Interests

Section 1124 states that claims and interests are impaired if the legal, equitable, and contractual rights of the holder of such claims or interests are altered, any defaults are not cured, and damages are not compensated for by the debtor.

To make a reorganization plan work, claims and interests may have to be impaired, but the impact of this leads to another significant consideration, which is discussed later in this chapter.

Development of the Reorganization Plan

A reorganization plan is created with a sequence of steps, starting with its development and ending with its implementation. Aside from the various technical provisions mandated by the Bankruptcy Code, the key issue is *feasibility*. Will the plan, if effected, really work? This question is addressed formally by the court, at the confirmation hearing. Some practitioners will go out of their way to avoid the feasibility issue until the confirmation hearing (which is at the end of the sequence of steps taken). If the issue is properly addressed in the early development of a plan, much time, cost, and frustration can be avoided later. Feasibility should be the first major issue studied in the development of a reorganization plan, and the issue should be openly addressed in the disclosure statement and the plan-approval hearings.

With this in mind, the plan development begins by addressing some very basic questions:

- Where have we (the debtor) been?
- Where are we now?

- How did we get here?
- What do we have to work with?
- Where do we want to go?
- How do we get there?

Each question must be addressed from several viewpoints: economic (financial), marketing, and managerial. Each viewpoint is dependent upon the other. The greatest product is of little value, if it cannot be economically produced and marketed; this, in turn, cannot be accomplished without competent management. These questions can be answered only after the debtor has developed a complete business plan. Cash and income projections for at least the next five years should be included in the business plan.

Once it has been determined that there are some aspects of the debtor's operation that can in fact be profitable, the structure of the reorganized entity must be considered. For the plan to be feasible, the debtor must be able to make the debt payments required under the plan. To determine the structure (amount of debt and amount of stockholders' equity) of the reorganized entity, the reorganization value of the entity must be determined. This value is often determined by discounting the future cash flows, which have been projected in the business plan.

For example, if it is determined that the reorganization value of the surviving business is $10.5 million, a plan that provides for the issuance of $10 million in new debt, in settlement of prepetition claims, will most likely not be feasible.

Various alternative plans may be considered, based on factors considered in developing the business plan and assumptions made regarding the structure of the reorganized debtor. Each of these alternatives should be analyzed, by showing the pro forma effect on the current balance sheet, in conjunction with the appropriate cash flow forecast over the subsequent life of the plan (the time it takes to complete all terms of the proposed plan). Financial forecasts must also be considered for the time between the current balance sheet date and the expected effective date of the plan (the date when the plan goes into effect following its confirmation by the court).

After considering the various alternatives, a plan is proposed. Such decisions must be a team effort, between the debtor or trustee and its attorneys and accountants, and hopefully, between the debtor and the creditor and equity security holder committees.

Disclosure Statement

A *disclosure statement* is a report, which is presented, together with the proposed reorganization plan, to the creditors and equity security holders when their vote is requested on the acceptance or rejection of the proposed plan. It is similar to a prospectus, in its nature and intended use. The Bankruptcy Code does not specify in detail the required content of the disclosure statement, leaving this to the judicial discretion of the court. The Bankruptcy Code in section 1125 does, however, define "adequate information" as

> ". . . information of a kind, and in sufficient detail, as far as is reasonably practical in light of the nature and history of the debtor and the condition of the debtor's books and records, that would enable a hypothetical reasonable investor typical of holders of claims or interests of the relevant class to make an informed judgment about the plan. . . ."

The issues that should be included in a disclosure statement will vary, depending on the specific case. Inclusion of all of the following matters should be given serious consideration:

1. Opinions, disclaimers, assumptions, and risks concerning the content of the financial statements, including forecasts and projections (here lies a special reporting issue for an accountant).
2. A brief description of the debtor and a history of its past and current business activities.
3. A description of the proposed management team, with individual profiles and current and proposed compensation.
4. A summary of the proposed reorganization plan, including a description of the classes of creditors and equity security holders, and the treatment the plan affords each class.
5. Disclosure of related parties, affiliates, and major equity security holders, under terms of the proposed plan, and a description of any transactions with such parties.
6. Both reorganization and liquidation values.
7. Special risk factors.
8. Income tax issues.
9. Financial information including: historical operating results for pre- and postpetition periods; current financial position; cash flow forecast for the plan life; pro forma effect of the plan and the forecast.
10. A statement indicating how the plan will be accomplished.
11. A brief description of pending legal proceedings.
12. A valuation of the specific assets and the surviving business as a going concern.
13. Marketing plans.
14. Major postpetition events and transactions, including information concerning the appointment of and reports from the trustee, examiner, and official creditor or equity security holder committees.

15. Terms of new debt or security instruments issued, or to be issued, under terms of the plan.

The disclosure statement must be approved, after a noticed hearing, by the court, before its release. The accountant's presence may be required, as an expert witness, on matters concerning the content of the disclosure statement and its adequacy.

Acceptance or Rejection of the Plan

After the disclosure statement has been approved by the court, the statement, the plan, and an approved ballot are sent to each holder of a claim or interest. This is the formal solicitation for approval of the plan, in accordance with section 1126 of the Bankruptcy Code. Prior and unauthorized solicitation activities can result in severe consequences. Promises, representations, and terms of treatment, which are not included in the approved plan and disclosure statement, are improper and not authorized; the plan and the disclosure document should include a statement of this fact.

Each holder of a claim or interest is entitled to vote for the acceptance or rejection of a proposed plan of reorganization. However, a class of claims or interests that is not impaired is presumed to have accepted the plan and its formal solicitation and vote is not required. A class of creditor claims has accepted a plan, if claims representing at least two-thirds of the value of the claims and more than one-half of the number of allowed claims vote to accept the plan. A class of interests has accepted a plan, if claims representing at least two-thirds of the value of allowed interests vote to accept the plan.

A very important element of the acceptance or rejection of a plan is that the required vote computations are based on the total claims or interests, by each class that actually cast votes (as opposed to the entirety of the amount and number of allowed claims or interests making up a defined class).

The bankruptcy court fixes the time within which the voting takes place. Generally, this is done in conjunction with the approval of the form of the ballot and related procedures.

Confirmation of the Plan

Following the voting process for a proposed plan of reorganization, the proponent of the plan will seek its confirmation by the court. Certain requirements must be met before the bankruptcy court will confirm a plan. The section 1129 requirements are:

1. The plan complies with the applicable provision of the Bankruptcy Code (Title 11, United States Code).

2. The proponent of the plan complies with the applicable provisions of the Bankruptcy Code.

3. The plan has been proposed in good faith and not by any means that is forbidden by law.

4. Payments made, or to be made, in connection with the case or the plan are reasonable and have been approved by the court, or are subject to such approval.

5. The plan makes disclosure of management or proposed management, insiders, and affiliates.

6. Approval of government regulatory bodies, concerning rate changes.

7. The plan, for each impaired class of claims and interests, has been accepted or will receive or retain under the plan, value (as of the effective date of the plan) that is not less than the amount such holders would receive or retain, if the debtor were liquidated under Chapter 7 of the Bankruptcy Code. This is sometimes known as the *best interest test.*

8. Each class of claims or interests has accepted the plan (or, if not impaired, is deemed to have accepted the plan).

9. The plan provides for the treatment of priority claims.

10. Acceptance by at least one class of impaired claims, other than a class held by insiders.

11. The plan will not likely be followed by liquidation or the need for further reorganization of the debtor (or its successor), not provided for in the plan. This is known as the *feasibility test.*

12. All fees payable under section 1930 of the U.S. Code, Title 28 have been paid or provided for.

13. The plan provides for the continuation of all benefits to retirees as defined.

Notwithstanding requirement number 8, the court may, under certain circumstances and upon request by the plan proponent, confirm the plan, if the plan does not discriminate unfairly, and if the plan is fair and equitable, with respect to an impaired class of claims or interests who rejected the plan. This is known as the *cram-down* provision. Section 1129(b) specifies tests for determining if a plan is fair and equitable.

Postconfirmation Activities

Following the confirmation of a reorganization plan by the court, the plan must be implemented. The date on which the plan is implemented is known as the effective date of the plan. Upon completion of the plan implementation, in accordance with its terms, the plan is referred to as consummated, and the case is considered closed.

FOR FURTHER READING

Altman, Edward J., *Corporate Financial Distress: A Complete Guide to Predicting, Avoiding, and Dealing with Bankruptcy* (New York: John Wiley & Sons, 1983).

Collier Bankruptcy Code and Rules, parts 1 and 2 (New York: Matthew Bender & Co., 1997).

Dykeman, Francis C., *Forensic Accounting—The Accountant as Expert Witness* (New York: John Wiley & Sons, 1982).

Frank, Peter B., Michael J. Wagner, and L. W. Roman, eds., *Litigation Services Handbook, The Role of the Accountant as Expert Witness* (New York: John Wiley & Sons, 1996).

Myers, Leo O., *Debtor–Creditor Relations—Manual and Forms* (New York: McGraw-Hill Book Co., 1986).

Newton, Grant W., *Bankruptcy and Insolvency Accounting Practice and Procedures*, 2 vols. including forms and exhibits, 4th ed. (New York: John Wiley & Sons, 1994, updated annually).

Newton, Grant W. and Gilbert D. Bloom, *Bankruptcy and Insolvency Taxation* (New York: John Wiley & Sons, 1994, updated annually).

Pratt, Shannon, *Valuing Small Businesses and Professional Practices* (Homewood, IL: Dow Jones Irwin, 1986).

Sulmeyer, Irving, D. M. Lynn, et al., *Collier Handbook for Trustees and Debtors in Possession* (New York: Matthew Bender & Co., 1987).

Wagner, Michael S. and Peter B. Frank, *Litigation Services MAS Technical Consulting Practice Aid #7* (American Institute of CPAs, 1986).

GLOSSARY

Account, duty to: The obligation of an agent or employee to keep accurate records of and turn over to his/her principal or employer any property received on behalf of said principal or employer.

Accounting exposure: Increases or decreases in assets and liabilities, resulting from exchange rate movements, that may not be associated with either current or prospective cash inflows or outflows. Accounting exposure is distinguished from economic exposure where cash inflows and outflows are expected to be associated with exchange rate movements.

Acquisition: Taking control of a business owned by another company (or division of another company) by purchasing either the assets or from 51 to 100% of the common stock of the company (or division).

Activity-based cost system: Accounting cost information system that focuses on the underlying activities that are necessary to produce the product and, in turn, consume the resources.

Adequate protection: Holders of secured claims, lessors, co-owners, conditional vendors, consignors, and so forth, are entitled to adequate protection of their interest in the property, when such holders request relief from the automatic stay. Adequate protection is also required, before the debtor or trustee can see, sell, or lease certain kinds of collateral, or before a lien that is prior to or equal to the creditor's lien can be granted.

Adjusted gross income: The taxpayer's gross taxable income, diminished by certain deductions (mostly relating to the conduct of a business). This concept serves as a basis for calculating the deductibility of certain itemized deductions, such as medical expenses, casualty losses, and miscellaneous employee expenditures.

Administrative expenses: The actual, necessary costs of preserving the estate, including wages, salaries, and commissions for services rendered after the commencement of the case, are considered administrative expenses. Compensation awarded a professional person, including accountants and attorneys, for postpetition services, is an expense of administration.

Affiliation: An acquisition of from 51 to 100% of another company's (or division's) common stock, following which the acquiree is established as an affiliate, or subsidiary, of the acquiror and continues to exist as a legal entity.

AICPA: The American Institute of Certified Public Accountants. This is the national professional association of certified public accountants (CPAs).

All-current method: A method for translating foreign currency financial statements whereby all assets and liabilities are translated at the current (balance sheet date) exchange rate, contributed capital accounts are translated at historical exchange rates (rates in existence when the account balances first arose), and all revenues and expenses are translated at the average exchange rate in existence during the reporting period. Translation differences (foreign-exchange gains and losses) resulting from fluctuating exchange rates are accumulated and reported as a separate component of stockholders' equity. (See also **Temporal (remeasurement) translation procedure.**)

Allocation: Process by which costs are charged to products. Traditionally, allocation processes are volume-based (e.g., direct labor hours, machine hours, or material dollars); this is appropriate only for process-type production systems.

Alternative minimum tax: An alternative method of calculating a taxpayer's income tax liability, which results in higher tax if the taxpayer has made excessive use of certain tax deductions and tax credits.

Annuity: A regular series of cash receipts or payments.

Apparent authority: The power of an agent to bind his/her principal to contracts with third parties, based, not upon express authority granted by the principal, but upon an appearance of authority created by the principal's acts or omissions.

Application software: The software that allows the end user to perform a useful function, such as word processing or creation of a spreadsheet. It is the software that is closest to the user.

Asset purchase: An acquisition of the assets used in the business of another company (or division), after which an offer usually is made to hire most, or all, of the business's employees.

Assets: Resources, owned or controlled by a company, that have future benefits. These benefits must be quantifiable in monetary terms.

Assignability: The ability to transfer the benefits and/or obligations under a contract to a third party without the consent of the other party to the contract.

Asymmetric risk: An exposure that results in profits or losses only if the underlying price or economic variable moves in one direction.

At-the-money: The condition of a call or put option when the strike price equals the stock price. Some economists define at-the-money as being the case when the stock price equals the present value of the strike price.

Attribution rules: The treatment, for certain purposes, of securities owned by relatives and affiliates of a taxpayer, as if they were owned by the taxpayer.

Audit committee: A committee of the board of directors that is responsible for assuring that the financial statements are fairly presented, that the internal control system is effective, and that allegations of misconduct or other irregularities are investigated promptly. The SEC requires that audit committee members be outside directors.

Auditor: A person or group that examines the validity of financial information and also, in many companies, recommends ways of improving performance. An external auditor is an outside firm of certified public accountants. This firm gives an audit opinion, stating either that the financial statements are fairly presented in accordance with GAAP principles (a clean opinion), or the reasons why they are not (a qualified opinion). An internal auditor is a company employee.

Automatic stay: A petition, filed under the Bankruptcy Code, that automatically stays virtually all actions of creditors to collect prepetition debts. As a result of the stay, no party, with minor exceptions, having a security or adverse interest in the debtor's property, can take any action that will interfere with the debtor or the debtor's property, regardless of where the property is located or who has possession, until the stay is modified or removed.

Balance sheet: A list of a company's assets, liabilities, and owner's equity at a particular point in time.

Bankruptcy: The proceedings initiated voluntarily by a financially troubled debtor, or involuntarily by creditors when the debtor is generally not paying debts as they become due, and involving the filing of a petition in a federal court under the Bankruptcy Code.

Bankruptcy Code: A federal statute, enacted October 1, 1979, as Title 11 of the United States Code, by the Bankruptcy Reform Act of 1978, which is applicable to all cases filed on or after its enactment and which provides the basis for the federal bankruptcy system in effect today.

Bankruptcy Court: The United States Bankruptcy Court of trial jurisdiction, that is, a unit of the district court. Responsible for all cases filed under Chapters 7, 11, 12, and 13 of the Bankruptcy Code.

Basis: The cost to a taxpayer of a capital asset, adjusted upward by later capital investment in it and adjusted downward by various forms of return of capital such as depreciation. Used to calculate the taxpayer's gain or loss upon disposition of the asset.

Bearish: Pessimistic. Anticipating a decrease in an asset value.

Blue-sky laws: State laws regulating securities, coordinated with federal laws, many of which provide for licensing brokers and dealers and registration of new securities.

Board of directors: The body that is responsible to shareholders and other outside parties for the overall governance of a corporation.

Boot: Cash or property received in exchange for a capital asset that does not qualify as like-kind property.

Breakeven: The unit volume where total revenue equals total cost, and there is neither profit nor loss.

Budget: A comprehensive, quantitative plan for utilizing the resources of an entity for some specified period of time—showing planned revenues, expenses, and resulting earnings—together with a planned balance sheet and cash flow statement. If budgets adjust for volume they are called flexible; otherwise, they are static.

Budget entity: Any accounting entity, such as a firm, division, department, or project, for which a budget is prepared.

Budget performance report: An internal accounting report that shows the difference between actual results and expected performance planned in a budget.

Budget review process: The process of evaluating budget proposals and arriving at the master budget.

Budget variance: The difference between budgeted data and actual results.

Bullish: Optimistic. Anticipating an increase in an asset value.

Business unit: An organization that is responsible for both the production and the marketing of a product or a family of related products; it is also called a division or profit center.

Call option: An asset that gives the owner the right but not the obligation to purchase some other asset for a set price on or up to a specified date.

Capital budget: A financial plan for the finance and acquisition of long-term investments.

Capital budgeting: The systematic process of identifying and evaluating capital investment projects to arrive at a capital expenditure budget.

Cash collateral: Cash, negotiable instruments, documents of title, securities, deposit accounts, or other cash equivalents, where the estate and someone else have an interest in the property. Also included would be the proceeds of noncash collateral, such as inventory and accounts receivable, if converted to proceeds of the type defined as cash collateral, provided the proceeds are subject to the prepetition security interests.

Cash flow statement: A presentation of the cash inflows and outflows for a particular period of time. These flows are grouped into the major categories of cash from operations, cash-investing activities, and cash-financing activities.

Cash settled: A future contract that does not require delivery of the underlying asset upon expiration. Instead of actual delivery, the contract is marked to market, so that one party is compensated in cash by the other for the change in the underlying asset price.

CD ROM: A digital, optically readable compact disk that is used for storing data. This data may be in the form of text, audio (music), pictures, or video.

Central processing unit (CPU):   The CPU is the "brain" of the computer. It is the hardware of the computer that makes all of the decisions and performs all of the calculations. Today, most CPU chips are approximately 2 inches by 2 inches and hold millions of electronic components. The vast majority of CPU chips are produced by Intel, which has established the chip standard for the personal computer.

Chairman: A person who presides over the board of directors. Increasingly called chairperson or simply chair, to avoid gender implications.

Chapter 7 proceeding: A liquidation, voluntarily or involuntarily initiated under the provisions of the Bankruptcy Code on or after October 1, 1979, that provides for an orderly liquidation of the business or debtor's estate.

Chapter 11 proceeding: A reorganization action, either voluntary or involuntary, initiated under the provisions of the Bankruptcy Code, on or after October 1, 1979, that provides for a reorganization of the debt structure of the business and allows the business to continue operations.

Chapter 12 proceeding: A reorganization, voluntarily initiated, under the provisions of the Bankruptcy Code, for family farmers with regular income.

Chapter 13 proceeding: A voluntary action, initiated under the provisions of the Bankruptcy Code, on or after October 1, 1979, that provides for the settlement of debts of individuals with regular income. Some small individually owned businesses may file a petition under Chapter 13.

Charging order: The right of a partner's creditors to have all distributions from the partnership which would otherwise by payable to that partner paid to the creditors.

Chief executive officer (CEO):   A person who is responsible to the board of directors for the management of an organization; often combined with another title, such as president and CEO.

Claim: Section 101(4) of the Bankruptcy Code defines claim as (1) right to payment, whether such right is reduced to judgment, liquidated, unliquidated, fixed, contingent, matured, unmatured, disputed, undisputed, legal, secured, or unsecured; or (2) right to an equitable remedy for breach of performance, if such breach gives rise to a right to payment, whether such right to an equitable remedy is reduced to judgment, fixed, contingent, matured, unmatured, disputed, undisputed, secured, or unsecured.

Clip art: Artwork in a line-drawing format, usually of a symbol or caricature. This artwork may be imported into any of the applications such as word processing, spreadsheets, or graphics presentations.

Close corporation: A corporation, all of the stock of which is owned by a small group of individuals who are usually directly involved with the operation of its business.

COBOL: A programming language used prior to the early 1990s to program most business applications.

Comfort letter (letter for underwriters):   Communication from the independent auditor to the underwriter, at the time of registration of the securities, which includes information about the auditor's role, auditor's independence, compliance of the financial statements with the Securities Acts, and any changes in the financial statements, subsequent to those included in the registration statement.

Committed fixed costs: The fixed costs of providing production facilities and other relatively long-term commitments or resources. Fixed costs that cannot be easily or quickly eliminated.

Compensation committee: A committee that recommends to the full board the compensation of the CEO and other principal executives. Usually, its members are outside directors.

Confirmation: An official approval by the court of a plan of reorganization, under Chapter 11 proceedings that makes the plan binding upon the debtor and creditors. Before a plan is confirmed, it must satisfy 11 requirements in section 1129(a) of the Bankruptcy Code. Plans may also be confirmed in Chapters 12 and 13. The requirements for confirmation differ in some respects from the confirmation requirements under Chapter 11.

Constant-dollar method: A method of inflation accounting whereby accounts, which are measured according to historical cost accounting principles, are expressed in units of the same purchasing power, that is, using the same general price index.

Constructive receipt: A doctrine requiring a taxpayer to pay income tax on income unconditionally available to the taxpayer, even though such income is not yet received.

Contribution: Total revenue less total variable costs.

Control: The concept of monitoring activities and taking action to correct undesirable performance or to ensure that goals and objectives are achieved, often using budgets as a basis for measuring performance.

Core earnings: Earnings exclusive of the effects of nonrecurring items (see **Sustainable earnings base**).

Corporation: An organization that is a legal entity with rights, privileges, and responsibilities that are separate from those of its owners, that is, its shareholders.

Cost driver: Vehicle used to trace (or "drive") cost-pool dollars to cost objects. For instance, a setup cost pool might be used to cost a production run on a simple driver basis (setup cost is $30) or on a more detailed basis (complex setup is $45; typical setup is $15).

Cost hierarchy: Various levels within an organization to which one can directly trace a cost. As one moves up the hierarchy from the organization as a whole, to a division, product line, and ultimately a product or customer, it becomes more and more difficult to trace the cost directly. Often, decisions do not require that all costs be directly traced to the top of the hierarchy.

Cost object: Level within the hierarchy for which a separate determination of cost is desired; may be a customer, an individual product, a distribution channel, a product line, or an organizational unit. For all decisions, one should start by identifying the relevant cost object.

Cost of capital: Weighted average after-tax amount of earnings required to maintain the value of the firm's securities.

Cost pool: An aggregation of costs. Traditionally, costs are aggregated along a functional orientation consistent with general ledger accounts (e.g., indirect labor, repairs and maintenance, material handling). Activity-based cost systems pool costs by activity across functional lines (e.g., setup, order process, machining process). This orientation demands a horizontal view of a company (costs grouped through integration of activities across functions) rather than a vertical one (costs grouped by isolated functions).

C+, C++: Programming languages used in the 1990s to program many personal computer and UNIX-based applications.

CPV (cost-profit-volume) analysis: Technique for estimating the contribution and profit at various levels of volume, or determining the unit volume for given levels of profit.

Cram-down: For a plan to be confirmed, a class of claims or interests must either accept the plan or not be impaired. However, the Bankruptcy Code allows the court, under certain conditions, to confirm a plan, even though an impaired class has not accepted the plan. The plan must not discriminate unfairly, and must be fair and equitable, with respect to each class of claims or interests impaired under the plan that has not accepted it. The Bankruptcy Code states conditions for secured claims, unsecured claims, and stockholder interests that would be included by the fair and equitable requirement. It should be noted that, because the word *included* is used, the meaning of *fair and equitable* is not restricted to those conditions.

Creditors' committee: In a Chapter 11 case, a committee of creditors holding unsecured claims shall be appointed as soon as practicable after the order for relief is granted. The U.S. Trustee has the responsibility for appointing the committee without any authorization from the court. The committee will ordinarily consist of the seven largest creditors willing to serve or, if a committee was organized before the order for relief, such committee may continue, provided it was fairly chosen and is representative of the different kinds of claims to be presented.

Credit risk: The loss potential that would result from the inability of a counterparty to satisfy the terms of the foreign-currency contract.

Currency swap: An exchange of currencies between two parties with an agreement to reexchange the currencies at a future date at the same rate.

Current-cost method: A method of inflation accounting, which replaces historical cost accounting principles with current (replacement) cost, as the basis for financial-statement measurement.

Cutoff rate: Minimum rate of return that must be earned by a proposed investment in order for it to be accepted.

Data warehouse: A repository for data transactions, in a database format. This technology is frequently used as a stopgap to replace older legacy systems in order to allow greater access to data.

Debtor-in-possession: Refers to a debtor in a Chapter 11 case, unless a trustee has been appointed. The debtor will remain in possession of its assets in a Chapter 11 case, unless a trustee is appointed.

Decision support system: An application used by middle-level and senior management to make management decisions.

Deferred tax valuation allowance: An amount equal to that portion of a deferred tax asset that is judged unlikely to produce a realized tax benefit.

Derivative: A financial instrument that derives its value from its relationship to some other asset or economic variable (for example, financial contract, currency, commodity, index).

Derivative suit: A lawsuit brought by a stockholder of a corporation on the corporation's behalf in order to pursue alleged rights of the corporation which its directors have refused to pursue. Usually these rights are asserted against the directors themselves.

Device driver: The software that interfaces the operating system to a specific hardware device. This software is usually supplied with the equipment (e.g., printer). It is installed the first time the device is used.

Dilution: Relative loss or weakening of equity position.

Director: A member of the board of directors.

Discontinued operations: Operations that constitute an entire segment of the firm's operations and not, for example, simply one product line in segment made up of a number of related product lines.

Discounted cash flow (DCF) rate of return: See **Internal rate of return.**

Discounting: The process of reducing the amounts of a stream of future cash flows to their present value.

Discretionary fixed cost: Fixed costs that can be eliminated at management's discretion in a relatively short period of time (for example, some administrative salaries, research and development, new systems development).

Dividend: A payment made to shareholders at a stated amount per share, usually quarterly, and usually in cash.

Dumping: Selling in a given country by a foreign producer at a price below the price in the home market.

Duration gap: A situation in which assets are more sensitive to interest rates than are liabilities. As interest rates rise, assets fall more than liabilities, wiping out equity.

Earnings: The difference between the revenues and the expenses for an accounting period. Also called net income.

Economic benefit: A doctrine requiring a taxpayer to pay income tax on income not yet received, if the eventual receipt of such income has been collateralized in such a way as to confer a present economic benefit on the taxpayer.

Economic exposure: ". . . [D]erived from the risk that currency fluctuations could affect the dollar value of future cash flows at the operating income level" (Dow 1995 Annual Report, p. 36).

Economies of scale: The decline of the total cost per unit as volume increases, often due to the existence of fixed costs.

EDI: Electronic data interchange, used by business to transact commerce electronically. These transactions include purchase orders, shipping notifications, invoices, and the like.

Effectiveness: The degree to which a goal is met; efficiency measures the inputs needed to produce a given level of output in pursuit of a goal.

Efficient search sequence: A pattern of searching for nonrecurring items that is designed to maximize their discovery in an efficient manner.

Employee stock ownership plan: A form of qualified deferred compensation plan in which the plan's assets are invested almost exclusively in the securities of the sponsoring employer.

Equity security: A share in a corporation (whether transferable or denominated stock) or similar security; interest of a limited partner in a limited partnership; or warrant or right (other than a right to convert) to purchase, sell, or subscribe to a share or interest.

Estate: The commencement of a case under the Bankruptcy Code creates an estate composed of the property of the debtor.

Examiner: An official appointed by the Bankruptcy Court in a Chapter 11 reorganization, if no trustee is serving, to conduct an investigation of the debtor, including an investigation of any allegations of fraud, dishonesty, incompetence, misconduct, mismanagement, or irregularity in the management of the affairs of the debtor by current or former management of the debtor, if (1) such appointment is in the interests of creditors, any equity security holders, and other interests of the estate, or (2) the debtor's fixed, liquidated, unsecured debts, other than debts for goods, services, or taxes, or owing to an insider, exceed $5 million.

Executive committee: A committee of the board of directors that is empowered to act between board meetings, and that brings to the board proposals that are not within the jurisdiction of other committees.

Executory contract: A contract in which something other than payment itself must be performed, wholly or in part, to complete the original agreement. Unexpired leases or purchase commitments are examples of executory contracts, typically found in cases under the Bankruptcy Code.

Exempt assets: Property of an estate that by federal or state laws is not liable for any debt of the debtor that arose before the commencement of the case. The debtor may maintain possession of exempt assets.

Exercise price: Same as **Strike price.**

Exotics: Engineered derivatives that contain unusual features, or nonstandard contingent cash flow formulas.

Expenses: Outflows of resources to generate revenues.

Extraordinary gains and losses: Revenues or gains and expenses or losses that are both unusual and nonrecurring.

FAQ: Frequently asked questions—a file of questions that are frequently asked about a specific product or topic that is available to users through the Internet or local intranets.

FIFO: A method of computing cost of sales that charges the oldest inventory costs into cost of sales. The costs purchased first, first-in, go into the cost of sales computation first. That is, the oldest costs are the first to go into cost of sales. Hence, first-in, first-out, or FIFO.

Finance committee: A committee of the board of directors that is responsible to the shareholders for monitoring the corporation's financial health and for assuring that its financial viability is maintained.

Financial Accounting Standards Board (FASB): The primary private-sector organization with the responsibility to establish and promulgate U.S. generally accepted accounting principles (GAAP).

Financial budget: The set of budgets including capital expenditures budget, cash budget, budgeted balance sheet, and budgeted statement of changes in financial position.

Financial flexibility: The ability of a company to raise funds (cash) to expand operations, pay off debt, or reduce stockholders' equity.

Fire wall: Computer systems security method used to prevent unauthorized outsiders from accessing data in a company's computer when the user enters through the Internet.

Fixed assets: Equipment.

Fixed budget: A budget prepared for a single expected level of activity. Also called a static budget.

Fixed costs: Those costs that are not responsive to changes in volume over the relevant range, but which may respond to factors other than volume. Fixed costs are sometimes known as "period costs" when they depend on time (for example, rent, depreciation, insurance).

Flexible budget: A budget prepared for more than one level of activity, covering several levels within the relevant range of activity. Also called a dynamic budget.

Foreign Corrupt Practices Act of 1997:   An act of Congress, which, among other things, explicitly prohibits the bribery of foreign governments or political officials and requires firms to keep accurate and detailed records of company financial activities and maintain an adequate system of internal controls.

Foreign-currency transaction: Any transaction (for example, the sale or purchase of inventory, the lending or borrowing of money) that creates a balance-sheet account that is denominated in foreign currency. Examples include foreign-currency-denominated receivables and loans, and foreign-currency-denominated payables and long-term debt.

Forward: A contract in which two parties agree to a deferred transaction. One party is obligated to deliver an underlying asset or commodity, the other party is obligated to take delivery and pay for it. The terms of the deferred transaction are fully specified in the forward contract.

Forward-exchange contract: A privately negotiated agreement to purchase foreign currency for future receipt or to sell foreign currency for future delivery. The amount of foreign currency, the rate of exchange, and the future date of settlement are established at the time the contract is made.

Fraudulent transfer: A transfer of an interest or an obligation incurred by the debtor, within one year prior to the date the petition was filed, with the intent to hinder, delay, or defraud creditors, or whereby the debtor received less than fair equivalent value and the debtor (1) was insolved before or became insolvent as the result of such transfer, (2) was left with unreasonably small business capital, or (3) intended to incur debts beyond the ability to pay such debts as they matured. Fraudulent transfers may be voided. Certain transfers considered fraudulent under state law may be voided, even if the transfer occurred more than one year before the petition was filed.

Functional currency: The currency of the primary economic environment in which the entity operates. Typically, this is the currency of the environment in which it generates and expends cash.

Futures contract: An exchange-traded instrument with a preestablished expiration date, whose market value is linked to the relative exchange rates between two currencies. A futures contract can be purchased (a long position), resulting in a gain if the foreign currency appreciates and a loss if it depreciates. A contract can also be sold (a short position), resulting in a gain if the foreign currency depreciates or a loss if it appreciates.

GAAP: Generally accepted accounting principles.

General utilities doctrine: The doctrine (since repealed) exempting from income taxation at the corporate level, gain from the sale of a corporation's assets, if the sale was done in the context of a corporate liquidation and dissolution.

Geographical information system: A computer application that uses a mapping system display on a terminal or a printer. Data, such as sales data or census data, are overlaid over the geographical information for decision-making purposes.

Hard disk: The device in the computer where information and programs are stored. As the computer requires data, it is loaded into RAM for processing and manipulation. The hard disk acts merely as a repository for the data when it is not in use. Today disk-drive capacities are typically measured in gigabytes (billions of bytes of data).

Headquarters: The CEO and the control, finance, legal, personnel, and other staff units. Usually these persons work in the same building or building complex. Also refers to the headquarters of a business unit.

Hedging: Steps taken to protect the dollar value of a foreign-currency asset or to hold constant the dollar burden of a foreign-currency liability, in the presence of fluctuating exchange rates, by maintaining offsetting foreign-currency positions. Also, more generally, to reduce risk by taking a position that offsets some preexisting risk exposure.

HTML: Hypertext markup language (HTML) is the language used for programming Web pages on the Internet. It facilitates the hypertext links that allow users to skip from one Web page to the next.

Hurdle rate: See **Cutoff rate.**

Impairment of claims: In determining which classes of claims or stockholders' interest must approve the plan, it is first necessary to determine if the class is impaired. A class of claims or interest is impaired under the plan, unless the plan provides for the following: (1) leaves unaltered, the legal, equitable, and contractual right of a class; and (2) cures defaults that led to acceleration of debts or equity interest.

Income statement: A matching of a company's accomplishments (that is, sales) with effort (expenses of operations) during a particular period of time. (Revenues – expenses = net income.)

Independent auditor (accountant):   An outside public accountant, having no financial stake or other interest in the person or company on whose financial statements a professional opinion is to be rendered.

Inside director: A director who is not an outside director, usually an employee of the company.

Insider: A corporate director, officer, person in control, relative of management, partner, affiliate, managing agent of a firm, or owner of more than 10% of a registered security whose position allows access to information on the security before the information is available to the other stockholders.

Insolvency: In the equity sense, the inability of the debtor to pay obligations as they mature. In the bankruptcy sense, a condition where liabilities of the debtor exceed the fair valuation of its assets.

Internal rate of return: The rate of discount that makes the present value of a stream of future net cash inflows equal to the amount of the investment that produces them.

International Accounting Standards Committee (IASC):   An organization representing accounting bodies from over 70 countries whose mission is to harmonize accounting standards internationally.

In-the-money: An option is in the money when exercise would be profitable. For a call option, this is when the underlying stock price is above the strike price; for a put option, this is when the stock price is below the strike price.

Intrinsic value: The amount of money earned when an option is exercised, or zero, whichever is greater. For a call option, intrinsic value is the maximum of zero or the stock price minus the strike price. For a put option, it is the maximum of zero or the strike price minus the stock price.

Investment banker: An organization that buys bond or stock issues in their entirety from the issuing corporation.

Involuntary petition: A petition filed under Chapters 7 or 11, by creditors forcing the debtor into bankruptcy court.

Joint and several liability: Each potentially responsible party is responsible for the entire amount of the liability, not just his/her proportionate share.

Labor variances: Measure the change in the cost of labor, analyzed according to wage changes and changes in labor productivity.

Leading and lagging: A foreign-currency hedging technique, which involves the matching of cash flows associated with foreign-currency payables and receivables, by speeding up or slowing down their payment or receipt.

Legacy systems: Older systems that were developed prior to the 1990s using older technologies. Usually mission-critical systems, they are both costly and difficult to replace.

Liabilities: Commitments to pay out assets (typically cash) to or render services for creditors.

LIBOR: The London Interbank Offer Rate. The interest rate used in Euromoney transactions between London banks. It is widely used as the benchmark floating rate in swaps.

LIFO inventory method: A method of computing cost of sales that charges the most recent inventory costs into cost of sales. The most recent, first-in, inventory items go into the cost of sales computation first. That is, the most recent costs in are the first to go out into cost of sales. Hence, last-in, first-out, or LIFO.

LIFO liquidation: A reduction in the physical quantity of inventory by a firm using the LIFO method. Typically older, lower costs will be associated with the liquidated quantities. This has the effect of reducing cost of sales and increasing earnings. This earnings increase is treated as nonrecurring in the computation of sustainable earnings.

Like-kind exchange: The exemption from taxation of gain from the disposition of a business or investment-use capital asset, if such asset is exchanged for a similar asset.

Local area network (LAN): The networking or interconnecting of computers in a building to allow for the exchange and sharing of data and resources.

Long (Go long in a future or forward): To enter a future or forward as the long party. Also known as "buying" the future or forward.

Long party: The party in a forward or future contract that will take delivery of the underlying asset and make payment, that is, the buying party. The party in a forward or future contract that benefits from a rise in the price of the underlying asset.

Management: A loosely defined term for all the managers of a company or a subdivision of a company. Senior managers are the managers at the top of the organizational hierarchy. Division managers are all the managers in a division.

Management's Discussion and Analysis of Results of Operations and Financial Condition (MD&A): A required report under Securities and Exchange Commission regulations. The discussion of operations is required to discuss material nonrecurring items of revenue or gain and expense or loss.

Manager: The leader of a group of individuals who work together to accomplish part of the organization's goals. These individuals are subordinates. A manager does not personally do the work; he or she ensures that the work gets done by others.

Mark to market: The process by which at the end of each trading day, a payment is made from one party in a futures contract to the other, based on that day's movement in the futures price. When the futures price rises, the short party pays the long party the amount of the price rise. When the futures price falls, the long party pays the short party the amount the price fell.

Master budget: The total budget package of an organization, including both the operating and financial budgets. Sometimes referred to as the profit plan.

Material items: Items of sufficient size to have the potential to influence decision makers or other users of financial statements.

Material participation: The level of activity necessary by an equity owner to escape characterization of the enterprise as a passive activity. Absent special circumstances, such activity must exceed 500 hours in the tax year.

Material variances: Measure the change in cost of materials used, analyzed according to price changes and changes in material efficiency.

MD&A: See **Management's Discussion and Analysis of Results of Operations and Financial Condition.**

Modem: An acronym for *mo*dulator + *dem*odulator, a modem converts the digital signals of a computer to the analog signals of the telephone system and back again, to allow computers to communicate with each other over the telephone system.

Monetary assets and liabilities: Assets and liabilities that represent a fixed number of monetary units. Monetary assets include cash and accounts receivable; monetary liabilities include accounts and notes payable. During inflationary periods, monetary assets (liabilities) result in purchasing power gains (losses), respectively.

Multistep income statement: An income statement format that includes one or more profit subtotals such as gross profit and operating profit (see **Single-step income statement**).

NASDAQ: National Association of Securities Dealers Automated Quotation System. An organized, electronically linked over-the-counter market for stocks. The NASDAQ stock index comprises stocks that trade on NASDAQ. These stocks are generally smaller, less-capitalized stocks than those that compose the S&P 500.

Net operating loss carryforward: Under U.S. tax law, operating losses can be carried back and set off against profits in the three previous years. A refund of taxes can be obtained. If the loss is greater than the profits in the three previous years, then the loss can be carried forward for 15 years and set off against the profits of future years. This produces a future tax savings.

Net present value (NPV): The difference between the amount of an investment and the present value of the future net cash inflows it will produce. For a proposed acquisition, the difference between (1) the present discounted value of the equity cash flows (earnings less investment) that the acquiree is expected to generate over time; and (2) the present cost in equity capital of the acquiree.

NetWare: The network operating system standard through the early and mid-1990s. Developed by Novell.

Network operating system: The software that runs a local area network. This software runs mostly on the network file server, but there is also a small component that runs on the network client.

Nonrecurring items: Items of revenue or gain and expense or loss that appear in earnings on only an infrequent or irregular basis, fluctuate significantly in terms of amount and/or sign, and often are not related to the core operational activities of the firm.

Notional principal: The principal amount specified in a swap agreement that, although not exchanged, serves as the benchmark to determine all cash flows. The cash flows generally equal the difference between two interest rates, multiplied by the notional principal.

Offering proceeds: Proceeds from the initial public offering and sale of securities of a company.

Operating budget: The set of budgets for the normal operations of a business, including all activities involved in generating operating income.

Operating income: An intermediate and pretax earnings total. Only the most operations-related (or core) items of revenue or gain and expense or loss are included in the computation of operating income.

Operating system: The software that tells the computer how to perform its most basic operations. It communicates between all of the components of the computer, ensuring that each of the components delivers the right information and calculations as they are needed and presents the display of its basic functionality to the user.

Operational control system: A system that runs a company's day-to-day operations.

Opportunity cost: A benefit forgone as a result of pursuing an alternative action.

Option contract: The right, but not the obligation, to purchase foreign currency at a fixed price (a call option), or the right, but not the obligation, to sell foreign currency at a fixed price (a put option).

Order for relief: An order, whether by decree or by position of law in a case with the Bankruptcy Code (filed on or after October 1, 1979), granting relief to (or against) the debtor. In a voluntary case, the entry of the order for relief is the filing of the petition. The court must enter the order for relief in an involuntary case, if the petition is uncontested or if the court determines that (1) the debtor is generally not paying debts as they become due, or (2) within 120 days before the petition was filed, a custodian was appointed for substantially all of the debtor's property.

Out-of-the-money: An option is out of the money when exercise would generate a loss. For a call option, this is when the underlying stock price is below the strike price. For a put option, this is when the stock price is above the strike price.

Outside director: A director who is not an officer or employee of the corporation on whose board he or she sits.

Overhead variances: Measure the change in the cost of overhead items, analyzed according to price and salary changes and changes in labor productivity.

Over-the-counter: Description of contracts that are negotiated between two parties, often with the help of an intermediary. Over-the-counter derivatives are custom-tailored to meet the needs of the parties involved, but are not traded on exchanges.

Owner's equity: Represents the owner's investment in a business either by direct investment or profitable operations.

Participative budgeting: The process of preparing the budget using input from managers who are held responsible for budget performance.

Passive income and loss: Income and loss generated by a passive activity, that is, a business activity in which the taxpayer does not materially participate. Such loss normally cannot be used to offset active or portfolio income, such as wages, salaries, bonuses, interest, and dividends.

Pass-through entity: A form of business entity, which is not itself subject to income taxation, but which, instead, passes all its taxable income and loss through to its owners' tax returns. Examples include limited liability companies, subchapter S corporations, and limited partnerships.

Payback period: The time it takes to recover an investment.

Pension: A promise to make regular payments to an employee after he or she has retired. The pension may be an amount fixed by the corporation (a defined-benefit plan); or it may be an amount that depends on the amount contributed to the pension fund by the employee, by the company, or by both (a defined-contribution plan).

Performance reporting: The comparison of actual results with the expected results embodied in the budget, often resulting in the reporting of variances.

Personal service corporation: A corporation, virtually all of whose revenues are derived from the personal services of its shareholders.

Petition: A document filed in a court of bankruptcy, initiating proceedings under the Bankruptcy Code.

Physical delivery: A future contract that stipulates actual delivery of the underlying asset upon expiration of the contract.

Plain-vanilla: The most common type of swap. It is fixed for a floating-interest-rate swap, where LIBOR is the floating rate. The fixed rate is the current rate of the Treasury bond with the same maturity as the swap.

Plan: An agreement that, when confirmed by the bankruptcy court, provides for the rehabilitation or liquidation of the debtor in a bankruptcy case under Chapters 11, 12, or 13. The plan may affect secured creditors and stockholders as well as unsecured creditors' interests.

Planning: The process of developing the set of budgets used in achieving organizational goals. A design or scheme for achieving specific goals or objectives.

Predatory pricing: Slashing selling prices below variable cost in order to drive out competitors.

Preference: A transfer of property on account of a past debt within 90 days (one year for insiders) prior to filing the petition, while the debtor is insolvent, to a creditor who receives more than would be received if the debtor's estate were liquidated under Chapter 7. The Bankruptcy Code provides exceptions for certain transactions that are substantially contemporaneous or in the ordinary course of business.

Premium: The difference between the price paid or asked for a public company's common stock and the price at which the stock was selling prior to the actual or prospective acquiror's decision to purchase a controlling interest in this stock. Also, the option price.

Present value: The sum of a stream of future cash receipts discounted at a positive interest (discount) rate.

Priority claim: A claim or expense that is paid after secured claims and before unsecured claims are satisfied, in accordance with statutory categories. The discharge is a privilege and the bankruptcy laws provide exceptions to discharge, in whole or in part, for certain wrongdoing, such as concealment of assets, or certain types of debts, such as alimony. Under the Bankruptcy Code (cases filed after October 1, 1979), a corporation that liquidates all (or substantially all) of its assets is ineligible for a discharge.

Process maps: Visual depiction of the manufacturing processes, which allows one to "see" activities that cause costs and, thus, to develop cost pools. Process maps should be developed for all aspects of the manufacturing process, from design through customer service.

Productivity: Output divided by input. Productivity rates measure the input required for a unit of output.

Profitability: For a proposed acquisition, the net present value (NPV) of an equity investment in the acquiree, where a profitable acquisition is one with a positive NPV, and the degree of profitability varies directly with the magnitude of the NPV.

Profit plan: A company's total budget used in achieving a desired profit goal. Sometimes the term refers only to the operating budget, and sometimes it is used synonymously with the term master budget.

Pro forma statement: A financial statement detailing management's predictions.

Promoter: An individual who intends to form a corporation for the conduct of his/her business.

Proof of claim: The Bankruptcy Code permits a creditor or indenture trustee to file a proof of claim and an equity holder to file a proof of interest. The filing of the proof is not mandatory in a Chapter 11 case, and the debtor may obtain a discharge for debts that were listed on the schedules filed with the court, even though a proof of claim is not filed. The debtor or trustee has the power to file a claim on behalf of the creditor, if the creditor did not file a timely claim. Thus, for debts that are nondischargeable, the debtor may file a proof of claim to cause the creditor to receive some payment from the estate and avoid having to pay all of the debt, after the bankruptcy proceedings are over.

Prospectus: A document issued for the purpose of describing a new security issue.

Proxy: The grant by a shareholder to another party of the right to vote the stockholder's shares of stock.

Put option: An asset that gives the owner the right but not the obligation to sell some other asset for a set price on or up to a specified date.

Qualified deferred compensation plans: Varieties of retirement plans, such as pension plans, profit-sharing plans, and employee stock ownership plans, which, due to their having met various stringent requirements, provide employers with deductions for contributions, while deferring employee taxation on such contributions and the earnings therefrom, until funds are withdrawn from the plans.

Random access memory (RAM):   The place in the computer where programs are executed and data are processed. Data and programs are brought from permanent storage on either disk or CD into RAM, where the data are then manipulated.

Rate of return: The ratio expressing the relationship between the amount of an investment and the income it will produce.

Red herring: An announcement describing a proposed issue of securities. Called a "red herring" because of the disclaimer emblazoned in red on the document.

Registration statement: A formal statement filed with the SEC by a company, containing financial information and other information for buyers of a proposed security issue.

Regression analysis: A mathematical technique for finding the line that best fits points on a chart. The result is a line that minimizes the sum of the squared distances of the points from the line, and is also known as the "least squares" line.

Relevant range: The range of unit volume which lies within recent experience, and which can therefore provide reasonably reliable cost information.

Remeasurement: See **Temporal (remeasurement) translation procedure.**

Reorganization: Proceedings under Chapter 11 of the Bankruptcy Code (cases filed on or after October 1, 1979), where a debtor attempts to reach an agreement with creditors, secured and unsecured, and continue in business.

Reporting currency: The currency in which a firm prepares its financial statements.

Restructuring charges: Expenses recognized typically in conjunction with downsizing, reengineerings, reorganizations, and comparable activities. The expenses are usually made up of cash costs, accruals of obligations for future expenditures, as well as the write-down of assets.

Revenues: Inflows of resources (assets) into a business generated through operations.

Roll over: To enter a new future or forward contract to replace a contract that is expiring.

Schedules: The detailed lists of debts and assets that the debtor is required to file with a petition in bankruptcy court, or shortly thereafter.

Secured claim: A claim against a debtor that is secured by collateral, which may be used to satisfy the debt in the event the debtor defaults. Under the Bankruptcy Code, a creditor's claim is secured only to the extent of the value of the collateral, unless the creditor selects, in a Chapter 11 proceeding [section 1111(b)(2)], to have the entire debt considered secure.

Securities and Exchange Commission (SEC):   A U.S. government body, with a large staff, which regulates the conduct of listed corporations and the conduct of the exchanges in which securities are traded (stock exchanges), so as to protect investors from fraud and misleading or inadequate financial information.

Semifixed costs: Costs which remain fixed over a certain range of volume, but then increase in a step fashion, at one or more trigger points.

Senior management: A loosely defined term for the chief executive officer and his or her principal subordinates.

Shareholder: An owner of a corporation, as evidenced by ownership of shares of the corporation's stock; also known as stockholder.

Short (Go short in a future or forward):   To enter a future or forward as the short party. Also known as "selling" the future or forward.

Short party: The party in a forward or future contract that will deliver the underlying asset and receive payment, that is, the selling party. The party in a forward or future contract that benefits from a decline in the price of the underlying asset.

Short-swing profits: Profits realized by insiders who take advantage of inside information for personal gain.

Single-step income statement: An income-statement format that simply deducts expenses and losses from revenues and gains in arriving at a single measure of earning before the following: discontinued operations, extraordinary items, and the cumulative effect of accounting changes (see **Multistep income statement**).

Solvency: The ability of a company to meet its short-term cash needs.

Speculate: Attempt to profit by taking on a risk exposure.

Spot market: The market in which transactions are executed for immediate delivery of an asset.

Spot price: The price to be paid for immediate delivery of an asset or commodity.

Standard and Poor's 500:   A stock portfolio consisting of 500 large corporations. The composition and value of the stock portfolio is tracked and reported by the Standard and Poor's publishing company. The S&P 500 value is widely used as a benchmark index of overall stock market performance.

Standards: Predetermined, expected levels of efficiency or measures of desired performance (for example, a budget amount, a standard cost, or a nonquantitative statement of desired performance). A standard cost is the predetermined cost of an input per unit of output. Standards may be unchanging (basic), perfect (ideal), or currently attainable.

Statement of affairs: A report filed with a petition under Chapter 11 and consisting of answers to 21 questions concerning the debtor's past operations. Also used to refer to a statement of a debtor's financial condition, as of a certain date, based on the assumption that the business will be liquidated. The statement consists of an analysis of the debtor's financial position and the status of the creditors with respect to the debtor's assets.

Statements of Financial Accounting Standards (SFAS):   The principal elements of generally accepted accounting principles. The standards are issued by the Financial Accounting Standards Board (FASB).

Statutory merger: An acquisition of from 51 to 100% of another company's (or division's) common stock, following which the acquired unit (the acquiree) is fused into the acquiring company (the acquiror) and ceases to exist as a legal entity.

Strategic information system: An application used by senior management to create a company's strategy.

Strategy: A broad course of action that the board of directors and CEO have adopted, as the best way to attain the organization's goals.

Strike price: The prespecified price at which an underlying asset may be either purchased (call) or sold (put) in an option contract.

Subchapter S corporation: A corporation that, having met various definitional requirements, has elected not to be taxed on the corporate level and to have all its taxable income or loss pass through to its stockholders, in proportion to their stock holdings.

Sustainable earnings base: A revised historical earnings series from which the effects of all nonrecurring items have been removed (see **Core earnings**).

Swap: An agreement between two parties to exchange cash flows over a period of time. Cash flows are determined by an agreed-upon formula specified in the swap agreement, a formula that is contingent on the performance of other underlying instruments.

Symmetric risk: An exposure that results in profits when an underlying price or economic variable moves in one direction, and proportional losses if the variable moves in the opposite direction.

Synthetic stock portfolio: A portfolio that consists of Treasury bills and a long position in equity futures contracts. A properly constructed synthetic stock portfolio behaves the same as a portfolio consisting of actual stocks.

Takeover: Acquisition of one company by another, or an attempt to do so. The company that is potentially being acquired is the target company. In an unfriendly or hostile takeover attempt, the target company resists the efforts of the acquiring company.

Tau: The amount of time remaining prior to an option's expiration.

Tax credit: Taxpayer expenditures, such as certain payments of foreign taxes or childcare expenses, which entitle the taxpayer to dollar-for-dollar reductions in his or her income tax liability. It is different from a tax deduction, which allows a reduction only in the taxpayer's taxable income.

Tax preference: One of various tax deductions or tax credits that, when employed excessively by a taxpayer, may expose such taxpayer to the alternative minimum tax.

Tax shield: A noncash tax-deductible expense, such as depreciation.

TCP/IP: Terminal Control Protocol/Internet Protocol (TCP/IP) is the communications standard that is used by the Internet. A protocol is the understanding that computers have for how information will be delivered over the communications network, which enables computers with different operating systems to communicate with each other and to eliminate errors in data transmission.

Temporal (remeasurement) translation procedure: A method for translating foreign currency financial statements, whereby monetary assets (including assets valued at market) and liabilities are translated at the current (balance sheet date) exchange rate, other assets, liabilities, and contributed capital accounts are translated at historical exchange rates (rates in existence when the account balances first arose), cost of goods sold and depreciation expense are translated at the rates in existence when the related inventory or fixed asset was purchased, and the revenues and other expenses are translated at the average exchange rate in existence during the reporting period. Translation differences (foreign exchange gains and losses) resulting from fluctuating exchange rates are reported as a component of net income. (See also **All-current method.**)

10-K, 10-Q, 8-K: Principal periodic reports filed by most companies registered under the Securities Acts.

Time-adjusted rate of return: See **Internal rate of return.**

Torts: Any of a series of civil wrongs committed by one party against another. Examples include: assault, battery, libel, slander, interference with contractual relations, unfair competition, negligence, and so forth.

Traceability: The ability to directly associate a cost with a cost object, as opposed to allocation, which often involves an arbitrary association. The foundation of activity-based cost systems is traceability.

Transaction exposure: The potential for gains and losses as foreign-denominated assets and liabilities (for example, accounts receivable, accounts payable, notes payable, and so forth) increase or decrease in value with changes in exchange rates.

Transfer prices: Prices charged when goods or services are transferred either within firms (for example, from one division of a firm to another) or between related firms (for example, between a parent and its subsidiaries).

Translation exposure: Typically, the excess of foreign-currency assets over foreign-currency liabilities of foreign subsidiaries. Translation gains result from increases in the value of the foreign currency and losses in the event of decreases.

Translation of foreign currency financial statements: The conversion of the financial statements of a foreign entity (typically, a subsidiary) from that entity's local (foreign) currency to the reporting currency (typically, the parent company's currency).

Trustee: The Bankruptcy Code refers to four categories of trustees: U.S. trustee; interim trustee; trustee under a Chapter 7, 11, 12, and 13 case; and standing trustee. *U.S. trustee:* A trustee appointed by the attorney general in 21 regions to establish, maintain, and supervise a panel of private trustees who are eligible and available to serve as trustees in a case under Chapters 7, 11, 12, or 13. The U.S. trustee is responsible for the administrative aspects of the bankruptcy case. Among other duties, the U.S. trustee approves fee applications, appoints trustees and committees, and reviews operating statements. *Interim trustee:* As soon as the order for relief has been entered in a Chapter 7 case, the court will appoint a disinterested person, from a panel of private trustees, to serve as the interim trustee. *Chapter 7 trustee:* At a meeting of creditors called under section 341, a trustee may be elected if an election is requested by at least 20% in amount of qualifying claims. The interim trustee will continue to serve if a trustee is not elected. *Chapter 11 trustee:* The Bankruptcy Code provides in Chapter 11 cases that a trustee can be either appointed or elected in certain situations, based on the facts of the case and not related to the size of the company or the amount of unsecured debt outstanding. The authorization for the appointment of a trustee is made only at the request of a party-in-interest, after a notice and hearing. Once the authorization has been made, at a meeting called under section 341, the creditors may elect a trustee. *Chapter 12 or*

13 case: The U.S. trustee may appoint an individual trustee to a Chapter 12 or 13 case, where a standing trustee has not been appointed. *Standing trustee:* In districts where warranted, the U.S. trustee may appoint one or more individuals to serve as standing trustees, for cases filed under Chapter 12 or 13. In addition to most of the duties of a trustee in a Chapter 7 or 11 case, the standing trustee collects payments under the plan and distributes them to the creditors. A percentage fee, based on payments under the plan, will be collected by the standing trustee to cover trustee's costs.

Ultra vires: Actions by a corporation that violate or go beyond the purposes expressed in its corporate charter.

Undersecured claim: A secured claim, where the value of the collateral is less than the amount of the claim.

Universal resource locator (URL):   A naming convention used for finding sites on the World Wide Web.

UNIX: An open operating system running on many manufacturers' computers. The first successful nonproprietary operating system, it was developed by Bell Labs in the 1970s.

Unsecured claim: A claim that is not secured by any collateral. In the case of an undersecured creditor, the excess of the secured claim over the value of the collateral.

Unwind: To close out a future or forward position.

Value bargain: An acquiree whose market value to the acquiror is greater than the acquiree's stand-alone (preacquisition) market value.

Value creation: A sustainable increase in an acquiror's market value relative to what the value would have been in the absence of the acquisition.

Variable costs: Those costs that are directly responsive to changes in volume over the relevant range. Variable costs may increase in direct proportion to volume, or may increase at a slower rate due to bulk discounts or other savings that relate to volume. Although variable costs are responsive to volume, they can also respond to other factors, including changes in wage rates or prices of raw materials used in the production process.

Variances: Measure the difference between actual costs and standard costs. Actual costs might be the company's or manager's performance; standard costs might be a budget, the costs for the same period in the preceding period, the costs for another organization, or the average costs of other organizations. Variances are favorable if costs are less than expected and unfavorable otherwise; they may be analyzed by looking at the effect of changing prices (price variances) or changing usage (quantity or usage variances).

Volume-based cost system: Traditional cost system in which costs are allocated to products using functionally aggregated cost pools and volume drivers. For instance, material dollars are often used to drive a material-related cost pool to the unit level; machine hours, to drive a machine-related cost pool; and labor hours, to drive a labor-related cost pool. The more diverse the production process, the more likely it is that this system will distort individual product costs.

Wide area network (WAN):   The interconnection of computers and LANs over a long distance to create a network for the exchange and sharing of data and resources. Long distance may be several miles or across state or country borders. The Internet is the largest WAN.

Windows NT: A network operating system, developed by Microsoft, that is quickly becoming the industry standard.

Working capital: Current assets less current liabilities.

World Wide Web: The part of the Internet that delivers information to users using a series of Web pages created in HTML or an equivalent language.

Write an option: Sell an option. The writer is paid the option premium up front. The writer of a call must later sell the underlying asset if the call option owner exercises. The writer of a put must later buy the underlying asset if the put option owner exercises. The writer of the option is essentially liable for any future payoffs received by the option owner. Also known as shorting the option.

ABOUT THE AUTHORS

William W. Alberts is a professor emeritus of business economics at the Graduate School of Business Administration of the University of Washington in Seattle. His teaching and research have been concentrated in the areas of industrial economics (including competitive analysis), business strategy (including product pricing analysis), and diversification strategy (including acquisition analysis). In the last few years, he has published papers on the profitability of growth by acquisition, the profitability of businesses operating in oligopolistic markets, the experience curve doctrine, ROE "drivers" in commercial banks, the profitability of U.S. commercial banks over the last decade, and the nature of value-based investment planning. Professor Alberts is also a partner and cofounder of Marakon Associates, a management consulting company with offices in Stamford (Connecticut), Chicago, and London. The company has pioneered in the development of value-based management and its application to the never-ending task faced by every shareholder-oriented business organization of identifying and then successfully implementing those competitive and diversification strategies that will serve the objective of maximizing the organization's market value.

Charles A. Anderson's career includes academic and business experience. He has been a faculty member of both the Harvard Business School and the Stanford Business School. He was the president, chief executive officer, and a director of Walker Manufacturing Co., J.I. Case, and the Stanford Research Institute. He has served on a number of corporate boards of directors, including NCR Corp., Owens-Corning Fiberglas Corp., Boise-Cascade Corp., and the Eaton Company.

Robert N. Anthony is Ross Graham Walker Professor of Management Control, Emeritus, at Harvard Business School. He has been a director and chairman of the audit committee of Carborundum Company and Warnaco, Inc. He has been a director of several smaller organizations and a trustee (including chairman of the board) of Colby College, and of Dartmouth-Hitchcock Medical Center. He is the author or coauthor of some 20 books and 100 articles on management subjects, especially management control; his books and articles have been translated into 12 languages. He is a past president of the American Accounting Association.

Eugene E. Comiskey received his Ph.D. from Michigan State University and his professional qualifications include both certified public accountant (C.P.A.) and certified management accountant (C.M.A.). Professor Comiskey taught for 15 years at the Krannert Graduate School of Management at Purdue University and also as a visiting faculty member at the University of California,

609

Berkeley. While at Purdue, he twice received the Salgo Noren Foundation Award, as the most out-standing professor in the Graduate Management Program. Since arriving at Georgia Tech in 1980, he has six times been recognized as Professor of the Year by the graduate students in management. Professor Comiskey has published over 50 papers in a wide range of professional and scholarly journals. His current research interests center on earnings forecasts, the relationship between accounting and market-based risk measures, the role of financial data in credit decisions, and international financial reporting practices. Professor Comiskey served for two years in the elective position of director of research for the American Accounting Association.

Steven Feinstein is an assistant professor of finance at Babson College. He holds a Ph.D. in economics from Yale University. Prior to joining the faculty of Babson College, Dr. Feinstein taught at Boston University, and before that he served as an economist at the Federal Reserve Bank of Atlanta. Dr. Feinstein's primary area of research is the use and pricing of derivatives. He has presented his research at numerous academic conferences, including the American Finance Association meetings. His book *Finance and Accounting for Project Management* is published by the American Management Association, and his articles have appeared in the Federal Reserve's *Economic Review*. He has consulted for a wide variety of institutions. Current and former clients include Analysis Group, Bankers Trust, Boston Security Analysts Association, Cho Hung Bank of Korea, Chrysler, Honeywell, ITT, Lehman Brothers, the law firm of Leonard, Street, and Deinard (Minneapolis), Michel/Shaked Group, Nippon Life Insurance, the law firm of Phillips and Cohen (Washington, DC), and Travelers Insurance.

Michael L. Fetters is a certified public accountant and earned M.B.A. and Ph.D. degrees from the University of Wisconsin–Madison. He is the chairperson of the Accounting and Law Division at Babson College. He previously worked for Arthur Andersen & Co. and currently consults with a variety of businesses, in the area of financial statement analysis. He has published numerous articles in accounting and management journals.

Theodore Grossman is a member of the faculty of Babson College, where he teaches information technology and accounting. He lectures on various information technology topics such as the use of information systems and technology in retailing, strategic information systems, as well as generic systems analysis and design, and accounting information systems. He also performs extensive consulting for both food and nonfood retailers, suppliers of technology products for retailers, and litigation support services in matters relating to technology and retailing. Prior to joining Babson College, he was the founder and CEO of a computer software company for the retail industry. He holds a B.S. degree in engineering from the University of New Hampshire and an M.S. in management from Northeastern University.

Les Heitger is a professor of accounting at the Indiana University Graduate School of Business in Bloomington, Indiana. He received his B.S.B.A. from the Ohio State University, his M.S.B.A. from the University of Denver, and his Ph.D. from Michigan State University. Professor Heitger has written six textbooks and numerous articles for academic and professional journals. He is a certified public accountant who worked for the Denver office of Arthur Young & Company. Dr. Heitger has consulted with over 50 companies on cost/managerial accounting systems and has extensive experience in developing effective planning and control systems. He has also served as an expert witness on financial matters in numerous litigations.

Paul G. Joubert, in addition to his client service responsibilities, is partner-in-charge of the Middlemarket Business Services Group at Cooper & Lybrand's Boston office. He manages a staff of over 150 professionals who provide a full range of auditing, tax, and business advisory services to companies throughout New England. Major services, in addition to reporting on financial statements and tax advice, include business and financial information systems, business strategy, productivity improvements, cash management programs, employee benefit plans, and merger and acquisition assistance. Mr. Joubert joined Coopers & Lybrand in 1971, after graduating from Northeastern University with a degree in finance and accounting. He was admitted to the partnership in 1981 and subsequently served a two-year term as staff director for Coopers & Lybrand's vice chairman of domestic operations. Mr. Joubert has worked extensively with both start-up and mature companies, especially in the manufacturing, high technology, telecommunications, and financial services industries. He has substantial experience in SEC reporting, mergers and acquisitions, and international operations.

William C. Lawler, Ph.D., is an associate professor of accounting and director of the Consortium for Executive Development at Babson College's School of Executive Education. His research and teaching interests focus on developing an awareness in operational managers on how they impact the financial performance of their company. He has run seminars on this topic for such diverse groups as TelCom managers in China, production managers in the Czech Republic, and R&D managers in the United States. Dr. Lawler has consulted with a number of companies concerning the design and use of cost information systems for management decision support rather than external financial reporting. He did his undergraduate work at the University of Connecticut and his graduate studies at the University of Massachusetts.

John Leslie Livingstone has been a principal in an international management consulting firm, with offices in Boston, Chicago, San Francisco, Washington DC, London, Paris, Rome, Frankfurt, Madrid, Hong Kong, and Tokyo. He has consulted on business strategy for major corporations as well as government agencies, including the U.S. Securities and Exchange Commission, U.S. Department of Health and Human Services, and U.S. Postal Service. Previously, he was a senior partner in the "Big Six" international accounting firm of Coopers & Lybrand. He is a CPA, with MBA and Ph.D. degrees from Stanford University. Dr. Livingstone is an adjunct professor at Babson College, and before that he held endowed professorships at the University of Southern California, Georgia Institute of Technology, and Ohio State University. He has published 10 books, more than 50 articles in professional periodicals, and many chapters in authoritative handbooks.

Richard P. Mandel is an associate professor of law at Babson College, where he teaches a variety of courses in business law and taxation and serves as chair of the Finance division. He is also a partner in the law firm Bowditch and Dewey, of Worcester and Framingham, Massachusetts, where he specializes in the representation of small businesses and their executives. Mr. Mandel has written a number of articles regarding the representation of small businesses. He holds an A.B. from Cornell University and a J.D. from Harvard Law School.

Kenneth S. Most has been a professor in the School of Accounting, College of Business Administration, Florida International University, since 1975. He has also taught at other universities in the United States, Europe, and Asia. He received his L.L.B. from the University of London, and his M.A. (accounting) and Ph.D. (economic theory) from the University of Florida. He is a chartered accountant, England & Wales (F.C.A.) and a certified public accountant (C.P.A.) in Texas. Dr. Most was in practice as a public accountant and management consultant for 17 years, before becoming an educator. He is the author of 20 books and over 200 articles.

Charles W. Mulford received his doctorate in accounting, with a support area in finance, from the Florida State University in Tallahassee. He is professionally qualified as a certified public accountant (C.P.A.) in Florida and Georgia. In 1983, he joined the faculty of the School of Management at Georgia Institute of Technology. At Georgia Tech, he is a KPMG Peat Marwick Faculty Fellow and associate professor of accounting. In 1985, 1989, 1990, and 1991, he was recognized as the Core Professor of the Year by the graduate students in management. Prior to joining Georgia Tech faculty, Dr. Mulford practiced public accounting with the firm of Coopers & Lybrand. He was an audit senior in the firm's Miami office. Professor Mulford has published numerous papers in scholarly as well as professional accounting and finance journals. His research interests center on the effects of accounting standards on investment and credit decision making, earnings forecasts, and relationship between accounting-based and market-based measures of risk, and international accounting and reporting practices. Professor Mulford is a member of the American Institute of C.P.A.s and the American Accounting Association.

Grant W. Newton, C.M.A., C.P.A., Ph.D., is professor of accounting at Pepperdine University, Malibu, California. Grant is the author of *Bankruptcy and Insolvency Accounting: Practice and Procedure,* 4th edition and coauthor with Gilbert D. Bloom of *Bankruptcy and Insolvency Taxation,* published by John Wiley and Sons. His articles have appeared in *Journal of Accountancy, Management Accounting, Practical Accountant, C.P.A. Journal, Commercial Law Journal,* and other professional periodicals. Grant was a member of the AICPA's Task Force on Financial Reporting by Entities in Reorganization Under the Bankruptcy Code that resulted in the issuance of the Statement of Position 90-7. Grant received his Ph.D. degree from New York University and his masters from the University of Alabama. He is currently a member of the board of directors and vice president of the Association of Insolvency Accountants and is a member of the board of directors of the American Bankruptcy Institute.

Ronald J. Sutter, C.F.E., C.I.R.A., C.P.A., is a litigation consultant practitioner who specializes in bankruptcy matters in San Diego, California. He has written and lectured on matters related to the CPA's role in bankruptcy and insolvency proceedings and has served in various related professional capacities, including that of an expert witness, an examiner, and as a Chapter 7 and Chapter 11 trustee. He has for over 35 years been an active member and served on the board of directors of a number of professional organizations.

Jeffry A. Timmons currently holds the Franklin W. Olin distinguished professorship at Babson College. In 1989 he became first holder of a new Harvard professorship in New Ventures, from which he resigned in 1994 to return to Babson College. In 1995 The Price Institute and Babson faculty and friends endowed The Jeffry A. Timmons Professorship in recognition of his contributions to Babson and the field. He has authored several books, including *New Venture Creation* (1994) and *Venture Capital at the Crossroads* (1992). He is cofounder and investor in several companies, including Boston Communications Group and Cellular One in southern Maine and New England, and is an advisor to Fax International, Internet Securities, Ernst & Young's National Entrepreneurial Services Group, BCI Advisors, Inc., and Spectrum Equity Partners. Since 1991 he has served as a special advisor and member of the board of The Center for Entrepreneurial Leadership, Inc. of the Ewing Marion Kauffman Foundation of Kansas City, a large U.S. foundation renowned for its support of entrepreneurship. He conceived of and is dean of the Kauffman Fellows Program. He received his MBA and doctorate from Harvard Business School and is a graduate of Colgate University, where he has served as a trustee since 1991.

Michael F. van Breda teaches at Southern Methodist University, where he was chairman of the Accounting Department from 1987 to 1991. His courses have included cost and managerial accounting at the graduate level. He obtained his Ph.D. in accounting from Stanford University and was previously on the faculty of M.I.T. He is the author of numerous scholarly publications, one of which won the Lybrand silver medal for its contribution to managerial accounting. He is the coauthor (with Eldon S. Hendriksen) of the 5th edition of *Accounting Theory* (Richard D. Irwin, 1991). In addition, he has consulted for a number of major corporations.

INDEX